# Behavioral Modeling for Embedded Systems and Technologies:
## Applications for Design and Implementation

Luís Gomes
*Universidade Nova de Lisboa, Portugal*

João M. Fernandes
*Universidade do Minho, Portugal*

T0345094

**Information Science**
**REFERENCE**

**INFORMATION SCIENCE REFERENCE**

Hershey · New York

| | |
|---|---|
| Director of Editorial Content: | Kristin Klinger |
| Senior Managing Editor: | Jamie Snavely |
| Assistant Managing Editor: | Michael Brehm |
| Publishing Assistant: | Sean Woznicki |
| Typesetter: | Jeff Ash, Michael Brehm, Carole Coulson, Chris Hrobak, Jennifer Johnson, Sean Woznicki |
| Cover Design: | Lisa Tosheff |
| Printed at: | Yurchak Printing Inc. |

Published in the United States of America by
Information Science Reference (an imprint of IGI Global)
701 E. Chocolate Avenue
Hershey PA 17033
Tel: 717-533-8845
Fax: 717-533-8661
E-mail: cust@igi-global.com
Web site: http://www.igi-global.com/reference

Library of Congress Cataloging-in-Publication Data

Behavioral modeling for embedded systems and technologies : applications for design and implementation / Luis Gomes and Joao M. Fernandes, editors.

p. cm.

Includes bibliographical references and index.
Summary: "This book provides innovative behavior models currently used for developing embedded systems, accentuating on graphical and visual notations"-- Provided by publisher.

ISBN 978-1-60566-750-8 (hardcover) -- ISBN 978-1-60566-751-5 (ebook) 1. Embedded computer systems. 2. System design. 3. Mathematical models. I. Gomes, Luis, 1958- II. Fernandes, Joao M., 1968-
TK7895.E42B42 2009
004.16--dc22
                    2009005273

British Cataloguing in Publication Data
A Cataloguing in Publication record for this book is available from the British Library.

All work contributed to this book is new, previously-unpublished material. The views expressed in this book are those of the authors, but not necessarily of the publisher.

# Table of Contents

### Section 1
### Model-Based Approaches

**Chapter 1**
UML as Front-End Language for Embedded Systems Design ........................................................ 1
> *Lisane Brisolara de Brisolara, Universidade Federal de Pelotas (UFPEL), Brazil*
> *Márcio Eduardo Kreutz, Universidade de Santa Cruz do Sul (UNISC), Brazil*
> *Luigi Carro, Universidade Federal do Rio Grande do Sul (UFRGS), Brazil*

**Chapter 2**
Model-Driven Design and ASM-Based Validation of Embedded Systems ..................................... 24
> *Angelo Gargantini, Università di Bergamo, Italy*
> *Elvinia Riccobene, Università degli Studi di Milano, Italy*
> *Patrizia Scandurra, Università di Bergamo, Italy*

**Chapter 3**
Abstract and Concrete Data Type Optimizations at the UML and C/C++ Level for Dynamic
Embedded Software ..................................................................................................................... 55
> *Christos Baloukas, Democritus University of Thrace, Greece*
> *Marijn Temmerman, Karel de Grote Hogeschool, Belgium*
> *Anne Keller, University of Antwerpen, Belgium*
> *Stylianos Mamagkakis, IMEC, Belgium*
> *Francky Catthoor, IMEC, Belgium*
> *Dimitrios Soudris, National Technical University of Athens, Greece*
> *Serge Demeyer, University of Antwerpen, Belgium*

## Section 2
## Aspect-Oriented Approaches

## Section 3
## Verification & Model Checking

### Section 4
### Design Automation

## Section 5
## Industrial Applications

# Detailed Table of Contents

### Section 1
### Model-Based Approaches

The first section is about model-based approaches to support some of the development activities associated with embedded systems. Due to the huge popularity of the UML (Unified Modeling Language), model-based approaches are nowadays available in almost all software and hardware engineering branches, and the embedded field is obviously no exception.

**Chapter 1**

*Lisane Brisolara de Brisolara, Universidade Federal de Pelotas (UFPEL), Brazil*
*Márcio Eduardo Kreutz, Universidade de Santa Cruz do Sul (UNISC), Brazil*
*Luigi Carro, Universidade Federal do Rio Grande do Sul (UFRGS), Brazil*

This chapter presents the use of the unified modeling language (UML) as a modeling notation for designing embedded systems. The authors also discuss the need to extend the UML through profiles in order to address the specific mechanisms associated with embedded computing.

**Chapter 2**

*Angelo Gargantini, Università di Bergamo, Italy*
*Elvinia Riccobene, Università degli Studi di Milano, Italy*
*Patrizia Scandurra, Università di Bergamo, Italy*

This chapter describes a model-driven approach based on UML and on abstract state machines (ASM) for supporting the design process system-on-chip (SoC). The approach supports also the generation of SystemC code, thus facilitating and speeding the implementation phase.

**Chapter 3**

    *Christos Baloukas, Democritus University of Thrace, Greece*

    *Marijn Temmerman, Karel de Grote Hogeschool, Belgium*

    *Anne Keller, University of Antwerpen, Belgium*

    *Stylianos Mamagkakis, IMEC, Belgium*

    *Francky Catthoor, IMEC, Belgium*

    *Dimitrios Soudris, National Technical University of Athens, Greece*

    *Serge Demeyer, University of Antwerpen, Belgium*

This chapter discusses how to optimize data types for dynamic embedded systems. It also describes UML transformations at the modeling level and C/C++ transformations at the software implementation level. These two types of transformations focus on the data types of dynamic embedded software applications and provide optimizations guided by the relevant cost factors (e.g., memory footprint and the number of memory accesses).

## Section 2
## Aspect-Oriented Approaches

The second section includes three chapters on approaches that use aspect-oriented concepts, namely the separation of concerns, to address the modeling of embedded systems.

**Chapter 4**

    *Jeff Gray, University of Alabama at Birmingham, USA*

    *Sandeep Neema, Vanderbilt University, USA*

    *Jing Zhang, Motorola Research, USA*

    *Yuehua Lin, Honda Manufacturing of Alabama, USA*

    *Ted Bapty, Vanderbilt University, USA*

    *Aniruddha Gokhale, Vanderbilt University, USA*

    *Douglas C. Schmidt, Vanderbilt University, USA*

This chapter presents a model-driven approach for generating quality-of-service (QoS) adaptation rules in distributed real-time embedded systems. Their approach creates graphical models representing QoS adaptation policies, which are expressed with the adaptive quality modeling language (AQML), a domain-specific modeling language that helps in separating common concerns of an embedded system via different views.

This chapter, written by researchers from UFRGS, Brazil, introduces an approach, based on concepts from model-driven engineering (MDE) and aspect-oriented design (AOD), for exploring the design space of embedded systems. The authors show how their approach achieves better reusability, complexity management, and design automation by exploiting simultaneously ideas and principles from MDE and AOD.

This chapter introduces a model-based framework for embedded real-time systems, proposed by researchers affiliated with CMU. Their approach enables a decomposition structure that reduces the complexity of both functional and parafunctional aspects of the software. This decomposition enables the separation of the functional and parafunctional aspects of the system into semantic dimensions (e.g., event-flow, timing, deployment, fault-tolerant) that can be represented, manipulated, and modified independently of the others from an end-user perspective.

**Section 3**
**Verification & Model Checking**

The third section tackles issues related with verification, a development activity that focuses on formally proving that the system implementation is in accordance with the respective specification. In particular, model-checking techniques for real-time embedded systems are addressed.

This chapter is devoted to modeling clocks in distributed embedded systems using the timed automata formalism. The discussion is centered around the UPPAAL model checker, which is based on the theory of timed automata. The different computer clocks that may be used in a distributed embedded system and their effects on the temporal behavior of the system are discussed, together with a systematic presentation of how the behavior of each type of clock can be modeled.

### Chapter 8

      *Libor Waszniowski, Czech Technical University in Prague, Czech Republic*
      *Zdeněk Hanzálek, Czech Technical University in Prague, Czech Republic*

This chapter shows how a multitasking real-time application, consisting of several preemptive tasks and interrupt service routines potentially synchronized by events and sharing resources, can be modeled by timed automata. As in chapter 7, the UPPAAL model checker is used, but in this case to verify the timing aspects and the logical properties of the proposed model.

### Chapter 9

      *Héctor Posadas, University of Cantabria, Spain*
      *Juan Castillo, University of Cantabria, Spain*
      *David Quijano, University of Cantabria, Spain*
      *Victor Fernández, University of Cantabria, Spain*
      *Eugenio Villar, University of Cantabria, Spain*
      *Marcos Martínez, DS2, Spain*

This chapter focuses on a framework based on SystemC for platform modeling, software behavioral simulation, and performance estimation of embedded systems. With the framework, the application software running on the different processors of the platform can be simulated efficiently in close interaction with the rest of the platform components. Therefore, design-space exploration can be supported by fast and sufficiently accurate performance metrics.

### Section 4
### Design Automation

The fourth section concentrates on several topics related with automating the development process (also named design process or design flow).

This chapter discusses the use of software specifications at higher abstraction levels and the need to provide tools for software automation, because quality issues, like reliability, safety, and time-to-market, are important aspects that have a great impact in the development of many embedded applications. The complete design flow for embedded software, from its modeling to its deployment is presented.

This chapter, authored by researchers from UC Irvine, addresses automation issues for multicore systems based on well-defined transaction level model (TLM) semantics. TLMs replace the traditional signal toggling model of system communication with function calls, thereby increasing simulation speed. TLMs play a pivotal role in the development activities before the final prototype is implemented. The authors discuss important topics in TLM automation and also provide an understanding of the basic building blocks of TLMs.

This chapter provides an overview of reconfigurable computing concepts and programming paradigms for the reconfigurable computing architectures. Two major aspects are taken into consideration; the first one is how the programming model can aid on the mapping of computations to these architectures, and the second one is how the programming models can be used to develop applications to these architectures.

## Section 5
## Industrial Applications

The fifth and last section includes three chapters that present and discuss several issues that are relevant in real industrial contexts, especially in the automotive domain.

### Chapter 13

> *Mohamed Khalgui, Martin Luther University, Germany*
> *Hans-Michael Hanisch, Martin Luther University, Germany*

This chapter discusses reconfiguration issues in the context of industrial control applications and in particular the development of safety reconfigurable embedded control systems following the international industrial standard IEC61499. The authors define a new semantic of the reconfiguration, by considering the improvement of the system performance at run-time as a major criterion.

### Chapter 14

> *Sébastien Faucou, Université de Nantes, France*
> *Françoise Simonot-Lion, Nancy Université, France*
> *Yvon Trinquet, Université de Nantes, France*

This chapter, written by Faucou, Simonot-Lion, and Trinquet, deals with the EAST-ADL, an architecture description language dedicated to the automotive domain, with a focus on the support provided concerning the validation and verification activities. The chapter concentrates mainly on the capabilities offered by EAST-ADL to support the validation and verification activities in order to fulfill the safety requirements associated with the system under consideration.

### Chapter 15

> *Justyna Zander, Fraunhofer Institute FOKUS, Germany*
> *Ina Schieferdecker, Fraunhofer Institute FOKUS & Technische Universität Berlin, Germany*

This chapter, authored by Zander-Nowicka and Schieferdecker, introduces model-based testing methods for embedded systems in the context of the automotive domain. A new test method, called model-in-the-loop for embedded system test (MiLEST), is proposed. This method is realized within the MATLAB®/Simulink®/Stateflow® environment and its main contribution lies on the functional black-box testing based on the system and test models.

# Foreword

*"A good model can advance fashion by ten years."*
*Yves Saint-Laurent*

I am very pleased to introduce here a comprehensive and well-balanced guide into model-based approaches for embedded system design, validation, and implementation.

Embedded systems design is rapidly evolving through its own fashions and trends. It is an expanding area of development in computer-based systems engineering. This is caused by both the demand of widening applications for embedded systems in many sectors of economy and people's daily life, and the availability of enormous computing resources on a single chip. Billion transistor systems-on-chip (SoCs) with multiple processor cores and complex communication networks are already becoming a reality. New design paradigms such as reconfigurable networks on chip and IP core reuse help tackle the biggest challenge of all, the problem of a widening "productivity gap" between what is available on a die for building a system and what can be absorbed by a design process with existing tools. As never before the role of software is increasing in SoCs because it helps to facilitate the incorporation of more complex features into these increasingly more miniaturized devices to render them more reactive and dependable, concurrent and user-friendly etc. In the scope of embedded applications, such as industrial control and automotive, the aspects of heterogeneity, reconfiguration, multi-functionality are paramount, too.

Let's turn our attention to the 2007 edition of International Technology Roadmap for Semiconductors (ITRS): "Software aspects of IC design can now account for 80% or more of embedded systems development cost, especially as we have fully entered the era of multi-core designs, with both homogeneous and heterogeneous architectures…Embedded software design has emerged as the most critical challenge to SOC productivity…"

Systems are now so complex that designers must use tools and must reuse existing blocks to reduce the cost of the design, time-to-market, and to make the systems meet requirements in performance and reliability. They must use abstractions, too. To facilitate these, models are an intrinsic part of these tools and practices. The concept of design flow is basically a concept of tool flow, and, in turn, a concept of model flow. As much as the models are important, the semantic relationships between these models are crucial too, because of the needs for model transformation and compositionality.

The need for the use of behavioral models is again emphasized by ITRS: "For decades, designers have reasoned about systems at various levels of abstraction (block diagrams, incomplete state charts, program models, etc.) with little support from design automation tools. This situation must change in the near future if necessary advances in productivity are to be achieved. To simplify the specification, verification, and implementation of systems including hardware and software, and to enable more efficient design space exploration, a new level of abstraction is needed above the familiar register-transfer level."

Much like in the above quotation from the famous couturier, the success in *how* we design hardware and software for our complex computer-based systems depends on how good our models are and how well we apply them in our engineering practice. Building complex embedded systems without using behavioral models is unimaginable today. In the past, the scope of models was rather limited–finite state machines, timing diagrams, algorithm flow-charts…Those models were mainly used to capture the essential characteristics of some parts of the system, usually with the aim to improve the designer's understanding of the behavior of the system, and help him/her to search for a good solution for a circuit or a program by looking at the behavior of the model. Today, the diversity and variety of models and their combinations, as they cover different aspects or views of the system, is such that their presence in the design practice is imperative. Indeed the models are used as a foundation of methods and algorithms of the very process of the construction of systems, their testing and evaluation.

The cost of developing design automation tools based on models is also an important measure. So is the issue of investing a research engineer's time into development of good models. What is a good model then? What is the model that can help the design flow sustain several years of evolution? Such a model must, first of all, be powerful in terms of its intended (perhaps, even theoretical) use, and at the same time it should be manageable in terms of its practical use. These general truths about good models are eternal. Can we be more specific and argue about the qualities of the models that we need for designing modern embedded systems? Well, those must certainly be models that are universal in capturing the behavior of both hardware and software. In fact the question today is more and more about model-based frameworks rather than individual modeling languages and analysis methods. The frameworks are like environments where the existing algorithmic solutions can be plug-ins. To cope with the productivity crisis, reuse is needed in modeling terms as much as it is in terms of the system designs.

*"Behavioral Modeling for Embedded Systems and Technologies: Applications for Design and Implementation"* is a book which specifically addresses the issues of what modeling languages are good for embedded systems design and how model-based design can be put into use through correspondence between transformations of models and their system implementations.

I particularly like the structure of this book. Its fifteen chapters are written by individual groups of authors who are experts in their specific fields. The chapters are organized in five sections according to larger themes–Model-based Approaches, Aspect-based Approaches, Verification and Model-checking, Design Automation, and Industrial Applications. Each of these sections includes the chapters which are more basic and more specialized–this should suit the readership with different levels of expertise.

For example, the book has an excellent cover of the fundamental modeling issues relevant to embedded systems and their model-based design approaches. The modern views and recent research developments come into play along with more established material. This gives the book both a good tutorial value as well as a state-of-the-art reference item. The readers who are new in the field can familiarize themselves with UML, use of abstract state machines, model-based optimization for power and performance, principles of separation of concerns, and aspect-oriented design, the latter being absolutely vital in developing complex distributed real-time systems.

Embedded systems design as any system design would be incomplete without validation. This issue is addressed in the book through sections on the modeling of clocks and timed automata for distributed systems, the use of model checking techniques for timed automata, as well as more practical verification methods, which use SystemC platforms for behavioral simulation and performance evaluation.

The book is spot-on about the addressing the most important developments in the design automation for embedded systems and SoCs. My eye has been immediately caught by its in-depth and systematic treatment of the topics of embedded software synthesis, transaction level model automation, as well as programming models for reconfigurable architectures.

Finally, what is often missing from existing texts on embedded systems are solid and comprehensive guides on real-life applications. This book is unique in presenting applications in terms of serious industrial case studies coming from automotive and industrial control domains. These practical match nicely the whole spectrum of the issues discussed in the preceding theoretical material. The reader will find here examples of the practical use of modeling and descriptive languages, temporal logics, extensions of Petri nets, model-checkers and model-based testing methods.

Summing up my overall impression about this book, I strongly recommend it to anyone who likes to use behavioral models in systems design, cares about their interrelationship and diversity, and their role in computer-aided design and validation of complex embedded systems. The book serves as an excellent reference source and may be used as a text for advanced courses on the subject.

*Alex Yakovlev*
*Professor of Computing Systems Design*
*School of Electrical, Electronic and Computer Engineering*
*Newcastle University, UK*
*January 2009*

**Alexandre (Alex) Yakovlev** *was born in 1956 in Russia. He received DSc from Newcastle University in 2006, and MSc and PhD from St. Petersburg Electrical Engineering Institute in 1979 and 1982 respectively, where he worked in the area of asynchronous and concurrent systems since 1980, and in the period between 1982 and 1990 held positions of assistant and associate professor at the Computing Science department. He first visited Newcastle as a postdoc British Council scholar in 1984/85 for research in VLSI and design automation. After coming back to Britain in 1990 he worked for one year at University of Glamorgan. Since 1991 he has been at the Newcastle University, where he worked as a lecturer, reader and professor at the Computing Science department until 2002, and is now heading the Microelectronic Systems Design research group (http://async.org.uk) at the School of Electrical, Electronic and Computer Engineering. His current interests and publications are in the field of modelling and design of asynchronous, concurrent, real-time and dependable systems on a chip. He has published four monographs and more than 200 papers in academic journals and conferences, has managed over 20 research contracts. He has chaired programme committees of several international conferences, including the IEEE Int. Symposium on Asynchronous Circuits and Systems (ASYNC) and DATE, and is currently a chairman of the steering committee of the Conference on Application of Concurrency to System Design. He is a senior member of the IEEE and Member of IET. In April 2008 he was general chair of the 14th ASYNC Symposium and 2nd Int. Symposium on Networks on Chip.*

# Preface

Embedded systems development requires integration of a variety of hardware and software components. This field, due to its multifaceted nature, has received contributions from different disciplines, namely computer science, computer engineering, software engineering, hardware-software codesign, and system modeling, not to mention mechanical engineering and materials sciences and engineering.

Model-driven development techniques are gaining importance, especially in the software community, and are expected to become a mainstream engineering approach in the near future, due to the benefits that they offer. Model-driven approaches offer a higher degree of abstraction, which is a crucial characteristic to tackle the growing complexity of the modern computer-based systems. This implies that in the next couple of years the application of model-driven approaches to develop embedded systems is likely to be not only useful, but a real necessity to address the growing complexity of those systems and fight against what is commonly called as the "productivity gap" (as far as methods and tools support are evolving at a small pace than chip complexity does, according with Moore's law). Therefore, system developers are supposed to master modeling techniques to perform their development tasks.

This book is about embedded computer systems. This book is also about how to model the behavior of those systems, for design and implementation purposes. Its technical contents focus on providing a state-of-the-art overview on behavioral models currently used for developing embedded systems, emphasizing on graphical and visual notations. You can find an excellent set of chapters, written in a tutorial-like style by leading and respected researchers and industry practitioners in the field of behavioral modeling of embedded systems. The chapters of this book cover a wide range of the important topics related to modeling embedded systems and were carefully selected and reviewed to give a coherent and broad view of the field.

## CHARACTERISTICS OF EMBEDDED SYSTEMS

Defining succinctly and precisely what is an embedded computing system seems literally impossible, since embedded devices are very diverse and encompass a big variety of different applications. As Koopman, et al. assert, *"embedded computing is more readily defined by what it is not (it is not generic application software executing on the main CPU of a "desktop computer") than what it is"* (1996). Thus, personal computers are not considered to be embedded systems, even though they are often used to build embedded systems (Wolf, 2001).

An embedded system can be defined as a combination of computer hardware and software, and perhaps additional mechanical and others parts, developed to perform a specific or dedicated function.

Embedded systems are computer-based systems conceived for a specific application, using software and hardware components (Kumar, et al., 1996).

Generally, an embedded system is part, as its designation suggests, of a more complex system in which it is physically incorporated. The term "embedded," which was popularized by the U.S. Department of Defense, refers to the fact that those systems are included in bigger systems, whose main function is not computation. Therefore, a system can be understood as embedded, if its observer foresees its use within the context of a broader system or environment.

Embedded systems are typically built to control a given physical environment, by directly interacting with electrical and electronic devices and indirectly with mechanical equipments. For this purpose, an embedded system uses a set of sensors and actuators that allow, respectively, to receive information from and to send commands to the surrounding environment.

The class of embedded systems represents a very large percentage of the systems we daily use, either at home and at industrial facilities. Typical examples of embedded systems are control systems for cars, home appliances, printers or industrial machines; systems to acquire data from laboratorial equipments; systems to support medical diagnosis; or systems to control or supervise industrial processes.

The most relevant characteristics of embedded systems are the following (Camposano and Wilberg, 1996):

- An embedded system is usually developed to support a specific function for a given application. In some cases, only a single system is put into work; in others, the system is supposed to be a mass-market product.
- Embedded systems are expected to work continuously, that is they must operate while the bigger system is also operating.
- An embedded system should keep a permanent interaction with its surrounding respective. This means that it must continuously respond to different events coming from the environment, whose order and timing of occurrence are generally unpredictable.
- Embedded system need to be correctly specified and developed, since they typically accomplish tasks that are critical, both in terms of reliability and safety. A unique error may represent severe losses, either financial or, even worse, in terms of human lives.
- Sometimes, embedded systems must obey some temporal restrictions. Thus, real-time issues must be dealt with. As pointed out by Zave: "*Embedded is almost synonymous with real-time*" (1982).
- Nowadays, almost all computer-based systems are digital, and embedded systems also follow this trend (at least at their core).

## CATEGORIES OF EMBEDDED SYSTEMS

Embedded applications vary so much in characteristics: two embedded systems may be so different, that any resemblance between both of them is hardly noticed. In fact, the term "embedded" covers a surprisingly diverse spectrum of systems and applications, including simple control systems, such as the controller of a washing machine implemented in a 4-bit microcontroller, but also complex multimedia or telecommunication devices with severe real-time constraints or distributed industrial shop-floor controllers.

Embedded systems can be found in applications with varying requirements and constraints such as (Grimheden, et al., 2005):

- Different production units, from a unique system for a specific client to mass market series, implying distinct cost constraints.
- Different types of requirements, from informal to very stringent ones, possibly combining quality issues, such as safety, reliability, real-time, and flexibility.
- Different operations, from short-life to permanent operation.
- Different environmental conditions in terms of radiation, vibrations, and humidity.
- Different application characteristics resulting in static versus dynamic loads, slow to fast speed, compute vs. interface intensive tasks.
- Different models of computation, from discrete-event models to continuous time dynamics.

Koopman, et al. divide, from an application point of view, embedded computing in the following twelve distinct categories (2005): (1) small and single microcontroller applications, (2) control systems, (3) distributed embedded control, (4) system on chip, (5) networking, (6) embedded PCs, (7) critical systems, (8) robotics, (9) computer peripherals, (10) wireless data systems, (11) signal processing, and (12) command and control.

This large number of application areas, with very distinct characteristics, leads us to the inevitable conclusion that embedded systems are quite hard to define and describe. This clearly makes generalizations difficult and complicates the treatment of embedded systems as a field of engineering.

One possible solution is to agree on a division of the embedded field, and consider, for example, four main categories: (1) signal-processing systems, (2) mission critical control systems, (3) distributed control systems, and (4) small consumer electronic devices (Koopman, et al., 1996). For each category, different attributes, such as computing speed, I/O transfer rates, memory size, and development costs apply. Furthermore, distinct models of computation, design patterns and modeling styles are also associated with those categories.

An alternative and simpler classification is proposed in (Edwards, et al., 1997): (1) reactive, (2) interactive, and (3) transformational embedded systems. The important message to retain here is that generalization about embedded systems may sometimes only apply to a specific category.

## TYPES OF EMBEDDED SYSTEMS

Even though some computing scientists consider very naïvely or arrogantly that embedded software is just software that is executed by small computers, the design of this kind of software seems to be tremendously difficult (Wirth, 1997). An evident example of this is the fact that PDAs must support devices, operating systems, and user applications, just as PCs do, but with more severe cost and power constraints (Wolf, 2002). In this section, we argue that embedded software is so diverse from conventional desktop software that new paradigms of computation, methods and techniques, specifically devised for developing it, need to be devised and taught.

The principal role of embedded software is not the transformation of data, but rather the interaction with the physical world, which is apparently the main source of complexity in real-time and embedded software (Selic, 1999). The role of embedded software is to configure the computer platform in order to meet the physical requirements. Software that interacts with the physical environment, through sensors and actuators, must acquire some properties of the physical world; it takes time to execute, it consumes power, and it does not terminate (unless it fails). This clearly and largely contrasts with the classical notion of software as the realization of mathematical functions as procedures, which map inputs into outputs. In traditional software, the logical correctness of the algorithm is the principal requirement, but this is not sufficient for embedded software (Sztipanovits & Karsai, 2001).

Another major difference is that embedded software is developed to be run on machines that are not just computers, but rather on cars, radars, airplanes, telephones, audio equipments, mobile phones, instruments, robots, digital cameras, toys, security systems, medical devices, network routers, elevators, television sets, printers, scanners, climate control systems, industrial systems, and so on. An embedded system can be defined as an electronic system that uses computers to accomplish some specific task, without being explicitly distinguished as a computer device. The term "embedded", coined by the U.S. DoD, comes actually from this characteristic, meaning that it is included in a bigger system whose main (the ultimate) function is not computation. This classification scheme excludes, for example, desktop and laptop computers from being embedded systems, since these machines are constructed to explicitly support general-purpose computing. As a consequence of those divergent characteristics, the embedded processors are also quite different from the desktop processors (Conte, 2002).

The behavior of embedded systems is typically restricted by time, even though they may not necessarily have real-time constraints (Stankovic, 1996). The correctness of a real-time system depends not only on the logical results of the computation, but also on the time at which those results are produced (Stankovic, 1998). A common misconception is that a real-time system must respond in microseconds, which implies the need to program it in a low-level assembly language. Although some real-time systems do require this type of answer, this is not at all universal. For example, a system for predicting the weather for the next day is a real-time system, since it must give an answer before the day being forecasted starts, but not necessarily in the next second; if this restriction is not fulfilled, the prediction, even if correct, is useless from a practical point of view.

A *real-time system* is a system whose behavior must respect the intended functionality but also a set of temporal restrictions, externally defined (Benveniste & Berry, 1991). A critical aspect or a real-time system, as it name clearly suggests, is the way temporal issues are handled. When developing a system of this type, the temporal requirements must be identified and the development team must make sure that they will be fulfilled when the system is in operation.

It is common to classify real-time systems in terms of the reaction time that they exhibit with respect to the needs of the environment where they are located. Thus, the temporal restrictions that affect the systems can be divided into three main categories, each one corresponding to a different type of real-time systems:

- **Hard real-time systems:** An answer to be correct needs to take into account also the instant when it occurs. A late answer is incorrect and constitutes a failure of the system. For example, if a moving robot takes more time than required to decide what to do when avoiding an obstacle a disaster may occur.
- **Soft real-time systems:** The requirements in this category are specified with a medium value for the answer. If an answer comes late, the system does not fail; instead the performance of the system degrades. For example, if a file takes too long to open (i.e. takes more time than expected), the user might become dissatisfied (or even desperate), but no failure results from this fact.

- **Firm real-time systems:** This represents a compromise between the two previous categories, where a low probability is tolerated in the non-fulfillment of a response time that conducts to a failure of the system, mostly affecting associated quality of service.

Embedded systems are also typically influenced in their development by other constraints, rather than just time-related ones. Among them one can include: liveness, reactivity, heterogeneity, reliability, and distribution. All these features are essential to guarantee the correctness of an embedded program. In particular, embedded systems are strongly influenced in their design by the characteristics of the underlying computing platform, which includes the computing hardware, an operating system, and eventually a programming framework (such as .NET or EJB) (Selic, 2002). Thus, designing embedded software without taking into account the hardware requirements is nearly impossible, which implies that, at least currently, "write once run anywhere" (WORA) and the model-driven architecture (MDA) principles are not easily or directly applicable.

*Reactive systems*, a class of systems in which embedded systems can be included, maintain a permanent or frequent interaction with their respective environment and respond based on their internal state to the external stimulus to which they are subject to. Reactive systems cannot be described by specifying the output signals in function of the input signals; instead, specifications that relate inputs and outputs along the time are required. Typically, descriptions of reactive systems include sequences of events, actions, conditions and flows of information, combined with temporal restrictions, to define the global behavior of the system.

Using terminology borrowed from the classical discipline of digital systems, a reactive system is classified as a sequential system (and not as a combinational system). A *combinational logic system* is described by logical functions, has a set of inputs and outputs, and the values of the latter depend exclusively on the values of the inputs and on the internal constitution of the system. In a *sequential logic system*, the output values, in a given moment, do not depend exclusively on the input values at that moment, but also on the past sequences of the values that were present in the inputs (Wakerly, 2000). It may happen that, for equal combinations of the inputs, different values in the outputs are obtained, in different points in time. Sequential systems contain the notion of memory, contrarily to what happens with combinational systems.

Reactive systems have concurrency as their essential feature (Manna & Pnueli, 2002). Put in other words, development of embedded software requires models of computation that explicitly support concurrency. Although software must not be, at all, executed in sequence, it is almost universally taken for granted that it will run on a von Neumann architecture and thus, in practice, it is conceived as a sequential process. Since concurrency is inherent in all embedded systems, it must be undoubtedly included in every development effort.

With all these important distinctions, one clearly notices that the approaches and methods that are used for traditional software are not suitable for embedded software. Embedded software requires different methods, techniques, and models from those used generically for software. The methods used for non-embedded software require, at a minimum, major modifications for embedded software; at a maximum, entirely new abstractions are needed that support physical aspects and ensure robustness (Lee, 2002).

The inadequacy of the traditional methods of software engineering for developing embedded systems appears to be caused by the increasing complexity of the software applications and their real-time and safety requirements (Balarin, et al., 2002). These authors claim that the sequential paradigm, embodied in several programming languages, some object-oriented ones included, is not satisfactory to adequately model embedded software, since this type of software is inherently concurrent.

One of the problems of object-oriented design, in what concerns its applicability for embedded software, is that it emphasizes inheritance and procedural interfaces. Object-oriented methods are good at analyzing and designing information-intensive applications, but are less efficient, sometimes even inadequate, for a large class of embedded systems, namely those that utilize complex architectures to achieve high-performance (Bhatt & Shackleton, 1998).

According to Lee, for embedded software, we need a different approach that allows us to build complex systems by assembling components, but whose focus is concurrency and communication abstractions, and admits time as a major concept (Lee, 2002). He suggests the term "actor-oriented design" for a refactored software architecture, where the components are not objects, but instead are parameterized actors with ports.

Actors provide a uniform abstract representation of concurrent and distributed systems and improve on the sequential limitations of passive objects, allowing them to carry out computation in a concurrent way (Hewitt, 1977; Agha, 1986). Each actor is asynchronous and carries out its activities potentially in parallel with other actors, being thus control distributed among different actors (Rens & Agha, 1998). The ports and the parameters define the interface of an actor. A port represents an interaction with other actors, but does not necessarily have call-return semantics. Its precise semantics depends on the model of computation, but conceptually it just represents communication between components.

## BEHAVIORAL MODELING

Abstraction and modeling are two related techniques for reasoning about systems. Abstraction is a process that selectively removes some information from a description to focus on the information that remains. It is an essential part of modeling where some aspect or part of the real world is simplified. Thus, abstraction is related to the notion of simplicity.

Modeling is the cost-effective use of something in place of something else for a given purpose. A model represents reality for the considered purpose and allows engineers and developers to use something that is simpler, safer or cheaper than reality. A model is an abstraction of reality, since it cannot represent all its aspects. Therefore, the world is dealt in a simplified manner, avoiding the complexity, the danger and the irreversibility of reality.

To be useful and effective, a model of a given system must possess the following five key characteristics (Selic, 2003):

- **Abstract:** The model must concentrates on the crucial aspects of reality for the purpose at hand. The aspects that are not important in a given situation must be neglected or hidden.
- **Understandable:** The reduced form of the model, when compared with reality, must still be sufficiently expressive to allow us to reason about the properties of the system.
- **Accurate:** The key features of the system under consideration must be represented by the model.
- **Predictive:** The model must permit the system's properties to be predicted, either by experimentation or by formal analysis.

- **Inexpensive:** The model must be significantly cheaper to build and analyzed that the system that it represents.

According to Sgroi, et al. (2000), usage of behavioral modeling in embedded system design may contribute:

- To unambiguously capture the required system's functionality.
- To verify the specification correctness against intended proprieties.
- To support synthesis into specific platforms.
- To support usage of different tools based on the same model, allowing interoperability and coverability of different development phases, including designing, producing, and maintaining the system.

In the previous paragraphs, some of the major advantages of model-based development were highlighted. Availability of a model for the system promotes a better understanding of the system, even before starting its design, and allowing the comparison of different approaches, forcing desired proprieties to be present, and detect and remove undesired proprieties in advance. This model-based development attitude is supported by adequate modeling formalisms.

A multitude of modeling formalisms have been proposed for embedded systems design emphasizing their behavior description, ranging from those formalisms heavily relying on a graphical representation to those supported by textual languages. Another dichotomy for classification of modeling formalisms relies on control versus data dominated formalisms. Another possible classification is based on emphasizing specific aspects, like the reactive nature of the system's behavior, the real-time response constraint, or the data processing capabilities.

Independently of the way we prefer to classify modeling formalisms, one crucial decision that the designer of embedded systems needs to take is the selection of the "right" formalism to use. This decision potentially constrains all the development steps and imposes the level of sophistication of the tools that support the process.

Some modeling formalisms for embedded systems are control-dominated, where data processing characteristics and computation are minimal, emphasizing the reactive nature of the system's behavior. Other modeling formalisms emphasize the data processing characteristic, integrating complex data transformations, and are normally described by data flows. For example, reactive control systems are clearly in the first group, while digital signal processing applications are clearly in the second, as they emphasize the usage of data flow models.

Additionally, it is also common to build distributed embedded systems, where one needs to face heterogeneity in terms of implementation platforms, as the different components of the system need to be mapped into different platforms due to cost and performance issues. In these situations, it is not easy to find a unique formalism to model the whole system, so the goal is to decompose the system into components, to model them using submodels and pick up the right formalism for the different submodels. In this situation, communication and concurrency enter into the picture and verification of the properties of the whole system could become more difficult to handle. It has to be stressed that model-based development adequately supports verification of properties, which is a subject of major importance in embedded system design, especially when the system complexity is high.

## BOOK CONTENTS

This book is composed of 15 chapters that are divided into five main sections.

The first section is about model-based approaches to support some of the development activities associated with embedded systems. Due to the huge popularity of the unified modeling language (UML), model-based approaches are nowadays available in almost all software and hardware engineering branches, and the embedded field is obviously no exception. Brisolara, Kreutz, and Carro present in **Chapter 1** the use of the UML as a modeling language for designing embedded systems. The authors also discuss the need to extend the UML through profiles in order to address the specific mechanisms associated with embedded computing. In **Chapter 2**, Gargantini Riccobene, and Scandurra deal with a model-driven approach based on UML and on abstract state machines (ASM) for supporting the design process system-on-chip (SoC). The approach supports also the generation of SystemC code, thus facilitating and speeding the implementation phase. **Chapter 3**, written by Baloukas and other colleagues, discusses how to optimize data types for dynamic embedded systems. The chapter describes UML transformations at the modeling level and C/C++ transformations at the software implementation level. These two types of transformations focus on the data types of dynamic embedded software applications and provide optimizations guided by the relevant cost factors (e.g., memory footprint and the number of memory accesses).

The second section includes three chapters on approaches that use aspect-oriented concepts, namely the separation of concerns, to address the modeling of embedded systems. Gray and others present in **Chapter 4** a model-driven approach for generating quality-of-service (QoS) adaptation rules in distributed real-time embedded systems. Their approach creates graphical models representing QoS adaptation policies, which are expressed with the adaptive quality modeling language (AQML), a domain-specific modeling language that helps in separating common concerns of an embedded system via different views. **Chapter 5**, written by researchers from UFRGS, Brazil, introduces an approach, based on concepts from model-driven engineering (MDE) and aspect-oriented design (AOD), for exploring the design space of embedded systems. The authors show how their approach achieves better reusability, complexity management, and design automation by exploiting simultaneously ideas and principles from MDE and AOD. **Chapter 6** introduces a model-based framework for embedded real-time systems, proposed by de Niz, Bhatia, and Rajkumar, all affiliated with CMU. Their approach enables a decomposition structure that reduces the complexity of both functional and parafunctional aspects of the software. This decomposition enables the separation of the functional and parafunctional aspects of the system into semantic dimensions (e.g., event-flow, timing, deployment, fault-tolerant) that can be represented, manipulated, and modified independently of the others from an end-user perspective.

The third section tackles issues related with verification, a development activity that focuses on formally proving that the system implementation is in accordance with the respective specification. In particular, model-checking techniques for real-time embedded systems are addressed. **Chapter 7**, authored by Rodriguez-Navas, Proenza, Hansson, and Pettersson, is devoted to modeling clocks in distributed embedded systems using the timed automata formalism. The discussion is centered around the UPPAAL model checker, which is based on the theory of timed automata. The different computer clocks that may be used in a distributed embedded system and their effects on the temporal behavior of the system are discussed, together with a systematic presentation of how the behavior of each type of clock can be modeled. In **Chapter 8**, Waszniowski and Hanzálek from the Czech Technical University show how a multitasking real-time application, consisting of several preemptive tasks and interrupt service routines potentially synchronized by events and sharing resources, can be modeled by timed automata. Again, the UPPAAL model checker is used, but in this case to verify the timing aspects and the logical properties of the proposed model. In **Chapter 9**, Posadas and his colleagues focus on a framework based on SystemC for platform modeling, software behavioral simulation, and performance estimation of embedded systems. With the framework, the application software running on the different processors of the platform can be simulated efficiently in close interaction with the rest of the platform components. Therefore, design-space exploration can be supported by fast and sufficiently accurate performance metrics.

The fourth section concentrates on several topics related with automating the development process (also named design process or design flow). **Chapter 10**, written by Ferreira and other coauthors, discusses the use of software specifications at higher abstraction levels and the need to provide tools for software automation, because quality issues, like reliability, safety, and time-to-market, are important aspects that have a great impact in the development of many embedded applications. This chapter discusses the complete design flow for embedded software, from its modeling to its deployment. In **Chapter 11**, Yu, Abdi, and Gajski address automation issues for multicore systems based on well-defined transaction level model (TLM) semantics. TLMs replace the traditional signal toggling model of system communication with function calls, thereby increasing simulation speed. TLMs play a pivotal role in the development activities before the final prototype is implemented. The authors discuss important topics in TLM automation and also provide an understanding of the basic building blocks of TLMs. Cardoso and his coauthors provide in **Chapter 12** an overview of reconfigurable computing concepts and programming paradigms for the reconfigurable computing architectures. Two major aspects are taken into consideration: (1) how the programming model can aid on the mapping of computations to these architectures, and (2) how the programming models can be used to develop applications to these architectures.

The fifth and last section includes three chapters that present and discuss several issues that are relevant in real industrial contexts, especially in the automotive domain. Khalgui and Hanisch discuss in **Chapter 13** reconfiguration issues in the context of industrial control applications and in particular the development of safety reconfigurable embedded control systems following the international industrial standard IEC61499. The authors define a new semantic of the reconfiguration, by considering the improvement of the system performance at run-time as a major criterion. **Chapter 14**, written by Faucou, Simonot-Lion, and Trinquet, deals with the EAST-ADL, an architecture description language dedicated to the automotive domain, with a focus on the support provided concerning the validation and verification activities. Finally, in **Chapter 15**, Zander-Nowicka and Schieferdecker introduce model-based testing methods for embedded systems in the context of the automotive domain.

*Luis Gomes and João M. Fernandes*
*Lisbon and Braga, Portugal*
*January 2009*

## REFERENCES

Agha, G. (1986). *Actors: A model of concurrent computation in distributed systems*. MIT Press.

Balarin, F., Lavagno, L., Passerone, C., & Watanabe, Y. (2002). Processes, interfaces, and platforms. Embedded software modeling in metropolis. *2nd International Workshop on Embedded Software (EMSOFT 2002)* (pp. 407-421). Springer.

Benveniste, A., & Berry, G. (1991). The synchronous approach to reactive and real time systems. In *Proceedings of the IEEE, 79*(9), 1270-1282.

Bhatt, D., & Shackleton, J. (1998). A design notation and toolset for high-performance embedded systems development. Lectures on embedded systems. *European Educational Forum School on Embedded Systems* (pp. 249–267). Springer.

Camposano, R. & Wilberg, J. (1996). Embedded system design. *Design Automation for Embedded Systems, 1*(1/2), 5–50.

Conte, T. M. (2002). Choosing the brain(s) of an embedded system. *IEEE Computer 35*(7),106–107.

Edwards, S., Lavagno, L., Lee, E. A., & Sangiovanni-Vincentelli, A. (1997). Design of embedded systems: Formal models, validation, and synthesis. In *Proceedings of the IEEE, 85*(3),366–390.

Grimheden, M., & Törngren, M. (2005). What is embedded systems and how should it be taught?—results from a didactic analysis. *ACM Transactions on Embedded Computing Systems, 4*(3),633-651.

Hewitt, C. (1977). Viewing control structures as patterns of passing messages. *Journal of Artificial Intelligence, 8*(3), 323-364.

Koopman, P. (1996). Embedded system design issues (the rest of the story). *IEEE International Conference on Computer Design (ICCD '96)* (pp. 310–317).

Koopman, P., Choset, H., Gandhi, R., Krogh, B., Marculescu, D., Narasimhan, P., Paul, J. M., Rajkumar, R., Siewiorek, D., Smailagic, A., Steenkiste, P., Thomas, D. E., & Wang, C. (2005). Undergraduate embedded system education at Carnegie Mellon. *ACM Transactions on Embedded Computing Systems, 4*(3), 500-528.

Kumar, S., Aylor, J. H., Johnson, B. W., & Wulf, W. A. (1996). *The codesign of embedded systems: A unified hardware/software representation.* Kluwer Academic Publishers.

Lee, E. A. (2002). Embedded software. *Advances in Computers, 56.*

Manna, Z., & Pnueli, A. (1992). *The temporal logic of reactive and concurrent systems: Specification.* Springer.

Ren, S., & Agha, G. (1998). A modular approach for programming embedded systems. Lectures on embedded systems. *European Educational Forum School on Embedded Systems* (pp. 170-207). Springer.

Selic, B. (1999). Turning clockwise: Using UML in the real-time domain. *Communications of the ACM, 42*(10), 46-54, 1999.

Selic, B. (2002). Physical programming: Beyond mere logic. *Embedded Software, 2nd International Workshop on Embedded Software (EMSOFT 2002)* (pp. 399-406). Springer.

Selic, B. (2003). The pragmatics of model-driven development. *IEEE Software, 20*(5),19-25.

Sgroi, M., Lavagno, L., & Sangiovanni-Vincentelli, A. (2000). Formal models for embedded systems design. *IEEE Design and Test of Computers, 17*(2), 14-17.

Stankovic, J. A. (1996). Real-time and embedded systems. *ACM Computing Surveys, 28*(1), 205–8.

Stankovic, J. A. (1988). Misconceptions about real-time computing: A serious problem for next-generation systems. *IEEE Computer, 21*(10), 10-19.

Sztipanovits, J., & Karsai, G. (2001). Embedded software: Challenges and opportunities. 1st International Workshop on Embedded Software (EMSOFT 2001) (pp. 403-415). Springer.

Wakerly, J. F. (2000). *Digital design: Principles and practices, 3rd ed.* Prentice-Hall International.

Wirth, N. (2001). Embedded systems and real-time programming. *1st International Workshop on Embedded Software (EMSOFT 2001)* (pp. 486-492). Springer.

Wolf, W. (2001). *Computers as components: Principles of embedded computing system design.* San Francisco: Morgan Kaufmann.

Wolf, W. (2002). What is embedded computing? *IEEE Computer, 35*(1), 136-137.

Zave, P. (1982). An operational approach to requirements specification for embedded systems. *IEEE Transactions on Software Engineering, SE-8*(3), 250-269.

# Acknowledgment

To make this book a reality, many persons contributed with their best skills and efforts. First of all, we would like to thank all the authors of chapter proposals, rejected chapters, and accepted chapters for collaborating with us and for the enthusiasm that they put in this project. Without their contribution, this book would not be now in your hands.

We would like also to acknowledge the superb work produced by our reviewers. All submitted full chapters were reviewed by 2 or 3 reviewers, who generally were able to produce very impressive comments that were a fundamental source for the authors to greatly improve their chapters.

The reviewers for this book were: Christos Baloukas, Manuel Barata, João P. Barros, Frederic Boulanger, Lisane Brisolara, José C. Campos, João M. Cardoso, Luigi Carro, Lucía Costas, Arnaud Cuccuru, J. Michael Duebner, João Canas Ferreira, Georg Frey, Lidia Fuentes, Aniruddha Gokhale, Jeff Gray, Roman Gumzej, Hans Hansson, Zdeněk Hanzálek, Leandro Indrusiak, Daniel Jackson, Peter G. Larsen, José Lastra, Luciano Lavagno, Johan Lilius, Ricardo J. Machado, Paulo Maciel, Grant Martin, Stephan Merz, José Carlos Metrôlho, Miguel Monteiro, Chokri Mraidha, Horácio Neto, Arnaldo Oliveira, José N. Oliveira, Ana Paiva, Hiren Patel, Carlos E. Pereira, Paul Pettersson, Luís M. Pinho, Elvinia Riccobene, Juan J. Rodríguez-Andina, Ella Roubtsova, Françoise Simonot-Lion, Isabel Teixeira, Dragos Truscan, Eugenio Villar, Valery Vyatkin, Flávio R. Wagner, Libor Waszniowski, Marek Wegrzyn, Fabian Wolf, Justyna Zander-Nowicka, and Dieter Zöbel.

We are also in debt to Alex Yakovlev for kindly agreeing to prepare a foreword to the book.

We must also extend our gratitude to the persons at IGI Global for their active support, namely Heather Probst in the first period and Christine Bufton during the last phases of the preparation of the book.


*Luis Gomes and João M. Fernandes*
*Lisbon and Braga, Portugal*

# Section 1
# Model–Based Approaches

The first section is about model-based approaches to support some of the development activities associated with embedded systems. Due to the huge popularity of the UML (Unified Modeling Language), model-based approaches are nowadays available in almost all software and hardware engineering branches, and the embedded field is obviously no exception.

# Chapter 1

# UML as Front-End Language for Embedded Systems Design

**Lisane Brisolara de Brisolara**
*Universidade Federal de Pelotas (UFPEL), Brazil*

**Márcio Eduardo Kreutz**
*Universidade de Santa Cruz do Sul (UNISC), Brazil*

**Luigi Carro**
*Universidade Federal do Rio Grande do Sul (UFRGS), Brazil*

## ABSTRACT

*This chapter covers the use of UML as a modeling language for embedded systems design. It introduces the UML language, presenting the history of its definition, its main diagrams and characteristics. Using a case study, we show that using the standard UML with its limitations one is not able to model many important characteristics of embedded systems. For that reason, UML provides extension mechanisms that enable one to extend the language for a given domain, through the definition of profiles covering domain-specific applications. Several profiles have been proposed for the embedded systems domain, and some of those that have been standardized by OMG are presented here. A case study is also used to present MARTE, a new profile specifically proposed for the embedded system domain, enabling designers to model aspects like performance and schedulability. This chapter also presents a discussion about the effort to generate code from UML diagrams and analyses the open issues to the successful use of UML in the whole embedded system design flow.*

## INTRODUCTION

Embedded systems design has become an important research area due to the high complexity of the new generations of such systems. This increased complexity derives from the amount of functionality that is associated with those systems, which evolved from simple, dedicated applications (like motor control) to portable multimedia devices (like modern portable phones). Efforts in all areas of system level design, like specification, modeling, synthesis, simulation, and verification are required to cope with this increasing complexity.

At the same time, the life cycle of embedded products has become increasingly tighter. Current research on embedded systems design emphasizes

DOI: 10.4018/978-1-60566-750-8.ch001

that the use of techniques starting from higher abstraction levels is crucial to the design success. Some authors like Selic (2003) and Gomaa (2000) argue that this approach is the only viable way to cope with the complexity that is found in the new generations of embedded systems. Using abstraction, models of embedded systems should evolve from high level views into actual implementations, ensuring a relatively smooth and potentially much more reliable process as compared to traditional forms of engineering.

The Unified Modeling Language (UML) (OMG, 1997) is a standard notation for modeling and documentation of object-oriented software. UML2 (OMG, 2007c), the current version of the language, supports thirteen different diagrams, which allows one to model system structure (e.g. class, deployment) and behavior (e.g. collaboration, sequence and timing diagrams). UML has gained popularity as a tool for specification and design of embedded systems, mainly due to the abstraction provided by this language (Lavagno, Martin & Selic, 2003; Martin & Mueller, 2005). The first investigation in this direction has been conducted by Grant Martin, Luciano Lavagno, and Jean Louis-Guerin in 2001 (Martin, Lavagno & Louis-Guerin, 2001). After that, several efforts that describe the use of UML during the different phases of an embedded system design process can be found in (Lavagno, Martin & Selic, 2003), including the investigation of the use of UML for modeling hardware by Edwards and Green (2003). Such popularization comes from the fact that UML is by far the most-used modeling notation for conventional computational systems. An advantage of UML is that it provides extension mechanisms that allow customization of the language, enabling the definition of profiles for specific domains. UML-SPT (OMG, 2002) and MARTE (OMG, 2007a) are examples of profiles proposed by OMG to model schedulability, performance, time and other implementation aspects that are paramount to the development of embedded products. Besides the language extension, UML also improves the clarity, readability and communicability amongst designers in the same domain.

This chapter introduces the UML language as a strong candidate for being the specification formalism for embedded system design, and discusses its usage in the embedded field, including limitations and the evolution of the application of this language in this domain.

The remaining parts of the chapter are divided in the following way. First, we present the history and evolution of the UML language, and the main supported diagrams in the *Background* section. An embedded system example is used to explain different diagrams and discuss limitations of the language, which have motivated extension proposals to support embedded systems design. The *Modeling Embedded Systems with UML* section addresses the use of UML for embedded systems modeling and presents MARTE through of a case study. The section *Code Generation from UML diagrams* discusses some weaknesses of UML that must be further tackled to allow complete code generation from an UML front-end. Future trends are discussed in the sequence followed by the main conclusions of this chapter.

## BACKGROUND

Models provide a way to cope with complex systems by letting designers work at a higher abstraction level. A model can hide details and provide a visual representation for the system. Several modeling approaches have been proposed in the software engineering domain (Atlee et al., 2007). With the popularity of object-oriented approach, the community decided to define a default modeling language. In this context, UML was proposed, and since October 1994 has been under development. The intention behind the definition of the language was to consolidate the various OO languages, methods, and notations in a single modeling language, in a vendor independent fashion. UML was based on the OMT method of Rumbaugh et al. (1991), the Booch method (Booch, 1993), and the OOSE (Jacobson et al., 1992). UML was hence defined to support specification, visualization, construction, and documentation of conventional computational systems.

In January 1997 the first version of the UML specification was released, and in July 1997 UML1.1 was offered to OMG, which assumed the formal responsibility for the language maintenance and revisions. When OMG observes a need for a new technology, the organization makes a request for proposal (RFP), opening a technology adoption process. OMG can have the assistance from academy members, industry and tool vendors, and all members can propose new features and vote for new solutions. According to Pender (2004), UML has become a pattern for modeling of object-oriented software and has been applied into 70% of IT center designs. Nowadays, UML is considered the *de facto* modeling language for software systems.

An editorial revision, UML 1.2, was released in November of 1997. After that, the language evolved until the UML 1.4.1 version. However, UML1.X, the first versions of the language presented some limitations, mainly with respect to the lack of formal semantics, and consequent ambiguous specification. These ambiguities in the model might incur into different interpretations, requiring extra implementation effort for tools and designers concerning model capturing and code generation. To automate these steps, some vendors defined more precise semantics, but the problem was that these semantics varied from vendor to vendor. Recently, a major revision of UML was coordinated by OMG and the new version of the language (UML2) was defined, with enhanced semantics. The main objective of this revision is to eliminate the ambiguities, facilitating design automation and giving support for Model Driven Architecture (MDA) (OMG, 2003). The first minor revision of the original UML 2 specification has resulted in UML 2.1.2 (OMG,

2007c). Although this revision adds fixes to the abstract syntax to eliminate minor inconsistencies and ambiguities, existing UML-tools still have limited capabilities regarding automatic code generation, and these will be explained later in the following sections.

The UML2 Specification was split into two complimentary specifications: *Infrastructure* and *Superstructure*. The *UML infrastructure* defines the foundational language constructs, which is complemented by *UML Superstructure*, which defines the user level constructs. The UML language specification follows a meta-modeling approach, which facilitates the definition of domain-specific modeling languages. In a complementary effort, OMG has defined the MOF (*Metamodel Object Facility*)(OMG, 2006a) to facilitate the definition of a formal meta-model to improve the interoperability of model and metadata driven systems. MOF has contributed significantly to some of the core principles of the Model Driven Architecture.

## UML Diagrams

UML 2.0, the last version of the language, defines thirteen types of diagrams, divided into two categories, as shown in Figure 1. The Structure diagrams represent static application structure. Class diagram, Object diagram, Component diagram, Composite Structure diagram, Package diagram, and Deployment diagram are classified as structure diagrams. The Use Case diagram, Activity diagram, and State Machine diagram represent general types of behavior. Four interaction diagrams, including the Sequence diagram, Communication diagram, Timing diagram, and Interaction Overview Diagram, represent different aspects of interactions.

The class model is at the core of object-oriented development and design. Class diagrams represent the classes of objects that will be used during the system execution, including relationships between classes, like inheritance, aggregation and com-

*Figure 1. UML2 diagram types*

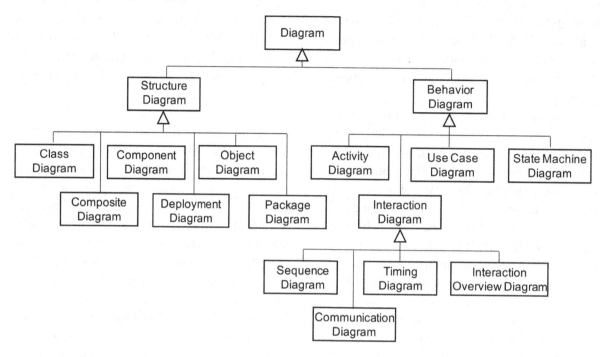

position. The relationship can be bidirectional or unidirectional, and a multiplicity can be indicated for a relationship in order to indicate the amount of objects that can be linked. Object diagrams allow the representation of the relationship between instances of object classes. These diagrams are available since the initial version of UML. The Component diagram allows one to represent the software components that will be used to build the system, focusing on the representation of the physical implementation of the application components that perform and provide the required functionality. The Composite diagram is proposed in UML2.0, and shows the internal structure (including parts and connectors) of a structured classifier or collaboration. The Package diagram describes the organization of packages and its elements, while the Deployment diagram represents the necessary environment for the components to execute in.

A Use Case diagram provides a high-level description of functionality that is achieved through interaction among systems or system parts. It represents the system boundary and the interac-

tion of the system with users and other systems. The Activity diagram represents the flow of data and control between activities. The State Machine diagram describes the state transitions and actions that a system or its parts perform in response to events. This diagram also represents the states that an object may be and the transitions between those states. An object's state is determined by the value of its attributes and transitions are the result of a method invocation that causes an important change in its state.

A Sequence diagram represents the interaction between collaborating objects. This diagram is not new, and has been used to model usage scenarios, the logic of methods, and logic of services. The diagram's name comes from the fact that it describes a sequence of method calls or messages in a logic and natural way. The ordering of the messages assumes that the first message is in the top left corner. The Communication diagram (formerly known as Collaboration diagram until UML1.4), like the Sequence diagram, is an interaction diagram, which shows the messages changed between objects. However, differently from the Sequence diagrams, its primary focus is on object relationships and associations between classes that are required for exchanging messages, and not in the ordering of messages. However, this diagram can also represent the message ordering (see Figure 4) and represents exactly the same dynamic behavior that could be described by a Sequence diagram.

The Timing diagram and the Interaction Overview diagram are new artifacts also added to UML2.0. The Timing diagram shows the behavior of one or more objects in a given period of time. When considering only one object, the Timing diagram can be similar to the State Machine diagram, because it can be used to represent the states that an object can be. However, differently from the State Machine diagram, it indicates the period of time during which the object is in each state.

The Interaction Overview diagram is a variant of the Activity diagram, and its focus is on the control flow of the interactions. Instead of activities, the nodes within the diagram are frames. A frame is a general concept defined to diagrams in UML2 notations. Once a diagram is encapsulated in a frame, it has a name, a type (e.g. *sd* for Sequence diagrams, *cd* for Class diagrams, etc.) and parameters. The name defined in the frame enables one to nest this diagram inside another diagram or frame. In the Interaction Overview diagram there are two types of frames: the interaction frames, which depict any type of UML interaction diagram (Sequence diagram, Communication diagram, Timing diagram, and Interaction Overview diagram) or interaction occurrence frames, which indicate an activity or operation to invoke. The interaction occurrence frames are of type *ref*. The concept of a frame allows a diagram to reference another diagram described in another frame, indicating that reference through the combined fragment *ref*.

## Case Study

In order to better illustrate the concepts underlying the UML language, we have developed a case study, which consists of a crane control system, proposed as a benchmark for system level modeling (Moser & Nebel, 1999). The crane moves a load to some desired position by moving the car in the track, and the load is plugged to the car through a cable. Once the user defines a position for the load, the control system should activate the motor and move the car to the desired point. Special care must be taken with speed and position limits while the crane is moving, to guarantee the safety of the transported load. Therefore, constant monitoring is needed to avoid unexpected situations. This system incorporates hard real time constraints and presents mixed behavior. Figure 2 gives an overview of the system.

UML allows designers to represent the system's needs or functionalities before their actual implementation through the Use Case diagram, where actors represent the external elements that interact with the system (I/O device or human user), and each use case represents a specific functionality that must be provided. The Use Case diagram for the crane system is presented in Figure 3. Usually, each use case also includes a textual specification to detail its related responsibility, which due to space limitations is not presented in Figure 3.

To describe the communication among objects that participate in each use case, the interactions are further detailed using UML interaction diagrams. Figure 4 illustrates the Communication diagram (called collaboration diagram before the UML2) used to represent the *NominalOperationMode* use case of the crane system. This diagram represents the communication among objects that are responsible to perform the crane control in the *NominalOperationMode*. The message number helps one to see the order of the exchanged messages and also identify nested messages. For instance, the messages 3.1.1, 3.1.2 and 3.1.3 are nested to message 3.1.

*Figure 2. Crane System inspired in Moser & Nebel, 1999*

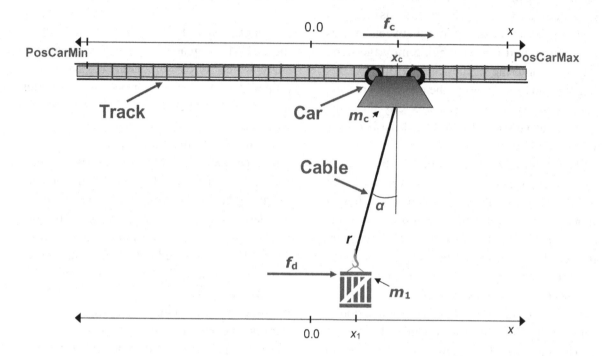

Figure 5 depicts the class diagram of the Crane system, where the classes used to represent the objects that compose the system are presented, as well as the relationship between them. The main classes are *Initialize, Sensorchecker, Controller,* and *Diagnoser*. Initializer initiates several objects that compose the system when the system is turned on. The *Sensorchecker* encapsulates a procedure responsible to check the position sensors responsible to indicate the car position, including the check whether the car is in the lower or upper limit of the track. The *Controller* class encapsulates the control algorithm for the crane system, which is used to determine the voltage to be applied to the motor in order to achieve the desired position. The *Diagnoser* runs in parallel to the control algorithm, and observes the position and angle sensors, setting *EmergencyStop* or *EmergencyMode* if some conditions are not satisfied.

Additionally, in this model there are classes to represent the interface between sensors or other I/O devices. The classes *AngleSensorInterface* and *PositionSensorInterface* represent the interface to cable angle and car position sensors, respectively. *ConsoleInterface* models the user interface used to define the desired position. The classes *MotorInterface* and *BreakInterface* represent the interfaces to the motor and break of the Crane system, respectively. Other classes are used to represent other resources used by the application, as for example *DesiredPosition* that represents the position indicated by user, while *PosCarMin* represents the lower limit for the car.

In order to detail the behavior of a system or an object, a State Machine diagram (know as statechart or state diagram before UML2) can be used. In this case study, the instance of the *Controller* class has an associated State Machine diagram, which is presented in Figure 6.

To detail the dataflow behavior inside the *control()* method from *Controller* object, we have used an Activity diagram (Figure 7), which allows one to describe a flowchart with conditions, loops and concurrency. This method is responsible to

*Figure 3. UML use case diagram of the Crane system*

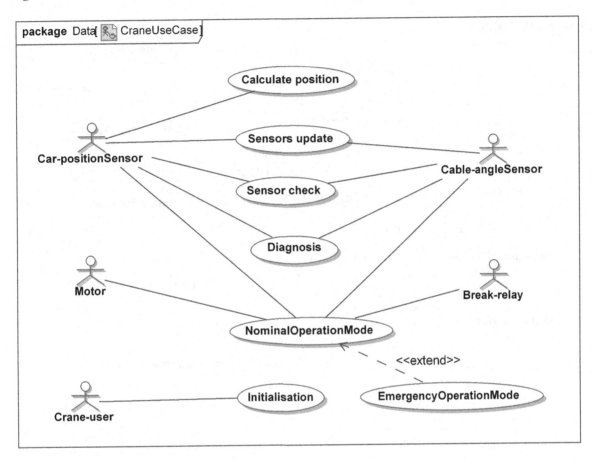

compute the voltage to supply the Crane motor using a control equation presented in (Moser & Nebel, 1999).

Although UML provides a rich notation for system modeling, as shown in the case study, it does not provide support to the detailed design of real-time and embedded systems. Aspects related to timing and concurrency of the crane system cannot be expressed using the default UML notations. For example, the crane control algorithm should determine a new result each 10ms, but this information cannot be described in the UML model presented here. In the same way, the main routines encapsulated by *Diagnoser* and *Controller* objects should be performed in parallel, but this model does not specifies these objects as being

concurrent. Later in this chapter we will explain how to overcome this limitation.

## UML Modeling Limitations

UML was proposed as a general purpose modeling language. However, it is not possible to define a language that can support all kind of systems that one can possibly design. UML is known as being more indicated to model event-based systems (Brisolara, Becker, Carro, Wagner, & Pereira, 2005a) (Douglass, 2004).

Some researchers observe that UML is not suitable for representing other models of computation (MoCs) besides the event based one. Bichler, Radermacher and Schürr (2004) proposed a new

*Figure 4. UML communication diagram of the Nominal Operation Mode use case*

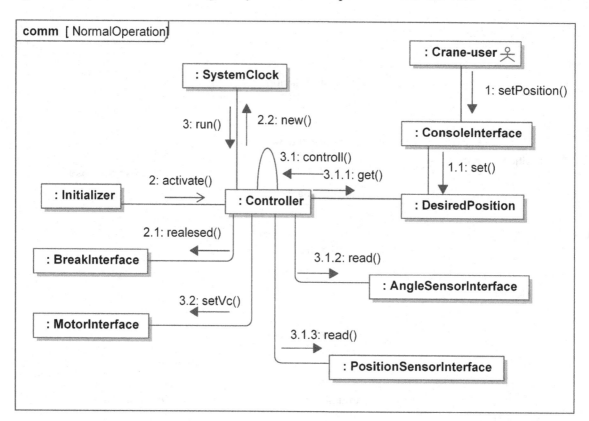

approach to support dataflow modeling, which is based on the inclusion of a dataflow mechanism coupled with mathematical equations in UML-RT. Hence, this proposal is named D-UML. A comparison among the D-UML, UML and a functional-block approach is presented in (Brisolara et al., 2005b), where the authors show that D-UML is not yet the appropriate way to solve this limitation. To solve the same problem, Green and Essa (2004) included the support of dataflow model into UML Activities diagrams. Axelsson (2000) proposes an UML extension to represent continuous time relationships, such as continuous variables, equations, time, and derivatives. A similar work has been conducted by Berkenkötter, Bisanz, Hannemann and Peleska (2003), where the authors extended UML with basis on a programming language suitable for hybrid systems.

Following Douglass (2004), although UML being a discrete modeling language, it is possible to model continuous behavior by specifying actions on Activity diagrams or statecharts. Since the UML does not define an action language, the continuous aspects are outside of the auspices of the UML. However, it is necessary to indicate in the model which component should be associated to a continuous behavior.

In present applications like a cell phone or even in the crane example shown here, embedded systems present a mix of several models of computation. Moreover, besides the heterogeneous behavior, embedded systems usually have real-time constrains (soft or hard) that should be specified in the system model, detailing aspects as concurrency, timing and usage of resources required for the embedded application. As exem-

*Figure 5. UML class diagram of the Crane system*

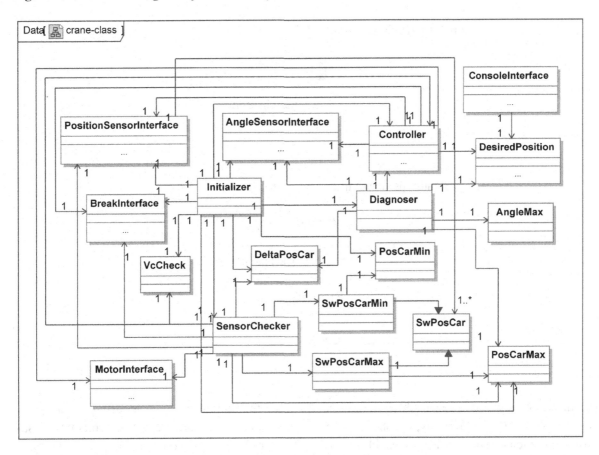

plified by the case study, UML does not provide notations to model those aspects, what indicated the need to extend the language for the real-time domain.

As stated before, UML was defined for general purpose software systems and cannot fully support modeling and design for any kind of systems. Usually, specific domains require additional modeling features, thus domain-specific languages must be adopted. In order to allow the use of UML in a wide range of domains, OMG provides mechanism to extend the language through the definition of a profile. Thanks to the UML meta-modeling-based approach and the MOF architecture, the definition of profiles or domain-specific modeling languages has become easier, what represents the strength of current UML-based approaches. Following,

we present the extension mechanism provided by UML and also the main profiles developed by OMG for different domains.

## UML Extension Mechanism

UML provides a mechanism for defining domain-specific models by extending the language through a profile. According to Pender (2004), an UML profile is a set of stereotypes, constrains, and tagged values that work together to extend the language for a specific domain. Once the UML language is defined by a meta-model that contains all model elements of the language, a profile is allowed to contain specialized versions (called *stereotypes*) of the meta-model elements (defined in the UML meta-model itself), user-defined values

*Figure 6. UML state machine diagram of the Controller object*

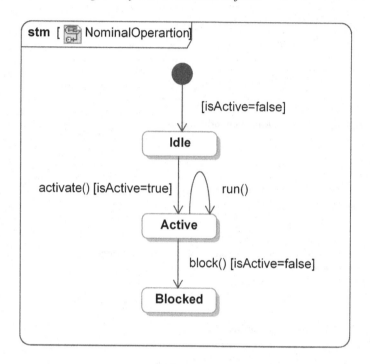

(properties or tags) attached to these elements, (Douglass, 2004). Additionally, constraints can be used as extension mechanisms to enable one to refine the semantics of a UML model element. A constraint refines a model element by expressing a condition or a restriction in a textual statement to which the model element must conform.

Stereotypes are used to create new model elements that can be used in specific domains, allowing one also to create new properties, and specifying new semantics. Using stereotypes defined by a profile, a designer can indicate that an object is of a specialized type, applying a different treatment for that. Tagged values are used to add an additional property for any kind of element from the model. A tag-value par indicates the property and the value for that, being useful to specify, for example, timing information like deadlines, throughput or period for a periodic task when modeling a real-time embedded system. A tagged value is represented in UML as a string that is enclosed by brackets {}. Constraints are used to add new rules, or modify existing ones, in order to extend the UML semantics. Usually, constraints are represented using the Object Constraint Language, OCL for short (Warmer & Kleppe, 1998), which is a declarative language for describing rules. A natural language like English also can be used to express constraints, although its use will make the automatic model verification very difficult.

The next section presents the main profiles defined by OMG that are related to the embedded systems domain. In the *Modeling embedded systems with UML* section, an example of the use of a profile defined for the embedded systems domain is presented.

## UML Profiles

As stated before, a profile is a meta-model of some particular domain of interest, which is expressed using a coherent set of UML stereotypes (Douglass, 2004). These stereotypes can have associated

*Figure 7. UML activity diagram of the control method*

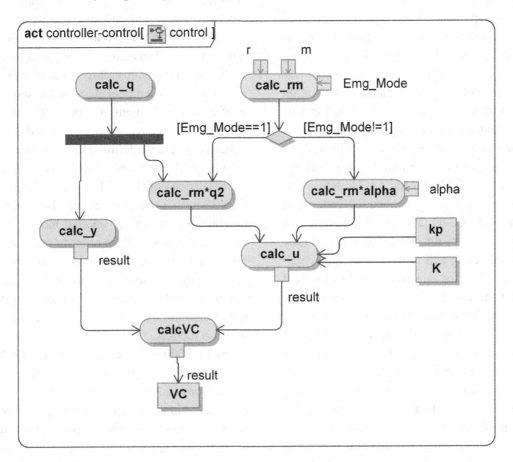

tagged values that are used via constraints, and are possibly accompanied by a model library specific to the domain(s) of interest. This section presents the main profiles related to the embedded systems area, presenting profiles from UML-SPT for real-time systems, and MARTE, the newer profile dedicated to real-time embedded systems.

The UML Profile for Schedulability, Performance and Time, in short UML-SPT, (OMG, 2002) allows one to build models that can be used to make quantitative predictions regarding schedulability, performance and time. Additionally, the use of this profile enables the specification of timing and concurrency aspects like deadlines for tasks and period for periodic tasks, as well as schedulable objects. UML-SPT supports both timing

and performance requirements specification. In a complementary effort, the UML Profile for Modeling QoS and Fault Tolerance Characteristics and Mechanisms, known as QoS&FT, (OMG, 2004) extends UML to represent Quality of Service (QoS) and Fault-Tolerance concepts, reducing the limitations of UML 2.0 for describing such properties, and integrates the extensions in two basic general frameworks (QoS Modeling Framework, and FT Modeling Framework). These profiles are interesting for the embedded system design because they support the specification of the system's Quality of service (QoS) requirements – performance, timing, power consumption, and cost.

There are however, some key points not covered by these profiles, which are important when designing embedded systems, such as explicitly modeling of applications and architectures, mapping of tasks to processing elements, definitions of HW-dependent SW as well as RTOS (Real-time Operation System) services. Although these services are not fully implemented, their main features and necessities can be modeled and be used as input for a synthesis tool, able to create the appropriate services, based on the requirements of a given application. These points are covered by the UML Profile for Modeling and Analysis of Real-time and Embedded Systems, in short MARTE (OMG, 2007a), which is a major revision over them for embedded and real-time systems modeling and analysis and adds capabilities to UML for model-driven development of Real Time and Embedded Systems (RTES). This profile is intended to replace the existing UML-SPT and supports the explicit modeling of processing elements and communication, as well as tasks mapping onto them. As a consequence, models for computation and communication can be analyzed for schedulability and performance. Besides the modeling of performance and timing aspects, MARTE supports the non-functional requirements (NFR) specification and the modeling of embedded platforms. This profile will be discussed in more detail in the section *UML profile for MARTE*.

Another effort from OMG defined a new visual language called Systems Modeling Language (SysML), which was standardized by OMG in 2007. SysML is an extension of UML 2.0 to satisfy the requirements for systems engineering (SE) domain (OMG, 2007b). The SysML language provides graphical representations with a semantic foundation for modeling system requirements, behavior, structure, and parameters, which are used to integrate with other engineering analysis models such as cost models, safety models, and others. In SysML, the activity diagram is extended to support the traditional SE functional flow block diagrams (dataflow) and continuous behaviors. The Requirement diagram was introduced to provide a bridge

between the typical requirements management tools and the system models. The Requirement diagram captures requirements hierarchies and requirements derivation. The satisfying and verifying relationships allow a modeler to relate a requirement to a model element that satisfies or verifies the requirements. For the system structure specification, SysML also modified the UML2 structure diagrams defining the block definition diagram and the internal block diagram, which are extensions of the UML2 Class diagram and Composite diagram, respectively. The Parametric diagram, a new type of internal block diagram, was defined in SysML in order to provide a representation of constraints (equations) between system property values such as performance and reliability, and serves as a means to integrate the specification and design models with engineering analysis models.

Since 2000 some efforts can also be found for supporting the modeling and specification of System-on-a-Chip (SoC) using UML. These have culminated in the specification of a UML profile for this specific domain (OMG, 2006b), which extends UML 2.0 in order to support modeling and specification of SoC designs. In the UML profile for SoC, stereotypes for each UML metaclass were defined by introducing a special notation and constraint for each SoC element. This profile provides the following representation capabilities: (a) hierarchical representation of modules and channels, which are the fundamental elements of SoC; (b) roles of modules; and (c) information transferred between modules using only one type of diagram. Structure diagrams are extended in this profile and are the most used diagram for SoC design. Even convenient for many characteristics of SoCs modeling, this profile lacks some important aspects in SoCs modeling such as non-functional requirements specification and the adoption for more Models of Computations. The main reason for this gap is that the proposed SoC profile targets SystemC-based applications, and is tightly coupled with SystemC modeling principles (actor-oriented, communication by ports and channels and support for event oriented MoC only). Nevertheless, OMG argues that SystemC is used only for illustration, since whole examples present in the official documentation are based on SystemC. The main effort that has motivated this profile was launched by a Japanese project with the objective to define a design flow which integrates UML and SystemC (Zhu et al., 2004).

Finally, the UML Testing Profile defines a language for designing, visualizing, specifying, analyzing, constructing and documenting the artifacts of test systems. It is a test modeling language that can be used with all major object and component technologies and applied to test systems in various application domains. The UML Testing Profile can be used in stand-alone mode for the handling of test artifacts, or in an integrated manner with UML for the joint handling of system and test artifacts.

## MODELING EMBEDDED SYSTEMS WITH UML

As already mentioned, due to their various applications, many embedded systems can be considered heterogeneous from the problem domain perspective. This applies to systems whose respective implementation require different models of computation (MoCs) (Edwards, Lavagno, Lee, & Sangiovanni-Vincentelli, 1997), like stream processing, control flow, and continuous time, in order to capture and express their behavior. For example, the specification of a mobile phone requires not only digital signal processing for the telecommunication domain, which is a discrete time MoC, but also sequential logic programs to describe several available applications (e.g. contacts and alarm clock). Such requirements contrast with the characteristics of UML, which was originally designed for the specification of event based systems.

This issue has already been discussed in (Brisolara, Becker, Carro, Wagner & Pereira, 2005a), where the object-oriented approach provided by UML and the functional-block approach provided by Simulink are compared. This comparative analysis demonstrated that UML is more suitable to be used in a platform-based embedded system design methodology. This is due to the following reasons: (i) UML is a recognized standard and is becoming very popular especially in industry; (ii) UML offers extension mechanisms (stereotypes, tagged values, profile), allowing one to implement specific additional semantics and to add it into UML; (iii) UML is modeled by a meta model, so that the conformity of models exchanged between tools is ensured. UML does not depend on any particular methodology, allowing one to use it together with an appropriate methodology. Moreover, UML provides all benefits from the object oriented paradigm like modularity, encapsulation, reusability, concurrency.

## UML Profile for MARTE

Recently, the UML profile for Modeling and Analysis of Real-Time and Embedded systems, or in short MARTE, was proposed as a profile to support modeling and analysis in the embedded systems domain. Embedded systems are usually characterized by their hard-constrained resources (memory, performance, and energy consumption), and so the non-functional requirements modeling is fundamental. Model-based design tools should take special care on non-functional requirements (NFR) in the embedded domain. Additionally, embedded systems are ever more being required to execute in real-time, indicating the need to model timing aspects such as deadlines, task period and throughput. Moreover, MARTE offers the concepts that are necessary to model hardware/software platforms for executing real-time embedded applications, which include supporting for modeling hardware resources (memory, processors, communication channels, etc) and software aspects like real-time operating system. The allocation concept is used to indicate that an application element is allocated into a processing platform element. Using the MARTE model libraries, one can specify, for instance, the processor type (RISC, CISC, DSP, etc.) and detail properties for hardware resources components that can be later useful for analysis purposes.

MARTE consists in defining foundations for model-based description of real time and embedded systems, which include concepts concerning both model and analysis. Modeling support provides mechanism (stereotypes and tagged values) to detailed design of real-time and embedded characteristics of systems, allowing the specification of non-functional requirements (NFRs), time, general resources and allocation. For model-based analysis support, MARTE provides facilities to annotate models with information required to perform specific analysis. The profile definition especially focuses on performance and schedulability analysis, but it provides also a general analysis framework which intends to refine/specialize any other kind of analysis.

Following OMG (2005), the main benefits offered by this profile are (i) providing a common way of modeling both hardware and software aspects of a RTES in order to improve communication between designers; (ii) enabling interoperability between development tools used for specification, design, verification, code generation, etc.; (iii) fostering the construction of models that may be used to make quantitative predictions regarding real-time and embedded features of systems taking into account both hardware and software characteristics.

MARTE integrates concepts of time and behavior that are strongly coupled in the embedded domain. In this profile, three different time abstractions can be used to represent the temporal ordering for behavioral flows that are causal/temporal, clocked/synchronous and physical/real-time. In the causal/temporal, the relations of precedence/

dependency are used to determine behavior. In this model, cooperation between concurrent entities takes place as communications that can be fully asynchronous, blocking, or hand-shake synchronization. The clocked/synchronous adds a notion of simultaneity, and divides the time scale in a discrete succession of instants. This class of time abstraction can be used for hardware and software modeling. The physical/real-time offers a way to specify the accurate modeling of real-time duration values, for scheduling issues in critical systems. Physical time models can also be applied to synchronous model, for instance to derive the admissible speed of a reaction.

MARTE is compliant with the UML and model-driven architecture (MDA) that has been proposed by OMG to support mode-based design (OMG, 2003). This profile defines the language constructs and provides model libraries with advanced types, and does not force specific execution models, analysis techniques or implementation technologies. MARTE is already implemented in PapyrusUML (Papyrus, 2008) and IBM RSA 7 (IBM, 2008), both based on Eclipse, and prototyped in MagicDraw14. For analysis purposes MARTE has been integrated to analysis tools such as RapidRMA (Tri-Pacific Software, 2008) and Cheddar (Singhoff, Legrand, Nana & Marcé, 2004). Thales RT has developed a set of Eclipse plugins which allows one to perform scheduling analysis (RMA style) with Cheddar on UML/MARTE models.

Although very convenient for embedded systems modeling, the MARTE profile still lacks some features that are essential in systems design and analysis. For instance, there is no support for code generation, or to analysis tools based on the domain of the target application and simulation of the system. As for now, MARTE can be used for the understanding of the whole system, with aspects such as architectural/application separation view, system tasks partitioning, non-functional requirements specification and models of computation employed. However, to all these

*Figure 8. UML class diagram of the Crane system using MARTE profile*

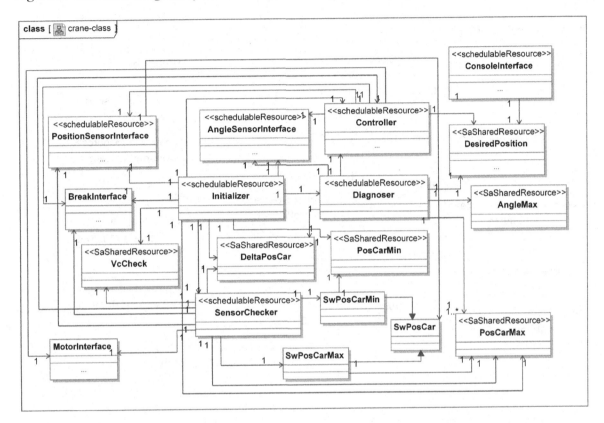

aspects one needs to add a semantic, allowing an executable model of the entire system to be created, simulated and checked against the application constraints. To that, specific tools and methods still have to be defined.

## Case Study

The Crane system has been modeled using standard UML, without stereotypes from any profile, as described in a previous section. The same application is used here as a case study to show the advantages of the MARTE profile. The class and communication diagrams decorated with stereotypes from the MARTE profile are used to model the system, showing some additional features provided by the profile, which facilitate the embedded system modeling and analysis. Figure

8 and Figure 9 illustrate the class diagram for the crane system and the communication diagram for the *NominalOperationMode* use case. Differently from the Class diagram depicted in Figure 5, the diagram depicted in Figure 8 illustrates the use of stereotypes from MARTE to specify the Crane objects.

In Figure 8, the «*SchedulableResource*» stereotype is used to indicate that the objects *Initalizer, Controller, Diagnoser, PositionSensorInterface, AngleSensorInterface* and *ConsoleInterface* are schedulable resources. When a real-time operating system is used, these objects represent a unit of concurrent execution, such as a task, a process, or a thread. The «*SaSharedResource*» stereotype is used in objects *DesiredPosition, VCCheck, AngleMax, DeltaPosCar, PosCarMax* and *PosCarMin,* indicating that these classes

*Figure 9. UML communication diagram of the NominalOperationMode using MARTE profile*

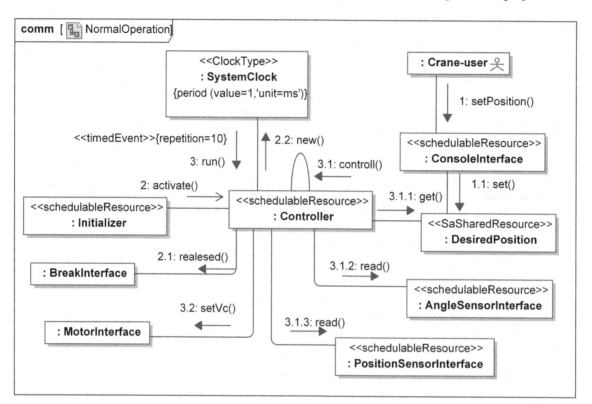

represent a shared resource, which is dynamically allocated to schedulable resources by means of an access policy. This stereotype is used to indicate I/O devices, DMA channels, critical sections or network adapters.

In the Communication diagram of Figure 9, stereotypes are also used to specify timing aspects for the messages changed among the Crane system objects. The message *run()* invoked from the *Controller* is marked with the stereotype «*TimedEvent*», to indicate that it is a periodic task with a period equal to 10ms. The *Controller* object represents a periodic task having the activation pattern obtained by the *repetition* property of «*TimeEvent*» stereotype. Since *Controller* is bounded the clock defined by the stereotype «*ClockType*» in *SystemClock* (with period of 1 ms) *repetition* = 10, means that *run()* executes periodically at every 10 ms. Comparing Figure 9 to Figure 4, one can

observe that the diagram in Figure 9 differs from the other by the application of stereotypes in the Crane object and messages.

Once modeled, the Crane Class and Communication diagrams could be used for analysis purposes. This is a very necessary task in embedded systems, since all system's functionality and constraints have to be met as early as possible during the application design cycle. In complex systems, comprised by hardware (HW) and software (SW) elements, it is very interesting to involve both the SW and HW teams to be concerned with the system's functionalities, in order to overcome possible errors that could arise during the integration/implementation phase.

In order to add useful analysis information to specifications, MARTE defines the SAM (Schedulability Analysis Model) sub-profile (OMG, 2007a). In this sub-profile, stereotypes are defined to cope with semantics related to resources specification, ability of resources to be shared, policies for scheduling and schedulability analysis (if a component is schedulable or not). In the SAM sub-profile Processing and Communication resources are also defined, so application tasks (resources) can be mapped to them, during analysis, in order to deploy the system solution.

Following the Crane example, the SAM sub-profile was applied to the class and communication diagrams, as can be observed in Figures 8 and 9. These stereotypes of the profile add the necessary semantics required by the model to be observable by a designer or by a tool. A tool can then be used to extract relevant informations and proceed with the system implementation.

In this direction, the «*SaSharedResource*» stereotype defines shareable objects, while the «*schedulableResource*» stereotype stands for objects that have to be scheduled (by a specific policy) during execution. Schedulable objects are allocated to processing resources, being subject to a scheduling policy. All such policies are also defined in the SAM sub-profile by an "enumeration". The "allocation" process is defined in another MARTE sub-profile, "*Alloc*" as can be seen in MARTE specification (OMG, 2007a). The Class and Communication diagrams were annotated with the stereotypes cited above for resources that have to be controlled during execution. For instance, it is possible for a tool to query the description and generate code to control the crane application, taking into account the scheduling policy for its objects. Besides - during the application optimization phase - after system simulation and analysis, it is possible for a designer to determine what should be the most suitable policy for each "schedulable" object. Last but not least, the designer can decide whether an object should execute as software or as hardware in a dedicated unit.

By using the MARTE profile it is possible to specify aspects related to timing and non-functional requirements required when specifying real-time embedded systems, allowing the building of a more complete model that can be used as input for analysis and synthesis tools. The profile provides modeling constructs covering the development process of real time embedded systems, including features categorized into qualitative (parallelism, synchronization, communication) or quantitative (deadline, periodicity). The stereotypes applied to the diagrams make explicit how useful a profile can be during the specification or analysis of embedded applications. Without the semantics added by the profiles, it would not be possible for a designer or a tool to interpret the exact meaning of some functionalities or how the object should behave during execution.

## CODE GENERATION FROM UML DIAGRAMS

### Synthesis from Dedicated Models

Several tools based on UML are available for software modeling and code generation. The tools proposed for code generation from UML models can be divided in two classes, structural and behavioral. This division was initially proposed by Björklund, Lilius & Porres (2005). In a structural code generation, only structural diagrams are used, i.e. class diagrams, where classes have attributes and relations. The tools that follow this approach generate only a skeleton of the code, and the strategy has been available since the first UML tools. For example, most tools can map all constructions (elements) in a class diagram to Java or C++ programs. On the other hand, the behavioral code generation is based on behavioral UML diagrams, such as state, sequence and collaboration diagrams. Most of the available tools provide code generation only from UML state diagrams, as for example, Artisan Studio, Rhapsody, UniMod and BridgePoint UML Suite.

To be able to generate complete code from UML diagrams, designers are asked to add information to the model, e.g. specifying the action correspondent to state (activity) in a state (activity) diagrams or specifying the method behavior in sequence diagrams. Some code generators use the target implementation language to describe these methods and actions, which make the model dependent on the target language. Other tools use action languages to complement the state and activity diagrams in order to generate complete code. However, as the Actions Semantics proposed for UML 1.5 defines only an abstract syntax, tool vendors use proprietary action languages. Such approach is used in iUML (Carter, 2005), BridgePoint UML Suite (Mentor Graphics, 2005), and Telelogic Tau Architect/Developer (Telelogic, 2004). As an example, BridgePoint uses the Object Action Language (OAL) and provides full code generation, in which the designer uses State diagrams to represent the system behavior and specifies actions correspondent to all states using OAL.

UML2 provides some constructions that aid the modeling of the complete execution flow, as for example the *ref* operator that allows to link fragments in different sequence diagrams. This new version of UML also provides the operators *alt*, *opt* and *loop*, which permit representing conditions and loops in sequence diagrams. These new constructions allow the proposal of code generation approaches based on sequence diagrams, as in (Babu, Malinowski & Suzuki, 2005) and (Reichmann, Kühl, Graf, & Müller-Glaser, 2004). Matilda (Babu, Malinowski & Suzuki, 2005) is a model-driven development platform that accepts the UML2.0 class and sequence diagrams as input. This platform, besides code generation, provides capabilities for model checking against the UML meta-models for syntax and semantic correctness.

## UML and Other Languages

The multidisciplinary nature of advanced embedded systems requires a combined usage of different tools and modeling languages. Several efforts have been made towards proposing the integration between UML and embedded systems domain languages and frameworks like Simulink and Scade.

As stated in (Vanderperren & Dehaene, 2006) and (Mueller et al., 2006), two different approaches for integration of UML and Simulink have been proposed so far: co-simulation and integration based on the target implementation language. As an example of the co-simulation approach, the Exite tool (Extessy, 2007) allows the coupling of a Simulink model with ARTiSAN Software Real-Time Studio or I-Logix Rhapsody. In another effort, the Rhapsody UML2.0 tool has been integrated with Matlab/Simulink, enabling the construction of UML mixed models that allow for modules to be described in Simulink (Boldt, 2007).

The alternative approach is the use of a common execution language. This solution is adopted in the Constellation framework (Real-Time Innovation, 2007) and in the GeneralStore integration platform (Reichmann, Kühl, Graf, & Müller-Glaser, 2004). Although the authors claim that a bidirectional mapping between UML and Simulink is provided in the GeneralStore framework, only the capturing of a Simulink model in an UML model is supported, and the integration is effectively made at the code-level.

Both approaches focus on the use of different modeling languages to specify each system module. Differently from these approaches, Brisolara et al. (2008) proposes using UML as the single modeling language for initial specification, which provides the benefits of a standard language that is widely accepted in the software engineering community. Brisolara 2008 reports an approach that directly derives the Simulink model from the UML modeling strategy chosen by the designer, hence allowing a single modeling language environment.

To couple the high-level structuring capabilities of UML with the precision semantic and expressive power of SCADE behavioral descriptions, a proposal for combining UML and the SCADE tool is presented in (Le Guennec & Dion, 2006). This proposal is intended to help deliver clear and correct-by-construction software artifacts targeting safety-critical systems for application domains such as aeronautics or automobile. In this approach, UML is used to describe the overall architecture of the application, while SCADE is used to formally describe the behavior of safety-critical software parts (note that less critical, or communication intensive sub-systems can remain in UML). The verification tools provided by SCADE can be used to prove the correctness of the SCADE parts of the system, and to generate certifiable C code from the specifications.

## FUTURE TRENDS

UML is already a standard language for modeling object-oriented systems and it is widely used in several application domains. The widely use of UML as a standard language also contributed for the definition of software development approach that shifts the focus from code to models, which is called model-driven development, MDD for short (Selic, 2006). MDD aims to make models the primary resource in all aspects of system engineering, and provide benefits of cost reduction and quality improvement.

Recently, OMG has proposed the MDA (*Model Driven Architecture*) that represents the OMG solution to support MDD. Software development in the MDA starts with a Platform-Independent Model (PIM) of an application's functionality and behavior, constructed using a modeling language. Following MDA, a PIM model should be mapped to a Platform model in order to obtain a Platform Specific Model (PSM). MDA relies on guided model transformations starting from high-level models until detailed models are obtained. Following MDA approaches, UML is not only used for specification, but also for analysis, synthesis and deployment. Nevertheless, stronger semantic

and specific profiles are required to enable the development of theses tools, since a formal semantic avoids ambiguity in the model capturing and interpretation, and a profile enables the use of model elements that have a specific role in the domain. This specific element can have a translation to a component in the final implementation, or follow a known pattern, facilitating synthesis and analysis.

We believe that the formal semantic defined by the UML2 meta-model will facilitate the implementation of complete code generation, and the use of profiles like MARTE will enable the development of analysis tools also for non functional requirements specifications. Since MARTE supports the detailed platform modeling, its usage together with UML enables one to use model-driven development approaches into the embedded systems design. However, MARTE does not cover methodological aspects: interface-based design, design space exploration, means to manage refinement of NFP measurement models, concrete processes to storage, bind, and display NFP context models, mapping to transform model of computation and communication into analysis models. Additionally, as of today there is a small number of tools that support the MARTE profile, but we believe that more tools will be available in the close future, and that the more formal semantic supported by UML2 will enable one to use models to achieve a complete system implementation and the definition of complete model-driven design methodologies.

## CONCLUSION

This chapter presented the UML language, the language evolution, the main supported diagrams and discussed UML usage in the embedded field, including limitations of the application of this language in this domain. A case study was developed in order to show the main UML diagrams through a real modeling example. Throughout this case study, we discuss the limitations of the language and we presented the main extensions proposed for the embedded domain, which are UML-SPT, SysML, UML profile for SoC and MARTE, and commented the progress obtained by these profiles. We discussed the modeling of embedded systems with UML and the UML profile for MARTE extending the previous case study. Since UML is proposed to be used for model-driven development, the model should be used not only for specification, but also for synthesis and deployment. This chapter also presented a discussion about the effort to generate code from UML diagrams and discussed the open issues to the successful use of UML in the embedded system design flow.

Several current projects in the embedded system domain apply UML as specification language. Therefore, its use should be widely expanded in the new generation of embedded systems thanks to the improvements of UML2 and the new UML profiles. The formal semantic of UML2 and the features provided by MARTE enable one to develop a powerful design flow for embedded systems. The MARTE modeling features enables one to specify an application model, and a detailed HW/SW embedded platform, as well as the allocation of software elements into hardware resources, allowing an effective model-based design. This separation of concerns aided by analysis tools enables the definition of design space exploration tools, which should be able to automatically explore different system solution, helping embedded systems designers to achieve an optimized solution for a system with limited resources.

## REFERENCES

Atlee, J. M., France, R., Georg, G., Moreira, A., Rumpe, B., & Zschaler, S. (2007). Modeling in software engineering. In *Proceedings of the International Conference on Software Engineering*.

Axelsson, J. (2000, December). Real-world modeling in UML. In *Proceedings of the 13th International Conference on Software and Systems Engineering and their Applications, Paris*.

Babu, E. M. M., Malinowski, A., Suzuki, J., & Matilda. (2005). A distributed UML virtual machine for model-driven software development. In *Proceedings of the World Multi-Conference on Systemics, Cybernetics, and Informatics*.

Berkenkötter, K., Bisanz, S., Hannemann, U., & Peleska, J. (2003). Hybrid UML profile for UML 2.0. In *Proceedings of the UML Workshop on Specification and Validation of UML Models for Real Time and Embedded Systems (SVERTS), San Francisco, USA*.

Bichler, L., Radermacher, A., & Schürr, A. (2004). Integrating data flow equations with UML/realtime. *Real-Time Systems, 26*, 107–125. doi:10.1023/B:TIME.0000009308.63403.e6

Björklund, D., Lilius, J., & Porres, I. (2005). Code generation for embedded systems. In S. Gérard, J. Babau & J. Champeau (Eds.), *Model driven engineering for distributed real-time embedded systems*. London: Hermes Science.

Boldt, R. (2007). Combining the power of Math-Works Simulink and Telelogic UML/SysML-based rhapsody to redefine the model-driven development experience. June, 2006. Telelogic white paper. Retrieved on February 23, 2007, from http://www.ilogix.com/whitepaper-overview.aspx

Booch, G. (1993). *Object-oriented analysis and design with applications, 2nd ed.* San Francisco: Benjamin Cummings.

Booch, G. (1999). *The unified modeling language user guide*. Boston: Addison Wesley.

Brisolara, L., Becker, L., Carro, L., Wagner, F., & Pereira, C. E. (2005a). A comparison between UML and function blocks for heterogeneous SoC design and ASIP generation. In G. Martin & W. Müller (Eds.), *UML for SoC design* (pp. 199-222). Dordrecht, The Netherlands: Springer.

Brisolara, L. B., Becker, L. B., Carro, L., Wagner, F. R., Pereira, C. E., & Reis, R. A. L. (2005b). Comparing high-level modeling approaches for embedded systems design. In *Proceedings of the Asia South Pacific Design Automation Conference, ASP-DAC,* Shanghai, China (pp. 986-989).

Brisolara, L. B., Oliveira, M. F. S., Redin, R., Lamb, L., Carro, L., & Wagner, F. (2008, March). Using UML as front-end for heterogeneous software code generation strategies. In *Proceedings of the Design, Automation and Test Conference, DATE,* Munich, Germany (pp. 504-509).

Carter, K. (2005). *iUML: Intelligent UML*. Retrieved on May 5, 2005, from http://www.kc.com

Douglass, B. P. (2004). *Real time UML: Advances in the UML for real-time systems, 3rd ed.* Boston: Addison Wesley.

Edwards, M., & Green, P. (2003). UML for hardware and software object modeling. In L. Lavagno, G. Martin & B. Selic (Eds.), *UML for real: Design of embedded real-time systems* (pp. 127-147). Norwell, USA: Kluwer Academic Publishers.

Edwards, S., Lavagno, L., Lee, E. A., & Sangiovanni-Vincentelli, A. (1997, March). Design of embedded systems: Formal models, validation, and synthesis. In *Proceedings of IEEE* (pp. 366-390).

Extessy (2007). Exite tool. Retrieved on May 25, 2007, from http://www.extessy.com/

Gomaa, H. (2000). *Designing concurrent, distributed, and real-time applications with UML*. Boston: Addison-Wesley.

Green, P. N., & Essa, S. (2004). Integrating the synchronous dataflow model with UML. In *Proceedings of the Design, Automation, and Test in Europe, DATE*. IEEE Press.

IBM. (2008). *IBM rational software architect, version 7.0*. Retrieved on May 10, 2008, from www.ibm.com

Jacobson, I., Christerson, M., Jonsson, P., & Overgaard, G. (1992). *Object-oriented software engineering: A use case driven approach*. Boston: Addison-Wesley.

Lavagno, L., Martin, G., & Selic, B. (Eds.). (2003). *UML for real: Design of embedded real-time systems*. Dordrecht, The Netherlands: Kluwer Academic.

Le Guennec, A., & Dion, B. (2006). Esterel technologies, bridging UML and safety-critical software development environments. In *Proceedings of the European Congress Embedded Real Time Software, ERTS*.

Martin, G., Lavagno, L., & Louis-Guerin, J. (2001). Embedded UML: A merger of real-time UML and codesign. In *Proceedings of the International Workshop on Hardware/Software Codesign, CODES* (pp. 23-28).

Martin, G., & Mueller, W. (Eds.). (2005). *UML for SoC design, v. 1*. Dordrecht, The Netherlands: Springer.

Mentor Graphics. (2005). *BridgePoint UML suite*. Retrieved on January 25, 2005, from http://www.projtech.com

Moser, E., & Nebel, W. (1999). Case study: System model of crane and embedded control. In *Proceedings of the Design, Automation, and Test in Europe, DATE*, Munich, Germany.

Mueller, W., Rosti, A., Bocchio, S., Riccobene, E., Scandurra, P., Dehaene, W., & Vanderperren, Y. (2006). UML for ESL design–basic principles, tools, and applications. In *Proceedings of the International Conference on Computer Aided Design, ICCAD* (pp. 73-80).

NoMagic. (2008). Retrieved on June 10, 2008, from www.magicdraw.com

OMG. Object Management Group. (1997). *Unified modeling language specification, v. 1.0*. Retrieved on May 2002, from http://www.omg.org

OMG. (2002). *UML profile for schedulability, performance, and time*. (OMG document no. ptc/02-03-02). Retrieved on March 15, 2004, from http://www.omg.org

OMG. (2003). *Model driven architecture*. (OMG document om/03-06-01) Retrieved on January 5, 2007, from http://www.omg.org/mda/

OMG. (2004). QoS&FT: *UML profile for modeling quality of service and fault tolerance characteristics and mechanisms*. (OMG document ptc/04-09-01). Retrieved on January 5, 2007, from http://www.omg.org

OMG. (2006a, January). *MOF: Metaobject facility (MOF) 2.0 specification*. Retrieved October 20, 2008, from http://www.omg.org/mof

OMG. (2006b, August). *UML profile for SoC specification, v1.0.1*. Retrieved on May 5, 2008, from http://www.omg.org/technology/documents/formal/profile_soc.htm

OMG. (2007b, September). *Systems modeling language (SysML) specification, version 1.0*. Retrieved on December 15, 2007, from http://www.omgsysml.org/

OMG. (2007c, November). *UML specification, version 2.1.2*. (OMG document: formal/2007-11-04). Retrieved on February 25, 2008, from www.omg.org/

OMG. (2007a). *MARTE specification beta 1*. (OMG document: ptc/07-08-04). Retrieved on June 2, 2008, from http://www.omg.org

Papyrus, U. M. L. (Ed.). home page. (2008). *Papyrus for MARTE*. Retrieved on June 2, 2008, from http://www.papyrusuml.org/

Pender, T. (2004). *UML bible*. New York: Wiley publishing.

Real-Time Innovation. (2007). *Constellation framework*. Retrieved on March 25, 2007, from http://www.rti.com/

Reichmann, C., Kühl, M., Graf, P., & Müller-Glaser, K. D. (2004). GeneralStore-a CASE-tool integration platform enabling model level coupling of heterogeneous designs for embedded electronic systems. In *Proceedings of the IEEE International Conference and Workshop on the Engineering of Computer-Based Systems, ECBS* (pp. 225- 232).

Rumbaugh, J., Blaha, M. R., Lorensen, W., Eddy, F., & Premerlani, W. (1991). *Object-oriented modeling and design*. New Jersey: Prentice Hall.

Selic, B. (2003). *Models, software models, and UML. UML for real: Design of embedded real-time systems* (pp. 1-16). Boston: Kluwer Academic Publishers.

Selic, B. (2006). UML 2: A model-driven development tool. Model-driven software development. *IBM Systems Journal, 45*(3), 607–620.

Singhoff, F., Legrand, J., Nana, L., & Marcé, L. (2004). Cheddar: A flexible real time scheduling framework. *ACM SIGAda Ada Letters, 24*(4), 1-8. New York: ACM Press.

Telelogic (2004). *Telelogic tau architecture/development*. Retrieved on October 24, 2004, from http://www.telelogic.com/

Telelogic (2008). *Telelogic rhapsody*. Retrieved on June 24, 2008, from http://www.telelogic.com/

Tri-Pacific Software. (2008). *RapidRMA*. Retrieved on June 20, 2008, from http http://www.tripac.com/

Vanderperren, Y., & Dehaene, W. (2006). From UML/SysML to Matlab/Simulink: Current state and future perspectives. In *Proceedings of the Design, Automation, and Test in Europe Conference, DATE* (pp.93-93).

Warmer, J., & Kleppe, A. (1998). *The object-constraint language: Precise modeling with UML* (p. 112). Boston: Addison-Wesley.

Zhu, Q., Nakata, T., Mine, M., & Kuroki, K. Endo, & Hasegawa, T. (2004). Integrating UML into SoC design process. In *UML for SoC Design Workshop*.

# Chapter 2
# Model–Driven Design and ASM–Based Validation of Embedded Systems

**Angelo Gargantini**
*Università di Bergamo, Italy*

**Elvinia Riccobene**
*Università degli Studi di Milano, Italy*

**Patrizia Scandurra**
*Università di Bergamo, Italy*

## ABSTRACT

*In the embedded system and System-on-Chip (SoC) design area, the increasing technological complexity coupled with requests for more performance and shorter time to market have caused a high interest for new methods, languages and tools capable of operating at higher levels of abstraction than the conventional system level. This chapter presents a model-driven and tool-assisted development process of SoCs, which is based on high-level UML design of system components, guarantees SystemC code generation from graphical models, and allows validation of system behaviors on formal models automatically derived from UML models. An environment for system design and analysis is also presented, which is based on a UML profile for SystemC and the Abstract State Machine formal method.*

## INTRODUCTION

In the Embedded System (ES) and System-on-Chip (SoC) design area, conventional system level design flows usually start by writing the system specification and developing a functional executable model. The system is refined through a set of abstraction levels, toward a final implementation in hardware and software. Nowadays it is an emerging practice to develop the functional model and refine it with the C/C++/SystemC languages (Gröetker et al., 2002). The hardware part of the system goes down to the Register Transfer Level (RTL) for the synthesis flow, while the software part can be either simulated at high (functional or transactional) level or compiled for an Instruction Set Simulator (ISS).

Recently, the increasing technological complexity coupled with requests for more performance

DOI: 10.4018/978-1-60566-750-8.ch002

and shorter time to market have caused a high interest for new methods, languages and tools capable of operating at higher levels of abstraction in the design process. Such an improvement has been achieved by exploiting visual software modeling languages like Unified Modeling Language (UML) (UML, 2005) to describe system specifications and generate from them executable models in C/C++/SystemC.

In the embedded system domain, the UML has been used mainly for documentation purposes. There are, indeed, some criticisms that are widely shared towards the use of the UML as modeling language. The UML includes a rich set of modeling elements that can be used for a wide range of applications, whereas modeling specific applications, as embedded systems and SoCs, would be easier using a more specialized (domain-specific) notation representing the basic elements and patterns of the target domain. Furthermore, the UML offers the possibility of designing the same system from different views (by different UML diagrams). Even if such a feature can be used to capture related aspects of a design from different prospective, it may result in inconsistencies between diagrams, when the use of UML is not coupled with a rigorous design discipline (Chen et al, 2003). Therefore, the use of the UML for the specific application domain of embedded system and SoC design requires:

- A domain specific language, called *profile*, built on the basic UML infrastructure and including domain-specific building blocks (defined using stereotypes) to model common design elements and patterns,
- A methodology defining how and when the profile notation should be used.

According to these requirements, in (Riccobene et al., 2005a, Riccobene et al., 2005b, Riccobene et al., 2007a) a UML2 profile for SystemC is presented, which lifts the SystemC language to the UML modeling level. It represents a set of structural and behavioral constructs for designing at system-level with automatic encoding in SystemC. With this approach, the standard UML language is applied as high-level system modeling language and operates in synergy with a lower-level system language. To foster the methodology in a systematic and seamless way, in (Riccobene et al., 2007b) a SoC design process, called UPSoC (Unified Process for SoC), is presented as extension of the conventional Unified Process (Arlow & Neustadt, 2002) for the SoC refinement flow. The UPSoC process has been developed following the principles of the Object Management Group (OMG) Model-driven Architecture (MDA) (Mellor et al., 2004) -- a framework for Model-driven Engineering (MDE) (Bezivin, 2005), according to which a system development process should rely on modeling, model transformations and automated mapping of models to implementations. Indeed, the UPSoC is based on *model-to-model* and *model-to-code* model transformations from abstract models towards refined (but still abstract) models and/or SystemC code models.

Even if modeling methods based on the UML and UML profiles have receiving increasing interest in the embedded system and SoC contexts as they allow modeling at a higher level of abstraction than that of system-level languages, UML-based design methods still suffer the lack of effective formal analysis (validation & verification) techniques. Formal methods and analysis tools have been most often applied to low level hardware design. But, these techniques are not applicable to system descriptions given in terms of programs of system-level languages (like SystemC, SpecC, etc.), since such languages are closer to concurrent software than to traditional hardware description (Vardi, 2007), and the focus in the literature so far has been mainly on traditional code-based simulation techniques. Moreover, classical analysis techniques are not directly applicable to UML-based design methods that lack of a strong mathematical foundation necessary for formal model analysis.

We tackle the problem of formally analyzing high-level UML SoC descriptions by joining the SystemC UML modeling language with a formal method, capable of eliminating ambiguities in the UML semantics, and using analysis techniques applicable to formal models. Therefore, we have complemented our UPSoC design process with a formal analysis process allowing system components to be functionally validated and verified early at high levels of abstraction, and even in a semi-transparent way (i.e. no strong skills and expertise on formal methods are required to the user) by the use of the Abstract State Machine (ASM) formal method (Börger & Stärk, 2003) and its related tools (Asmeta, 2007).

In this chapter, we present a model-driven methodology for the SoC design, which involves the SystemC UML profile as major system modeling notation and the Abstract State Machines as formal support for validation of system behavior. The modeling activity can be performed at different levels of abstraction, from a high functional level down to the Register Transfer Level (RTL). Model-to-code transformations allow automatic mapping of UML models to SystemC code, while model-to-model transformations provide automatic mapping of SystemC UML graphical model to formal models suitable for application of model analyses standard techniques.

A supporting environment for both processes of SoC design and validation is also presented. The *modeling kit* of this environment assists the designer along the modeling activity and provides SystemC code generation/back-annotation from/to UML modes. The validation process is supported by an *analysis kit* built upon the ASMETA toolset – a set of tools around ASMs --, which operates on the formal specification of the system.

As case study, the Counter system taken from the standard SystemC distribution will be considered to illustrate how to design and validate a SoC by our approach. The design model is developed using the SystemC UML profile. We then show how the UML model of the underlying system is automatically mapped into a corresponding ASM model, and how to validate the system functionality by techniques based on simulation and scenarios construction.

The remainder of this chapter is organized as follows. Sect. *Background* quotes some related work and provides an overview of the SystemC UML profile explaining the rationality behind the development of a UML profile for the SoC design. It also briefly summarizes the application of formal methods to specify and analyze embedded systems, and presents and justifies the choice of the ASMs as formal support for our design methodology. Sect. *Model-driven SoC design and analysis flow* describes the overall SoC design and analyses flow, at the light of the MDA principles. It also comments on the advantages of a model-driven methodology with respect to a code design for the development of SoCs. Sect. *SoC modeling & validation environment* describes the architecture and the tool components of the supporting design and validation environment. Sect. *The Counter case study* presents the application of our design methodology to the case study. Sect. *Industrial application* discusses some industrial case studies. Sect. *Future Trends* sketches some future directions. Finally, Sect. *Conclusion* provides some concluding remarks.

## BACKGROUND

This section provides an overview of existing work concerning model-driven approaches for embedded system and SoC modeling using UML and UML profiles, and on the formal analyses of UML design models. It also introduces the reader to the main notations used in our approach, namely the UML profile of the SystemC language and the Abstract State Machines. It also justifies the choice of the formal method we use for analyses purposes, in relation to the models of computation most commonly used in the area of embedded system and SoC modeling.

## Related Work

The possibility to use UML 1.x for system design (Martin, 1999) started since 1999, but the general opinion at that time was that UML was not mature enough as a system design language. Nevertheless significant industrial experiences using UML in a system design process soon started leading to the first results in design methodology, such as the one in (Moore et al., 2002) that was applied to an internal project for the development of a OFDM Wireless LAN chipset. In that project, SystemC was used to provide executable models.

More integrated design methodologies were later developed. The authors of (Zhu et al., 2004) propose a methodology using UML for the specification and validation of SoC design. They define a flow, parallel to the implementation flow, which is focused on high-level specs capture and validation. In (Lavagno et al., 2003), a UML profile for a *platform-based* approach to embedded software development is presented. It includes stereotypes to represent platform services and resources that can be assembled together. The authors also present a design methodology supported by a design environment, called Metropolis, where a set of UML diagrams (use cases, classes, state machines, activity and sequence diagrams) can be used to capture the functionality and then refine it by adding models of computation. Another approach to the unification of UML and SoC design is the HASoC (Hardware and Software Objects on Chip) (Edwards & Green, 2003) methodology. It is based on the UML-RT profile (Selic, 2003) and on the RUP process (Kruchten, 1999). The design process starts with an *uncommitted model,* then a *committed model* is derived by partitioning the system into software and hardware, which is finally mapped onto a system platform. From these models a SystemC skeleton code can be also generated, but to provide a finer degree of behavioral validation, detailed C++ code must be added by hand to the skeleton code. All the works

mentioned above could greatly benefit from the use of UML2 (UML, 2005).

In (do Nascimento et al., 2007), the authors present a model-driven framework, called ModES (Model-driven Design of ES), made of metamodels definition and APIs to integrate, by model transformations, several model-based design tools. However, this framework is more related to the design space exploration at a high abstraction level than to model refinement, model validation, and automatic code generation from models, which are, instead, our main concerns.

SysML (SysML, 2007) is an extension of the UML2 for a domain-neutral representation of *system engineering* applications. It can be involved at the beginning of the design process, in place of the UML, for the requirements, analysis, and functional design workflows. So it is in agreement with the SystemC UML profile, which can be thought (and effectively made) as customization of SysML rather than UML. Unluckily, when we started the SysML specification was not yet finalized and there were no tools yet supporting it. Similar considerations apply also to the recent MARTE (Modeling and Analysis of Real-Time Embedded Systems) profile initiative (Rioux et al., 2005; MARTE, 2008).

The standardization proposal (USoC, 2005) by Fujitsu, in collaboration with IBM and NEC, has evident similarities with the SystemC UML profile, like the choice of SystemC as a target implementation language. However, their profile does not provide building blocks for behavior modeling, neither any time model.

Some other proposals already exist about extensions of UML towards C/C++/SystemC. All have in common the use of UML stereotypes for SystemC constructs, but do not rely on a UML profile definition. In this sense, it is appreciable the work in (Bruschi & Sciuto, 2002) attempting to define a UML profile for SystemC; but, as all the other proposals, it is based on the previous version of UML, UML 1.4. Moreover, in all the proposals we have seen, no code generation, except in (Nguyen et al., 2005), from behavioral diagrams is considered.

Concerning the analysis (i.e. the validation and verification) of UML-based embedded system descriptions, in (Patel & Shukla, 2007) the authors present a model-driven development and validation process which begins by creating (from a natural language specification of the system requirements) a functional abstract model and (still manually) a SystemC implementation model. The abstract model is described using the Abstract State Machine Language (AsmL) – another implementation language for ASMs. Our methodology, instead, benefits from the use of the UML as design entry-level and of model translators that provide automation and ensure consistency among descriptions in different notations (such those in SystemC and ASMs). In (Patel & Shukla, 2007), a designer can visually explore the actions of interest in the ASM model using the Spec Explorer tool and generate tests. These tests are used to drive the SystemC implementation from the ASM model to check whether the implementation model conforms to the abstract model (*conformance testing*). The test generation capability is limited and not scalable. In order to generate tests, the internal algorithm of Spec Explorer extracts a finite state machine (FSM) from ASM specifications and then use test generation techniques for FSMs. The effectiveness of their methodology is therefore severely constrained by the limits inherited from the use of Spec Explorer. The authors themselves say that the main difficulty is in using Spec Explorer and its methods for state space pruning and exploration. The ASMETA ATGT (Asmeta, 2007) tool that we intend to use for the same scope exploits, instead, the method of model checking to generate test sequences, and it is based on a direct encoding of ASMs in PROMELA, the language of the model checker SPIN (Holzmann, 1997).

The work in (Habibi & Tahar, 2006) also uses AsmL and Spec Explorer to settle a development

and verification methodology for SystemC. They focus on assertion based verification of SystemC designs using the Property Specification Language (PSL), and although they mention test case generation as a possibility, the validation aspect is largely ignored. We were not able to investigate carefully their work as their tools are unavailable. Moreover, it should be noted that approaches in (Patel & Shukla, 2007; Habibi & Tahar, 2006), although using the Spec Explorer tool, do not exploit the scenario-based validation feature of Spec Explorer.

In (Mathaikutty et al., 2007), a model-driven methodology for development and validation of system-level SystemC designs is presented. The design flow is entirely based on the specification of a functional model (reference model) in the ESTEREL language, a state machine formalism, and on the use of the ESTEREL Studio development environment for the purpose of test generation. This approach provides coverage-directed test suite generation for system level design validation.

Authors in (Bruschi et al., 2005) provide test case generation by performing *static analysis* on SystemC designs. This approach is limited by the strength of the static analysis tools, and the lack of flexibility in describing the reachable states of interest for directed test generation. Moreover, static analysis requires sophisticated syntactic analysis and the construction of a semantic model, which for a language like SystemC (built on C++) is difficult due to the lack of formal semantics.

The SystemC Verification Library (Open SystemC Initiative, 2008) is a standard for developing test-benches for SoC designs. It provides API for transaction-based verification, constrained and weighted randomization, exception handling, and HDL-connection. These techniques are applicable at SystemC code level, while we aim at developing formal techniques for validation of SystemC system designs at model level.

The Message Sequence Chart (MSC) notation (MSC, 1999), originally developed for telecom-

*Figure 1. SystemC Language Architecture*

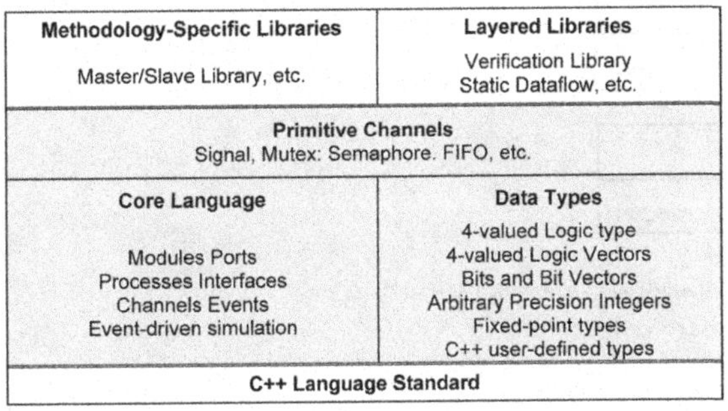

| Methodology-Specific Libraries | Layered Libraries |
|---|---|
| Master/Slave Library, etc. | Verification Library<br>Static Dataflow, etc. |

| Primitive Channels |
|---|
| Signal, Mutex: Semaphore. FIFO, etc. |

| Core Language | Data Types |
|---|---|
| Modules Ports<br>Processes Interfaces<br>Channels Events<br>Event-driven simulation | 4-valued Logic type<br>4-valued Logic Vectors<br>Bits and Bit Vectors<br>Arbitrary Precision Integers<br>Fixed-point types<br>C++ user-defined types |

| C++ Language Standard |
|---|

munication systems, can be adapted to embedded systems to allow validation. For instance, in (Kogel et al., 2004) MSC is adopted to visualize the simulation of SystemC models. The traces are only displayed and not validated, and the authors report the difficulties of adopting a graphical notation like MSC. Our approach is similar to that presented in (Haroud et al., 2004), where the MSCs are validated against the SDL model, from which a SystemC implementation is derived. MSCs are also generated by the SDL model and replayed to cross validation and regression testing.

## The SystemC UML Profile: An Overview

The UML has been used in areas for which it was not originally intended. Many proposals have been arisen for extending the UML for specific domains as banking, telecommunications, aerospace, real-time systems, etc. These extensions are called *profiles*. UML profiles provide a standard and generic extension mechanism for customizing UML models for particular domains and platforms. Since a complete coverage of the UML is beyond the scope of this chapter, we suppose the reader familiar with UML2 (UML, 2005). We here provide some background information on the SystemC standard and on the UML extension mechanism based on profiles, and then present the SystemC UML profile.

## SystemC

SystemC (Open SystemC Initiative, 2008; SystemC, 2006) is an IEEE standard controlled by the major companies in the Electronic Design Automation (EDA) industry. It is a system-level design language intended to support the description and validation of complex systems in an environment completely based on the C++ programming language. SystemC is defined in terms of a C++ class library, organized according to a layered-architecture shown in Figure 1 (adapted from Gröetker et al., 2002).

The *Core Language* and *Data Types* are the so called *core layer* (or layer 0) of the standard SystemC, and consists of the event-based and discrete-timed SystemC simulation kernel, the core design primitives (modules, ports, channels, etc.) and data types. The *Primitive Channels* represents, instead, the layer 1 of SystemC; it comes with a predefined set of interfaces, ports and channels for commonly used communication mechanisms such as signals and fifos. Finally, the external libraries layer on top of the layer 1 are not considered as part of the standard SystemC language.

A design of a system in SystemC is essentially given by a containment hierarchy of *modules*. A *module* is a container class able to encapsulate *structure* and *functionality* of hardware/software blocks. Each module may contain *variables* as simple data members, *ports* for communication with the surrounding environment and *processes* for performing module's functionality and expressing concurrency in the system. Two kinds of processes are available: *method* processes and *thread* processes. They run concurrently in the design and may be sensitive to *events* which are notified by other processes. A port of a module is a proxy object through which the process accesses to a *channel* interface. The *interface* defines the set of access functions for a channel, while the channel provides the implementation of these functions to serve as a container to encapsulate

*Figure 2. sc_port stereotype*

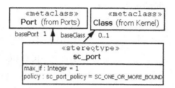

*English:* A port can have exactly one required interface and no provided interfaces.
*OCL:* basePort.required->size()=1 and basePort.provided->size()=0

the *communication* of blocks. There are two kinds of channels: *primitive channels* and *hierarchical channels*. Primitive channels do not exhibit any visible structure, do not contain processes, and cannot (directly) access other primitive channels. A hierarchical channel is a module, i.e., it can have structure, it can contain processes, and it can directly access other channels.

## UML Profiles

A UML profile is a set of *stereotypes*. Each stereotype defines how the syntax and the semantics of an existing UML construct (a class of the UML metamodel) is extended for a specific domain terminology or purpose. A stereotype can define additional semantic *constraints* – the *well-formedness rules* – expressed as OCL (Object Constraint Language) formula over the base metaclass to enforce a semantic restriction of the extended modeling element, as well as *tags* to state additional properties. Figure 2 shows an example of stereotype definition for the concept of "port" in SystemC (sc_port) together with an example of OCL constraint.

At model level, when a stereotype is applied to a model element (an instance of a UML metaclass), an instance of a stereotype is linked to the model element. From a notational point of view, the name of the stereotype is shown within a pair of guillemets above or before the name of the model element and the eventual tagged values displayed inside or close as name-value pairs. Examples of

stereotypes application are provided in Sect. *The SystemC UML profile* (see Figure 6, e.g., for the sc_port stereotype).

## The SystemC UML profile

The UML2 profile for SystemC (Riccobene et al., 2005b) is a consistent set of modeling constructs designed to lift both structural and behavioral constructs of SystemC (including events and time features) to the UML modeling level.

The profile is defined at two distinct levels, reflecting the layered-architecture of SystemC: the *basic SystemC profile* for the core layer (or layer 0) of SystemC, and the *extended SystemC profile* for the SystemC layer of predefined channels, ports and interfaces (or layer 1). This last is provided either as a UML class library, modelled with the basic stereotypes of the basic SystemC profile, or as a group of standalone stereotypes – – specializing the basic SystemC profile.

Figure 3 summarizes the essential UML diagrams used in the profile.

Below, we briefly present the most significant modeling elements of the basic SystemC profile. It is logically structured in three parts: structure and communication, behavior and synchronization, and data types.

The **Structure and Communication** part defines stereotypes for the SystemC basic structural modeling elements (modules, interfaces, ports and channels) for use in UML structural diagrams like UML class diagrams and composite

*Figure 3. UML diagrams in the SystemC profile*

| Diagram | Purpose |
|---|---|
| **Class Diagram** | To define modules, channels, interface, port types |
| **Composite Structure Diagram** | To describe how parts of modules and channels are connected to each other to form the internal structure of a container module |
| **State Diagram** | Used as method state machine to describe the reactive behavior of processes/operations of modules and channels |
| **Object Diagram** | Derived from a composite structure diagram by instantiating parts and connectors, to describe a particular configuration (also partial) of the system |

*Figure 4. Structure and Communication Stereotypes*

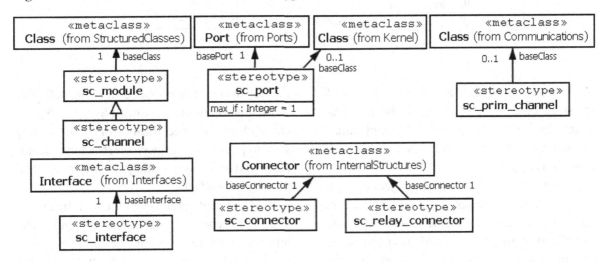

structure diagrams. Figure 4 shows the stereotypes definition using the standard notation of UML profiles, while Figure 5 shows the concrete notation of these stereotypes when applied at model level.

The sc_module stereotype defines a SystemC module as extension of a UML structured class.

As structured class, a composite structure (diagram) can be further associated to a module to represent its internal structure (if any) made of channel and other module parts[1]. Furthermore, modules containing reactive processes are considered *active* classes (and hence shown by a class box with additional vertical bars).

*Figure 5. Structure Stereotypes Notation*

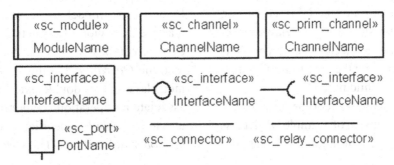

*Figure 6. Modules, ports and interfaces*

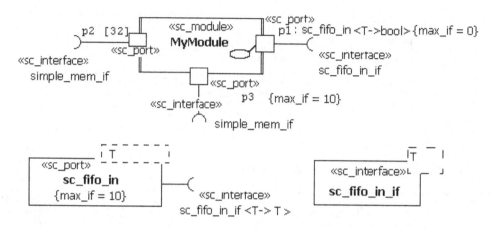

In SystemC, an interface defines the set of access functions (methods) for a channel. The sc_interface stereotype defines a SystemC interface as a UML interface, and uses its (longhand/shorthand) notation.

A port of a module is a proxy object through which a process accesses to a channel interface. The sc_port stereotype maps the notion of SystemC port directly to the notion of UML port, plus some constraints to capture the concepts of simple, multi and behaviour port. The tag max_if defined for the port stereotype specifies the maximum number of channel interfaces that may be attached to the port. The type of a port, namely its required interface, is shown with the socket icon attached to the port. Figure 6 shows an example of a SystemC module exposing a multi-port, an array port, and a simple port, together with the port type and the interface definitions of the simple port.

Since UML ports are linked by connectors, a SystemC connector (binding of ports to channels) is provided as extension of the UML connector, by the sc_connector stereotype. A relay connector -- the sc_relay_connector stereotype -- is also defined to represent the port-to-port binding between parent and child ports[2].

The sc_prim_channel stereotype defines a primate channel as extension of a simple UML class that implements a certain number of interfaces (i.e. the provided interfaces of the channel). The sc_channel stereotype defines a SystemC hierarchical channel as specialization of the sc_module stereotype as it may further have structure (including ports) and may contain processes other than providing interfaces.

UML class diagrams are used to define modules, port types, interfaces and channels. The internal structure of composite modules (or of hierarchical channels), especially the one of the topmost level module (for the structure of the overall system), is captured by UML composite structure diagrams; then, from these diagrams several UML object diagrams can be created to describe different configuration scenarios. This separation allows the specification (also partial) of different HW platforms as instances of the same parametric model (i.e. the composite structure diagram).

The **Behavior and Synchronization** part defines special state and action stereotypes (see Figure 7) to model the control flow and the reactive behavior of SystemC processes. The two stereotypes sc_method and sc_th-read extend the *Operation* and the *StateMachine* UML metaclasses. This double extension allows us to associate an operation (i.e. a process of a module) to its behavior specified in terms of a UML *method* state machine[3]. These stereotypes lead to

*Figure 7. Behavioral Stereotypes*

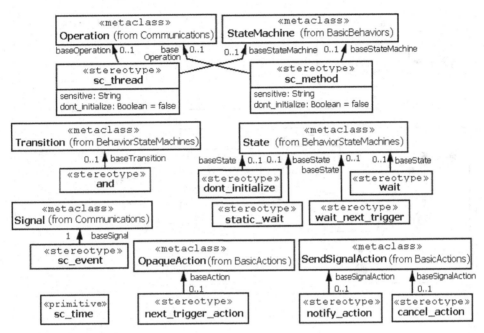

a new formalism, called *SystemC Process State Machines*, defined as extension of the UML state machines.

Each kind of process has a slight different behavior, but basically all processes: run concurrently, are sequential, and are activated (if terminated or simply suspended) on the base of their own sensitivity, which consists of an initial list of zero, one or more events -- the *static sensitivity* of a process (specified as a list attached to the process operation in the container module) -- and can dynamically change at run time realizing the so called *dynamic sensitivity* mechanism. Stereotypes wait, static_wait, and, wait_next_trigger, next_trigger_action, and dont_initialize model the dynamic sensitivity mechanism of a process behavior (a thread or a method).

The sc_event stereotype models a SystemC event in terms of a UML signal (instance of the class *SignalEvent*). The notify_action stereotype can be applied to an UML action to model the SystemC function notify used to notify events. The cancel_action stereotype can be applied to an UML action to model the SystemC function

cancel used to eliminate a pending notification of an event.

The sc_time type is used to specify concrete time values used for setting clocks objects, or for the specification of UML time triggers.

In addition to these stereotypes, a finite number of *abstract behavior patterns* of process state machines have been identified. Figure 8 depicts one of these behavior patterns together with the corresponding SystemC pseudo-code for a thread that: (i) is not initialized, (ii) has both a static (the event list $e_{1}, ..., e_{Ns}$) and a dynamic sensitivity (the wait state), and (iii) runs continuously (by the infinite while loop). Note that activities a1 and a2 stand for blocks of sequential (or not) code without wait statements. Moreover, the notation used for the wait state in the pattern in Figure 8 stands for a shortcut to denote a generic wait(e*) statement where the event e* matches one of the cases reported in Figure 9 (each arc is a *run to completion* step of UML state machines).

It should be noted that the state machine pattern depicted in Figure 8 can be more complex in case of one or more wait statements are enclosed

*Figure 8. A thread process pattern*

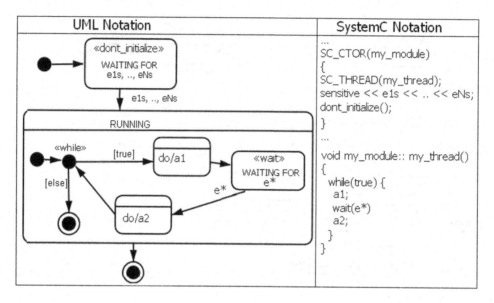

*Figure 9. Dynamic Sensitivity of a Thread*

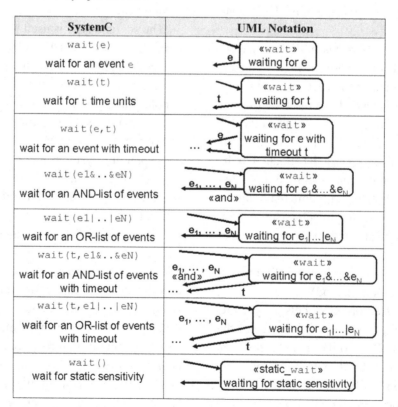

in the scope of one or more nested control structures. In this case, as part of the UML profile for SystemC, the control structures while, if, etc. need to be explicitly represented in terms of special stereotyped junction or choice pseudostates[4] combined together in order to stand out the state-like representation of the wait calls. The infinite loop mechanism of the thread process in Figure 8, for example, is modelled with a while stereotyped pseudostate with a true guard on the outgoing transition. These control stereotypes allow us to effectively generate code from state diagrams in a style that reflects the nature of constructs of the target implementation language, despite to well know techniques (like state pattern, stable table pattern, etc.) existing to achieve this goal.

The **Data types** part defines a UML class library to represent the set of SystemC data types.

## Formal Methods for Embedded System Design

The embedded systems and SoCs design approach currently used in the industry, is still informal and system requirements and functionality are expressed in natural language. The inherent ambiguities of an informal specification prevent a meaningful analysis of the system and may result in misunderstandings with customers and in incorrect or inefficient decisions at the time when the design is partitioned and the tasks are assigned to different teams. Therefore, it is nowadays widely acknowledged that an abstract mathematical model is an essential ingredient for a sound system-level design methodology (Sgroi et al., 2000). Indeed, a formal model permits (a) to unambiguously capture the required functionality and other nonfunctional constraints (e.g., performance, cost, power consumption, and quality of service); (b) to verify the correctness of the functional specification with respect to its desired properties (e.g., satisfaction of temporal logic properties or expected simulation behav-

ior); (c) model refinement to include stepwise design decisions and implementation details to synthesize part of the specification onto the chosen architectural and communication resources, and the possibility to verify the correctness of the refinement; (d) the use of different tools, all understanding (possibly different aspects of) the model. In literature, there exist different Models of Computation (MOCs) that have been used for system design. Among the main MOCs, we can cite: discrete event models, data flow process networks, Petri nets, synchronous and asynchronous finite state machines together with their extensions. For a complete and detailed presentation and comparison of them, we refer the reader to (Edwards et al., 1997), while in the rest of this section, we introduce the concept of Abstract State Machines (ASMs) (Börger & Stärk, 2003) that represent an extension of Finite State Machines and have been widely applied as high-level system design and analysis method in the area of the embedded systems. A complete mathematical definition of the ASM method can be found in (Börger & Stärk, 2003), together with a presentation of the great variety of its application.

Certainly, ASMs could be themselves used as systems engineering method, and thanks to the notion of model refinement (Börger, 2003), which allows mapping abstract specifications into code through a sequence of refinement steps (Beierle et al., 1995; Börger et al., 2000), they are able to guide the development of embedded hardware/software systems seamlessly from requirements capture to their implementation. However, this is not the view of ASMs that we prefer to give here. Indeed, we like to integrate this formal method into a system development process where design models are developed using a graphical front-end conforming to the current industrial standard, i.e. the UML targeted for the SoC application domain, and the ASMs can be adopted to provide formal intermediate representations of the intended system, which can be used for several goals (abstract representation, models refinement, behavioral validation, properties verification, etc.) according to the designer needs.

The choice of the ASM as formal support for model analyses in intentional and due to the following main reasons:

a. ASMs capture the principal models of computation and specification in the literature (Börger & Stärk, 2003 (cap 7)), and therefore, ASMs have the potentiality to smoothly integrate useful concepts and techniques which have been tailored and are successfully applied for specific goals or application domains.

b. Although the ASM method comes with a rigorous scientific foundation, the practitioner needs no special training to use it since it can be understood correctly as pseudo-code or Virtual Machines working over abstract data structures.

c. ASM models are executable specifications, therefore suitable for high-level model validation, and they are supported by a set of tools for model simulation, testing, and verification.

d. It is endowed with a metamodel (Asmeta, 2007) defining the ASM abstract syntax in terms of an object-oriented representation. The metamodel availability allows automatic mapping of SystemC UML models into ASM models by exploiting MDE techniques of automatic models transformation (Zhang et al., 2008).

## Abstract State Machines and the ASMETA toolset

Abstract State Machines (Börger & Stärk, 2003) are an extension of Finite State Machines, where unstructured "internal" control states are replaced by states comprising arbitrary complex data. The *states* of an ASM are multi-sorted first-order structures, i.e. domains of objects with functions

*Figure 10. The ASMETA tool set*

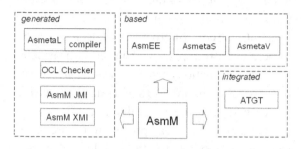

and predicates defined on them. The *transition relation* is specified by "rules" describing the modification of the functions from one state to the next. The basic form of a transition rule is the *guarded update* having form **if** *Condition* **then** *Updates*, where *Updates* are a set of function updates of the form $f(t_1, ... t_n) := t$ and are simultaneously executed[5] when *Condition* is true.

An ASM $M$ is a finite set of rules for such guarded multiple function updates. State transitions of $M$ may be influenced in two ways: *internally*, through the transition rules, or *externally* through the modifications of the environment. A *computation* of $M$ is a finite or infinite sequence $S_0, S_1, ... S_n$ of states of $M$, where $S_0$ is an initial state and each $S_{n+1}$ is obtained from $S_n$ by firing simultaneously all of the transition rules which are enabled in .

The notion of ASMs moves from a definition which formalizes simultaneous parallel actions of a single agent, either in an atomic way, *Basic ASMs*, and in a structured and recursive way, *Structured or Turbo ASMs*, to a generalization where multiple agents interact *Multi-agent ASMs*. Appropriate rule constructors also allow non-determinism (existential quantification) and unrestricted synchronous parallelism (universal quantification).

The *ASMETA* (ASM mETA modeling) toolset[6] (Gargantini et al., 2007; Asmeta, 2007) is a set of tools around ASMs developed according to the model-driven development principles. At the core of the toolset (see Figure 10), the *AsmM metamodel* is a complete meta-level representation of ASMs concepts based on the OMG's Meta-Object-Facility (MOF). AsmM is also available in the meta-language EMF/Ecore thanks to the ATL-KM3 plug-in which allows model transformations both in the EMF and MOF modeling spaces.

The ASMETA toolset includes, among other things,

- A textual notation, *AsmetaL*, to write ASM models (conforming to the AsmM) in a textual and human-comprehensible form;
- A text-to-model compiler, *AsmetaLc,* and the *OCL Checker*, to parse respectively AsmetaL models and check for their consistency w.r.t. the AsmM OCL constraints;
- An XMI (XML Metadata Interchange) interchange format for ASM models, JMI (Java Metadata Interfaces) APIs for the creation, storage, access and manipulation of ASM models;
- A simulator, *AsmetaS*, to execute ASM models,
- The *Avalla* language and the *AsmetaV* validator for scenario-based validation of ASM models
- The *ATGT* tool for automatic test case generation from ASM models, which is based upon the SPIN model checker (Holzmann, 1997);
- An Eclipse plug-in called *ASMEE* (ASM Eclipse Environment) which acts as graphical front-end to edit, manipulate, and export ASM models by using all tools/artifacts listed above.

More details on these tools and on how we have targeted them for our goal are provided in Sect. *SoC Modeling and validation environment*.

## MODEL-DRIVEN SOC DESIGN AND ANALYSIS FLOW

The *model-driven design methodology* we are presenting, has been developed (Riccobene et al., 2005a; Riccobene et al., 2007a) according to the principles of the MDA approach, namely (a) high-level modeling, (b) automated mapping of models to implementations, and (c) model transformations.

Our design process starts by applying the SystemC UML profile presented in Sec. The SystemC UML profile, to develop a high-*level UML model of the system* from its informal requirements or from its higher-level description in terms of a platform independent model (which can be developed by, for example, SysML or MARTE).

The modeling activity can be performed at different levels of abstraction. It is possible to create a pure *functional model*, or to add timing information in a *functional-timed model*. A *transactional model* describes abstract communication by transactions, which are protocols exchanging complex data with associated timing information. It is possible modeling the details of the implementation platform with a *behavioural model* (which is pin and functionally accurate), by a *Bus Cycle Accurate model* (which is also cycle accurate at its boundaries), or by a *RTL model* (the model is described as transfer of information between registers). Each model is an instance of the SystemC UML profile metamodel.

*Model-to-code* transformations allow automatic mapping of SystemC UML models into SystemC executable code, at a fixed abstraction level.

The SystemC UML profile provides in a graphical way all modeling elements for SoC design, and exactly resembles the modeling primitives of SystemC. Indeed, the intention of defining this profile was to lift SystemC at the UML level so to use the UML for platform-specific modeling of SoCs. Through different case studies (see Sect. *Industrial application*), we performed an evaluation of modeling with our UML based methodology compared to coding. An immediate benefit is a significant reduction in the effort to produce the final code (there is a big saving in the number of lines that are written by hand, especially redundant lines of code due to the C++ syntax are avoided), but the greatest benefits are in terms of model documentation, maintenance and reuse. Furthermore, high-level SystemC UML modeling allows more flexibility than coding. Indeed, well-established abstraction/refinement patterns coming from hardware/system engineering and till now only used at code level with great difficulty, can be easily managed (possibly automatically by appropriate model transformation engines) as *model-to-model transformation* steps along the modeling process from a high functional level model down to a RTL model. Their application at the UML level, by the use of the SystemC UML profile, guarantees (possibly) automatic and traceable evolution of the system. Furthermore, proving correctness of the refinement process and system properties is a very hard, and we can say impossible, activity at code level, whereas, it is feasible at model level with the aid of suitable formal analysis tools.

Automatic *model-to-model* transformations are at the base of the *formal analyses flow* that we propose. The process starts by automatically mapping a SystemC UML model into an ASM, moving from a visual graphical view of the system to a formal view. Once the ASM specification of the system is generated, several analyses activities can be performed, i.e. validation, verification, and conformance testing.

Validation is intended as the process of investigating a model (intended as formal specification) with respect to its user perceptions, in order to ensure that the specification really reflects the user needs and statements about the application, and to detect faults in the specification as early as possible with limited effort. Techniques for validation include *scenarios generation,* when the user builds scenarios describing the behavior

of a system by looking at the observable interactions between the system and its environment in specific situations; *simulation,* when the user provides certain input and observes if the output is the expected one or not (it is similar to code debugging); model-based *testing,* when the specification is used as oracle to compute test cases for a given critical behavior of the system at the same level of the specification. These abstract test cases cannot be executed at code level since they are at a wrong level of abstraction. Executable test cases must be derived from the abstract ones and executed at code level to guarantee *conformance* between model and code. In any case, validation should precede the application of more expensive and accurate methods, like requirements formal analysis and verification of properties, which should be applied only when a designer has enough confidence that the specification captures all informal requirements. Formal verification has to be intended as the mathematical proof of system properties, which can be carried on by hand or by the aid of model checkers (which are usable when the variable ranges are finite) or of theorem provers (which require strong user skills to drive the proof).

Currently, system validation is fully supported in our framework, as described in the next section, through simulation and scenarios construction. Future advanced analyses features have been planned, as explained in Sect. *Future Trends*.

## SOC MODELING & VALIDATION ENVIRONMENT

The Modeling & Validation environment works as front-end for consolidated lower level co-design tools, and is intended to assist the designer across the refinement steps in the modeling activity, from a high-level functional UML model of the system down to the SystemC RTL level. Figure 11 shows the general architecture of the proposed environment. It consists of two major parts: a

*Figure 11. Modeling and Analysis tool*

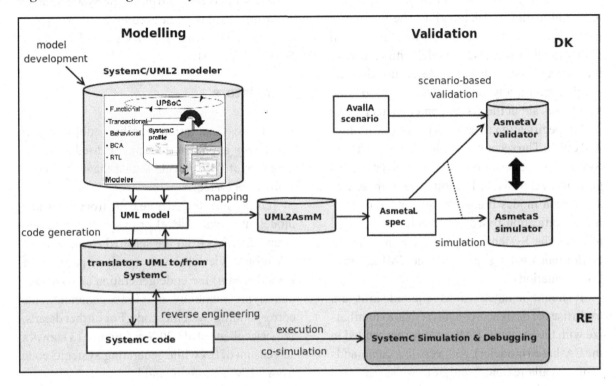

runtime environment (RE) that is the SystemC execution engine, and a development kit (DK) consisting of a UML2 *modeler* supporting the UML profile for SystemC and for multi-thread C, *translators* for forward/reverse engineering to/from C/C++/SystemC, and a *Validation toolset* based on the ASM formal method. The modeler is based on the Enterprise Architect (EA) UML tool by Sparx Systems. The validation toolset is built upon the ASMETA toolset (Asmeta, 2007).

Figure 11 also shows the phases (denoted with a label) the designer undertakes in the overall SoC modeling and validation process. The modeling process starts by *developing a model* written with the SystemC UML profile going through a sequence of refinement steps from a high-level functional UML model down to a UML model at RTL level, as already explained in the previous section. At each abstraction level, by automatic *code generation*, a unique SystemC specification (for both the structural and behavioural aspects)

is obtained from the UML model. The resulting code can be executed in the SystemC simulation environment at suitable abstraction levels (from transactional downto RTL). The code generation flow is complemented by a *reverse engineering* flow to transform SystemC programs into UML models.

The validation process starts by applying the *mapping* of the SystemC-UML model of the system (exported from the EA-based modeler) into a corresponding ASM model (written in AsmetaL). This transformation has been defined (once for all) by establishing a set of semantic mapping rules between the SystemC UML profile and the AsmM metamodel. The UML2AsmM transformation is completely automatic by means of the ATL engine developed within the Eclipse Modeling Project as implementation of the OMG QVT (QVT, 2007) standard.

Two different levels of model execution for analysis are supported by our environment: (i) the simulation based on AsmetaS; (ii) the SystemC simulation and debugging. The first one is more abstract and aimed at high-level functional validation to investigate a model with respect to the desired system behavior to ensure that the specification really reflects the user needs and statements about the system, and to detect faults in the specification as early as possible with limited effort. The second one is low-level, based on SystemC code, and necessary to deliver correct system-level designs. The joint use of these two simulation modes brings the advantage of having specification-based test oracles to be used to drive the SystemC implementation code for conformance testing (and to test the UML2AsmM transformation).

It should be noted that as required skills and expertise the designer (or analyst) has to familiarize with the SystemC UML profile (embedded in the EA-based modeler), with very few commands of the Avalla textual notation to write pertinent ASM validation scenarios, and with property specification notations like temporal logics.

A brief description of each tool component follows.

## The Modeler

It is built upon the Enterprise Architect (EA) tool by SparxSystems, but any other tool supporting UML2 with the standard extension mechanism of UML profiles can be also used and easily customized. We decided to rely on tools supporting UML2. The SystemC UML profile can be imported into an EA design project for use in the UML modeling process. The available stereotyped modeling elements will appear in the Resource View page of the project browser of EA and can be dragged and dropped into UML diagrams. The EA tool attaches automatically all the extensions (tagged values, default values, etc.) provided by the related profile. Figure 12 shows a screenshot of EA while attaching a port to a module in a class diagram. The SystemC data types and predefined

channels, interfaces, and ports (the SystemC layer 1) are modelled with the core stereotypes, and are also available in the Project View with the name SystemC_Layer1.

## Translators

The Code Generation Facility adopts a *full generation* approach. SystemC is used as action language at UML level, so that the source code is fully generated.

It is possible to generate code from the whole model, at package level or even for single diagrams. Starting from the selected element in the EA project view browser (project, package or class diagram) the code generation analyzes the underlying hierarchy of views generating the corresponding SystemC code. For further details, see (Riccobene et al., 2006m). Figure 13 shows a screenshot of EA while generating SystemC code from a UML-SystemC model.

The Reverse Engineering component is made of three parts: a parser, a data structure and a XMI writer. We developed a parser for SystemC using the JavaCC tool. The component accepts SystemC code which is translated into a UML model conforming to the UML profile. The internal data structure of this engine captures the main structures of the SystemC model and their relations. The XMI writer finally produces a UML model that can be imported in the EA tool.

The reverse engineering facility allows us to import existing models into the modeling environment and to achieve rapidly a high number of design cases. It is also indispensable to allow round trip engineering, that is the synchronized cooperation with code generation (forward engineering) to complete the description of a model working on both the UML model and the code. It is also useful in practice as a tool to inspect the structure of a source code graphically. Currently, the reverse facility is limited to the generation of the design *skeleton*[7] only, and some open problems still exist in the layout of the resulting graphi-

*Figure 12. Using the SystemC UML profile in EA. (Adapted from Scandurra 2005.)*

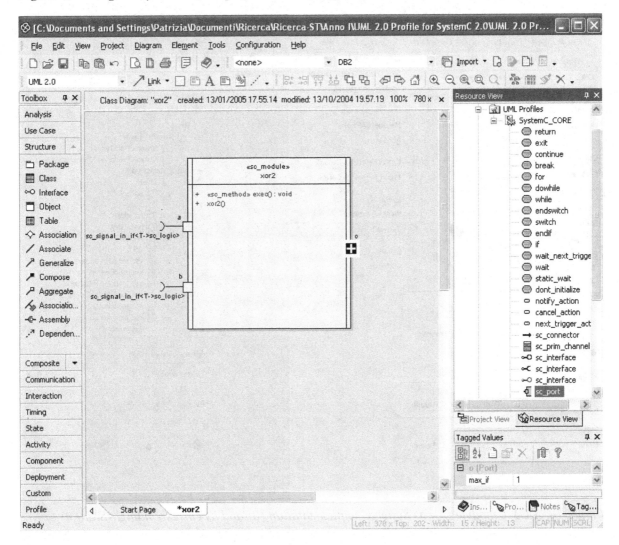

cal UML model, that have been left for further development.

## Mapping from SystemC UML Profile to AsmM

A SystemC UML model provided in input from the EA tool is transformed into a corresponding ASM model (an instance of the AsmM meta-model). In order to provide a one-to-one mapping (for both the structural and behavioral aspects), first we had to express in terms of ASMs the SystemC discrete (absolute and integer-valued)

and event-based simulation semantics. To this goal, we considered the ASM specification of the SystemC 2.0 semantics in (Müller et al., 2003) to define a precise and executable semantics of the SystemC UML profile (Gargantini et al., 2008a; Riccobene et al., 2005c) and, in particular, of the SystemC scheduler and the *SystemC process state machines*. We then proceeded to model in ASMs the predefined set of interfaces, ports and primitive channels (the layer 1 of SystemC), and SystemC-specific data types. The resulting SystemC-ASM component library is therefore available as target of the UML2AsmM transformation process.

*Figure 13. Generate SystemC code from EA. (Adapted from Scandurra 2005.)*

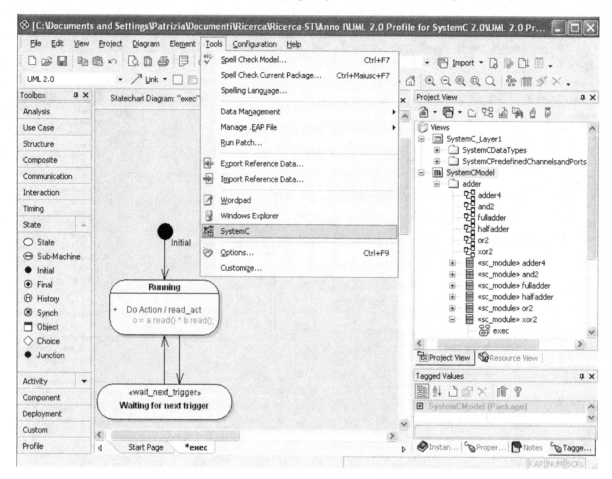

*Figure 14. A UML module (A), its SystemC implementation (B) and its corresponding ASM (C)*

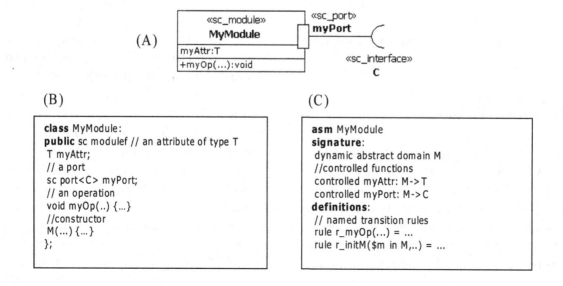

Since a complete coverage (Gargantini et al., 2008a) of the transformation rationale is beyond the scope of this chapter, we limit to provide in Figure 14 an example of application of such mapping by showing the UML notation, the corresponding SystemC code, and the resulting ASM (in AsmetaL notation) for a module.

## Validation by Simulation

The AsmetaS simulator (Gargantini et al., 2007) interprets ASM models written in AsmetaL. It can be used in a standalone way to provide basic simulation of the overall system behavior. As key features for model validation, AsmetaS supports *axiom checking* to check whether axioms expressed over the currently executed ASM model are satisfied or not, *consistent updates checking* for revealing inconsistent updates, *random simulation* i.e. an environment provides (when needed) random values for "monitored functions"[8], *interactive simulation* to validate a system component separately (or even the entire system) by providing the required input to the component interactively during simulation, and configurable *logging* facilities to inspect the machine state. Axiom checking and random simulation allow the user to perform a draft system validation with minimal effort, while interactive simulation, although more accurate, requires the user interaction. These simulation modes are illustrated in practice in Sect. *The Counter case study* for the Counter system.

## Scenario-Based Functional Validation

The AsmetaV validator is based on the AsmetaS tool and on the Avalla language (Gargantini et al., 2008b). This last provides constructs to express execution scenarios in an algorithmic way as interaction sequences consisting of *actions* committed by the *user actor* to set the environment (i.e. the values of monitored/shared functions), to check the machine state, to ask for the execu-

tion of certain transition rules, and to enforce the machine itself to make one step (or a sequence of steps by step until) as reaction of the actor actions. An example of scenario written in Avalla is given for the Counter case study.

AsmetaV reads a user scenario written in Avalla (see Figure 11), it builds the scenario as instance of the Avalla metamodel by means of a parser, it transforms the scenario and the AsmetaL specification which the scenario refers to, to an executable AsmM model. Then, AsmetaV invokes the AsmetaS interpreter to simulate the scenario. During simulation the user can pause the simulation and watch the current state and value of the update set at every step, through a watching window. During simulation, AsmetaV captures any check violation and if none occurs it finishes with a "PASS" verdict. Besides a "PASS"/"FAIL" verdict, during the scenario running AsmetaV collects in a final report some information about the coverage of the original model; this is useful to check which transition rules have been exercised.

## THE COUNTER CASE STUDY

To give an idea on how the UML profile for SystemC can be used in practice, we show here part of the model of a simple Counter system consisting of: one module count, that represents an integer counter of stimuli; one module count_stim, that provides stimuli to the counter; one module display, that shows simulation results; and one clock object which propagates activities within the system.

Moreover, as part of the analysis process, we apply to the Counter system (relying on its corresponding ASMs-based representation) two forms of validation techniques: basic simulation and scenario-based validation. Note that, even if the proposed case study could seem a toy example, it covers all the essential communication aspects between process state machines and it is didactic to illustrate the proposed validation techniques.

*Figure 15. The count_stim module*

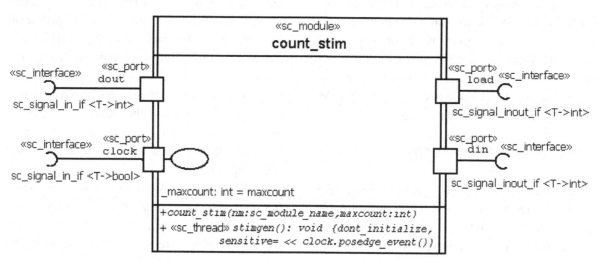

Major case studies from industrial design projects have been taken in consideration (see Sect. *Industrial Application* for a brief description), but cannot be reported in depth since protected by confidential information.

## Modeling

The count_stim module is shown in Figure 15. This module contains one thread process stimgen, two input ports dout and clock, and two output ports load and din. In particular, clock is a behavior port since it provides events that trigger the stimgen thread process within the module. The stimgen thread state machine is shown in Figure 16. It is a realist example of the behavior pattern presented in Figure 8. The stimgen thread drives the load and din inputs of the count module. It can initialize the count_val of the count module by setting the load port to true; the value loaded into the count module is the value of din. It can set, instead, the counter to the counting mode putting load to false. It also receives back the value from the counter in the dout port, and may restart the counter when it reaches the value specified by the local _maxcount attribute.

The count module (see Figure 17) has a private attribute count_val of type integer that stores the

actual value of the counter, and three input ports: one clock behaviour port to receive stimuli coming from the system's clock; one boolean input port load that, when set to true at the next rising edge of the clock, loads the data into the counter; one integer input port din; and one integer output port dout, which gives out the actual value of the counter. The count functionality is implemented inside the body of the count_up method process (see Figure 16), which is sensitive to the positive edges of the clock. If the load input is true, the signal value from port din is loaded into the counter. Otherwise, the counter increments its value by 1.

Finally, the display module (see Figure 18) prints out any new data from the counter. This function is computed by its internal method process display_count which is activated at any new value on the input port. The state machine for this process is straightforward.

The top level container is shown by the composite structure diagram in Figure 19. It represents the internal structure of the module top used to assemble the whole system. This module contains parts of instances of the inner modules count, count_stim and display, and of the clock and sc_signal channels (predefined SystemC channels) used to connect the module's parts.

*Figure 16. The stimgen and the count_up process state machines*

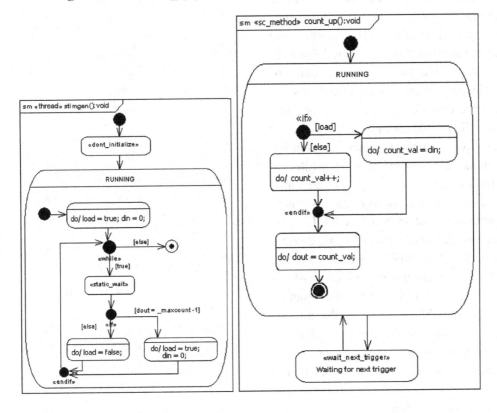

*Figure 17. The count module*

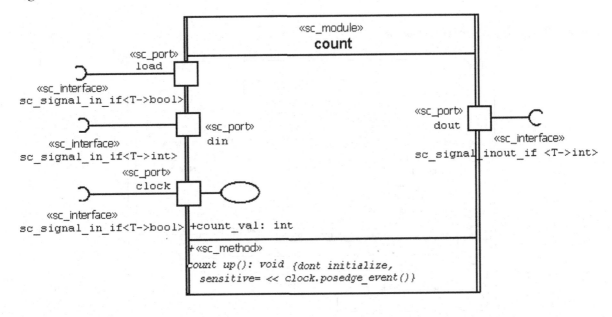

Part of the SystemC code for the Counter system is reported below. The C++ header files (.h) for the definition of modules, channels and interfaces are automatically generated from the UML class diagrams. The C++ body files (.cpp) are determined by the process state machines that implement the behavior of SystemC processes. The header file named count_stim.h (see below on the left), for example, is generated from the count_stim module class in Figure 15, while, the body section (see below on the right) is determined by the process state machine in Figure 16, where the C++ notation is put on top of the UML action semantics and the control structures are directly derived from the stereotyped pseudostates while, if-then, etc., of the state machine diagram. Moreover, by an analysis of the composite structure diagram it is possible to discover the internal structure of the module to determine how internal parts are connected to each other. The constructor body of the enclosing top module of the Counter system is therefore derived by the composite structure diagram in Figure 19.

*Figure 18. The display module*

```
«sc_interface»
sc_signal_in_if < T->int >

            «sc_module»
              display
         «sc_port»
         dout

         «sc_method»
         +display_count():void { sensitive = << dout }
```

```
public:
sc_port<sc_signal_inout_if<bool> > load;
sc_port<sc_signal_inout_if<int> > din;
sc_port<sc_signal_in_if<bool> > clock;
sc_port<sc_signal_in_if<int> > dout;
void stimgen();
SC_HAS_PROCESS(count_stim);
count_stim(sc_module_name nm,int max-
count):
 sc_module(nm), _maxcount(maxcount){
  SC_THREAD(stimgen);
  dont_initialize();
  sensitive << clock.posedge_event();
 }
private: int _maxcount; };
#include ``count_stim.h''
void count_stim::stimgen(){
 load = true; din = 0;
```

```
#include ``systemc.h''
class count_stim: public sc_module {
```

*Figure 19. The Top composite structure*

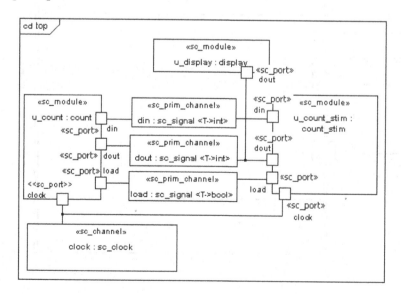

```
while(true){
 wait();
 if(dout == _maxcount-1){
   load =true;
   din = 0; }
 else load = false;
 }
}
```

## Validation: Simulation and Scenario-Based Validation

According to the mapping from SystemC UML to ASM, the SystemC UML model of the Counter system is provided in input from the EA tool to the UML2AsmM component and therefore automatically transformed into a corresponding ASM model in textual form in the AsmetaL notation. Below we report the ASM r_count_up rule of the count module; it corresponds to the count_up process state machine shown in Figure 16.

```
macro rule r_count_up =
  seq
    if read(load(self)) then
      count_val(self):= readInt(din(self))
    else
      count_val(self):= count_val(self) + 1
    endif
    r_writeInt(dout(self), count_val(self)]
    r_wait_next_trigger[self]
  endseq
endlet
```

### Simulation

We started with the simulation of the entire system. In this case, the user executes the system and observes the output produced by the display module and checks that it is correct with respect to the input provided by the counter_stim module.

Axiom checking The user can increase and decrease the verbosity of the output produced during simulation either by modifying the logging configuration for the simulator or by inserting logging messages directly in the ASM specifications. However, this activity can be time consuming and several errors may pass unnoticed. For this reason, the user should insert appropriate axioms which will be automatically checked by the simulator. For example the following axiom:

```
axiom inv_count_val over count_val:
    (forall $c in Count with count_val($c)
!= undef implies count_val($c) >= 0)
```

was added to the Count module. It states that the value of the internal variable count_val is always greater than or equal to zero. The following axiom:

```
axiom inv_max over dout: (forall $c in Count_
stim with
    let ($out = readInt(dout($c))) in ($out
!= undef implies $out < maxcount($c)) endlet)
```

was added instead to the counter_stim module and states that the value read from the dout channel from the counter is always less than maxcount.

By running the counter example again, this axiom is falsified, and the simulator prints a trace like:

```
<UpdateSet>
...
INFO - axiom (name inv_max) violated
FATAL - UpdateSet:
value(dOUT)=8
</UpdateSet>
INFO - State:
...
maxcount(u_count_stim)=8
```

The right axiom states that the value read can be less or equal to maxcount.

Interactive simulation The user can validate a system component separately by providing the input interactively. The component must be connected with the external environment by means of monitored variables. For example, the counter_stim module, the user can slightly modify the counter_stim signature as follows. First the following monitored variables can be added to the count_stim signature

```
monitored load_cmd: Count_stim_user ->
Boolean // the user wants to set the counter
  monitored din_value: Count_stim_user ->
Integer // the desired value
```

and then the rule, which transfers the information to the counter ports load and din.

```
if load_cmd($d) then seq
  r_write[load($d), true]
  r_writeInt[din($d), din_value($d)]
endsdeq
```

By running this example, the simulator will ask the user to provide the value of load_cmd and, if needed, also for din_value. The user must type the value directly on the console and the simulator will show the response of the system.

Random simulation The random simulation is easy to perform, since it does not require any user interaction. The simulator executes the ASM specification with a random environment, i.e. by providing random values to assign to the monitored functions. During random simulation the axioms are checked and possible violations are displayed. For example, the fact that the axiom inv_count_val is false, can be discovered by random simulation when the din_value becomes less than zero and the counter is set to that negative value. Random simulation is complementary with

user guided simulation: it is cheaper and it can discover faults in correspondence to input the user forgets, possible because of implicit assumptions he/she assumes.

## Scenario Validation

To be able to rerun scenarios, to avoid repeating the interactive simulation with the same inputs over again, the user can write scenario in which specifies the input to system and the expected outputs. The correctness of the output is no longer of the user to judge, but it is formally specified in the scenario. For example, the following scenario written in Avalla sets the value to write to the counter to 10, it checks that the value read from the dOut channel is 10, then it lets the counter increment the value and it checks that the new value read from the dOut channel is 11.

```
scenario test1
 // set the counter to 10
 load ./main_user.asm
 set load_cmd(u_count_stim) = true;
 set din_value(u_count_stim) = 10;
 step until time = 30 and phase = TIMED_
NOTIFICATION;
  check readInt(dOUT) = 10;
 set load_cmd(u_count_stim) = false;
 step until time = 50 and phase = TIMED_
NOTIFICATION;
  check readInt(dOUT) = 11;
```

## INDUSTRIAL APPLICATION

The design methodology has been tested on several different case studies, some taken from the SystemC distribution like the Simple Bus design (Bocchio et al., 2008), and some of industrial interest.

The Simple Bus system was entirely developed in a forward engineering manner. The code generator has been tested primarily on this example, and it produced an executable and complete (i.e. including both structural and behavioral parts) SystemC code. On this example we performed also an evaluation about the benefits of modeling with our UML based methodology compared to coding. Even if our methodology is oriented to the implementation and the modeling style strictly resembles the structure of the target SystemC language, by analyzing the produced SystemC code we find out that 652 of the 1018 lines are automatically inferred from the structural diagrams of the UML model, the remaining 366 lines of code are derived from the behavioral description in the Process State Machines diagrams or produced from actions introduced manually in the model. Therefore, we unexpectedly concluded that there is a significant reduction in the effort to produce the final code and there is also a benefit in documentation, maintenance and reuse. For instance one benefit compared with SystemC is that all the header files are completely and consistently generated from the UML structural diagrams.

The reverse engineering flow was tested by modeling the On Chip Communication Network (OCCN) library (OCCN). This library is made of about 14.000 lines of code and implements an abstract communication pattern for connecting multiple processing elements and storage elements on a single chip. We understood that the reverse engineering component is useful in practice as a tool to inspect the structure of a source SystemC code graphically, which is typically hierarchical with modules containing sub-modules and so on. Starting from a bunch of source code header files, it is therefore possible to obtain immediately a graphical representation of the most important design changes introduced at code level including structure, relations, variables, functions, etc.

In (Bocchio et al., 2005), an application example related to an 802.11.a physical layer transmitter and receiver system described at instruction level is presented. The hardware platform is composed of a VLIW processor developed in STM, called LX, with a dedicated hardware coprocessor that implements an FFT (Fast Fourier Transform) operation.

We tested also advantages and indispensability of a round trip engineering -- based on a synchronized cooperation between code generation (forward engineering) and reverse engineering -- in order to have a complete description of a system design on both the UML abstract level and the code level. Finally, the adoption of formal analysis techniques at model level helped to discover errors or inconsistencies early in the design process before producing a more detailed implementation in SystemC code.

## FUTURE TRENDS

Our model-driven methodology for the design and analysis of embedded systems can be further improved. As future aims, we want to provide model-based testing, conformance testing and property verification for the SystemC UML models.

By using the ATGT tool (Gargantini et al., 2003) that automatically generates test cases from the specification by exploiting the counter example generation of the SPIN (Holzmann, 1997) model checker, it is possible to build functional tests on the same level of abstraction as the model. These test cases are known as the *abstract test suite*. We also plan to integrate AsmetaV with the ATGT tool in order to be able to automatically generate some scenarios by using ATGT and ask for a certain type of coverage (rule coverage, fault detection, etc.). Test cases generated by ATGT and the validation scenarios can be transformed in concrete SystemC test cases to test the conformance of the implementations with respect to their specification. This requires the implementation of a SystemC code instrumenter which should map the abstract test cases to concrete test cases suitable for execution. Selected behavioural aspects of the system can be studied, therefore, by *conformance testing*, i.e. by instrumenting the SystemC implementation code from the model.

We plan to support system properties formal verification by model checking techniques. Every model-checking tool comes with its own modeling language. By model transformations, appropriate links can be provided from AsmetaL to model checkers like the well-known SPIN/Promela, and therefore encoding ASM models into Promela communicating automata. The user has therefore to specify only the properties (linear temporal logic (LTL) formulas, in the case of SPIN) that the final system is expected to satisfy. The model checker then outputs yes if the given ASM model satisfies the given properties, or generates a counterexample otherwise. By studying the counterexample, you can pinpoint the source of the error, correct the model, and try again. The idea is that by ensuring that the model satisfies enough system properties, we increase our confidence in the correctness of the model.

Beyond code generation, the MDA-style separation of models demands automatic model transformations as support to evolution activities (Mens et al., 2005) in general like refinement/abstraction, model refactoring, model inconsistency management, etc. Refinement, in particular, is a key issue in the model-driven engineering approach. Compared with the refinement techniques available for formal methods like Z, B, and ASMs (Börger & Stärk, 2003), few work has been carried out for visual modelling languages like UML. At the time of writing, very few proposals exist in literature. Some proposals that we are considering in our process can be found in (Catalysis; Pons & Kutsche, 2004; Pons & Garcia, 2006; Pons & Kutsche, 2003; Paige et al., 2005). The general idea is to collect and reuse precise abstraction/refinement transformation patterns, coming from industry best practices. Once the transformation patterns have been proved correct and complete, they may be used during the modeling activity for guiding a refinement process or for pointing out missing elements in a particular refinement schema. By applying the model transformations defined for a given pattern, a UML system design may automatically and correctly evolve to an abstract/refined model reflecting the abstraction/refinement rules defined for the applied pattern.

To this purpose, in the future we aim at identifying characteristics of reusable transformations and ways of achieving reuse by collecting in a library precise abstraction/refinement transformation patterns according to the levels of abstraction: functional, transactional, behavioral, BCA, and RTL. In particular, we are focusing on the *transactional-level modeling* to model the communication aspects at a certain number of TLM sub-levels according to the OSCI TLM 1.0 library (Open SystemC Initiative, 2008). We believe the use of fine-grained transformations that are being composed (chaining) would be beneficial, both increasing the productivity and the quality of the developed systems.

## CONCLUSION

This work is part of our ongoing effort to enact *design flows* that start with system descriptions using UML-notations and produce C/C++/SystemC implementations of the SW and HW components as well as their communication interfaces, and that are complemented by *formal analysis flows* for system validation and verification.

In this paper, we proposed a model-driven system-level design and analysis methodology by the use of the SystemC UML profile (for the modeling part) and the ASM formal method and its related ASMETA toolset (for the analysis part). We have been testing our methodology on case studies taken from the standard SystemC distribution and on some of industrial interest.

Thanks to the ease in raising the abstraction level using the UML and ASMs, and considering the results obtained by applying our methodology to case studies, we believe that our approach scales effectively to industrial systems.

# REFERENCES

Arlow, J., & Neustadt, I. (2002). *UML and the Unified Process*. Addison Wesley.

The ASMETA toolset. (2007). http://asmeta. sf.net/

Beierle, C., Börger, E., Durdanovic, I., Glässer, U., & Riccobene, E. (1995). Refining abstract machine specifications of the steam boiler control to well documented executable code. In Abrial, J.-R., Börger, E., and Langmaack, H., editors, *Formal Methods for Industrial Applications*, volume 1165 of *Lecture Notes in Computer Science*, pages 52–78. Springer.

Bezivin, J. (2005). On the unification power of models. [SoSym]. *Software and System Modeling*, *4*(2), 171–188. doi:10.1007/s10270-005-0079-0

Bocchio, S., Riccobene, E., Rosti, A., & Scandurra, P. (2005) A SoC design flow based on UML 2.0 and SystemC. In *Proc. of the International DAC Workshop UML- SoC'05*. IEEE press.

Bocchio, S., Riccobene, E., Rosti, A., & Scandurra, P. (2008). An Enhanced SystemC UML Profile for Modeling at Transaction-Level. In Villar, E., editor, *Embedded Systems Specification and Design Languages*, pages 211-226. Springer.

Börger, E. (2003). The ASM refinement method. *Formal Asp. Comput, 15*(2-3), 237–257.

Börger, E., Riccobene, E., & Schmid, J. (2000). Capturing requirements by Abstract State Machines: The light control case study. *J.UCS . Journal of Universal Computer Science, 6*(7), 597–625.

Börger, E., & Stärk, R. (2003). *Abstract State Machines: A Method for High-Level System Design and Analysis*. Springer Verlag.

Bruschi, F., Ferrandi, F., & Sciuto, D. (2005). A framework for the functional verification of systemc models. *International Journal of Parallel Programming, 33*(6), 667–695. doi:10.1007/s10766-005-8908-x

Bruschi, F., & Sciuto, D. (2002). SystemC based Design Flow starting from UML Model. In *Proc. of European SystemC Users Group Meeting.*

Carioni, A., Gargantini, A., Riccobene, E., & Scandurra, P. (2008). A Model-driven Technique for Embedded System Validation. In *FDL 08: Proceedings of Forum on Specification and Design Languages,* pp. 191-196. IEEE press.

Catalysis. The Catalysis process: www.catalysis. org

Chen, R., Sgroi, M., Martin, G., Lavagno, L., Sangiovanni-Vincentelli, A. L., & Rabaey, J. (2003). Embedded System Design Using UML and Platforms. In *System Specification and Design Languages* (Eugenio Villar and Jean Mermet, eds.), CHDL Series, Kluwer.

do Nascimento, F. A. M., Oliveira, M. F. S., & Wagner, F. R. (2007). ModES: ES Design Methodology and Tools based on MDE. In *Fourth International workshop on Model-based Methodologies for Pervasive and Embedded Software (MOMPES'07)*. IEEE Press.

Edwards, M., & Green, P. (2003). UML for hardware and software object modeling. *UML for real design of embedded real-time systems*, pp. 127–147.

Edwards, S., Lavagno, L., Lee, E., & Sangiovanni-Vincentelli, A. (1997). Design of Embedded Systems: Formal Models, Validation, and Synthesis. Proc. IEEE, vo. 85, n. 3, 1997, pp. 366–390.

Gargantini, A., Riccobene, E., & Rinzivillo, S. (2003). Using Spin to Generate Tests from ASM Specifications. In *Proc. of the 10th Int. Workshop on Abstract State Machines*. LNCS 2589, p. 263-277. Springer.

Gargantini, A., Riccobene, E., & Scandurra, P. (2007). A metamodel-based simulator for ASMs. In *Proc. of the 14th Int. ASM Workshop*.

Gargantini, A., Riccobene, E., & Scandurra, P. (2008a). A language and a simulation engine for abstract state machines based on metamodelling. In [Springer.]. *Journal of Universal Computer Science, 14*(12), 1949–1983.

Gargantini, A., Riccobene, E., & Scandurra, P. (2008b). A scenario-based validation language for ASMs. In *Proc. of First International Conference on Abstract State Machines, B and Z (ABZ 2008)*. LNCS 5238, pp. 71–84, Springer.

Gröetker, T., Liao, S., Martin, G., & Swan, S. (2002). *System Design with SystemC*. Kluwer Academic Publisher.

Habibi, A., & Tahar, S. (2006). Design and verification of systemc transaction-level models. *IEEE Transactions on VLSI Systems, 14*, 57–68. doi:10.1109/TVLSI.2005.863187

Haroud, M., Blazevic, L., & Biere, A. (2004). HW accelerated ultra wide band mac protocol using sdl and systemc. In *IEEE Radio and Wireless Conference*, pp. 525–528.

Holzmann, G. J. (1997). The model checker SPIN. *IEEE Transactions on Software Engineering, 23*(5), 279–295. doi:10.1109/32.588521

Kogel, T., Doerper, M., Kempf, T., Wieferink, A., Leupers, R., Ascheid, G., & Meyr, H. (2004). Virtual architecture mapping: A systemc based methodology for architectural exploration of system-on-chip designs. In Pimentel, A. D. and Vassiliadis, S., editors, *Computer Systems: Architectures, Modeling, and Simulation, Third and Fourth International Workshops, SAMOS*, volume 3133 of *Lecture Notes in Computer Science*, pp. 138–148.

Kruchten, P. (1999). *The Rational Unified Process*. Addison Wesley.

Lavagno, L., Martin, G., Vincentelli, A. S., Rabaey, J., Chen, R., & Sgroi, M. (2003). UML and Platform based Design. *UML for Real Design of Embedded Real-Time Systems*.

MARTE (2008). OMG, UML Profile for Modeling and Analysis of Real-time and Embedded Systems, ptc/08-06-08.

Martin, C. (1999). UML and VCC. White paper, Cadence Design Systems, Inc.

Mathaikutty, D., Ahuja, S., Dingankar, A., & Shukla, S. (2007). Model-driven test generation for system level validation. *High Level Design Validation and Test Workshop, 2007. HLVDT 2007. IEEE*, pp. 83–90.

Mellor, S., Scott, K., Uhl, A., & Weise, D. (2004). *MDA Distilled, Principles of Model Driven Architecture*. Addison-Wesley Professional.

Mens, T., Wermelinger, M., Ducasse, S., Demeyer, S., Hirschfeld, R., & Jazayeri, M. (2005). Challenges in Software Evolution. In *Proc. of the International Workshop on Software Evolution*. IEEE.

Moore, T., Vanderperren, Y., Sonck, G., van Oostende, P., Pauwels, M., & Dehaene, W. (2002). A Design Methodology for the Development of a Complex System-On-Chip using UML and Executable System Models. In *Forum on Specification and Design Languages, ECSL*.

MSC. (1999). Message Sequence Charts (MSC). ITU-T Recommendation Z.120 International Communication Union.

Nguyen, K., Sun, Z., Thiagarajan, P., & Wong, W. (2005). Model-Driven SoC Design: The UML-SystemC Bridge. *UML for SOC Design*.

OCCN. OCCN Project: http://occn.sourceforge.net/

Open SystemC Initiative. (2008). http://www.systemc.org.

Paige, R. F., Kolovos, D. S., & Polack, F. A. (2005). Refinement via consistency checking in MDA. *Electronic Notes in Theoretical Computer Science, 137*(2), 151–161. doi:10.1016/j.entcs.2005.04.029

Patel, H. D., & Shukla, S. K. (2007). Model-driven validation of systemc designs. In *DAC '07: Proc. of the 44th annual conference on Design automation*, pp. 29–34, New York, NY, USA. ACM.

Pons, C., & Garcia, D. (2006). An OCL-Based Technique for Specifying and Verifying Refinement-Oriented Transformations in MDE. In *MoDELS*, pp. 646–660.

Pons, C., & Kutsche, R.-D. (2003). Using UML-B and U2B for formal refinement of digital components. In *Proc. of Forum on specification and design languages, Frankfurt, 2003*.

Pons, C., & Kutsche, R.-D. (2004). Traceability Across Refinement Steps in UML Modeling. In *Proc. of WiSME@UML 2004*.

QVT (2007). OMG, MOF Query/Views/Transformations, ptc/07-07-07.

Riccobene, E., Scandurra, P., Rosti, A., & Bocchio, S. (2005a). A SoC Design Methodology Based on a UML 2.0 Profile for SystemC. In *Proc. of Design Automation and Test in Europe (DATE 05)*, IEEE Computer Society.

Riccobene, E., Scandurra, P., Rosti, A., Bocchio, S. (2005b). A UML 2.0 Profile for SystemC. STMicroelectronics Technical Report, AST-AGR-2005-3.

Riccobene, E., Scandurra, P., Rosti, A., & Bocchio, S. (2005c). A UML 2.0 profile for SystemC: toward high-level SoC design. In *EMSOFT '05: Proceedings of the 5th ACM international conference on Embedded Software* (pp. 138-141). ACM Press.

Riccobene, E., Scandurra, P., Rosti, A., & Bocchio, S. (2006). A Model-driven Design Environment for Embedded Systems. In *DAC '06: Proc. of the 43rd annual conference on Design automation* (915-918). ACM Press.

Riccobene, E., Scandurra, P., Rosti, A., & Bocchio, S. (2007a). A Model-driven co-design flow for Embedded Systems. In (Sorin A. Huss ed.) *Advances in Design and Specification Languages for Embedded Systems*. Springer.

Riccobene, E., Scandurra, P., Rosti, A., & Bocchio, S. (2007b). Designing a Unified Process for Embedded Systems. In *MOMPES '07: Proceedings of Fourth international workshop on model-based methodologies for pervasive and embedded software*. IEEE Press.

Rioux, L., Saunier, T., Gerard, S., Radermacher, A., de Simone, R., Gautier, T., et al. (2005). MARTE: A new Profile RFP for the Modeling and Analysis of Real-time ES. In *UML for SoC Design workshop at DAC'05*.

Scandurra, P. (2005). Model-driven Language Definition: metamodelling methodologies and applications. PhD thesis, Catania (Italy), December 2005.

Selic, B. (2003). A Generic Framework for Modeling Resources with UML. In *Proceedings of the 16th Symposium on Integrated Circuits and Systems Design (SBCCI'03)*. 33:64–69, IEEE Computer Society.

Sgroi, M., Lavagno, L., & Sangiovanni-Vincentelli, A. (2000). Formal Models for Embedded System Design. *IEEE Design & Test Magazine. Special Issue on System Design*. IEEE press.

SysML (2007). OMG, SysML, Version 1.0, formal/2007-09-01. http://www.omgsysml.org/.

SystemC (2006). SystemC Language Reference Manual. IEEE Std 1666-2005, 31 March 2006.

UML. (2005). Unified Modeling Language, Version 2.0, 2005. http://www.uml.org/

USoC (2005). Fujitsu Limited, IBM, NEC. A UML Extension for SoC. Draft RFC to OMG, 2005-01-01.

Vardi, M. Y. (2007). Formal techniques for SystemC verification; position paper. In *DAC '07: Proc. of the 43rd annual conference on Design automation*, (pp. 188–192). IEEE.

Zhang, T., Jouault, F., Bézivin, J., & Zhao, J. (2008). A MDE Based Approach for Bridging Formal Models. In Proc. 2nd IFIP/IEEE *International Symposium on Theoretical Aspects of Software Engineering*. IEEE Computer Society.

Zhu, Q., Oishi, R., Hasegawa, T., & Nakata, T. (2004). System-on-Chip Validation using UML and CWL. In *Proc. of CODES*.

## ENDNOTES

[1] A property (or part) denotes a set of instances (in case of a property multiplicity greater than 1) that are owned by the structured module. These instances are instances (just a subset of the total set of instances) of the classifier (a module or a channel) typing the property.

[2] A port-to-port connection is the binding of a module port (parent port) to a lower level module port (child port).

[3] In UML, a *method* state machine is a state machine associated to a behavioral feature (such as an operation of a class) to specify the algorithm or procedure for the behavioral feature.

[4] Choice pseudostates must be used in place of junction pseudostates whenever the head condition of the while loop is a function of the results of prior actions performed in the same run-to-completion step.

[5] $f$ is an arbitrary $n$-ary function and $t_1,...,t_n$, $t$ are first-order terms. To fire this rule to a state, $i \geq 0$, evaluate all terms $t_1,...,t_n$, $t$ at and update the function $f$ to $t$ on parameters $t_1,...,t_n$. This produces another state which differs from in the new interpretation of $f$.

[6] http://asmeta.sourceforge.net

[7] The skeleton describes only the static structure of the system. For OO technologies, this means generating classes, attributes, relations and operations, but not method bodies.

[8] *Monitored* functions are dynamic functions of the ASM signature which provide input from the external environment. Monitored functions are also named *read-only* functions of the ASM program since they must not be updated by the ASM itself.

# Chapter 3

# Abstract and Concrete Data Type Optimizations at the UML and C/C++ Level for Dynamic Embedded Software

**Christos Baloukas**
*Democritus University of Thrace, Greece*

**Marijn Temmerman**
*Karel de Grote Hogeschool, Belgium*

**Anne Keller**
*University of Antwerpen, Belgium*

**Stylianos Mamagkakis**
*IMEC, Belgium*

**Francky Catthoor**
*IMEC, Belgium*

**Dimitrios Soudris**
*National Technical University of Athens, Greece*

**Serge Demeyer**
*University of Antwerpen, Belgium*

## ABSTRACT

*An embedded system is a special-purpose system that performs predefined tasks, usually with very specific requirements. Since the system is dedicated to a specific task, design engineers can optimize it by exploiting very specialized knowledge, deriving an optimally customized system. Low energy consumption and high performance are both valid optimization targets to increase the value and mobility of the final system. Traditionally, conceptual embedded software models are built irrespectively of the underlying hardware platform, whereas embedded-system specialists typically start their optimization*

DOI: 10.4018/978-1-60566-750-8.ch003

*crusade from the executable code. This practice results in suboptimal implementations on the embedded platform because at the source-code level not all the inefficiencies introduced at the modelling level can be removed. In this book chapter, we describe both novel UML transformations at the modelling level and C/C++ transformations at the software implementation level. The transformations at both design abstraction levels target the data types of dynamic embedded software applications and provide optimizations guided by the relevant cost factors. Using a real life case study, we show how our transformations result in significant improvement in memory footprint, performance and energy consumption with respect to the initial implementation. Moreover, thanks to our holistic approach, we are able to identify new and non-trivial solutions that could hardly be found with the traditional design methods.*

## INTRODUCTION

Modern embedded systems are a combination of software and hardware, which perform a single or a few dedicated functions. In the context of this chapter, we will focus on embedded systems that perform more than one function and more specifically on the category of *nomadic embedded systems*. These are mobile devices that have multimedia or wireless communication functionality (or both) and provide to the end user the ease of rich multimedia content anytime, anywhere. To provide this functionality, they rely on hardware platforms, which integrate a number of processing elements, communication infrastructure and memory hierarchy on a single chip (or multiple chips on a board). The processing elements are programmable, which means that they can perform more than one function according to the embedded software that accompanies those (Catthoor & Brockmeyer, 2000). We classify embedded software as application software and system software, as can be seen in Figure 1. Application software performs some tasks relevant to the end user and the system software interfaces with hardware to provide the necessary services for application software. The embedded system designers are responsible for the design, integration and optimization of the hardware, application software and system software components.

In embedded systems, the software is gaining an ever increasing importance. Because hardware

becomes more programmable, multiple applications can run on the same hardware platform through dedicated software. In this context, we define as embedded software applications the different programs, which are written for each one of these applications (from now on, we will simply refer to them as *applications* in the text). It is important to note that applications receive input from and serve directly to the end user of the embedded system. This means that the actions of the user have significant impact on the control flow of the algorithms in the applications, thus making the execution dynamic and event-driven.

The proposed optimization methodology is part of a general design flow. This flow targets a

*Figure 1. Hardware and software components in an embedded system*

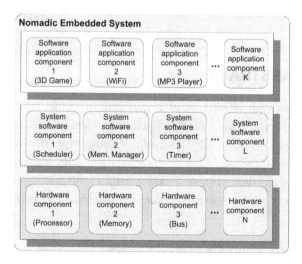

56

*Figure 2. Proposed optimization methodology in the general design flow (seen as part of the metaflow) (Catthoor & Brockmeyer, 2000)*

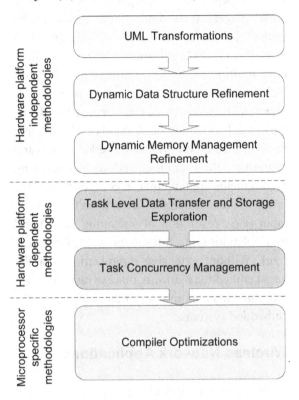

very broad application domain, thus not all of its (sub) steps are important for every type of design. In fact, it represents a *meta* flow (Figure 2 (Catthoor F, de Greef, Wuytack, 1998)) which is to be instantiated by omitting those (sub) steps which are irrelevant from the viewpoint of the specific type of application to be designed. Moreover, depending on the type of application domain which is considered, a specific step in the generic but abstract metaflow will be instantiated in a partly different way. The strict separation between different abstraction layers allows the designer to deal with the issues on each level more clearly and in a more decoupled fashion, and provides feedback as early as possible, avoiding large scope iterations through the entire design process. As seen in Figure 3, we illustrate an instance of the metaflow focusing on the higher abstraction level design stages for dynamic software applications.

In the context of this book chapter, we deal with the first two steps of the hardware independent methodologies. More precisely, we discuss UML model transformations which deal with Abstract Data Type optimizations and Dynamic Data Structure refinement, which deals with Concrete Data Structure optimizations at the source code

*Figure 3. (a) Introducing the ADT modeling level in the design process and (b) the need for an ADT-specific modeling language*

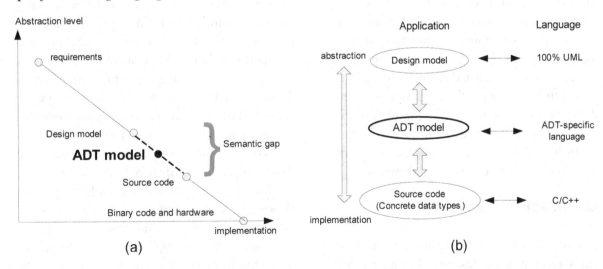

level (i.e. C++). These stages should be performed before the subsequent ones because in each of the next stages, several main steps depend on knowledge of the implementation cost for the major data types. And that cost cannot be accurately estimated or determined without a refinement of the initial abstract data types (either in the dynamic or static case). Also the dynamic memory allocator (Atienza D., Mendias, J. M., Mamagkakis, S., Soudris, D., & Catthoor 2006) functionality has to be decided in order to get a reasonable idea of the allocation cost in the virtual memory space for the dynamic data structures.

Then, the *Data Transfer and Storage Exploration (T-DTSE)* stage should be executed where the DTSE steps related to the physical memory management (Catthoor F., de Greef, E., & Wuytack S., 1998) are applied to the data selected at this task-level abstraction (Marchal P., Gomez, J., Atienza, D., Mamagkakis, S., & Catthoor, F., 2005). The purpose of the subsequent *task concurrency management (TCM)* (Zhe Ma, 2007) stage is to determine an optimal constraint-driven scheduling, allocation and assignment of the various threads and tasks to one or more abstract Processing Elements. Constraints are derived from both the DDSR/DMMR and T-DTSE stages. These platform dependent optimization methodologies as well as any compiler optimizations are out of the context of this book chapter.

In this chapter, we focus on the multimedia and wireless network application domains, which on top of increased dynamic behavior display also increased data transfer and storage activity. These two particular characteristics make the targeted domains good candidates for the optimization methodology introduced in this chapter.

In the two following subsections, we will give an overview of the two targeted domains.

## Multimedia Applications

Multimedia embedded applications have experienced recently a very fast growth in their variety,

complexity and functionality. In the context of this chapter we consider as multimedia applications, video (Mpeg4, 2002; Sodagar I., et al 1999) and music players, three-dimensional games (Moby Games, 2003; Cosmas G., et al, 2002), or Voice-Over-IP (VOIP) applications. Nowadays, these new multimedia applications (e.g., MPEG4) include complex algorithms, written in object-oriented languages (e.g., *C++* or *Java*), and thus they largely increase the demand of memory and performance of traditional embedded software. Moreover, their graphic and data processing requirements are unknown at compile time. This is due to the fact that they depend on the specific input (e.g., resolution of streaming video) and user behavior (e.g., full screen or small window size). Without extensive optimizations for the target embedded platform, this can result in unaffordable high cost and power consumption in the embedded systems.

## Wireless Network Applications

In the context of this chapter, we use the term wireless network applications to refer to the C or C++ source code that is running on an embedded system and is responsible for the connection and communication of this embedded system with another embedded system (Access/Mobile Point) or with a server. The basis of the networking theory for wireless embedded systems is derived from the networking theory for general purpose computing systems (Tannenbaum, 2005), which can be split into 7 layers according to the Open Systems Interconnection (OSI) Basic Reference Model. The introduced methodologies are relevant for the Data link, Network, Transport, Session, Presentation and Application layers (i.e., every layer except the Physical layer).

The chapter organization is as follows: section 4 presents related work regarding the proposed methodologies of this chapter. Section 5 presents the abstract data type optimizations, taking place at the modeling level, while section 6 deals with concrete data type optimizations that happen at the source code level. In section 7, a case study is presented, which demonstrates the applicability of the two types of optimizations presented in the previous sections. Finally, in section 8 there is a discussion about future trends, while in section 9 we draw our conclusions.

## BACKGROUND

Regarding research at the design abstraction level of Abstract Data Types (ADTs), UML model refactorings are considered a suitable candidate for design improvements (e.g. (SUNYÉ G. et al, 2001)). In particular, refactoring of class diagrams has been investigated by various researchers. From a practical point of view, very few tools provide integrated support for model refactoring. Boger, M., Sturm, T., & Fragemann, P., (2003) developed a refactoring browser integrated with a UML modeling tool. It supports refactoring of class diagrams, state chart diagrams and activity diagrams. When it comes to reasoning about the behavior-preservation properties of models, we need to rely on behavioral models (e.g., state diagrams, interaction diagrams or activity diagrams), OCL (Warmer J., 1998) constraints, or program code. With respect to refactoring of behavioral models, not much work is available. In (Gorp P. V., Stenten, H., Mens, T., & Demeyer, S., 2003), Van Gorp proposes an UML extension for automating the consistency between the model and the code. Gheyi R., Massoni, T., & Borba, P. (2005) suggests specifying model refactorings in Alloy (Alloy Website, 2007), an object-oriented modeling language used for formal specification. It can be used to prove semantics-preserving properties of model refactorings.

Our ADT optimization approach is mainly inspired by the above work from the software refactoring community. There are, however, three main differences. First, we concentrate on restructuring application models to map them ef-ficiently onto an embedded platform as opposed to restructuring existing applications to improve their internal structure for readability, re-use, or maintenance. Second, we explicitly intend to explore the design space of efficient data models in contrast to the "re-use of good OO practice" approach of the software-refactoring community. Third, we exploit application specific knowledge to obtain optimal implementations, which restricts the usage of our transformations to specific application domains, as opposed to the more general purpose techniques of software refactoring and re-engineering.

Regarding research at the design abstraction level of Concrete Data Types, data management and data optimizations for traditional (i.e., non-dynamic) embedded applications have been extensively studied in the related literature (Benini L. et al, 2000; Green et al, 1997; Kandemir M. et al, 1999; Steinke S. et al, 2002). The works presented in (Benini L. et al, 2000; Steinke S. et al, 2002) are good overviews about the vast range of proposed techniques to improve memory footprint and decrease energy consumption in statically allocated data. Also, from the methodology viewpoint, several approaches have been proposed to tackle this issue at the different levels of abstraction (e.g., memory hierarchies), such as the Data Transfer and Storage Exploration (DTSE) methodology (Catthoor F. et al, 1998).

In contrast to the above, in modern applications the behavior of many algorithms is heavily determined by the input data. This often means that multiple and completely different execution paths can be followed, leading to complex, dynamic data usage according to the behavior of the users. Therefore, our approach focuses on optimizing the *dynamic* Concrete and Abstract Data Types for modern network application with run-time memory allocation needs, contrary to the aforementioned static (i.e., compile-time) data allocation optimizations.

## ABSTRACT DATA TYPE OPTIMIZATIONS AT THE MODELING LEVEL (UML)

Nowadays several tools exist to assist the embedded-system designer in the trade-off investigation of the platform-related cost factors of data-intensive applications. However, these tools mainly start from source code, where a lot of data-related design decisions are already taken. This poses an inherent limitation on the number of alternatives investigated. In essence, this kind of analysis is able to find optimal solutions close to the original data structures, but is never able to jump beyond a local optimum to find even better ones. Moreover, it is widely accepted that design decisions taken at higher abstraction levels can lead to significantly superior results (Guttag, 1977). Therefore, we decided to move up in abstraction layer, namely to the ADT modeling level, where the details of the concrete data types are abstracted into domain-specific concepts. We introduce this ADT level between the *abstract* UML design model of the application and its refinement in source code (Figure 3.a).

At the ADT modeling level, we aim to optimize the data-related aspects of the application with respect to the memory footprint and the number of memory accesses. These two factors have an important impact on the performance and energy consumption of data-dominant applications. To achieve our goal, we explore the ADT-level design space taking into consideration the application-specific dynamic (i.e. run time) access behavior for the dominant scenarios.

For now, due to the lack of appropriate tools (i.e. due the complexity of the ADT transformations and the necessity for careful and scrupulous encoding), we manually transform the ADT models and refine them afterwards in executable code. However, considering the recent evolutions in model-driven design (e.g., the OMG Model Driven Architecture), the (semi)automation of our ADT transformations and source-code generation become feasible.

In the following sections we present an ADT-level modeling language in the form of a UML profile, a formal description of the ADT design space, and an initial catalog of optimizing ADT-level transformations.

## A UML Profile for ADTs at the Modeling Level

At this new abstraction level, we need an appropriate modeling language that enables precise formulation of the application in terms that reflect the fundamental ADT-level concepts.

By creating an ADT language as an extension of the UML (OMG, 2007), we facilitate a smooth transition from the design model, expressed in pure UML, to the ADT model as shown in Figure 3.b. Because the ADT-specific concepts are still closely related to the standard UML modeling elements, we can formulate our ADT language as a UML profile, which we call the *ADT profile* (Temmerman, 2008).

### Features of an ADT Modeling Language

The features of our ADT modeling language are deduced from its interfaces with the two surrounding abstraction levels. Namely, an ADT model is on the one hand a refinement of a UML design model, and on the other hand an abstraction of its various implementations in source code at the concrete data-type level (cf. Figure 3.b).

This brings us to the following lists of requirements. To refine a design model, the ADT profile needs to provide: (a) the modeling elements for the precise refinement of multi-valued multiplicities in the UML design model into custom ADTs, and (b) the syntax to specify the semantics of the configuration (i.e. a structural or functional relationship) of the elements inside a collection. To make abstraction of the concrete data types, the ADT profile needs to provide: (a) the modeling elements to represent the data records of data structures in a way that allows reasoning about the

*Figure 4. (a) Structure of the ADT profile, (b) a multi-valued association end in a UML design model, and (c) a refining ADT model*

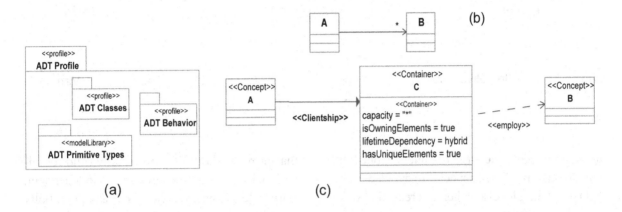

platform-related cost factors at the ADT modeling level, (b) the syntax for specifying the interface of the custom ADTs in terms of ADT-specific operations such as add, remove, lookup, and traverse, and (c) the syntax for specifying the memory-related properties of ADTs: i.e., sharing, cloning, redundant storage, and lifetime dependency.

In the next section, we present an overview of our ADT profile that meets all the requirements stated here.

## Structure of our ADT Profile

We organized the elements of the ADT profile into three packages (Figure 4.a). The *ADT Classes* profile offers the stereotypes for the ADT-level class diagrams. The primitive data types of the reference hardware platform are collected in the model library named *ADT Primitive Types*. Finally, to annotate the dynamic (i.e. the application-specific behavior at run time) properties of the data in sequence diagrams, the *ADT Behavior* profile is supplied.

The ADT Classes profile contains 15 stereotypes. We discuss the four most significant stereotypes: *Concept*, *Container*, *Clientship*, and *employ* that serve the refinement of associations in the UML design model (Figure 4.b).

UML associations can vary in many ways, but at the concrete data-type level (i.e. the source-code level) there are only a few variations to relate objects. Therefore, our ADT profile offers just a directed, binary association between classes: the *Clientship*. In essence, a *Clientship* (together with a Container) is used to eliminate from the design model the multi-valued multiplicities of the association ends that represent collections of objects (Figure 4.c). *Concepts* model the atomic data elements (i.e. data records) with which the run-time data structures are composed. *Containers* show explicitly the collections of data elements at the ADT modeling level. The relationship between a container and its type of elements is indicated by means of the stereotyped dependency *employ*. The stereotype *Container* offers six tags (e.g. *lifetimeDependency*) to indicate the memory-related properties of an ADT.

## ADT Design-Space and Exploration

As stated before, since we aim at reducing the data-memory related cost factors of the application, both the memory footprint of the data elements and their number of data accesses are the driving forces behind our optimization process. However, at the ADT level, we deal with more

*Figure 5. Decision trees: (a) a binary decision tree, (b) a multiple-choice decision tree, and (c) a hybrid tree*

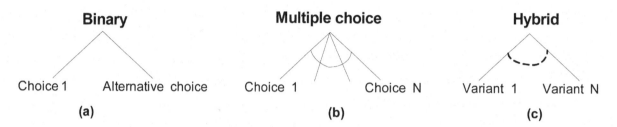

abstract concepts such as Containers, Concepts, and Clientships. These aspects are decided at the ADT-modeling level and, hence, create the ADT-level design space.

The ADT profile gives also our definition of well-formed ADT models and thus demarcates the limits of the ADT design space within which we work. Namely, every ADT model that is obtained during design-space exploration must conform to the ADT profile.

## Specifying the ADT Design Space

Optimizing a design model is traditionally based on the experience and inspiration of the designer. Consequently, only a limited number of ad-hoc design alternatives are considered. This is mainly due to the lack of a systematic methodology to explore the design space. Therefore, we reach a solution by formally specifying the ADT design space by means of decision trees.

**Decision trees:** The data that is internally managed by an application can be modeled in many different ways. These variations include the set of concepts, the set of their attributes, the configurations into containers, and their dynamic aspects (i.e. run-time memory usage and data-access patterns). We classified the most relevant design options that constitute the ADT design space in multiple constrained-orthogonal (corthogonal) decision trees (Catthoor, 2007). The orthogonal aspect means that any decision in any tree can be combined with any decision in another tree and

that the result should be a potentially valid combination. However, these trees are not independent. Earlier decisions propagate strict and potentially complex constraints to the next decision trees. Therefore, they are constrained orthogonal.

Figure 5 shows the three types of discrete decision trees that we use: (a) a binary tree that proposes two alternative options, (b) a multiple-choice decision tree with a finite number of enumerated alternatives, and (c) a tree that offers two or more variants with all their possible hybrid combinations.

We clustered the decision trees into so-called categories according to the following three classes of kindred decisions that can be distinguished in data modeling: the category *Modeling Concepts*, the category *Modeling Relations*, and the category *Dynamic Aspects*. We discuss the first two categories in more detail.

**Modeling concepts:** The category Modeling Concepts (Figure 6) assembles the decision trees a designer applies when modeling the pure data information of an application. For each distinguished Concept in an ADT model, its attributes have to be identified first. Then, for each attribute, the following decisions are to be made: the unit of the attribute value, the range of the possible values, whether its values are relatively or absolutely encoded, the fact that the value is read-only or not, and finally, whether the attribute is essential to the Concept or not (i.e. its value is derivable from other data in the model).

*Figure 6. The category of decision trees that deal with modeling concepts*

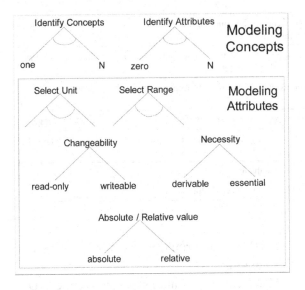

design model is larger than one. The subcategory Grouping holds the decision trees that deal with Containers and contains three decision trees. The instances of a Concept can be collected in one or more Containers. For each Container, we have to determine if its elements bear a structural or functional role to each other or to the Concept they constitute. This issue is decided by means of the HasConfiguration decision tree. If the instances of a Concept are organized into multiple Containers then the Grouping Criterion decision tree indicates which choice has to be made for the partitioning of the parts. These choices include grouping by lifetime dependency, by access pattern, by attribute value(s), or a combination of these alternatives (i.e. hybrid). The partitions can be homogeneous or heterogeneous.

## ADT Design-Space Exploration

Exploration of the ADT design space concerning memory footprint and number of data accesses consists in the systematic search for equivalent ADT models for which their run-time instances differ (i) in the set of their object types and attributes, (ii) in the quantity of their composing objects, and (iii) in their access patterns. ADT models are equivalent if their implementations exhibit the same global I/O behavior. We reach our goal by exploiting specific characteristics of the objects in the application, taking into consideration the most likely values of the non-deterministic (e.g. user input via the keyboard) input for the scenario under investigation.

It should be clear that the complete set of equivalent ADT models can be very large. However, we aim at identifying solely the subset of ADT models that yields new Pareto-optimal implementations with respect to the considered cost metrics. Therefore, we transform the original ADT model incrementally into a number of equivalent models at the same level of abstraction by means of behavior-preserving model transformations (i.e. model refactorings or restructur-

**Modeling relations:** The decision trees of the category Modeling Relations (Figure 7) are used to decide whether the instances of the Concepts are related to each other and how. If a relationship exists and we decide to save this information in the system, then a Clientship relation is inserted. In addition, a Container has to be introduced if the multiplicity value of the related objects in the

*Figure 7. The category modeling relations that deals with clientships and containers*

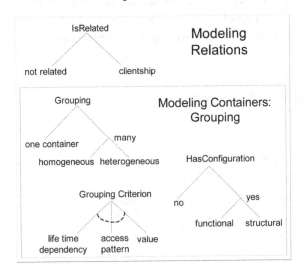

*Table 1. Overview of the catalog of generic ADT transformations with their name and intention*

| Name | Intention |
|---|---|
| Fuse Attributes | combine two attributes of a concept into one single attribute to reduce the memory footprint and to increase the data rate |
| Raise Attribute | move an attribute from a part concept to the enclosing concept to reduce the memory footprint and the number of data accesses |
| Add Computable Attribute | store a computed value as an attribute of a concept to reduce the number of data accesses |
| Partition Concept | split up a concept into two separate concepts to exploit application-specific knowledge |
| Partition Container | split up a container into two disjoint containers to exploit application-specific knowledge |
| Compress Container | compress a container to reduce the memory footprint |
| Remove Redundant Container | remove a container to reduce the memory footprint |

ings) and this steered by the system cost factors (Temmerman, Daylight, Catthoor, Demeyer, & Dhaene, 2007).

## A Catalog of Atomic ADT Transformations

To enable a systematic and incremental exploration of the ADT design-space derived in the previous subsection, we propose an initial catalog of generic and atomic behavior-preserving ADT transformations. We are inspired by transformation techniques from the software-refactoring community, e.g. (Fowler, 1999). This catalog is the outcome of our experiences in the multimedia application domain. We are aware that the exploration of other application domains is necessary to refine and discover

the ADT transformations that will complete this catalog.

This catalog contains seven atomic ADT transformations. For every transformation in this catalog, there also exists the reverse transformation. In Table 1 the names of the transformations and their intentions are listed next to give an overview.

We want to emphasize that we do not consider the memory footprint of the source code (that can increase by adding classes), but only the memory footprint of the data objects at run time. For the application domain that we target the data memory cost is more important than the program memory. The latter is namely stored typically in a huge off-chip flash memory, and only the *active* part will be loaded on-chip. Hence, both the area and energy overhead of the proposed transformations are

*Figure 8. Partition concept transformation to split up the collection of Part objects into two separate collections*

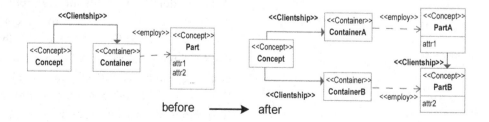

*Table 2. Consequences of the partition concept transformation*

| Pros | Cons |
|------|------|
| If the access patterns to the attributes *attr1* and *attr2* differ, then this can be exploited by the splitting. Hence, this transformation enables distribution of data accesses over two containers. | The splitting of *Part* decreases the spatial locality for the data fields *attr1* and *attr2*. |
| This transformation enables compaction in the implementations of the two new containers. | If the accesses to *attr1* and *attr2* are temporally correlated, then this partitioning can increase the pressure in the smaller memories closer to the processor. |
| If the accesses to attribute *attr1* are temporally correlated, then this transformation increases the data rate for the parts of *ContainerA* and thus also the execution time. | The overall memory footprint may be augmented due to the extra clientship between *PartA* and *PartB*. However, this depends on the implementation of this link. |
| This transformation enables implementations with a smaller memory footprint. Hence, considering the optimized access behavior, this partitioning can lead to solutions with lower energy consumption. | |
| After the splitting, we have to find for each container a cost-efficient implementation. This transformation, therefore, widens the solution space drastically, due to the multiple combinations that exist at the concrete data type level. | |

minimal. However, for the data memory, typically several layers of hierarchy are required to make the access latency acceptable and to reduce the data transfer overhead (by exploiting data reuse). In order to enable more data to stay local to the processors, i.e. be stored lower in the memory hierarchy, the proposed transformations are really crucial and they have a large impact.

What follows is a more detailed description of three ADT transformations from this catalog. The other four transformations are briefly explained to give the reader a basic idea of their usability. Inspired by the software design-patterns literature, e.g. (Gamma, Helm, Johnson, & Vlissides, 1995), we use a template to describe them in a consistent way. To enable the re-use of the transformations, we give their intention and trade-offs that exist.

## Partition Concept

### Intention
The intention of this ADT transformation is to split up concept *Part* (see Figure 8) into two separate concepts. Therefore we divide the original *Container* into two new containers, one for each new type of concept. This transformation enables the exploitation of application-specific behavior and reduces the memory footprint of the data of each resulting collection of objects.

*Figure 9. Partition container transformation to split a collection of part object into two disjoint collections*

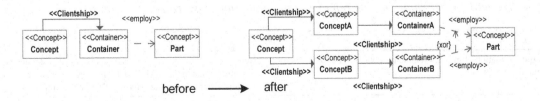

before ⟶ after

*Table 3. Consequences of applying the partition container transformation*

| Pros | Cons |
|---|---|
| If the access patterns of the two partitions differ, then this can be exploited by the splitting. Hence, the partitioning enables the distribution of the data accesses over the two new Containers. | If the partitioning has no direct impact on the dominant access patterns of the application, then this transformation increases the number of data accesses due to the introduction of an extra level in the structural hierarchy of the ADT model. |
| If the splitting criterion is well chosen, then this transformation distributes the *Part* elements over the partitions. Although the total number of elements in the containers remains the same, the splitting enables greater compaction in the implementation of each partition. Hence, considering also the (optimized) access behavior of the containers, this transformation leads to solutions with lower energy consumption. | By partitioning the container, we have two separate data structures. This may result in an increase of the total memory footprint of the data. |
| After the splitting, we have to find for each partition a cost-efficient implementation. This transformation, therefore, widens the solution space drastically, due to the multiple combinations that exist at the concrete data type level. | |

## Consequences

In Table 2, we present the tradeoffs that exist when applying this ADT transformation. The first column contains the benefits. The drawbacks are listed in the second column.

We want to emphasize that we do not consider the memory footprint of the source code (that can increase by adding classes), but only the memory footprint of the data objects at run time.

## Partition Container

### Intention

The intention of this ADT transformation is to partition a Container of *Part* objects (see Figure 9) into two disjoint containers according to a certain splitting criterion. This criterion exploits the clustering of the *Part* objects. Each of these containers can then be further refined, exploiting their specific properties, to reduce the memory footprint and/or the number of data accesses.

*Figure 10. Remove redundant container transformation to remove a collection of redundant parts*

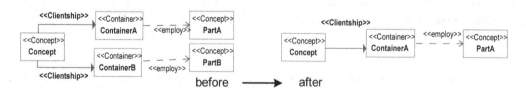

before → after

*Table 4. Tradeoffs when applying the remove redundant container transformation*

| Pros | Cons |
|---|---|
| This transformation eliminates redundant data and, hence, reduces the memory footprint. | However, when the removed data is needed, it must be deduced from the remaining data in the ADT model. This leads to an increase in the number of data accesses and thus also the execution time. |

**Consequences**

Table 3 presents the tradeoffs that have to be taken into consideration when applying this ADT transformation. The first column contains the benefits. The drawbacks are listed in the second column.

## Remove Redundant Container

**Intention**

The intention of the Remove Redundant Container transformation is to eliminate a Container that stores redundant Part objects to reduce the memory footprint. Figure 10 shows a generic ADT model before and after the transformation.

**Consequences**

The tradeoffs that exist for this ADT transformation are gathered in Table 4.

## Fuse Attributes

The intention of this ADT transformation is to compress two attributes of a Part class into one single attribute, to reduce the memory footprint of the Part instances.

If it is possible to encode the fused attribute into a value that requires less memory space, then we reduce the memory footprint of the Part instances and increase the data rate when a Part object is read or written. However, this comes at a cost in processing time when the original attributes need to be consulted.

## Raise Attribute

The intention of this transformation is to remove an attribute from a Part class and insert it into a Container, in order to reduce the memory footprint of each Part object.

This transformation only preserves the behavior if all the instances of Part have simultaneously the same value for the raised attribute. With this transformation, the attribute becomes a shared (or global) value for the whole collection.

## Add Computable Attribute

The intention this transformation is to store a computed value as an attribute that, otherwise, has to be re-derived from the Part objects, in order to reduce the number of data accesses.

This transformation increases only the memory footprint of the Container object (i.e. for a global, computable value) or enlarges the memory footprint of every Part instance (for an individual value). If the stored value is fairly stable and frequently consulted, then we reduce the number of data accesses and thus also the execution time.

## Compress Container

The intention of the Compress Container transformation is to compress a collection of Part objects into one single object, to reduce the number of elements in the collection.

If the Part instances exhibit a long-lasting and exploitable regularity, then compression makes sense and results in a reduction of the data (and, hence, also of the memory footprint) in the collection. Access operations that concern the whole collection of objects, such as a traverse, require now only one data access. On the contrary, the extraction (and also insertion and look up) of a single Part object from the compressed Container consumes an extra cost in computation time.

## CONCRETE DATA TYPE OPTIMIZATIONS AT THE SOURCE CODE LEVEL (C/C++)

### Concrete Data Types at the Source Code Level

In modern applications, data is stored in concrete data structure entities. These entities are refinements from the initial ADTs that have been specified at the UML abstraction level, and that can be transformed by the exploration described

*Figure 11. Componentized library of CDTs*

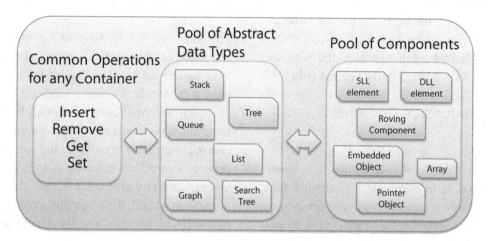

in section 5 above. In the rest of the chapter, we are going to focus only on the dynamic concrete data structures referred to from now on as *Concrete Data Types(CDTs)* like arrays, lists or trees, (Wood, 1993). These containers are realized at the software architecture level (Leeman, et al., 2005) and are responsible for keeping and organizing the data in the memory and also servicing the application's requests at run-time. These services require to include abstract data type operators for storing, retrieving or altering any data value, which is not tied to a specific container implementation and shares a common interface (as in STL (SGI, 2006)). The implementation of these operators depends on the chosen container and each one of them can favor specific data access and storage patterns.

Each application can host a number of different containers according to its particular data access and storage pattern in the algorithm. Choosing an improper operator and container implementation for an abstract data type will have significant negative impact on the dynamic memory subsystem of the embedded system (Bartzas, et al., 2006). On the one hand, inefficient data access and storage operations cause performance issues, due to the added computational overhead of the internal CDT mechanisms. On the other hand, each access of the

CDTs to the physical memory (where the data is stored) consumes energy and unnecessary accesses can comprise a very significant portion of the overall power of the system (Daylight, Demoen, & Catthoor, 2004; Bartzas, et al., 2006)

## Concrete Data Types Design Space and Exploration

In today's object oriented application designs, a modular way of building the software is adopted and this also includes the application's data handling. Libraries like STL show a modern trend of componentized design that has many advantages over the more classical monolithic approach. A CDT can be implemented by combining several modules of some basic data structures. Based on this componentization strategy, we present a library of ADTs and corresponding CDT modules that offers the designer a wide range of choices in the ADT implementation. Depending on the application a customized CDT can be a better choice than usual solutions like arrays or simple lists.

As depicted in Figure 11, the library consists of two pools of components. First, we have the ADTs, where we should provide support for a number of abstract data types, in order for the library to support many applications. The ADT is strongly

*Figure 12. A singly linked list (SLL) with roving pointer. This pointer remembers the last accessed position so traversals begin from that point instead starting from the beginning*

# SLL(O)

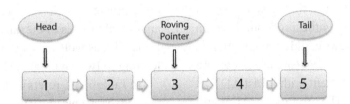

connected to the application's functionality, so a designer cannot simply change the ADT. Instead, one can work on ADT transformations, like the one's presented in chapter 5.3. However, we are free to change the underlying implementation of the ADT. For example, a List ADT can be implemented using an array or a linked list.

As an example of the design space created by the wide range of ADT implementation choices, we present the basic CDT modules used to concretize all ADTs of Figure 11.

*Figure 13. CDT synthesis procedure*

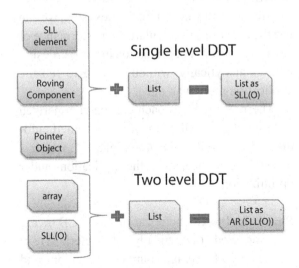

- Array (AR): is a set of sequentially indexed elements of size. Each element of the array is a record of the application.
- Single Linked List (SLL): SLL is a singly linked list of pointers. Each element of the list is connected with the next element through a pointer.
- Double Linked List (DLL): DLL is a doubly linked list of pointers. Each element of the list is connected with the next and the previous element with two separate pointers.

In addition, we should include the fundamental variations of these basic CDTs, regarding their key value (Atienza, et al., 2007), to cover effectively the design space of CDT implementations, namely:

- Pointer (P): in the pointer variation of each basic CDT, the record of the application is stored outside the CDT and is accessed via a pointer. This leads to a smaller CDT size, but also to an extra memory access to reach the actual data.
- Roving Pointer (O): The roving pointer is an auxiliary pointer useful to access a particular element of a list with fewer accesses in case of iterator-based access patterns.

For instance, for an array if you access element $n + 1$ immediately after element n, your average access count is $1 + 1$ instead of $n/2 + 1$. Figure 12 presents a singly linked list with a roving pointer.

All these components can be combined to form customized CDTs. The library is realized in a modular way for easy synthesis of complex data structures. For example we could combine a Single Linked List (SLL) element, a Roving Pointer and a Pointer Object component with a List ADT as depicted in Figure 13. The produced CDT would be a singly linked list, integrating an optimization for sequential access (roving pointer), where all elements contain pointers to the actual data

By taking advantage of object oriented design techniques, all DDT implementations can be re-used to construct multilevel data structures. For instance, as depicted in Figure 13, in the place of an object we could have a single-level DDT implementation. In the example, each array element is in fact a singly linked list (SLL(O)) under the List ADT, forming a two-level data structure. The number of levels we can add to the DDT implementations is not limited by the design of the library, rather than the applicability and usefulness of such complex implementations.

## Design Space Exploration

Normally, a designer would have to test all possible CDT implementations for an ADT to identify which one suits best the targeted application. However, this is not feasible in most modern complex applications, as the number of ADTs to optimize is too great. For example, for an application that has 10 ADTs and considering 10 CDT candidates for each one, we should run $10^{10}$ times our application to see which CDT combination performs best.

To tackle with this situation another approach is proposed. This approach is based on an analytical pre-characterization of CDT implementations.

The behavior of basic CDTs is analytically characterized in terms of average number of memory accesses needed to perform certain operations and average memory size. In other words, equations that describe the average number of memory accesses for sequential and random access patterns to the elements of each CDT implementation are extracted. Table 5 presents the whole set of analytical models of the basic CDTs presented in Figure 11, as well as some combinations of them leading to two layered CDTs.

In Table 5, $NA_r$ refers to the number of accesses needed to retrieve one value with a random access pattern to the CDT, $NA_s$ relates to the total number of accesses required to access all the values stored in the CDT with an iterator-based access pattern. Then, $S_{av}$ indicates the average memory footprint used by the CDT during the execution of the application. Furthermore, $N_e$ is the number of valid or initialized elements in the CDT, $N_a$ is the number of reserved or allocated positions that can be used to store elements in the CDT, $s_w$ is the width of a word on the architecture and $s_T$ the size of one element of type $T$.

To use these equations, we also need a trace of the application's data accesses. In order to obtain that, we need to integrate a profiling library like (Poucet C., Atienza, D., & Catthoor, F., 2006) with the application. Such a trace would record and discern between sequential and random accesses and memory allocations. In the next step, we can use the equations to calculate the performance of each possible CDT combination in various design metrics analytically, without having to run the application more than once.

The proposed approach can be summarized in three phases. All of them are executed automatically, except for the initial phase 1, which is executed only once, for all the applications under optimization:

**Phase 1:** Pre-characterization. All CDTs are modeled (analytically characterized) in terms of average number of random and

*Table 5. Analytical characterization of basic and two layered CDTs*

| CDT Implementation | Sequential (NAs) Access Count | Random (NAr) Access Count | Average Size (Sav) |
|---|---|---|---|
| SLL(AR) | $3 \times N_e + N_a$ | $\dfrac{N_e}{2 \times N_a} + 3$ | $5s_w + \dfrac{N_e}{N_a}$ |
| SLL(ARO) | $3 \times N_e + N_a$ | $\dfrac{N_e}{2 \times N_a} + \dfrac{3 \times N_a}{N_e} + 1$ | $7s_w + \dfrac{N_e}{N_a} \times (3s_w + s_T)$ |
| DLL(AR) | $3 \times N_e + N_a$ | $\dfrac{N_e}{4 \times N_a} + 3$ | $6s_w + \dfrac{N_e}{N_a} \times (4s_w + s_T)$ |
| DLL(ARO) | $3 \times N_e + N_a$ | $\dfrac{N_e}{4 \times N_a} + \dfrac{N_a}{5 \times N_e} + \dfrac{5}{4}$ | $8s_w + \dfrac{N_e}{N_a} \times (4s_w + s_T)$ |
| SLL | $3 \times N_e$ | $\dfrac{N_e}{2} + 1$ | $4s_w + N_e(2s_w + s_T)$ |
| SLL(O) | $3 \times N_e$ | $\dfrac{N_e}{2} + \dfrac{1}{N_e}$ | $6s_w + N_e(2s_w + s_T)$ |
| DLL | $3 \times N_e$ | $4N_e + 1$ | $5s_w + N_e(3s_w + s_T)$ |
| DLL(O) | $3 \times N_e$ | $\dfrac{N_e}{4} + \dfrac{2}{N_e} + \dfrac{1}{4}$ | $7s_w + N_e(3s_w + s_T)$ |
| AR | $N_a$ | $1$ | $N_a \times s_T$ |
| AR(P) | $2 \times N_a$ | $2$ | $N_a(s_T + s_w)$ |

*Figure 14. Shows an overview of the different phases (in light gray) and the inputs (in dark gray) required to perform the overall CDTs optimization*

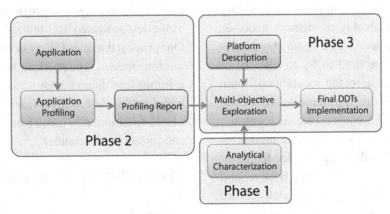

sequential accesses, and average size for a given number of elements. This phase happens only once. The models are required by the multi-objective algorithm to analytically calculate the performance of each DDT implementation, for various cost factors, i.e. execution time, memory footprint and energy consumption.

**Phase 2:** Profiling. Here, the initial profiling of the iterator-based access methods to the different CDTs used in the application takes place. A detailed report is produced, which comprises all the accesses to the CDTs done by the application. This report, along with the analytical models and the platform description are fed to our multi-objective evolutionary algorithm during the third phase.

**Phase 3:** Evaluation. Exploiting the characteristics of the final platform, we perform an exploration of the design space of CDTs implementation using multi-objective computation. (Figure 14)

## CASE STUDY FOR COMBINED ADT/ CDT EXPERIMENTAL RESULTS

In modern embedded systems, due to their energy-efficient nature, the most typical memory architecture available consists of several memory levels (i.e. on-chip and off-chip memories) to try to make use of the locality of memory accesses in real-life applications. As a result, hardware-controlled caches are used to try to map all of the most frequently accessed locations of main memories in smaller on-chip memories very close to the processor. The energy cost in accessing and communicating with these cache memories is much smaller than that required for fetching/ storing information from/into large background memories. In the first memory architecture (marked as option a), we consider one level of on-chip hardware-controlled cache (i.e. L1) and

the main memory for our dynamic memory management subsystem. With this architecture, all the accesses to the data pass through the cache. Hence, when the microprocessor requests the access to certain dynamic data (both the dynamic data generated in the application and the maintenance dynamic data structures), the hardware takes care of transparently moving the data from the main memory to the cache. After this, the processor accesses the data from the cache memory and any later access to the same data is fetched from the hardware-controlled cache.

In the second type of architecture (labelled as b in Figure 15), we have software controlled on-chip SRAM memories (i.e. scratchpad memories) for the dynamic memory management subsystem instead of on-chip hardware controlled caches. To efficiently transfer data between main memory and the scratchpad, which is rather costly in just a line-based copy scheme, we consider extra available hardware, i.e. a Direct Memory Access controller (DMA), to be able to transfer also bursts of data (i.e. several lines in the same copy process). If the DMA is not programmed for a certain transfer of data, then the microprocessor directly fetches the dynamic data from the main memory using the global bus of the system (i.e. bypassing the scratchpad). In the context of this book chapter, results are demonstrated by using the second processor-scratchpad memory architecture. Nevertheless, our methodologies work also for the processor-cache memory architecture as we demonstrated in (Mamagkakis, et al 2004). Our proposed methodology is independent of the microprocessor type and frequency used because it minimizes data accesses and data footprint at a higher abstraction level (and thus less data accesses automatically mean less memory accesses and higher performance).

### The Spell-Checker Application

The spell-checker application is a popular embedded software application found in most of

*Table 6. Characterization of input texts*

|  | Text-1 | Text-2 | Text-3 |
|---|---|---|---|
| Number of Words | 303 | 1 107 | 7 764 |
| Erroneous Words | 41 | 152 | 1 239 |
| Error Rate [%] | 13.5 | 13.7 | 15.92 |

*Figure 15. Typical processor-cache/scratchpad memory architecture*

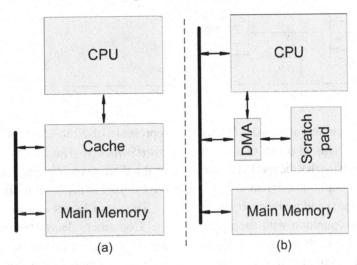

today's mobile phones with email client ((Absar & Catthoor, 2006) and (Kukich, 1992)). The functionality is simple: to determine whether a word is spelled correctly, the spell checker compares each input word against its internal dictionary. If a word is not found in the dictionary, it is added

to a list of misspelled words. At startup of the application the dictionary is loaded into memory, i.e., a new dictionary is created with words from an external word list.

The dictionary of the spell checker is created from a word list provided by (Kelk, 2003). For the presented experiments a dictionary consisting of 20 833 words was used.

The results of the profiling are obtained by spell checking different texts taken from various newspapers and news magazines. In order to make the texts comparable a common genre (i.e., daily news) was chosen (See Table 6 for details of three representative input texts.).

Originally, the dictionary of the spell-checker application is modeled with one Trie ADT (Fred-

*Figure 16. Conceptual trie ADT*

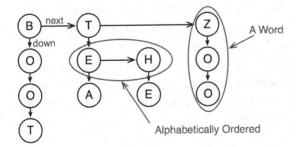

*Figure 17. ADT model of spell-checker application*

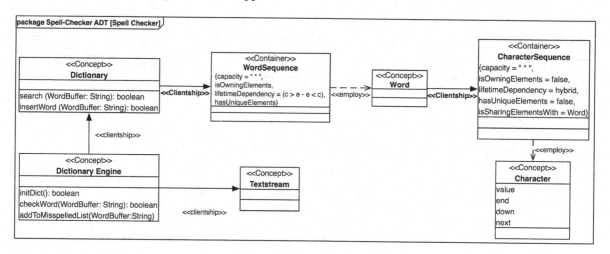

kin, 1960). A Trie is a commonly used ADT to represent dictionaries. This specific choice is motivated by the observation that the spell-checker application receives a continuous, dynamic input stream (i.e., the input text) and performs both an insertion and a search operation with each part of the input stream (i.e., each word) on a large data set (i.e., the dictionary). Thus the main abstract data type needs to be space efficient as well as algorithmically efficient in lookups and inserts. The Trie ATD meets both requirements. It is space efficient by sharing tree branches for words starting with the same letters and allows fast insertion and lookup by using the alphabet as index. Figure 16 shows how sharing of characters and alphabetical ordering is conceptually realized in a Trie ATD.

The design of the spell-checker is modeled using the ADT profile (Temmerman M., 2008). Figure 17 shows the ADT model of the spell-checker and specifically the Trie. When modeling the Trie it is crucial to model what characterizes the Trie at the modeling level, i.e., a word is unique in the dictionary yet it might share a sequence of letters with other words.

The set of words in the dictionary is represented by the Container *WordSequence* associated with the Concept *Dictionary*. A single word is represented by the Concept *Word* contained in *WordSequence*. The fact that a word is unique in the dictionary is expressed by the constraint *hasUniqueElements* set to its default, i.e., true.

The set of letters in a word is represented by the Container *CharacterSequence* containing the individual letters as the Concept *Character*. Sharing of letters in the Trie is modeled by the constraint *hasUniqueElements* set to false and *isSharingElementsWith = Word* indicates who the characters are shared with.

The attributes *end*, *down* and *next* represent parts of the unique structure of the Trie. *End* denotes the end of a word. *Down* refers to the next possible character in a word as shown in Figure 16. While *next* establishes the alphabetical order within the Trie. This is relevant since it represent the knowledge of each character of its position in the dictionary.

The initial Trie implementation is realized with a single-linked list concrete data type (CDT). The experimental results taken in the context of this work assume a 2-layer hierarchy of single-port on-chip SRAM memories (L1 up to 64Kbytes and L2 up to 1MByte) for single microprocessor systems. Energy consumption is calculated based on the energy model provided by (Papanikolaou, et al., 2003).

*Figure 18. Fuse attribute ADT transformation*

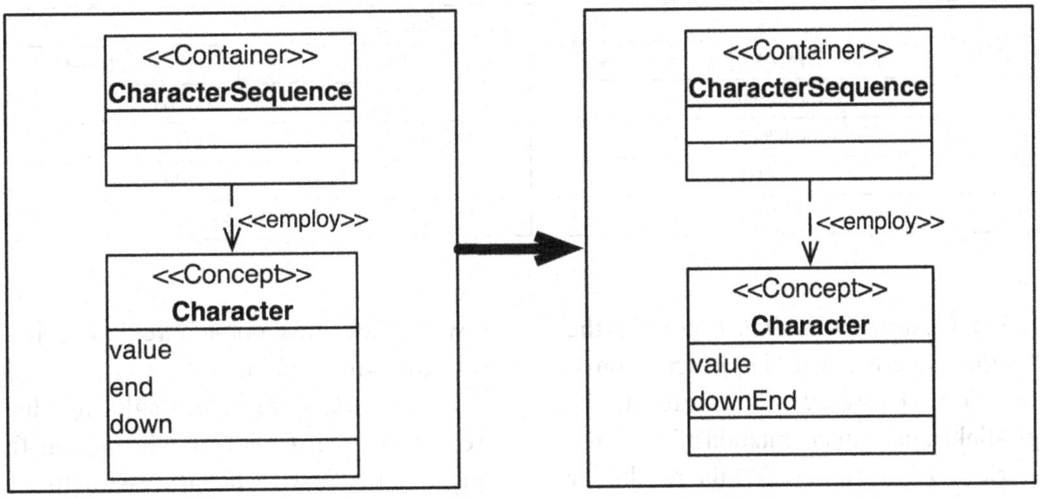

## Fuse Attributes ADT Transformation

The Fuse Attribute transformation replaces two attributes by one attribute. The values of both attributes are accessible through the new attribute. The transformation is applied in order to reduce the memory footprint of the concept, while an increase in processing effort is to be expected when the values of each attribute need to be consulted individually.

In the spell-checker the transformation was applied to fuse the *down* and *end* attributes into *downEnd* in the concept *Character* as shown in Figure 18. The *end* attribute determines whether the end of a word is reached in order to stop lookup

in the dictionary. The *down* attribute refers to the next character in a word. When the end of a word is reached the down attribute is not necessary anymore. Thus *downEnd* acts as the down attribute within the word, while it refers to the last character itself in order to denote the end of the word. Removing end accounts to removing a 4 Byte integer from each Character, i.e., from every node in the Trie.

## Results

Table 7 shows the experimental results for accesses and memory footprint of the Fuse Attribute transformation. The table presents the results for three

*Table 7. Fuse Attribute results for accesses and memory footprint*

| | Accesses | | | Mem[B] | | |
|---|---|---|---|---|---|---|
| | Text-1 | Text-2 | Text-3 | Text-1 | Text-2 | Text-3 |
| adt1(cdt1) | 2633928 | 2712209 | 3364289 | 859744 | 862408 | 888496 |
| adt2(cdt1) | 2580257 | 2658538 | 3310618 | 645060 | 647724 | 673812 |
| adt2(cdt2) | 870273 | 890341 | 1063109 | 7085580 | 7088244 | 7114332 |
| Gain | 66.96% | 67.17% | 68.4% | -724.15% | -721.91% | -700.72% |

adt1(cdt1) Original Implementation, single-linked list Trie
adt1(cdt2) Trie ADT with fused attributes, single-linked list Trie
adt2(cdt2) Trie ADT with fused attributes, array-structured Trie
Gain Gain from adt2(cdt2) to adt1(cdt1)

*Table 8. Fuse attribute results for energy*

| | Energy [nJ] | | |
| --- | --- | --- | --- |
| | **Text-1** | **Text-2** | **Text-3** |
| adt1(cdt1) | 4988660 | 5136924 | 6371963 |
| adt2(cdt1) | 4887007 | 5035271 | 6270310 |
| adt2(cdt2) | 7279834 | 7447702 | 8892907 |
| Gain | -45.93% | -44.98% | -39.56% |

different input texts. Row *adt1(cdt1)* presents the results for the single-linked list implementation of the initial Trie ADT, row *adt2(cdt1)* the results for the single-linked list implementation of the transformed Trie ADT, and *adt2(cdt2)* the results for the array-based implementation of the transformed Trie ADT. The gain is calculated by comparing the initial single-linked list Trie implementation (*adt1(cdt1)*) with the ADT and CDT transformed implementation (*adt2(cdt2)*).

Rows *adt1(cdt1)* and *adt2(cdt1)* represent the ADT Transformation Fuse Attribute. For this transformation the number of accesses is reduced. The access scheme of the spell-checker application consists of two phases: setting up the dictionary by loading all words into memory and checking a given input text. A reduction of accesses is due to the fact that in the setup phase only the *downEnd* attribute is written for each character instead of two attributes. In phase two, the lookup, the number of accesses is not decreased. The memory footprint is reduced since both the end attribute

as well as the down pointer are now represented by one downEnd pointer.

In row *adt2(cdt2)* the results for the concrete data type (CDT) transformation from a single-linked list to an array-structured Trie are shown. The CDT transformation decreases the number of accesses additional to the ADT transformation. Accesses are mainly saved since each access to the Trie required a traversal of the single-linked list Trie, while an array implementation provides direct access to the array cells. The memory footprint that was decreased by the ADT Fuse Attribute transformation is increased by the CDT transformation. This is explained by the need to allocate a full array of possible next letters in a word even in cases where cells of the array might stay empty. E.g., a Trie for the two words 'Trie' and 'Tree' contains six cells in the linked-list (one for each letter minus the shared letters, in this case 't' and 'r'). In the array-structured Trie implementation one array of 26 cells is allocated for each letter position

*Figure 19. Fuse attribute results for accesses and memory footprint*

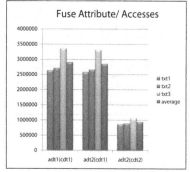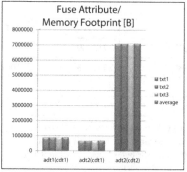

*Figure 20. Fuse attribute results for energy*

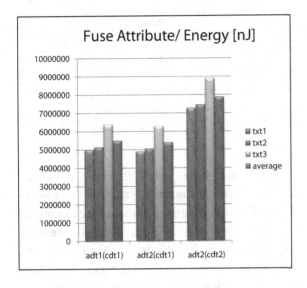

in a word, i.e., four arrays for the word 'Trie' and since the letters 't' and 'r' are shared two more arrays for the last two letters of 'Tree'. (The array cells contain pointers to the next letter of the word.)

Table 8 shows the results for energy consumption of both the ADT and CDT transformation. The ADT Fuse Attribute transformation applied on the single-linked list Trie reduces the overall energy consumption due to the decrease in both number of accesses as well as memory footprint (Figure 19). The increase in memory footprint of the CDT transformation weights heavy enough to increase the overall energy consumption (Figure 20) of the spell-checker application.

## Partition Container ADT Transformation

The Partition Container transformation suggests splitting a Container into two new Containers according to a splitting criterion. In the spell-checker example the Container *WordSequence* is split into two new containers, namely *WordSequence1* and *WordSequence2*. This is motivated by the different access behavior due to the varying occurrence frequency of different words in a language. Thus

*Figure 21. Partition container ADT transformation*

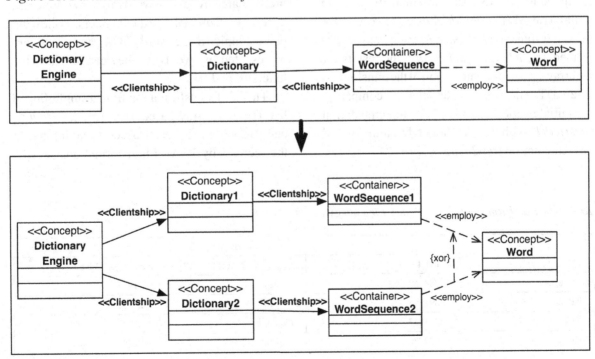

*Table 9. Partition container results for accesses and memory footprint*

| | Accesses | | | Mem[B] | | |
|---|---|---|---|---|---|---|
| | **Text-1** | **Text-2** | **Text-3** | **Text-1** | **Text-2** | **Text-3** |
| adt1(cdt1) | 2633928 | 2712209 | 3364289 | 859744 | 862408 | 888496 |
| adt2(cdt1) | 2560338 | 2646210 | 3400178 | 950480 | 953144 | 979232 |
| adt2(cdt2) | 1039158 | 1062633 | 1268965 | 14005720 | 14008384 | 14034472 |
| Gain | 60.55% | 60.82% | 62.28% | -1529.06% | -1524.33% | -1479.57% |

the splitting criterion is the occurrence frequency. In the presented example, the most frequent words (3219 words with the highest occurrence frequency) are assigned to the Container *WordSequence1* while the majority of the words (17614 words) are assigned to *WordSequence2*. Figure 21 shows the ADT transformation on the conceptual spell-checker ADT model.

## Results

Table 9 shows the experimental results for accesses and memory footprint of the Partition Container transformation for the three different input texts. Row *adt1(cdt1)* presents the results for the single-linked list implementation of the initial Trie ADT, row *adt2(cdt1)* the results for the single-linked list implementation of the transformed Trie ADT, and *adt2(cdt2)* the results for the array-based implementation of the transformed Trie ADT. The gain is calculated by comparing the initial single-linked list Trie implementation (*adt1(cdt1)*) with the ADT and CDT transformed implementation (*adt2(cdt2)*).

Rows *adt1(cdt1)* and *adt2(cdt1)* represent the ADT Transformation Partition Container. Through partitioning the *WordSequence* Container the number of accesses is reduced. This is easily explained by the fact that in the search phase the smaller dictionary is accessed more often than the large dictionary, i.e., the small dictionary is accessed every time a word is looked up while the larger dictionary is only accessed if a word is not found in the small dictionary. Due to the Trie's structure, traversals of a smaller Trie are less costly than traversals of a larger Trie. The memory footprint is increased because some of the sharing of characters is split between the two new containers. That is, characters that were formerly shared by several words are now duplicated in the two *WordSequence* containers. Following our example, if the words 'Trie' and 'Tree' are represented by two Tries, they cannot share the letters 't' and 'r'.

The CDT transformation from a single-linked list Trie to a array-based Trie (row *adt2(cdt2)*) decreases the number of accesses additional to the decrease by the ADT transformation. Here the

*Table 10. Partition container results for energy consumption*

| | Energy [nJ] | | |
|---|---|---|---|
| | **Text-1** | **Text-2** | **Text-3** |
| adt1(cdt1) | 4988660 | 5136924 | 6371963 |
| adt2(cdt1) | 2891956 | 2975648 | 3527252 |
| adt2(cdt2) | 7743247 | 7794270 | 8363287 |
| Gain | -55.22% | -51.73% | -31.25% |

*Figure 22. Partition concept results for accesses and memory footprint*

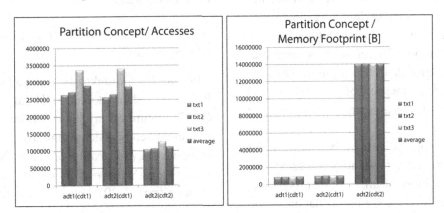

direct access behavior of the arrays is added to the benefit of often accessing a smaller container. As explained earlier, the memory footprint of a array-structured Trie implementation is increased compared to a single-linked list Trie implementation, due to the allocation of full arrays. Further the already applied ADT splitting transformation and thus the duplication of formerly shared characters adds to this effect.

Table 10 presents the results of the Partition Container transformation in terms of overall energy consumption. The ADT transformation Partition Container reduces the overall en-

ergy consumption while after applying the CDT transformation the overall energy consumption increases again resulting in negative gains (see Figures 22, 23).

## FUTURE TRENDS

Future trends in respect with abstract and concrete data types are pointing towards: (i) increased automation and code generation, (ii) faster exploration mechanisms and, finally, (iii) more run-time optimizations based on system scenarios. Today, each abstract or concrete data type must be individually conceived, manually developed and then inserted in a software library. This limits the amount of data types that can be used by the exploration mechanisms and thus limit the customization potential of our approach. Automatic code generation from a higher level of abstraction description would solve this problem, thus enabling more exploration options, which eventually lead to finer grain customizations and bigger optimizations.

Additionally, faster exploration mechanisms would need to be developed in order to select the correct optimized solution in a limited timeframe. The combinations, which are available from the current search space, are already exploding for

*Figure 23. Partition concept results for energy*

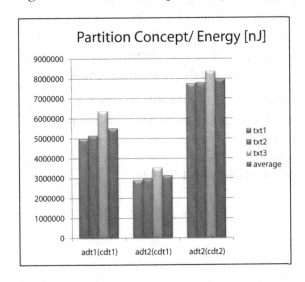

data storage and access intensive software applications and, as noted earlier, the search space is only going to increase with automatic code generation solutions. Therefore, new heuristics and methodologies that reduce the design time needed for the exploration of the abstract and concrete data type design search space are going to be developed.

Finally, as applications are becoming more dynamic we are going to identify and select and implement a number of different data types according to the different scenarios that are being manifested. These scenarios will depend both on input and on the situation of the whole hardware and software system. These system scenarios will address the need for finer grain optimization according to the different run time situations of the system and avoid a single worst case data type implementation.

## CONCLUSION

To conclude, since a software application of an embedded system is dedicated to a specific task, design engineers can optimize it by exploiting very specialized knowledge, deriving an optimally customized system. In this book chapter, we describe both novel UML transformations at the modeling level and C/C++ transformations at the software implementation level that utilize the application specific knowledge to deliver optimizations and trade-offs for relevant cost factors. Using real life case studies we show how our individual and combined transformations result in significant improvement in memory footprint, performance and energy consumption with respect to the initial implementation. Moreover, thanks to our holistic approach, we are able to identify new and non-trivial solutions that could hardly be found with the traditional design methods.

## REFERENCES

Alloy Website. Retrieved from http://alloy.mit.edu/index.php

Atienza, D., Baloukas, C., Papadopoulos, L., Poucet, C., Mamagkakis, S., Hidalgo, J. I., et al. (2007). Optimization of dynamic data structures in multimedia embedded systems using evolutionary computation. *Proceedings of the 10th International Workshop on Software & Compilers for Embedded Systems* (pp. 31-40). Nice, France: ACM.

Atienza, D., Mendias, J. M., Mamagkakis, S., Soudris, D., & Catthoor, F. (2006). Systematic dynamic memory management design methodology for reduced memory footprint. *ACM Transactions on Design Automation of Electronic Systems*, *11*(2), 465–489.

Baloukas, C., Papadopoulos, L., Mamagkakis, S., Soudris, D. (2007, October 4-5). Component based library implementation of abstract data types for resource management customization of embedded systems. *Embedded Systems for Real-Time Multimedia (ESTIMedia 2007), IEEE/ACM/IFIP Workshop* (pp. 99–104).

Bartzas, A., Mamagkakis, S., Pouiklis, G., Atienza, D., Catthoor, F., Soudris, D., et al. (2006). Dynamic data type refinement methodology for systematic performance-energy design exploration of network applications. *DATE '06: Proceedings of the Conference on Design, Automation, and Test in Europe* (pp. 740--745). Munich, Germany: European Design and Automation Association.

Benini, L., & de Micheli, G. (2000). System-level power optimization: Techniques and tools. *ACM Transactions on Design Automation of Electronic Systems*, *5*(2), 115–192. doi:10.1145/335043.335044

Boger, M., Sturm, T., & Fragemann, P. (2003). Refactoring browser for UML. In *NODe '02: Revised Papers from the International Conference NetObjectDays on Objects, Components, Architectures, Services, and Applications for a Networked World* (pp. 366–377).

Catthoor, F. (2007). *Course on metaconcepts and unified system design flow*. Retrieved from http://www.imec.be/tcmwebapp/internet/platform/index.htm

Catthoor, F., & Brockmeyer, E. (2000). Unified metaflow summary for low-power data-dominated applications. In *Unified low-power design flow for data-dominated multimedia and telecom applications*. Boston: Kluwer Academic Publishers.

Catthoor, F., de Greef, E., & Wuytack, S. (1998). *Custom memory management methodology: Exploration of memory organisation for embedded multimedia system design*. Kluwer Academic Publishers.

Cosmas, G., et al. (2002). *3D murale*. Retrieved from http://www.brunel.ac.uk/project/murale/home.html

Daylight, E. G., Demoen, B., & Catthoor, F. (2004). Formally specifying dynamic data structures for embedded software design: An initial approach. *SPACE 2004: Semantics, Program Analysis, and Computing Environments for Memory Management (Proceedings not published)*. Venice, Italy.

Fowler, M. (1999). *Refactoring: Improving the design of existing code*. Boston: Addison-Wesley Longman Publishing Co., Inc.

Fredkin, E. (1960). Trie memory. *Communications of the ACM*, 3(9), 490–499. doi:doi:10.1145/367390.367400

Gamma, E., Helm, R., Johnson, R., & Vlissides, J. (1995). *Design patterns: Elements of reusable object-oriented software*. Boston: Addison-Wesley Longman Publishing Co., Inc.

Gheyi, R., Massoni, T., & Borba, P. (2005). A rigorous approach for proving model refactorings. In *ASE '05: Proceedings of the 20th IEEE/ACM International Conference on Automated Software Engineering* (pp. 372–375).

Gorp, P. V., Stenten, H., Mens, T., & Demeyer, S. (2003). Towards automating source-consistent UML refactorings. In *Proceedings of UML* (pp. 144–158).

Green, P. A., Jr. (1997). The art of creating reliable software-based systems using off-the-shelf software components. In *SRDS '97: Proceedings of the 16th Symposium on Reliable Distributed Systems (SRDS '97)*, Washington, D.C. (p. 118). IEEE Computer Society.

Guttag, J. (1977). Abstract data types and the development of data structures. *Communications of the ACM*, 20(6), 396–404. doi:doi:10.1145/359605.359618

Kandemir, M., Ramanujam, J., & Choudhary, A. (1999). Improving cache locality by a combination of loop and data transformations. *IEEE Transactions on Computers*, 48(2), 159–167. doi:10.1109/12.752657

Kotz, D., & Essien, K. (2005). Analysis of a campus-wide wireless network. *Wireless Networks*, 11(1-2), 115–131. doi:doi:10.1007/s11276-004-4750-0

Leeman, M., Atienza, D., Deconinck, G., Florio, V., Mendias, J. M., & Ykman-Couvreur, C. (2005). Methodology for refinements and optimisation of dynamic memory management for embedded systems in multimedia applications. *VLSI Signal Processing*, 40, 383–396. doi:10.1007/s11265-005-5272-4

Mamagkakis, S., Atienza, D., Poucet, C., Catthoor, F., Soudris, D. & Mendias, J. M. (2004). Custom design of multilevel dynamic memory management subsystem for embedded systems. *In Proceedings of the IEEE Workshop on Signal Processing Systems (SIPS)* (pp. 170-175). IEEE Press.

Marchal, P., Gomez, J., Atienza, D., Mamagkakis, S., & Catthoor, F. (2005). Power aware data and memory management for dynamic applications. *IEE Proceedings. Computers and Digital Techniques, 152*(2), 224–238. doi:10.1049/ip-cdt:20045077

Memik, G., Mangione-Smith, W. H., & Hu, W. (2001). NetBench: A benchmarking suite for network processors. *ICCAD '01: Proceedings of the 2001 IEEE/ACM International Conference on Computer-aided Design* (pp. 39-42). San Jose, CA: IEEE Press.

Moby Games. *A game documentation and review project*. Retrieved from http://www.mobygames.com/

Mpeg4. *Iso/iec jtc1/sc29/wg11 mpeg-4 standard features overview*. Retrieved from http://www.chiariglione.org/mpeg/standards/mpeg-4/mpeg-4.htm

OMG. (2007). *Unified modeling language specification 2.1.1*. Retrieved from http://www.omg.org/spec/UML/2.1.1/

Poucet, C., Atienza, D., & Catthoor, F. (2006). Template-based semiautomatic profiling of multimedia applications. *Proceedings of the International Conference on Multimedia and Expo (ICME 2006)* (pp. 1061 - 1064). Toronto, Canada: IEEE Computer, IEEE Signal Processing, IEEE System & IEEE Communications Society.

SGI. (2006). *Standard template library*. Retrieved from http://www.sgi.com/tech/stl

Shreedhar, M., & Varghese, G. (1995). Efficient fair queuing using deficit round robin. *SIGCOMM*. Cambridge.

Smaragdakis, Y., & Batory, D. (2001). Mixin-based programming in C++. (LNCS 163).

Sodagar, I. (1999, March). Scalable wavelet coding for synthetic and natural hybrid images. *IEEE Transactions on Circuits and Systems for Video Technology, 9*(2), 244–254. doi:doi:10.1109/76.752092

Steinke, S., Wehmeyer, L., Lee, B., & Marwedel, P. (2002). Assigning program and data objects to scratchpad for energy reduction. In *DATE '02: Proceedings of the Conference on Design, Automation, and Test in Europe*, Washington, D.C. (p. 409). IEEE Computer Society.

Sunye, G., Pollet, D., Traon, Y. L., & Jezequel, J.-M. (2001). Refactoring UML models. In *UML 200-the unified modeling language: Modeling Languages, Concepts, and Tools. 4th International Conference* (LNCS 2185, pp. 134–148).

Tannenbaum, A. S. (2005). *Modern operating systems* (p. 992). Upper Saddle River, NJ: Prentice-Hall, Inc.

Temmerman, M. (2008). *An ADT Profile*. Retrieved from http://www.lore.ua.ac.be/Research/Artefacts/

Temmerman, M. (2008). *Optimizing abstract data type models for dynamic and data-dominant embedded applications*. Unpublished doctoral dissertation, Antwerp.

Temmerman, M., Daylight, E., Catthoor, F., Demeyer, S., & Dhaene, T. (2007). Optimizing data structures at the modeling level in embedded multimedia. [JSA]. *Journal of Systems Architecture, 53*(8), 539–549.doi:doi:10.1016/j.sysarc.2006.11.008

Vandevoorde, D., & Josuttis, N. M. (2003). *C++ templates, the complete guide.* London: Addison Wesley.

Warmer, J., & Kleppe, A. (1998). *The object constraint language: Precise modeling with UML.* Addison-Wesley.

Wood, D. (1993). *Data structures, algorithms, and performance.* USA: Addison-Wesley Longman Publishing Co.

Zhe, M., Marchal, P., Scarpazza, D., Yang, P., Wong, C., Gomez, J. I., et al. (2007). *Systematic methodology for real-time cost effective mapping of dynamic concurrent task-based systems on heterogeneous platforms.* Springer.

# Section 2
# Aspect–Oriented Approaches

The second section includes three chapters on approaches that use aspect-oriented concepts, namely the separation of concerns, to address the modeling of embedded systems.

# Chapter 4

# Concern Separation for Adaptive QoS Modeling in Distributed Real-time Embedded Systems

**Jeff Gray**
*University of Alabama at Birmingham, USA*

**Sandeep Neema**
*Vanderbilt University, USA*

**Jing Zhang**
*Motorola Research, USA*

**Yuehua Lin**
*Honda Manufacturing of Alabama, USA*

**Ted Bapty**
*Vanderbilt University, USA*

**Aniruddha Gokhale**
*Vanderbilt University, USA*

**Douglas C. Schmidt**
*Vanderbilt University, USA*

## ABSTRACT

*The development of distributed real-time and embedded (DRE) systems is often challenging due to conflicting quality-of-service (QoS) constraints that must be explored as trade-offs among a series of alternative design decisions. The ability to model a set of possible design alternatives—and to analyze and simulate the execution of the representative model—helps derive the correct set of QoS parameters needed to satisfy DRE system requirements. QoS adaptation is accomplished via rules that specify how to modify application or middleware behavior in response to changes in resource availability. This chapter*

DOI: 10.4018/978-1-60566-750-8.ch004

*presents a model-driven approach for generating QoS adaptation rules in DRE systems. This approach creates high-level graphical models representing QoS adaptation policies. The models are constructed using a domain-specific modeling language—the adaptive quality modeling language (AQML)—which assists in separating common concerns of a DRE system via different modeling views. The chapter motivates the need for model transformations to address crosscutting and scalability concerns within models. In addition, a case study is presented based on bandwidth adaptation in video streaming of unmanned aerial vehicles.*

## INTRODUCTION

The ability to adapt is an essential trait of distributed real-time and embedded (DRE) systems, where quality-of-service (QoS) requirements demand a system adjust to external evironment changes in a timely manner. A DRE system typically consists of a stack of software layers that are coupled to a physical system (e.g., a control system within an automotive factory or avionics subsystem). Several capabilities are needed to provide adaptability within DRE systems, including (1) the ability to express QoS requirements in some manipulatable form, (2) a mechanism to monitor important conditions associated with the environment and physical system, and (3) a causal relation between the monitoring of the environment and the specification of the QoS requirements (Karr et al., 2001). Addressing QoS concerns via software adaptation has a concomitant effect on the physical system, such that a feedback loop is established between the physical parts of the system and the corresponding software.

Recent advances in middleware technologies have enabled a new generation of object-oriented DRE systems based on platforms such as Real-time CORBA and the Real-time Specification for Java (Dibble, 2008). Although middleware solutions promote software reuse resulting in higher development productivity (Schantz & Schmidt, 2001), provisioning and satisfying QoS requirements, such as predictable end-to-end latencies, remains a fundamental challenge for DRE systems,

due to their distributed nature, unpredictable resource loads, and resource sharing. Moreover, specifying and satisfying QoS requirements in DRE systems often uses *ad hoc* problem-specific code optimizations, which impede the principles of reuse and portability.

To satisfy QoS requirements in the presence of variable resource availability, programmable QoS adaptation layers atop the middleware infrastructure have been proposed (Schantz et al., 2002). These QoS adaptation layers implement QoS adaptation policies, which include rules for modifying application or middleware behavior in response to a change in resource availability. The key idea behind such adaptation layers is to *separate concerns* with respect to QoS requirements. This separation provides improved modularization for separating QoS requirements from the functional parts of the software.

For example, the Quality Objects (QuO) project, developed by BBN, is an adaptation layer (Sharma et al., 2004) that extends the Object Management Group's (OMG) Interface Definition Language (IDL). This extension, known as the Contract Definition Language (CDL), is a textual language that supports the specification of QoS requirements and adaptation policies in the style of a state-machine. QuO contracts written in CDL are compiled to create stubs that are integrated into the QuO kernel and are used to monitor and adapt the QoS parameters when the system is operational.

## Common QoS Implementation Problems

Although QuO's use of CDL works well from a software engineering perspective, there are drawbacks to using these approaches as the sole source for systems adaptation, including:

1. The control-centric nature of the programmatic QoS adaptation extends beyond software concepts, e.g., issues such as stability and convergence become paramount. In a DRE system, QoS is specified in software parameters, which have a significant impact on the dynamics of the overall physical system. Due to complex and non-linear dynamics, it is hard to tune the QoS parameters in an *ad hoc* manner without compromising the stability of the underlying physical system. The QoS adaptation software is, in effect, equivalent to a controller for a discrete, non-linear system. Sophisticated tools are therefore needed to design, simulate, and analyze the QoS adaptation software from a control system perspective.

2. Programmatic QoS adaptation approaches offer a lower level of abstraction, i.e., textual code-based. For example, implementing a small change to CDL-based adaptation policies requires manual changes that are scattered across large portions of the DRE system, which complicates ensuring that all changes are applied consistently. Moreover, even small changes can have far-reaching effects on the dynamic behavior due to the nature of emergent crosscutting properties, such as modifying the policy for adjusting communication bandwidth across a distributed surveillance system, as shown in the case study of this chapter.

3. QoS provisioning also depends on the performance and characteristics of specific algorithms that are fixed and cannot be modified, such as a particular scheduling algorithm or a specific communication protocol. These implementations offer fixed QoS and offer little flexibility in terms of tuning the QoS. Consequently, any QoS adaptation along this dimension involves structural adaptation in terms of switching implementations at run-time, which is highly complex, and in some cases infeasible without shutting down and restarting applications and nodes. Moreover, issues of state management and propagation, and transient mitigation, gain prominence amid such structural adaptations. Programmatic QoS adaptation approaches often offer little or no support for specifying such complex adaptations.

## A Solution: Aspects for Supporting Model-Driven Engineering

Addressing the challenges previously outlined requires raising the level of abstraction for reasoning about the systemic properties of DRE systems, including how the crosscutting QoS adaptations are effected and how they impact different parts of the DRE system. Model-Driven Engineering (MDE) (Bézivin et al., 2006; Schmidt, 2006) offers a promising approach to address these problems. From a modeling perspective, expressive power in software specification is gained from using notations and abstractions that are aligned to a specific problem domain (Mernik et al., 2005). This domain-specific approach can be further enhanced when graphical representations are provided to model the domain abstractions.

In domain-specific modeling, a design engineer describes a system by constructing a visual model using the terminology and concepts from a specific domain (Gray et al., 2007). Analysis can then be performed on the model and/or the model can be synthesized into an implementation. A key application area for MDE is in DRE systems that are tightly integrated between the computational structure of a system and its physical configuration (Sztipanovits and Karsai, 1997),

*Figure 1. Model-Driven Design of Adaptive QoS for DRE Systems*

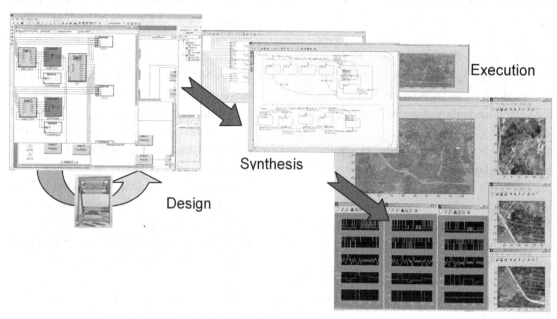

such as the so-called cyber-physical systems typified by embedded computing. In such DRE systems, MDE has been shown to be a powerful paradigm for providing adaptability in evolving environments.

The Generic Modeling Environment (GME) (Lédeczi et al., 2001) is a domain-specific modeling tool that provides metamodeling capabilities that can be configured and adapted from meta-level specifications (representing the modeling paradigm) that describe the domain. GME provides a unified software architecture and framework for creating a customized domain-specific modeling environment (Balasubramanian et al., 2006; Lédeczi et al., 2001). The core components of the GME infrastructure are: a customizable *Generic Model Editor* for creation of multiple-view, domain-specific models; *Model Databases* for storage of the created models; and, a *Model Interpretation* technology that assists in the creation of domain-specific, application-specific model interpreters for transformation of models into executable/analyzable artifacts.

In this chapter, the challenges of QoS imple-

mentation are addressed by applying Aspect-Oriented Software Development (AOSD) (Kiczales et al., 1997; Tarr et al., 1999) techniques to MDE tools. Aspects have been effective at the programming language level to assist in modularizing concerns that were tangled within a single module, as well as other concerns scattered throughout multiple modules. Aspects provide a new construct to modularize such concerns in a manner not possible with the primary constructs in the paradigm of the development language, e.g., object-oriented languages such as Java cannot modularize many concerns that exhibit a cross-cutting representation. Examples of crosscutting concerns at the implementation (i.e., source code) level include the canonical logging example, systems issues such as caching and prefetching, and web concerns like session expiration. The case study of this chapter demonstrates the application of aspects to MDE.

Figure 1 shows how MDE and aspects can be used to develop a DRE system. It involves the following three activities:

- **Design**. A domain-specific modeling tool is used to specify the structural composition and behavioral semantics of the DRE system. For example, as shown in Figure 1, the approach described in this chapter uses the *Generic Modeling Environment* (GME) to assist designers in modeling the DRE system and the QoS adaptation policy using standardized notations, such as Statecharts (Harel, 1987) and Dataflow (this is the Design phase of Figure 1). The modeling language is partitioned among various perspectives that allow model engineers to focus on specific related views of the design. Aspect-oriented weavers at the modeling level assist model engineers in rapidly changing crosscutting properties of a model that are traditionally hard to change due to the scattering of their specification. For example, a policy for adapting bandwidth usage could span multiple models in a language whose semantics is based on a finite state machine (FSM), as demonstrated in the case study section of this chapter.

- **Synthesis**. The next stage is model transformation. MDE tools provide model interpreters associated with the domain-specific languages that can be used to traverse model instances to transform them into different kinds of artifacts, such as source code, input to analysis tools or metadata for configuration. In our example, as represented by the "Synthesis" part of Figure 1, a generator tool synthesizes artifacts for Matlab Simulink/Stateflow® (a popular commercial simulation tool), providing the ability to simulate and analyze the QoS adaptation policy. This tool enhances assurance that the system will perform as desired without having to deploy the actual system in the field. This generator tool has been implemented as a model interpreter for GME (Neema et al. 2002). The

generator computes a mapping of the QoS adaptation policy represented in the modeling language into a semantically equivalent FSM representation in the Stateflow tool. In addition, the generator constructs a closed-loop control model in Simulink, in which the generated Stateflow model acts as the "controller," while the underlying computational system is abstracted as the "plant."

- **Execution**. The final step is run-time QoS adaptation, which is performed via feedback. In our example, a second generator tool creates CDL specifications from the QoS adaptation models. The generated CDL is then compiled into executable artifacts (the "Execution" phase of Figure 1). The right side of Figure 1 shows the screenshots taken from the execution of a military target recognition system that was generated by a model representation using our approach. By modeling DRE systems at a higher level of abstraction, model engineers can evolve their designs without incurring the accidental complexities of specific implementation techniques. A previous study showed that small changes to an abstraction represented at the modeling level resulted in large changes across the corresponding CDL representation (Neema et al., 2002).

A growing body of literature is forming around the topic of aspect modeling and is perhaps best chronicled by the annual workshops on Aspect-Oriented Modeling (AOM) (www.aspect-modeling.org). A representative selection of publications in the AOM area can be found in (Reddy et al., 2006; Stein et al., 2006; Clarke & Baniassad, 2005), which focus on developing notational conventions that assist in documenting concerns that crosscut a design. These notational conventions advance the efficiency of expressing these concerns in the model. Moreover, they also have the important trait of improving traceability from design to implementation. The Motorola WEAVR (Cottenier et al., 2007) is similar to our approach, i.e., it is a real tool for aspect modeling, rather than simply a new notation. The Motorola WEAVR only works with UML static diagrams, however, whereas our model weaver used in this chapter is applicable to any modeling language.

Although current efforts do well to improve the cognizance of AOSD at the design level, they generally tend to treat the concept of aspect-oriented modeling primarily as a specification convention. The focus has therefore been on the graphical representation, semantic underpinnings, and decorative attributes concerned with aspects and their representation within UML. A contribution of this chapter is to consider AOM more as an operational task by constructing executable model weavers, i.e., AOSD is used as a mechanism to improve the modeling task itself by providing the ability to quantify properties across a model throughout the system modeling process (Filman & Friedman, 2000). This action is performed by utilizing a model weaver that has been constructed with the concepts of domain-specific system modeling in mind. This chapter focuses attention on the Design phase of DRE systems, as shown in Figure 1. The approach described in this chapter has benefits that are similar to those of model-driven middleware (MDM) (Gokhale et al., 2008) and adaptive and reflective middleware (ARM) (Schantz and Schmidt, 2001). The primary contribution of the chapter is the utilization of an aspect-oriented weaver that performs model transformations across higher level abstractions to separate policy decisions that were previously scattered and tangled across the model.

## VIEWPOINT MODELING FOR QOS ADAPTATION IN DRE SYSTEMS

The Adaptive Quality Modeling Language (AQML) is a GME-based modeling language that assists in modeling key aspects of a DRE system. Each area of concern in the model is partitioned into a specific view that slices through a particular perspective of the overall model. The separation of concerns provided by a GME view is similar in intent to previous research on viewpoints (Nuseibeh et al., 1994) in requirements engineering. AQML defines the following three views defined in the metamodel (Neema et al, 2002) as follows:

1. **QoS adaptation modeling**, which models the adaptation of QoS properties of the DRE system. Designers can specify the different state configurations of the QoS properties, the legal transitions between the different state configurations, the conditions that enable these transitions (and the actions that must be performed to enact the change in state configuration), the data variables that receive and update QoS information, and the events that trigger the transitions. These properties are modeled using an extended finite-state machine (FSM), which is useful for specifying actions in a control-centric environment. Other Models of Computation (MoC) may be useful in different contexts (e.g., queuing models are useful for performance estimation).

2. **Computation modeling**, which models the computational aspect of a DRE system. A Dataflow MoC is employed to specify the various computational components and their interaction. The Dataflow MoC is chosen because it is well-suited to a particular class of DRE systems, namely streaming distributed multimedia application, which is the focus of this chapter. It should be noted, however, that the approach of QoS adaptation presented in this chapter is general, and can be composed with other MoCs for computational modeling.

3. **Middleware modeling**, which models the middleware services, the system monitors, and the tunable "knobs" (i.e., the parameters

*Figure 2. Metamodel of QoS Adaptation Modeling*

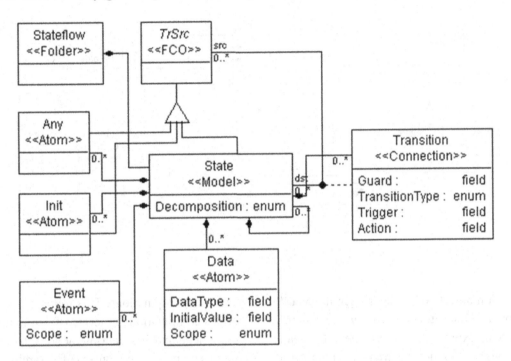

being provided by the middleware) in such a way that the parameters are specified for possible analysis. This category of modeling ensures the many configuration parameters offered by middleware are used correctly, so the deployment of an application is optimal rather than suboptimal due to the selection of a collection of parameters that have opposing effects or should not be used together.

The next four sub-sections describe the metamodel of each of these modeling categories and their interaction in AQML. Each metamodel represents a view of the overall system and each metamodel is linked together through interactions.

## QoS Adaptation Modeling

Stateflow models capture the adaptive QoS behavior of DRE systems. A discrete FSM representa-tion, extended with hierarchy and concurrency, is provided for modeling the QoS adaptive behavior of the system. This representation has been selected due to its scalability, universal acceptability, and ease-of-use in modeling. Figure 2 shows the QoS adaptation view of AQML.

The main concept in an FSM representation is a *State*, which defines a discretized configura-tion of QoS properties. Hierarchy is enabled in the representation by allowing States to contain other States. Attributes define the decomposition of the State. The State may be an *AND* state (when the state machine contained within the State is a concurrent state machine), or, the State can be an *OR* state (when the state machine contained within the State is a sequential state machine). If the State does not contain child States, then it is specified as a *LEAF* state. States are stereotyped as *models* in GME.

*Transition* objects are used to model a transi-tion from one state to another. The attributes of

*Figure 3. Metamodel of Computation Architecture Modeling*

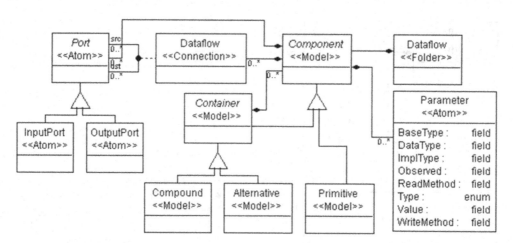

the transition object define the trigger, the guard condition, and the actions. The trigger and guard are Boolean expressions. When these Boolean expressions are satisfied, the transition is enabled and a state change (accompanied with the execution of the actions) takes place. Transitions are stereotyped as a *Connection* in the GME tool. To denote a transition between two States, a connection has to be made from the source state to the destination state.

In addition to states and transitions, the FSM representation includes data and events. These can be directly sampled external signals, complex computational results, or outputs from the state machine. In the AQML, *Event* objects capture the Boolean event variables, and the *Data* objects capture arbitrary data variables. Both the Events and Data have a Scope attribute that indicates whether an event (or data) is either local to the state machine or is an input/output of the state machine.

## Computation Modeling

This view is used to describe the computational architecture. A dataflow representation, with extensions for hierarchy, has been selected for modeling computations. This representation describes computations in terms of computational components and their data interactions. To manage system complexity, the concept of hierarchy is used to structure the computation definition. Figure 3 shows the computation view of the AQML.

The computational structure is modeled with the following classes of objects: *Compounds*, *Alternatives*, and *Primitives*. These objects represent a computational component in a dataflow representation. *Ports* are used to define the interface of these components through which the components exchange information. Ports are specialized into *InputPorts* and *OutputPorts*.

A Primitive is a basic modeling element that represents an elementary component. A Primitive maps directly to a processing component that will be implemented as a software object or a function. A Compound is a composite object that may contain Primitives or other Compounds. These objects can be connected within the compound to define the dataflow structure. Compounds provide the hierarchy in the structural description that is necessary for managing the complexity of large designs. An Alternative captures "design choices" – functionally equivalent designs for a rigorously defined interface, providing the abil-

*Figure 4. Metamodel of Middleware Modeling*

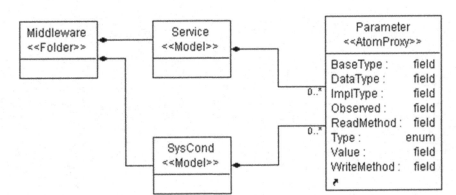

ity to model design spaces instead of a single design. The use of Alternatives allows capturing discrete combinatorial design spaces in a highly compact and scalable representation. The large design space thus modeled, however, must be explored to determine the subset of designs that satisfy requirements. An automated Design Space Exploration Tool (DESERT), assists the user in performing this exploration. A detailed description of DESERT is beyond the scope of this chapter; the interested reader is referred to (Neema et al., 2003).

An important concept relevant to QoS adaptive DRE systems is the notion of parameters, which are the tunable "knobs" used by the adaptation mechanism to tailor the behavior of the components so the desired QoS properties are maintained. Parameters can be contained in Compounds, Primitives, and Alternatives. The Type attribute defines whether a Parameter is read-only, write-only, or read-write. The DataType attribute defines the data type of the parameter.

## Middleware Modeling

In this view, the concerns of the middleware are modeled, which include the services and the system conditions provided by the middleware.

Example services include an Audio-Video Streaming service, Bandwidth reservation service, Timing service, and Event service. *System conditions* are components that provide quantitative diagnostic information about the middleware. Examples of these include observed throughput, bandwidth, latencies, and frame-rates. Figure 4 shows the middleware modeling view of the AQML.

The *Service* object represents the services provided by the middleware. Services can contain parameters that are the configuration points provided by the service. In addition to being tunable "knobs," parameters play a second role as instrumentation, or probes, by providing some quantitative information about the service. The *SysCond* object represents the system condition objects present in the middleware layer. SysConds can also contain parameters.

We do not facilitate a detailed modeling of the middleware components or the dataflow components because the focus of AQML is on the QoS adaptation. We model only those elements of the dataflow and middleware that facilitate the QoS adaptation (namely, the tunable and observable Parameters).

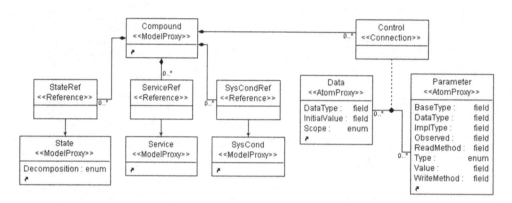

## Interaction of QoS Adaptation with Middleware and Computation Modeling

This category specifies the interaction of the previous three modeling categories, as shown in Figure 5. As described earlier, the Data/Event objects within the Stateflow model form the interface of the state machine. Within the Computation and the Middleware views, Parameters form the control interfaces. The interaction of the QoS adaptation (captured in Stateflow models), and the middleware and application (modeled in the Middleware/Computation models), is through these interfaces. The interaction is modeled with the *Control* connection class, which connects the Data object of a State model to a Parameter object of a Middleware/Computation model.

In GME, connections between objects that are not contained within the same model are specified as references, which are equivalent to a "reference" or a "pointer" in a programming language (Karsai et al, 2004). These are contained in the same context (model) such that a connection can be drawn between them. The *StateRef, ServiceRef*, and the *SysCondRef* objects are the reference objects that are contained in a Compound (Computation) Model. All the views mentioned in this section partition the concerns of a larger model

space into cohesive units that make the modeling activity more manageable.

In addition to the physical interactions specified in the metamodel of Figure 5, there are deeper and indirect interactions across the different views that are not expressed in the models, yet must be accounted for by the designer of the QoS adaptations. The aggregate QoS space of the system is in essence a subset of the cross product of the (potentially continuous and infinite) state-space of the Computation, the Middleware, and the Resource. The states in the QoS Adaptation aspect represent an abstraction and partitioning of the QoS space into discrete states. Similarly, there are linkages between Computation, and Middleware, through direct utilization of APIs, scheduling of resources, and communication. In the approach presented, some of these interactions must be accounted for in the plant model (e.g., when simulating the QoS adaptation policies). In general, however, QoS adaptation designers must consider these latent interactions when designing the QoS adaptation policies.

The three metamodels defined in this section correspond to specific views of a DRE system. At the instance model level, this multidimensional view perspective provides model engineers with multiple perspectives for separating different concerns of the model such that details not pertinent to the modeling task at hand are abstracted into other views. Although this approach offers a valuable modeling construct, viewpoints alone are not sufficient for capturing certain types of crosscutting concerns, as shown later in this chapter. Before describing that issue, however, the next section introduces the problem domain used in the case study of the chapter, which is built as an instance of the AQML metamodel.

## SPECIFYING QOS POLICIES FOR ADAPTATION OF VIDEO BANDWIDTH

The case study used in this chapter demonstrates an application of QoS modeling as applied to a conceptual scenario involving a number of Unmanned Aerial Vehicles (UAVs) conducting surveillance, e.g., in support of disaster relief efforts. Each UAV streams video back to a central distributor that forwards the video on to several different displays (Loyall et al., 2001). The feedback cycle for utilizing UAVs as surveillance devices includes (1) video from each UAV is sent to the distributor that is located in a command center located on a ground station, (2) the distributor broadcasts the video to numerous video display hosts at the command center, (3) the video is received by each host and displayed to various operators, and (4) each operator at a display observes the video and sends commands, when deemed necessary, to control the UAVs (Karr et al., 2001). The UAV prototype used for our case study was developed by researchers from BBN as an integration testbed and experimental platform for the DARPA Program Composition for Embedded Systems (PCES) project.

The concept of operation for the scenario can be summarized briefly as follows. Initially, several UAVs are conducting surveillance in a region of interest. UAV imagery must be transmitted in real-time to ground stations, ensuring an acceptable image quality. The latency of the transmission of

an image and its reception at the ground station must be low enough to provide a continuous update of the region of interest as the UAVs loiter above. The available bandwidth must be shared uniformly over all of the collaborating UAVs and each UAV must adapt its transmission rate to the available bandwidth such that the timeliness requirement of the delivered imagery is met.

The scenario advances to the next stage when one or more of the UAVs observe a target in their field-of-view. In this next stage of the scenario, QoS requirements evolve as the UAVs observing the target acquire primary importance with respect to the collective goals of the system. It is required that the UAVs observing a potential target receive preferential treatment in bandwidth distribution such that the transmission of the critical information they observe is not delayed. All other UAVs that are not observing a target must reduce their bandwidth usage. In this case study, attention is restricted to just these two stages of the scenario in order to keep the description comprehensible (although there are additional stages that exercise a broader spectrum of QoS adaptation).

In the presence of changing conditions in the environment, the fidelity of the video stream must be maintained according to specified QoS parameters. The video must not be stale, or be affected by jitter to the point that operators cannot make informed decisions. Within the BBN implementation of the QuO project, a *contract* assists the system developer in specifying QoS requirements that are expected by a client and provided by a supplier. Each contract describes operating regions and actions that must be taken when QoS measurements change.

A textual domain-specific language (DSL) was developed by BBN to assist in the specification of contracts; the name of this DSL is the *Contract Description Language* (CDL) (Karr et al., 2001; Schantz et al., 2002). A code generator translates the CDL into code that is integrated within the run-time kernel of the application. The textual intention of a CDL specification is similar to the

*Figure 6. Top-Level Computational Components for One UAV*

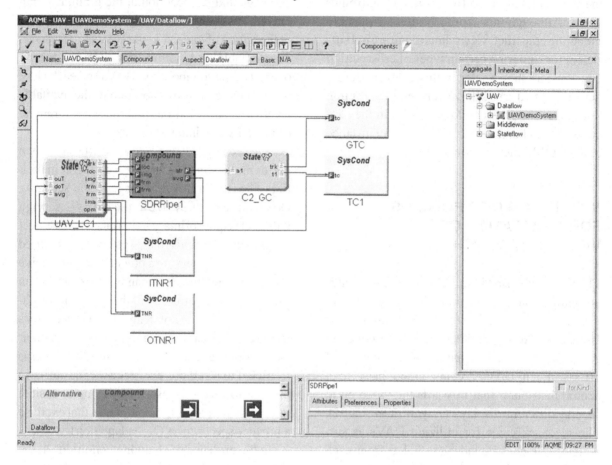

semantics of a hierarchical state machine. The overall approach adopted by BBN for implementation of QoS adaptation is aspect-oriented (Duzan et al., 2004).

Several things make the UAV case study a complex and challenging problem, including its real-time requirements, resource constraints, and distributed nature. In addition, there are other interesting observations to consider, including (1) the link between the UAVs to the host command center is a wireless link imposing some strict bandwidth restrictions, (2) there is a need for prioritization between different video streams coming from different UAVs owing to the region of interest, (3) latency is a higher concern than throughput because it is important to get the latest changes in the threat scenario at the earliest possible time,

(4) there may be a wide-variety of computational resources (e.g., processors, networks, switches) involved in the entire application, and (5) the scenario is highly dynamic, because UAVs frequently enter and leave regions of interest.

To address these complex requirements, a QoS-enabled middleware solution has been designed for this application (Sharma et al., 2004). AQML was developed in response to the need for a modeling language to represent QoS specification for the UAV application (Neema et al., 2002). The next sub-section introduces some instances of the AQML metamodel applied to the UAV case study.

*Figure 7. Concurrent States within one UAV*

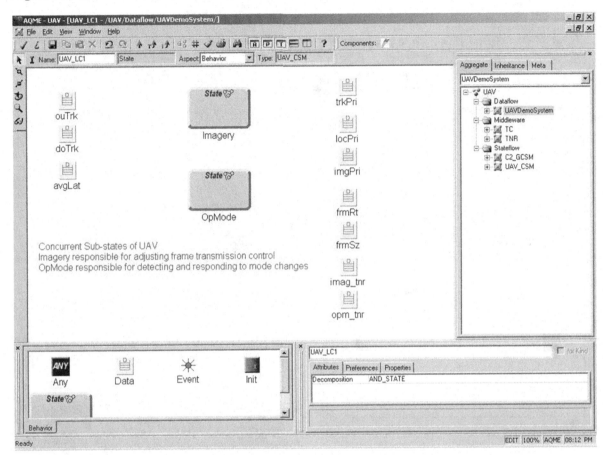

## AQML Modeling of UAV Interactions

Figure 6 shows the top-level computational components for one UAV and its interactions. The view shown is a dataflow diagram with interactions between the UAV adaptation controller, the middleware system condition variables, and the computational components responsible for transmission of video content. This view represents the integration of the different concerns (i.e., Qos Adaptation, Application Computation, and Middleware), which are captured in separate diagrams and merged together in the integrated view. The box labeled SDRPipe1 represents the top-level of the hierarchical composition of the Sender-Distributor-Receiver components that are responsible for production, distribution, and

display of the video stream. The UAV_LC1 component represents the top-level of the UAV QoS adaptation controller (detailed further in the following). The C2_GC component represents the top-level of the Ground Station's QoS adaptation controller, which is responsible for coordinating between UAVs for distribution of bandwidth according to the tactical importance of each UAV.

This particular view reveals only a single UAV. The OTNR1, ITNR1, GTC, and TC1 are system condition variables, which are middleware objects responsible for communicating QoS information across different objects in a distributed system. The OTNR/ITNR represents time in region, which keeps track of the time the UAV has been in a particular mode of operation. The TC1 and GTC keep track of the observation of a target by

*Figure 8. Model of QoS Adaptation within Imagery State*

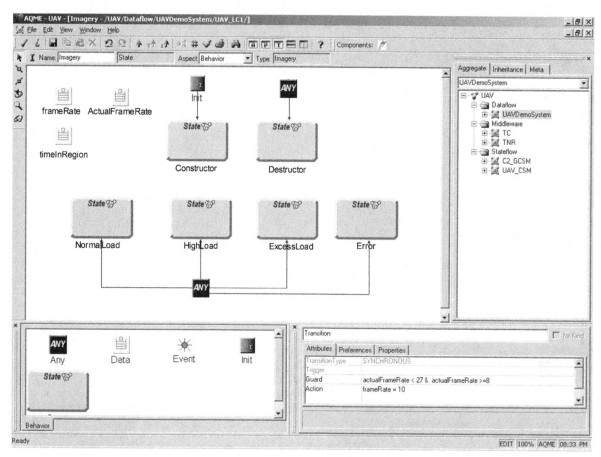

the UAVs. The TC1 is a variable set by UAV1 when it sees a target. The GTC is a logical-OR of all the TC variables, indicating if one or more of the UAVs have observed a target. All the lines shown in the view represent flow of information among these components. The UAV_LC1 controls the video stream parameters such as frame rate, frame size, and image quality, which is indicated by the connections between the UAV_LC1's and the SDRPipe1's appropriately named ports.

Figure 7 and Figure 8 show a model of the QoS-adaptive behavior of the UAVs as modeled in AQML. Figure 7 shows the top-level behavior consisting of two concurrent states: Imagery and OpMode. The OpMode state represents the operational modes of the UAV related to the observation of a target. The Imagery state manages the adaptation of imagery transmission based on the available bandwidth and the operational mode. Figure 8 shows the sub-states of the Imagery state.

In this application, the goal of QoS adaptation is to minimize the latency on the video transmission. When the communication resources are nominally loaded, it may be possible to transmit the video stream at the full frame rate with a minimal basic network delay. When the communication and computational resources are loaded, however, the delays in transmission expand for the same frame rate resulting in increased latencies. The adaptation scheme attempts to compensate for the increased load by reducing the rate of transmission, thus improving the latency again.

There are several ways to reduce the transmission rate, including (1) reducing the frame rate by dropping frames, (2) reducing the image quality per frame, or (3) reducing the frame size. Depending on the actual scenario, one or more of these situations may apply. In the example of this chapter, dropping the frame rate is the only option considered, but other alternatives are possible, e.g., changing the video from color to black and white.

Figure 8 shows a QoS adaptation model of the UAV scenario in the AQML. The three states NormalLoad, ExcessLoad, and HighLoad capture three different QoS configurations of the system. A few data variables (actualFrameRate, frameRate, timeInRegion) can also be seen in this figure. These data variables provide the state machine with sensory information about the network. At the same time, other data variables may enact the adaptation actions that are being performed in the transitions.

The attribute window at the bottom-right corner of Figure 8 shows the trigger, guard, and action attributes of a transition. An example guard expression is visible in the attribute window of the figure (i.e., "actualFrameRate < 27 and actualFrameRate >= 8"). When this expression evaluates to true, the transition is enabled and the modeled system enters the HighLoad state. An example action expression can be seen in this figure (i.e., "frameRate = 10"). This sets the frameRate data variable to a value of 10.

The next section provides a UAV case study modeled in AQML that uses model transformations to address challenges of modeling that frequently occur in the modeling process. The case study highlights the benefits that model transformations provide to adapt a DRE system in the presence of crosscutting concerns and scalability requirements.

## TRANSFORMATIONS FOR RAPID EVOLUTION OF MODELS

Although viewpoints provide a valuable mechanism for managing disparate concepts within a design, these views are not without interactions. Designers are typically responsible for maintaining consistency among views. Moreover, maintaining this consistency is a non-trivial task as the system evolves. Aspect modeling offers a mechanism to automate these interactions.

The Constraint-Specification Aspect Weaver (C-SAW) is a model transformation engine that unites the ideas of aspect-oriented software development (AOSD) (Kiczales et al., 1997; Tarr et al., 1999) with MDE to provide better modularization of model properties that are crosscutting throughout multiple layers of a model (Gray et al., 2001; Gray et al., 2004). In the same manner that code can be scattered across the boundaries of source modules, the same emergent behavior occurs at the modeling level. For example, the addition of a black box data recorder into the model of a mission computing avionics system requires modeling changes across the whole collection of model entities (Gray et al., 2006). C-SAW is available as a GME plug-in and provides the ability to explore numerous modeling scenarios by considering crosscutting modeling concerns as aspects that can be inserted and removed rapidly from a model. The next two sections provide examples of transformations that address the separation of crosscutting modeling aspects and scalability issues within large models for DRE systems.

Within the C-SAW infrastructure, the language used to specify model transformation rules and strategies is the Embedded Constraint Language (ECL), which is an extension of the Object Constraint Language (OCL). ECL provides many of the common features of OCL, such as arithmetic operators, logical operators, and numerous operators on collections (e.g., size, forAll, exists, select). It also provides special operators to support model aggregates (e.g., models, atoms,

*Figure 9. Dataflow for UAV Prototype*

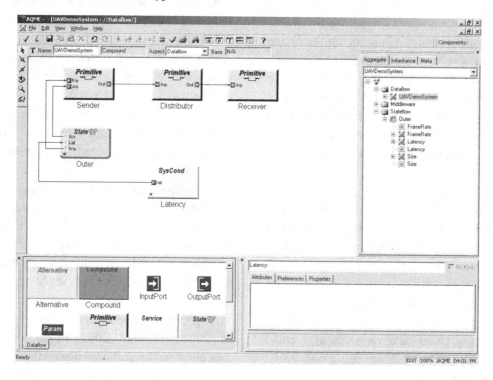

attributes), connections (e.g., source, destination) and transformations (e.g., addModel, setAttribute, removeModel) that provide access to modeling concepts that are within GME.

There are two kinds of ECL specifications: (1) a modeling specification that describes the binding and parameterization of strategies to specific entities in a model and (2) a strategy that specifies elements of computation and the application of specific properties to the model entities.[1] C-SAW interprets these specifications and transforms the input source model into the output target model. The C-SAW web site (www.cis.uab.edu/gray/Research/C-SAW) is a repository for downloading papers, software, and several video demonstrations that illustrate model transformation with C-SAW in GME. The following sections provide representative examples of ECL and the concept of aspect model weaving and model transformation applied to behavioral modeling of embedded systems.

## Weaving Across Finite State Machines

When writing a specification for QoS adaptation, there typically arises one dimension of the adaptation that is treated as a dependent variable. There are numerous other independent variables that are adjusted to adapt the dependent variable according to some QoS requirement. For example, the end-to-end latency of video stream distribution may be a dependent variable that drives the adaptation of other independent variables (e.g., the size of a video frame, or even the video frame rate). In such cases, a *policy* is defined that represents the process for performing QoS adaptation.

The actions prescribed by a policy often cross-cut the structure of a hierarchical state machine. Changing the policy requires modifying each location of the state machine that is affected by the policy. Elrad et al. have also reported on scenarios where state machine models are cross-

*Figure 10. Top-Most View of Parallel State Machine*

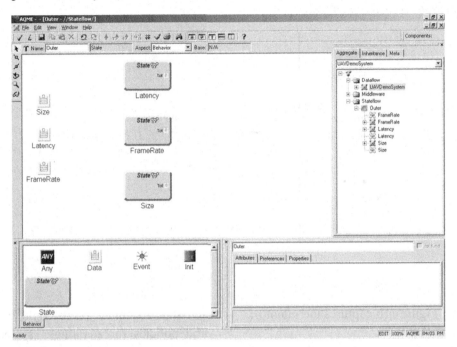

cutting (Elrad et al., 2002), but their approach is notational in nature and does not utilize a weaver at the modeling level. The Motorola WEAVR (Cottenier et al., 2007) represents one of the most mature aspect modeling implementations. The WEAVR is also focused on state machines, but is limited in application to UML. The weaving described in this chapter can be integrated with other modeling languages.

The C-SAW weaver has been applied to the AQML language to assist in weaving properties according to the semantics of an adaptation policy. Several strategies have been created to support the modeling of state machines that represent the behavior of a contract. The first strategy focuses on issues related to the creation of state machines and their internal transitions. The view of the model shown in Figure 9 pertains to the dataflow of the UAV case study.

The model in Figure 9 is an instance of the AQML metamodel. In this case, the latency concern is the dependent variable that represents a system condition object whose value is monitored from the environment. The latency is an input into a hierarchical state machine called Outer. Within Outer, there are internal state machines that describe the adaptation of identified independent control variables (e.g., FrameRate and Size, as shown with the dependent Latency variable in Figure 10).

As shown in Figure 11, there are two ways that a state machine model can be extended to address QoS adaptation. Along one axis of extension, the addition of new dependent control variables often can offer more flexibility in adaptation toward the satisfaction of QoS parameters. It could be the case that other variables in addition to FrameRate and Size would help in reducing the latency, e.g., color, video format, and compression. Figure 11a captures the intent of this extension by introducing new control variables. It may also be the case that finer granularity of the intermediate transitions within a particular state would permit better adaptation to QoS

*Figure 11.* ***Axes of Variation within a State Machine*** *(a) Adding New Control Variables (b) Adding More Intermediate Transitions in States*

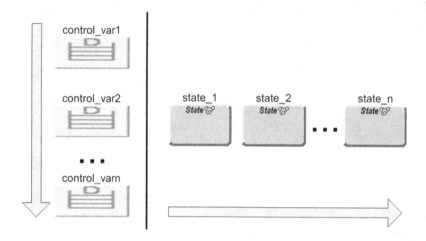

requirements. Figure 11b captures the intent of this extension.

In addition to the strategy for creating control variables and their intermediate states, an additional strategy was written to provide assistance in changing the adaptive policy that spans across each state machine. There could be numerous valid policies for adapting a system to meet QoS requirements. Two possibilities are shown in Figure 12. The realization that each of these policies is scattered across the boundaries of each participating state machine suggests that these

*Figure 12. Policies for Adapting to Environment (a) Priority Exhaustive (b) Zig-zag*

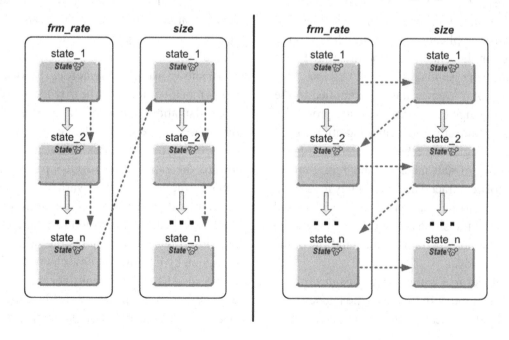

*Figure 13. Latency Adaptation Transition Strategy*

```
1    defines AddTransition, FindConnectingState, ApplyTransitions;
2
3    strategy AddTransition(stateName, guard : string;
4                           prev: object; prevPri : integer)
5    {
6
7      declare pri, minVal, maxVal, avgVal : integer;
8      declare end : object;
9      declare aConnection : object;
10     declare action : string;
11
12     pri:= findAtom("Priority").getIntAttribute("InitialValue");
13
14     if(pri == prevPri + 1) then
15
16       end := self;
17       minVal := findAtom("Min").getIntAttribute("InitialValue");
18       maxVal := findAtom("Max").getIntAttribute("InitialValue");
19       avgVal := (minVal + maxVal) / 2;
20
21       action := stateName;
22       action := action + "=" + intToString(avgVal);
23
24       aConnection := parent().addConnection("Transition", end, prev);
25       aConnection.addAttribute("Guard", guard);
26       aConnection.addAttribute("Action", action);
27
28     endif;
29
30   }
31
32   strategy FindConnectingState(stateName, guard : string)
33   {
34
35     declare pri : integer;
36     declare start : object;
37
38     pri:= findAtom("Priority").getIntAttribute("InitialValue");
39     start := self;
40
41     if(pri < 4) then
42
43       parent().models("State")->
44                  AddTransition(stateName, guard, start, pri);
45
46     endif;
47
48   }
49
50   strategy ApplyTransitions(stateName, guard : string)
51   {
52
53     declare theModel : object;
54
55     theModel := findModel(stateName);
56     theModel.models("State")->FindConnectingState(stateName, guard);
57
58   }
```

*Figure 14. Internal Transitions within the Size State*

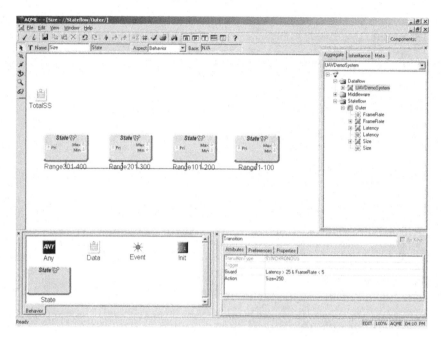

protocols represent a type of crosscutting concern that should be separated to provide an ability to change the policy rapidly.

The left side of Figure 12 specifies a protocol that exhausts the effect of one independent variable (frm_rate) before attempting to adjust another independent variable (size). The semantics of this protocol pertain to the exhaustive reduction of one variable before attempting to reduce another one. The size variable is therefore of a higher priority in this case because it is not reduced until there is no further reduction possible to the frame rate. The dotted-arrow in this figure indicates the order in which the transitions fire based upon the predicate guards.

The right side of Figure 12 represents a more equitable strategy for maintaining the latency QoS requirement. In this protocol, a zig-zag pattern suggests that the reduction of a variable is staggered with the reduction of a peer variable. Observe that Figure 12 involves only two control variables. The ability to change the protocol (by

hand) becomes complicated when many variables are involved, or when there are numerous intermediate states. This crosscutting nature suggests that a C-SAW strategy would be beneficial to assist in the exploration of alternative policies. Figure 13 contains a strategy that supports the protocol highlighted in Figure 12a.

There may be several different variables that can be the focus of QoS adaptation, depending on the contract and goals of an application. In the scenario specified in the strategy of Figure 13, a smaller frame rate is tolerated to maintain a desired latency. The transitions between two sub-states with different priorities will be inserted by the strategies specified in Figure 13. The strategy *ApplyTransitions* in line 50 retrieves the *stateName*, finds out the corresponding sub-state model, and calls another strategy "*FindConnectingState*" (line 32) that will then retrieve the priority of this sub-state. If the current priority is less than 4, another strategy *AddTransition* will be invoked in order to insert the transition from the current sub-state to the next sub-state with a higher priority. Line 12 through Line 14 determine the next sub-state whose priority is just 1 higher than the current state. Line 16 through Line 26 represent the implementation for the insertion of the transition, along with associated attributes.

As a result, the weaving of the strategy from Figure 13 into the model of Figure 10 produces the internal view of the size state, shown in Figure 14. Each state progressively reduces the size of the video frame. The guard condition for the selected transition appears in the lower-right side of the figure. The guard condition states that the transition fires when the latency is not at the desired level, and also when the frame rate has been reduced to its smallest possible size.

Related work on modeling aspects for DRE systems propose notations for modeling time using UML (Zhang & Liu, 2005). Likewise, the GenER-TiCA tool assists in separating various concerns of a DRE system into aspects within UML and generating code that weaves in the non-functional concerns identified in the models (Wehrmeister et al., 2008). This related work differs from the approach described in this chapter because they are tied to a single modeling language (i.e., UML), as opposed to a more general approach that can be used for multiple domain-specific modeling languages. Moreover, the tool support for weaving at the modeling level itself is not supported in these other works as available in C-SAW.

The Virginia Embedded Systems Toolkit (VEST) (Stankovic et al., 2004)—which is also built as a GME metamodel—is a research effort that has similar goals to the ideas presented in this chapter. VEST supports modeling and analysis of real-time systems and introduces the notion of prescriptive aspects within a design that are programming language independent. A distinction between VEST and the aspect modeling approach presented in this section concerns the generalizabilty of the weaving process. All the modeling aspects possible within VEST can also be specified in C-SAW, but the type of aspect shown in Figure 13 is not possible in VEST. The structure of a prescriptive aspect is limited to the form, "for <some conditional statement on a model property> change <other property>," which is comparatively less powerful than the type of model weaving shown in this chapter.

## Scaling a Base Model to Include Multiple UAVs

In addition to the ability to capture crosscutting concerns in models as aspects, C-SAW can assist in transformations that address scalability concerns. In this case study, all the UAVs must share bandwidth and communicate with a ground station that is responsible for allocating bandwidth share to the UAVs according to their operational modes. The behavior of the ground station, as well as its interaction with each UAV, is also modeled in AQML.

It is a relatively modest effort for a user to develop a scenario involving two UAVs that are interacting with one ground station. A challenge arises, however, when the scenario must scale up to production systems containing thousands of UAVs and hundreds of Ground Stations. The models and the synthesis tools available in AQML may assist in mitigating the complexity to some extent by synthesizing a large fraction of the software. A significant share of complexity would be transferred over to model engineers who would need to build models of the larger production scenario.

Consider the single-UAV model of Figure 6. The difficulty of scaling a model to include additional UAVs is rooted in the implicit relationships between a UAV and the modeled control adaptation. The control logic to perform the requisite adaptation is scattered across numerous entities such that the addition of a new UAV necessitates changes to many other locations to attach the UAV into the model. A model transformation engine like C-SAW applies exceedingly well to this situation. The general solution separates all the complexities of interaction into a strategy that can be reused in many design choices to scale to larger numbers of UAVs.

Figure 15 shows the ECL strategies for inserting two additional UAVs into the modeled system that was originally described in Figure 6. The aspect *Start* (Line 3) is the initiation point of the model weaving process. The strategy *addUAV_r* (Line 8) recursively invokes the strategy *addUAV* (Line 16) that will then call the strategy *updateDF* (Line 21) in order to replicate the UAV and its interactions with the other components in the

*Figure 15. ECL Strategies for Replication of UAVs*

```
1     defines Start, addUAV_r, addUAV, updateDF;
2
3     aspect Start()
4     {
5        addUAV_r(3,2);
6     }
7
8     strategy addUAV_r(max,idx: integer)
9     {
10       if (idx <= max) then
11         addUAV(idx);
12         addUAV_r(max,idx+1);
13       endif;
14     }
15
16     strategy addUAV(idx: integer)
17     {
18     rootFolder().findFolder("Dataflow").findModel("UAVDemoSystem").updateDF(idx);
19     }
20
21     strategy updateDF(idx:integer)
22     {
23         //The declaration of the local variables are omitted here
24
25         id_str := intToString(idx);
26         uav_csm := rootFolder().findFolder("Stateflow").findModel("UAV_CSM");
27         uav_ins := addInstance("State", "UAV_LC" + id_str, uav_csm);
28
29         tnr := rootFolder().findFolder("Middleware").findModel("TNR");
30         itnr_ins := addInstance("SysCond", "ITNR" + id_str, tnr);
31         otnr_ins := addInstance("SysCond", "OTNR" + id_str, tnr);
32
33         tc := rootFolder().findFolder("Middleware").findModel("TC");
34         tc_ins := addInstance("SysCond", "TC" + id_str, tc);
35
36         sdr := findModel("SDRPipe");
37         sdr_ins := addInstance("Compound", "SDRPipe" + id_str, sdr);
38
39         uins_itnr := uav_ins.findAtom("imag_tnr");
40         itins_tnr := itnr_ins.findAtom("TNR");
41         addConnection("Control", uins_itnr, itins_tnr);
42         addConnection("Control", itins_tnr, uins_itnr);
43
44         // The creations of other connections between the components are omitted
45     }
```

*Figure 16. System with 3 UAVs after Weaving*

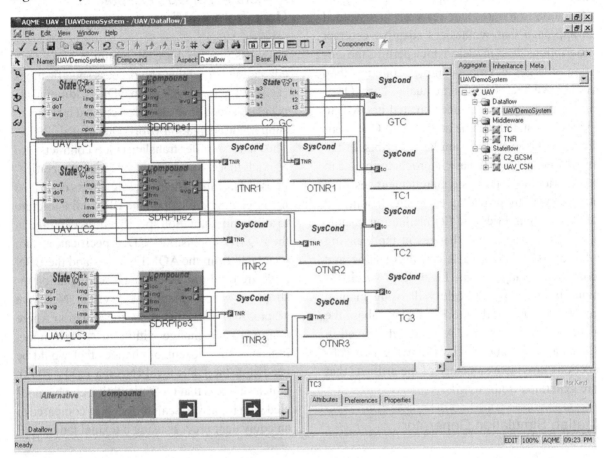

system. The UAV reference is created from Line 25 to Line 27, which is followed by the creation of the related components such as "*TNR*" (Lines 29 to Line 31), *TC* (Lines 33 and 34), *SDRPipe* (Lines 36 and 37), as well as the connections between the UAV and *TNR* (Line 39 to Line 42). Many other connections are performed in the actual strategy, but they have been omitted here for the sake of brevity (the addition of other interactions follow similarly to those specified here).

As a result, Figure 16 shows the evolved system with three interacting UAVs. This model can be compared to the original single-UAV model of Figure 6. Without the capability to separate the intent of UAV replication, the ability to scale a model to multiple UAVs presents a manual modeling task that is too burdensome in practice. The

use of C-SAW to automate the process permits rapid exploration of a base-line model in order to investigate alternative scenarios involving multiple UAVs. The concept of adding multiple ground stations is not shown here, but would be a similar burden if left solely to manual adaptation of a model. Other examples of scalability of these types of models for several different domains and modeling languages are presented in (Lin et al., 2008).

## Synthesis of AQML Models for Simulation and Execution

Using a model-based representation and employing generators to successfully synthesize low-level artifacts from models raises the level of abstraction and provides better tool support for analyzing the adaptation software. Our research has yielded an approach that synthesizes adaptive contract descriptions from models, which permits the creation of larger and more complex contracts than could have been specified manually. The AQML modeling language has been created in GME to synthesize state machine models into CDL contracts, and also Matlab simulation scripts. Initial results suggest an increase in productivity due to (1) shortening of the design, implement, test, and iterate cycle by providing early simulation, and analysis capabilities and (2) facilitating change maintenance: minimal changes in the weaving of properties into models can make large and consistent changes in the lower level specifications that would not scale well using manual reconfiguration of the models. Details about the generation process from AQML is described in (Neema et al., 2002). The following two sub-sections provide a summary of the artifacts that are generated from AQML.

## Matlab Simulation Generator

A primary goal of the modeling approach described in this chapter is to provide integration with tools that can analyze the QoS adaptation from a control-centric viewpoint. A model interpreter for AQML has been created that can translate the QoS adaptation specifications defined in AQML into a Simulink/Stateflow model. Matlab provides an API that is available in the Matlab scripting language (M-file) for procedurally creating and manipulating Simulink/Stateflow models. The simulation generator produces an M-file that uses the API to create Simulink/Stateflow models. Analyses are possible in terms of the time spent in different states, the latency from the time of a change in excitation, to the time of change in outputs in the state machine, and stability of the system. Many details of synthesis to Matlab are documented in (Neema et al., 2002).

## Generation of QoS Adaptation Code from AQML

BBN has produced a CDL compiler and a QoS adaptation kernel that can process specifications (i.e., contracts) expressed in CDL. Additional aspect languages have also been created by BBN to support the adaptation effort (Duzan et al., 2004). The CDL compiler translates QoS contracts into artifacts that can execute the adaptation specifications at run-time. The modeling efforts described in this chapter build upon the BBN infrastructure to affect the adaptation specifications captured in the AQML models, i.e., CDL specifications are generated from the AQML models and the BBN tools are used to instantiate these adaptation instructions at run-time in a real system. Neema et al. present results that show the situation where a simple state change within an AQML model translates into dozens of changes that would be needed at the CDL level (Neema et al., 2002), which suggests that QoS adaptation can be modeled with improved scalability when compared to an equivalent process using a textual language.

## CONCLUDING REMARKS

Composition of artifacts across the software life-cycle has been the focus of several recent research efforts (Batory, 2006; Gray et al., 2004; Rashid et al., 2003). The synergistic power resulting from a combination of modeling and aspects enables rapid changes to a high-level system specification, which can be synthesized into a simulation or implementation. This chapter described an approach based on MDE for simulating and generating QoS adaptation software for DRE systems using modeling aspects. Our approach focuses on raising the level of abstraction in representing QoS adaptation policies, and providing a control-centric design for the representation and analysis of the adaptation software.

Our approach has been tested and demonstrated on a UAV Video Streaming application described as a case study in this chapter. Although the case study presented a relatively simple scenario, C-SAW enables the modeling of much larger scenarios with a high degree of variability and adaptability. In our experience, the simulation capabilities have been particularly helpful in fine-tuning the adaptation mechanism. In addition to the UAV case study presented in this chapter, the GME and C-SAW have been applied also to Bold Stroke (Roll, 2003), which is a mission avionics computing platform described further in (Gray et al., 2006) in the context of using C-SAW on GME models representing Bold Stroke event channels.

Our investigation into model-driven QoS adaptation of DRE systems has led us to the following observations, which serve as the lessons learned from this contribution:

- *Separation of QoS logic from application source code*: Our experience with QuO and the UAV case study from BBN suggests that separation of QoS adaptation rules into a textual language like CDL offers improvements over QoS adaptation that is otherwise hard-coded directly into the application source code. By separating the QoS adaptation from the source code, it is possible to evolve the QoS adaptation layers more flexibly because the logic relating to each QoS concern can be found in one location, rather than spread across multiple source files.

- *Higher level modeling of QoS concerns*: Although textual languages like CDL can provide improved modularization over source code in a general-purpose programming language (GPL), higher level abstractions associated with domain-specific modeling languages offer even further improvements by assisting developers in specifying QoS concerns and their associated interactions across the components of the underlying application. In several cases, a single modification within the AQML modeling language was found to be equivalent to multiple changes in the corresponding CDL.

- *Adaptation of DRE models through model transformation and aspect weaving*: There are some modeling tasks that are traditionally associated with manual changes to the modeling structure (e.g., concerns like the bandwidth adaptation policy and scalability example from the case study). Such manual changes often require much clicking and typing by the model engineer, such that the modeling task does not scale well (e.g., modifying a single UAV to 10 UAVs would require thousands of mouse clicks); furthermore, issues of correctness emerge when a large number of structural changes are made to a model manually. This chapter presented a contribution toward automated evolution of QoS modeling concerns through model transformation and aspect weaving.

- *Generation of analysis and corresponding artifacts from models:* After the QoS policy has been modeled, it is desirable to simulate the QoS adaptation policy and to analyze various characteristics of the model. Model interpreters, such as those possible within the GME, can generate the necessary files needed to transform the model representation into the format expected by other tools. Furthermore, model interpreters can also translate the model representation into other artifacts, such as CDL and source code in a GPL, for integration within the execution platform of a DRE system. The contribution of this chapter is a justification for treating models as an important artifact for describing QoS adaptation in DRE systems.

We have identified several enhancements as future areas for investigation. We plan to integrate

*Figure 17. Summary of Concern-Driven QoS Modeling*

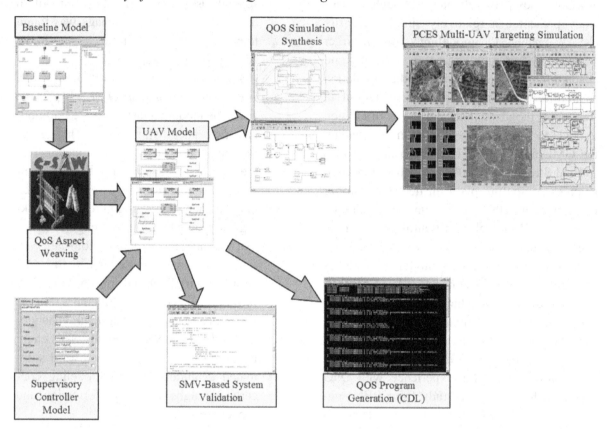

a symbolic model-checking tool, such as SMV (Burch et al., 1992), to enable formal reasoning about the adaptation mechanism. With the aid of this tool, various properties can be established (e.g., liveness, safety, and reachability) about the state machine implementing the adaptation policy. We also plan to strengthen the computation and middleware modeling to facilitate analysis of the application and middleware components. The topic of testing a model transformation rule is another area that will be explored in the future. As model transformations become a large part of the MDE process, it is desirable to have a testing framework that can be used to verify the correctness of each transformation rule. We are currently developing a GME-based testing framework to execute and compare model transformations with C-SAW (Lin et al., 2007; Lin et al., 2005).

A summary of the benefits of concern-driven modeling are shown in Figure 17. A viewpoint is an important concern separation technique that allows different perspectives to be modeled through partitioning mechanisms provided by the GME tool. With viewpoints, attention can be focused on related segments of a model without being overwhelmed by details unrelated to the concern of interest. From the base model, an aspect model weaver can be used to perform global transformations that span the hierarchy of the base model. Aspects at the modeling level enable various design alternatives (e.g., properties related to QoS specification) to be explored rapidly. From a transformed model, techniques from generative programming (Czarnecki & Eisenecker, 2000) can be applied to synthesize the model into a form suitable for simulation or model checking.

After verification of the models, code can be generated that captures the execution semantics of the modeled system (along with the specified QoS). The iterative nature of the process enables the evaluation of numerous system configurations before actual deployment.

## ACKNOWLEDGMENT

This work was previously supported by DARPA under the Program Composition of Embedded System (PCES) program and is partially supported by NSF CAREER (CCF-0643725). The authors thank Joseph Loyall and Richard Schantz of BBN Technologies for valuable discussions and comments.

## REFERENCES

Balasubramanian, K., Gokhale, A., Karsai, G., Sztipanovits, J., & Neema, S. (2006). Developing applications using model-driven design environments. *IEEE Computer*, *39*(2), 33–40.

Batory, D. (2006). Multilevel models in model-driven engineering, product lines, and metaprogramming. *IBM Systems Journal*, *45*(3), 527–540.

Batory, D., Sarvela, J. N., & Rauschmayer, A. (2004). Scaling stepwise refinement. *IEEE Transactions on Software Engineering*, *30*(6), 355–371. doi:10.1109/TSE.2004.23

Bézivin, J., Kurtev, I., Jouault, F., & Valduriez, P. (2006). Model-based DSL frameworks. *Companion to the 21st Annual ACM SIGPLAN Conference on Object-Oriented Programming, Systems, Languages, and Applications (OOPSLA)*, Portland, OR (pp. 602-616).

Burch, J., Clarke, E., McMillan, K., Dill, D., & Hwang, L. (1992). Symbolic model checking: 10^20 states and beyond. *Information and Computation*, *98*(2), 142–170. doi:10.1016/0890-5401(92)90017-A

Clarke, S., & Baniassad, E. (2005). *Aspect-oriented analysis and design: The theme approach.* Addison-Wesley.

Cottenier, T., van den Berg, A., & Elrad, T. (2007). Motorola WEAVR: Aspect and model-driven engineering. *Journal of Object Technology*, *6*(7), 51–88.

Czarnecki, K., & Eisenecker, U. (2000). *Generative programming: Methods, tools, and applications.* Addison-Wesley.

Dibble, P. (2008). *Real-time specification for Java.* Addison-Wesley.

Duzan, G., Loyall, J., Schantz, R., Shapiro, R., & Zinky, J. (2004). Building adaptive distributed applications with middleware and aspects. *International Conference on Aspect-Oriented Software Development (AOSD)*, Lancaster, UK (pp. 66-73).

Elrad, T., Aldawud, A., & Bader, A. (2002). Aspect-oriented modeling: Bridging the gap between modeling and design. *Generative Programming and Component Engineering (GPCE)*, Pittsburgh, PA (pp. 189-201).

Filman, R., & Friedman, D. (2000). Aspect-oriented programming is quantification and obliviousness. *OOPSLA Workshop on Advanced Separation of Concerns*, Minneapolis, MN.

Gokhale, A., Balasubramanian, K., Krishna, A., Balasubramanian, J., Edwards, G., & Deng, G. (2008). Model-driven middleware: A new paradigm for developing distributed real-time and embedded systems. *Science of Computer Programming*, *73*(1), 39–58. doi:10.1016/j.scico.2008.05.005

Gray, J., Bapty, T., Neema, S., & Tuck, J. (2001). Handling crosscutting constraints in domain-specific modeling. *Communications of the ACM, 44*(10), 87–93. doi:10.1145/383845.383864

Gray, J., Lin, Y., & Zhang, J. (2006). Automating change evolution in model-driven engineering. *IEEE Computer, 39*(2), 41–48.

Gray, J., Sztipanovits, J., Schmidt, D., Bapty, T., Neema, S., & Gokhale, A. (2004). Two-level aspect weaving to support evolution of model-driven synthesis. In *Aspect-Oriented Software Development*, (pp. 681-710). Addison-Wesley.

Gray, J., Tolvanen, J.-P., Kelly, S., Gokhale, A., Neema, S., & Sprinkle, J. (2007). Domain-specific modeling. In *Handbook on dynamic system modeling* (pp. 7-1–7-20). CRC Press.

Harel, D. (1987). Statecharts: A visual formalism for complex systems. *Science of Computer Programming, 8*(3), 231–274. doi:10.1016/0167-6423(87)90035-9

Karr, D., Rodrigues, C., Loyall, J., Schantz, R., Krishnamurthy, Y., Pyarali, I., & Schmidt, D. (2001). Application of the QuO quality-of-service framework to a distributed video application. *International Symposium on Distributed Objects and Applications*, Rome, Italy (pp. 299-309).

Karsai, G., Maroti, M., Lédeczi, A., Gray, J., & Sztipanovits, J. (2004). Composition and cloning in modeling and metamodeling languages. *IEEE Transactions on Control Systems Technology, 12*(2), 263–278. doi:10.1109/TCST.2004.824311

Kiczales, G., Lamping, J., Mendhekar, A., Maeda, C., Lopes, C., Loingtier, J.-M., & Irwin, J. (1997). Aspect-oriented programming. *European Conference on Object-Oriented Programming (ECOOP)*, Jyväskylä, Finland (pp. 220-242).

Lédeczi, A., Bakay, A., Maroti, M., Volgyesi, P., Nordstrom, G., Sprinkle, J., & Karsai, G. (2001). Composing domain-specific design environments. *IEEE Computer, 34*(11), 44–51.

Lin, Y. (2007). *A model transformation approach to automated model evolution.* Unpublished doctoral dissertation, University of Alabama at Birmingham, Department of Computer and Information Sciences. Retrieved from http://www.cis.uab.edu/softcom/dissertations/LinYuehua.pdf

Lin, Y., Gray, J., & Jouault, F. (2007). DSMDiff: A differentiation tool for domain-specific models. *European Journal of Information Systems, 16*(4), 349–361. doi:10.1057/palgrave.ejis.3000685

Lin, Y., Gray, J., Zhang, J., Nordstrom, S., Gokhale, A., Neema, S., & Gokhale, S. (2008). Model replication: Transformations to address model scalability. *Software, Practice & Experience, 38*(14), 1475–1497. doi:10.1002/spe.876

Lin, Y., Zhang, J., & Gray, J. (2005). A framework for testing model transformations. In *Model-driven software development*, (pp. 219-236). Springer.

Loyall, J., Schantz, R., Zinky, J., Pal, P., Shapiro, R., Rodrigues, C., et al. (2001). Comparing and contrasting adaptive middleware support in wide-area and embedded distributed object applications. *IEEE International Conference on Distributed Computing Systems (ICDCS)*, Phoenix, AZ (pp. 625-634).

Mernik, M., Heering, J., & Sloane, A. (2005). When and how to develop domain-specific languages. *ACM Computing Surveys, 37*(4), 316–344. doi:10.1145/1118890.1118892

Neema, S., Bapty, T., Gray, G., & Gokhale, A. (2002). Generators for synthesis of QoS adaptation in distributed real-time embedded systems. *Generative Programming and Component Engineering (GPCE)*, Pittsburgh, PA (pp. 236-251).

Neema, S., Sztipanovits, J., Karsai, G., & Butts, K. (2003). Constraint-based design-space exploration and model synthesis. *International Conference on Embedded Software (EMSOFT)*, Philadelphia, PA (pp. 290-305).

Nuseibeh, B., Kramer, J., & Finkelstein, A. (1994). A framework for expressing the relationship between multiple views in requirements specification. *IEEE Transactions on Software Engineering, 20*(10), 760–773. doi:10.1109/32.328995

Rashid, A., Moreira, A., & Araújo, J. (2003). Modularization and composition of aspectual requirements. *International Conference on Aspect-Oriented Software Development (AOSD)*, Boston (pp. 11-20).

Reddy, Y., Ghosh, S., France, R., Straw, G., Bieman, J., & McEachen, N. (2006). Directives for composing aspect-oriented design class models. *Transactions on Aspect-Oriented Software Development, 1*(1), 75–105. doi:10.1007/11687061_3

Roll, W. (2003). Towards model-based and CCM-based applications for real-time systems. *International Symposium on Object-Oriented Real-Time Distributed Computing (ISORC)*, Hokkaido, Japan (pp. 75-82).

Schantz, R., Loyall, J., Atighetchi, M., & Pal, P. (2002). Packaging quality of service control behaviors for reuse. *International Symposium on Object-oriented Real-time Distributed Computing (ISORC)*, Washington, D.C. (pp. 375-385).

Schantz, R., & Schmidt, D. (2001). Middleware for distributed systems: Evolving the common structure for network-centric applications. In *Encyclopedia of Software Engineering*. John Wiley and Sons.

Schmidt, D. (2006). Model-driven engineering. *IEEE Computer, 39*(2), 25–32.

Sharma, P., Loyall, J., Heineman, G., Schantz, R., Shapiro, R., & Duzan, G. (2004). Component-based dynamic QoS adaptations in distributed real-time and embedded systems. *International Symposium on Distributed Objects and Applications (DOA)*, Agia Napa, Cyprus (pp. 1208-1224).

Stankovic, J., Nagaraddi, P., Yu, Z., He, Z., & Ellis, B. (2004) Exploiting prescriptive aspects: A design time capability. *International Conference on Embedded Software (EMSOFT)*, Pisa, Italy (pp. 165-174).

Stein, D., Hanenberg, S., & Unland, R. (2006). Expressing different conceptual models of join point selections in aspect-oriented design. *International Conference on Aspect-Oriented Software Development (AOSD)*, Bonn, Germany (pp. 15-26).

Sztipanovits, J., & Karsai, G. (1997). Model-integrated computing. *IEEE Computer, 30*(4), 10–12.

Tarr, P. (2003). Toward a more piece-ful world. *Generative Programming and Component Engineering (GPCE)*, Erfurt, Germany (pp. 265-266).

Tarr, P., Ossher, H., Harrison, W., & Sutton, S. (1999). N degrees of separation: Multidimensional separation of concerns. *International Conference on Software Engineering (ICSE)*, Los Angeles, CA (pp. 107-119).

Wehrmeister, M., Freitas, E., Pereira, C., & Rammig, F. (2008). GenERTiCA: A tool for code generation and aspects weaving. *International Symposium on Object Oriented Real-Time Distributed Computing (ISORC)*, Orlando, FL (pp. 234–238).

Zhang, L., & Liu, R. (2005). Aspect-oriented real-time system modeling method based on UML. *International Conference on Embedded and Real-Time Computing Systems and Applications (RTAS)*, San Francisco, CA (pp. 373-376).

## ENDNOTE

[1] More details about ECL are available in (Lin, 2007).

# Chapter 5
# High-Level Design Space Exploration of Embedded Systems Using the Model-Driven Engineering and Aspect-Oriented Design Approaches

**Marcio Ferreira da Silva Oliveira**
*Universidade Federal do Rio Grande do Sul (UFRGS), Brazil*

**Marco Aurélio Wehrmeister**
*Universidade Federal do Rio Grande do Sul (UFRGS), Brazil*

**Francisco Assis do Nascimento**
*Universidade Federal do Rio Grande do Sul (UFRGS), Brazil*

**Carlos Eduardo Pereira**
*Universidade Federal do Rio Grande do Sul (UFRGS), Brazil*

**Flávio Rech Wagner**
*Universidade Federal do Rio Grande do Sul (UFRGS), Brazil*

## ABSTRACT

*Modern embedded systems have increased their functionality by using a large amount and diversity of hardware and software components. Realizing the expected system functionality is a complex task. Such complexity must be managed in order to decrease time-to-market and increase system quality. This chapter presents a method for high-level design space exploration (DSE) of embedded systems that uses model-driven engineering (MDE) and aspect-oriented design (AOD) approaches. The modelling style and the abstraction level open new design automation and optimization opportunities, thus improving the overall results. Furthermore, the proposed method achieves better reusability, complexity management, and design automation by exploiting both MDE and AOD approaches. Preliminary results regarding the use of the proposed method are presented.*

DOI: 10.4018/978-1-60566-750-8.ch005

# INTRODUCTION

An increasing number of hardware and software components are being incorporated into single embedded systems in order to enhance their functionality. This leads to a growing design complexity, which must be managed properly. Besides, the stringent requirements regarding power, performance, cost, and time-to-market also hinder the design of embedded systems. Designer's expertise is not enough to deal with this ever-growing challenge, where a very wide range of design alternatives must be evaluated in order to find the best trade-off among conflicting requirements. Therefore, new development methods are imperative, including efficient Design Space Exploration (DSE) approaches, which are used to quickly find an adequate design solution while coping with a wide design space and conflicting requirements.

In order to improve embedded system design, meet-in-the-middle strategies, such as Platform-based Design (PBD) (Sangiovanni-Vincentelli, 2001), are largely employed. These methods maximize the reuse of pre-designed components and achieve the best customization of the design platform concerning system requirements, by applying a layered design approach and a large library of components. In this strategy, a DSE step is required in order to optimize each mapping between layers, thus building a link from the initial specification until the final implementation. The increase in the number of reused components, together with the complex mapping between layers, reinforces the need for new DSE methods, which should enable the automation and optimization of design tasks. An appropriate DSE strategy should perform design decisions at the earliest development phases, at higher abstraction levels, where their impact on the final product quality is much larger than at lower levels.

Although the PBD approach is very valuable to the design of embedded system, developing applications for the existing complex platforms is a hard task. Furthermore, developing a new platform from the scratch is a big bet for companies (Goering, 2002). Moreover, Sangiovanni-Vincentelli (2002) highlights the difficulties in performing the mapping between layers, as well as in getting benefits from the optimization potential at higher abstraction layers.

In order to overcome the difficulty in rising the abstraction level and to improve the automation of the design from the initial specification until the final system, research efforts look for modelling methods, formalisms, and suitable abstractions to specify embedded systems in a fast and precise way. Approaches such as Model-Driven Engineering (MDE) (Schmidt, 2006) and Aspect-Oriented Design (AOD) (Filman, 2004) have been proposed in order to improve the complexity management and also the reusability of previously developed/specified artefacts. The MDE method, combined with a standard modelling language, such as UML or Simulink, raises the design abstraction level and provides mechanisms to improve the portability, interoperability, maintainability, and reusability of models. In addition, MDE helps abstracting platform complexity and also representing different system concerns, by exploiting well-accepted meet-in-the-middle development strategies, following the principles of the PBD approach.

However, embedded systems design must deal with non-functional requirements (NFRs), such as time constraints, memory footprint, energy consumption, communication bandwidth, etc., which are indirectly related to the functionality performed by the system. Traditional approaches, such as Object Orientation, do not offer adequate support for handling crosscutting NFRs, intermixing them with the handling of functional requirements (FRs). This situation produces tangled and scattered requirements handling, which negatively impacts the reusability (Wehrmeister, 2008a). Approaches such as AOD propose the separation of concerns in the handling of FRs and NFRs. The AOD approach initially addressed this problem at the implementation level. However, the handling of NFRs must be taken into account as soon as possible to enhance system design. This fact motivates pushing the separation of concerns to the early design phases, such as in the Early-Aspects approach (Rashid, 2002).

This chapter presents a DSE method to be used in the context of platform-based design. This DSE method takes advantage of the development process and modelling style to open new optimization opportunities and improve the overall result of system design, by applying both MDE and AOD approaches. MDE and AOD allow performing DSE much earlier, during the high-level design model specification, than other approaches that postpone it to a later and more expensive design step, after code generation and hardware synthesis, such as in SPADE (Lieverse, 2001), StepN (Paulin, 2002) and (Ascia, 2004). Moreover, MDE and AOD also provide mechanisms to represent the system concerns in a consistent and orthogonal way. In order to cope with the lack of methods to support requirements specification and improve the separation of concerns argued by PBD, the proposed method exploits the AOD approach during the development phase, by which the system FRs and NFRs can be separately specified. Furthermore, the use of MDE combined wit AOD increases the abstraction level of system models and achieves better system customization and design automation.

## BACKGROUND AND RELATED WORK

### Model-Driven Engineering

Previous attempts to rise the abstraction level in the software development process originated the Computer Aided Software Engineering (CASE) tools (Schmidt, 2006), which provided graphical representations for fundamental programming concepts. Moreover, they provide automatic generation of implementation code to decrease the complexity concerning programming details. However, one of the main problems with CASE tools was exactly the code generation process that, mainly due to the limitations of the existing platforms at those days, produced very inefficient implementations (Schmidt, 2006). Moreover, the graphical representations were too generic, i.e. they could not efficiently deal with many application domains, and were also not easily customizable.

Nowadays, the limitations have been drastically reduced, due to object-oriented languages with development frameworks, which make easier the reuse of software components. However, these development frameworks, or platforms, are extremely complex, such that it became very difficult to efficiently use the features provided by their APIs, for example.

One of the current approaches to deal with the complexity of platforms is Model Driven Engineering (MDE) (Schmidt, 2006), where two basic principles are adopted: *domain specific languages* (DSL), whereby an adequate language for each application domain is used; and *transformation engines*. By applying successive transformations starting from models, these engines can generate different kinds of artefacts that implement the specified application. The *transformations* between models can be used to incorporate details into a given model, converting different types of models by re-factoring their constructs. There are at least two types of transformations: from model to code and from model to model. Model-to-model transformations allow the replication of elements at different points of given models, as well as the replication of elements inside the same model. On the other hand, model-to-code transformations generate an implementation from a specification model.

There are at least two variants of MDE: the Model Driven Architecture (MDA) (OMG, 2007) that adopts UML (Unified Modelling Language) as standard modelling language (OMG, 2007a) and is oriented to the automatic code generation for many types of platforms (e.g. CCM - CORBA Component Model (OMG, 2006)); and the Model Integrated Computing (MIC) approach (Karsai, 2003) that adopts different modelling languages (one for each application domain) and allows the generation of implementations for specific platforms.

MDA is a standard proposed by the Object Management Group (OMG) for the software development process. Independently from the abstraction level, modelling languages are classified as: platform-independent languages, which are oriented to system specification; and platform-dependent languages, which are oriented to system implementation. MDA defines the concept of mapping, which establishes automatic or semi-automatic mechanisms to transform Platform-Independent Models (PIM) into Platform-Specific Models (PSM) that use specific languages. Thus, the development of systems can be focused on aspects that do not involve implementation details (OMG, 2007). The languages used to express these models are defined by means of meta-models, which are able to represent abstract and concrete syntaxes, as well as the operational semantics of the modelling language.

There are many recent research efforts on embedded systems design based on MDE. The adoption of platform-independent design and executable UML has been vastly investigated. For example, xtUML (Mellor, 2002) defines an executable and translatable UML subset for embedded real-time systems, allowing the simulation of UML models and C code generation oriented to different microcontroller platforms. The Model Execution Platform (MEP) (Schattkowsky, 2005) is another approach based on MDA, oriented to code generation and model execution. Our approach, instead, is more oriented to DSE at a higher abstraction level (using the notion of transformations between models) than to validation or code generation.

The Generic Modelling Environment (GME) (Davis, 2003) is oriented to the development of domain-specific visual modelling languages by specifying meta-models. In GME, meta-models are described as UML class diagrams. A visual editor, supporting the edition of diagrams and also code generation, is then automatically generated for the creation of models based on those meta-models. GME has been used to implement some model-based tools for embedded system design, such as MILAN (Model-based Integrated Simulation) (Bakshi, 2001), which allows simulation of embedded systems.

## Aspect-Oriented Design and Its Application to Embedded Systems Design

The concepts of Aspect-Oriented Design (AOD) presented in this chapter follow the terminology and glossary presented in (Van den Berg, 2005) and (Schauerhuber, 2006), which provide more comprehensive semantics for AOD concepts than those presented in (Kiczales, 1997), which focus on the Aspect-Oriented Programming (AOP). The main concept is the *Concern*, which represents an interest within the system development, system operation/use, or any other issues that are critical or otherwise important to one or more stakeholders. *Separation of Concerns* means to deal with each concern in isolation, in order to allow the creation of modular artefacts that handle them. Specifically in the embedded systems design literature, such as in (Keutzer, 2000), the *Separation of Concerns* usually deals with the orthogonal specification of the functional and architectural concerns of the system, or of the computation and communication concerns. In this chapter we adopt a more comprehensive use of these concepts, including also the separation of functional (FRs) from non-functional requirements (NFRs) and the separation of analysis from design models, which are related to, respectively, functional and architectural models. *Modularization* means the ability to group or partition artefacts into entities called *Modules* (i.e. an abstraction unit in the adopted language) that ideally must be loosely coupled and highly cohesive. *Composition* is the ability of integrating several modular artefacts into a coherent whole, while *Decomposition* is the division of a larger problem into smaller ones, which may be handled apart from each other.

An important concept is *Crosscutting*, which represents the occurrence of *Tangling* (i.e. multiple concerns mixed together in one module) and *Scattering* (i.e. the representation of one concern spread over multiple modules), which happen when the selected decomposition is unable to modularize concerns in an effective way. Therefore, *Crosscutting Concerns* are concerns that cannot be mapped to unique modules, thus leading to tangling and scattering. NFRs can be viewed as crosscutting concerns, because they are usually intermixed with FRs inside several modules.

In AOD, an *Aspect* represents a unit of modularization for crosscutting concerns, i.e. an aspect can encapsulate in a single entity all structure and/or behavioral elements of a crosscutting concern. These elements are specified by the *Adaptations*, which represent how the concern structure and/or behavior are adapted, i.e. enhanced, replaced, or even deleted, when an aspect affects the concern. Adaptations can be *Structural* and *Behavioral* ones. The former represent modifications in the structure of concerns, while the later represent modifications in the concern behavior. *Weaving* is the composition process that spreads aspect adaptations into other concerns. Another important concept is the *Join Point*, which represents a well-defined place in the structure or behavior of concerns where aspects perform adaptations. The association between aspect adaptations and join points receives the denomination *Pointcut*. Adaptations are applied in the associated join points at a *Relative Position*, which can be before, after, or around the join point.

AOD was initially proposed as a new paradigm in the implementation phase of the development of general systems. Programming languages such as AspectJ (Kiczales, 1997) and Aspect C++

(Spinczyk, 2002) are examples of languages that use concepts of AOD. However, researchers saw the potential of using aspects in other development phases, in order to obtain the same benefits of separation of concerns already achieved in writing source code. Considering the use of AOD concepts to handle NFRs at earlier design phases, works regarding requirements analysis such as (Araújo, 2002; Rashid, 2002; Sousa, 2004; Yu, 2004) and (Kaiya, 2004) must be cited. They mainly use template-like structures and use cases to specify FRs and NFRs. In a further step of requirements analysis, these approaches identify which NFRs affect functional ones and associate them with aspects. On the same direction, there are works that apply aspects at analysis and design phases, such as (Clarke, 2005; Jacobson, 2005; Klein, 2006; Stein, 2002; Zhang, 2005). Those works apply aspects within UML diagrams, or use Domain Specific Modelling Languages (DSML), or even use their own modelling languages.

However, in spite of the works referenced above, there are few efforts aiming at the use of AOD in the context of embedded systems design, as for example (Kishi, 2004; Stankovic, 2003; Zhang, 2005). The first one presents a toolset to help in the composition of component-based embedded systems. Two new concepts have been introduced: (i) *aspects checking*, which checks the dependence among components; and (ii) *prescriptive aspects*, which are "general aspects" that adjust component properties in the reflective information (Stankovic, 2003). The second one proposes an extension to UML for specifying timing requirements, while the last one uses AOD concepts to model the context in which the embedded system is intended to operate. The work presented in this chapter differs from all the above in various aspects: (i) our approach uses standard and well accepted modelling languages, such as UML and its MARTE profile (OMG, 2007d), instead of using "home-made" languages; (ii) aspects are used to specify the handling of NFRs from earlier design phases, such as requirements analysis; (iii) a high-level aspect library for the embedded systems domain has been created to be used at modelling level; and (iv) due to the abstract nature of this library, aspects can have different implementations, which affect the trade-off (e.g. execution time vs. memory usage vs. energy consumption) to be evaluated by the DSE tool.

## Design Space Exploration for Embedded Systems Development

In a definition that is appropriate for high-level system design, *Design Space Exploration* (DSE) is the design activity by which we look for different solutions for the mapping between an application and an architectural platform, such that each one corresponds to a different trade-off regarding design requirements and constraints (Keutzer, 2000). From the development process point of view, DSE can be seen as a set of development activities that look for the best refinement of the analysis model into a design model of the system. The analysis model represents concepts from the problem domain (e.g. wheels, steer, and transmission in automotive systems), for which the FRs and NFRs are defined. During this refinement, the *analysis model* should be mapped to some architecture in the solution domain (e.g. scheduler, processors, classes, and objects in an embedded system), represented by the *design model*.

As a single problem (analysis model) can be solved by (mapped to) alternative solutions (design models), a design space is composed by all these available alternatives, which should be manually or automatically explored in order to find the best one according to the design goals and constraints (e.g. measured by performance and energy consumption). Therefore, the design space is the set of all alternative design decisions for all existing design activities, which can be performed in a serial or parallel fashion. Due to the different abstraction levels, development activities and DSE can be performed at each level of refinement, until achieving the final implemented system.

Through the years, many methods have been proposed in order to automate DSE for different design activities. Some methods investigate DSE in a coarse grain fashion, as presented in (Balarin, 2003; Bakshi, 2001; Blickle, 1998; Bondé, 2004; Dick, 1998; Dwivedi, 2004; Erbas, 2003; Kangas, 2006; Ledeczi, 2003; Mihal, 2002; Pimentel, 2006). These methods concentrate on global decisions such as hardware allocation, hardware and software partitioning, task mapping, and scheduling. Other methods investigate a special case of DSE called platform tuning, by which the established architecture is fine tuned (adjusted) according to system requirements. The methods proposed in (Givargis, 2002) and (Ascia, 2004) are examples of platform tuning. Platform tuning usually involves system evaluation using lower abstraction level models in order to establish values for local configuration parameters, for instance cache configuration, bus width, and buffer sizes. Some design tools (Mohanty, 2002) cover both DSE and platform tuning.

In order to improve design automation, some proposals focus on system-level design decisions, due to the fact that global optimizations have more impact on the final system properties. However, these proposals require very detailed specifications at low abstraction levels and use programming languages, such as C and C++ (Bomtempi, 2002; Lieverse, 2001), or hardware description languages, such as Verilog (Russel, 2003). Exploiting the fact that the design at high abstraction levels improves the productivity and the quality of DSE, the works described in (Sciuto, 2002) and StepN (Paulin, 2002) use SystemC to model the application. Following the change on the focus from implementation code to model, new methods change the specification input from programming to model languages, thus raising even more the abstraction level. Some of these proposals use Simulink, as in (Neema, 2003) and (Reyneri, 2001); UML, as proposed by Metropolis (Chen, 2003), DaRT (Bondé, 2004), and Koski (Kangas, 2006); and SysML, an extension of UML

(SysML is not a profile) for system modelling, as in (Ganesan, 2006).

The main impact of the abstraction level regarding DSE concerns the flexibility and the easier evaluation of alternative designs. Higher abstraction levels reduce the evaluation effort, but at the same time reduce the estimation accuracy. Providing both a better abstraction level and an estimation method with an adequate balance between speed and accuracy is one of the main challenges for new DSE methods. The right combination of specification languages and Models of Computation (MoC) with exploration and estimation methods is essential. The approach proposed in MILAN (Bakshi, 2001) uses DSML and a MoC specialized for Digital Signal Processing to capture design details with less design effort. It also exploits MDE concepts using a meta-modelling infrastructure, which allows model refinement, and, in combination with different evaluation tools, DSE at different abstraction levels. However, some designer's effort is required to model the available design space, and the early estimation method is heavily based on datasheets or designer's expertise. Another method, which also exploits MDE concepts, is proposed in the DART project (Bondé, 2004), which uses a Y-chart (Kienhuis, 1997) based approach together with MDA to simulate and generate code for data-flow applications.

Despite the fact that some methods select a more abstract language as input for the DSE phase, none of those methods exploits a modelling approach in order to improve the DSE process. Exploiting the modelling approach regards not only the use of a more abstract language, but also the improvement of design methods for different development phases, until the input for the automatic DSE step is reached. In the proposed method, the development phases before the DSE step (requirements specification, analysis and design) are improved by using the AOD and MDE approaches, which not only rise the abstraction level but also provide several additional advantages: i) improve the requirements analysis, allowing better

guidelines for DSE; ii) extend the separation of concerns, mainly regarding FRs and NFRs, thus highlighting new optimization opportunities; and iii) allow early and fast DSE without performing costly synthesis-and-simulation cycles at lower abstraction levels.

## MODELLING FOR AUTOMATED DESIGN SPACE EXPLORATION

It is widely known that the choice of abstraction levels and the separation of concerns have deep influence on the DSE process (Sangiovanni-Vincentelli, 2001). And they are determined by modelling concepts such as language, Model of Computation (MoC), and modelling style. By adequately handling those concepts, one can improve reusability and the exploration of reused artefacts. They may also improve the design flexibility and allow one to find new optimization opportunities. Moreover, modelling issues are also strongly related to design automation, since an adequate systematization of inputs and outputs for a design task is essential for its automation during the DSE process.

In all current DSE methods, the modelling of functional and NFRs is not especially considered, concerning the influence of requirements analysis and specification modelling on the DSE process. Most of the current methods, such as in (Kangas, 2006; Lieverse, 2001; Neema, 2003; Pimentel, 2006), propose a specification approach for FRs and present some mechanism to specify at least the constraints in order to prune the design space and avoid infeasible designs, since this systematization and information are minimally required for DSE. Besides approaches for software code generation and hardware synthesis, such as (Coyle, 2005) and (Lu, 2003), no work was found that exploits the model concepts to improve the DSE process and automate at least non-creative design tasks, which can be performed by an heuristic search on the design space, such as selecting the number of processors and mapping tasks onto the selected processors.

We believe that the automation of non-creative design tasks and the optimization of design decisions are the best approaches to improve design productivity, reduce time-to-market, and achieve fast and high quality designs. To reach these goals, we propose to improve the DSE process by exploiting the requirements analysis and the modelling approach during the analysis and design phases.

The requirements analysis process is important due because DSE is essentially a requirements-driven activity. Since in the early design phases it is more difficult to have the big picture of the system and a good understanding of all its requirements, an adequate requirements analysis becomes essential to improve the inputs, namely FRs and NFRs, for DSE. Moreover, we should also improve the separation of concerns, by specifying functional requirements orthogonally to the non-functional ones. We should also provide a systematized path to identify constraints, which guide the DSE process. For this reason a specific development process based on AOD was tailored for DSE and applied to the development process of embedded systems. This method is called RT-FRIDA (Real Time – From Requirements to Design using Aspects) (Freitas, 2007), which provides a set of templates and specification guidelines, in order to help the designer to identify and specify the system requirements.

The modelling approach defines how flexible is the DSE process and isolates the distinct domains of design decisions (design space). Also the different abstraction levels depend on the adopted modelling approach. They define the model reusability and how detailed the models should be, constraining the alternatives in the lower level models and the possibilities to automate design decisions.

Through AOD, we improve simultaneously the abstraction and the separation of concerns, by separately handling NFRs through aspects, thus opening new design automation and optimization opportunities. Besides the requirements analysis process, the development process provides also the guidelines to specify the analysis and design models using the AOD concepts. Thus, the aspect framework DERAF (Distributed Embedded Real-time Aspects Framework) (Freitas, 2007), containing high-level aspects models, is provided to rise even more the abstraction and improve the reuse of models. More specifically, it specifies pre-defined handling elements for common NFRs of embedded, real-time and distributed systems.

The proposed MDE/AOD approach provides several advances for model-based DSE. Firstly, the MDE approach changes the development focus from implementation code to design models, where the development effort is now concentrated and modelling decisions can lead to substantially superior improvements. Secondly, MDE allows the coherent representation of different concerns of the system through meta-modelling, in order to capture the specification models and make them available to other design automation tools. The MDE/AOD approach is supported by the MDE-framework MODES (MOdel-Driven Embedded System design) (Nascimento, 2007), which provides an efficient meta-modelling infrastructure to capture the system structure and behaviour. It represents system concerns in distinct dimensions that correspond to the Y-chart: application, platform, mapping, and implementation. Moreover, MODES provides a transformation engine, which interacts with the exploration tools to allow both verification of requirements and generation of the final model after the DSE step.

A DSE tool called H-SPEX (High-level design SPace EXploration) (Oliveira, 2008) has been developed to exploit the MDE and AOD approaches in the requirements, analysis and design phases of the development process. H-SPEX allows a designer to concentrate the effort on problem domain concepts and on creative activities, instead of dealing with design decisions that can be automatically optimized by tools. Early and fast

*Figure 1. Design methodology*

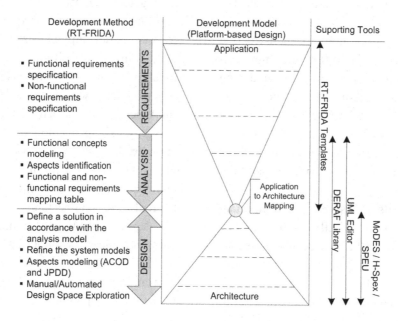

evaluation is achieved by using a model-based estimation tool called SPEU (System Properties Estimation with UML) (Oliveira, 2006).

The proposed DSE method is weakly dependent on a specific development process and may be easily adapted to different development processes, such as RUP-SE (Cantor, 2003), ROPES (Douglass, 2003), HASoC (Green, 2002), SHE (Geilen, 2001), MIDAS (Fernandes, 2000), Ptolemy (Kalavade, 1993), and others. In the proposed DSE method, the requirements specification, analysis and design phases (commonly proposed on the referenced process) are extremely important, because they produce the input for the DSE process.

Figure 1 illustrates the proposed design methodology and highlights the main activities and the supporting tools. On the left column the basic activities are shown, following the RT-FRIDA development method. The development method has three main phases: (i) identification and specification of requirements; (ii) mapping requirements onto system elements; and (iii) system design. These phases correspond to the main development phases (i.e. requirements specification, analysis

and design), which refine the system specification by performing different activities. The schema in the middle column illustrates the PBD approach, the abstraction levels, and the mapping from application to architecture performed during the refinement from the analysis to the design phase. The right column indicates which supporting tools are used during each development phase.

It is important to highlight that the focus of this chapter is on the specification and design space exploration of embedded systems. However, the research effort in progress at the Embedded System Lab of UFRGS (www.inf.ufrgs.br/~lse) considers the complete development process, which includes different tools to cover the whole embedded system development, from the requirements specification until the lower level of implementation. The complete tool chain includes code generators from UML models, such as as GeneRTICA (Wehrmeister, 2008b), estimation and simulation tools for multiple abstraction levels, such as (Oyamada, 2008) and CACO-PS (Beck, 2003), and the synthesis tool SASHIMI (Ito, 2001). Some of these tools are integrated to or make uses of well known third-party tools, such as Telel-

*Figure 2. Wheelchair control system overview*

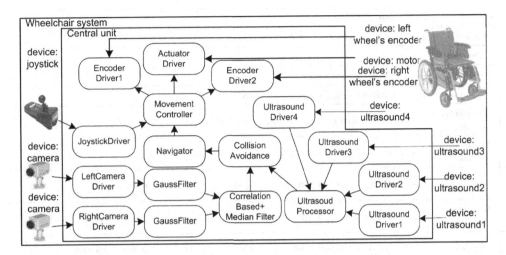

ogic Doors (www.telelogic.com/Products/doors/), Magic Draw (UML Editor) (www.magicdraw. com), Eclipse (www.eclipse.org), oAW (www. openarchitectureware.org), Polis (Balarin, 1997), and Uppaal (Larsen, 1997), in order to support a wide range of development tasks.

The next sub-sections describe the proposed design methodology in the context of a general development process for embedded systems, from the requirements specification, going through analysis and design modelling, until the automated DSE during the design phase. These sections explain (with the help of a case study) how the AOD and MDE approaches are applied in the development process to improve the DSE method and also how they are exploited by H-SPEX.

In each sub-section, samples of produced artefacts (forms and models) are given. The presented case study is a real application, concerning the automated control of an automated wheelchair with functions such as movement control, collision avoidance (ultrasound and stereo vision), and navigation. Figure 2 gives an overview of the wheelchair control system.

## Requirements Specification

The requirements identification phase is divided into two steps: FRs and NFRs specification. The former means the specification of the desired functionality through forms to provide detailed information on the use cases specified in the UML Use Cases Diagram. A template form is provided to guide the FRs specification. Table 1 shows such template with explanations on how to use it, while Table 2 shows a filled form used to specify the movement control of the wheelchair case study.

In order to help the designer to assess the NFRs, the method provides a checklist, which is a set of pre-defined questions related to the domain of embedded and real-time systems. Table 3 shows an example of such checklist. Following, NFRs template forms are filled with the information gathered in the checklists. Such form is similar to those created for FRs specification. Table 4 presents the template for NFR specification, while an example of a filled form specifying a NFR called NFR-1 is shown in Table 5.

Upon reaching this point, a developer can iterate to improve information on the requirements specification or go on with the development pro-

*Table 1. Template of FR form*

| | Item | Description |
|---|---|---|
| **Identification** | **Identifier** | Allows traceability over the whole project. |
| | **Name** | Use case name. |
| | **Goal** | Description of the use case goals. |
| | **Author** | The person responsible for the use case description. |
| **Context** | **Pre-condition** | A condition that must hold **before** the execution of use case. |
| | **Pos-condition** | A condition that must hold **after** the execution of use case. |
| **Actors** | **Primary Actor** | Actors who are the sources of the events that stimulate the main scenario. |
| | **Secondary Actor** | Passive actors who interact with the use case, but do not execute any action over it. |
| **Decision and evolution** | **Priority** | Levels of relative importance among use cases: **Maximum, Medium, and Minimum.** |
| | **situation** | A requirement can have one of the following status: 0-identified; 1-analysed 2-specified; 4-cancelled; 3-approved; 5-finished; |
| **Paths** | **Main (normal)** | Describes the main flow of the use case considering only positive results, and without error conditions. |
| | **Alternative** | Describes the alternative flow to the use case. |
| | **Exceptional** | Describes a flow on exceptional situation of the use case. |
| **Scenario** | **Main** | Describes the main steps of the use case scenario. |
| | **Variations** | Describes steps that modify one or more steps within the main scenario. |

cess, which means to perform the mapping of FRs and NFRs into concepts in the analysis model and the successive refinement of the analysis model into the design one. All requirements identified during this phase can be seen using UML Use Case Diagrams extended with stereotypes to differ FRs from NFRs. Figure 3 shows a sample Use Case Diagram and the two additional stereotypes (<<*crosscut*>> and <<*non-functional*>>). Tools such as Telelogic Doors and Magic Draw help in the task of linking and organizing the requirement forms in the development environment, as the information gathered in the requirements specification is used during different phases of the development process. Especially for the DSE process, this information is used to evaluate the alternative designs and to verify their feasibility. Moreover, in the case where different alternative

designs are candidates, this information is used to guide the designer in finding the best trade-off between the alternatives.

## Analysis and Design Modelling

Following the development process, after the requirements specification phase, FRs and NFRs were fully or partially (depending on the adopted development process) specified and are available to be refined. In the first refinement, the analysis model is specified using the elements that represent concepts in the problem domain, and the FRs and NFRs should be mapped into these elements. Then, the resulting analysis model is refined into a design model. Models in the analysis and design phase are specified using UML diagrams.

*Table 2. Example of filled FR form*

| | Item | Description |
|---|---|---|
| **Identification** | **Identifier** | FR-2 |
| | **Name** | Wheelchair Movement Control |
| | **Goal** | Control the basic movements of the wheelchair. |
| | **Author** | Smith |
| **Context** | **Pre-condition** | The data from sensors and the joystick must be available. |
| | **Pos-condition** | The movement parameters must be updated. |
| **Actors** | **Primary Actor** | Navigation Control |
| | **Secondary Actor** | -- |
| **Decision and evolution** | **Priority** | Maximum |
| | **situation** | Finished |
| **Paths** | **Main (normal)** | Periodically it calculates movement parameters based on the data from sensors and joystick. |
| | **Alternative** | |
| | **Exceptional** | |
| **Scenario** | **Main** | (1) Reads the data from the movement sensors and the joystick. (2) Calculates new movement parameters. (3) Makes available the new parameters to be used by the actuators. |
| | **Variations** | (2) In case of malfunction of any system element, the parameters must be calculated following the emergency policy. |

The design phase searches for the software and hardware architecture that supports the elements that handle FRs and NFRs that were specified during the previous phases. The specification approach is based on the Y-chart approach, where the application model should have no architectural implications as much as possible. Therefore, the languages should raise the abstraction level in

*Table 3. Example of checklist for NFRs*

| | Relevance | Priority | **Restrictions / Conditions / Description** |
|---|---|---|---|
| **Time** | | | |
| **Timing** | | | |
| Is there any periodic activity or data sampling? | X | 8 | Joystick sensing, Movement Control and Movement Sensing |
| Is there any sporadic activities? | -- | -- | -- |
| Is there any aperiodic activity? | X | 7 | Alarm |
| Is there any restriction in relation to the latency to start an execution of a system activity? | X | 9 | Deal with maximum latency overrun: Corrective action |
| Is there any specific instant to start or finish an execution of a system activity? | -- | -- | -- |
| Was any WCET specified? Or at least, is there any concern about this? | | | The sampled data from joystick and movement sensors must be read at a maximum of 10 ms. |

*Table 4. Template model for NFRs*

| | Item | Description |
|---|---|---|
| **Identification** | **Identifier** | Allows traceability over the whole project. |
| | **Name** | NFR name. |
| | **Author** | The person responsible for NFR specification. |
| **Specification** | **Classification** | Class to which the NFR belongs. |
| | **Description** | Description of how the NFR affects system functionality. |
| | **Affected Use Cases** | List of the use cases affected by the NFR. |
| | **Context** | Determines when the NFR is expected to affect a use case. |
| | **Scope** | (Global/Partial) The requirement is global if it affects the whole system, and is partial if affects only a part of the system. |
| **Decision and Evolution** | **Priority** | A number used to decide the relative importance among non-functional concerns. |
| | **Status** | A requirement can have one of the following status: 0-identified; 1-analysed 2-specified; 4-cancelled; 3-approved; 5-finished; |

order to allow maximal flexibility in the DSE.

During the design specification, computational/engineering issues (e.g. scheduling, memory, communication mechanism, processors, instructions, and others) arise as the relevant problems. In order to find the appropriate software and hardware architecture, different design activities must be performed. We can organize these activities along the design space domains, which represent the axes on the Y-chart approach.

In the Application Domain, a designer may investigate issues such as:

*Table 5. Sample of filled NFR form*

| | Item | Description |
|---|---|---|
| **Identification** | **Identifier** | NFR-1 |
| | **Name** | Periodicity |
| | **Author** | Smith |
| **Specification** | **Classification** | Time/Timing/Period |
| | **Description** | The system has some activities that must be executed periodically: (1) data acquisition from joystick; (2) data acquisition from sensors; and (3) the control of wheelchair movement. |
| | **Affected Use Cases** | (1) Joystick Sensing; (2) Movement Sensing; (3) Movement Control |
| | **Context** | When the system needs to update the data collected from (1) the joystick position and (2) movement information, as well as (3) during the wheelchair movement control |
| | **Scope** | Global |
| **Decision and Evolution** | **Priority** | 8 |
| | **Status** | 5 |

*Figure 3. Sample of use case diagram showing FRs and NFRs*

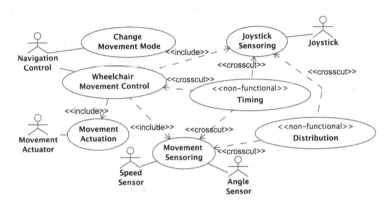

- **Algorithm implementation:** How will the FR be implemented? Should it be optimized for power saving or for performance improvement?
- **Data structures definition:** How should the data be organized and stored?
- **Responsibility distribution:** Which classes and how many objects should implement a given FR?
- **Functionality encapsulation:** How are the interactions between objects?
- **Task definition:** How many schedulable or parallel tasks should the system have?
- **Task scheduling:** When should each task be executed?

In the Architectural Domain, a designer can explore:

- **Hardware and software partitioning:** Which function should be implemented in software and which one in hardware?
- **Communication mechanisms and protocols definition:** How should the components be interconnected? Which protocol should be used in each interconnect?
- **Component / service implementation:** Considering a platform repository, which component that implements a given service should be used in the system?

- **Component configuration:** How should the parameters, such as processor voltage or bus width, be set?

The Mapping Domain expresses the alternative mappings between application and architecture concepts. In this domain, a designer may explore:

- **Task mapping:** In which processor should each task be executed?
- **Hardware allocation:** Where in the physical communication structure should the hardware components be located?
- **Software binding:** Which memory should the software be stored in?

Depending on the development approach and on the required abstraction level, those and other design decisions can be postponed to be performed by automated tools or performed manually only based on a designer's expertise.

Using the information gathered in the previous phases, FRs are specified using standard UML diagrams and the MARTE profile (OMG, 2007d). A non-intrusive set of modelling guidelines should be followed to allow the design automation tools to capture and handle the UML models. Figure 4-A shows the partial class diagram for the wheelchair movement control, which shows classes

*Figure 4.Functional specification: (a) class diagram (b) sequence diagrams*

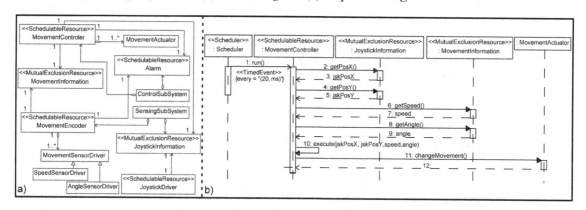

annotated with the <<*SchedulableResource*>> stereotype representing classes of active objects, and with the <<*MutualExclusionResource*>> stereotype representing classes whose objects are accessed concurrently by active classes. Figure 4-B shows the movement controller active object behaviour.

The specification of the NFRs handling is done by reusing aspects provided by the DERAF aspects framework. DERAF contains extensible high-level aspect models, which provide aspects that encapsulate all issues related to the handling of one or more NFRs. The main idea is to provide aspects that enhance the modelled system by adding specific behaviour and structure for handling NFRs during the design phase. The framework also provides a set of join points, which specify places where aspects apply adaptations. *Join Point Designation Diagrams* (JPDD) (Stein, 2006) are used to describe the join point selection at modelling level. The use of high-level join point descriptions improves their reuse, allowing that

the same join point may be reused with different adaptations. We use the UML sequence diagram to specify a behavioural JPDD, which captures control flow join points. However, it could also be modelled by using activity and state-chart diagrams capturing data flow and state models. Figure 5 shows three sample join points:

- *ActiveClass* (Figure 5-A) represents the selection of all active object classes (i.e. those annotated with the <<*SchedulableResource*>> stereotype)
- *ActObjConstructor* (Figure 5-B) selects the action that constructs all active objects
- *PeriodicActivation* (Figure 5-C) represents the selection of all messages that are annotated with the <<*TimedEvent*>> stereotype, sent by the scheduler to some active object

Based on their high-level semantics, aspects are chosen from the aspects framework to deal

*Figure 5. Three samples of Join Point selection*

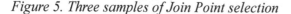

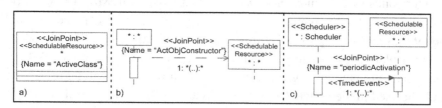

*Figure 6. Sample of ACOD to specify the handling of NFRs*

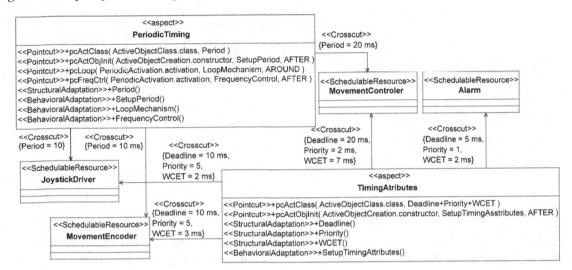

with the NFRs gathered in checklists and forms of the requirements specification phase. These aspects are described using the *Aspects Crosscutting Overview Diagram* (ACOD) (Wehrmeister, 2007), which is a special class diagram that shows aspects, as well as the crosscutting relationships between aspects and elements that handle FRs. ACOD also specifies pointcuts, which represent the links between join points and aspect adaptations. Figure 6 shows a fragment of a sample ACOD.

Aspects (classes annotated with the *<<Aspect>>* stereotype) are shown affecting classes that handle FRs. Associations among aspects and classes, those stereotyped with *<<Crosscut>>*, represent crosscutting concerns, which are handled through aspects adaptations. When some aspect affects the class structure by adding a new attribute, the crosscut relation is used to specify the value for the newly inserted attribute. Figure 6 shows that *TimingAttributes* and *PeriodicTiming* aspects insert new attributes with their respective values (tagged values of the *<<Crosscutting>>* stereotype) in active objects. As can be seen, attributes related to deadline, priority and WCET are inserted by *TimingAttributes*, while the *PeriodicTiming* aspect inserts the activation period. It is important

to highlight that crosscutting associations do not insert by themselves new attributes into participating elements (class or aspect), like UML normal associations do.

*Pointcuts* are specified with the *<<Pointcut>>* stereotype and show the link between join points defined in JPDDs and adaptations, which are defined as operations tagged with *<<StructuralAdaptation>>* or *<<BehavioralAdaptation>>* stereotypes in the aspects. As shown in Figure 6, the *PeriodicTiming* aspect links *ActiveClass*, *ActObjContructor* and *PeriodicActivation* JPDDs with its adaptations, while the *TimingAttributes* aspect reuses the first two JPDDs and links them with its own adaptations. The selection of which element is affected by this aspect is obtained through the evaluation of the associated JPDD, which is performed by a tool. Therefore, the designer does not need to specify crosscutting relations for all aspects, but just for those that insert new structural elements that need initialization of values.

After specifying the elements that handle FRs and NFRs (in the UML model), a mapping table that links requirements with one or more handling elements is created. This table is very important because it allows the requirements traceability. A fragment of such table is shown in Table 6. As one

*Table 6. Mapping table that shows NFRs affecting FRs*

| | | Non-functional Requirements | | | | Classes for the FRs treatment |
|---|---|---|---|---|---|---|
| | | NFR_1 | NFR_2 | NFR_3 | ... | |
| Functional Requirements | FR_1 | X | X | X | | JoystickDriver |
| | FR_2 | X | X | | ... | MovementControler |
| | FR_3 | X | | | ... | Alarm |
| | ... | ... | ... | ... | ... | ... |
| | Aspects for NFRs treatment | Timing Attributes | Periodic Timing | Tolerated Delay | ... | |

can see, FRs are shown in rows, while the elements handling them are shown in the last column. On the other hand, NFRs are depicted in columns and the corresponding handling elements in the last line. In addition, when NFRs affect functional ones, a mark is written in the intersection of the related requirements.

The AOD approach improves the separation of concerns by isolating design decisions related to NFRs, such as defining schedulable or parallel tasks, selecting communication mechanism, and others. Therefore, those design decisions can be explored in two different ways: i) by selecting which design element should be affected by a specific aspect; and ii) by selecting how the applied aspects should be implemented. In the first exploration opportunity, a designer or an automated DSE tool can select, for example, which objects will be implemented as a thread, by collapsing or dividing schedulable tasks in order to deal with power or performance requirements. The second opportunity takes advantages of MDE premises (followed by the aspects framework) that postpone the decision on how an aspect will be implemented. This improves the component reuse and system customization. As an example, consider an aspect that defines the communication between two elements. Different alternative implementations could be available in a repository, as in the PBD approach, and the exploration step would decide which communication mechanism should be implemented (e.g. shared memory or

message passing), depending on other design issues to be defined, such as hardware allocation, task mapping, and software binding.

The deployment diagram may be used for a manual definition of system architectural issues, such as the number of processors, the types of processors, the task mapping, and the hardware communication structure. By using the proposed DSE method, some of these activities can be automated by H-SPEX and the designer is not required to specify the deployment diagram. However, even in the case of an automated design, the deployment diagram may be used to specify particular design constraints, such as a specific processor that must be used.

## SUPPORTING TOOLS FOR AUTOMATIC DESIGN SPACE EXPLORATION

The H-SPEX tool implements the automatic model-based and multi-objective DSE. The proposed MDE/AOD method produces the models used as input for H-SPEX during the automated DSE process. It uses SPEU, a model-based estimation tool, in order to evaluate the alternative designs during the search on the design space. Finally, the model-based design is supported by MODES, an MDE-framework, which provides the MDE infrastructure to store, transform the models, and make them available to the model-based tools.

*Figure 7. Tool interaction to implement the DSE methodology*

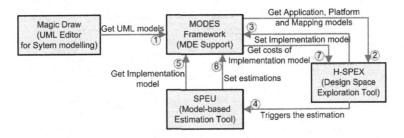

Figure 7 shows the tool interactions during the automated DSE process in the design phase. The process starts by (1) loading the UML models from a UML editor into the MODES meta-modelling infrastructure. After (2) the H-SPEX tool reads the system models for application, platform and mapping, this information is used to search for an alternative design in the design space. For the selected alternative design, H-SPEX (3) writes in the Mapping models the conditions and the design choices to set up the Implementation model according to the selected alternative design. After that, the SPEU tool (4) is triggered in order to perform the model-based estimation. SPEU (5) reads the resulting Implementation Model from the MODES framework, (6) performs the estimations and writes the result back in the MODES infrastructure. By using the estimated values in the Implementation Model, H-SPEX (7) evaluates the design alternative and iterates again from step (2) to generate another alternative design,

if the selected set does not meet the design constraints. Each tool is explained in the following sub-sections.

## MDE Infrastructure

The MODES framework is a method and a corresponding set of tools that implement our MDE/AOD approach. MODES includes a meta-modelling infrastructure to support model-based design tasks such as DSE, estimation, code generation, and hardware synthesis.

As shown in Figure 8, in our design flow the application is specified independently from the platform. A mapping defines how application functions are partitioned among architectural components. Accordingly, four internal meta-models have been proposed in order to allow the independent application and platform modelling.

The MDE approach is used to generate the internal representations, by performing model-to-

*Figure 8. Meta-modelling infrastructure*

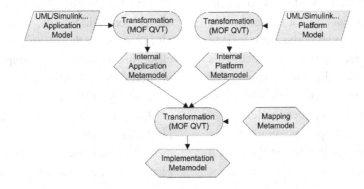

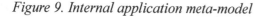

*Figure 9. Internal application meta-model*

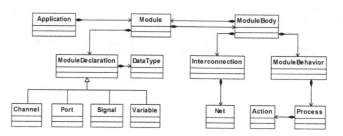

model transformations using QVT (Query, Views, and Transformations) resources, standardized by OMG (OMG 2007b). In the current version of the MODES framework, we use the Eclipse Modelling Framework (EMF) (www.eclipse.org/emf) features to implement the meta-modelling infrastructure.

We have Ecore representations for our meta-models, and a designer can use the UML2 editor plug-in, Magic Draw, or other UML editor compliant with UML/EMF, to create application, platform, and mapping models, which are also stored in an Ecore-based repository. This repository also stores the implementation model that is generated by the transformation engine during the design process. Our meta-models are based on the Meta Object Facility (MOF) standard from OMG (OMG 2007c). In the following, we describe the meta-models introduced in Figure 8.

In order to represent an application in a standard way, a model that is captured according to some application meta-model (e.g., Simulink or SystemC meta-models) is translated into a common application model defined by the Internal Application Meta-model (IAMM), shown in Figure 9. Thus, from different application modelling formalisms, a uniform model with a well-defined syntax and operational semantics is obtained. This translation corresponds to the traditional steps of a compiler, but it is implemented in MODES by means of transformations between models.

Using IAMM, a system specification captures the functionality of an application in terms of a set of modules that are composed of concurrent communicating processes and/or sub-modules. The module behaviour is captured in terms of actions represented by a Control Data Flow Graph (CDFG) that captures the data and control flow between the actions. The CDFG corresponds to the UML actions of the scenarios (sequence diagrams) that are related to the process, according to its active object. Therefore, our IAMM captures structural information of the Application Model by using a hierarchy of modules and processes, as well as behavioural information by means of the CDFGs. These concepts of modules, intercommunicating processes and CDFGs, adopted by the IAMM, correspond to CSP-like languages, which are able to describe any kind of concurrent, distributed system.

Moreover, IAMM represents NFRs handling through the use of AOD concepts, as shown in Figure 10. *Aspects* provide structural and behavioural adaptations, respectively *StructuralAdaptations* and *BehavioralAdaptations*, which modify system elements that were selected through *Joinpoints*. Pointcuts represent the link between aspects adaptations and join points, i.e. they define the *RelativePosition* of a *Joinpoint* where adaptations are performed. Finally, *Crosscuting* represents all information that is inserted by an aspect in a class through structural adaptations in terms of properties and their values.

Usually, different Platform Meta-models (PMM) are required for the specification of platform models, corresponding to the platform modelling languages that are commonly employed in the description of system architectures,

*Figure 10. IAMM aspects representation*

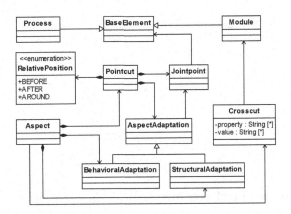

such as SystemC and VHDL. As for application models, in order to have a standard representation, the PMM is translated into an Internal Platform Meta-Model (IPMM), shown in Figure 11.

In our methodology, the available hardware/software components and the meta-information about them are stored in a platform repository, whose meta-model is based on the General Resource Model from UML-SPT (OMG 2005). This meta-information can correspond to physical properties such as performance or energy consumption, logical dependencies between components, or versioning information. It will be used to support design tasks such as estimation, simulation, and DSE. Therefore, the Internal Platform Meta-model corresponds to a taxonomy of hardware and software elements with characterization properties. The meta-model can be easily enhanced by extensions to its meta-classes.

The Mapping Meta-model describes the rules used to transform instances of IAMM and IPMM into an instance of the Implementation Meta-model (IMM), as shown in Figure 12. These rules define the possible transformations between the involved models and include the mapping from application into architecture. Each rule has a condition for its firing – when the condition is true, the transformation can be applied to the model. The Mapping Model thus guides the exploration tool or a designer to build a candidate Implementation Model. The main function of the Mapping Model is to allow H-SPEX to automatically optimize the transformation of a PIM (an instance of IAMM and IPMM) into a PSM (instance of IMM).

The Implementation Meta-model allows the representation of the models that can implement the system specification without violating the system requirements. Figure 13 shows the class diagram of the Implementation Meta-model. An

*Figure 11. Internal platform meta-model*

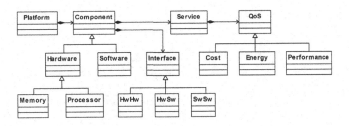

*Figure 12. Mapping meta-model*

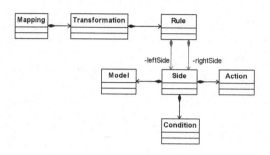

instance of the IMM can be described as a list of selected platform components, application components, and associations between them. Furthermore, it also represents the design decisions about component configuration, task mapping, and resource allocation.

The information contained in an instance of IMM and in the instances of the other proposed meta-models is used by a design tool to generate: (i) partial embedded software source code; (ii) scripts for hardware synthesis; and (iii) system deployment scripts. As explained in the next subsection, other tools, such as SPEU, use an instance of the Implementation Meta-model in order to estimate the properties of a candidate implementation model, before the subsequent steps of the development process are performed.

The allocation, partitioning, and binding tasks of the DSE process must adopt some deterministic or heuristic approach, such as dynamic programming or genetic algorithms, to investigate the space of possible implementations. For each possible implementation to be considered, the exploration tool or designer takes some design decisions and incorporates the corresponding information into

the conditions of the transformation rules of the Mapping Model.

At this point, the transformation engine can be invoked to traverse the set of transformation rules, so as to select and apply the ones that are enabled at that moment, thus generating a hardware/software mapped architecture in the form of an Implementation Model.

## Model-Based Estimation Tool

In order to support a fast DSE process in the early design phases, the SPEU estimation tool is used by H-SPEX to evaluate alternative model solutions and to guide the designer's decisions. SPEU provides analytical estimates about physical system properties (execution cycles, energy/power consumption, volume of communication data, and memory footprint). These properties are directly obtained from instances of the meta-models in the MODES framework repository, with estimation errors as low as 5%, comparing to results extracted by cycle-accurate simulation, when the reuse of repository components is largely employed by a platform-based design (PBD) approach.

*Figure 13. Implementation meta-model*

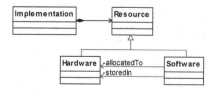

The estimation is performed by using the information that is extracted from UML application structure/behaviour models and stored in the Internal Application Meta-model as a CDFG (Control and Data Flow Graph). Additionally, the estimation of implementations of the used aspects is also performed. To obtain a more precise estimation, aspects adaptations are woven into the affected model elements before starting the estimation process. To improve the estimation accuracy, the information specified in the platform repository is used to compute the costs of pre-designed components and added in the final estimation. An ILP (Integer Linear Programming) formulation is used to identify the best- and worst-case execution paths in the CDFG. In order to reduce the complexity, each ILP formulation is solved in a hierarchical fashion, such that each task has one ILP formulation to be solved. This avoids problems for MPSoCs with a large number of tasks. The SPEU tool allows H-SPEX to rapidly evaluate each candidate solution during the DSE process, without depending on costly synthesis-and-simulation evaluation cycles. After each evaluation, the estimated properties are stored in the MODES framework repository and used to compute the solution cost during the multi-objective optimization, performed by the exploration algorithm implemented in H-SPEX.

## Automated Design Space Exploration Tool

Since most of the DSE activities correspond to a multi-objective (multi-criteria) optimization problem, an algorithm to search for alternative solutions on the design space and to optimize the parameterized multi-objective cost function, which qualifies the alternatives, should be employed. Hence the H-SPEX tool employs the Crowding Population-based Ant Colony Optimization for Multi-objective (CPACO-MO) (Angus, 2008) algorithm. In each iteration this algorithm generates a set of candidate solutions, from where the best

candidates are selected to compose a population. This population is a set of non-dominated design points (Pareto-optimal), with which the designer can take a decision by considering design trade-offs and system requirements. H-SPEX uses an abstraction layer in order to detach the exploration algorithm from the design space, such that any other multi-objective heuristic, as in the case study presented in (Oliveira, 2008), can be used.

This abstraction layer uses a categorical graph product (Weichsel, 1962) to build a logical graph that represents the design space, in which the exploration algorithm searches for alternative designs. The graph product is formed by a set of graphs, each one related to a given design issue (e.g. tasks, processors, communication structure, configuration parameters, and others), extracted from the model instances in the MDE infrastructure provided by MODES. The product between these graphs represents design activities, where the nodes from the resulting graph are pieces of an alternative design and outgoing edges are the available design options at a specific node. By using this approach, the DSE process is performed as a search for the sub-graph on the resulting graph product (design space) which presents the best trade-off for each objective. As the graph product simultaneously represents two or more graphs, the simultaneous multi-activity exploration arises naturally. Moreover, as the search can be started from any node on the resulting graph product, this abstraction also deals with the situation where there is no specific order to perform design activities, which assures the best result.

As mentioned in the section "Analysis and Design Modelling", the designer must perform several design activities until reaching the final system implementation. Some of these activities can be automatically performed by H-SPEX, thus helping the designer to reach the most appropriate design in a shorter time. Currently, the activities performed by H-SPEX in the context of an MPSoC design are: (i) selecting the number and type of processors, (ii) mapping tasks into processors,

*Table 7. Part of the Mapping Model*

| Source IAMM | Target IPMM | Condition | Action |
|---|---|---|---|
| mod:Module | p:Processor, m:Memory, b:Bus | p.name=processor1 or p.name=processor2 | new Processor(), new Memory(), new Bus() |
| proc:Process | a:API | a.name=Math or a.name=RTTrhead | new API() |
| threadctrl:Action | s:Service | s.name=waitNextPeriod or s.name=waitForCycles | new Service() |
| interaction: Action | s:Service | s.name=interactionStatic or s.name= interactionDynamic | new Service() |
| getObjectField:Action | s:Service | s.name=getStaticObjectField or s.name=setStaticObjectField or s.name=setDynamicObjectField | new Service() |
| mathoper:Action | s:Service | s.name=sqrt or s.name=sin or s.name=cos or s.name=s.atan | new Service() |
| sched:OS | s:OS | s.schedtype=EDFScheduler or s.schedtype=FixedPriority or s.schedtype=RMScheduler | new OS() |

(iii) allocating processors in a communication structure, and (iv) selecting processor voltage operation. The automation of the selection of the number of tasks is in progress and was enabled after the introduction of the AOD approach, by encapsulating into aspects the adaptations related to scheduling and time. The result of the automated DSE is written back to the MODES infrastructure and can be seen again as UML models to be refined or used as input to the code generation and synthesis tools. In the MPSoC design context, H-SPEX can be used to optimize performance, energy or power consumption, communication bandwidth, memory footprint, or any combination of the above.

## Preliminary Results

In order to illustrate the proposed DSE method, this section presents preliminary results for the current automated process. For this purpose, a DSE scenario for the automated control of a wheelchair case study has been developed. The initial phases of the proposed method, i.e. requirements specification, the application analysis and design modelling, were presented in section "Modelling for Automated Design Space Exploration." This section goes further showing the DSE step.

As the AOD approach has been applied, the specification of schedulable tasks can be performed just by configuring the crosscutting information on the ACOD diagram to inform which design element should be affected by the *TimingAttributes* and *PeriodicTiming* aspects. One sample ACOD illustrating the task specification for the case study can be seen in Figure 6. For this specific experiment, our application model contains 17 tasks, which have communication dependencies between them. The platform model is based on a Java microcontroller (Ito, 2001), upon which an API and operating system components (Wehrmeister, 2005) for real-time behaviour and communication support are available. The platform may have any number of processors, connected through a bus that can be split into two segments.

Table 7 lists some of the transformation rules of the Mapping Model. These rules specify the possible mappings from elements of the wheelchair Application Model to elements of the target platform, including the actions that will generate elements in the Implementation Model.

*Figure 14. DSE results for different objectives*

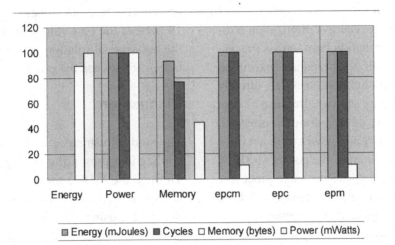

As specified by the transformation rules, modules can be implemented either by a simple *processor1* or by a more complex *processor2*. In the Implementation Model, a memory component will be instantiated for program code and data, and a bus will be instantiated to connect the processor to the memory. Other transformation rules state that: a) processes in the application can make use of the *Math* and *RTThread* APIs; b) actions in the thread of the processes may use services to suspend the execution (*waitForNextPeriod* and *waitForCycles* services); c) actions can have access to static and dynamic object attributes (*get/set Static/Dynamic ObjectField* services); d) mathematical operations can be implemented by the *Math API*; and e) scheduling of processes and threads can be implemented by different kinds of schedulers from a given operating system.

The H-SPEX tool selects the number of processors and maps tasks to them in order to minimize the overall communication costs between tasks. Communicating tasks requiring higher bandwidth tend to be grouped in the same processor, if possible. The candidate task partitioning can neither violate the task deadlines nor exceed the node processing capacity. If necessary, H-SPEX adds another processor to the system. Simultaneously, H-SPEX maps processors to the communication

structure, such that the overall communication cost is again minimized. Again, processors with higher communication (because of the tasks assigned to them) tend to be mapped to the same bus segment. In order to reduce the energy consumption, H-SPEX also selects the minimal voltage for each processor, but avoiding task deadline violations. Realistic energy, voltage, performance, and memory costs for HW and SW platform components and services (such as task scheduling), extracted by using the SPEU estimation tool, have been used to guide the exploration.

The results were obtained after evaluation of 1000 candidate solutions. In our experiments, H-SPEX takes 1 hour to evaluate each 1000 solutions, using an AMD Athlon 1.8 GHz with 512 Mbytes of RAM and the SPEU tool. The number of design alternatives in this DSE scenario is huge, so that the utilization of an automated DSE approach at very high abstraction level is fully justified.

Figure 14 shows a chart with the final solution found by H-SPEX for different combinations of optimization objectives. In this chart, the values of solution properties were normalized with regard to the worst solution, so that they could be presented in the same chart. The horizontal axis is organized by optimization objective, e.g. energy, power, memory, energy-power-cycles-memory (epcm), energy-power-cycles (epc), and energy-power-memory (epm).

The DSE results for energy optimization present a good load distribution between six processors selected by H-SPEX. This parallel execution reduces the number of execution cycles, directly contributing to energy savings. Because of data and code replication in the various processors, the values for memory and power were not optimized. In order to minimize the power, H-SPEX has mapped simple tasks to the same processor with low voltage settings. Processors with high utilization require higher voltage settings.

In order to reduce the memory size, H-SPEX has mapped tasks that exchange large amounts of data to the same processor, reducing in this way the data replication and communication structures (packages and messages).

In the last three results in Figure 14, the chart presents DSE results using multi-objective functions. Due to the hard real-time constraints, H-SPEX could not reduce the cycles by mapping many tasks to the same processor and thus reducing the communication cost, because this would cause task deadline violations. However, by distributing tasks in different processors and setting low voltages for each processor, H-SPEX could get better results for power, which dominates the optimization process.

Figure 15 shows the properties values estimated for the population of 19 candidate solutions found by H-SPEX. It shows the values for energy, cycles, memory, and power, respectively, used in the multi-objective exploration. In each chart, the vertical axis shows the property values for the entire system. The horizontal axis identifies the candidate solutions. Observing each graph individually, designers can select one specific candidate solution to follow the development process with. However, observing all graphs together, it is easy to observe the conflicting nature of NFRs. Candidates 7-19 present almost the same value of energy, and candidates 4 and 11 present the best figures for cycles. Considering the memory, candidates 12,

14 and 19 present good values and candidate 17 presents the best one. Finally, candidates 18 and 19 present the best values for power. However, the best overall solution must be selected after a trade-off between the evaluated figures.

## Discussion

The study illustrates a DSE scenario for a real application presenting a large design space. Through the MDE approach for multi-objective DSE presented in this work, a designer can specify the system using UML models at high abstraction level (without source coding/generation) and look for the best alternative to be implemented, very early in the development process, without relying on costly synthesis-and-simulation evaluation cycles.

Better optimizations could be achieved if the Application Domain was also explored by the H-SPEX tool. This exploration could result in reduced values for execution cycles, for instance by changing the interaction between objects and the interaction of the objects with the platform services (e.g. reducing service calls), or by looking for a new distribution of responsibilities (e.g. unifying/splitting classes, reducing object instantiation, and changing method distribution). Another exploration in the Application Domain could specify different schedulable tasks in order to arrange the functionality in a way to improve or reduce the parallelism, thereby dealing with the trade-off between power and performance or avoiding wasting resources with overload communication. Some of these exploration activities in the Application Domain may be automatically performed, by taking even more advantage from the AOD modelling approach, as the information required to implement tasks are encapsulated inside aspects. This avoids spreading the information on timing requirements, schedulability, and other related issues within the entire model. Such ability facilitates the adaptation of models (performed by H-SPEX) to a different set of tasks. This follows

*Figure 15. Physical properties for 19 best candidate solutions: (a) energy values; (b) execution cycles (c) memory size; and (d) power value*

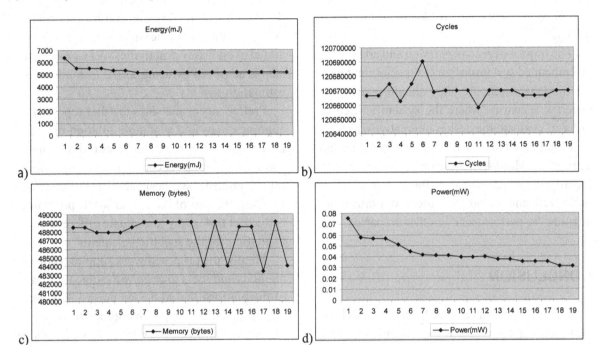

the principle of the Y-chart, by which different concerns (e.g., application and architecture) are separately specified. In this way, the exploration of architectural solutions without modifying the application model is allowed.

## FUTURE TRENDS

Currently, several efforts look for an efficient method for design space exploration. However, few information can be extracted from reports on the application of these methods in order to assess their pros and cons. The main problem for this assessment is the lack of standard evaluation metrics and benchmarks to measure design space exploration approaches. Thereby, some effort should try to identify how to quantify the optimization and evaluation (estimation/simulation) techniques, as well as the specification of inputs and outputs for the DSE process, abstraction level/design effort, automation, and others.

After years of research and improvements on hardware design, the current industrial standards and the state-of-the-art provide efficient ways to design, integrate, and manufacture embedded hardware. On the other hand, despite the improvements on the Software Engineering methods, the embedded software development has increased in complexity by adding new features, but current methods still do not provide consolidated techniques. New Software Engineering methods, such as MDE and AOD, help embedded system designers to cope with design complexity and improve the design automation, including the DSE process.

In a scenario of increasing design complexity, reusable components are employed raising the challenge between reuse and optimization. The embedded system modelling approaches increase the abstraction level to improve the reuse and design space exploration opportunities. In turn, the reuse involves some overhead, due to the generalization of each component. Future design exploration methods should provide means for optimizing systems by reducing the overhead of reused components, but still keeping their reusability.

The impact of reconfiguration and adaptation on embedded system design is a special challenge for the DSE methods. They should predict the different scenarios where the system is used in order to evaluate the design alternatives, as well as to optimize the system without strangling the adaptation. Moreover, these new methods should identify for which scenarios the system must be optimized and avoid that these optimizations degrade the performance in other scenarios.

## CONCLUSION

This chapter presented a high-level method for DSE, which takes advantage from the AOD and MDE approaches, in order to provide an efficient development framework with focus on automated DSE. Through this framework, DSE can be performed at earlier development phases with a higher abstraction level, thus leading to substantially superior improvements.

Separating the handling of NFRs from FRs, through the AOD approach, improves the abstraction level used during design, thus opening new opportunities for design automation and optimization. The MDE approach provides a coherent representation of different system concerns through meta-modelling. The combination of both approaches reduces the development complexity and improves the reusability.

By applying the RT-FRIDA development method, the proposed approach covers the requirements specification, analysis and design phases of a development process, providing a systematic form to specify constraints to guide the model-based DSE process. While the development method guides the development process, the MDE-framework, supported by MODES, provides an efficient meta-modelling infrastructure to capture

system structure and behaviour, thus supporting model-based DSE. Automating the DSE step using the H-SPEX tool, a designer is able to concentrate efforts on concepts of the target application domain and also on creative activities. A fast evaluation step is achieved by using SPEU as model-based estimation tool.

Preliminary results show that the proposed DSE approach may find a suitable solution regarding the design requirements and constraints in a very short time, with an acceptable accuracy, without relying on costly synthesis-and-simulation cycles. Besides, the use of AOD and MDE promotes a better and faster way to evaluate different implementation for the specified elements.

Finally, the proposed work supplies powerful methods and tools to cope with some drawbacks of the platform-based design approach, since it: (i) improves the requirements analysis, allowing better guidelines for DSE; (ii) extends the separation of concerns, mainly regarding FRs and NFRs, thus highlighting new optimization opportunities; and (iii) allows early and fast DSE, which benefits from optimization potentials at higher abstraction layers.

One of the future directions to be considered is the improvement of the meta-modelling infrastructure, in order to represent more complex applications, platforms, and mappings. Moreover, we intend to extend the exploration tool, by adding new architectural exploration activities and automating the exploration activities to the Application Domain.

## REFERENCES

Angus, D. (2007). Crowding population-based ant colony optimisation for the multiobjective travelling salesman problem. In *Proceedings of IEEE Symposium on Computational Intelligence in Multicriteria Decision Making* (pp. 333-340). Los Alamitos: IEEE Computer Society Press.

Araújo, J., et al. (2002, October). *Aspect-oriented requirements with UML*. Paper presented at Workshop on Aspect-oriented Modeling with UML, Dresden, Heidelberg.

Ascia, G., Catania, V., & Palesi, M. (2004). A GA-based design space exploration framework for parameterized system-on-a-chip platforms. *IEEE Transactions on Evolutionary Computation, 8*(4), 329–346. doi:10.1109/TEVC.2004.826389

Bakshi, A., Prasanna, V. K., & Ledeczi, A. (2001). MILAN: A model based integrated simulation framework for design of embedded systems. *ACM SIGPLAN Notices, 36*(8), 82–93. doi:10.1145/384196.384210

Balarin, F., et al. (1997). *Hardware-software codesign of embedded systems: The polis approach*. Kluwer Academic Publishers.

Balarin, F., Watanabe, Y., Hsieh, H., Lavagno, L., Passerone, C., & Sangiovanni-Vincentelli, A. (2003). Metropolis: An integrated electronic system design environment. *IEEE Computer, 36*(4), 45–52.

Beck, A. C. S., Mattos, J. C. B., Wagner, F. R., & Carro, L. (2003). CACO-PS: A general purpose cycle-accurate configurable power simulator. In *Proceedings 16ᵗʰ Symposium on Integrated Circuits and Systems Design* (pp. 349-354). Los Alamitos: IEEE Computer Society Press.

Blickle, T., Teich, J., & Thiele, L. (1998). System-level synthesis using evolutionary algorithms. *Design Automation for Embedded Systems, 3*(1), 23–58. doi:10.1023/A:1008899229802

Bondé, L., Dumoulin, C., & Dekeyser, J.-L. (2004, September). *Metamodels and MDA transformations for embedded systems*. Paper presented at Forum on Design Languages, Lille, France.

Bontempi, G., & Kruijtzer, W. (2002). A data analysis method for software performance prediction. In *Proceedings of the Design, Automation, and Test in Europe Conference and Exhibition* (pp. 971-976). Los Alamitos: IEEE Computer Society Press.

Cantor, M. (2003). *Rational unified process for systems engineering*. Retrieved on August 15, 2007, from http://www.therationaledge.com/content/aug 03/f rupse mc.jsp

Chen, R., Sgroi, M., Lavagno, L., Martin, G., Sangiovanni-Vincentelli, A., & Rabaey, J. (2003). Embedded system design using UML and platforms. In L. Lavagno, G. Martin, B. Selic (Eds.), *UML for real: Design of embedded real time systems* (pp. 107-126). Dordrecht: Kluwer Academic Publishers.

Clarke, S., & Banaissad, E. (2005). *Aspect-oriented analysis and design the theme approach*. Boston: Addison-Wesley.

Coyle, F. P., & Thornton, M. A. (2005, April). *From UML to HDL: A model driven architectural approach to hardware-software codesign*. Paper presented at Information Systems: New Generations Conference, Las Vegas, NV.

Davis, J. (2003, October 26-30). GME: The generic modeling environment. In R. Crocker & G. L. Steele, Jr. (Eds.), *Companion of the 18ᵗʰ Annual ACM SIGPLAN Conference on Object-Oriented Programming, Systems, Languages, and Applications, OOPSLA 2003, Anaheim, CA* (pp. 82-83). New York: ACM Press.

Dick, R. P., & Jha, N. K. (1998). MOGAC: A multiobjective genetic algorithm for hardware-software cosynthesis of distributed embedded systems. *IEEE Transactions on Computer-Aided Design of Integrated Circuits and Systems, 17*(10), 920–935. doi:10.1109/43.728914

Douglass, B. (2003). *Real-time design patterns: Robust scalable architecture for real-time systems.* Boston: Addison Wesley.

Dwivedi, B. K., Kumar, A., & Balakrishnan, M. (2004). Automatic synthesis of system on chip multiprocessor architectures for process networks. In A. Orailoglu, P. H. Chou, P. Eles & A. Jantsch (Eds.), *Proceedings of the 2nd IEEE/ACM/IFIP International Conference on Hardware/Software Codesign and System Synthesis* (pp 60-65). New York: ACM Press.

Erbas, C., Erbas, S. E., & Pimentel, A. D. (2003). A multiobjective optimization model for exploring multiprocessor mappings of process networks. In R. Gupta, Y. Nakamura, A. Orailoglu & P. H. Chou (Eds.), *Proceedings of the 1st IEEE/ACM/IFIP International Conference on Hardware/Software Codesign and System Synthesis* (pp 182-187). New York: ACM Press.

Fernandes, J., Machado, R., & Santos, H. (2000). Modeling industrial embedded systems with UML. In F. Vahid & J. Madsen (Eds.), *Proceedings of the Eighth International Workshop on Hardware/Software Codesign* (pp. 18-22). New York: ACM Press.

Filman, R. E., Elrad, T., Clarke, S., & Aksit, M. (2004). *Aspect-oriented software development.* Boston: Addison-Wesley.

Freitas, E. P., Wehrmeister, M. A., da Silva Junior, E. T., Carvalho, F., Pereira, C. E., & Wagner, F. R. (2007, March 13). DERAF: A high-level aspects framework for distributed embedded real-time systems design. In A. Moreira (Ed.), *Early Aspects: Current Challenges and Future Directions, 10th International Workshop on Early Aspects,* Vancouver, Canada (LNCS 4765, pp. 55-74). Berlin, Heidelberg: Springer-Verlag.

Ganesan, S., & Prevostini, M. (2006). *Bridging the gap between SysML and design space exploration.* Paper presented at Forum on Design Languages, Darmstadt, Germany.

Geilen, M. C. W. (2001). Modeling and specification using SHE. *Journal of Computer Languages, 27*(1-3), 19–38. doi:10.1016/S0096-0551(01)00014-5

Givargis, T., & Vhid, F. (2002). Platune: A tuning framework for system-on-a-chip platforms. *IEEE Transaction on Computer-aided Design of Integrated Circuits and Systems, 21*(11), 1317–1327. doi:10.1109/TCAD.2002.804107

Goering, R. (2002, November). Platform-based design: A choice, not a panacea. *EEDesign of EE-Times.* Retrieved in September 2008, from http://www.eetimes.com/story/OEG20020911S0061

Green, P. N., & Edwards, M. D. (2002). The modeling of embedded systems using HASoC. In *Proceedings of the Design, Automation, and Test in Europe Conference and Exhibition* (pp. 752-759). Los Alamitos: IEEE Computer Society Press.

Ito, S., Carro, L., & Jacobi, R. (2001). Making java work for microcontroller applications. *IEEE Design & Test of Computers, 18*(5), 100–110. doi:10.1109/54.953277

Jacobson, I., & Ng, P.-W. (2005). *Aspect-oriented software development with use cases.* Boston: Addison-Wesley.

Kaiya, H., & Saeki, M. (2004). Weaving multiple viewpoint specification in goal-oriented requirements analysis. In *Proceedings of the 11th Asia Pacific Software Engineering Conference* (pp. 418-427). Washington, D.C.: IEEE Computer Society.

Kalavade, A., & Lee, E. A. (1993). Hardware/software codesign using ptolemy: A case study. In *Proceeding of First IFIP International Workshop Hardware/Software Codesign* (pp. 84-87). Los Alamitos: IEEE Computer Society Press.

Kangas, T., Kukkala, P., Orsila, H., Salminen, E., Hännikäinen, M., & Hämäläinen, T. D. (2006). UML-based multiprocessor SoC design framework. *Transactions on Embedded Computing Systems*, 5(2), 281–320. doi:10.1145/1151074.1151077

Karsai, G., Sztipanovits, J., Ledeczi, A., & Bapty, T. (2003). Model-integrated development of embedded software. [Washington, D.C.: IEEE Computer Society.]. *Proceedings of the IEEE, 91*, 145–164. doi:10.1109/JPROC.2002.805824

Keutzer, K., Newton, A. R., Rabaey, J. M., & Sangiovanni-Vincentelli, A. (2000). System-level design: Orthogonalization of concerns and platform-based design. *IEEE Transactions on Computer-Aided Design of Integrated Circuits and Systems, 19*(12), 1523–1543. doi:10.1109/43.898830

Kiczales, G., et al. (1997). Aspect-oriented programming. In M. Aksit & S. Matsuoka (Eds.), *Proceedings of European Conference for Object-Oriented Programming* (pp. 220-240) (LNCS 1241). Berlin, Heidelberg: Springer-Verlag.

Kienhuis, B., Deprettere, E., Vissers, K., & van der Wolf, P. (1997). An approach for quantitative analysis of application-specific dataflow architectures. In *Proceedings of 11th International Conference on Application-specific Systems, Architectures, and Processors* (pp. 338-350). Los Alamitos: IEEE Computer Society Press.

Kishi, T., & Noda, N. (2004, March). *Aspect-oriented context modeling for embedded systems*. Paper presented at Early Aspects 2004: Aspect-Oriented Requirements Engineering and Architecture Design Workshop, Lancaster, Lancashire.

Klein, J., Hélouët, L., & Jezequel, J.-M. (2006). Semantic-based weaving of scenarios. In R. Filman (Ed.), *Proceedings of the 5th International Conference on Aspect-Oriented Software Development* (pp. 27-38). New York: ACM Press.

Larsen, K. G., Pettersson, P., & Yi, W. (1997). UPPAAL in a nutshell. *International Journal on Software Tools for Technology Transfers, 1*(1-2), 134–152. doi:10.1007/s100090050010

Ledeczi, A., Davis, J., Neema, S., & Agrawal, A. (2003). Modeling methodology for integrated simulation of embedded systems. *ACM Transactions on Modeling and Computer Simulation, 13*(1), 82–103. doi:10.1145/778553.778557

Lieverse, P., Wolf, P. V., Vissers, K., & Deprettere, E. (2001). A methodology for architecture exploration of heterogeneous signal processing systems. *Journal of VLSI Signal Processing Systems, 29*(3), 197–207. doi:10.1023/A:1012231429554

Lu, T., Turkay, E., Gokhale, A., & Schmidt, D. C. (2003, October). *CoSMIC: An MDA tool suite for application deployment and configuration*. Paper presented at Workshop on Generative Techniques in the Context of Model Driven Architecture in Conference on Object Oriented Programming Systems Languages and Applications, Anaheim, CA.

Mellor, S., & Balcer, M. (2002). *Executable UML: A foundation for model driven architecture*. Boston: Addison-Wesley.

Mihal, A., Kulkarni, C., Moskewicz, M., Tsai, M., Shah, N., & Weber, S. (2002). Developing architectural platforms: A disciplined approach. *IEEE Design & Test of Computers, 19*(6), 6–16. doi:10.1109/MDT.2002.1047739

Mohanty, S., Prasanna, V., Neema, S., & Davis, J. (2002). Rapid design space exploration of heterogeneous embedded systems using symbolic search and multigranular simulation. In P. Marwedel & S. Devadas (Eds.), *Proceedings of the Workshop on Languages, Compilers, and Tools for Embedded Systems* (pp. 18-27). New York: ACM Press.

Nascimento, F. A., Oliveira, M. F. S., & Wagner, F. R. (2007). ModES: Embedded systems design methodology and tools based on MDE. In *Fourth International Workshop on Model-Based Methodologies for Pervasive and Embedded Software -MOMPES* (pp.6-76). Los Alamitos: IEEE Computer Society Press.

Neema, S., Sztipanovits, J., & Karsai, G. (2003, October 13-15). Constraint-based design-space exploration and model synthesis. In R. Alur & I. Lee (Eds.), *Embedded Software: Third International Conference, EMSOFT 2003,* Philadelphia, PA (pp 290-305) (LNCS 2855). Berlin, Heidelberg: Springer-Verlag.

Oliveira, M. F. S., Briao, E. W., Nascimento, F. A., & Wganer, F. R. (2008). Model driven engineering for MPSoC design space exploration. *Journal of Integrated Circuits and Systems, 3*(1), 13–22.

Oliveira, M. F. S., Brisolara, L. B., Carro, L., & Wagner, F. R. (2006). Early embedded software design space exploration using UML-based estimation. In *Proceedings 17th IEEE International Workshop on Rapid System Prototyping: Vol. 1. Shortening the Path from Specification to Prototype* (pp. 24-30). Los Alamitos: IEEE Computer Society Press.

OMG. (2005). *UML SPT–UML profile for schedulability, performance, and time v1.1.* Retrieved on December 2, 2005, from http://www.omg.org

OMG. (2006). *CCM–CORBA component model.* Retrieved on December 12, 2006, from http://www.omg.org

OMG. (2007). *Model driven architecture guide.* Retrieved on December 15, 2007, from http://www.omg.org/mda

OMG. (2007a). *UML–Unified modeling language.* Retrieved on November 15, 2007, from http://www.omg.org/uml

OMG. (2007b). *MOF QVT-queryviews/transformations.* Retrieved on December 4, 2007, from http://www.omg.org

OMG. (2007c). *Meta object facility (MOF) 2.0 core specification.* Retrieved on December 4, 2007, from http://www.omg.org

OMG. (2007d). *UML profile for modeling and analysis of real-time and embedded systems (MARTE).* Retrieved on March 4, 2008, from http://www.omgmarte.org/

Oyamada, M. S., Zschornack, F., & Wagner, F. R. (2008). Applying neural networks to performance estimation of embedded software. *Journal of Systems Architecture, 54*(1-2), 224–240. doi:10.1016/j.sysarc.2007.06.005

Paulin, P. G., Pilkington, C., & Bensoudane, E. (2002). StepNP: A system-level exploration platform for network processors. *IEEE Design & Test of Computers, 19*(6), 17–26. doi:10.1109/MDT.2002.1047740

Pimentel, A. D., Erbas, C., & Polstra, S. (2006). A systematic approach to exploring embedded system architectures at multiple abstraction levels. *IEEE Transactions on Computers, 55*(2), 99–112. doi:10.1109/TC.2006.16

Rashid, A., Sawyer, P., Moreira, A., & Araujo, J. (2002). Early aspects: A model for aspect-oriented requirements engineering. In S. Greenspan, J. Siddiqi, E. Dubois & K. Pohl (Eds.), *IEEE Joint International Conference on Requirements Engineering* (pp. 199-202). Washington, D.C.: IEEE Computer Society.

Reyneri, L. M., Cucinotta, F., Serra, A., & Lavagno, L. (2001). A hardware/software codesign flow and IP library based on simulink. In J. Rabaey (Ed.), *Proceedings of the 38th Design Automation Conference* (pp. 593-598). New York: ACM Press.

Russell, J. T., & Jacome, M. F. (2003). Architecture-level performance evaluation of component based embedded systems. In I. Getreu, L. Fix & L. Lavagno (Eds.), *Proceedings of the 40th Design Automation Conference* (pp. 396-401). New York: ACM Press.

Sangiovanni-Vincentelli, A. (2002, February). Defining platform-based design. *EEDesign of EETimes*. Retrieved in August 2007, from http://www.gigascale.org/pubs/141.html

Sangiovanni-Vincentelli, A., & Martin, G. (2001). Platform-based design and software design methodology for embedded systems. *IEEE Design & Test of Computers, 18*(6), 23–33. doi:10.1109/54.970421

Schattkowsky, T., Muller, W., & Rettberg, A. (2005). A generic model execution platform for the design of hardware and software. In G. Martin & W. Müller (Eds.), *UML for SoC design* (pp. 33-68). New York: Kluwer Academic Publishers.

Schauerhuber, A., et al. (2006, March). *Towards a common reference architecture for aspect-oriented modeling*. Paper presented at 8th International Workshop on Aspect-Oriented Modeling, Bonn, North Rhine-Westphalia.

Schmidt, D. C. (2006). Model-driven engineering. *IEEE Computer, 39*(2), 25–31.

Sciuto, D., Salice, F., Pomante, L., & Fornaciari, W. (2002, May). *Metrics for design space exploration of geterogeneous multiprocessor embedded systems*. Paper presented at 10th International Symposium on Hardware/Software Codesign, Estes Park, USA.

Sousa, G., Soares, S., Borba, P., & Castro, J. (2004, March). *Separation of crosscutting concerns from requirements to design: Adapting a use case driven approach*. Paper presented at Early Aspects 2004: Aspect-Oriented Requirements Engineering and Architecture Design Workshop, Lancaster, Lancashire.

Spinczyk, O., Gal, A., & Schröder-Preikschat, W. (2002). AspectC++: An aspect-oriented extension to the C++ programming language. In J. Potter, J. Noble, & B. Meyer (Eds.), *ACM International Conference Proceeding Series: Vol. 21. Proceedings of the Fortieth International Conference on Tools Pacific: Objects for Internet, Mobile, and Embedded Applications* (pp. 53-60). Darlinghurst, NSW: Australian Computer Society.

Stankovic, J. A., et al. (2003). VEST: An aspect-based composition tool for real-time system. In R. Bettati, D. Locke, G. Bollella & D. Schmidt (Eds.), *9th IEEE Real-Time and Embedded Technology and Applications Symposium* (pp. 70-77). Washington, D.C.: IEEE Computer Society.

Stein, D., Hanenberg, S., & Unland, R. (2002). A UML-based aspect-oriented design notation for aspect. In H. Ossher & G. Kiczales (Eds.), *Aspect-oriented software development: Proceedings of the 1st International Conference on Aspect-oriented Software Development* (pp. 106-112). New York: ACM Press.

Stein, D., Hanenberg, S., & Unland, R. (2006). Expressing different conceptual models of join point selections in aspect-oriented design. In R. Filman (Ed.), *Proceedings of 5th International Conference on Aspect-Oriented Software Development* (pp. 15-26). New York: ACM Press.

van den Berg, K., Conejero, J. M., & Chitchyan, R. (2005). *AOSD ontology 1.0-public ontology of aspect-orientation* (Tech. Rep. AOSD-Europe-UT-01). Retrieved in June 2008 from http://eprints.eemcs.utwente.nl/10220/

Wehrmeister, M. A., Becker, L. B., Wagner, F. R., & Pereira, C. E. (2005). An object-oriented platform-based design process for embedded real-time systems. In *8th IEEE International Symposium on Object-Oriented Real-Time Distributed Computing–ISORC* (pp. 125-128). Los Alamitos: IEEE Computer Society.

Wehrmeister, M. A., Freitas, E. P., Orfanus, D., Pereira, C. E., & Rammig, F. J. (2008a). A case study to evaluate pros/cons of aspect- and object-oriented paradigms to model distributed embedded real-time systems. In *5th International Workshop on Model-based Methodologies for Pervasive and Embedded Software–MOMPES* (pp. 44-54). Los Alamitos: EEE Computer Society Press.

Wehrmeister, M. A., Freitas, E. P., Pereira, C. E., & Rammig, F. J. (2008b). GenERTiCA: A tool for code generation and aspects weaving. In *11th IEEE Symposium on Object Oriented Real-Time Distributed Computing–ISORC* (pp. 234-238). Los Alamitos: IEEE Computer Society.

Wehrmeister, M. A., Freitas, E. P., Pereira, C. E., & Wagner, F. R. (2007). An aspect-oriented approach for dealing with nonfunctional requirements in a model-driven development of distributed embedded real-time systems. In *10th IEEE International Symposium on Object and Component-Oriented Real-Time Distributed Computing* (pp. 428-432). Washington: IEEE Computer Society.

Weichsel, P. M. (1962). The Kronecker product of graphs. *Proceedings of the American Mathematical Society, 13*(1), 47–52. doi:10.2307/2033769

Yu, Y., Leite, J. C. S. P., & Mylopoulos, J. (2004). From goals to aspects: Discovering aspects from requirements goal models. In N. Aoyama, M. Saeki & N. Maiden (Ed.), *12th IEEE International Requirements Engineering Conference* (pp. 38-47). Los Alamitos, CA: IEEE Computer Society.

Zhang, L., & Liu, R. (2005). Aspect-oriented real-time system modeling method based on UML. In R. Bettati, D. Locke, G. Bollella & D. Schmidt (Eds.), *11th IEEE International Conference on Embedded and Real-Time Computing Systems and Applications* (pp. 373-376). Washington, D.C.: IEEE Computer Society.

# Chapter 6
# Separation of Concerns in Model-based Development of Distributed Real-time Systems

**Dionisio de Niz**
*Carnegie-Mellon University, USA*

**Gaurav Bhatia**
*Carnegie-Mellon University, USA*

**Raj Rajkumar**
*Carnegie-Mellon University, USA*

## ABSTRACT

*Software is increasingly being used to enable new features in systems in multiple domains. These domains include automotive, avionics, telecomunication, and industrial automation. Because the user of these systems is not aware of the presence of the software, this type of software is known as embedded software. More importantly, such a software, and the whole system in general, must satisfy not only logical functional requirements but also parafunctional (a.k.a. nonfunctional) properties such as timeliness, security, and reliability. Traditional development languages and tools provide powerful abstractions such as functions, classes, and objects to build a functional structure that reduces complexity and enables software reuse. However, the software elements responsible for the parafunctional behaviors are frequently scattered across the functional structure. This scattering prevents the easy identification of these elements and their independent manipulation/reuse to achieve a specific parafunctional behavior. As a result, the complexity of parafunctional behaviors cannot be reduced and even worse, the construction of those behaviors can corrupt the functional structure of the software. In this chapter, we propose a model-based framework for designing embedded real-time systems to enable a decomposition structure that reduces the complexity of both functional and parafunctional aspects of the software. This decomposition enables the separation of the functional and parafunctional aspects of the system into semantic dimensions (e.g., event-flow, timing, deployment, fault-tolerant) that can be represented, manipulated, and modified independent of one another from an end-user point of view. The realizations of these dimensions, however, do interact on the target platform since they consume common resources and impose constraints. These interactions can be captured during model construction and resource demands*

DOI: 10.4018/978-1-60566-750-8.ch006

*mediated during platform deployment. The use of semantic dimensions results in three significant benefits. First of all, it preserves the independence of the functional structure from parafunctional behaviors. Secondly, it enables the user to manipulate different parafunctional concerns (e.g., timeliness, reliability) independent of one another. Lastly, it enables the reuse of compositions along any dimension from other systems. The second core abstraction in our modeling approach is an entity called a coupler. A coupler expresses a particular relationship between two or more components, and can also be used recursively. Couplers enable the hierarchical decomposition of functional as well as parafunctional aspects. Aided by semantic dimensions and multiple coupler types, our framework enables the auto-generation of glue code to produce a fully deployable system. Our framework can also construct a detailed timing and resource model. This model in turn is used to optimize the usage of a given hardware configuration, or synthesize a configuration to suit a given software model. Our framework is implemented in a tool (de Niz, Bhatia & Rajkumar 2006) called SysWeaver that had been used to generate glue code and analyze the timing behavior of avionics, automotive, and software-radio pilot systems.*

## INTRODUCTION

Embedded systems can be found in a large variety of products with which we interact daily. These systems take their name from the fact that even though they are enabled by software (called *embedded software*), this software is concealed inside the physical device. The user then relates to the system as if it were an smart and flexible device. The key appeal of software is its flexibility and the potential for low-cost functional upgrades. Due to this appeal, the functionality delivered previously by hardware and mechanical artifacts is steadily migrating to software. Examples of this migration are software radios (Mitola, 2002) and automotive drive-by-wire (Isermann, Schwarz, & Stolzl, 2002) capabilities. These efforts are looking to leverage software to improve and reuse functionality in the most cost-effective manner.

Unfortunately, the flexibility of software is also a problem given that it is possible to express incorrect behaviors that a more inflexible system would not allow. For instance, to test whether a switch is in the *On* position in software, a test needs to be encoded, e.g., *switch == On*. However, a typo can transform such a test into an assignment, e.g., *switch = On*. In contrast, when that test is encoded into an electrical system, the switch could be implemented as current getting into the circuit where an error would be easily detectable and diagnosed by perhaps the blowing of a fuse. As a result, the development of embedded software requires a verification process more complex than the one used to develop the analog system being replaced.

Embedded systems need to be functionally equivalent to the analog systems they replace along with being able to achieve that in a timely manner. This is because such analog systems interact with physical phenomena as can be the case of a braking system or a signal analyzer. This timeliness requirement is known as a real-time

*Figure 1. Anti-lock braking system*

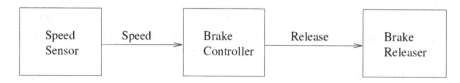

requirement and systems with these requirements are called real-time systems. These types of embedded systems are known as embedded real-time systems.

As an example, consider the system depicted in Figure 1. This system depicts a simplified version of an Anti-Lock Braking System (ABS). This system works as follows. The speed sensor samples the speed of the wheel and sends the samples to the brake controller. The brake controller looks for abnormal deceleration that only happens an instant before the wheel will start to skid. If such deceleration is detected, then the controller sends a command to release the pressure on the brake to prevent the wheel from skidding.

Two timing requirements are important in this ABS braking system. First, the frequency at which the speed of the wheel is sampled must be high enough to observe the physical feature that signals the start of skidding. Secondly, the reaction time between the discovery of the abnormal deceleration and the release of the brake must be fast enough to ensure that skidding is avoided. These two requirements, known in the real-time theory as *period* and *deadline*, must then be verified. To do this verification, it is necessary to know the worst-case execution time (*WCET*) of the software functions being executed. Given the *WCET*, it is possible to answer whether such software can be executed periodically as defined by the *period* and if it can complete before its *deadline*.

In addition to timing requirements, other requirements such as reliability and security may need to be satisfied in an embedded real-time system. We identify these requirements, typically known as non-functional requirements, as *para-functional* requirements to avoid a negative connotation of the non-functional term. The implication of these para-functional requirements is that the development process requires designing, implementing and testing of not only functionality but also of constructs (e.g., replication for reliability) that ensure that para-functional requirements are satisfied. Para-functional requirements complicate

the addition and reuse of functionality. The addition of new functionality can break para-functional assumptions, such as the WCET, and the reuse of functionality in another application has to be verified against both the functional specification and the para-functional requirements.

## EMBEDDED SOFTWARE: BEYOND FUNCTIONAL BEHAVIOR

In this section we introduce the problems in software development due to para-functional requirements of embedded real-time system as well as our approach to solve these problems. Two fundamental factors increase the complexity of the development of embedded real-time systems beyond other types of systems: constrained hardware and timely interaction with the environment. For instance, in an automotive system, the hardware consists of networks of small microcontrollers. The configuration of this hardware is restricted by multiple constraints such as power, space, and cost. On the other hand, the software running on this hardware control mechanical, electrical, or chemical phenomena, such as avoiding the skidding of the tires while braking or ensuring the proper air-to-fuel ratio in the combustion chambers of the engine. These software controllers require sensing and actuating in a timely manner to avoid instability.

The timeliness requirement of embedded real-time systems conflicts with the traditional view of programming languages where the execution of program statements is timeless and the only concern is their logical sequencing. Due to this conflict, the translation of control algorithms, perhaps from control-theoretic tools, to code in a programming language is prone to timing errors. The traditional approach for non-embedded systems of increasing the size and performance of hardware to reduce the execution time cannot be used in embedded systems due to the multiple constrains they are subject to. In fact, in embed-

*Figure 2. Fault-tolerance construct*

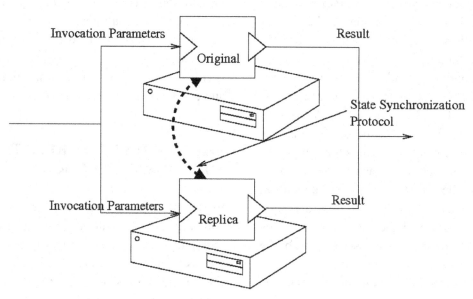

ded systems, the opposite direction is more likely, i.e., the reduction of hardware to save cost, space and/or power.

Beyond timing, embedded real-time systems have other requirements such as reliability, throughput, modality, etc. We identify these requirements as *para-functional* requirements as opposed to the functional requirements that are focused on functional transformations of data such as mathematical operations and control structures that guide these operations. In embedded real-time systems, both functional and para-functional requirements are part of the correctness of the final system.

To satisfy para-functional requirements, specific design and implementation decisions must be made. For instance, if a function must be executed despite hardware failures, then a replica of this functional module can de deployed to run on two (or more) processors. To make this possible, a synchronization protocol must be added to ensure that both modules keep their internal state synchronized (e.g., using atomic multicast). In this way, if one of the replicas fails because its processor breaks down, the other(s) can continue to work and the overall system functions as if

no failure had occurred. Figure 2 depicts such a configuration.

Replication in this case is added to satisfy the specific para-functional requirement of fault-tolerance. As such, this type of construct is referred to as a *para-functional* construct. As this example shows, these constructs involve adding mechanisms to the existing functional construct (e.g., data transformation and execution sequence among the modules). Specifically, in the replication construct, atomic multicast and remote communication mechanisms are added while deploying the replicas on different processors. Unfortunately, in traditional programming languages such as $C$ and $C++$, the addition of such mechanisms involves disassembling the functional construct to insert code and/or calls to libraries for remote communication, synchronization, and other support code. In addition, as software and performance requirements evolve, new functional and para-functional requirements need to be added that further complicates the development, maintainance, and upgrade processes of these systems.

Two main issues are intrinsic to the evolutionary software process: Finding which elements to change, and manipulating those elements at different levels of granularity. For instance, consider the ABS braking system presented in Figure 1. If we want to change the speed threshold upon which the controller decides to release the brakes, we would need to search for the place where that condition is tested. From the structure of the system, we can guess that such a decision is inside the Controller component. Two potential modifications at different levels of granularity can happen. On the one hand, if the interface of the component module includes an input parameter for the speed threshold, we would only need to modify that parameter. On the other hand, if such a parameter does not exist, then we would need to search inside the module for the statement that tests against the threshold (e.g., if (speed > 100)) and then proceed with the modification.

To address the issues of finding elements to modify and their granularity, software hierarchies have been introduced over the years. Simplification of the search process has been achieved through hierarchical structures in programming languages (e.g., functions, data structures, classes etc.) that can reduce the complexity of the search to a search-tree. At the same time, this structure can present each module as a composition of a number of sub-modules (children in the tree) that can be managed manually.

Even though software hierarchies have enabled the construction of large and complex software systems, they still need to be designed to suit a single goal. For instance, in the ABS braking system, to simplify the modification of the functional concerns of the system, we may want to create functional classes such as *Speed Sensor*, *Brake Releaser*, *Brake Coordinator*, etc. However, if we want to simplify the modification of the replication process, we may want to use classes such as: *Primary Replica*, *Backup Replica*, *Response Merger*, etc. to build a primary-backup replication construct (Budhiraja, 1993). This illustrates that different classification hierarchies might be required depending on the concerns of the system

at hand we may want to have different classification hierarchies.

The current state of the art in embedded systems development lacks structures to reduce complexity and manipulate para-functional constructs at different levels of granularity. The core of our approach is to propose and evaluate new structures which facilitate the provisioning and verification of para-functional properties in embedded real-time systems.

## A NEW APPROACH TO DESIGN FUNCTIONAL AND PARA-FUNCTIONAL CONSTRUCTS

This section presents a model-based framework that enables multiple parallel structures to reflect functional and para-functional concerns. These structures provide encapsulation units and recursive encapsulation capabilities along each concern. The framework exploits this structure to provide multiple ways to navigate and analyze the system behavior.

### Semantic Dimensions

The multiple hierarchies proposed by our framework are presented in different views called *semantic dimensions*. Semantic dimensions present the software elements and the system structures or constructs formed by these elements relevant to a specific concern of the system (such as timeliness, fault-tolerance, concurrency, etc.). For instance, consider the system in Figure 1. It has a functional dimension, a faul-tolerant dimension and a deployment dimension. In the functional dimension, the software elements would consist of the functional modules (e.g., *SpeedSensor*, *BrakeController* and *BrakeReleaser* for this system), and the structures would be constructed with the connection and sequencing of these modules. In the fault-tolerant dimension, the elements would consist of an atomic multicaster, the response

*Figure 3. Aggregating unit for para-function code*

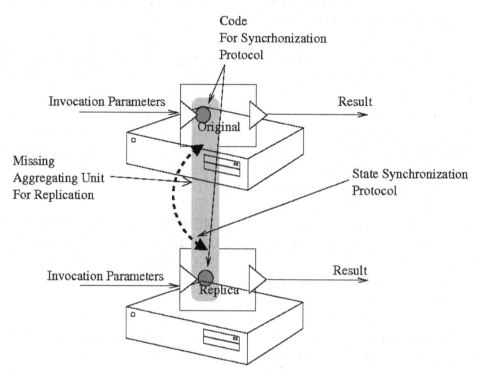

mergers and deployment restrictions such as a disjoint deployment restriction to ensure that the modules run on different processors to enable hardware failure independence. The structures, on the other hand, would assemble these elements into fault-tolerant replicas that are related to the functional elements. Finally, in the deployment dimension, the execution platform elements such as processors and networks would be used to assemble structures that describe the hardware in terms of connectivity and number of processors and networks. In addition, this dimension can contain the binding between the functional elements and the execution platform.

## Couplers

New abstractions are needed to enable the recursive encapsulation of para-functional constructs. A fundamental challenge in the design of these abstractions is the cross-cutting nature across

functional and para-functional constructs. Figure 3 depicts an example of such cross-cutting. In the figure, if an aggregating (or encapsulating) unit is to be used for the synchronization protocol, it would cross-cut the functional modules (*Original* and *Replica*). In other words, the elements that the synchronization protocol contains will also be contained in the modules *Original* and *Replica*.

We use two fundamental strategies to deal with the cross-cutting issue among functional and para-functional constructs. Firstly, we encapsulate all the functional modules in a component-based framework, where all functional modules are components that interact with other components through ports. Secondly, a new abstraction called a *coupler* is introduced as an encapsulating abstraction for para-functional elements. A coupler captures the relationship between two or more components. Couplers of different types are used to capture different kinds of relationships. For instance, a *Data Coupler* is used to capture the

*Figure 4. Couplers*

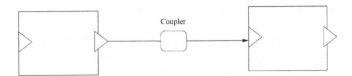

communication of events across components; a *Parametric Coupler* captures the relationship between periodic activations of components; and *Deployment Constraint Couplers* capture restrictions on the bindings of a component to a processor.

Couplers are located between ports of components and are used as constructs to link ports together as shown in Figure 4.

Each coupler can have a code fragment element referred to as a *state manager*. When a coupler has a state manager, this state manager is inherited by all component ports linked to this coupler. In addition, an association between the state managers of the ports linked to this coupler is built. This association is referred to as a *synchronization group*. The state manager inside the port acts as a filter for events that passes through such a port. This filtering function is coordinated among the members of the synchronization group enabling the composition of synchronization protocols among specific ports. For instance, consider the example depicted in Figure 2. In this example, the

*Figure 5. Coupler with code elements*

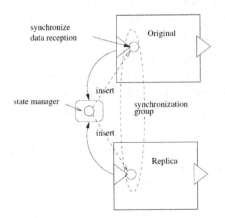

synchronization protocol depicted as a dashed line between the *Original* and *Replica* modules can be encapsulated into a state manager in a coupler linking the input ports of both components. This state manager can encapsulate the code for the *Atomic Multicast* protocol and the synchronization group can give network addresses and global parameters to the participating parties. An important consequence of this construct is that the state manager of the coupler can be modified (even replaced) while the functional construct (data coupling between the replicas and the other components) remains intact. Figure 5 depicts an example of a coupler with a state manager.

An important property of couplers is that they enable components to be involved in multiple relationships. For instance, Figure 6 depicts the input ports of components *Original* and *Replica* involved in a coupler to synchronize data reception. At the same time, these same ports are involved in a data coupler along with the output port of a *Data Source* component to encode the data exchange between them.

Two strategies are used to automatically resolve conflicts that arise from applying multiple couplers over a single port. Firstly, for couplers with state managers, a total processing order is imposed among the state managers to rule out unwanted sequences such as a circular wait for a mutex lock. Secondly, assumptions about the hardware, such as independence of failure (due to binding of components to different processors), or shared memory (e.g., for a mutex implemented with shared memory) are expressed as constraints honored by our automatic binding algorithms to satisfy the resource demands (e.g., processing, network bandwidth).

*Figure 6. Multiple couplers*

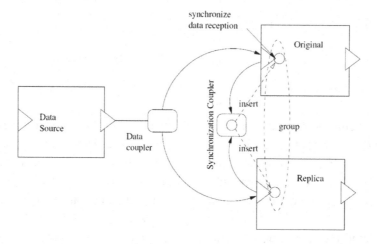

## RELATED WORK

### Composition Languages

Substantial work has been performed in recent years in the area of composition languages. The CL language (Ivers, Sinha, & Walnau, 2002) is part of the Predictable Assembly from Certifiable Components Initiative at the Software Engineering Institute. This work has a strong focus on the functional correctness of a system composed of software components. It defines a formal description of components and interconnections that enables formal analysis. Darwin (Magee, Dulay, & Kramer, 1993) is a compositional language that has a strong focus on the behavior of the system diminishing its concern for its structure, i.e., it does not represent explicity the boundaries and interfaces of the developed components. Koala (van Ommering, van der Linden, Kramer, & Magee, 2000) is a tool based on Darwin developed for the consumer electronics market. It addresses concurrency by the addition of primitives called *thread pumps* and *pump engines*. PECOS (Nierstrasz, Arevalo, Cucasse, Wuyts, Black, Muller, et al., 2002) is a component model for field devices. It defines components and connectors along with annotation mechanisms to enable different types of

analysis. The behavior of components is defined formally using Petri nets. It is specialized for memory constrained devices and has a built-in cyclic scheduler. Piccola (Achermann, Lumpe, Jean-Guy, & Oscar, 2001) is a composition language that adds to an ADL-type (Architecture Description Language) of description scripting. It uses a process algebra to specify both component and assembly behavior. Its scripting language has the role of a glue language that is used to adapt components to remove interface and behavior mismatches among components.

### UML

The Unified Modeling Language (UML) unifies the modeling proposals of multiple software development methodologies based on the object-oriented paradigm. It proposes the use of multiple views to capture different perspectives of the system. Unfortunately these views lack both precise semantics (operational semantics) and consistency across views. However, the idea of having multiple perspectives of the system marked an important step forward in software modeling. At its core, UML enables the representation of the static structures of an object-oriented system (e.g. classes) and the interactions of the objects of these clases that constitute an instance of the system. In our work, we also use different views, but we ensure the consistency of the views and provides them with well-defined semantics. A related work important to us is the MARTE Profile (OMG, 2008). However, this is still a work in progress where the finalization task force group is expected to do final recommendations to the profile by April 2009. Hence, it is still not clear the impact of this work on ours.

## AIRES

AIRES (Wang & Shin, 2000) is an architecture where systems are modeled as components comunicating through events. The inside of the component is described as a Finite State Machine (FSM). The final system is therefore integrated as a nested finite state machine triggered by a control plan. The timing of this control plan can be verified with rate-monotonic analsys techninques (RMA) (Klein, Ralya, Pollak, & Obenza, 1993). In contrast our framework is not limited to FSMs and is aimed more to the decomposition techniques to separate functional and para-functional modeling elements.

## AADL

The Architecture Analysis and Design Language (AADL) is an Society of Automotive Engineers (SAE) standard language (SAE, 2004) designed to model analyzable runtime architectures. Runtime architectures are defined as the runtime structures that defined the operational quality attributes of a software system. Such an architecture is composed of processes, threads, subprograms and the processors and busses over which they run. The language has well-defined execution semantics aimed at specifying precise task models to be analyzed with RMA. The language is extensible in the sense that new sublanguages can be added to create new constructs that can be combined with the core language to enable new analyses.

Our work is different from this work in the sense that we are interested in separating the different aspects of the para-functional concerns while AADL keeps all the descriptions together. In addition, our model has constructs that increase the tool automation where, given a high-level decision of the designer, the tool will automatically propagate such a decision to the proper places. This is the case of communication scopes and automatic propagation and conflict resolution among the different concerns.

## Ptolemy II

Ptolemy II (Bhattacharyya, et al., 2003) is a tool that enables the modeling of systems with multiple models of computations. The use of these models are limited to a single hierarchy. These models of computation are based on actors (somewhat related to the Agha and Hewitt model (Agha, 1986), (Hewitt, 1977). These actors are port-based software modules that communicate among each other through events. The interpretation of the execution of a model in a system is contained in a description called *director*. To enable hierachical composition, an actor can contain a model. Along with this model both an interface and the director are defined. Ptolemy can simulate the behavior of its models and some code generators have also been developed. In our work we separate the functional from the para-functional constructs while Ptolemy bundles both together into elements of its models of computation.

## Aspect-Oriented Programming

Aspect-Oriented Programming (Lieberherr, 1997) triggered new ways to think about concerns. It recognizes the fact that many requirements do not decompose neatly into behaviors centered on a single locus. It specifies these behaviors separately with some description of their relationships, and enables the tool environment to compose them into a coherent program. AOP mainly deals with cross-cutting concerns and the various ways to encapsulate them into a single unit, with a strong emphasis on programming mechanisms and abstractions. A new abstraction called *aspect* was created to encapsulate the description of cross-cutting concerns that can later be properly inserted into the corresponding traditional methods in OOP languages. An aspect specifies both a description of the *pointcuts* and the code to be inserted in those points. Pointcuts are typically described as a parsing expression (e.g., regular expression) over source code. This specification creates a strong dependency of the aspect specification not only on the program syntax but also on the specific program source code, i.e., how the methods were named. This issue has resonated with the community and additional work has been done to address this problem. One example of this work is (Griswold, et al., 2006) where the authors decompose the point cuts to decrease the dependency of the pointcut to the code. However, even in this work one part of the pointcut is still dependent on the source code of the implementation. In addition, aspects cannot be composed, i.e., you cannot create an aspect out of other aspects.

Our motivation is similar, but we differ in the way we approach the solution. We believe that for an embedded real-time system the para-functional concerns are as important as the functional aspect, and appropriate support for complexity reduction is a must. Furthermore, the specification of the para-functional concerns should not depend on the functional ones, as the specification of pointcuts do. Closer to our work is the work on Aspect-Oriented Modeling (AOM) where a higher level description of the system composition is used (as we do) to reason about crosscutting concerns. In particular, in (Iqbal & Elrand, 2006) the authors present an approach to model timing constraints as a crosscutting concerrn. In their work they use real-time statecharts to model these constraints that are later woven into a final hierarchical timed automaton. Their final view is a global

time implemented in a centralized controller. In contrasts our timing model is that of a set of tasks with different arrival patterns (e.g., periodic, aperiodic) that execute a flow of jobs. In addition, pieces of our timing model are included as part of the modeling of the components that are later integrated into a global model, instead of having the timing completely separate. Additional work from the AOM community such as (Bakre & El-rad, 2007), (Heidenreich, Johannes, & Zschaler, 2007), (Klein & Kienzle, 2007), extend UML modeling to incorporate aspects. However, their final models fall-back to the semantics of UML with dimished role of the hardware model and its impact on the para-functional aspects of the systems. Moreover, while some of the models talk about some para-functional aspects, e.g., security, no specialized notion for the whole class of these aspects is proposed.

## Meta-Model Tools

Other modeling approaches for embedded systems use meta-models to define a style or patterns commonly used in embedded systems. The purpose of this approach is to enable the designer to define their own constructs that better adapt to them. This is the case of tools such as the Generic Modeling Environment (GME) (Ledeczi, et al., 2001) and some Domain-specific modeling tools such as MetaEdit+ (Tolvanen & Rossi, 2003). Our approach has a different focus than these ones. In particular, we focus on the interactions of constructs needed to address the different concerns of embedded real-time systems with a well-defined set of constructs, while the meta-model approach focuses on enabling the creation of additional constructs.

## PARA-FUNCTIONAL BEHAVIORS AND SOFTWARE STRUCTURES

A common problem faced in the development of software systems and in particular in embedded systems is the need to use different abstractions for different goals. For instance, consider the design of a large-scale signal processing system such as a wideband surveillance system. This system receives unidentified transmissions and attempts to decode them. To build this system, signal engineers need to use a language and simulation environment that can abstract away the timing behavior of the software (e.g., execution time) to be able to focus on the mathematical transformations (e.g., Matlab). Once the objective of this abstraction is fulfilled, the functionality is transformed into another language (e.g., C++). After this new program is verified, its timing behavior is evaluated. Based on this evaluation, synthesis decisions are made, i.e., hardware sizing, deployment, and insertion of remote communication mechanisms (RCMs) such as remote procedure calls.

The transformation across these different descriptions (Matlab, C++, timing model) is done manually. This involves an error-prone process with numerous opportunities for errors in addition to the large cost of the manual process. Furthermore, any modification to one of the descriptions needs to be verified against the other descriptions.

A second problem faced by this system structure is the scattering of the para-functional elements across functional modules such as program functions. In other words, to be able to use an RCM such as CORBA, additional code needs to be added. In the example of CORBA, this code can include statements to localize the remote module (object), marshal the method parameters and invoke the middleware to perform the remote invocation. This code needs to be modified if the functional structures (dataflow connections) are modified, or if the deployment decisions are modified.

One solution that has been explored in the past is middleware-based para-functional constructs (e.g., (Narashimhan, 1999)) and constitutes a powerful form of transparent reuse. However, to be able to use them, functional modules must be adapted with special runtime code for their integration with the middleware. Once this adaptation is in place, additional para-functional constructs can be added transparently (e.g., fault-tolerance). However, this approach hides the para-functional constructs and therefore cannot be evaluated for timing behavior or conflicts with other constructs. As a result, the need for explicit modeling and analysis of para-functional constructs persists.

## Separating Functional and Para-Functional Concerns

In this section, we discuss our two novel composition schemes, couplers and semantic dimensions, with full detail. We start by defining our components and then move to couplers and semantic dimensions to complete the discussion of our composition model.

A system in our framework is the description of both the software and the execution platform (hardware and software system, e.g., operating system, middleware) over which the software runs. This dual description enables timing analysis and synthesis of mechanisms to enable the splitting of the system across multiple processors (e.g., remote communication mechanisms).

In our framework, software modules are called *components*. Three types of code units reside inside components: *application agents*, *state managers*, and *protocol agents*. In addition, *couplers* are design-time abstractions that manipulate these types of code units to construct the final running system.

Components communicate with other components through *ports*. Ports are either input or output ports. *Input ports* receive data and *output ports* send data. Components communicate *events* to other components. Events are occurrences that

*Figure 7. Component structure*

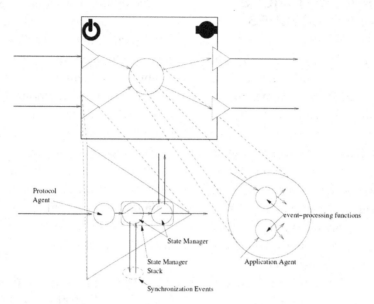

need to be communicated across components and can embed any data structure, e.g., a single variable, as in a parameter for a function call or an array with the full set of parameters for the function call. This communication is synchronous by default, but can be made asynchronous with port properties. Events are typed, and the ports through which such events are communicated inherit that type. As a result, ports are typed and can only send or receive events of that type.

Inside a component, the application code is localized in an element called an *application agent*. An application agent is structured as a set of functions where each function processes a type of event and generates a set of events. Components contain additional elements that support the construction of para-functional behaviors. The organization of the elements inside a component is depicted in Figure 7. Ports contain a protocol agent that is responsible for getting events from one component to another. As a result, communication happens from one protocol agent to another. In other words, protocol agents implement the necessary mechanism to achieve the inter-component communication. Protocol agents also encode the

concurrency elements of the component. This means that each protocol agent can contain a thread of execution that can run concurrently with any previous one before the event was delivered to this protocol agent.

After events are received through protocol agents, a series of state managers implement the synchronization protocol that may be necessary for different para-functional constructs. For instance, consider the replication example depicted in Figure 2. In this example, a state manager in the input port of each replica verifies that both replicas receive an event before giving it to the application agent. This implies that such state managers exchange messages that inform the other of the reception of events so each can verify that an event has been received by both.

Because components can be involved in multiple para-functional constructs, ports can contain multiple state managers. These state managers are organized in series, where the first state manager passes the event to the next one until the final one in the series passes it to the application agent. For instance, when accessing multiple mutually exclusive resources, a component needs to synchronize

*Figure 8. Multiple state managers*

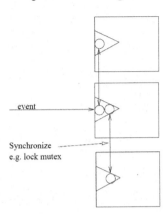

event

Synchronize
e.g. lock mutex

with other components. This example is depicted in Figure 8. When an event is delivered to the application agent, it executes and generates a set of zero or more events. These generated events traverse a set of output state managers and gets to the protocol agents of the output ports to be communicated to the components connected to the output ports.

Components have two optional special ports: *activation port* and *completion port*. The activation port is used to encode the self-activation of the component. Its protocol agent can be made active (with a thread inside) and the periodicity of the activation can be chosen. Because it has the same structure as the other ports, it can also participate in para-functional synchronization protocols (e.g., mutual exclusion, modal activation). This port generates a reserved type of event known as a *tick*. The completion port acts as a sink that marks the completion of the processing of the component when no output events are generated. This port can participate in para-functional synchronization protocols as any other regular port. It generates a reserved type of event called *completion*.

## Couplers

Couplers manipulate the component elements (state managers, protocol agents, concurrency, etc.) to build inter-component relationships.

Different types of couplers are used to capture the different types of relationships required to describe a system.

Data couplers build event communication relationships among component ports. This relationship has publish-subscribe semantics (Rajkumar, Gaglardi, & Sha, 1995). In this semantics, the output port acts as a publisher of a type of event and the associated input ports act as subscribers. In such an association, the publisher can have many subscribers enabling one to many communication relationships.

Synchronization couplers encapsulate a state manager that is inherited by the state manager stack of associated ports. In addition, a synchronization group is built among the state managers of the associated ports setting up the participants in the synchronization protocol. Note that the semantics of this protocol is embedded in the code and only its design-time configuration parameters and its timing model (to be discussed later) are exposed to the designer. The timing model is then an interpretation of the semantics of the code to enable the analysis of the timing concerns at hand. This shapes the component nature of the couplers enabling the designer to limit himself to connect the coupler to other components and configure its parameters. In other words, it is not the intention of the framework to be expressive enough to describe a large range of possible behaviors but rather to enable the composition of well-understood architectural patterns. Figure 9 depicts a synchronization coupler to synchronize the processing of events in a replication scheme for the Brake Controller of the ABS system. In this figure, the input ports of both copies of the Brake Controller inherit the *Atomic Multicast* state manager. The synchronization group is built among the inherited state managers to be able to exchange synchronization events. The inheritance and automatic synchronization group construction enable a single location for the protocol code: the synchronization coupler.

*Figure 9. ABS system: Synchronization coupler*

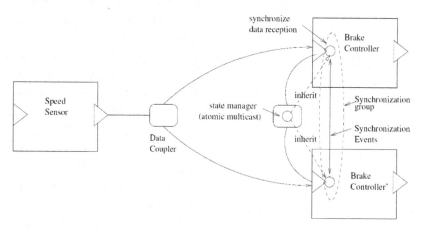

Components are parameterized with properties. Parametric couplers define properties that can be propagated to the components associated with them. For instance, the period of a group of active components that execute periodically can be defined by using one coupler. In a recursive form, couplers build trees of recursive property propagation. This scheme enables hierarchical relationships between component properties.

### Deployment Restrictions

Deployment restrictions are encoded with aggregating couplers between components to ensure specific patterns of parallelism. Basic restriction couplers include the following:

- **Junction:** Specifies that the associated components should be deployed together on the same hardware element.
- **Disjunction:** Specifies that the group of components associated with this constraint should not be deployed together on the same hardware element.
- **Isolation:** Specifies that the group of components associated with this constraint should have exclusive use of a hardware element all by themselves.
- **Binding:** Specifies that the group of components associated with this constraint

should be deployed to a specific hardware element.

### Couplers for the Execution Platform

The description of the execution platform is defined with a type of coupler known as a *Hardware Coupler*. Hardware couplers capture two important parts of the execution platform: processors and communication scopes.

### Communication Scopes

We define a communication scope as an execution environment where a specific communication mechanism is used. For instance, a process is a communication scope where a shared-memory communication mechanism (e.g., invocation) is used. Correspondingly, the communication between components that are not in the same scope (e.g., same process) cannot use such a mechanism. Instead, a common communication scope must be defined among them, e.g., Unix pipes among processes in the same processor. The communication mechanism to be used in a communication scope is specified by a protocol agent. Communication scopes have a strong relationship with the hardware and system software (e.g., operating system and middleware). Hence, *hardware couplers* are used to encode both the parallelism capabilities and the communication scopes.

The basic types of hardware couplers are:

- *Process.* It defines a scope of shared memory and provides a default invocation protocol agent.
- *Processor.* It defines a scope of operating-system-mediated communication such as Inter-Process-Communication (IPC) and a protocol agent must be defined if it couples more than one process. It is also a unit of parallelism, i.e., code associated with this coupler can execute in parallel with that associated with other processors.
- *Network.* A network coupler associates a group of processors and defines the protocol agent to use to communicate across processors.
- *System.* It defines all the hardware elements that belong to the system. It can be considered the root of the hardware hierarchy.

In summary, hardware couplers are used to describe the hardware available to the system. This description is organized as a hierarchy where the *System* coupler is the root. The system coupler couples a set of networks that in turn can couple more networks or processors. Finally, processors couple processes.

**The Timing Model**

The timing model used in our framework is based on the task model of the Rate-Monotonic Analysis (RMA) framework (Liu & Layland, 1973). In this model we need three pieces of information: the periodicity (period) of execution of the code, the deadline upon which the execution should have finished and the worst-case execution time (WCET) of the code. The period and deadline are linked to active ports. In particular, active port abstractions have both of these properties and can be specified by the user. Other timing models, such as the Time-Triggered Architecture (Kopetz & Bauer, 2003) can be supported very easily. Our choice of the RMA framework as the initial timing

model was motivated by its successful use in the industry supported by commercial analysis tools and real-time operating systems that support the model. This use includes distributed systems that, even though the utilization of hardware may not be optimal, provides an analyzable behavior.

The characterization of the WCET of the component requires a more detailed specification of its execution. Components in our framework are event-processing components with a reactive nature, i.e., they react to the arrival of an event by executing a piece of code. This reactive nature is encoded in the application agent, state managers, and protocol agent with a transition table. The transition table maps an input event to a sequence of output events. This mapping contains a WCET for each of the reactions.

Integrating the timing behavior of multiple components that are coupled together consists of identifying execution threads (active ports) and the actions that such threads execute. This information is part of a model known as *response chain* (Klein, Ralya, Pollak, & Obenza, 1993) where a thread is represented as a trigger that activates periodically and executes a chain of actions. A deeper discussions of the analysis techniques is beyond the scope of this chapter and we refer the reader to (Klein, Ralya, Pollak, & Obenza, 1993) for a initial introduction to the topic.

## MULTIPLE HIERARCHIES

Hierarchies are the key structures to reduce complexity in software. However, in order for a hierarchy to work properly, the software artifact it organizes must address a single concern. In this section, we present our approach to compose multiple hierarchies and later we will discuss the resolution of conflicts among hierarchies.

*Figure 10. Functional composition*

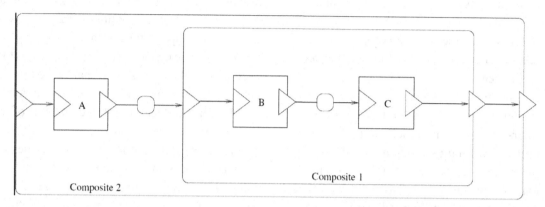

## Functional Hierarchies

Functional hierarchies are composed of the sequencing and data communication between functional modules. As presented previously, our framework encapsulates functional modules in port-based components and connect their ports through couplers to encode their transfer of data and control. Synchronization between data reception and control transfer is encoded with state managers. These state managers are bundled into *composite ports*. An example of this synchronization is the synchronization of function invocations where the callee and the caller need to synchronize their transfer of data and control. As a result, functional hierarchies are built by aggregating connected components into a composite component that presents its input and output port to the outside for further (recursive) composition. These components are called *encapsulators* and they aggregate multiple ports into *protocol ports*. Figure 10 depicts an example of functional composition. In this example, components *B* and *C* compose *Composite1*. This composite is used, in turn, with component *A* to compose *Composite2*.

Couplings between protocol ports are implemented by the construction of *Typed Channels*. A single data coupler can compose multiple typed channels when it associates two protocol ports, i.e., if more than one component port with a dif-

ferent type is associated with each protocol port, then the data coupler creates a typed channel for each of the types in these protocol ports. Typed channels compose recursively to support multiple levels of encapsulation.

Typed protocol ports complement component port type checking by encoding a more elaborate type checking at the level of the protocol port as a whole. Examples of these protocol ports are the facets and receptacles of the CORBA Component Model (CCM) (OMG, 2006). Facets and receptacles are two classes of typed protocol ports with a type-checking algorithm that verifies that a facet is the inverse of a receptacle (i.e., same type with complementary ports).

## Para-Functional Hierarchies

Our model, as discussed earlier, captures each para-functional element in a separate but consistent view. Each view may then be structured differently based on its needs and expressive power. We shall discuss these structures next.

### Parametric Structures

The para-functional elements (e.g., threads, periodicity, deadlines, etc) are parameterized with port properties. Parametric structures relate the port properties of different components. Parametric

*Figure 11. Parametric pipeline*

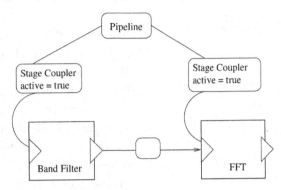

structures can be used to construct structures for threads, activation patterns and timing behavior. For threads, the *active* property of the port can be inherited from a *parametric coupler*. A structure of couplers, i.e., a coupler aggregating a set of couplers, can be built to define parts of the processing that must happen concurrently. This way pipeline stages can be encoded in *stage* couplers which state that specific ports must be active. These stage couplers in turn can be associated with the final *pipeline* coupler. This example is depicted in Figure 11.

## Role-Based Synchronization Protocols

Synchronization couplers can be composed of multiple roles. Different subsets of these roles can compose different synchronization groups that together support a desired para-functional construct. For instance, Figure 12 depicts a role-based replication coupling construct. In this figure, a *Replication Coupler* is built with two roles. In one role, an *Atomic Multicast* state manager is added to synchronize the processing of the events arriving to the replicas (B and B') coupled to this role. In the second role, an *Event Merger* state manager is added to merge the two responses from the replicas into one that component C can process.

*Figure 12. Role-based replication coupling*

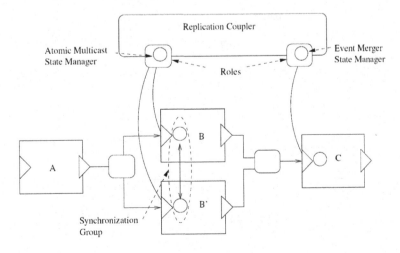

*Figure 13. State manager layers*

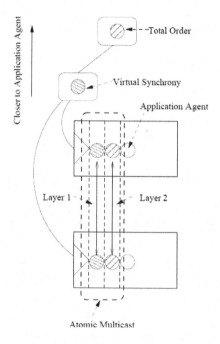

## Synchronization layers

Synchronization layers are built on a coupling hierarchy as depicted in Figure 13. In such a construct, state managers are inherited from couplers at all levels of the hierarchy. The higher the coupler is in the hierarchy, the closer the location of its state manager is to the application agent.

The layering construct enables the decomposition of complex synchronization protocols into simpler structures to incrementally build the desired behavior. For instance, in the example depicted in Figure 13, the *Atomic Multicast* protocol is decomposed into two layers: *Virtual Synchrony* and *Total Order*. Virtual synchrony implements an agreement protocol to ensure that all components process the same events. Total order, on the other hand, ensures that such events are processed in the same order. Such a layering structure provides a decomposition scheme that can reduce complexity and improve reuse.

Synchronization groups can also be created across different roles in a role-based coupling. These groups are formed by adding a common type of state manager to the roles to be involved in the group and a common parent coupler. In this way, each of the state managers in the different roles can have different property values to characterize their role in the synchronization protocol.

To support scalability of couplers, we enable both the application of couplers to protocol ports (from the functional hierarchy) and the construction of groups of functional components into composites with protocol ports to which couplers roles are connected. For instance, a functional component can be associated with a large group

*Figure 14. Communication scopes hierarchy*

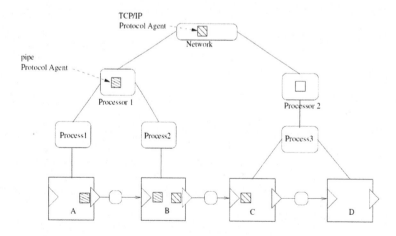

of replicas all of them included in a composite component associated to a single coupler role.

## Hardware Description

Hardware is described as a hierarchy of hardware couplers. As discussed previously, these couplers define both the hardware and the communication scopes. This description is composed in a hierarchy. An example of a communication scope hierarchy is depicted in Figure 14.

The communication scopes defined by the hardware couplers is another key abstraction to support scalability of the design process. These scopes in particular define the mechanism (e.g., communication protocol) that is to be used by a potentially large set of components. To see this, imagine a modified version of Figure 14 where we replace each of the individual components (A,B,C, and D) with one thousands of them, i.e., associated to the same process and with multiple connections. In such a case, the selection of the proper communication mechanism (i.e., protocol agent) is automatic without any modification to the decisions taken when defining the hardware model. In other words, the design decisions taken to model the hardware hierarchy can scale from a few components to thousands or more. In addition, the decision of where to deploy (associate components to hardware) can be done with an optimization algorithm (to be explained later), increasing further the scalability of design decisions.

## SEMANTIC DIMENSIONS

Couplers enable the clean separation of the hierarchies of different concerns. As a result, views can be implemented with a simple filter to hide couplers not belonging to a concern. However, it is very important to note that the modification to one view can impact other views.

Our modeling framework takes a two-fold approach to preserve the value of multiple views

in a model. First, a user may modify a view locally without regard to other views. Secondly, the impact of any such changes in other views is accounted for by the framework automatically. In other words, changes in one view are automatically projected to other views and its coupling interactions handled accordingly. This automatic projection creates stronger semantics than just isolated views. We refer to our views as *semantic dimensions* as they automatically preserve the semantics (intended behavior) of the couplings. Note that this approach contrasts with other approaches with a single composition view such as the more traditional models of computation. That is, with models of computation either a single view is used to compose the system or different models of computation are arranged into a single hierarchy (Bhattacharyya, et al., 2003).

The coupler interactions between dimensions handled by our framework are classified into coupling ordering and resource interactions. Coupling ordering refers to the order in which the state managers in a port perform their synchronization. These different orders can yield different behaviors as presented in Figure 15 where the order of state managers from different couplers is undefined (it can be *Order 1* or *Order 2*). To prevent this problem, our framework allows the addition of a sequencing number to state manager types. With this order, when two state manager-based couplers are associated with a port and no order is specified among the couplers, i.e., they are not part of a coupling hierarchy, an automatic reordering of these state managers is performed. This order is defined by the sequencing numbers associated with their type. This order is defined by the creator of state manager libraries.

Resource interactions derive from the fact that components require computing resources (e.g., CPU cycles, memory) and couplings can constrain the choices to satisfy such requirements. For instance, consider the replication example depicted in Figure 16. For the replication construct to work, each of the replicas needs to be deployed

*Figure 15. Ordering conflicts*

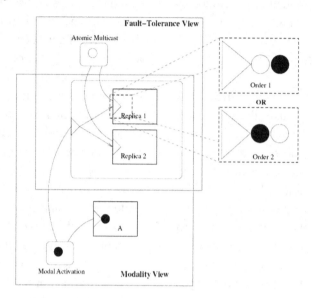

on different processors to ensure that the failure of a processor only shuts down one replica.

Given such constraints and a hardware description, these resource interactions are managed by deploying each component to a processor such that they have enough CPU to satisfy their deadlines and all the constraints are respected. An automatic deployment algorithm to optimize the required hardware is used to address this issue.

We have defined a set of core semantic dimensions for embedded real-time systems. These dimensions constitute the fundamental concerns around which the behaviors of such systems are built. These dimensions are as follows:

- **The Functional dimension** deals with the typical functional transformations described by popular languages such as C, or Matlab.
- **The Deployment dimension** deals with:
  - the description of the deployment platform (hardware, operating system, middleware, etc.),
  - the definition of the communication scopes (processes, processors,

networks, etc.) and their respective communication mechanism,
  - the assignment of components to the deployment entities,
- **The Timing dimension** deals with the relationships between the periods and deadlines of active components,
- **The Fault-tolerance dimension** deals with the constructs to provide redundant

*Figure 16. Deployment constraint of replication coupling*

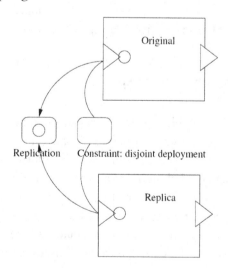

computation,

- **The Modality dimension** deals with constructs that enable the system to change its configuration over time to satisfy changing objectives, and the

- **Concurrency dimension** deals with enabling and synchronizing parallel activities.

Even though we define a set of common embedded system dimensions, we believe different application domains may need to define new dimensions. Dimensions are defined by, first, the set of coupling constructs and its elements (state managers) that are the building blocks to address the concern of this new dimension. Secondly, we need to define over which constructs the concern is to be built on. For instance, most dimensions are built on top of the functional dimension but new dimensions may require other constructs as well. One example of the latter is the deployment dimension that builds its constructs (e.g., component-to-processor assignments) over components from all the other dimensions. Finally, the projections to and from the other dimensions need to be considered and configured. For example, if specialized components are added, they need to be projected to the deployment dimension.

## CODE GENERATION

Central to our objective of keeping a faithful model of the runtime image is the ability to generate executable glue code. By glue code, we mean the code that combines the application code together to form the final running system. Our code generation framework is composed of two main parts: an inter-component communication library and the generator of code that performs the inter-component connections and initializes the application. The framework generates a runtime application consisting of a network of computing elements connected through a table-driven publish-subscribe mechanism. In this latter mechanism, one publisher (at an output port) maintains a list of subscribers for each event type it generates. When an event must be generated, the publisher chooses the appropriate list of subscribers based on the type of the event, and delivers the event to all of them. Execution paths begin at activation ports that generate *tick* events according to the selected activation pattern. This event is sent to the application agent to indicate that a new activation event has occurred. The application agent then reacts to this event.

The code generated in our framework is glue code since we glue together application code provided by the designers. The glue code consists of two parts: the connection of the subscribers to the publishers, and the initialization of the system.

A primary goal of our system is to support multiple execution platforms (e.g., operating system and middleware). Therefore, all calls to the target platform are hidden inside a library. This library is then changed appropriately when a different platform is desired. As a result, differences between different platforms are hidden and the generated glue code makes calls to a standard programming interface.

Our framework supports multiple target languages. The selection of the target language does not need to be the same for the different parts of an application. In other words, one part of the system can be generated in one language, say C, while the other part can be generated in another language such as Java. Because the communication across components happens through a well-contained element (protocol agent), the only condition to enable this mixture is to provide cross-language protocol agents.

Multiple optimizations are possible for the generation of glue code. A simple optimization is the elimination of dead-code elements (state managers and protocol agents) that do not add any value. Perhaps the most interesting ones are those that have a compact code representation due to the possibility of producing optimized glue code that is not possible to embed in a library. This is the case for Data Flow Components where components operate over a stream of input data that is transformed into an output stream. The processing paths built with these components are typically static. This allows us to encode the dataflow as a simple sequence of function calls with the proper data transfer across the parameters of the called functions when the components are deployed on a common process and thread. However, when the communicated components are deployed on different processors, we keep the protocol agents. Our framework had been used to generate code for multiple automotive, software radio, and robotic pilot systems on multiple languages, hardware, and operating systems. Furthermore, we were able to compare the efficiency of the generated glue code against CORBA-based glue code in a software radio project and found that the generated code improved the execution time of the system by 16.77%.

## Deployment Synthesis Algorithms

Our framework allows automatic synthesis of a complete system that binds software modules to hardware resources. In particular, we have extended the traditional Best-Fit-Decreasing bin-packing algorithm to work with a network of computers. This extension casts the bin-packing problem as the deployment of *partitionable* composite objects, where these objects are sets of components that communicate with each other. In a previous publication we have shown that partitioning lead to gains in the number of bins needed. Based on the analysis in this publication, we developed two algorithms called *Best-Fit-Decreasing with Partitioning* and *Best-Fit-Decreasing with Excess Bin Partitioning*. In addition, we have developed two additional heuristics to trade off network bandwidth requirements against the number of bins required. These algorithms defer object partitioning as much as possible (to avoid creating network

load), and can choose from two different selection orderings of the objects to be partitioned.

## SUMMARY

The fundamental motivation for our approach is the growing need to reduce the complexity of designing embedded real-time systems. We proposed that this reduction in complexity along with an increase in usability can be obtained by separating functional from para-functional concerns. This separation enables the designer to focus on different concerns of the system at different times, making decisions pertinent to a particular concern while deferring decisions that interact with other concerns. Interactions across the various concerns are automatically projected and managed. Various analysis and synthesis techniques are enabled. Finally, we treat the problem at the system-level by developing a set of algorithms that near-optimally bind software modules to underlying hardware resources and provide a glue-code generation framework to ensure the compliance of the model to the code.

Our work addresses the complexity of embedded real-time systems with a component-based framework that concurrently constructs timing and deployment model as the runtime system is modeled. This simultaneous construction ensures that the analysis/synthesis models do not deviate from the actual running code. This approach targets marked improvements in the state of the practice where project deadlines and the fast pace of commercial software production breaks well-known best practices. Our framework also enables and promotes the simultaneous reuse of compositions in three areas: functional composition, para-functional constructs (e.g., pipelines, replication schemes, caches, etc.), and analytical model composition.

# REFERENCES

Achermann, F., Lumpe, M., Jean-Guy, S., & Oscar, N. (2001). Piccola-a small composition language. *Formal methods for distributed processing-a survey of object-oriented approaches*, (pp. 403-426).

Agha, G. A. (1986). *Actors: A model of concurrent computation in distributed systems*. Boston: MIT Press.

Bakre, S., & Elrad, T. (2007). Scenario based resolution of aspect interactions with aspect interaction charts. *Aspect-Oriented Modeling*.

Bhattacharyya, S., Cheong, E., Davis, J., Goel, M., Kienhuis, B., Hylands, C., et al. (2003). *Ptolemy II heterogeneous concurrency modeling and design in java*. Berkeley, CA: University of California Berkeley.

Budhiraja, N. (1993). *The primary-backup approach: Lower and upper bounds*. Ithaca, NY: Cornell University.

de Niz, D., Bhatia, G., & Rajkumar, R. (2006). Model-based development of embedded systems: The sysweaver approach. *IEEE Real-Time and Embedded Technology and Applications Symposium 2006*, San Jose, CA.

Griswold, W., Shonie, M., Sullivan, K., Song, Y., Tewari, N., & Cai, Y. (2006). Modular software design with crosscutting interfaces. *IEEE Software*, *23*(1), 51–60. doi:doi:10.1109/MS.2006.24

Heidenreich, F., Johannes, J., & Zschaler, S. (2007). Aspect orientation for your language of choice. *Aspect-Oriented Modeling*.

Hewitt, C. (1977). Viewing control structures as patterns of passing messages. Journal of Artificial Intelligence.

Iqbal, A., & Elrand, T. (2006). Modeling timing constraints of real-time systems as crosscutting concerns. *Aspect-Oriented Modeling Workshop*.

Isermann, R., Schwarz, R., & Stolzl, S. (2002). Faul-tolerant drive-by-wire systems. *Control Systems Magazine, IEEE*, 64-81.

Ivers, J., Sinha, N., & Walnau, K. (2002). *A basis for composition language CL*. Pittsburgh, PA: Software Engineering Institute-Carnegie Mellon University.

Klein, J., & Kienzle, J. (2007). Reusable aspect models. *Aspect-Oriented Modeling*.

Klein, M. H., Ralya, T., Pollak, B., & Obenza, R. (1993). *A practitioners' handbook for real-time analysis: Guide to rate monotonic analysis for real-time systems*. Pittsburgh, PA: Kluwer Academics Publishers.

Kopetz, H., & Bauer, G. (2003). The time-triggered architecture. *Proceedings of the IEEE*, *91*(1), 112–126. doi:10.1109/JPROC.2002.805821

Kruchten, P. (1995). Architectural blueprints-the "4+1" view model of software architecture. *IEEE Software*, *12*(6), 42–50. doi:doi:10.1109/52.469759

Ledeczi, A., Bakay, A., Maroti, M., Volgyesi, P., Nordstrom, G., & Sprinkle, J. (2001). Composing domain-specific design environments. *Computer*, *34*(11), 44–51. doi:10.1109/2.963443

Lieberherr, K. (1997). Demeter and aspect-oriented programming. *STJA*.

Liu, C., & Layland, J. (1973). Scheduling algorithms for multiprogramming in hard real-time environment. Journal of the ACM.

Magee, J., Dulay, N., & Kramer, J. (1993). Structuring parallel and distributed programs. *IEEE Software Engineering Journal*.

Mitola, J. I. (2002). *Software radio architecture*. Wiley InterScience.

Narashimhan, P. (1999). *Transparent fault-tolerance for CORBA.* Unpublished doctoral dissertation, Santa Barbara, CA: Electrical and Computer Engineering, University of California Santa Barbara.

Nierstrasz, O., Arevalo, G., Cucasse, S., Wuyts, R., Black, A., Muller, P., et al. (2002). A component model for field devices. *First International IFIP/ACM Working Conference on Component Deployment,* Berlin, Germany (LNCS).

OMG. (2006). *CORBA component model specification version 4.0.* Object Management Group.

OMG. (2008, January 23). *The official OMG MARTE Web site.* Retrieved on November 3, 2008, from www.omgmarte.org

Rajkumar, R., Gaglardi, M., & Sha, L. (1995). The real-time publisher/subscriber interprocess communication model for distributed real-time systems: Design and implementation. *Real-Time Technology and Application Symposium.* IEEE.

SAE. (2004). *Architecture analysis & design language (AADL).* SAE.

Stewart, D., Volpe, R., & Khosla, P. (1997). Design of dynamically reconfigurable real-time software using port-based objects. *IEEE Transactions on Software Engineering.*

Tolvanen, J., & Rossi, M. (2003). MetaEdit+: Defining and using domain-specific modeling languages and code generators. *Conference on Object Oriented Programming Systems Languages and Applications,* Anaheim, CA (pp. 92-93). ACM.

van Ommering, R., van der Linden, F., Kramer, J., & Magee, J. (2000). The koala component model for consumer electronics software. *Computer, 33*(3), 78–85.doi:doi:10.1109/2.825699

Wang, S., & Shin, K. (2000). An architecture for embedded software integration using reusable components. *International Conference on Compilers, Architecture, and Synthesis for Embedded Systems,* San Jose, CA.

# Section 3
# Verification & Model Checking

The third section tackles issues related with verification, a development activity that focuses on formally proving that the system implementation is in accordance with the respective specification. In particular, model-checking techniques for real-time embedded systems are addressed.

# Chapter 7
# Using Timed Automata for Modeling the Clocks of Distributed Embedded Systems

**Guillermo Rodríguez-Navas**
*Universitat de les Illes Balears, Spain*

**Julián Proenza**
*Universitat de les Illes Balears, Spain*

**Hans Hansson**
*Mälardalen University, Sweden*

**Paul Pettersson**
*Mälardalen University, Sweden*

## ABSTRACT

*Model checking is a widely used technique for the formal verification of computer systems. However, the suitability of model checking strongly depends on the capacity of the system designer to specify a model that captures the real behaviour of the system under verification. For the case of real-time systems, this means being able to realistically specify not only the functional aspects, but also the temporal behaviour of the system. This chapter is dedicated to modeling clocks in distributed embedded systems using the timed automata formalism. The different types of computer clocks that may be used in a distributed embedded system and their effects on the temporal behaviour of the system are introduced, together with a systematic presentation of how the behaviour of each kind of clock can be modeled. The modeling is particularized for the UPPAAL model checker, although it can be easily adapted to other model checkers based on the theory of timed automata.*

## INTRODUCTION

The importance of adopting formal verification techniques in order to assess the correctness of embedded systems is nowadays beyond discussion. Through the use of formal methods, an embedded system can be precisely and unambiguously specified, and the specification can go through a systematic analysis that indicates whether the system behaves according

DOI: 10.4018/978-1-60566-750-8.ch007

to its requirements or not. This facilitates the early detection of design errors, which could reduce the development costs, and also causes a significant increase in the level of confidence of the system (Baier & Katoen, 2008).

Among the existing formal verification techniques, this chapter primary concerns *model checking*. Model checking is an automated technique that, given a model of a system and a logical property (a requirement), systematically checks whether this property holds for that model. Moreover, whenever the system does not fulfill the property, model checking provides a counter example (in the form of a trace) which can be extremely useful in order to find flaws in the system design.

Model checking was introduced in the eighties (Clarke & Emerson, 1981; Queille & Sifakis, 1982; Clarke, Emerson & Sistla, 1986) and has since then gained wide acceptance. Many advances have been reported and, as a consequence, several model checking tools (also known as *model checkers*) have been made available. Nevertheless, the usefulness of model checking still depends on the ability of the system designer to realistically express the behaviour of the system under verification. In fact, in the literature about formal verification it is often pointed out that "model checking is only as good as the model to be checked" (Baier & Katoen, 2008).

For the model checking of real-time systems, *timed automata*, (Alur & Dill, 1994) is a well established and widely used formalism. A timed automaton is a finite-state machine extended with real-valued variables, called *clocks*. The main advantage of timed automata is that they incorporate a quantitative notion of time, which makes this technique especially suitable for those systems in which the requirements are characterized by quantitative timing properties, i.e. by time bounds. Note that this is the case for most embedded systems, since they usually have to fulfill real-time requirements that are specified in the form of periods, deadlines, etc.

Nevertheless, the mechanism for time representation in timed automata exhibits a particularity that is sometimes regarded as a limitation to the modeling: it assumes that all the clocks in a model increase at the same rate. In other words, it assumes that only one time base is available in the system. Although such an assumption can be suitable for modeling most single-processor embedded systems, in which actually only one computer clock exists, it is not acceptable for the modeling of many distributed embedded systems. In a distributed embedded system, each node usually works with its own computer clock, and since the computer clocks may not tick at exactly the same rate, the perception of time among the nodes is not consistent. Even when some kind of clock synchronization mechanism is used by the nodes, the drift of the computer clocks cannot be perfectly corrected and thus certain residual degree of inconsistency (the so-called *precision*) always persists among them.

Due to this, it might seem that the timed automata formalism is not suitable for modeling and verifying distributed embedded systems with such clocks. However, various modeling techniques can actually be used in order to circumvent this limitation and specify different time bases in the timed automata that compose a system model. Descriptions of these techniques can be found in the literature, but since they are scattered in different publications, for instance in (Alur, Torre & Madhusudan, 2005; Daws & Yovine, 1995; Rodriguez-Navas, Proenza & Hansson, 2006), it is unfortunately difficult to have a general perspective of what can be done, and how.

The aim of this document is to shed some light on this issue, by describing these modeling techniques in a more systematic way. We believe that such a description can be a valuable help for any system designer interested in using timed automata and model checking for formal verification. In our experience, the modeling of drifting computer clocks is one of the most challenging aspects when specifying a model with timed automata.

The descriptions of the techniques are particularized for the UPPAAL model checker, which is one of the most successful model checkers relying on the theory of timed automata (Larsen, Pettersson & Yi, 1997; Behrmann, David & Larsen, 2004). Nevertheless, they could be easily adapted to other model checkers, such as Kronos (Yovine, 1997), if required.

The chapter is divided into three sections. In Section 1 we introduce the main concepts of the UPPAAL model checker, including a brief review of the timed automata theory. Section 2 deals with the properties of the computer clocks used in distributed embedded systems, whereas Section 3 is devoted to discussing the different techniques that can be used for modeling such computer clocks. This discussion pays special attention to the specific temporal implications of the different modeling techniques.

## MODELLING WITH TIMED AUTOMATA

In this section we introduce the main concepts of the UPPAAL model checker (Larsen, Pettersson & Yi, 1997; Behrmann, David & Larsen, 2004), including a brief review of the timed automata theory (Alur and Dill, 1994).

### Timed Automata

The model of *timed automata* extends the model of finite-state automata with a finite collection of real-valued clocks (Alur & Dill, 1994). The clocks are assumed to proceed synchronously (i.e. at the same rate) and measure the time since they were last reset. Syntactically, the edges of timed automata are labeled with action names as in finite-state automata, but extended with clock constraints to test the clock values, and "reset sets" indicating the reset of clock values to zero. To model progress, each location is labeled with a local progress condition in the form of a clock

constraint, called a location invariant (Henzinger, Nicollin, Sifakis & Yovine, 1992).

As an example consider the timed automaton shown in Figure 1(a). It has two clocks, $x$ and $y$, two control locations $l_0$ and $l_1$, and an edge from control location $l_0$ to $l_1$ labeled with the guard $y \geq 1$, the action name $a$, and the reset set $\{x\}$. Location $l_0$ is labeled with the location invariant $x \leq 2$.

A *state* of a timed automaton is in the form $(l, v)$, where $l$ is a control location and $v$ is an assignment mapping clock variables to non-negative real numbers. The initial state is the pair $(l_0, v_0)$, where $l_0$ is the initial location of the timed automaton, and $v_0$ is the time assignment assigning 0 to all clock variables.

Consider again the timed automaton shown in Figure 1(a). Assuming that all of the clock variables are initially set to zero and that the initial control location is $l_0$, the automaton starts in the state $(l_0, \{x = y = 0\})$. As the clocks increase synchronously with time, it may evolve to all states of the form $(l_0, \{x = y = t\})$, where $t$ is a non-negative real number less than or equal to 2. At any state with $t \in [1,2]$ it may change to state $(l_1, \{x = 0, y = t\})$ by following the edge from $l_0$ to $l_1$, that resets $x$. The values of clocks $x$ and $y$ in two possible traces are illustrated in Figure 1(b). Note that the timed automaton may not idle forever in location $l_0$ since the location invariant $x \leq 2$ forces it to leave location $l_0$ within 2 time units.

More formally, the semantics of a timed automaton is defined as a transition system that can perform two types of transitions:

- *Discrete transitions*: $(l, v) \xrightarrow{a} (l', v')$ if there is an edge $l \xrightarrow{g, a, r} l'$ in the timed automaton, the clock assignment $v$ satisfies the guard $g$, and $v'$ is the result of resetting clocks $r$ in $v$.
- *Delay transitions*: $(l, v) \xrightarrow{t} (l, v')$ where $t$ is a non-negative real number, if $v'$ is the result of adding $t$ to all clocks in $v$, time assignment $v'$ satisfies the location

*Figure 1.(a) A timed automaton, and (b) The values of clocks x and y in two possible traces*

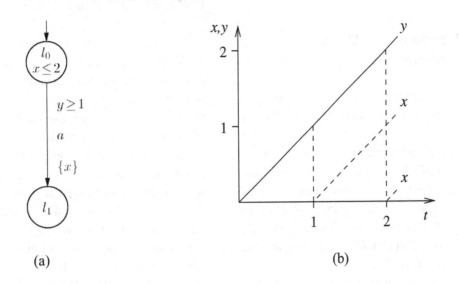

(a)  (b)

invariant of location $l$, and all delay $t'$ transitions with $0<t'<t$ are also possible.

A *network of timed automata* is the parallel composition $A_1|...|A_n$ of a finite collection $A_1,...,$ $A_n$ of timed automata for a given synchronization function $|$. The UPPAAL tool uses networks of timed automata composed with a CCS-like parallel composition operator (Milner, 1989). It allows for individual components to perform internal actions (i.e. interleaving), and for pairs of components to synchronize on actions.

To describe the notion of a network $\bar{A}$ of timed automata more formally, we define the state of a network as a pair $(\bar{l},v)$, where $\bar{l}$ is a location vector in $\bar{A}$ and $v$ is a clock valuation over all clocks in $\bar{A}$. We further define the set of actions over alphabet $\Sigma$ to be $\{ a! \mid a \in \Sigma \} \cup \{ a? \mid a \in \Sigma \} \cup \{ \tau \}$ where $\tau$ is a distinct silent action. The network can perform two types of transitions:

- *Discrete transitions*:
  ○ $(\bar{l},v) \xrightarrow{\ \tau\ } (\bar{l}\left[l'_i/l_i\right]',v')$ if there is an edge $l_i \xrightarrow{\ g,\tau,r\ } l_i'$ in a timed automaton $A_i$, the clock assignment

$v$ satisfies the guard $g$, and $v'$ is the result of resetting clocks $r$ in $v$.
  ○ $(\bar{l},v) \xrightarrow{\ a\ } (\bar{l}\left[l'_i/l_i,l'_j/lj\right]',v')$
    if $i \neq j$, there are edges $l_i \xrightarrow{\ g_i,a!,r_i\ } l_i'$ and $l_j \xrightarrow{\ g_j,a?,r_j\ } l_j'$ in the timed automaton $A_i$ and $A_j$, respectively, the clock assignment $v$ satisfies the guard $g_i \wedge g_j$, and $v'$ is the result of resetting clocks $r_i \cup r_j$ in $v$.
- *delay transitions*: $(\bar{l},v) \xrightarrow{\ t\ } (\bar{l},v')$ where $t$ is a non-negative real number, if $v'$ is the result of adding $t$ to all clocks in $v$, time assignment $v'$ satisfies the location invariant of all locations in $\bar{l}$, and all delay $t'$ transitions with $0<t'<t$ are also possible.

The first rule describes that an individual automaton can perform a $\tau$-transition if there is an enabled edge labeled with action $\tau$. The second rule describes how two automata in the network can synchronize if they have enabled edges with complementary synchronization actions, e.g. $a!$ and $a?$. The delay transition in the third rule is possible as long as the conjunction of the location invariants of all automata in the network is satisfied.

## UPPAAL Extensions Used in the Modeling

The modeling language of the UPPAAL tool features a number of extensions. In this chapter we shall make use of (global) bounded integer variables, committed locations, and broadcast synchronization. *Bounded integer variables* are simply data variables declared with bounded domains that can be assigned integer values in their domain. UPPAAL supports integer arithmetic expressions over data variables, constants, and the arithmetic operators +, -, *, and /.

*Committed locations* are used to model atomic behaviours in UPPAAL by declaring a subset of the locations of an automaton as *committed* (denoted © or with prefix c:). If in a state ($\bar{l}$,$v$) some locations $l_i \in \bar{l}$ is committed, then the next transition of the network must be a discrete transition involving automaton $A_i$, otherwise the network is deadlocked. It is not possible to delay in a committed location. The notion of committed locations is defined formally and described in detail in (Bengtsson *et al.*, 2002).

*Broadcast synchronization* has been introduced in UPPAAL to extend the pair-wise synchronization described in Section 1.1. The broadcasting synchronization involves one sender performing an action transition labeled *c!*, where c $\in \Sigma$, and an arbitrary number of receivers performing complementary action transition *c?*. Any automaton (except the sender) that has an enabled transition labeled *c?* must take part in the broadcast synchronization. The number of receivers can be zero or more, hence, the sender can execute the *c!* action transition even if there are no receiving automata.

## CLOCKS IN EMBEDDED SYSTEMS: PROPERTIES AND USES

In the previous section, we have seen that the theory of timed automata includes the notion of clock as a very useful mechanism to model the progress of time. The question we address hereafter is: does this notion of clock correspond to the notion of clock that we have in an embedded system? Or in other words, can the computer clocks used for designing embedded systems be directly modeled with the clocks of a timed automaton?

Answering this question is not straightforward. First of all, there are several definitions of what a computer clock is. In any computer system, there are several things that can be called a "clock". Does it refer to the local oscillator of the system? Does it refer to the register used for counting cycles of the local oscillator? Should a timer be considered a clock? Also, in a distributed embedded system in which every node uses a different clock, which one should be considered the system clock? In our opinion, this confusion on the terminology is one of the aspects that cause difficulties when modeling distributed embedded systems with timed automata.

The purpose of this section is to establish the basic terminology on clocks. We first present the various types of clocks that can be found in a computer system, and discuss the properties they exhibit. Then, the ways in which these clocks are used by system designers are also discussed. The techniques for modeling such clocks and their properties with timed automata will be discussed in Section 3.

### The Ideal Clock

The function of any clock is to measure time. Therefore, prior to any discussion on clocks, we should establish what *time* is, or more properly speaking, what model of time we will consider.

In this document we assume the Newtonian concept of time, as is usually done for computer systems. I.e., time is considered an external and continuous dimension that is perceived equally everywhere. This notion of time, which is often referred to as *real time,* can be represented by the set of positive real numbers. Any time instant belonging to this external dimension is usually denoted with the letter *t*.

An *ideal clock* is the clock that always reflects the value of real time. This clock does not have physical existence, and can be considered only theoretically.

## The Physical Clock

In order to physically measure real time, computers rely on devices that exhibit a regular behaviour over time: the local oscillators. A local oscillator is an electronic device that makes use of piezoelectric material, such as a quartz crystal or a ceramic resonator, to provide a periodic electrical signal of very precise frequency.

Every pulse of the local oscillator is called a *microtick*. Given that the nominal frequency of the local oscillator is known a priori, measuring time would be equivalent to counting microticks. However, since the frequency of the local oscillators is too high for what needs to be measured, the local oscillator is usually connected to a frequency divider and the output of the frequency divider is connected to a counter. The value of this counter is the value of the *physical clock*, and each pulse of the frequency divider's output is called a *tick* of the physical clock.

At a given time instant *t*, the value of the physical clock is denoted as $C(t)$. Note that the value of $C(t)$ increases in discrete steps (tick by tick), but it can be satisfactorily approximated with a linear function of rate $C'(t) = dC(t)/dt$.

Due to factors such as manufacturing imperfections, aging, temperature changes or variations of the power supply, local oscillators inevitably deviate from their nominal frequency. Therefore, the rate of a physical clock actually corresponds to $C'(t) = 1 + \rho(t)$, where $\rho(t)$ is called the *drift* of the physical clock. The absolute value of the drift of a non-faulty physical clock is always bounded by a value known as the *maximum drift*, which is denoted as $\rho_{max}$. The value of $\rho_{max}$ is usually in the order of $10^{-4}$ to $10^{-6}$.

In a distributed embedded system, every node is provided with its own physical clock to measure time locally. But, since each physical clock exhibits an individual and different drift, their values tend to diverge, even if they had the same value initially. Due to this, the physical clocks by themselves cannot guarantee that the nodes of the system share a common perception of real time.

## The Global Clock

Some distributed embedded systems are built upon the assumption that all the nodes have access to a time reference which is perceived equally everywhere within the system. The clock that provides the value of this absolute time reference is called the *global clock.*

An important characteristic of the global clock is that it does not map real time perfectly, but may deviate from real time. Moreover, the global clock may have physical existence or not. It does exist physically when the global clock is chosen among the available physical clocks in the system. This is the case, for instance, in the master/slave approach for clock synchronization. In that approach, one of the physical clocks (usually the one with the best-quality local oscillator) becomes the global clock, or *master*, and the other physical clocks become *slaves* and try to follow the master's clock as close as possible.

In contrast, the global clock does not exist physically when it is defined as a function of the values of a number of physical clocks. For instance, for certain time instant *t*, the value of the global clock $GC(t)$ may be calculated by averaging the values of four physical clocks as follows

$$GC(t) = [C_1(t) + C_2(t) + C_3(t) + C_4(t)]/4.$$

The specific function that is used for calculating the value of the global clock is called the *convergence function*. Several convergence functions have been proposed in the literature –for instance, see (Schneider, 1987; Anceaume & Puaut, 1997) –, but discussing them is out of the scope of this chapter. Note that the rate of the global clock may be obtained in an analogous way, for instance by averaging the rates of a number of physical clocks.

## The Virtual Clock

The main advantage of using a global clock in a distributed system is that the nodes can all rely on this common reference in order to coordinate their operations. Nevertheless, it is important to remark that this approach works only if every node is able to estimate the value of the global clock very closely. For example, a TDMA scheme for communication is useful only as long as the nodes approximately agree on the beginning and the end of every transmission window. Otherwise, the transmission windows would not be respected, and collisions that make communication impossible could occur.

As already indicated, the physical clocks by themselves cannot be used to approximate the value of the global clock, because their different drifts make them diverge as time passes by. To solve this problem, every node must periodically execute a procedure to estimate its deviation with respect to the global clock and correct it. This procedure is called the *clock synchronization algorithm*. The clock that node *i* obtains after applying the clock synchronization algorithm on its physical clock is called the *virtual clock of node i*, and is denoted as $VC_i(t)$.

The clock synchronization algorithm is executed in three steps by each node (Anceaume & Puaut, 1997):

- Detection of the periodical synchronization instant.

- Estimation of the value of the global clock at that time instant, and therefore of the error between the virtual clock and the global clock.
- Correction of the error of the virtual clock.

The result of applying a clock synchronization algorithm is the fulfilment of the property known as *internal clock synchronization*, which is stated as follows. For any time instant *t*, the absolute value of the difference between any pair of non-faulty virtual clocks may not differ more than a given amount Π, which is called the *precision*. Therefore, $|VC_i(t) - VC_j(t)| \leq \Pi$ for any time instant *t*, and any pair of nodes *i, j*.

## Clocks and the Paradigms for the Design of Distributed Embedded Systems

In the previous subsections, the different types of clocks that can be found in a distributed embedded system have been presented and discussed. Table 1 summarizes the properties of such clocks. In order to build the formal model of a distributed embedded system it is important to understand not only what kind of clocks the system uses, but also how they are used. Next, we describe how system programmers use these clocks for the design of distributed embedded systems.

As indicated in (Veríssimo, 1997), distributed systems (embedded or not) can be divided into two groups, according to the way in which clocks are used by the nodes. The systems belonging to the first group are called *timer-driven* systems, whereas the systems belonging to the second group are called *clock-driven* systems.

In a timer-driven system, it is assumed that the clock of every node is independent of the clocks of the rest of the nodes. This corresponds to having only physical clocks. In this kind of systems, each node can only measure durations that are relative to its own physical clock.

The main disadvantage of a timer-driven sys-

*Table 1. Clock types and their properties*

| Clock name | Other names | What it measures | Exists physically |
|---|---|---|---|
| Ideal clock | Newtonian clock, Perfect clock | The external and continuous dimension we call *real time*. | No, it is a theoretical construction. |
| Physical clock | Hardware clock | It counts ticks of a local oscillator, attempting to approximate the value of the ideal clock. | Yes. It consists of a local oscillator, a frequency divider and a counter. |
| Global clock | Absolute clock, Reference clock, System-wide clock | An absolute reference time, common to all nodes. | It may exist physically or not. |
| Virtual clock | Logical clock, Synchronized clock | It approximates the value of the global clock. | Yes. It is a physical clock, plus a mechanism for clock correction. |

tem is that, due to the lack of an absolute reference time, timestamps do not give any information about the order of events if such events have happened in different nodes, and thus the timestamps have been taken with different physical clocks. Moreover, it is not possible to measure the duration of actions that start at one node and finish at another one, i.e., actions that are distributed. In order to achieve some level of coordination among a subset of nodes, timer-driven systems usually rely on using local timers that are set by the nodes upon the occurrence of a given event, such as the transmission or reception of certain messages, that may be detected by the nodes of the subset.

In contrast, clock-driven systems assume the existence of a global clock that represents an absolute reference time for the nodes, and every node is supposed to have a virtual clock that approximates the value of the global clock with certain precision $\Pi$. Thanks to this, any timestamp taken by one node can be used by the rest of the nodes for determining the order of events happening in different nodes[1], or to measure the duration of distributed actions.

Moreover, the existence of a global clock allows the nodes to consistently schedule tasks at predefined instants of time. These time instants are indicated by means of *time marks,* which are just clock values internally used by the nodes to decide when to perform a given task. For instance,

let us assume a distributed system that requires each individual node to perform a certain periodic task, with period T, and also requires that all of the nodes agree on the time to perform said tasks. In the clock-driven paradigm, this can be implemented by having each node *i* to trigger the task when $VC_i(t) = kT$, where k is a natural number that indicates the round number. Therefore, the values T, 2T, 3T, etc. would be the internal time marks used by the nodes. Since the virtual clocks are synchronized, this mechanism guarantees temporal consistency among the nodes: they would all trigger the tasks at approximately the same instants. However, perfect simultaneity cannot be achieved because of the limited precision of the clock synchronization algorithm.

Clock-driven systems may also use timers in the same way as the timer-driven systems use them, although the timers will be defined over the virtual clocks and not over the physical clocks.

## Common Challenges when Modeling Computer Clocks

In the programming of distributed embedded systems, the term *local clock* has been coined to refer to the clock that each node uses for its own computations. Unfortunately, such a term gives little information about the properties of the clock itself, and does not indicate whether the system is timer-driven or clock-driven.

For instance, in some distributed embedded systems, the term local clock is used to indicate that the node does not have any access to a global clock. In such a case, the local clock would correspond to what we described as a physical clock and the system would be timer-driven. In other occasions, however, the term local clock refers to the *local view* that one node has of the global clock. In this case, the local clock would be what we called a virtual clock, and the system would be clock-driven.

This ambiguity in the definition of the local clock is mainly caused by the fact that, from the programmer's perspective, it is very good that the details of the clock synchronization algorithm remain hidden. In fact, in a well-designed software architecture, the clock synchronization service should be transparent to the application. Nevertheless, when it comes to modeling a distributed embedded system for formal verification, such an ambiguity may constitute a problem.

To give just an example, the POSIX standard states in (IEEE, 2004) that a Timer is *"a mechanism that can notify a thread when the time as measured by a particular clock has reached or passed a specified value, or when a specified amount of time has passed."* Note that this definition does not take into account whether this *particular clock* is synchronized or not with the other clocks of the system, so it can be applied both to a physical clock and to a virtual clock.

However, let us consider the node of a distributed embedded system executing a specific algorithm that requires the use of timers as defined by the POSIX standard. Would the formal model of the node remain unchanged if the node uses the timers with a (synchronized) virtual clock instead of an (unsynchronized) physical clock? Note that, regardless of the type of clock used, the algorithm would not change at all, and then the application code might not change either. However, the key point is that the use of different clocks does change the underlying assumptions of the system, and

therefore the formal model should be different in each case. To formally verify a real-time system, it is fundamental that the model captures the actual temporal behaviour of the system, and therefore a change of the clock properties will usually cause a change of the model.

System designers are frequently not aware of these subtleties in the specification of their formal models. And when they are, the difficulty of expressing the desired temporal behaviour with the timed automata formalism sometimes discourages them from attempting such a formal verification. For this reason, many systems are verified only under the assumption that the drift of the computer clocks is negligible. Other realistic assumptions, such as having clocks of bounded drift or having clocks of variable drift are seldom considered.

We believe that this problem could be diminished if the system designers had better knowledge of the techniques available for specifying any kind of computer clock. But this firstly requires a clear and systematic description of these techniques. In next section we carry out such a description, paying special attention to the temporal implications of each modeling technique.

## MODELLING COMPUTER CLOCKS WITH UPPAAL

For the sake of clarity, in this section we restrict ourselves to the modeling of the temporal properties of a system, without considering other functional aspects. This aim is fulfilled through the study of the so-called UPPAAL timers, which are very useful artefacts to represent the temporal properties of any computer system.

The idea of using timers for this purpose is borrowed from the UPPAAL tutorial in (Behrmann, David & Larsen, 2004). In that tutorial, the characteristics of a basic timer are specified for the UPPAAL language, although only for the case of an ideal clock. We use the same definition

*Figure 2. Temporal behaviour of an ideal timer*

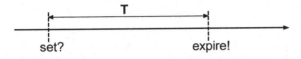

*Figure 3. Timed automata modeling an ideal timer*

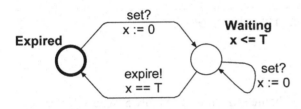

of timer, with some slight changes, and extend it in order to embrace all the types of clocks that were discussed in Section 2.

## Modeling Ideal Timers with UPPAAL

As indicated in (Behrmann, David & Larsen, 2004) a timer in UPPAAL is defined basically as a process that measures some time duration, with respect to a certain UPPAAL clock, and signals the instant when that duration has elapsed. The operation of a timer is simple: at a given time instant it is reset and counts up until it reaches a predetermined value. At that moment, the timer is said to have expired and generates a timeout notification. In principle, timers can be reset at any time instant.

The operation of a timer can thus be modeled with two primitives: set(T) and expire(), where T is the predetermined duration of the timer. The expected temporal behaviour of such a timer is depicted in Figure 2, and the timed automaton that is used for specifying this behaviour is shown in Figure 3. This timed automaton is defined with two locations (Expired and Waiting) and one clock (x). Moreover, it uses a global variable T, which may be written by other processes in order to indicate the duration of the timer.

The automaton starts initially in the location Expired, in which the timer is not set. The transition to the location Waiting may be fired at any instant through the synchronization channel set. Note that in this transition the value of the clock x is set to zero. After that, and due to the invariant and the guard defined over clock x, the automaton remains in the location Waiting for exactly T time units, provided that the synchronization channel set is not activated again. As soon as clock x reaches the value of T, the transition to Expired is fired and is signalled through the channel expire. Notice that while being in location Waiting, the timer can be reset again through channel set.

To illustrate the use of the proposed timer in the modeling of a system, let us consider an application that periodically executes a certain task. This application is specified with the timed automaton of Figure 4.

The execution of the automaton depicted in Figure 4 in parallel with the timed automaton of Figure 3 would result in the following behaviour.

*Figure 4. Example of an application executing a periodic task*

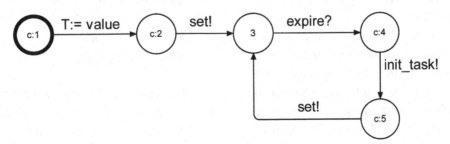

*Figure 5. Scheme of the model of a set of nodes executing periodic tasks*

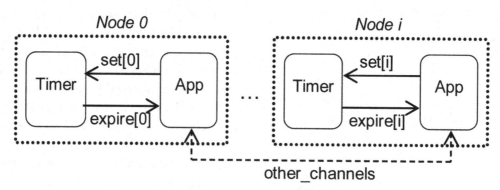

The initial location (location 1) is committed and thus it is left as soon as the automaton is initiated. In the edge to location 2, the value of the global variable T is overwritten with the value of the local variable value, which serves to set the duration of the timer. After that, the application immediately sets the timer through channel set (location 2 is also committed) and steps into location 3. Then, the system remains in location 3 until the timer expires, which causes the immediate execution of the task.

The details of the executed task are irrelevant for the model and are not discussed. The task is simply abstracted away with the synchronization channel init_task, which is signalled in the transition from location 4 to location 5. We assume that this signalling will trigger the required actions somewhere else in the model.

Note that location 4 and location 5 are both committed. This means that the timer is set again with no delay, when the transition to location 3 is taken. In this way, this automaton enforces a periodic behaviour for the system: init_task is signalled every T time units.

This modeling technique can be easily adapted for the case of a distributed embedded system made up of several nodes that execute periodic tasks. It would require two timed automata for every node of the system, one to model the timer and one to model the application. The resulting

scheme is depicted in Figure 5, where Timer represents an automaton such as the one of Figure 3 and App represents an automaton such as the one of Figure 4. Note that each node *i* requires two channels (set[i] and expire[i]) to make the interaction between App and Timer possible. As indicated in the figure, other channels might be used to specify any kind of communication among the applications.

Nevertheless, the modeling of the temporal behaviour of nodes with ideal timers, like the one described in Figure 3, has important limitations. In particular, this timer does not take into consideration the potential deviation that may exist among the computer clocks used by the nodes. Instead, all the nodes would be in perfect synchrony, without suffering any drift. For this reason, using this kind of timer always implies one of the following assumptions:

1)  The system is timer-driven and the drifts of the physical clocks with respect to the ideal clock are negligible, or
2)  The system is clock-driven and the drifts of the virtual clocks with respect to the global clock are negligible.

In order to specify systems that do not fulfill these assumptions, we need to use more sophisticated modeling techniques than the one just presented. They are to be described in the next subsections.

## Modeling Timers of Bounded Drift with UPPAAL

By definition, all the clocks of a timed automaton evolve at the same rate. Any automaton not fulfilling this property is not a timed automaton and, in principle, would not be verifiable with a model checker like UPPAAL. However, as discussed next, the perturbed timed automata formalism provides a way to circumvent this limitation.

## Perturbed Timed Automata

In the paper by (Alur, Torre & Madhusudan, 2005) it is shown that any automaton whose clocks have bounded rates can be translated into an equivalent timed automaton, as long as the bounds are constant and known a priori. The obtained timed automaton would then be verifiable. An automaton fulfilling these restrictions on the clocks' rates is called a *perturbed timed automata* (Alur, Torre, Madhusudan, 2005).

The rationale behind the translation from perturbed timed automata to timed automata is that having a clock of bounded rate is equivalent to having an ideal clock and defining the occurrence instants as time intervals whose lengths depend on the rate boundaries. Therefore, to obtain a timed automaton, the modeler must place the uncertainty of the clock rate into the guards and invariants.

*Figure 6. Temporal behaviour of a timer defined over a drifting physical clock*

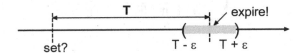

This is better explained with an example. Let us consider a timer defined over a physical clock that ticks with a rate that lies within the range $[1 - \rho_{max}, 1 + \rho_{max}]$ (note that this is consistent with the definition of physical clock given in Section 2.2). Assuming that the timer counts T time units, the effect of the physical clock's drift would be that the timer would expire after $\Delta$ time units, with $T/(1 + \rho_{max}) \leq \Delta \leq T/(1 - \rho_{max})$. Therefore, the expiration instant would actually happen within a time interval $[T-\varepsilon, T+\varepsilon]$ after the timer has been set, with $\varepsilon = \rho_{max} T$. This temporal behaviour is depicted in Figure 6. In this figure, the grey area indicates the time interval in which the timer expiration may be signaled. The expiration may only occur once within the interval.

The timed automaton that models this kind of behaviour is shown in Figure 7. Notice that it is similar to the timer of Figure 3, but in this case, clock x is not compared to the same value in the guard and in the invariant of location Waiting. In this way, if the application that sets the timer makes T_min:= T-ε and T_max:= T+ ε then the behaviour would be as indicated in Figure 6.

A significant advantage of this approach is that the states generated during the model checking

*Figure 7. A timed automaton that models a drifting timer*

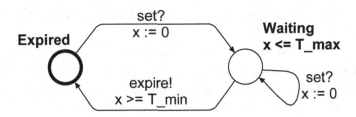

*Figure 8. Timer-driven application executed by node i*

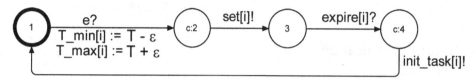

process would take into account the effect of *all* possible rates in the range $[1 - \rho_{max}, 1 + \rho_{max}]$. Therefore, the results are not only valid for one specific clock rate, but for the whole range of possible rates.

The notion of perturbed timed automata is very useful to specify a system with computer clocks, since it may be applied to a physical clock that drifts from real time as well as to a virtual clock that drifts from the global clock. This is discussed in the following two examples.

## Example 1: A Timer-Driven System with Drifting Physical Clocks

Let us assume a timer-driven system made up of N nodes, each one having a physical clock with different drift from real time. Let us also assume that upon detection of a certain common event, each node sets a timer to measure T time units and that, once the timer expires, the corresponding node performs some kind of task. In order to simplify the model, we will assume that the common event is simultaneously detected by all the nodes, but the same technique can be applied in the (more realistic) case in which the event is detected with different latency by each node.

To model the behaviour of this system, it is possible to use the scheme shown in Figure 5, although the automata Timer and App of every node should be changed. First of all, the automaton Timer should be a timer like the one of Figure 7, which models the effect of bounded drift. Second, the automaton App should be like the one depicted in Figure 8. Note that this automaton assumes that there is a broadcast channel e to signal the occurrence of the common event (channel e would be

one of the *other channels* appearing in Figure 5). The behaviour of the automaton is very simple: it starts in location 1; as soon as the event is signaled through channel e, the automaton overwrites the boundaries of its timer (namely T_min[i] and T_max[i]) and steps into location 2. Location 2 is committed, so it is left immediately, setting the local timer through channel set[i]. The automaton waits in location 3 until the expiration of the timer is signaled with expire[i]. After that, the task is initiated with init_task[i] and the automaton goes back to the first location.

Since we have supposed that the event is detected simultaneously by all the nodes, the setting of the timers is simultaneous as well. In contrast, the expiration may not be simultaneous because of the individual drift of each timer (ε is a local variable of each automaton App). Therefore, the temporal behaviour exhibited by these nodes would correspond to the one in Figure 9. Notice that the model allows the nodes to initiate their tasks at different time instants, yet all around T time units after the event occurrence, which is exactly what we were interested in modeling.

This example shows that the notion of perturbed timed automata may be useful to realistically model timer-driven systems with drifting physical clocks.

## Example 2: A Clock-Driven System with Drifting Virtual Clocks

In Section 2.5 it was explained that clock-driven systems may work either with timers, in exactly the same way as timer-driven systems do, or with time marks. When using timers, the modeling techniques that were adopted for the previous

*Figure 9. Temporal behaviour of three nodes with drifting physical clocks, when using timers that are set by a simultaneous event*

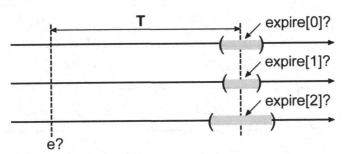

example are also applicable. The only difference would be that the individual deviation of each automaton App (the local variable $\varepsilon$) should be calculated with respect to the global clock, and not with respect to the real time.

Due to this, this second example will only discuss the modeling of clock-driven systems that work with time marks. It will be shown that the notion of perturbed time automata can also be applied to this kind of systems, although the modeling becomes a little bit more complex than in the previous example.

An important characteristic of these clock-driven systems is that the nodes do not use any timer internally. The virtual clock of each node keeps running indefinitely and as soon as a time mark is reached, the node performs the corresponding action and recalculates (or obtains in an equivalent way) the next time mark to wait for. There is no need to reset the virtual clocks.

Nevertheless, in a model made up of timed automata it is not possible to have clocks increasing indefinitely together with an infinite number of time marks that are to be compared with the clock values. This would make the state-space of the system blow up, and would make model checking unfeasible. Due to this, the modeler has to specify the operation of the system on the basis of rounds, with clocks that are reset in every round. However, this round-based modeling must guarantee that, although the clocks are not

allowed to increase indefinitely, the evolution of the system model still satisfies the expected temporal behavior.

The round-based modeling of a clock-driven system can be performed with the UPPAAL timers described so far. Nevertheless, it is important to understand that the timers used in the model do not actually exist in the system; they are just a "modeling trick" to specify the evolution of the nodes over time. This is different from the case discussed in Example 1, in which the timers really existed as components of the system to be modeled.

To illustrate our modeling, we consider here the distributed system described in Section 2.5., in which each node $i$ is assumed to trigger a periodic task whenever $VC_i(t) = kT$. Figure 10 shows the expected behaviour of the nodes of such system. Each timeline corresponds to the behaviour of a node with respect to the global clock. The grey areas depict the time intervals in which the tasks are triggered by the corresponding nodes (only one task is triggered in each time interval). For simplicity, in this example we have assumed that the global clock is provided by node 0. Due to this, the virtual clock of node 0 does not drift with respect to itself, which means that (as shown in the first timeline) this node executes the task with a period of exactly T time units. The other nodes, which have drifting virtual clocks, may execute their tasks a little earlier or a little later than node

*Figure 10. Temporal behaviour of three clock-driven nodes, when driven by the first node's virtual clock*

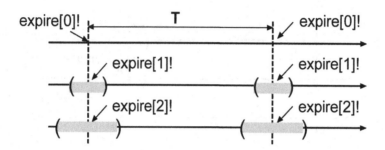

0. Thanks to the clock synchronization algorithm, the imprecision is kept low and, moreover, the imprecision of one round is not accumulated for the next rounds.

As in the previous models, the way to specify this system behaviour will require the use of an UPPAAL timer for each node. Since the expiration of these timers will trigger the execution of the tasks, the model must enforce the expiration of each timer within the allowed time intervals, which correspond to the grey areas of Figure 10. This is highlighted in Figure 10 with the arrows that indicate when the channel expirations must happen (labeled with expire[i]!).

At first sight, this behaviour could be specified with a scheme similar to the one used for the periodic application discussed in Section 3.1. In principle, the scheme depicted in Figure 5 could be applied, although with some changes. Since

the main difference concerns the fact that one of the timers is the global clock, and thus dictates the passage of time, we have to define some kind of mechanism to model the synchronization with respect to this global clock. An easy way to do it is by having only one broadcast channel (named set) to set all the timers simultaneously. This would slightly change the automaton App of the nodes, which would turn into the automaton of Figure 11.

Apparently, the automaton of Figure 11 is very similar to the periodic application with ideal timers discussed in Section 3.1 (see Figure 4), but there are four aspects that merit special attention. Firstly, for the node that keeps the global clock, the value of the local variable ε is 0, whereas for the rest of virtual clocks it must be calculated according to the assumed bounds on the drift with respect to the global clock. Secondly, only the

*Figure 11. Example of an application executing a periodical task, triggered by a drifting virtual clock*

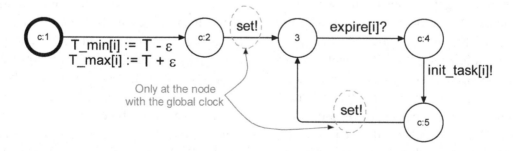

*Figure 12. The automaton App, without the previous flaw, assuming drifting virtual clocks*

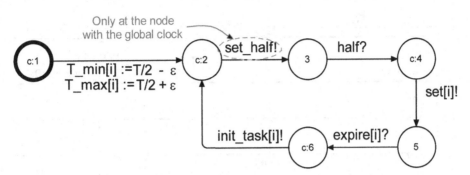

node keeping the global clock should include the synchronization through channel set that appears in the transition from location 2 to location 3 and in the transition from location 5 to location 3. The other nodes will have an unconditional transition instead. Given that set is defined as a broadcast channel and every automaton Timer is waiting for this signal, this synchronization will cause all the other timers to be reset as well. Thirdly, the expiration of the timers is still individual, and therefore each node $i$ waits for the expiration of its timer, signaled through expire[i], to trigger its task. Fourthly, this model does not guarantee that all timers will expire in every round, because the expiration of the global clock's timer may occur while some of the other timers are still in location Waiting (see Figure 7) and then the expiration of those timers would not be signalled.

In fact, the last aspect should be considered a flaw of the model, since it makes the model not correspond to the real behaviour of the system, shown in Figure 10, and has to be corrected. The technique that eliminates this flaw requires the addition of one more timer and one more broadcast channel to the model. The function of this additional timer, which is to be handled by the node keeping the global clock, is to delay the reset of the other timers, so that no expiration is prevented. Due to this, the duration of this timer must be greater than the maximum delay caused by the drift of the virtual clocks ($\varepsilon$). In the following,

and without losing generality, we assume that the duration of this timer is half of the period: T/2. For this reason, this timer will be called Half timer hereafter. The Half timer is set through channel set_half and signals the expiration through the broadcast channel half.

The Half timer will not drift with respect to the global clock and will be implemented as the ideal timer discussed in Section 3.1. The way in which the Half timer is used by the nodes can be observed in the new automaton App, which is depicted in Figure 12. As indicated in the figure, only the node keeping the global clock will set the Half timer when taking the transition from location 2 to location 3. In contrast, every automaton App waits for the expiration of the Half timer. Once the expiration is signalled, the automaton steps into location 4 and immediately sets its own individual timer (through set[i]) in the transition to location 5. As soon as the individual timer expires, the automaton goes to location 6, signals the execution of the task, steps into location 2 and then immediately goes to location 3, where it waits again for the expiration of the Half timer.

Notice that initially, in the transition from location 1 to location 2, the local timers are now set to measure just T/2 time units, since the first T/2 shall been counted by the Half timer. However, the value of $\varepsilon$ remains unchanged, as it accounts for the imprecision caused by the drift during the whole period (T). The resulting temporal

*Figure 13. Temporal behaviour enforced by the addition of the Half timer*

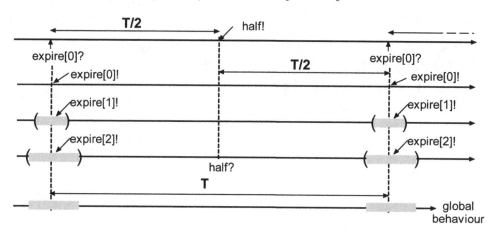

behaviour appears in Figure 13 for the case of three nodes, assuming that node 0 provides the global clock.

The first timeline of Figure 13 shows the behaviour of the Half timer. This timer is set whenever expire[0]? is signalled, and has a duration of T/2 time units. Since this timer does not drift with respect to the global clock, the notification through half is generated after exactly T/2 time units.

The following three timelines correspond to the individual timers of the three nodes considered. As discussed above, every timer is set upon expiration of the Half timer, which is signalled through the broadcast channel half, and measures T/2 time units. Note that the expiration instants of the individual timers vary according to their drifts with respect to the global clock, and that the imprecision of one round is not accumulated for the next round.

The global behaviour of the system is shown in the bottom timeline, in which we can observe that all the nodes initiate their tasks with a period of T time units, but with a certain imprecision (except for the node 0) caused by the drift of each virtual clock. This is exactly the expected behaviour presented in Figure 10.

It is important to remark that up to this point we have assumed that the global clock had physical existence, and corresponded to the virtual clock of one of the nodes in the system. Therefore, we have implicitly assumed that the nodes execute some kind of master/slave clock synchronization. Nevertheless, the discussed scheme for synchronizing the timers of the virtual clocks is also valid for the case in which the global clock does not exist physically. In such a case, the global clock must be specified by means of an additional node, which would include a *dummy* automaton app that does not initiate any task, but only resets the timers after every expiration.

## Modeling Timers of Variable Drift with UPPAAL: The Case of Clock Synchronization

In section 3.2 we showed that the notion of perturbed timed automata is very useful to realistically specify the temporal behaviour of a system with drifting physical clocks or drifting virtual clocks. Nevertheless, this formalism also exhibits some limitations. The main limitation of the perturbed timed automata is that they require the system designer to know the bounds of the clock rates in advance. Due to this, they do not work properly if the rates of some virtual clocks depend on the rates of other virtual clocks, and

*Figure 14. The new App automaton, assuming drifting virtual clocks and potentially inconsistent clock synchronizations*

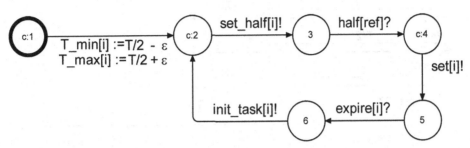

change dynamically.

Fortunately, system designers may usually know in advance the expected drift of the computer clocks they use, and then this limitation is not a problem for verifying a wide range of distributed embedded systems. However, this limitation turns out to be particularly cumbersome when trying to model and verify clock synchronization algorithms. When modeling a clock synchronization algorithm, it is important that the bounds on the clock rates may change dynamically, as a consequence of the actions performed by the algorithm. Otherwise, the model would not reflect the real operation of the nodes.

This problem was encountered during the formal verification of OCS-CAN (the *Orthogonal Clock Subsystem for the Controller Area Network*). OCS-CAN is a master/slave solution for clock synchronization over CAN networks, which is described in (Rodriguez-Navas, Roca & Proenza, 2008). OCS-CAN achieves tolerance to faults of the master through the use of master redundancy: in every synchronization round, a number of backup masters try to become the active master by sending a synchronization message called the Time Message (TM). In this way, whenever the active master fails and does not send its TM, one of the backup masters takes over.

In the absence of channel errors, it is guaranteed that all the nodes of OCS-CAN receive the same TM in every synchronization round and thus agree on which the active master is. Therefore, all the

virtual clocks would follow the same global clock. However, when considering channel errors, some specific scenarios appear in which the reception of the TM might be inconsistent (Rodriguez-Navas, Roca & Proenza, 2008). This undesirable situation makes it possible that different slaves follow different masters, which in practice implies that various virtual clocks may not follow the same global clock.

In (Rodriguez-Navas, Proenza & Hansson, 2006) it is discussed how to model the effect of such inconsistent clock synchronizations in OCS-CAN, and is showed how to measure the impact that these inconsistencies may have on the precision of the clock synchronization algorithm. We will here discuss the techniques that were developed to model virtual clocks with variable drift for the formal verification of OCS-CAN. Again, we do not show the complete model, but we only focus on the techniques that enforce the expected temporal behaviour.

The techniques developed are based on the scheme for modeling drifting virtual clocks described in the Example 2 of Section 3.2, but the model is extended in order to allow the nodes to have different global clocks. This is done by having one Half timer for each node in the system, instead of only one for the whole system. Therefore, in the model each node includes two timers plus the automaton App to handle them. The new behaviour of the automaton App is shown in Figure 14.

Before describing the new automaton it is im-

*Figure 15. Temporal behaviour of three nodes after a consistent synchronization round.*

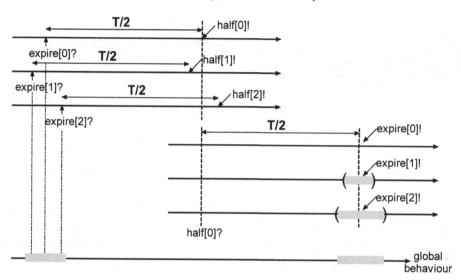

portant to remark that each automaton App keeps in a local variable, named ref, the identifier of the node to which it has synchronized in the previous round. A synchronization round is said to be *consistent* if all the nodes agree on the value of ref, whereas it is said to be *inconsistent* if at least two nodes disagree on the value of ref. The way to obtain the value of ref is irrelevant at this point and will not be explained, but it is related to the reception of the message TM mentioned above. Inconsistent synchronization rounds are always caused by channel errors that lead to inconsistent omissions of the TM (Rodriguez-Navas, Roca & Proenza, 2008).

The new automaton App, depicted in Figure 14, exhibits only two differences compared to the automaton of Figure 12: (1) every automaton App sets its own Half timer in the transition from location 2 to location 3, as indicated by the synchronization set_half[i]!, and (2) the automaton waits in location 3 until the expiration of the Half timer of the node to which the node has synchronized. This is signalled with the synchronization half[ref]?. Since more than one node may be waiting for the expiration, each channel half[i] has to be a broad-

cast channel. The temporal behaviour achieved with this modeling technique is illustrated with the examples of Figure 15 and Figure 16.

Figure 15 shows the behaviour of three nodes of the system when the synchronization round is consistent and then the nodes all agree on the value of ref. More specifically, the nodes agree that node 0 (the first timeline) is the active master and therefore they all use the expiration signalled through channel half[0] to reset their individual timers. Notice that the behaviour in this case would be exactly the same behaviour depicted in Figure 13.

In contrast, Figure 16 shows the behaviour of the same three nodes when node 1 is discrepant, and considers that its virtual clock is the global clock in the system (i.e., for node 1, the value of ref is 1). In this case, nodes 0 and 2 use the expiration signalled through channel half[0] to reset their timers, whereas node 1 uses the expiration signalled through channel half[1].

Notice that the effect of such an inconsistency is a displacement of the possible expiration instants of Timer 1 and that, due to this displacement, the distance between the initiation instants of the tasks

*Figure 16. Temporal behaviour of three nodes after an inconsistent synchronization round*

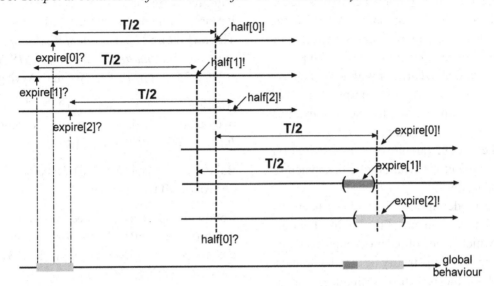

may be greater than it was in Figure 15. This is highlighted in Figure 16 with darker grey. This increment means that the nodes have lost precision due to the lack of consistency among the nodes. Therefore, the aim of modeling virtual clocks that may exceed their drift boundaries is accomplished. It is also possible to make the drift of one virtual clock depend on the drift exhibited by other virtual clock. For instance, it would be the case if both node 1 and node 2 considered that node 1 is the global clock and used half[1] to reset their individual timers.

Due to space limitations, it is not possible to discuss all the possibilities and implications of the modeling techniques used in the formal verification of OCS-CAN. Nevertheless, we think that the described examples are a good starting point for those interested in modeling systems with virtual clocks of variable drift.

## CONCLUSION

Timed automata is an established and widely used formalism that has proven very useful for specifying and formally verifying distributed embedded systems. However, the fact that all the clocks of a timed automaton must evolve at the same rate is often considered as a shortcoming for realistic modeling of distributed systems, since clocks with variable rate cannot be directly modeled. Fortunately, a number of modeling techniques exist that allow system developers to circumvent this limitation and specify clocks of variable rate. This chapter has been devoted to presenting and discussing these techniques in a systematic way.

Furthermore, and prior to the description of these techniques, a taxonomy of the types of clocks that may be found in a distributed embedded system has been presented. This taxonomy is useful for modeling distributed embedded systems because it allows system developers to fully understand the implicit assumptions of the computer clocks they use. As we have indicated, the fact that clock synchronization is a transparent service sometimes makes the system developers not really aware of certain subtleties that are important for the correct modeling of the system.

After the computer clocks taxonomy, the modeling techniques have been introduced in order of increasing complexity. First, we have discussed the modeling of ideal clocks, which is almost trivial with timed automata. After that, we have discussed the important cases in which the distributed embedded system works with physical clocks of bounded drift or with virtual clocks of bounded drift. Most of current distributed embedded systems belong to one of these two groups. Finally, we have discussed the modeling of virtual clocks of variable drift, as required for the modeling and verification of clock synchronization algorithms.

All the modeling techniques have been described with the elements of the UPPAAL model checker, which is one of the most popular model checkers based on the theory of timed automata. Nevertheless, the presented techniques can be adapted to similar model checkers, such as Kronos.

The basis of our discussion has been the so-called UPPAAL timers, since they allow us to specify the temporal properties of generic systems without having to provide further details about the executed applications. In our experience, dissociating the specification of the temporal properties from the application details is a significant help for the modeller. Given that the proposed techniques are application-independent, they can actually be used as a sort of predefined "modeling patterns" for reducing the time required for formal specification of many distributed embedded systems with computer clocks.

# REFERENCES

Alur, R., & Dill, D. (1994). A theory of timed automata. *ACM Theoretical Computer Science*, *126*(2), 183–235. doi:10.1016/0304-3975(94)90010-8

Alur, R., Torre, S. L., & Madhusudan, P. (2005). Perturbed timed automata. In M. Morari & L. Thiele (Eds.), *8th International Workshop, Hybrid Systems: Computation and Control, HSCC 2005* (LNCS 3414, pp. 70-85). Springer-Verlag.

Anceaume, E., & Puaut, I. (1997). A taxonomy of clock synchronization algorithms. *Publication Interne IRISA-PI-97-1103*. IRISA.

Baier, C., & Katoen, J. (2008). *Principles of model checking*. MIT Press.

Behrmann, G., David, A., & Larsen, K. (2004). A tutorial on UPPAAL. In *Formal methods for the design of real-time systems* (LNCS 3185, pp. 200-236). Springer Verlag.

Bengtsson, J., Griffioen, W., Kristoffersen, J., Larsen, K., Larsson, F., Pettersson, P., & Yi, W. (2002). Automated analysis of an audio control protocol using uppaal. *Journal of Logic and Algebraic Programming*, *52-53*, 163–181. doi:10.1016/S1567-8326(02)00036-X

Clarke, E. M., & Emerson, E. A. (1981). Design and synthesis of synchronization skeletons using branching time logics. In *Logics of Programs: Workshop* (LNCS 131). Springer.

Clarke, E. M., Emerson, E. A., & Sistla, A. P. (1986). Automatic verification of finite-state concurrent systems using temporal logics specifications. *ACM Transactions on Programming Languages and Systems*, *8*(2), 244–263. doi:10.1145/5397.5399

Daws, C., & Yovine, S. (1995). Two examples of verification of multirate timed automata with Kronos. In *Proceedings of the 16th IEEE Real-Time Systems Symposium (RTSS'95)*, Pisa, Italy (pp. 66-75).

Henzinger, T. A., Nicollin, X., Sifakis, J., & Yovine, S. (1992). Symbolic model checking for real-time systems. In *Proceeding of the 7th Annual IEEE Symposium on Logic in Computer Science.*

IEEE. (2004). Standard for information technology-portable operating system interface (POSIX). Base definitions, IEEE Std 1003.1, 2004 ed. *The Open Group Technical Standard Base Specifications, 6.*

Kopetz, H. (1997). *Real-time systems: Design principles for distributed embedded applications.* Kluwer Academic Press.

Larsen, K. G., Pettersson, P., & Yi, W. (1997). UPPAAL: Status & developments. In *Proceedings of the 9th International Conference on Computer Aided Verification*, Haifa, Israel (pp. 22-25).

Milner. (1989). *Communication and concurrency.* Prentice-Hall.

Queille, J.-P., & Sifakis, J. (1982). Specification and verification of concurrent systems in CESAR (LNCS 137). Springer-Verlag.

Rodriguez-Navas, G., Proenza, J., & Hansson, H. (2006). An UPPAAL model for formal verification of master/slave clock synchronization over the controller area network. In *Proc. of the 6th IEEE International Workshop on Factory Communication Systems,* Torino, Italy.

Rodriguez-Navas, G., Roca, S., & Proenza, J. (2008). Orthogonal, fault-tolerant, and high-precision clock synchronization for the controller area network. *IEEE Transactions on Industrial Informatics, 4*(2).

Schneider, F. (1987). *Understanding protocols for Byzantine clock synchronization* (Tech. Rep. 87-859). Dept of Computer Science, Cornell University.

Veríssimo, P. (1997). On the role of time in distributed systems. In *Proceedings of the 6th Workshop on Future Trends of Distributed Computing Systems.*

Yovine, S. (1997). KRONOS: A verification tool for real-time systems. [STTT]. *International Journal on Software Tools for Technology Transfer, 1*(1-2), 123–133.

## ENDNOTE

[1]     Although with some limitations: it is not possible to determine the order of two events whose timestamps are less than $2\Pi$ time units apart (Kopetz, 1997).

# Chapter 8
# Model Checking of Multitasking Real–Time Applications Based on the Timed Automata Model Using One Clock

**Libor Waszniowski**
*Czech Technical University in Prague, Czech Republic*

**Zdeněk Hanzálek**
*Czech Technical University in Prague, Czech Republic*

## ABSTRACT

*The aim of this chapter is to show how a multitasking real-time application running under a real-time operating system can be modeled by timed automata. The application under consideration consists of several preemptive tasks and interrupts service routines that can be synchronized by events and can share resources. A real-time operating system compliant with an OSEK/VDX standard is considered for demonstration. A model checking tool UPPAAL is used to verify time and logical properties of the proposed model. Since the complexity of the model-checking verification exponentially grows with the number of clocks used in a model, the proposed model uses only one clock for measuring execution time of all modeled tasks.*

## INTRODUCTION

This chapter deals with formal modeling of software applications running under real-time operating system (OS). The typical application under assumption is a complex controller consisting of periodic and aperiodic tasks. Tasks are constrained by deadlines and can be synchronized via inter-task communication primitives. Tasks are assumed to

be asynchronous and triggered by external events or by time events. An operating system compliant with the automotive standard OSEK/VDX (OSEK) is considered as an example. The objective is to use an existing model-checking tool for automatic verification of the model described in this chapter.

The proposed model is based on timed automata (Alur and Dill, 1994). It considers an operating system, application tasks and a controlled environment behavior. It assumes a fine-grain model of the task

DOI: 10.4018/978-1-60566-750-8.ch008

internal structure consisting of computations, OS calls, selected variables, code branching and loops. Therefore the model combines both, logic and timing characteristics of the discrete event system enabling one to check rather complex properties (safety and bounded liveness properties, state reachability or schedulability) by model checking tool (UPPAAL (Larsen, *et al.*, 1997) in our case) in finite time. Deadlock freeness of the application, occurrence of the race condition during access to shared data structures, a concrete value of some essential variable under certain conditions, end to end response time of an arbitrary event, proper ordering and timing of events in the control application or the controlled environment can be verified, for example.

Due to the composability of timed automata, models of different parts of the system can be combined together (under condition of syntactic and semantic compatibility of these models). For example, a single processor system model can be expanded to a distributed system model by adding a communication layer model. Since many real-time systems are safety-critical, they are often constructed as fault-tolerant systems. The proposed modeling methodology is flexible enough, to allow incorporation of many fault-tolerant methods used in this kind of application.

It is generally known that timed automata and model-checking are susceptible to the state space explosion. This fact restricts the size of verified application to a small size that seems to be unusable in practice. Therefore we try to show in this chapter, how to reach a compromise between a model of reasonable size on one side, and reasonable granularity on the other side. Model of proper granularity allows a detailed formal analysis of real-time properties that can not be made by response time analysis.

When modeling preemption in a multitasking application, it is necessary to stop a clock variable measuring the execution time of a preempted task and remember its value until the task is scheduled

again. This can be done in hybrid automata, but not in timed automata. On the other hand, it has been shown in (Henzinger, *et al.*, 1998) that the most general decidable hybrid automaton is the initialized rectangular automaton. The rectangular automata however, are not expressive enough to model preemption. Precise preemption modeling requires a so called stopwatch automata belonging to the undecidable class of hybrid automata (Henzinger, *et al.*, 1998).

For timed automata, however, the reachability problem is decidable and the verification algorithm is therefore guarantied to terminate. This is a motivation of our work providing a timed automata based over-approximate model of preemptive tasks. The over-approximation of the model means that besides the real behavior of the system, also some additional behavior is modeled. Therefore only properties preserved by this approximation can be verified by a model-checking tool. This does not degrade the usability of the model too much since the most important classes of properties (safety and bounded liveness) are preserved (Berard, *et al.*, 2001).

The complexity of the timed automata based model checking is exponential on the number of clocks and on the largest time constant appearing in the timing constraints. Even though the growing complexity due to time constants can be avoided by the symbolic representation of sets of states, the number of clocks remains a problem determining the feasibility of the model checking in practice (Daws & Yovine 1996). Even though a method for reducing the number of clocks of timed automata has been proposed in (Daws & Yovine 1996), we have minimized the number of clocks already in the phase of the model construction.

This approach is motivated by the fact that only one task can be running on the processor at any given time and only the running task can be finished. Therefore, only the clock of the task currently running can affect the progress of the model. Timed automata of the other tasks cannot change state. These facts have motivated us to share only one clock for all tasks sharing the processor.

The following text presents the main ideas of our approach and the most important properties of the model. The fine-grain model of a multitasking application is described; examples of a task model and an OS kernel model are presented. The *one-clock* approach to the preemption modeling is proposed and experimental results demonstrate performance improvement.

## BACKGROUND

One of the formal methods that can be used for verification is a method called model checking. Various formal models can be verified by model checking. We focus on timed automata in this chapter. This section provides the necessary background on model checking, timed automata and UPPAAL model checker modeling and specification formalisms. We also introduce the main features of an operating system compliant with the standard OSEK/VDX (OSEK Group, 2005), considered in this chapter as an example.

### Model-Checking

The basic idea of model checking is to use mathematically based algorithm, executed by a computer tool, to verify the correctness of the system according to specified correctness requirements. The user inputs a model of the system (representing the possible behavior) and a requirement specification (representing the desirable behavior) and leaves the verification up to the computer tool, which checks whether the required properties hold for the given initial state in the model. Notice that in this manner, the validation becomes a typical engineering task, which does not require deep knowledge of the mathematical background of any verification method. A very important property of model checking is its ability to provide a counter

example which shows under which circumstances the requirements are violated. It helps the designer to correct errors in the system.

Algorithms of model-checking are based on exhaustive state space search. Therefore, a finite state model is required and the system can be checked only for a fixed set of parameters. It means that successful verification for one set of parameters (e.g. given number of nodes or tasks) does not imply success for another set of parameters (e.g. lower or higher number of nodes or tasks).

A big problem of model-checking is that it is prone to state-space explosion resulting in memory requirements exceeding the possibilities of computers. Therefore, it is necessary to construct the model of reasonable size. Moreover, the theory of computability provides a limitation on what can be decided by an algorithm. For verifying real-time systems we use a model in the form of timed automata and verified properties are specified in timed computation tree logic. Such a verification problem is decidable (an algorithm decides in a finite time whether the specification is satisfied). There are models however, e.g. hybrid automata, for which the model checking algorithms termination is not guaranteed. For verification of such modes, an over-approximation may be used. It means that the undecidable model is substituted by an over-approximate decidable model.

The over-approximation means that the new model contains all behaviors of the original one, but in addition it can contain an additional behavior that is not contained by the original model. Over-approximation must be taken into account during verification, since not all kinds of properties are preserved by the over-approximation. Realize, for example, that adding a new behavior (new states and transitions) to the system containing deadlock can cause the new system to be deadlock free. Therefore, when an over-approximated system is deadlock-free, it cannot be concluded that the original system is also deadlock-free. It means that the deadlock-freeness is not preserved by the over-approximation (Berard, *et al.*, 2001). On the other hand, it is important from a practical point of view, that over-approximation preserves the safety and bounded liveness properties (Berard, *et al.*, 2001). A safety property states that, under certain conditions, an undesirable event never occurs. A bounded liveness property states that, under certain condition, some desirable event will occur within some deadline. When the safety or the bounded liveness property is satisfied by over-approximated model, it is also satisfied by the original model. On the other hand, when the safety or the bounded liveness property is not satisfied by the over-approximated model, we can not decide whether it is satisfied by the original model. We can only conclude that the property is "maybe not satisfied".

Even though properties of a model are verified automatically via model checking tool, there remains a lot of engineering work that must be done manually at the modeling and specification phase. The effort spend on formal verification of the system does not, however, increase the cost of the system under development since the formal verification can find errors that would become much more expensive in later phases of development. Results of verification can also guide the testing of the system. The most important benefit of the formal verification is the potential improvement of the developed system quality and the existence of a formal proof necessary for certification of a safety critical system.

## Real-Time Systems Model: Timed Automata

A timed automaton is a standard finite state automaton extended by a finite set of real valued clocks. Clocks are assumed to proceed at the same rate and measure the amount of time that has been elapsed since they were reset. Clock value may be tested (compared to natural numbers – see definition of clock constraints) and reset (assigned to 0 or another integer constant).

Clock constraints are formulas defined by:

$$\alpha ::= x \sim c \mid x\text{-}y \sim c \mid \neg\alpha \mid (\alpha \wedge \alpha)$$

where x,y are real valued clocks, c is a natural number and the relation $\sim$ is one of $\{\leq, \geq, =, <, >\}$.

Clock constraints can be used on edges of timed automata as an enabling condition of the edge (also called guard).

Clock constraints can also be assigned to locations of the timed automaton to define so called time invariant – the condition that must be satisfied by the clocks when the automaton resides in this location. An invariant in the form "$c<=U$", allows to stay in the location only when valuation of the clock variable c is smaller than or equal to integer U. When the location can not be quit and the invariant is not satisfied, a deadlock state is reached.

Informally, the system starts at initial location with all its clocks initialized to 0. The values of the clocks increase synchronously with time at a location as long as they satisfy the invariant condition. Therefore, invariants ensure progress. At any time, the automaton can change location by following an edge starting at this location, provided the current values of the clocks satisfy the enabling condition of the edge. With this transition the clocks specified on the edge get reset. Also a synchronization channel can be used for synchronization with another automaton in the model (Alur and Dill, 1994).

The UPPAAL notation is used in this chapter for graphical representation of timed automata. An example of timed automaton in this notation is on Figure 1. The location with double circle represents the initial location. Locations marked by "**c**" are so called committed locations providing atomicity of the in-coming and out-coming transitions (committed location is left immediately without any interference of other automaton that is

*Figure 1. UPPAAL notation of timed automata*

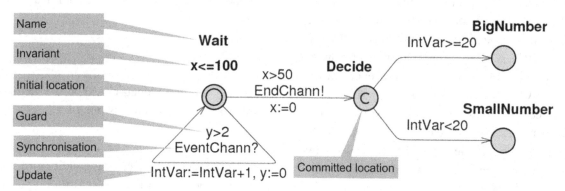

not in committed location). Each location can be labeled by its name and time invariant. Each edge can be labeled by guard (comma separated logical terms, e.g., *c>=L[1], State[1]==RUNNING*), synchronization (channel name with '?' or '!') and assignment (comma separated assignments by sign ':=').

The model used in UPPAAL is a net of timed automata synchronized via channels (an edge labeled by *ch!* is taken simultaneously with an edge of another automaton labeled by *ch?*). The automata can share integer and clock variables. Integer arrays can be defined. Access to elements of array is made by name of array (e.g. "*A*") and index (e.g. "*i*"): *A[i]*.

## UPPAAL Requirement Specification Language

The following temporal operators are used to specify properties in UPPAAL (Larsen, *et al.*, 1997):

E<> expression: Denotes possibly ("for some path future")

A<> expression: Denotes eventually ("for all paths future")

E[]expression: Denotes potentially always ("for some path globally")

A[]expression: Ddenotes invariantly ("for all paths globally")

p --> q: Denotes a formula A[] (p imply A<> q) ("whenever p holds, eventually q will hold as well")

Where expression is a side effect free logical expression constructed by operators. It is possible to test whether a certain automaton is in a given location while using expressions in the form "AutomatonName.LocationName".

UPPAAL does not define any quantitative time operators, but values of clocks can be explicitly tested in formulas. For example, formula *P1.Request --> P1.Response and t<10* express the property: "Whenever location labeled by *Request* in automaton *P1* is reached, location labeled by *Response* will be reached eventually and valuation of clock *t* will be smaller than ten". If clock *t* is reset whenever location *Request* is reached and it is not modified later, mentioned formula can be used to worst-case response time verification.

Another way how to express more complex properties is to define so called observer automaton. Observer automaton is synchronized with verified model and changes its states when observed events (synchronized transitions) occur. Then we simply verify reachability of a certain location of the observer automaton.

## OSEK/VDX Overview

An operating system compliant with the standard OSEK/VDX (OSEK Group, 2005), further called OSEK, is a simple static multitasking executive for electronic control units used in automotive applications. All objects of the system are created in compilation time. Therefore, they can be modeled by timed automata and static data structures. Small memory demand requires simple services, which can be modeled by timed automata of reasonable size.

## Task Management

OSEK provides static priority based, preemptive and non-preemptive scheduling (OSEK Group, 2005). Even though OSEK distinguishes basic and extended tasks, we consider only extended ones, since basic tasks are only a subset variant of extended ones and both are modeled in the same way.

Tasks, created as suspended at the system generation time, become ready after activation by OS service ActivateTask() called from ISR or another task. The highest priority ready task becomes running. The running task may terminate its execution by calling service TerminateTask() and become suspended or it may voluntarily relinquish processor by calling service Schedule() and become ready. If there is no higher-priority ready task, calling of service Schedule() does not affect tasks execution. Extended tasks are, moreover, allowed to use system call WaitEvent(), which may result in waiting state. The waiting task requires an event it is waiting for to be set, to become ready.

## Event Management

OSEK provides an event management for tasks synchronization. The event is represented by one bit in a byte assigned to an extended task - the event's owner. The event is, therefore, identified by its owner and its name (or mask specifying more than one event). The event owner may wait for the event and clear the event (services WaitEvent() and ClearEvent()). All tasks may set or get the binary value of a non-suspended task event (services SetEvent() and GetEvent()).

## Resource Management

A resource management is used to coordinate access of several tasks (and interrupt service routines (ISR)) to the critical section. The resource access protocol, called "OSEK priority ceiling" in the OSEK specification, is used to provide mutually exclusive access, to prevent priority inversion and deadlock. According to this protocol, the priority ceiling is statically assigned to the resource at the system generation time. Its value is equal to the highest priority of all tasks (or ISR) ever accessing the resource. At run time, the priority of the task occupying the resource is increased to the resource priority ceiling. Task priority is reset to the previous value after releasing the resource. Consequently, no task (or ISR) ever tries to access occupied resource and, therefore, no task can be blocked on the resource.

A task may get or release a resource (services GetResource() and ReleaseResource()). Services TerminateTask(), WaitEvent() and Schedule() cannot be called while resource is occupied. Nested access to the same resource is forbidden. In the case of multiple resource occupation, critical sections must be properly nested.

To prevent preemption within specified group of tasks, internal resource can be assigned to the task (statically at system generation time). This resource is automatically acquired when the task is started and automatically released when the task terminates or begins waiting. Consequently, the running task cannot be preempted by any task sharing the same internal resource.

*Figure 2. Overview of entire timed automata model*

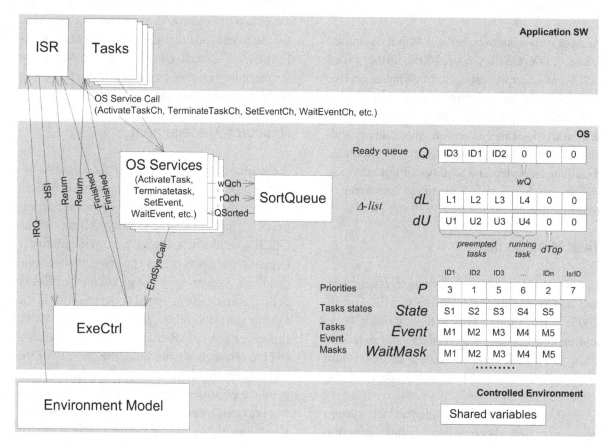

## Interrupt Management

OSEK distinguishes interrupt service routines (ISRs) of category 1 that do not use any OS services (no influence on the task management) and ISR of category 2 allowing all OS services except some services dedicated entirely to tasks (WaitEvent(), TerminateTask()). There is no difference between both categories from the modeling point of view.

## FINE-GRAIN MODEL OF A MULTITASKING APPLICATION

The proposed fine-grain model considers the internal structure of the tasks and the interrupt service routines (ISR), the OS functionality and the controlled environment behavior. All components are modeled by timed automata synchronized via channels and by shared variables. A simplified structure of the entire model is shown on Figure 2. Rectangular blocks represent particular timed automata. Synchronization is expressed by arc labeled by the name of the synchronization channel. The most important data structures are shown on the right side of the figure. The essential components are briefly explained in the following sections.

## Task Model

The task model consists of several blocks of code called *computations*, calls of OS services, selected variables, code branching and loops (affected by the values of the modeled variables). A *computa-*

*Figure 3. Example of a simple task pseudcode*

```
Task1()
{
    Comp1;
    WaitEvent(Event1);
    Comp2;
    TerminateTask();
}
```

*tion* represents a block of code that is not modeled in details but its execution time is considered. Since the *computations* execution time can be nondeterministic, it is specified by an interval covering all possible cases, i.e. ⟨BCET, WCET⟩, where BCET is the best-case execution time and WCET is the worst-case execution time. Considering the execution time as an interval ⟨BCET, WCET⟩, it allows one to incorporate the uncertainty of the execution time due to non-modeled code branching inside the *computations*, cycle stealing by a DMA device, or due to nondeterministic execution times of the code on modern processors (due to cache faults or deep pipelining).

Realize that a general property of the model is analyzed by an exhaustive state space search (made by a model checking tool). We cannot therefore simply suppose that WCET have always the worst influence on the verified property as in the schedulability analysis theory (Liu, 2000). Even, when a task response time is verified in the model considering the internal structure of the task, the WCET of *computations* does not always lead to

the worst-case response time of the whole task, due to a possibility of a scheduling anomaly.

Each task is modeled by one timed automaton synchronized with the OS model via channels (see Figure 2). We demonstrate the modeling methodology on an example of a simple task (compliant with the OSEK standard) executing *computations* *Comp1* and *Comp2* and calling the OS services *WaitEvent(Mask)* and *TerminateTask*. A pseudocode of this task is listed in Figure 3 and the corresponding model is depicted in Figure 4.

Each *computation* is represented by one location of the same name (e.g. *Comp1*). The time spent in this location represents *computation's* response time (i.e. the time necessary to its execution including preemption). BCET and WCET of the *computation* are assigned to the *dTop* position of the integer array *dL* and *dU* respectively (i.e. *dL[dTop]* and *dU[dTop]* respectively) at the transition leading to a computation location. According to these values (and scheduling policy) the *ExeCtrl* automaton determines the time when the computation is finished (taking preemption into account) and by synchronization via the channel *Finshed[ID]* (where index *ID* is a unique task identifier) makes the task model leave the location corresponding to the finished *computation*.

OS service calls are modeled by transitions synchronized via channels of corresponding names (e.g. *WaitEventCh!*) and by locations of the corresponding names (e.g. *WaitEvent*), where

*Figure 4. Example of a simple task model*

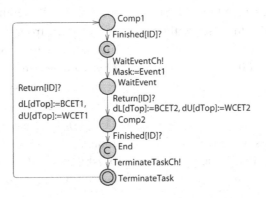

the task is waiting for the return from the service (channel *Return[ID]?*). OS service parameters, if they are needed, are assigned to the shared variables *ParTask* and *Mask* (OSEK never uses more than these two parameters). Notice that some OS services (e.g. *Schedule*, *SetEvent* or *ActivateTask*) can cause rescheduling. In this case, the return from the called service occurs after finishing all higher priority tasks. When the task is suspended, the corresponding automaton is in its initial location *TerminateTask* that simultaneously models the termination of the task execution by calling the *TerminateTask* OS service.

The return from an OS service causes the start of a new *computation*. When there are two successive calls of OS services without an intermediate *computation* in the task code, an intermediate location (dummy computation) with zero BCET and WCET must be used. Realize that the task can be interrupted in this place.

The modeling of language constructs, such as branching and loops, is straightforward. A committed location representing the statement (*if, for,...*) is used after a *Computation* or an OS service location and transition guards and assignments are used to determine which *Computation* or OS service should follow. This methodology allows us to model an arbitrary structure of the task e.g. loops and branching (non-deterministic or affected by values of variables).

Interrupt service routine (ISR) is modeled by a timed automaton representing an application dependent code in the same way as the task code. Moreover, there is an initialization part that prevents a rescheduling inside the ISR and a finalization part that provides the rescheduling at the end of the ISR (as is required by the OSEK specification (OSEK Group, 2005)).

## OS Kernel Model

The OS kernel model consists of some variables representing OS objects (e.g. ready queue, tasks states, events,...), timed automata representing OS

services functionality, timed automaton managing preemption (*ExeCtrl*) and timed automaton sorting ready queue according to the priority (*SortQueue*).

## Variables Representing OS Objects

Tasks priorities are stored in a global array *P*, indexed by a unique tasks identifier *ID*. The higher number represents the higher priority.

The task state is stored in the array *State* at the index corresponding to its *ID*. The task state is either *SUSPENDED, WAITING, READY, PREEMPTED* or *RUNNING*. The meaning of the states *SUSPENDED, WAITING* and *RUNNING* is the same as in common OS (before activation, waiting for an event, and currently executed). The state *PREEMPTED* represents state when the task is ready to execute, but it has been preempted by a higher priority task. The state *READY* therefore, represents only states after activation and before the first run.

Variable *RunID* stores the *ID* of the currently running task or interrupt service routine.

The *ID*s of all tasks, which are ready for execution (*State[ID]* equals to *READY* or *PREEMPTED*), are stored in the ready queue modeled as a global array *Q* (see Figure 2). Tasks are ordered in descending order according to their priorities in *Q*. *Q[0]* is the ready task with the highest priority and the first empty position in *Q* is stored in variable *wQ*. The queue must be reordered according to the tasks priorities after the new task is inserted. Moreover, the elements of the queue must be shifted to left after the highest priority ready task is extracted from the zero position. Both these mechanisms are provided by the automaton *SortQueue* (see Figure 5). The reordering mechanism is started via the synchronization channel *wQch* by an OS service writing the new *ID* to *Q[wQ]*. The *Q* shifting is started via the synchronization channel *rQch* by the OS service reading *Q[0]*. The finishing of both these mechanisms is announced by the channel *QSorted*.

*Figure 5. SortQ automaton*

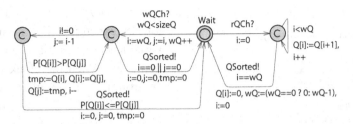

Notice that it would also be possible to implement the ready queue as a circular buffer. The top of the queue would not always be at position zero, but it would be pointed by a pointer (lets call it $rQ$) increased after reading the highest priority task. It would not be necessary to shift the elements of $Q$ in this case. The circular buffer would therefore be a more elegant approach from the programming point of view. But this approach is not appropriate for verification purposes, since such a model generates a bigger state space. Realize that the circular buffer containing the same tasks, even stored in different positions (different $rQ$ and $wQ$), represents the same situation from the application point of view and therefore allows the same future behavior. However, from the model checking point of view, these two configurations of the circular buffer are represented by two different states in the state space. Contrary to the circular buffer implementation, in our approach, all instances when $Q$ contains the same tasks are represented by only one state since the same set of tasks is always stored in the same position in $Q$ (from zero to $wQ-1$).

For inter-task communication purposes, the OSEK operating system (OSEK Group, 2005) provides some objects that are also modeled by variables. We only mention events here. Events are represented by the array *Event* associating one byte *Event[ID]* to each task identified by the *ID*. Each bit in *Event[ID]* represents one event that can be set or cleared. Moreover, the array *WaitMask* represents events, which the corresponding task is waiting for.

The data structure *Δ-list* consisting of two arrays *dU*, *dL* and integer *dTop* does not represent any object of the OS, but it is used to model the evolution of the tasks execution (will be explained later).

## OS Services

Each OS service is modeled by one timed automaton representing its functionality defined by the OSEK specification (OSEK Group, 2005). The automaton is waiting in its initial state until its function is called from the task model. Then it manipulates the tasks states, ready queue and other operating system objects (e.g. events), chooses the highest priority task to run and store its *ID* in the variable *RunID*. Then it invokes the *ExeCtrl* automaton modeling the context switch and providing the preemption control.

As an example of an OS service model, we introduce the *WaitEvent(Mask)* service that causes the calling task to wait for events corresponding to bits set in the parameter *Mask*. Figure 6 shows the *WaitEvent* OS service functionality in a pseudo-code and Figure 7 shows the corresponding automaton. It is supposed that interrupts are disabled within the whole service. All locations in the model, except the initial one, are committed locations. Therefore, the whole service is atomic from the point of view of the rest of the system (it takes zero execution time). The execution time of the OS service is involved in the execution time of the preceding *computation*. The OS service automaton waits in the initial state until

*Figure 6. WaitEvent service pseudo-code*

```
WaitEvent (Mask)
{
  if ((Event[RunID] & Mask) == 0)
  {
    State[RunID] := WAITING;
    WaitMask[RunID] := Mask;
    Release Internal Resource;
    RunID := Extract Top of ReadyQ;
    ContextSwitch;
    Get Internal Resource;
    State[RunID] := RUNNING;
  }
  return E_OK;
};
```

the synchronization via the channel *WaitEventCh*. The context switch is modeled by the *ExeCtrl* automaton invoked by the service via the channel *EndSysCall*.

## PREEMPTION MODELING

This section describes the basic idea of a preemptive multitasking application modeling by timed automata using only one clock.

### The Essential Problem with Preemption Modeling

Timed automata have been chosen due to the decidability of the model checking problem. They are, however, not expressive enough to model preemption. The essential problem is that it is impossible to stop a clock variable in timed automata.

When the execution of a *computation* (let us call it $Comp_{low}$) is modeled by a timed automaton, its execution time is measured by a clock variable (let us call it $c_{low}$) reset at the *computation* start. When the clock variable $c_{low}$ reaches an arbitrary value within the interval $\langle BCET_{low}, WCET_{low}\rangle$, where $BCET_{low}$, $WCET_{low}$ are the best and the worst case execution times of $Comp_{low}$, the *computation* is considered to be finished and the model progresses to the next statement. This mechanism is depicted in Figure 8.

Let us now consider that a higher priority task (let us call it $Task_{high}$) preempts $Comp_{low}$. Since $Comp_{low}$ is not executed during the preemption, $c_{low}$ should also be stopped as is depicted in Figure 9. This is, however, not possible in timed automata or any other known modeling formalisms for which the model checking problem is decidable.

This insufficiency of timed automata expressiveness must be solved by an over-approximation. One approach is to add execution time bounds of the preempting task $Task_{high}$ ($BCET_{high}$ and $WCET_{high}$) to the bounds of all preempted computations ($BCET_{low}$ and $WCET_{low}$ in our case) when the preemption occurs and the clock $c_{low}$ does not need to be stopped anymore. This approach is used, for example, in (Waszniowski & Hanzálek, 2005). We will refer to this approach as the *n-clock* approach, since $n$ clocks are used for $n$ tasks.

The resulting model is an over-approximation since it is loosing the information that the execution time of $Task_{high}$ equals to the duration of $Comp_{low}$ preemtion. It only holds in the model that both

*Figure 7. WaitEvent service automaton*

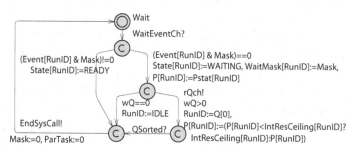

*Figure 8. Modeling execution time of a computation*

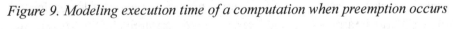

of these values are arbitrary (possibly different) values nondeterministically chosen from the interval $\langle BCET_{high}, WCET_{high} \rangle$. The model, therefore, contains all the real system behavior, but it also contains some additional behavior. The advantage of this approach is that the worst case response time of $Comp_{low}$ in the model and in the real system is equal (it is not pessimistic) (Waszniowski, 2006). The disadvantage of this approach is that a clock variable is used for each task. Since model checking complexity is exponential on a number of clocks, a reduction of the number of required clocks improves the applicability of the

model checking for realistically sized problem verification.

## Basic Idea of the One-Clock Approach

In this section we propose an over-approximate model using only one clock for all tasks. It is based on the idea that only one task can run on the processor at any given time instance. Therefore, only one clock (let as call it $c$) is necessary in order to measure the progress of the *computations* of the running task. Therefore we call this approach

*Figure 9. Modeling execution time of a computation when preemption occurs*

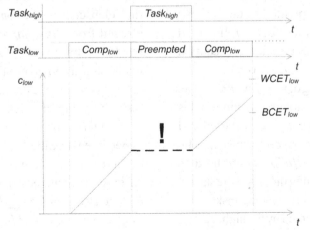

*Figure 10. Principle of sharing a clock and manipulating Δ-list in one-clock approach*

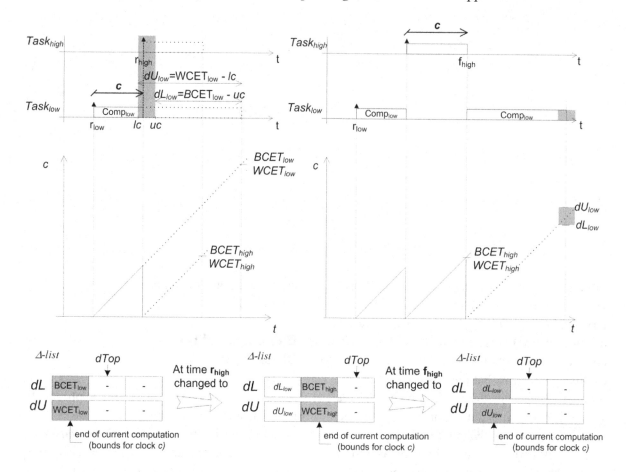

the *one-clock* approach. We will explain it on an example of task $Task_{low}$ executing *computation* $Comp_{low}$ (see Figure 10).

At the beginning of $Comp_{low}$, clock $c$ is reset and $BCET_{low}$ and $WCET_{low}$ are written to the arrays $dL$ and $dU$ to the position pointed by the variable $dTop$. We call this data structure *Δ-list*. It is used to store the bounds of the remaining execution times of the started *computations* (that is $BCET$ and $WCET$ at the beginning of a *computation*). The pointer $dTop$ is zero when no task is running; it is incremented when a *computation* is started and decreased when the *computation* is finished. The values $dL[dTop-1]$ and $dU[dTop-1]$ are used as bounds of clock $c$ determining the end of the started *computation* of the currently running task.

When $Comp_{low}$ is preempted by the higher prior-

ity task $Task_{high}$ at time $r_{high}$, we want to compute the new remaining execution time and use clock $c$ for the new running task ($Task_{high}$). The new remaining execution time is computed by decreasing the old one (its bounds are stored in the *Δ-list*) by the time elapsed from the *computation* start. The time elapsed from the *computation* start is measured by clock $c$ but its value is a real number that can not be stored and manipulated in timed automata, since it would make its state space infinite. Therefore, the value of clock $c$ is over-approximated by an interval bounded by the nearest lower and upper integer (called $lc$ and $uc$). The remaining execution time of the preempted *computation* is an interval bounded by $dL_{low}=max(0, BCET_{low}-uc)$ and $dU_{low}=WCET_{low}-lc$. The values $dL_{low}$ and $dU_{low}$ are written to $dL[dTop-1]$ and $dU[dTop-1]$

*Figure 11. Mechanism of modeling preemption by only one clock*

```
Clock2Int (clock c, int MaxC)
{
    int lc:=0;          // lover integer
    int uc:=MaxC;       // upper integer
    while ((uc-lc) > 1)
    {
        if ((lc+uc)/2 >= c)
            uc:= (lc+uc)/2;
        if ((lc+uc)/2 <= c)
            lc:= (lc+uc)/2;
    };
    if (lc == c)
        uc:=lc;
    if (uc == c)
        lc:=uc;
    return lc, uc;
};
```

```
NewCompStarted
{
    dL[dTop]:=BCET;
    dU[dTop]:=WCET;
    if (dTop>0)
    { //Preemption
        lc, uc := Clock2Int (c, dU[dTop]);
        if (dL[dTop-1] > uc)
            dL[dTop-1] := dL[dTop-1] – uc;
        else
            dL[dTop-1] := 0;
        dU[dTop-1] := dU[dTop-1] – lc;
    }
    c:=0;
    dTop++;
}
```

```
Current computation (started
computation of task RunID) is finished
when clock c∈(dL[dTop-1],dU[dTop-1])

CurrentCompFinished
{
    Finished[RunID]! // Progress in task
    dTop--;
    c:=0;
    if (dTop>0)
        Wait_ CurrentCompFinished;
    else
        Idle;
}
```

and clock $c$ is reset and used for measuring the execution time of $Task_{high}$. Therefore, $BCET_{high}$ and $WCET_{high}$ are written to $dL[dTop]$ and $dU[dTop]$ and $dTop$ is incremented.

The remaining execution times of the started *computations* of the preempted tasks are now stored at positions from 0 to $dTop-2$. Since the remaining execution times are written to the *Δ-list* in the LIFO (Last In First Out) order when preemption occurs, it holds that they are ordered according to the tasks priorities. Therefore, $dTop-1$ always points to the remaining execution time of a started *computation* of the task with the highest priority (*RunID*).

When $Task_{high}$ is finished at time $f_{high}$ ($c$ reaches a value between $dL[dTop-1]$ and $dU[dTop-1]$), $dTop$ is decreased, clock $c$ is reset and the preempted *computation* $Comp_{low}$ can continue in execution. Notice that even though the execution times of $Task_{high}$ and $Comp_{low}$ are deterministic ($BCET=WCET$), the over-approximation causes an uncertainty in the finishing time of $Comp_{low}$ (the shaded bar in Figure 10).

Figure 11 summarizes the described mechanism in a comprehensive form. There is an algorithm for modifying the *Δ-list* when a new *computation* is started (NewCompStarted) and an algorithm used when the current *computation* is finished (CurrentCompFinished). These algorithms call the algorithm Clock2Int computing integers $lc$ and $uc$ from clock $c$ by bisection. Its complexity is $O(log_2 MaxC)$ where *MaxC* is the upper margin of the clock $c$ valuation.

## Implementation of the One-Clock Approach by the Timed Automaton

The described mechanism of the preemption modeling by one clock only, is implemented by the *ExeCtrl* timed automaton depicted in Figure 12. It provides the following functions:

- models the context switch, i.e. send *Return[RunID]* to the scheduled task at the end of an OS service call (transitions related to locations *EndOSserv*, *ToTask* and *UpdateDlist*),

- manages the *Δ-list* when a preemption occurs (transitions related to locations *UpdateDlist*, *C2Int_Begin*, *C2Int_End* and *CompStarted*) and

- measures the execution time of the started *computation* of the currently running task by clock $c$ and synchronizes with the task automaton by the channel *Finished[RunID]* when the *computation* is finished (transitions related to locations *Wait* and *CompFinished*).

*Figure 12. ExeCtrl automaton*

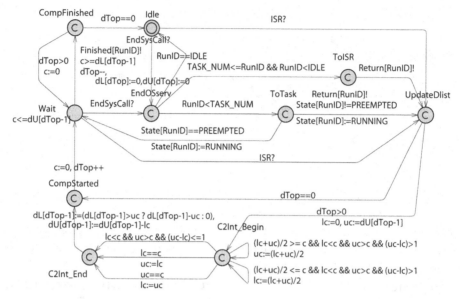

## Ad Context Switch Modeling

The context switch can occur from two reasons but always as a result of some OS service. The first reason is that the running task calls an OS service releasing higher-priority task (*AtivateTask*, *SetEvent* or *ReleaseResource*). The task model is in the location corresponding to the called OS service and it is waiting there until the synchronization *Return[ID]* occurs. The variable *State[ID]* is set to the value READY in this case.

The second reason of the context switch is related to the services called asynchronously from the interrupt service routine. The preempted task model is in the location corresponding to the currently processed computation and its remaining execution time is already written in the *Δ-list*. Since the task model is not waiting to the synchronization *Return[ID]*, the variable *State[ID]* is set to the value *PREEMPTED* distinguishing this situation from the previous case (this is made in ISR model before the OS service is called).

## Ad Δ-List Management after Preemption

When the new computation is started, the Δ-list content must be modified according to the mechanism described in Figure 11. The BCET and WCET of the started computation are written to the Δ-list arrays dL and dU respectively at the task automaton, at the transition synchronized by the Return[ID]. (see Figure 4).

The automaton ExeCtrl then modifies the remaining execution time of the preempted task. This is modeled by transitions beginning at location UpdateDlist and transitions between locations C2Int_Begin and C2Int_End implementing the algorithm computing the nearest lower and upper integers of clock *c*. The remaining execution time of the preempted task is modified on the transition incoming to the location *CompStarted* (see Figure 11).

## Ad Execution Time Measurement

When a new computation is started and the *Δ-list* content is modified, the *ExeCtrl* timed automaton

*Figure 13. An example of a preemption*

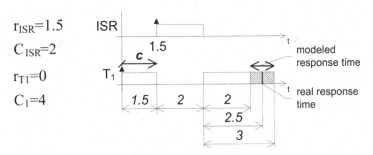

reaches the location *Wait* where the execution time of the currently executed computation is measured by clock *c*. When the execution time of currently executed computation expires (clock $c \in \langle dL[dTop-1], dU[dTop-1] \rangle$), the transition synchronized with the *RunID* task model by the channel *Finished[RunID]* is taken and the top of the *Δ-list* is decreased (*dTop--*). If the *Δ-list* is not empty (*dTop>0*), clock *c* is reset and the execution time of the next task from the *Δ-list* is measured. If the *Δ-list* is empty (*dTop==0*), the transition from the location *CompFinished* to *Idle* is taken and the automaton waits there until the interrupt service routine is started (transition synchronized by *ISR?*) or end of an OS system call occurs (transition synchronized by *EndSysCall?*). Notice that transitions synchronized by these channels also lead from the location Wait. These transitions are taken when preemption occurs.

## Over-Approximation of Preemption Modeling

It has been explained that the already executed time of the preempted computation (measured by clock *c*) is approximated by an interval bounded by the nearest lower and the nearest upper integers, *lc* and *uc* respectively (see Figure 10). The preemption of the currently executed *computation* can only be caused by an interrupt service routine (ISR) or by a task activated from this ISR. The over-approximation, therefore, increases the size of the interval of the possible execution times

$\langle BCET, WCET \rangle$ at most by one for each interrupt that occurs when the task model is in the location corresponding to a *computation*.

Figure 13 shows that even though the execution times of the ISR $C_{ISR}$ and the task $C_1$ are deterministic, the finishing time of the task is non-deterministic when interrupt occurs at time $r_{ISR} \in (1,2)$. When the interrupt occurs at an integer value of the clock *c* there is no over-approximation (*uc=lc*).

The following inequalities hold for the best case and the worst case response times (BCRT and WCRT) of each *computation*:

$$BCRT_{one\text{-}clock\,Model} \leq BCRT_{Real\,System}, \text{ and}$$

$$WCRT_{one\text{-}clock\,Model} \geq WCRT_{Real\,System}, \text{ and}$$

$$WCRT_{one\text{-}clock\,Model} - BCRT_{one\text{-}clock\,Model} \leq WCRT_{Real\,System} - BCRT_{Real\,System} + NumInt,$$

where *NumInt* is the number of interrupts that occur when the task model is in the location corresponding to the *computation*.

An example illustrating real behavior and its over-approximation by modeled behavior is shown on Figure 14 where task T is supposed to be once preempted by an ISR. The finishing time of the task T, depends on the moment of the preemption $t_{preemption}$.

Due to an additional non-determinism in the model, the set of system real behaviors is a sub-

*Figure 14. Relation of the finishing time ($F_T$) of a task T preempted by an ISR and the time of the pre-emption ($t_{preemption}$). $C_T = [2,3]$, $C_{ISR} = 2$*

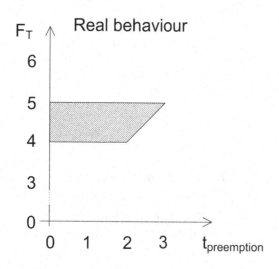
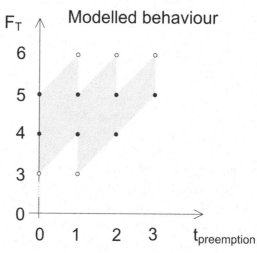

set of the set of modeled behaviors (the model is an over-approximation of the real system). It is important to keep this fact in mind during verification since the over-approximation does not preserve the satisfaction of all general properties. It is important from the practical point of view, that the over-approximation preserves the safety and bounded liveness properties (Berard, *et al.*, 2001). On the other hand, the over-approximation brings some pessimism to the model. Consider the example in Figure 13. Even though the property "Response time of task $T_2$ is always smaller or equal to 6" is satisfied in the real system, it is not satisfied in the model.

Notice that the accuracy of over-approximation depends on the chosen time units. When we express the time quantum 1s in the model by the number 1 (the chosen time units are seconds), the over-approximation is very coarse. When the time quantum 1s is expressed by the number 1000 (the chosen time units are milliseconds), the over-approximation is much more fine-grained because the interval of possible execution times is always increased by the dimensionless number one. Realize, however, that also the complexity of the verification process is increased by choosing

smaller time units. Our experience from experiments with UPPAAL shows that if we increase the time constants in the model ten times, also time and memory required for verification are increased ten times.

The relation of over-approximation and the clock constants granularity has a very important consequence. Since the duration of a task execution shorter than one is rounded to zero, when the remaining execution time of a preempted task is computed by the Clock2Int algorithm, the shortest time between two subsequent preemptions must be longer than one time unite. The preempted task would be never finished in the case of infinite number of preemptions with minimal inter-arrival time shorter than one time unite.

## EXPERIMENTAL RESULTS

In this section we compare the complexity of the *one-clock* approach with the *n-clock* approach (Waszniowski & Hanzálek, 2005) by measuring the memory and time required for verification of the following example. Tasks codes are listed in Figure 15. There is only one instance of TaskA

*Figure 15. Tasks code*

```
TaskA  // Only one instance T0
{
   Comp;              // ⟨0, 5⟩
   TerminateTask();
}
```

```
TaskB   // Instances T1, T2,...
{
   Comp1;             // ⟨0, 5⟩
   ActivateTask (T0);
   Comp2;             // ⟨0, 10⟩
   TerminateTask();
}
```

(T0) activated by several instances of TaskB (T1, T2, ...) that are periodically activated by an interrupt service routine (ISR). The instance of TaskA has the highest priority, instances of TaskB have priority assigned rate-monotonically. The ISR is periodically invoked with a period of 25 time units. It provides a computation taking from 0 to 5 time units and it activates instances of TaskB, each with its period.

Four cases (case1, case2, case3 and case4) are distinguished according to the number of executed tasks instances (4, 6, 8 or 10). Three instances T1, T2 and T3 (besides ISR and T0) activated with periods 600, 900, and 1800 are executed in case1. Five instances from T1 to T5 activated with periods 360, 450, 600, 900, and 1800 are executed in case2. Seven instances from T1 to T7 activated with periods 225, 300, 360, 450, 600, 900, and 1800 are executed in case3. Nine instances from T1 to T9 activated with periods 180, 200, 225, 300, 360, 450, 600, 900, and 1800 are executed in case4.

Besides the mentioned tasks instances a timer periodically generating an interrupt has been modeled (it contains one clock variable) and one additional clock has been used for verification of the bounded response time property (see property P3).

The following properties have been verified:

P1: Each task is finished before the end of its period

P2: Computation *Comp1* is executed mutually-exclusively by all task instances T1, T2,....

P3: The worst-case response time (WCRT) of task instance T3 is 76.

The mutual-exclusivity of execution *Comp1* (property P2) means that the *Comp1* of any instance of TaskB cannot be preempted by another instance of TaskB. The response time of a task instance is assumed to be the time from its activation to its completion (including preemption). Since properties P1 and P2 are safety properties and property P3 is the bounded liveness property, they are all preserved by the model over-approximation.

All properties have been formalized in the UPPAAL requirement specification language and successfully verified by UPPAAL 4.1 running on a AMD Opteron 2,21GHz, with 4GB RAM. Memory requirements and the time necessary for verification of properties of four models (Case 1, Case 2 Case 3 and Case 4) by the *one-clock* approach and the *n-clock* approach are listed in Table 1.

Both approaches use the same data structures to model the ready queue, tasks states, priorities, etc. While the *n-clock* approach model uses two arrays for the bounds of the response time of each task, the *one-clock* approach model uses the *Δ-list* consisting of the arrays *dL* and *dU* and the pointer *dTop*. Therefore the data structures used by the *one-clock* approach are slightly bigger. Moreover, managing preemption in the *one-clock* approach (computing *lc* and *uc*) is usually a little bit more demanding than in the *n-clock* approach (increasing response times of all preempted tasks). Therefore, the results of the comparison of the *one-clock* and the *n-clock* approach model verification (Table 1) show that the *one-clock* approach is a little bit more expensive in memory and time requirements than the *n-clock* approach for a small number of tasks (4 tasks). For 6 tasks

*Table 1. Time and memory requirements of verification by the one-clock and n-clock approach (\* less than 1 second, ⁺ more than 2 GB)*

| | Property | one-clock | | n-clock | |
|---|---|---|---|---|---|
| | | Time [min:sec] | Memory [MB] | Time [min:sec] | Memory [MB] |
| Case 1 (4 tasks) | P1 | 0:1 | 8.6 | 0:1 | 7.2 |
| | P2 | 0:1 | 8.3 | 0:0* | 7.1 |
| | P3 | 0:2 | 20.4 | 0:0* | 11.2 |
| Case 2 (6 tasks) | P1 | 0:4 | 17.6 | 0:14 | 68 |
| | P2 | 0:6 | 15.6 | 0:14 | 68 |
| | P3 | 0:4 | 36.5 | 0:11 | 134 |
| Case 3 (8 tasks) | P1 | 0:9 | 40.5 | 7:0 | 1788 |
| | P2 | 1:22 | 36 | 7:28 | 1811 |
| | P3 | 0:8 | 65 | --- | Out of mem.⁺ |
| Case 4 (10 tasks) | P1 | 8:17 | 1317 | --- | Out of mem.⁺ |
| | P2 | 12:46 | 1320 | --- | Out of mem.⁺ |
| | P3 | 10:06 | 1654 | --- | Out of mem.⁺ |

however, the higher number of clocks used in the *n-clock* approach causes that the *one-clock* approach wins the comparison of the time and memory requirements. The verification of the *one-clock* approach model consisting of 8 tasks is approximately six times faster (for P1 even forty times faster) and requires approximately forty-five times less memory than the verification of the corresponding *n-clock* approach model. Even then the verification of the model containing 10 tasks modeled by *one-clock* approach in the Case 4 is near the limit of memory which is 2GB in the mentioned version of UPPAAL.

The WCRT of T3 explored by the *n-clock* approach is 75. However, the WCRT of T3 explored by the *one-clock* approach is 76 due to over-approximation.

## CASE STUDY

In this section we briefly describe an example of modeling an automated gearbox control system. This system is described in (Waszniowski & Hanzálek, 2008) in details where tasks are non-

preemptive. In this section we present results of verification of preemptive version of this example while using *one-clock* approach.

The controlled system consists of a five-speed gearbox and a dry clutch. The gearbox mechanics consist of three shift rails and a shift finger actuated by *SelectServo* and *ShiftServo*. *SelectServo* can move the shift finger from a slot of one rail to another one. *ShiftServo* engages one of two gears (odd or even) or neutral by moving the selected rail by the shift finger. The direction of the shift finger movement is limited by a gait.

The gearbox is controlled by a single processor control unit running an OSEK compliant OS. The application software consists of three tasks (*SlipCtrlTask*, *SelectGearTask*, *GearBoxCtrlTask*) and four ISRs.

The ISRs are periodically invoked by a timer or by the clutch, *ShiftServo* or *SelectServo* when their position changes. According to the source of the interrupt, periodic tasks are activated (timer) or events are set (clutch, *ShiftServo* or *SelectServo*).

Task *SlipCtrlTask* is periodically activated by ISR. It provides slip control and torque tracking but its detailed functionality is not relevant to verification, therefore, it is not considered here. Only its computation time is modeled.

Task *SelectGearTask* is periodically activated by ISR. It selects the appropriate transmission rate and if the desired gear differs from the current one, it activates task *GearBoxCtrlTask* that controls changing of the gear. Also the model of this task is very rough.

Task *GearBoxCtrlTask* sends a command to open the clutch first, then it waits for the event *ClutchEvent* signaling that the clutch is open. If NEUTRAL is not currently engaged, it disengages the current gear by sending the command to the *ShiftServo* to move the shift finger to the neutral position and waits for the event *ShiftServoEvent*. Then the new gear, stored in variable *DesiredGear*, can be engaged. First, the rail and shift direction corresponding to the *DesiredGear* are computed and stored in the variable *DesiredRail* (Rail 0, 1, or 2) and *DesiredShift* (*ODD* or *EVEN*). Then if the *DesiredRail* is not currently selected, the command to the *SelectServo* is sent to move the shift finger to the position of the *DesiredRail*. When the *DesiredRail* is selected (signalled by the event *SelectServoEvent*) the *DesiredGear* is engaged by sending the command to the *ShiftServo* to move the selected rail to *DesiredShift* position. After finishing the *ShiftServo* movement (signalled by the event *ShiftServoEvent*), the command to close the clutch is sent and when the clutch is closed (signaled by the event *ClutchEvent*), the variable *CurrentGear* is updated and the task is terminated.

A model of the whole system consists of timed automata representing the controlled system (*Clutch*, *SelectServo* and *ShiftServo*), a hardware of a control unit (periodic timer generating interrupts), an OS (services *ActivateTask*, *TerminateTask*, *SetEvent*, *WaitEvent* and automaton *SortQueue* and *ExeCtrl*), three application tasks (*SlipCtrlTask*, *SelectGearTask*, *GearBoxCtrlTask*) and ISRs.

Pseudocodes of all tasks and ISRs and timed automata representing controlled system are

presented in (Waszniowski & Hanzálek, 2008) where they have been used in combination with non-preemptive task model. Models of OS, tasks and ISRs has been developed according to methodology presented in this chapter.

The following properties are required for proper function of the system.

Safety properties:

P1: Shifting is allowed only when the clutch is open

P2: Selecting is allowed only when the shift servo is in neutral

P3: Shifting is allowed only when a rail is selected

P4: Clutch cannot be open longer than 650 time units

Bounded liveness:

P5 – P11: When new desired gear (NEUTRAL, 1...5, R) is selected, it is engaged in 1020 time units

All the above mentioned properties of the system have been successfully verified within 732 seconds. The required memory is 1.2GB.

## RELATED WORKS

In (Fersman, *et al.*, 2002) and (Fersman, *et al.*, 2003) the timed automata are extended by asynchronous tasks (i.e. tasks triggered by events) to provide a model for event-driven systems. Each task is specified by its execution time and is associated to a timed automaton location. A transition leading to the location denotes an event releasing the task. Released tasks are stored in a queue and they are assumed to be executed according to a given scheduling strategy. The problem of system schedulability is transformed to the reachability problem in a timed automaton (Fersman, *et al.*, 2003).

Moreover, it is shown in (Fersman, *et al.*, 2003), that only two clocks are necessary to implement schedulability analysis of *n* independent tasks. However *n+1* clocks are necessary in the case of sharing variables between tasks and timed automata.

This approach provides an exact schedulability analysis for aperiodic tasks (due to the detailed model of the environment releasing the tasks) but contrary to our approach, it is not suited to model the task's internal structure. It would be possible to model the task's internal structure by a skeleton automaton representing the structure of the task with branching and loops and blocks of code would be modeled by *tasks* (the task in the meaning of approach (Fersman, *et al.*, 2002)). Completion of a *task* would be synchronized with the skeleton automaton. Results of (Krčál & Yi, 2004) show, however, that the model is decidable if non-preemptive scheduling is used, or no synchronization between the *tasks* and automaton is used, or if the execution time of all *tasks* is deterministic. Our model remains decidable in all these cases.

The approach of Fersman, *et al.* (2003) is therefore appropriate for exact schedulability of bigger sets of aperiodic tasks, but without considering their internal structure. The schedulability analysis is very efficient in this case, due to the abstract model of the task (the worst-case execution time of the whole task). The verification of the worst-case response time of ten tasks (properties P1 and P3 in section Experimental results) takes less than 1 second and requires approximately 5MB of memory. Times tool 1.3 beta (Fersman, *et al.*, 2002)) has been used for this experiment.

Corbet in (Corbett, 1996) provides a method for constructing models of multitasking programs based on hybrid automata. Since the reachability problem is undecidable for hybrid automata, the termination of the analyzing algorithm is not guaranteed in general.

Timed automata are used to model a multitasking system in (Lundqvist & Asplund, 2003). However, the variable used to measure the execution time of tasks ("system clock") is an integer,

which is periodically incremented by a timed automaton modeling system clock. Therefore, opposite to our approach where time is dense, the notion of time in the application is discrete. Discrete time for modeling a real-time application is used also in (Campos & Clarke, 1999) presenting a modeling language and a symbolic algorithm for quantitative analysis of synchronous real-time systems and also in (Fredette & Cleaveland, 1993) where a generalized approach to schedulability analysis based on process algebra is proposed. Even though the last two approaches consider a task's internal structure, the controlled environment affecting the release time of tasks is not modeled.

Krčál, *et al.* (2004) proposed time triggered automata, a subclass of timed automata, useful for time triggered systems modeling. The semantic of this formalism is based on the fact that a digital computer is driven by a system clock with a fixed granularity of time.

Extensions of Petri nets can also be used to model a multitasking application. Two basic extensions of Petri Nets considering explicit time exist, Timed Petri Nets (TPNs) (Merlin & Faber, 1976) and Timed Petri Nets (Ramchandani, 1974). Since all clocks progress at the same rate in these extensions, their semantic is, therefore, similar to timed automata. TPN's and Timed Petri Nets can not model preemption from this reason.

There are extensions of TPN's allowing one to model systems with preemption; Preemptive Time Petri Nets (pTPN) (Bucci, *et al.*, 2004), Scheduling Extended Time Petri Nets (SETPN) (Lime & Roux, 2004) and Time Petri Nets with Stopwatches (SwTPN) (Berthomieu, et al., 2007). However, these formalisms are undecidable. Therefore, decidable over-approximations that preserve safety properties are usually used for verification.

In addition, Bucci, *et al.* (2004) describes a method that does not suffer from the undecidability of the reachability problem. It generates the over-approximate reachability graph of a pTPN first and

*Table 2. Time and memory requirements of pTPN model over-approximate state space enumeration*

|  | Time [min:sec] | Memory [MB] | Num. of classes |
|---|---|---|---|
| Case1 (4 tasks) | 0:0.4 | 5 | 968 |
| Case2 (6 tasks) | 0:12 | 45 | 15038 |
| Case3 (8 tasks) | 17:58 | 634 | 278710 |
| Case4 (10 tasks) | no result after 44:04 | ---- | --- |

then refines execution sequences identified in this graph. The over-approximate reachability graph of pTPN is based on the smallest Difference Bounds Matrix (DBM) envelopes of general polytopes representing the states equivalence classes of the pTPN. Linear programming is used to derive an exact (not over-approximate) profile of feasible timings from timing constraints included in state classes visited in the execution sequences. The profile permits one to evaluate the exact minimum and the exact maximum time that can elapse between two events (Bucci, *et al.*, 2004).

As it is clear from pTPN semantic a "clock" (pTPN do not use explicit clocks on the syntax level but the time to fire used in semantic definition has similar definition) is needed to measure time to fire of each enabled transition of the pTPN. pTPN therefore needs a "clock" for each ready task. Experiments that we have conducted on the tool ORIS (tool implementing the pTPN analysis described in (Bucci, *et al.*, 2004)) show that pTPN model complexity is similar to *n-clock* approach.

We have generated the state space of the models from Section Experimental results via the ORIS plugin *tcAnalyzer2*. It enumerates the over-approximate state space that can be inspected later by other ORIS plugins. The time and memory requirements are listed in Table 2.

In fact, the comparison of pTPN and TA can not be done while comparing execution times of different tools. Notice that UPPAAL checks the state space of the model on the fly while ORIS enumerates and saves all the state space. We present this comparison for demonstration of the relation between the number of tasks and the state-space size.

## CONCLUSION

In this chapter, we have demonstrated how timed automata can be used for modeling of the multitasking preemptive application. The main advantage of this approach is that the proposed model only requires one clock variable for all tasks in the application. Since the complexity of the timed automata model checking is exponential on the number of clocks (Daws & Yovine 1996), reduction of the number of used clocks provides a very important reduction of the state space. The effect of the number of clocks reduction is slightly counter balanced by the complexity of the algorithm *Clock2Int* used to find the nearest lower and upper integer of the clock. Since the complexity of the *Clock2Int* algorithm is only $O(log_2\ MaxC)$ the reduction of the number of clocks provides a significant improvement of the complexity, especially for a higher number of tasks (more than four in our experiments).

Since an exhaustive analysis of the detailed timed automata model is subjected to a state space explosion (which is a general property of most formal methods (Corbett, 1996)), reduction of the model state-space size is one of the most important issues that must be solved prior to wide use of formal methods in practice. Therefore, the proposed model is abstract as much as possible and only contains information necessary for correct verification of the system specification.

The operating system model uses modest data structures and it does not use any clock variables (duration of the OS services and context switch is involved in the execution time of the *computations*). Notice also that OSEK is one of the most appropriate operating systems to be modeled by timed automata since it is static (all objects are created at the compilation time) and it is designed for a modest runtime environment of embedded devices. More complex OS can make the verification impossible due to the state space explosion. Also the model of application tasks must be designed as a compromise between the model precision and its state space size. It is necessary to limit the size of the modeled data, the non-determinism and the number of *computations* to obtain a model of reasonable size. The method is therefore appropriate for verification of critical parts of the system while the rest is modeled in abstract way.

Even though the model is an over-approximation of the real system behavior, complex time and logical properties considering application data and a controlled system model can be verified by a model-checking tool, since safety and bounded liveness properties (the most important classes) are preserved by over-approximation. On the other hand, the over-approximation decreases the precision of the model. Since the level of the over-approximation depends on the ratio of the number of preemptions and execution times of computations, the methods is not appropriate for systems with short computations and many preemptions.

The method has been demonstrated on the example of concrete OS. It can be generalized, however, for systems satisfying the following conditions:

- Single processor system. In the case of multiprocessor system, all application tasks must be dedicated to a processor with OS.

- The number of all OS objects (tasks, inter-task communication primitives, etc.) must be bounded and known in advance.
- Bounded execution times (lower and upper bounds),
- Fixed priority preemptive scheduling. It could be modified for any deterministic scheduling policy in principle, but any additional information necessary for scheduler decision (e.g. absolute deadlines in EDF) blows up the state space.
- Scheduler or interrupts provide stack-based interruption and restoration of tasks (first interrupted task is restored last).

## ACKNOWLEDGMENT

We would like to thank Gerd Behrmann from the Department of Computer Science at Aalborg University, Denmark for his advice related to reducing the complexity of the ready queue model.

This work was supported by the Ministry of Education of the Czech Republic under Project 1M0567 and by the Ministry of Industry and Trade of the Czech Republic under project FT-TA3/044.

## REFERENCES

Alur, R., & Dill, D. L. (1994). A theory of timed automata. *Theoretical Computer Science*, *126*, 183–235. doi:10.1016/0304-3975(94)90010-8

Berard, B., Bidoit, M., Finkel, A., Laroussinie, F., Petit, A., Petrucci, L., et al. (2001). *Systems and software verification. Model checking techniques and tools*. Berlin/New York: Springer-Verlag.

Berthomieu, B., Lime, D., Roux, O. H., & Vernadat, F. (2007). Reachability problems and abstract state spaces for time petri nets with stopwatches. *Discrete Event Dynamic Systems*, *17*(2), 133–158. doi:10.1007/s10626-006-0011-y

Bucci, G., Fedeli, A., Sassoli, L., & Vicario, E. (2004). Timed state space analysis of real-time preemptive systems. *IEEE Transactions on Software Engineering*, *30*(2), 97–111. doi:10.1109/TSE.2004.1265815

Campos, S., & Clarke, E. (1999). Analysis and verification of real-time systems using quantitative symbolic algorithms. *Journal of Software Tools for Technology Transfer*, *2*(3), 260–269. doi:10.1007/s100090050033

Corbett, J. C. (1996). Timing analysis of ada tasking programs. *IEEE Transactions on Software Engineering*, *22*(7), 461–483. doi:10.1109/32.538604

Daws, C., & Yovine, S. (1996). Reducing the number of clock variables of timed automata. In *Proceedings of the 17th IEEE Real Time Systems Symposium*. Washington, D.C.: IEEE Computer Society Press.

Fersman, E., Pettersson, P., & Yi, W. (2002). Timed automata with asynchronous processes: Schedulability and decidability. In *Proceedings of 8th International Conference on Tools and Algorithms for the Construction and Analysis of Systems TACAS 2002* (LNCS 2280, pp.67-82). Berlin/New York: Springer-Verlag.

Fersman, E., Pettersson, P., & Yi, W. (2003). Schedulability analysis using two clocks. In *Proceedings of 9th International Conference on Tools and Algorithms for the Construction and Analysis of Systems TACAS 2003* (LNCS 2619, pp. 224-239). Berlin/New York: Springer-Verlag.

Fredette, A. N., & Cleaveland, R. (1993). RTSL: A language for real-time schedulability analysis. In *Proceedings of the Real-Time Systems Symposium* (pp 274-283). IEEE Computer Society Press.

Henzinger, T. A., Kopke, P. W., Puri, A., & Varaiya, P. (1998). What's decidable about hybrid automata? *Journal of Computer and System Sciences*, *57*, 94–124. doi:10.1006/jcss.1998.1581

Krčál, P., Mokrushin, L., Thiagarajan, P. S., & Yi, W. (2004). Timed vs. time triggered automata. In *Proceedings of the 15th International Conference on Concurrency Theory CONCUR'04* (LNCS 3170, pp. 340-354). Berlin/New York: Springer-Verlag.

Krčál, P., & Yi, W. (2004). Decidable and undecidable problems in schedulability analysis using timed automata. In *Proceedings of 10th International Conference on Tools and Algorithms for the Construction and Analysis of Systems TACAS* (LNCS 2988, pp. 236-250). Berlin/New York: Springer-Verlag.

Larsen, K. G., Peterson, P., & Yi, W. (1997). UPPAAL in a nutshell. *International Journal on Software Tools for Technology Transfer*, *1*(1/2), 134–152.

Lime, D., & Roux, O. H. (2004). A translation based method for the timed analysis of scheduling extended time petri nets. In *Proceedings of the 25th IEEE International Real-Time Systems Symposium* (pp. 187-196). IEEE Computer Society Press.

Liu, J. W. S. (2000). *Real-time systems*. Upper Saddle River, NJ: Prentice-Hall.

Lundqvist, K., & Asplund, L. (2003). A ravenscar-compliant run-time kernel for safety-critical systems. *Real-Time Systems*, *24*(1), 29–54. doi:10.1023/A:1021701221847

Merlin, P., & Faber, D. J. (1976). Recoverability of communication protocols. *IEEE Transactions on Communications, 24*(9), 1036–1043. doi:10.1109/TCOM.1976.1093424

OSEK Group. (2005). *OSEK/VDX operating system specification 2.2.3*. Retrieved from http://www.osek-vdx.org/

Ramchandani, C. (1974). *Analysis of asynchronous concurrent systems by timed petri nets* (Tech. Rep. No. 120). Cambridge, MA: Massachusetts Institute of Technology.

Waszniowski, L. (2006). *Formal verification of multitasking applications based on a timed automata model*. Unpublished doctoral dissertation, Czech Technical University in Prague, Czech Republic.

Waszniowski, L., & Hanzálek, Z. (2005). Timed automata model of preemptive multitasking applications. In *Preprints of the 16th World Congress of the International Federation of Automatic Control* [CD-ROM]. Praha: IFAC.

Waszniowski, L., & Hanzálek, Z. (2008). Formal verification of multitasking applications based on timed automata model. *Real-Time Systems, 38*(1), 39–65. doi:10.1007/s11241-007-9036-z

# Chapter 9

# SystemC Platform Modeling for Behavioral Simulation and Performance Estimation of Embedded Systems

**Héctor Posadas**
*University of Cantabria, Spain*

**Juan Castillo**
*University of Cantabria, Spain*

**David Quijano**
*University of Cantabria, Spain*

**Victor Fernández**
*University of Cantabria, Spain*

**Eugenio Villar**
*University of Cantabria, Spain*

**Marcos Martínez**
*DS2, Spain*

## ABSTRACT[1]

*Currently, embedded systems make use of large, multiprocessing systems on chip integrating complex application software running on the different processors in close interaction with the application-specific hardware. These systems demand new modeling, simulation, and performance estimation tools and methodologies for system architecture evaluation and design exploration. Recently approved as IEEE 1666 standard, SystemC has proven to be a powerful language for system modeling and simulation. In this chapter, SCoPE, a SystemC framework for platform modeling, SW source-code behavioral simulation and performance estimation of embedded systems is presented. Using SCoPE, the application SW running on the different processors of the platform can be simulated efficiently in close interaction with the rest of the platform components. In this way, fast and sufficiently accurate performance metrics are obtained for design-space exploration.*

DOI: 10.4018/978-1-60566-750-8.ch009

# INTRODUCTION

Current integrated circuit technologies allow the implementation of general-purpose processors and application-specific HW in a single chip leading to what is called, Systems on Chip (SoC). The tendency continues towards SoC containing multiple processors executing SW in parallel. In this way, the SoC become Multi-Processing SoC (MPSoC) (Jerraya & Wolf, 2005). Moreover, the interactions among so many computational units make traditional bus-based architectures unscalable and unfeasible for efficient MPSoC communication. The increase of collisions and delays produced in buses obliges a move to Network on Chip (NoC) architectures (Benini & de Micheli, 2006).

Design productivity for these complex, integrated systems remains one of the Grand Challenges to the evolution of the semiconductor technology, as stated by the ITRS (ITRS, 2007A). In fact, "cost of design is the greatest threat to continuation of the semiconductor roadmap". An essential aspect to be highlighted is that "SW aspects of Integrated Circuit (IC) design can now account for 80% or more of embedded system development costs" (ITRS, 2007B, p. 1).

Correct dimensioning of the system at the beginning of the development process is a key design decision to ensure an optimized implementation. System design with an optimum trade-off in performance and cost requires the consideration of a wide set of parameters, such as number and type of processors, mapping of SW tasks and suitability of communication infrastructure. This wide set of system parameters implies a wide design space to be explored by the system designer.

Design Space Exploration (DSE) enables the designer to evaluate different possibilities in order to implement the design covering the requirements in an efficient way. Once the system specification has been developed, and before fine grain refinement, all the relevant possibilities have to be explored. This exploration of the design space consists in analyzing the characteristics of the possible system configurations in terms of performance, power, area, cost, etc.

Due to the large number of possibilities to be analyzed, fast and sufficiently accurate modeling and simulation techniques are required. As a consequence, fast simulation and performance analysis is necessary with enough accuracy in the metrics provided in order to enable an adequate system evaluation. Estimation errors of about 30-40% can be accepted for initial system assessments (ITRS, 2007).

System modeling, simulation, performance analysis and design-space exploration are fundamental Electronic, System-Level (ESL) design activities. ESL design is currently a very active area including any electronic design methodology that focuses on higher abstraction levels than RTL (Bailey, Martin, & Piziali, 2007). The basic premise is to model the behavior of the entire system using languages that support higher abstraction levels than VHDL or Verilog. Among them, C, C++, MatLab-Simulink, SystemVerilog and SystemC are the most popular ones. ESL is now an established market and most of the world's leading SoC CAD companies offer different tools tackling different design steps.

Currently, two different approaches to system modeling and simulation can be found (Milligan, 2005). On the one hand, high-level, behavioral models such as C/C++ or MatLab-Simulink are used. They are fast but do not provide information about the performance of a particular architectural solution. On the other hand, there are cycle-accurate models based on ISS simulation of the complete application SW and Real Time Operative System (RTOS) on each processor interacting with the application-specific HW using a Transaction Level Modeling (TLM) interface. They are precise but too slow for performance analysis and architectural exploration.

In this chapter, SCoPE, a SystemC framework supporting platform modeling for behavioral simulation and performance estimation of embedded systems is proposed. The execution of the application SW is simulated in the host using advanced, abstract models of the processor and the RTOS. This emulation provides a timed modeling of the SW from a common, untimed SW source code, in order to provide a timed executable model of the entire embedded system. Application-specific HW is easily integrated using TLM bus interfaces. SCoPE is based on a SystemC library that makes use of the SystemC features for system modeling and simulation. As will be shown in the case study, the framework is flexible enough to support any MPSoC architecture with any number of nodes in a NoC, each node with any bus architecture, either Symmetric and Heterogeneous Multi-Processing architectures and the complete system with any topology of memory spaces[2].

The content of the chapter is the following. First the state-of the art for system design modeling and simulation is analyzed. SystemC is introduced, presenting its benefits and identifying its advantages and disadvantages for SW source-code and platform simulation. Then, solutions for developing a fast and sufficiently accurate modeling infrastructure are presented. The SCoPE Framework implements these solutions, which will be presented in section III.4. Finally, the chapter ends with future trends and conclusions.

## BACKGROUND

The fundamental steps of the generic design process for complex, heterogeneous, embedded systems are shown in Figure 1 (Bailey, Martin, & Piziali, 2007). From the initial system specification using an appropriate language (such as Matlab-Simulink or SystemC), the architectural mapping is decided. In this step, functionality is allocated to specific platform resources such as a general-purpose processor or application-specific HW. Design space exploration is the process in which the platform architecture and the architectural mapping are optimized with the objective of ensuring the satisfaction of the design constraints.

Once the architectural mapping is finished, the HW and SW functions in each platform resource are extracted. SW can be compiled for each processor and HW synthesized.

## System Simulation and Performance Estimation

As commented above, system simulation is a key design task widely used for design verification. System simulation is twofold. On the one hand, the main objective is to ensure the functional correctness of the design at the different abstraction levels. On the other, system simulation is used for performance analysis, verifying the non-functional design constraints such as delays, throughput, utilization rates, bandwidths, etc. Power consumption is becoming an additional, increasingly important parameter to be estimated.

While HW simulation can be performed at different abstraction levels using appropriate languages such as VHDL, Verilog, System-Verilog and SystemC, efficient, sufficiently accurate SW simulation is still an unsolved problem.

Currently, the two main methodologies used for SW simulation are SW execution on a host computer and Instruction-Set Simulation (Bailey, Martin, & Piziali, 2007). As shown in Figure 2, the application SW can be directly executed on the host using the native compiler. The host OS can be used to emulate the target platform RTOS. Moreover, direct source-code execution eliminates any overhead caused by modeling techniques, providing very fast execution times. However, implementation details, such as time and power consumption cannot be estimated. SW execution can be linked to a model of the platform. Nevertheless, as the SW is not simulated, the actual interaction with the HW cannot be taken into account. Thus, the evaluation of the effect of any modification in any design parameter is not possible. This makes SW execution invalid for DSE.

Instruction Set Simulators (ISS) can be used to execute the SW binary code, together with

*Figure 1. Generic HW/SW embedded system design flow*

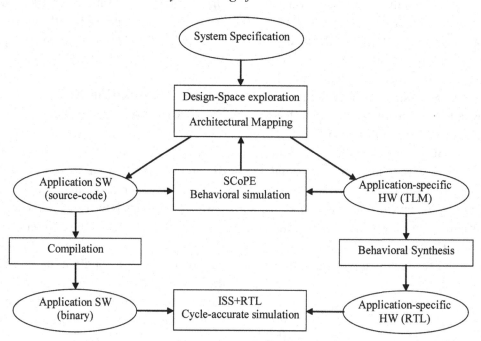

cycle accurate models of other platform components. As shown in Figure 3, the application SW including the RTOS is compiled and the corresponding binary code is simulated using an ISS as an additional component of the complete, cycle-accurate, platform model. However, these techniques require hours or even days to simulate relatively simple systems. Thus, although they are still needed for final system verification and refinement, they are not useful for DSE.

In order to ensure sufficiently accurate simulation with reasonable execution times, an intermediate solution is needed. The proposed solution, shown in Figure 4, is to perform SW source-code simulation, including accurate estimations of the performance parameters, running conjointly with a

high-level model of the HW platform. These models are not as accurate as cycle accurate models, but they are much faster. High-level descriptions of the platform components are used for this source-code, behavioral simulation. In this approach, the processor and the RTOS are modeled together, as a single high-level component, which replaces the ISS. This solution enables the designer to obtain sufficiently accurate system performance estimations with higher simulation speeds. Furthermore, it avoids the need of cross-compiling the source code for the target architecture.

The commercial modeling and simulation tools currently available are based on previous research activity in academia. In (Benini et al., 2003) a generic design environment for multiprocessor

*Figure 2. SW execution*

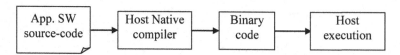

*Figure 3. Instruction-set simulation*

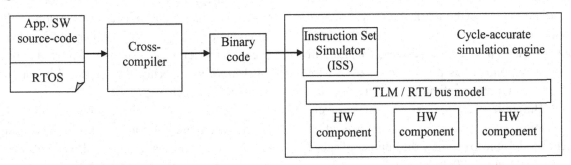

system modeling was proposed. The environment enables transparent integration of ISSs and prototyping boards. As an evolution of this work, in (Benini et al., 2005) a SystemC infrastructure was developed to model architectures with multiple ARM cores. This approach provides a varied set of tools that enables designers to efficiently design SW applications (OS ports, compilers, etc.). A fully operational Linux version for embedded systems was ported on the platform. SW simulation was based on an ISS for each processor, thus presenting the advantages and disadvantages commented above. Moreover, it cannot be easily used to evaluate platforms that do not contain ARM processors.

Several approaches have been proposed to improve the state-of-the-art of commercial tools. One of them is the modification of the OS running over the ISS. As the OS is in fact the interface between SW applications and the rest of the system, it can be used to save simulation time. In (Yi, Kim, & Ha, 2003), a technique based on virtual synchronization is presented to speed up execution of several SW tasks in the ISS. Only the application tasks run over the ISS. The OS is modeled in the co-simulation backplane thus accelerating its simulation. As the OS execution time is only part of the total execution time, the gain is limited. Authors provide improvements up to 38%.

As commented before, fast SW simulation requires direct execution of the source code. At this level, either using static (Balarin et al., 1997; Hergenhan & Rosenstiel, 2000) or dynamic techniques (Brandolese et al., 2001; Kempf et al., 2006; Posadas et al., 2004) the SW execu-

*Figure 4. Source-code SW simulation*

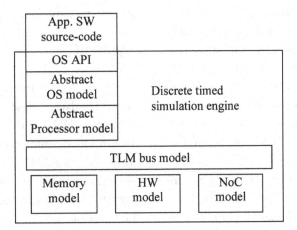

tion times are estimated and annotated to obtain timed simulations of the application SW. A simple version of this technique has been implemented in a commercial tool (Interdesign). This kind of analysis technique has proven to be useful for power consumption estimation (Laurent et al., 2002; Brandolese, 2000; Castillo, 2007) as well. Rosenstiel et al. have proposed an instruction cache model able to estimate the number of cache misses (Rosenstiel, 2008).

However, application SW cannot be adequately modeled alone. SW requires a RTOS for execution. When several SW tasks run in the same processor, they cannot run at the same time. They have to be scheduled adequately. Furthermore, SW/SW communication commonly uses mechanisms not directly supported by SystemC. As a consequence, a RTOS model is required as an integral part of the SW simulation environment. The previously mentioned approaches required the complete source code to operate, that is, the application SW and the RTOS. In order to model the target RTOS functionality on the host, an emulation using the host RTOS has to be provided.

Several approaches have been proposed for abstract OS modeling for SW source-code simulation, from generic (Yoo, 2002; Gerstlauer, 2003; He, 2005; Hassan, 2005) to real OS models (Hassan, 2005A; Posadas, 2006). This approach has two main advantages. On the one hand, as the RTOS functionality is abstracted, additional simulation time is saved. On the other hand, when efficiently exploited, a more accurate model of the underlying RTOS can be achieved. This additional efficiency is obtained by combining the source-code execution time estimation with the OS model providing more accurate results. These abstract RTOS techniques also dedicate a large effort to accurately integrate time annotation and OS modeling with HW/SW communication, especially for HW interrupt management. Very few of these approaches support a real OS application programming interface (API) such as TRON or POSIX (Hassan, 2005B)(Posadas, 2007). The

idea of integrating facilities for OS modeling in SystemC was proposed as a new version of the language (SystemC 3.x) [Grotker, 2002]. However, OS modeling at system level proved to be a much more complex task than expected, becoming an active research area.

However, none of these modeling methodologies are aimed at complex Multi-Processing systems. Dynamic task mapping, drivers and interrupt management required in MPSoC modeling and simulation are not covered by the previous techniques with the simulation speed required for performance estimations and system dimensioning. Moreover, a framework is required that supports a complete model of the platform that can easily integrate new components, either an application-specific HW or a programmable processor. In this chapter, a framework where these limitations are solved is proposed. Specifically, SCoPE includes abstract models of the RTOS and the multi-processing architecture that can easily integrate the application SW through the RTOS API (i.e. POSIX). The SW is annotated with estimates of the execution time and power consumption. In each node, the multi-processing architecture is connected through an abstract TLM model of the bus with the peripherals and application-specific HW components. Different nodes in the system are connected through a network-on-chip simulator. As a consequence, SCoPE provides the designer with a framework for holistic simulation and performance estimation of a complete, multi-processing embedded system.

## SystemC

As derived from the previous discussion, traditional Hardware Description Languages (HDLs) such as VHDL and Verilog lack the required features to accommodate the increasing functionality of current MPSoCs. HW/SW co-simulation is a clear case where these languages show their limitations. These languages also show limitations for behavioral synthesis, SW development

*Figure 5. SystemC structure*

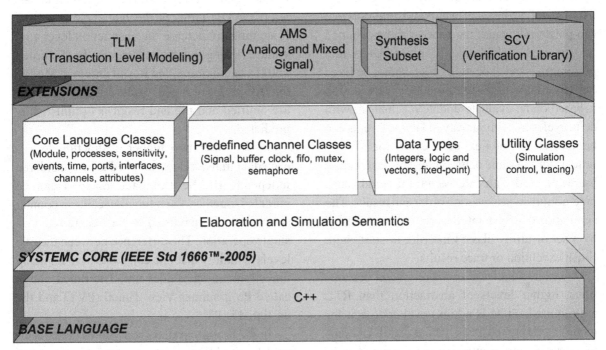

and SW compilation. These restrictions reduce their usefulness for system-level modeling. In this scenario, the OSCI (Open SystemC Initiative) developed SystemC™ as an open industry standard for system-level modeling, design and verification. SystemC™ is an ANSI standard C++ class library for ESL design (Swan, 2002). The goal of the language is to provide system designers and architects with the required facilities for the specification, modeling and design of complex MPSoCs including the parallel application SW and RTOS in each processor, the memory and bus architectures, DMAs, peripherals, the application-specific HW and the NoC. Although SystemC provides the required features for those tasks, additional effort is needed to provide the designer with a complete framework for MPSoC with NoC modeling, simulation and performance estimation.

SystemC can be structured as shown in Figure 5. The language relies on C++ as it is actually a C++ class library. The middle part of Figure 5 describes what is usually called the language core.

It is composed of two layers. The lower layer is a discrete-event (DE), event-driven simulator. Its implementation is undefined in order to allow the development of different simulators with the same functionality but not necessarily the same performance. The upper layer contains a varied set of C++ classes clearly defined in the IEEE Standard. Most of these classes provide the semantic, structural, functional, communication and data typing facilities required for HW/SW system modeling and design. These classes have simulation semantics, so they can be seen as the user facilities to program the underlying DE virtual machine. On top of the core part of the language, one can find several language extensions, which are being developed by different OSCI working groups. One of the main advantages of SystemC is its flexibility. Being a C++ library, the system designer can exploit the full language on top of the SystemC core with specific semantics for any particular application.

SystemC descriptions, once the hierarchy is flattened, can be seen as a set of parallel processes.

Such processes have static and dynamic sensitivity lists that define the set of events and time-outs that can potentially cause the process to be resumed or triggered. Scheduling of processes is non pre-emptive and execution order cannot be fixed directly by the user. The model of computation is based on an evaluate-update mechanism with delta cycles in a similar way to HDLs. Events can be notified for the next delta cycle, for a future time or for the same delta cycle. This last feature has to be used with care because it could cause indeterminism in execution order and results. The simulation of a SystemC description is controlled by a set of utility classes in order to start, stop, finish execution or trace results.

In order to increase speed of system descriptions, higher levels of abstraction than RTL are required. TLM is a high-level approach for modeling digital systems, where details of communication among modules are separated from the details of the implementation of functional units or of the communication architecture. This clear separation enables the simplification of the communication mechanisms, thus increasing the simulation speed (Ghenassia, 2005). In TLM, each transfer only requires a function call, instead of several signal accesses. In this way simulation speed is greatly improved. Several generic TLM bus models have been developed (Viaud, 2006; Klingauf 2006), as well as specific bus ones, such as AMBA (Pasricha, 2004), CAN (Schirner, 2007) or STBus (Moussa, 2003).

TLM does not represent a single abstraction level. Transfers can be applied at different levels of abstraction. Usually three levels are defined (Klingauf, 2006). In the first one, Bus-Cycle Accurate (BCA), each clock cycle is modeled independently. Thus, each transfer requires a different function call. This technique is suitable when executing SW code in processor models. Each time the SW wants to send a word through the bus, one transfer is done. As ISSs of specific processors are required, this level is commonly used with specific bus models. In (Pasricha, 2004),

Cycle Count Accurate at Transaction Boundaries (CCATB) replaces the bus cycle accuracy. It attempts to increase the abstraction level a bit without losing the cycle accuracy. In (Schirner, 2007) a technique called Result Oriented Modeling (ROM) is presented, where internal bus states are omitted and the end result is optimistically predicted.

In the other two higher abstraction levels, each data transfer does not need to be considered independently. Several data transfers can be modeled together. Each function call can contain several words (payload) to be transferred in a single operation. The difference between the two levels is mainly that one considers transfer delay times but the other does not. The timed one is called Programmer View Timed (PVT) and the un-timed is PV.

In PVT, approximate delay times are considered. Delays in transferring payloads can be caused by three elements: bus propagation delay, transfer time (time of single transfer x size of payload) and peripheral internal delay. Thus, a bus access does not finish until all these times have been applied. This provides approximately-timed simulations that allow system performance estimations to be obtained avoiding the overheads of clock-cycle based descriptions.

Although TLM extension provides functionality to use SystemC as a high-level language, it still lacks important features. SystemC is not capable of adding or even considering non-functional parameters for SW source-code. All sc_threads are handled to run completely in parallel, without considering any resource occupation or scheduling effect. In the same way, HW/SW interfacing, such as interruption handling or device driver management are not covered. Furthermore, the TLM library provides interfaces for modeling communication, but complete bus or network models are not provided. The TLM goal is just to define the interfaces to be used, but the models have to be developed by the user.

From the discussion above, it can be concluded that SystemC provides the fundamental features for complex, HW/SW embedded system modeling. Nevertheless, several SystemC extensions are required in order to provide fast, sufficiently accurate MPSoC with NoC modeling including application SW running in parallel. The proposed extensions are presented in the next section.

## SYSTEMC EXTENSIONS FOR TIMED-BEHAVIORAL SIMULATION

### Application SW Modeling

Performance (even behavior) of embedded systems depends significantly on execution times of application software. Functional, untimed simulation does not provide accurate enough information. Timing behavior of application SW may have an important impact. So, for instance, tasks can be rescheduled in a different way than predicted by the untimed simulation, suffer from priority inversion, hardware interrupts can be missed, unprotected shared memory or unpredicted interaction with peripherals and application-specific HW may cause non-deterministic behavior, etc. In order to detect and avoid these sources of error at early stages of the design process, it is necessary to obtain a fast, sufficiently accurate model of the application software taking into account the execution times of the different tasks and how these times affect the behavior of the SW running in interaction with the rest of the system.

If the simulation model of SystemC is considered, the code of "sc-threads" is executed in "zero time", advancing the time only when the "*wait (time)*" sentence is reached within the code execution. Nevertheless, this behavior does not correspond to what happens with real software, where time advances with every instruction executed by the processor.

In order to simulate real software behavior within a SystemC environment, it is necessary to obtain an executable model including the execution time estimations. The proposed approach uses a two-step model. First, the stand-alone execution time of SW tasks is estimated (this step must be performed before starting the SystemC simulation). These times are used in the second step, where they are back-annotated in the application code by inserting some extra code. The resultant code is simulated with the rest of the system, thus obtaining a HW-SW co-simulation environment which provides early performance estimations.

### Performance Estimation

As mentioned before, the first step of the proposed model is to estimate the execution times of application software. These times must be obtained *stand-alone*, assuming that all resources are available for the SW task and no interruptions arrive at the system. These and other collateral effects will be considered later during the SystemC simulation of the whole system. As an example, bus collisions will be considered within the bus model.

In order to estimate execution times, the embedded microprocessor must be previously modeled and characterized. This model must be light enough to allow fast simulations, in contrast to traditional ISS-based models providing cycle or instruction accuracy.

The proposed approach provides two techniques for processor modeling and performance estimation. Each technique can be located at a different level of abstraction. The highest level technique consists of assigning an average time to each C/C++ operator. These average values can be obtained with physical measurements, cycle-accurate simulators or analytical techniques. Thus, the estimated running time for a software task will be the sum of all operators executed, plus some extra operations such as loops or branches. This technique is valid for sufficiently large application codes, when average values can be applied for each operator without a great loss of accuracy.

*Figure 6. Annotation points*

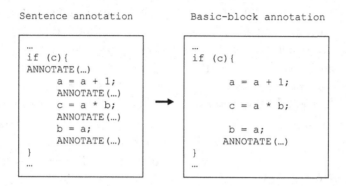

The estimated running time must be registered and increased with the execution of the SW tasks and annotated in the SystemC simulation. SystemC annotation is performed by means of *"wait (time)"* sentences at some pre-defined key points (we denominate the task execution between two consecutive "wait" sentences *segment*). To account for the execution time of each segment, the estimated time obtained from operator costs is back-annotated in the original source code. Thus, it is necessary to introduce some extra information at some places in order to store the execution time in a temporal variable and to increase it as simulation advances.

The execution of this extra information involves a penalty in the simulation performance since it is not functional user code, so it must be done as efficiently as possible. The proposed solution is to annotate the code at each basic-block (any piece of code without control sentences (Aho, 2007) as shown in Figure 6. The basic block minimizes the number of annotations without affecting the accuracy of the technique.

Figure 7 shows a basic example of the annotation technique.

The second model for time estimation is located at a lower level of abstraction, but it can provide better results in accuracy with a relative low penalty in performance. The application code is cross-compiled for the target architecture, and the resultant assembler code is analyzed, identifying and characterizing each basic block. This characterization is done in terms of number of instructions, so that execution time can be estimated multiplying by the average Cycles Per Instruction (CPI) of the processor. The information

*Figure 7. Example of extra code for annotating delays*

```
int a, b, c, i;
a = 1;
b = 2;
for (i=0;i<10;i++)
{
        c=a+b+i;
        a++;
}
i=0;
if (c>100) {
        b=0;
}
```

```
int a, b, c, i;
a = 1;
b = 2;
segment_time+=10; for (i=0;i<10;i++)
{
        c=a+b+i;
        a++;
segment_time+=40; }
i=0;
segment_time+=5; if (c>100) {
        b=0;
segment_time+=10; }
```

is back-annotated in the original source code in a similar way as in the previous technique based on the operators' cost.

Both techniques are complementary, in the sense that operator costs can be applied at very early stages of the design process, when the CPU has not yet been chosen. Assembler Machine Code (ASM) analysis can be applied at later stages, when higher accuracy is needed. In this case, a pre-processing stage after cross-compilation for the target architecture is required.

In parallel to time estimations, the proposed techniques are able to estimate the power consumption required by the processor to execute the application software. The same methods used for execution time estimation can be applied for power and energy modeling.

The first approach consists of assigning an average value of energy consumption to each C/C++ operator, so the account of estimated energy can be calculated in parallel with execution time (Castillo, 2007). The main difference is that, while time estimations are annotated within the SystemC simulation kernel, energy estimations must be stored, so they can be reported at the end of the simulation.

The second approach consists of assigning an average value of energy to each machine instruction. By analyzing the cross-compiled code, we obtain the number of instructions for each basic block, and this value is back-annotated in the original source code along with time annotations. When running the simulation, this extra code is executed so we can estimate the number of machine instructions executed. By multiplying this value by the average energy per instruction, we obtain an estimation of the total energy required by the processor. It should be noted that, while this approach is valid for all processors, the accuracy of the technique depends on the stability of the power consumption of the target core.

One important issue that must be considered when estimating software performance is the influence of cache memories. Models of both the data and instruction caches are now under refinement and will be included in a future version of SCoPE.

In order to parse and annotate systemC code, a C/C++ "*pseudo-compiler*" has been developed. This pseudo-compiler performs several internal steps. First, the application source code is preprocessed with a common pre-processor (*cpp*). The resultant code is parsed in order to detect operators or basic blocks, depending on the technique selected by the designer. If necessary, the code is cross-compiled and then, with another tool, basic blocks are characterized from its assembler code. Estimated parameters are back-annotated in the original source code. As a last step, this annotated code is compiled (*gcc* or *g++*) and linked with the rest of the SystemC simulation files. Figure 8 shows this process for the case of the assembler machine instructions technique.

## Execution Model

As mentioned before, to model the behavior of software in a SystemC simulation environment, the source code is characterized in terms of time and energy and instrumented with SystemC "*wait (time)*" statements. These "*wait (time)*" statements are inserted into the application code at some key points of the task code. The code between two consecutive waits is called a segment.

According to the SystemC simulation mechanism, segments are executed without preemption. At the end of the segment, a "*wait (time)*" sentence is executed, annotating the segment time in the SystemC simulation. Then, the scheduler is invoked to execute the remaining SystemC threads. Nevertheless, this is not the behavior of real software, where the control flow of a segment can be affected by external events, typically interruptions.

The proposed approach deals with this situation considering that the execution of some parts of the SW tasks is independent from the rest of the system. This is true while the application code

*Figure 8. Compilation (with parsing and annotation) process*

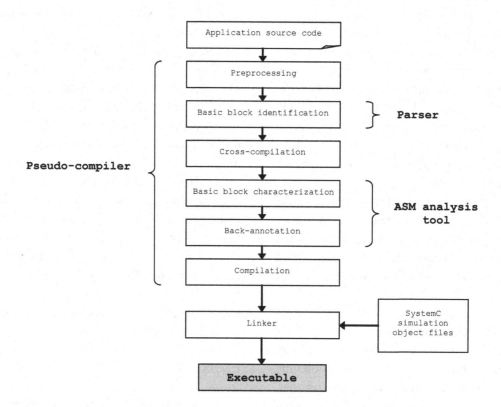

accesses only internal data and does not require any external information. Thus, we can map such local parts of code to segments. To identify local code, we have to detect the events at which we have an external access, such as I/O operations, IPC (Inter-Process Communication) or interruptions. While none of these events occur, we can obtain the same result with the twp annotation techniques commented above:

- Advancing the time with each assembler instruction executed, or
- Executing all the instructions and advancing the total time at the end of the segment

The proposed model uses the second technique, since it is much more time-efficient because the number of waits executed is dramatically reduced.

I/O operations and IPC system calls are explicitly inserted in the code, so they can be detected easily. These events will be used as the key points to insert the "*wait (time)*" sentences. Execution time of SW tasks is annotated in the SystemC simulation at the end of each segment, given that the segment code is entirely executed without pre-emption.

Interruptions are asynchronous and unpredictable events, so they must be detected dynamically during execution. When considering real software, external events (such as hardware interruptions) can pre-empt the current task and modify shared resources, so the behavior of the application can change. Nevertheless, if source code is deterministic, accesses to shared resources and critical regions are always performed through system calls, so the approach is still valid.

*Figure 9. Modeling of interruption*

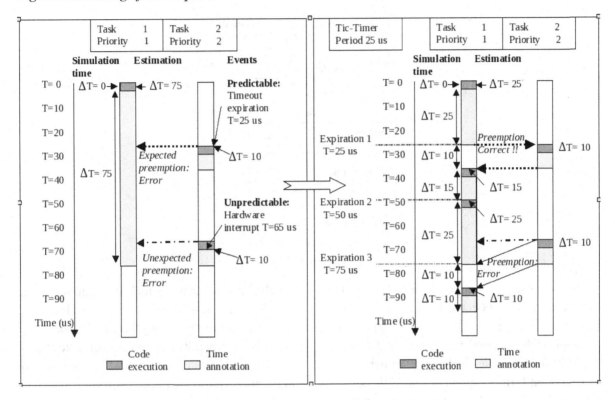

Hardware interruptions are modeled using SystemC events. Then, wait statements for SW tasks are conditioned to those events:

wait (time, event);

If the event is notified, the wait finishes immediately, even if the complete time has not elapsed. The OS model (see the following section of this chapter) is called to manage the preemption, adding the preempted thread to the ready queue and starting the interrupt manager. When the preempted task is rescheduled, it detects that there is still a remaining time from the last wait sentence, so it immediately executes a wait sentence again with the remaining time. Figure 9 illustrates the proposed approach:

RTOS delays are taken into account by considering the overhead of system calls and system services. System calls are those routines of the

RTOS which are executed at the request of application SW, while system services are those routines that are executed independently (interrupt service routines, task scheduler, etc). Each time these routines are executed, their associated delay is added to the total cost of the SW task. These associated costs should be provided by the operating system provider.

## RTOS Modeling

One of the most important points when transforming a high-level description into a real SW implementation is the inclusion of the OS. The SW code is gradually refined, mapping high-level facilities, such as communication and synchronization facilities, to the target OS facilities. Thus, the development infrastructure has to support the refined SW code, providing the target OS facilities inside the PVT model of the application SW.

*Figure 10. OS model architecture*

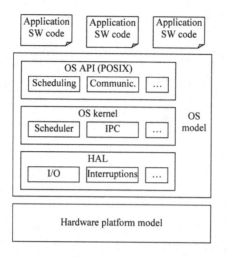

The proposed OS model is divided in a similar way to real OSs. An OS can be divided into several layers (Tanenbaum, 2001). In the upper part, we can find the system call handlers that support the API. In the middle, the layers for internal OS management form what can be called the kernel core. At the bottom, there are the layers oriented to hide the HW platform details (Hardware Abstraction Layer, HAL) from the rest of the system, such as low-level functions to access the bus, the interruption management or the context switch infrastructure. Thus, the proposed OS model will provide support for all of these common OS sections, as can be seen in Figure 10. In order to simplify the models, all the possible layers have been concentrated into three layers, following the classification above.

The kernel core is mainly in charge of process and thread execution management, memory management and task communication and synchronization. To model task scheduling characteristics, a new scheduler is placed on top of the original SystemC scheduler. The OS model scheduler controls task execution by maintaining only one unblocked thread per processor. This scheduler manages the priorities and policies as indicated in POSIX, integrating a two-level scheduler: process scheduling and thread scheduling. The scheduler

is called when a task is blocked or unblocked as an effect of a system call, or when an interrupt resumes a task preempting the current one.

This functionality has been implemented making use of the SystemC features. So, each thread in the application SW is associated to a SystemC thread ("SC_THREAD") running the corresponding code. In this way, the SystemC scheduler is in charge of managing the thread context switches. To model the OS thread scheduling the SystemC scheduler is hidden. All the SystemC threads are maintained stopped in SystemC "wait" statements. When the scheduler selects one of these threads, a "notify" call is performed to awake the corresponding thread. When the thread is preempted or blocked, it returns to the "wait" statement and a new thread is scheduled. Thus, the SystemC scheduler executes the only runnable thread each time, so scheduling is completely managed by the OS model scheduler through "wait" and "notify" statements. Thus, SystemC "wait" statements are used for two purposes: thread blocking for scheduling purposes, as explained here, and time annotation as explained in the previous section.

The proposed scheduler model is based on defining seven different states for each execution flow (Figure 11). This graph is similar to the graph commonly used in UNIX systems. Thus, the OS

*Figure 11. Task status graph*

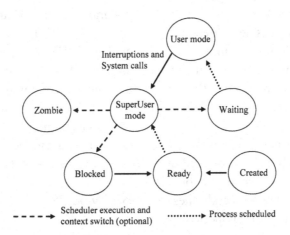

kernel model allows the tasks' execution order to be taken into account in the system simulation, providing much more accurate results than only using the standard SystemC facilities. Modeling the scheduling enables the designer to check and improve priorities and policies of the system SW tasks.

However, SW code refinement implies more than optimizing task scheduling characteristics. The proposed OS model has to provide a wide set of OS facilities, in order to allow the transformation of high-level descriptions into real executable SW codes. High-level features for communication, synchronization or time management have to be substituted by real OS features. In our proposal, a POSIX API has been implemented. POSIX facilities for communication, such as message queues or sockets, facilities for synchronization, such as semaphores, mutex or conditional variables, signals, timers, sleeps and many other facilities are provided. Thus, the designer can simulate the real SW code together with the rest of the system before moving to more accurate but time costly simulation infrastructures, such as ISS models.

Nevertheless, the OS kernel and the API are not enough to provide a complete OS model for software modeling and refinement. Although application code refinement is mostly supported,

Hardware dependent Software (HdS) (such as drivers) is not. A more complete model, capable of managing interruption handlers and drivers, is required. The HdS is usually critical in embedded systems and its analysis at the early stages of embedded system development can provide large benefits during the rest of the project.

HW/SW interface modeling requires an OS model capable of managing the I/O accesses from the processor to the peripherals, and the interruptions the peripherals send to the processor. To manage the I/O, Linux-based driver support is provided. Linux standard functions for registering, accessing and managing drivers are integrated in the OS model, allowing the creation and use of Linux drivers.

Interruptions are produced from the HW platform model and received by the application SW modeling infrastructure, as was explained in the previous section. When the timing effects have been established, the OS facilities for interrupt handling are called by the SW modeling infrastructure, calling the corresponding "wait" and "notify" statements. The standard or user defined handlers associated with the interruptions are executed, performing the proper operations, and calling the corresponding drivers. The HW timer interrupt is of special interest. It is used to manage timers, sleeps, alarms and time-based scheduling policies, such as Round-Robin.

The OS modeling technique is flexible enough to cover the most usual OS architectures. Each OS is associated to a memory space independently of the underlying processing architecture (bus or network). The complete MPSoC may contain as many memory spaces as needed.

To support several independent OS models the OS model information has been encapsulated in a C++ class. Thus, modeling several OSs only requires instantiating an OS class several times.

Multiprocessor management is supported by maintaining as many running threads as processors. When a process is created or preempted, the presence or not of an idle processor is verified. When a processor is delivered, a new thread is scheduled to run on this processor. In this way, all processes are maintained active, and tasks are scheduled as soon as a processor becomes empty.

As all threads are SystemC threads, and the SystemC kernel activates the threads sequentially, there is no real parallelism during the simulation. Parallelism is only emulated. As a consequence, no additional mechanism is required to ensure safe concurrency inside the OS model, in contrast to real Symmetric Multi-Processing (SMP) OSs, where mechanisms such as "spinlocks" are critical to handle concurrency safety.

## HW Platform Modeling

Once the software modeling has been defined, it needs to be connected to a HW platform for HW/SW co-simulation. For this purpose, an intermediate infrastructure is proposed. This infrastructure is placed in the OS model and in the target platform modeling facilities.

The SW modeling facilities presented above require a bus and, sometimes, a network interface to simulate a real communication of the SW with the rest of the platform. The bus model has to interact effectively and efficiently with the

HW, thus a simple and flexible HW interface is integrated. This interface allows connection not only of SCoPE HW components, but also user application HW written in SystemC. Furthermore, some auxiliary HW models are needed to create a complete communication framework. These HW modules are a network interface for node interconnection, a DMA for large data transfers and an abstract model of the physical memory to exchange data with the rest of the platform.

## Bus Modeling

The techniques explained for SW estimation are always focused on fast performance estimation. TLM models are very efficient in this kind of applications. In order to take advantage of the simulation performance that TLM can provide, PVT models are used instead of bus cycle-accurate models. These models use behavioral descriptions with simplified communication mechanisms to perform fast simulations.

The bus model developed uses the TLM library for fast data transmission. In this way, communications are modeled considering complete payload transfers instead of word-by-word transfers. The bus manages the simulation time of each transfer considering parameters such as bus bandwidth and packet priority and size. However, the bus needs another component to complete its functionality, an arbiter. This module performs the transfer scheduling based on packet priority and delivery order. Therefore, the threads that try to access the bus and are not scheduled are blocked in a queue.

Another feature to take into account is the possibility to create bus hierarchy to cover more platform designs. The bus interface is able to connect not only buses with HW models, but also with other buses. This is implemented making use of the standard TLM interface to communicate the different components. This interface can interconnect several modules transparently to the users.

*Figure 12. Wrapper for Bus/HW connection*

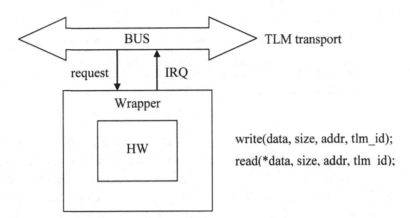

To facilitate the designer's use of the underlying technology (TLM), the HW model has a wrapper with a simple interface shown in Figure 12. With this technique, the bus implementation can be changed transparently. This wrapper transforms the TLM structures and functions to simple read and write functions with data, size and address as parameters. Therefore, the user does not see the complex TLM structures and can work with the relevant data.

## NoC Modeling

The bus or any bus structure does not scale with the number of processing components in a MPSoC. For this reason, SCoPE communication framework includes a NoC that simulates the transfers among different systems. In this way, the group behavior of several devices can be studied. The framework covers a SW driver, an interface HW module and an external network simulator. The driver is similar to the Virtual Point-to-Point network device of Linux (TUN). The TUN driver was designed as a low-level kernel support for IP tunneling. In SCoPE the TUN is used by the SW to send simple packets between two nodes. The HW module can be considered as a network interface that implements the necessary protocols to interconnect the simulated nodes. Furthermore, it synchronizes the kernel of the two simulators, SCoPE and the NoC simulator when a packet enters or exits the network. Finally, the NoC simulator performs the real connection between the nodes.

## HW Peripherals

HW platform modeling also requires taking into account the HW peripherals. Apart from the user-defined peripherals that can be integrated in the platform model making use of the facilities commented in previous sections, SCoPE includes some generic peripherals in order to simplify the designer's work. Generic models are provided for some usual components such as memory or DMA.

As SCoPE runs the application SW source code directly, data are stored on the host memory, and thus, a physical memory model is not needed. From the OS point of view, data manipulation is only done at functional level. For the HW platform, data have to be transported through the bus and processed by the HW memory. However, there is no need to copy real data to the memory or develop and simulate a complex memory model. As a result, the simulation is sped up again at HW level.

*Figure 13. HW wrapper interface*

```
class HW_module : public uc_generic_bus_if {
public :
        HW_module(sc_module_name module_name,int irq_num, int ret);

        int write(DATA data,int size,ADDRESS addr,int tlm_id);
        int read(DATA *data,int size,ADDRESS addr,int tlm_id);
};
```

In conclusion, this component is only used for simulating real traffic and to advance the simulation time depending on the type of access (read/write) and data size. This is commonly used by DMA and processor caches.

In most complex systems there are DMAs for transferring large amounts of data. The proposed DMA model is implemented first, in the OS driver facilities, and second, in the HW platform. Using the Linux driver facilities, the user can configure a HW DMA that performs data transfers. It is basically done configuring the initial and final addresses, the read/write mode and the number of bytes to transfer. In SCoPE, the DMA module models the real traffic with the devices and makes an abstract model of the traffic through the bus to the memory, as explained before. Currently, the DMA model can handle 16 channels simultaneously for data transfers in the same way as most commercial devices.

## SCoPE: SystemC Library for Platform Modeling

The SCoPE tool provides the technology to perform MPSoC HW/SW co-simulation with NoC. It provides the required metrics allowing the designer to explore the design space and select the most appropriate architecture for the embedded system. It also enables the simulation of different nodes connected through a NoC to analyze the behavior of large systems.

SCoPE is a C++ library that extends, without modification, the standard SystemC language to perform the co-simulation. On one hand, it simulates C/C++ software code based on two different operating system interfaces (POSIX, MicroC/OS). On the other hand, it co-simulates these pieces of code with hardware described in SystemC.

The use of SCoPE for system modeling by a designer is quite easy and can be summarized in the following points:

- SW: Applications based on POSIX or MicroC/OS APIs can be run without changes. Common Linux headers are accepted.
- HW: Specific application HW can be developed in SystemC inheriting the SCoPE HW interface. The only code that has to be added to the original module is the read and write functions (Figure 13). The peripheral receives read and write requests from the bus and has to store the data and return the number of bytes accepted. Then, other internal threads can emulate the real behavior of the peripheral. It can be treated as a HW register interface with its HW threads.
- Platform: Easy and flexible system configuration. Figure 14 shows a multiprocessor configuration (2 processors) connected to a single bus and a memory module. Moreover, each processor has an associated process (user_code_1/2).

The resulting timed simulation allows information about functional and non-functional parameters to be obtained from the system described. Using SystemC and the SCoPE features, the designer can collect the specific information required to analyze and optimize the system. Furthermore, the library provides generic reports with information about processor running time, usage

*Figure 14. Architectural description of the system in SystemC with SCoPE*

```
int sc_main(int argc, char **argv) {
        // the rtos with the number of cpus
        UC_rtos_class *rtos = new UC_rtos_class(2);

        // register new processes
        rtos->get_processor(0)->new_process(user_code_1, args1);
        rtos->get_processor(1)->new_process(user_code_2, args2);

        // creates the Hardware Abstraction Layer:
        UC_HAL_hw_class *hal = new UC_HAL_hw_class("HAL", 2, 1, 100);

        // Processor to HAL binding
        rtos->get_processor(0)->m_port(*hal);
        rtos->get_processor(1)->m_port(*hal);

        // HAL's irq to processor binding
        (*hal->get_irq_port(0))(*rtos->get_processor(0));
        (*hal->get_irq_port(1))(*rtos->get_processor(1));

        HW_module *mem = new HW_module("mem", 10, 100);
        (*hal->get_hw_port(0))(*mem->get_target_port());
        (*mem->get_irq_port())(*hal);
        hal->memory_map->add_peripheral(0, 0x5000000, 0x5ffffff, 1, "mem");

        sc_start(500, SC_MS); // simulation time
        return 0;
}
```

percentage, power consumption, RTOS context switches, etc. An example of a partial report can be found in Figure 15.

## Case Study and Results

To demonstrate the usefulness of the proposed approach, an example of a GSM system is proposed

*Figure 15. SCoPE output example*

```
processor_0_rtos_0
        Number of thread switches: 3000
        Number of context switches: 0
        Running time: 27167551026 ns
        Use of cpu: 90.5585%
        Instructions executed: 3667562959
        Instruction cache misses: 1224440
        Core Energy: 4.62113e+09 nJ
        Core Power: 154.038 mW
        Instruction Cache Energy: 5.5303e+09 nJ
        Instruction Cache Power: 184.343 mW
```

*Figure 16. Coder-decoder task graph*

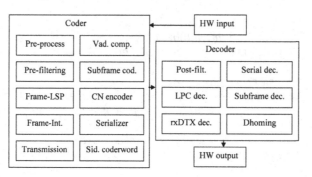

(Figure 16). The GSM system is composed of a coder and a decoder. Each part contains several tasks that can be executed concurrently.

To show the modeling possibilities of the library, four different platforms have been considered to run the same example: a mono-processor architecture, a SMP architecture, a Heterogeneous Multi-Processing (HMP) architecture and a networked architecture (Figure 17). Thus, performance results can be analyzed to select the best platform architecture for the GSM system.

- Mono-processor architecture: in this case, a single ARM runs the two coding and decoding processes. Communication

between coder and decoder is done using the OS message queue. Input values and output results are managed by a specific HW module that interacts with the environment. To model the processors, configuration files with the time and power costs of an ARM processor have been used (Castillo, 2007).

- SMP architecture: In this case, the system has been run on a platform with two symmetric ARM processors, a single bus and a shared memory. In this platform, coder and decoder share the OS, and thus, their threads can be moved between the processors by the OS depending on the processor

*Figure 17. Possible platforms to be evaluated*

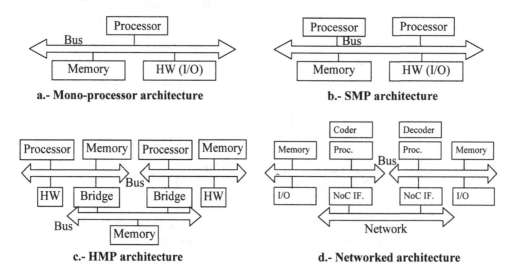

*Figure 18. Estimated performance of the GSM example in the different architectures*

|  |  | MonoP | SMP | HMP | Net |
|---|---|---|---|---|---|
| Estimated time (sec) | Proc 1 | 60.2 | 32.2 | 55.08 | 55.15 |
|  | Proc 2 | - | 28 | 5.2 | 5.5 |
|  | Total | 63.6 | 34.7 | 59.8 | 60 |
| Estimated Energy (mJ) | Proc 1 | 149 | 80 | 142 | 136 |
|  | Proc 2 | - | 69 | 77.4 | 13 |
|  | Total | 153.4 | 218.1 | 219.4 | 218.2 |
| Processor utilization | Proc 1 | 95% | 92% | 92% | 93% |
|  | Proc. 2 | - | 82% | 9% | 8% |

utilization. Coder and decoder are connected through message queues.

- HMP architecture: The third platform contains two processors in different buses. The two buses are connected with a third one that contains a shared memory. This shared memory is used to transfer the coded information between coder and decoder using polling techniques. The HW receiver is in the coder part and the HW transmitter next to the decoder. Tasks cannot be moved dynamically among processors.

- Networked architecture: Finally, the fourth simulation has been done considering a networked system. To follow the previous examples, a two-node network has been modeled with the mesh model described in section III.4. Each node has its own operating system. Although the experiment itself involves only the two nodes under consideration, the network simulator models the effect of the traffic among the rest of nodes in the complete system.

## Results

To compare the proposed target architectures with the GSM example, the performance estimations have been analyzed, in terms of time, power and processor utilization (Figure 18). Results show that source-code estimations at system level can provide valuable information at the first stages

of development, where the system architecture has to be decided.

By analyzing the results, it can be concluded that the SMP architecture is the best one, since tasks are optimally distributed between the two processors, avoiding the low utilization of processor 2 exhibited by the HMP and networked architectures. Furthermore, as the total execution time is doubled in the latter cases, the energy required is also increased. When processors are not executing application SW the idle task is running, with a lower but not null power consumption.

However, the most interesting result is the simulation time reduction, when compared with ISS-based simulation infrastructures. The simulation times required to code 10 GSM frames using the library in the mono-processor architecture with SCoPE and a SkyEye ISS (SkyEye, 2005), which is based on the ARMulator (ARM), are presented in Figure 19. The speed-up obtained from the library modeling any architecture with respect to SkyEye is about two orders of magnitude. It is expected that comparisons with multi-ISS infrastructures (to model MPSoCs) would provide even better results. Summarizing, the source-code technique presented proves to be faster than ISS-based techniques, as expected.

The improvement in simulation time is achieved by assuming a certain estimation error. In this case, comparing the number of assembler instructions executed by the SkyEye and the estimation obtained by SCoPE we found that

*Figure 19. Results obtained with SCoPE compared with the Skyeye*

|  | SkyEye | SCoPE | Diff. |
|---|---|---|---|
| Executed instructions | 148,423,081 | 139,798,607 | 6% |
| Simulation time | 2' 35" | 0.35" | x400 |

the error is around 6%. As a consequence, it can said that by sacrificing some accuracy much faster estimations can be obtained, which allows these techniques to be used in the early stages of development, and especially in Design Space Exploration frameworks.

A GUI has been developed to analyze the results of the previous example. The GUI is shown in the figure 20.

## CONCLUSION

As a general conclusion, SystemC has proven to be a powerful language for platform modeling. Nevertheless, its full exploitation for this purpose requires a very important research activity in order to cover all the modeling requirements. The SystemC framework SCoPE has been described taking advantage of the language capabilities for

*Figure 20. GUI of SCoPE*

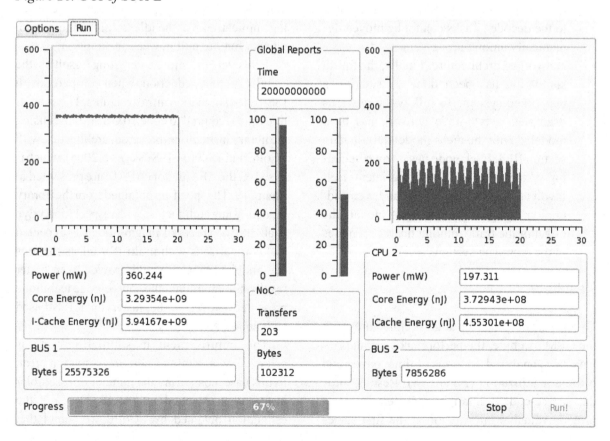

system modeling and simulation. A methodology and associated library has been developed providing a complete OS functionality that can produce accurate timed simulations of the SW components. Power and timing estimations of the application SW running on the multi-processing platform in close interaction with the rest of the platform components can be obtained from the system simulation.

To model the platform, a bus-timed model is provided, allowing some configuration options and the possibility of easily integrating HW components. Thus, SCoPE can be used for fast system modeling. This makes the library really useful for several design purposes, especially for design space exploration.

The results demonstrate that the source-code modeling techniques proposed constitute a sufficiently accurate technique that is much faster that ISS-based systems. This speed increase makes the technique optimal for fast system evaluation, covering the need to obtain effective metrics, which is necessary for efficient Design Space Exploration frameworks.

# REFERENCES

Aho, A. V., Lam, M. S., Sethi, R., & Ullman, J. D. (2007). *Compilers: Principles, techniques, and tools*. ED Pearson.

ARM. (2005). *ARM realview development suite*. Retreived from www.arm.com/products/Dev-Tools/RealViewDevSuite.html

Bailey, B., Martin, G., & Piziali, A. (2007). *ESL design and verification: A prescription for electronic system level methodology*. Morgan Kaufmann

Balarin, F., Giusto, P., Jurecska, A., Passerone, C., Sentovich, E., Tabbara, B., et al. (1997). *Hardware-software codesign of embedded systems: The POLIS approach*. Springer.

Benini, L., Bertozzi, D., Bruni, D., Drago, N., Fummi, F., & Ponzino, M. (2003). SystemC co-simulation and emulation of multiprocessor SoC design. *Computer, 36*(4). IEEE.

Benini, L., Bogliolo, A., Menichelli, F., & Oliveri, M. (2005). MPARM: Exploring the multiprocessor SoC design space with SystemC. *Journal of VLSI Signal Processing, 41*(2). Springer.

Benini, L., & de Micheli, G. (Eds.). (2006). *Networks on chip*. Morgan Kaufmann.

Brandolese, C., Fornaciari, W., Salice, F., & Sciuto, D. (2001). Source-level execution time estimation of C programs. In *Proc. of CoDes*. IEEE.

Brandolese, C., Fornaciari, W., & Sciuto, D. (2000). A multilevel strategy for software power estimation. In *Proc of ISSS*. IEEE.

Castillo, J., Posadas, H., Villar, E., & Martínez, M. (2007). Energy consumption estimation technique in embedded processors with stable power consumption based on source-code operator energy figures. In *Proc. of DCIS*.

Gerstlauer, A., Yu, H., & Gajski, D. D. (2003). *RTOS modeling for system level design*. In *Proc. of DATE*. IEEE.

Ghenassia, F. (2005). *Transaction-level modeling with SystemC*. Springer.

Hassan, M. A., Sakanushi, K., Takeuchi, Y., & Imai, M. (2005B). Enabling RTOS simulation modeling in a system level design language. *Proc. of ASP-DAC*. IEEE.

Hassan, M. A., Yoshinori, S. K., Takeuchi, Y., & Imai, M. (2005A). RTK-Spec TRON: A simulation model of an ITRON based RTOS kernel in SystemC. In *Proc of DATE*. IEEE.

He, Z., Mok, A., & Peng, C. (2005). Timed RTOS modeling for embedded system design. In *Proc. of RTAS*. IEEE.

Hergenhan, A., & Rosenstiel, W. (2000). Static timing analysis of embedded software on advanced processor architectures. In *Proc. of DATE*. IEEE.

IEEE. *1666-2005 standard LRM*. Retrieved from http://www.systemc.org/downloads/lrm

InterDesign Technologies. *FastVeri™ (SystemC-based high-speed simulator) product overview*. Retrieved from http://www.interdesigntech.co.jp/english/

ITRS. (2007A*). ITRS-executive summary*. Retrieved from http://www.itrs.net/Links/2007ITRS/Home2007.htm

ITRS. (2007B). *ITRS-design*. International Technology Roadmap for Semiconductors. Retrieved from http://www.itrs.net/Links/2007ITRS/Home2007.htm

Jerraya, A., & Wolf, W. (Eds.). (2005). *Multiprocessor systems on chip*. Morgan Kaufmann.

Kempf, T., Karur, K., Wallentowitz, S., & Meyr, H. (2006). A SW performance estimation framework for early SL design using fine-grained instrumentation. In *Proc. of DATE*. IEEE.

Klingauf, W., Gunzel, R., Bringmann, O., Parfuntseu, P., & Burton, M. (2006). GreenBus- a generic interconnect fabric for transaction level modelling. In *Proc. of DAC*. ACM.

Laurent, J., Senn, E., Julien, N., & Martin, E. (2002). Power consumption estimation of a c-algorithm: A new perspective for software design. In *Proc. of LCR*. ACM.

Milligan, M. (2005). *The ESL ecosystem-ready for deployment*. Retrieved from http://www.esl-now.com/pdfs/eco_presentation.pdf

Moussa, I., Grellier, T., & Nguyen, G. (2003). Exploring SW performance using SoC transaction-level modeling. In *Proc. of DATE*. IEEE.

Pasricha, S., Dutt, N., & Ben-Romdhane, M. (2004). Fast exploration of bus-based on-chip communication architectures. In *Proc. of CODES/ISSS*. IEEE.

Posadas, H., Adámez, J., Sánchez, P., Villar, E., & Blasco, P. (2006). POSIX modeling in SystemC. In *Proc. of ASP-DAC*. IEEE.

Posadas, H., Herrera, F., Sánchez, P., Villar, E., & Blasco, F. (2004). System-level performance analysis in systemc. In *Proc. of DATE*. IEEE.

Posadas, H., Quijano, D., Villar, E., & Martínez, M. (2007). TLM interrupt modelling for HW/SW cosimulation in SystemC. In *Proc. of DCIS*.

Schirner, G., & Domer, R. (2007). Result oriented modeling, a novel technique for fast and accurate TLM. *Transactions on Computer-Aided Design of Integrated Circuits, 26*(9). IEEE.

Schnerr, J., Bringmann, O., Viehl, A., & Rosenstiel, W. (2008). High-performance timing simulation of embedded software. In *Proc. of DAC*.

SkyEye. (2005). *SkyEye user manual*. Retrieved from www.skyeye.org

Swan, S., et al. (2002). *Functional specification for systemc 2.0*. Retrieved from http://www.systemc.org/

Tanenbaum, A. (2001). *Modern operating systems, 2nd ed*. Prentice Hall.

Viaud, E., Pecheux, F., & Greiner, A. (2006). *An efficient TLM/T modeling and simulation environment based on conservative parallel discrete event principles*. In *Proc. of DATE*. IEEE.

Yi, Y., Kim, D., & Ha, S. (2003). Fast and time-accurate cosimulation with OS scheduler modeling. *Design Automation of Embedded Systems, 8*(2-3). Springer.

Yoo, S., Nicolescu, G., Gauthier, L. G., & Jerraya, A. A. (2002). Automatic generation of fast timed simulation models for operating systems in SoC design. In *Proc. of DATE*. IEEE.

## ENDNOTES

[1]    This work has been funded by DS2 under the Medea 2A708 LoMoSa project.

[2]    In its current version, a function cannot be associated to processors of different kinds.

# Section 4
# Design Automation

The fourth section concentrates on several topics related with automating the development process (also named design process or design flow).

# Chapter 10
# Engineering Embedded Software
## From Application Modeling to Software Synthesis

**Ronaldo Ferreira**
*Universidade Federal do Rio Grande do Sul (UFRGS), Brazil*

**Lisane Brisolara**
*Universidade Federal de Pelotas (UFPEL), Brazil*

**Julio C.B. Mattos**
*Universidade Federal de Pelotas (UFPEL), Brazil*

**Emilena Spech**
*Universidade Federal do Rio Grande do Sul (UFRGS), Brazil*

**Erika Cota**
*Universidade Federal do Rio Grande do Sul (UFRGS), Brazil*

**Luigi Carro**
*Universidade Federal do Rio Grande do Sul (UFRGS), Brazil*

## ABSTRACT

*Since 1965, with Moore's law statement, industry is continually aggregating complex services into their products, enhancing people's life quality with decreasing prices. Despite the advances towards hardware integration, current electronic products are relying even more on software to offer distinguished functionalities to users. Hence, the embedded system industry is facing a paradigm shift from its old fashioned hardware driven development to a strong software based one, exposing to the embedded systems domain unforeseen software design challenges. Indeed, this domain must devise its own and very specialized software engineering techniques, in order to achieve sustainable market growth with quality in the scheduled time. Embedded software is distinct from the standard one, fundamentally in the sense that its development is driven by physical properties such as memory footprint and energy consumption. Furthermore, embedded systems are developed within a very tight time-to-market window, pushing design and development practices to their limit. In this chapter, we discuss the use of software specifications at higher abstraction levels and the need to provide tools for software automation, because reliability*

DOI: 10.4018/978-1-60566-750-8.ch010

*and safety are important criteria present in several embedded applications, as well as time-to-market. This chapter discusses the design flow for embedded software, from its modeling to its deployment in the embedded platform.*

## INTRODUCTION

For a long time now, personal and server computers amount to less than 2% of the processor market, where standard software executes on (Turley, 2002). Most of the developed software runs on the remaining 98% of the processors available in the market. The embedded system domain is driven by reliability, cost, and time-to-market factors (Graaf, Lormans, & Toetenel, 2003). It usually has hard constraints regarding performance, memory, and power consumption, among other physical properties. Embedded systems are also often used in life-critical situations, where reliability and safety are more important criteria than pure performance (Edwards, Lavagno, Lee, & Sangiovanni-Vincentelli, 1997; Koopman, 2007).

Embedded software has always been associated to a low-level, relatively simple code responsible for a few specific tasks, such as hardware configuration and device drivers. However, such a view is no longer a reality. In currently developed applications, software is advancing to constitute the main part of the system, and in many cases software solutions are preferred to hardware ones, because software is more flexible, easier to update, and can be reused (Graaf, Lormans, & Toetenel, 2003). In addition, industry statistics from (Venture Development Corporation, 2006) reveal that the amount of lines of embedded code is growing at about 26% yearly. Although this data cannot be considered alone, it is an important indicative of software complexity (Kan, 2002). Due to this growing complexity and short time-to-market window, statistics from (CMP Media, 2006) show that more than one half of current embed-

ded design projects are running behind schedule. This delay is mostly caused by the software productivity and testing gap, where hardware is almost being considered a commodity product, since the introduction of platform-based design (Sangiovanni-Vincentelli & Martin, 2001).

To cope with the increasing complexity, developers have been looking for higher levels of abstraction during system specification. Abstraction makes the development easier, and the final program becomes more readable and less hard to maintain. This fact is known by software engineers since the 1960's, when the software crisis was first discussed in the NATO conference (Naur & Randell, 1969), and important advances on the software development methods and techniques have been proposed since then. Such advances help tackle the complexity of a million-line code with the use of software languages, management approaches, testing tools, and modeling methods (Osterweil, 2007).

There are several well-established software development processes, such as the Unified Process and Agile Development Methods (Cockburn, 2001), whose usage is now supported by the standard system modeling language UML (OMG, 1997) and by CASE (Computer Aided Software Engineering) tools (Pressman, 2004). Today, one can think of *software product lines*, producing code and delivering software services in a rate that could never be imagined in 1968 during the NATO conference. Furthermore, software companies may now rely on certifications over the development process as a way to achieve software quality. This is the goal, for instance, of the Capability Maturity Model (CMM) and the Capability Maturity Model Integration (CMMI)

(Chrissis, Konrad, & Shrum, 2003). Thus, standard software can rely on well established techniques and processes that leverage manageability and, in some order, guarantee quality. However, the desired automation stage has not been reached yet. Software development is still being presented as a very complex activity, mainly because very few steps can be actually automated. We will show that this point is particularly important in the embedded systems domain.

In the embedded system domain coding is still implemented mostly by hardware engineers (as opposed to software engineers), whose basic education on software practices is rather weak. Such workers are usually educated to code in a lower-level programming language with specific hardware and optimization-related goals in mind. Thus, it becomes particularly difficult to re-educate those engineers to adapt and use traditional software engineering practices, specially the ones related to the process of software design before coding. For instance, hardware engineers are more receptive to visual and lightweight verification embedded on automatic tools than to written mathematical and formal processes.

On the other hand, the advances in the software development process were promoted for standard software, and do not explicitly consider the requirements and constraints present in the embedded software. For instance, non-functional requirements can be annotated in an UML model of the system, but its implementation cannot be assured. As another example, standard software quality is based on a detailed and very well documented process, which requires longer design times, usually not affordable in the embedded market with an average turnaround time of just a few months. Thus, simply reusing the available software models and tools in the embedded domain is not the answer to solve the current productivity gap.

This chapter addresses the software design intended for embedded hardware platforms *(from*

*modeling* to *synthesis),* including a review of the modeling and synthesis approaches used in the embedded domain. By modeling we mean specification of software behavior and requirements. By synthesis we mean not only code generation and verification, but design space exploration as well. We start by showing that standard software engineering processes and models are not enough to tackle the requirements and constraints of embedded software. Then, we present domain specific formalisms to model embedded systems and software synthesis approaches, both from industry and academia, followed by a discussion on *design space exploration* for selecting a final system solution. We finish by presenting a proposal that covers the whole process. We conclude the chapter with a discussion of future trends on this field.

## BACKGROUND

## Embedded Software Development Requirements

In early days, embedded software was written exclusively in the assembly language of the target processor, in order to meet the stringent memory and performance limitations of the application (Lee, 2000). In this approach, programmers have complete control of the processor and peripheral hardware, which ensures maximum optimization of the final code. On the other hand, the system designer has to deal with the well-known disadvantages of assembly languages, such as higher software development costs (including coding and debugging time) and reduced portability and code reuse. Nowadays, embedded software designers are also using high-level languages like C to code parts of the application, while still keeping some control over the hardware platform so as to meet the performance and cost requirements of the application. Despite the undeniable advantages of this language compared to the original assembly code, there are still important limitations in terms of abstraction, validation, and maintenance.

The high cost for hardware development has motivated the reuse of hardware platforms, and thus design derivates are mainly configured by software. Design derivate is the variability introduced between a company's product line. Commonality between products is manageable by maintaining an updated assets database, enabling reuse when designing a new product (Kim, 2006). As a consequence, software development is where most of the design time is spent, and it is the largest cost factor in embedded systems design (Graaf, Lormans, & Toetenel, 2003). This scenario together with time-to-market pressures has motivated the investigation of strategies to accelerate embedded software development.

The use of design methodologies and techniques based on higher abstraction specifications has proven to be the key to reduce (but not eliminate) the productivity gap of traditional software design. Similarly, for embedded software, current research shows that starting from higher abstraction levels is crucial to the design success. Some authors like (Selic, 2003), (Douglass, 1998), and (Gomaa, 2000) argue that this approach is the only viable way of coping with the complexity found in the new generation of embedded systems. The growing number of system functionalities and the complex interactions among modules of software and hardware cannot be properly considered without a design method supported by suitable higher abstraction languages and tools.

The use of higher abstraction levels hides details of implementation in the programming language, facilitating the system specification that will be on the model level, instead of code level. Using this approach, models of embedded systems should evolve from high level views into actual implementations, ensuring a relatively smooth and potentially much more reliable process as compared to traditional forms of software engineering. Furthermore, to deal with tight time-to-market, the

translation of the high-level model into an executable description should be automatic. Depending on the modeling notation, it may need different degrees of designer interaction.

The best technologies developed for standard software are based on layers of abstraction, elaborate algorithms, code reuse, and detailed documentation. In these approaches, the amount of memory and energy spent during the computation is not an issue, and program tasks do not have a specific deadline. There is, of course, a concern about program complexity, size, and performance, but the target execution memory is measured in mega or giga bytes, whereas the processor is constantly plugged in. In an embedded system, memory is measured in kilo bytes or a few mega bytes, and the processor, as well as any other peripheral hardware, operates on (expensive) batteries. In addition, performance is measured in terms of the exact number of execution cycles required for a task to complete, instead of an expected behavior for a number of input data. Moreover, the completion of certain tasks within a specific time (called real-time constraints) is usually related to safety and life-critical issues of the embedded application, which is rarely the case for traditional software. Thus, the use of a higher-level software design paradigm together with a fixed hardware platform allows designers to focus on the overall system functionality, which reduces design time and cost. However, non-functional aspects such as the ones mentioned above can be negatively affected, unless they are also considered since the beginning of the project. For instance, in the traditional software development process code reuse is crucial to reduce development time. For the embedded software the reuse can also potentially reduce design time and time-to-market. However, reusable code is usually generic and less prone to compiler optimizations. This means a potentially larger and slower target code that may not be acceptable to a number of embedded applications (Chatzigeorgiou & Stephanides, 2002; Mattos, Specht, Neves, & Carro, 2005).

*Table 1. Traditional software vs. embedded software*

| | Traditional software | Embedded software |
|---|---|---|
| **Time to market** | can be long | must be short |
| **Application Domain** | single | many |
| **Model of Computation** | single | multiple |
| **Software Automation** | mature | immature |
| **Code Reuse** | without restrictions | with restrictions |
| **Power dissipation** | not considered | must be considered |
| **Memory Footprint** | usually not considered | must be considered |
| **Real-time constraints** | usually not considered | usually must be considered |

The designer of an embedded system (of which the embedded software is the most flexible part) searches for the best tradeoff between memory, performance, power consumption, and time-to-market. Thus, a good design process must help the designer in this iterative task. These are the first reasons why traditional software development approaches are not directly applicable to embedded software (Lee, 2000).

Embedded systems are composed of several computational units offering services to other actors, both internal, such as processors, and external ones, like users. These components perform computations in distinct ways, having thus different underlying *models of computations* (MoC) (Martin, 2002). A MoC is an abstraction targeted to some computation domain; it does not relate to how the computation will be implemented, but it eases the representation of how computation is performed, allowing deep and focused problem analysis and solving. Two very common MoCs in the embedded domain are the *control-flow* (CF) and *data-flow* (DF) models. Data-flow models capture the data-intensive computations common in signal processing algorithms while control-flow focuses on modeling of control functions by using hierarchical finite state machines and synchronous/reactive languages. CF models usually represent *reactive systems*. These are computational systems that continuously respond to the

environment in the speed determined by the same environment (Halbwachs, 1993). These systems have a *finite state machine* (FSM) describing the system behavior. This FSM has an initial state where it waits for an internal or external event, after which it branches to some state (calculated by a next state function), performs some data processing and returns to the initial state where it waits for the next event. DF models represent the application of successive filtering stages, being usually modeled as diagram blocks where each block is connected to other ones through its input and output ports (Lee & Messerschmitt, 1987). Most complex embedded systems have a heterogeneous behavior, and multiple MoC are required to describe such behaviors. However, most of the academic and commercial solutions for software automation focus on the management of huge domain-specific systems, focusing in a single-domain (such as databases SQL, web-based systems, or XML-based data sources) and on a particular language. The reason for this is because conventional software is usually suited for a single domain. Table 1 summarizes the main differences between the traditional and the embedded software in terms of characteristics (rows 1 and 2), design process (rows 3 and 4), and constraints (rows 5 to 7).

According to (Tanenbaum, Herder, & Bos, 2006), a conservative estimation is that executable code may contain from six to sixteen errors per 1,000 lines of code. The cost of software testing and debugging can be as high as 50% of the system production cost and, the later the bugs are discovered, the higher the costs (Sommerville, 2006). These statements apply to both traditional and embedded software. Actually, because of less support and automation in embedded software design, the target code is likely to contain even more errors. Moreover, embedded systems are commonly used in safe-critical applications, where system failures are not tolerable. For such systems, safety and reliability can be more important than the other requirements such as performance and power. Thus, validation and verification (V&V) of the whole system is a major issue. However, V&V techniques are costly, and may represent 80% of the total software design cost in critical systems (Koopman, 2007), while the usual tradeoffs among design time and system constraints (on top of the quality requirement) are still sought by the designer (Sommerville, 2006). Specifically, the verification of the interaction between software and hardware is an important open problem that is not considered in traditional software. Thus, to guarantee the development of more reliable systems, a careful support for requirements and model verification is required.

Formal property verification can be very powerful for catching errors early in the design process, and tools that offer formal verification to designers and do not imply in an additional increase in development time are valuable contributions. However, tools responsible for these checking activities are often far apart from actual designs, either because of the inherent difficulty in using them, either because they are often too narrow focused.

To summarize, any software development methodology must be tailored within a well-founded software process. In the embedded software domain, this process must foresee elicitation and specification of functional and non-functional requirements, and provide facilities to allow model validation, as well as features that can be used to guide implementation and improve software design productivity.

Embedded systems are an area of active research, and several modeling and design approaches have been proposed for embedded software specification and design. These approaches are revised in the following section, where modeling language and synthesis tools from academia and industry are discussed.

## Embedded Software Modeling and Design

One way of managing complexity is to abstract away non important details, thus constructing a specific application view; this is accomplished by using *models*. Models contain only what is important and essential to capture from the application requirements and its interaction with other actors and systems. Models can be *formal, semiformal* and even completely *informal.* Examples of such models are paper prototypes of user interfaces (informal) (Snyder, 2003), UML models (semiformal) and formal specifications like Alloy (Jackson, 2006), Z (Hall, 1990) or VDM (Vienna Development Method; Bjørner & Jones, 1978). These specification formalisms (or the lack of them, when considering informal models) have distinct purposes within a software development process. Informal specifications are easy and fast to create, are usually preferred when communicating with stakeholders and users, and are cheaper than code prototypes in a new software design. Semiformal specifications perform well when there is some confidence that all important requirements were properly gathered from users, and are well suited for team communication and system documentation. Formal specifications are especially important when the target application is a very safe critical one, where specification and modeling flaws can cause serious catastrophes.

Code generators are based on at least semiformal models, where a subset of the modeling language has well defined *syntax* and *semantics*. Currently, there are plenty of tools capable of generating code from a defined UML subset, as described earlier; but restricting the UML model to perform code generation can be awkward in some situations. Indubitably, UML is a *de facto* standard for software and system modeling, being widespread used in industry. To take advantage of existing know-how in software modeling, one current proposal is to adapt *model driven architecture* (MDA) techniques to the embedded domain. MDA is a framework for *model transformation* and *refinement* (Miller & Mukerji, 2003). In MDA, an application model is actually a *meta-model* instance. A meta-model defines syntax and semantics of a given formalism like UML, defining all valid constructs that can occur in a specific model instance. The underlying idea is that one can start system modeling in high abstraction levels, and successively refine this model into a less abstract one.

Modeling and programming languages implementing a MoC are called *domain specific languages* (DSL). DSLs are suited for code generation because it is simpler to assume premises only valid in some specific domain; although being more restrictive, DSLs are more abstract than a general purpose language to their target domains. Considering the DF and CF models, there are available several DSL both from industry and academia, and many of them are discussed in this book and briefly revised in the following section. Unfortunately, to properly model and generate code from these DSLs, the designer must be aware of their specific syntax and semantics, what may increase overall design time. An interesting approach is to use UML as front-end to system modeling, and transform it into a DSL such as Simulink and Esterel. This approach follows the MDA principles, taking advantage of putting together the well-know syntax and semantics of UML, reaching a broader audience of designers, and the specific code generators and legacy components library modeled with

DSLs. For example, (Brisolara, Oliveira, Redin, Lamb, Carro, & Wagner, 2008) transform UML models into Simulink for the data-flow application portion, and to a FSM based language for the control-flow portion.

## Domain Specific Languages for Embedded Systems

Many modeling approaches and tools have been proposed for embedded software specification, but there is no model that is more appropriated or better for all applications. Some special features have been added to languages to give an appropriate support to the specification of some domain applications. Languages that adopt the synchrony hypothesis are called synchronous languages. These languages have been introduced to simplify reactive systems programming. Some examples are Esterel (Berry & Gonthier, 1992), Signal (Guernic, Gautier, Borgne, & Maire, 1991) and Lustre (Halbwachs, Caspi, Raymond, & Pilaud, 1991). Synchronous languages are also suited to design real time systems and reactive real-time embedded systems (Edwards, Lavagno, Lee, & Sangiovanni-Vincentelli, 1997). To provide graphical specification, StateCharts (Harel, 1987) was proposed as an extension to state machines for the specification of discrete event systems. Although these approaches have a formal model, and provide some mechanisms for formal verification, these languages do not provide high abstraction in comparison to traditional programming languages.

Traditionally, the functional block (FB) modeling approach has been used by the signal processing, industrial automation, and control engineering communities for the development of embedded systems (John & Tiegelkamp, 2001). These models are widely accepted in industrial design, driven by an extensive set of design tools, as for instance, Matlab/Simulink (Mathworks, 2008).

More recently, UML has gained popularity for embedded systems design mainly because it provides high abstraction and mechanisms to extend the language through a profile that can be seen as a domain specific language. Recently, OMG proposed the UML Profile for Modeling and Analysis of Real-time and Embedded Systems, in short MARTE (OMG, 2007) for the embedded domain.

Several tools capturing high-level specification into designs can be found in industry and academia, depending on the underlying model of computation (MoC) and language adopted. Commercial packages such as LabView (National Instruments, 2008), Simulink (Mathworks, 2008), ASCET-SD (Honekamp, Reidel, Werther, Zurawka, & Beck, 1999), and SCADE (Esterel Technologies, 2008) allow for modeling and development of embedded control systems based on functional-block specifications.

ASCET-SD (Honekamp, Reidel, Werther, Zurawka, & Beck, 1999), from ETAS, supports modeling, simulation, and rapid prototyping of automotive embedded software modules and, in addition, it provides optimized code generation for various microcontroller targets. SCADE provides modeling of data-flow and state machines and code generation for safety-critical applications, such as avionics and automotive. SCADE checks model completeness and determinism, including cycle detection in nodes. The Mathworks toolset allows one to model a system through functional block diagrams using Simulink and/or through finite state machines (FSM) described using Stateflow (Mathworks, 2008). The Simulink representation language handles discrete data-flow and continuous time, and also FSMs by the integration with the Stateflow tool. Many embedded applications have been successfully developed using these tools. However, these tools are domain-specific, and only support a fixed MoC.

Concerning academia, one can find POLIS (Balarin, et al., 1999), Metropolis (Balarin, Watanabe, Hsieh, Lavagno, Passerone, & Sangio-vanni-Vincentelli, 2003), and ForSyDe (Sander & Jantsch, 2004). Usually, these tools support model

simulation and code generation. POLIS provides code generation based on the model of Concurrent Finite State Machines (CFSM) created by the authors. Metropolis (Balarin, Watanabe, Hsieh, Lavagno, Passerone, & Sangiovanni-Vincentelli, 2003) was proposed as an extension of POLIS. The Metropolis MetaModel specification language is based on process networks and is targeted for system-level specification.

Academic research projects, like Ptolemy (Buck, Ha, Lee, & Messerschmitt, 1994) and UMoC++ (Mathaikutty, Patel, Shukla, & Jantsch, 2006) have addressed the heterogeneity of embedded systems, proposing multi-MoC modeling frameworks that support the simulation of heterogeneous systems. PtolemyII (Christopher, Edward, Xiaojun, Stephen, Yang, & Haiyang, 2008), the version currently under development in the Ptolemy project, includes a growing suite of domains, each of which realizes a MoC. It also includes a component library. The system model in Ptolemy can be described by the instantiation of pre-existing components through a graphic interface or components defined in Java by the user. The main advantage of this project is that it is open-source and supported MoC and components can be extended.

ForSyDe (Sander & Jantsch, 2004) is a framework for modeling and synthesizing embedded systems. Specifications in this framework are modeled in Haskell, to obtain high-level abstraction and formal semantics to the model. To provide abstraction for many domains, ForSyDe requires knowledge and classification of several different models of computation, which may increase development time. Moreover, the abstraction provided by Haskell is similar to OCaml, being close to standard programming languages.

## Formal Verification for Embedded Systems

To handle complex and critical embedded software, several projects from academia and industry have focused on the use of formal verification techniques to achieve a high level of assurance (Gu & Shin, 2005). Several recent works that investigate software model-checking can be found in (Klaus, Rupak & Jens, 2008).

POLIS (Balarin, et al., 1999), Metropolis (Balarin, Watanabe, Hsieh, Lavagno, Passerone, & Sangiovanni-Vincentelli, 2003) and ForSyDe (Sander & Jantsch, 2004) are examples of frameworks that have addressed this issue providing formal semantics and model-checking features to the embedded systems domain. POLIS uses a formal specification in order to enable a direct interface with existing formal verification algorithms based on FSMs. However, the set of applications generated and the scheduler (specifically generated for the set of tasks) compound a static set; hence no dynamic behavior is possible. Its successor Metropolis uses the Metropolis Meta-Model specification language, which is based on process networks and is targeted for system-level specification. Two verification techniques are implemented in Metropolis: formal verification using the model checker SPIN (Holzmann, 1997) and simulation trace checking (Chen, Hsieh, & Balarin, 2006). Some case studies for property verification using the SPIN model checker can be found in (Chen, Hsieh, Balarin, & Watanabe, 2003). When SPIN is used, a Promela (Holzmann 1997) specification is generated from a system level specification. SPIN is an automata-based model checker, which verifies the Promela model by performing random or iterative simulations or even generating a C program that performs a fast exhaustive verification of the system state space. Unfortunately, these formal verification techniques usually represent a boost in quality at the price of extra development time, something that cannot be afforded in current stringent time-to-market needs. ForSyDe uses the Haskell language, which provides a formal semantics to the model. In our approach, we use Alloy's lightweight verification mechanism to merge software quality with time-to-market

constraints. The Alloy language will be briefly introduced later.

Simulink is a widely used embedded software synthesis tool. However, formal verification of Simulink design models is being carried out manually, resulting in excessive time consumption during the design phase. To solve this problem, (Meenakshi, Bhatnagar, & Sudeepa, 2006) propose a tool that automatically translates certain Simulink models into the input language used by the NuSMV model checker, allowing the verification of the generated models against temporal logic requirements. Some other tools have been developed to formally verify Simulink models, as for instance the SCADE tool (Esterel Technologies, 2008).

As UML has gained attention from industry, UML-based approaches have been investigated for embedded systems design, including modeling, verification and synthesis as well. However, these approaches have been criticized due to the UML's lack of formal semantics. (Voros, Snook, Hallerstede, & Masselos, 2004) proposed to map UML models to the formal B language in order to allow formal proof of system properties. An approach to perform model-checking of UML models based on a mapping of these models into a framework of communicating extended timed automata was proposed in (Ober, Graf, & Ober, 2004). Timed automata is a widely used formalism in the real-time and embedded systems area, mainly for checking schedulability, and whether or not the real-time constraints are satisfied; the most famous tool based on timed automata is the model-checker UPPAAL (Bengtsson, Larsen, Larsson, Pettersson, & Yi, 1996). Our approach uses Alloy as modeling language providing at the same time abstraction and the formal semantics required to perform formal verification without mapping the initial specification to another model.

Some academic works have proposed the use of Alloy for formal verification of programs or system specifications. (Massoni, Gheyi, & Borba, 2004) proposes an approach that transforms UML class diagrams with OCL constraints to Alloy code in order to verify class diagrams. As behavioral diagrams are not analyzed, this approach only verifies the system structure. Recently, a method was proposed for translating sequential Java programs to DynAlloy in order to formally verify Java programs and their dynamic properties (Galeotti & Frias, 2007). DinAlloy checks pre and post conditions of a modeled behavior by extending the Alloy language and (Galeotti & Frias, 2007) checks if these conditions are reflected on the Java code by translating this code into DynAlloy. Another approach uses an annotation language based on Alloy for annotating Java code, allowing a fully automatic compile-time analysis (Khurshid, Marinov, & Jackson, 2002). Although these works also propose the use of Alloy for formal verification, they start with Java programs, and hence miss the higher abstraction mechanism that is required to produce more code with less describing effort for complex embedded software specification. In the opposite direction from these approaches, we propose to automatically generate Java code from verified Alloy models.

## Software Synthesis

Embedded software synthesis can be compared to target code generation (in Java, C or assembly) from synchronous languages such as Esterel (Berry & Gonthier, 1992), and Lustre (Halbwachs, Caspi, Raymond, & Pilaud, 1991). Although these programming languages are not intended as specification languages, they represent an improvement over standard imperative languages for implementing reactive systems. The concept of synthesis can be applied only if the precise mathematical meaning of a system specification is applied. It is then important to start the design process from a high-level abstraction that offers formal semantics (Sgroi, Lavagno, & Sangiovanni-Vincentelli, 2000).

Simulink and Ptolemy are examples of embedded software synthesis tools, which generate code

from functional blocks models. Regarding code generation functionality, Simulink with Real-Time Workshop (Mathworks, 2008), from Mathworks, is probably the most widely used environment in industry. The Real-Time Workshop takes a Simulink model as input and generates C code as output. The Real-Time Workshop Embedded Coder, which is an extension for RTW, generates C code from Simulink and Stateflow models, enabling code generation from data and control-flow models.

Ptolemy supports modeling and simulation of heterogeneous models, but it has limited implementation capabilities for models other than data-flow (Buck, Ha, Lee, & Messerschmitt, 1994). At present, Ptolemy II proposes two different code generation approaches (Zhou, Leung, & Lee, 2007). In the first one, the code generator called Copernicus generates Java code (.class) from non-hierarchical Synchronous Data-Flow (SDF) models, using a component-specialization framework built on top of a Java compiler. The second approach is a template based code generation system, in which a component called "codegen helper" is used to generate code for a Ptolemy II functional block (actor) in a target language. Currently, this template based code generator produces C code for synchronous data-flow (SDF), finite-state machines (FSM) and heterochronous data-flow models (HDF). The later is an extension of SDF that permits dynamic changes of production and consumption rates without sacrificing static scheduling. This code generator consists of actor templates (called helpers) that contain C code stubs that are stitched together. As mentioned before, only a subset of actors has helpers. Although this is an interesting approach, a large amount of work is yet required to implement templates (helpers) for other widely used components and templates for different target languages, before one has a powerful code generation environment.

Several UML-based tools have code generation capabilities, but some tools generate only code skeletons for class diagrams, while others generate also behavioral code from state diagrams. MagicDraw (No Magic, 2008) is an example of tool that supports only generation of code skeletons from the static structure. On the other hand, Artisan Studio, Rhapsody, UniMod and BridgePoint UML Suite (Mentor Graphics, 2008) are examples of tools that support generation of complete code from UML models. UniMod defines a methodology for designing object-oriented event-driven applications, focusing on execution and code generation from UML state diagrams. Rhapsody (Gery, Harel, & Palachi, 2002) allows for creating UML models for an application and then generates C, C++ or Java code for the application. These tools support complete code generation, but only based on UML state diagrams, so they are more appropriate for event-based systems. Recently, Telelogic launched the new version of Rhapsody that provides the code generation from flowcharts (activity diagrams) used to specify complex algorithms (Telelogic, 2008). These tools can provide great abstraction to the designer, but none of them embodies formal verification of the modeled solution.

Besides of code generation, synthesis for embedded software can include code optimization and some support for solutions meeting the application requirements. Non-functional requirements, such as power dissipation, energy consumption, program memory footprint, and processor selection are fundamental issues in the embedded design. The possible configurations/solutions formed by varying some of design decisions create a huge solution space. The process of selecting a proper solution to satisfy the application requirements is called *design space exploration* (DSE). DSE enables us to evaluate different configurations and to automatically find a proper solution. In order to support DSE, tools that enable one to estimate physical properties (memory footprint, performance and power consumption) from the software high-level specification are required. These estimation tools should consider the map of the application into a given platform in order to obtain physical properties.

Milan (Mohanty, Prasanna, Neema, & Davis, 2002) is a hierarchical design space framework based on Generic Modeling Environment (GME) (Ledeczi, et al., 2001), which is a framework for creating domain-specific modeling languages. For design space exploration, Milan uses DESERT (Neema, Sztipanovits, Karsai, Butts, & K, 2003) that is considered a semi-automated tool, because once the design space has been specified, it performs optimization and automatically indicates the optimal design.

Other examples of design space exploration environments are SPADE (Lieverse, van der Wolf, Deprettere, & Vissers, 2001), Artemis/Sesame (Pimentel, Hertzberger, Lieverse, van der Wolf, & Deprettere, 2001; Pimentel, Erbas, & Polstra, 2006) and Koski (Kangas, et al., 2006). They all abstract the application model using Kahn Process Network, KPN, (Kahn & MacQueen, 1977), whereby such application model is mapped to the architecture model during the design space exploration. SPADE (Lieverse, van der Wolf, Deprettere, & Vissers, 2001) is a system-level performance analysis methodology and tool which uses trace-driven simulation for exploration purposes. Based on SPADE, Pimentel *et. al.* proposed Artemis (Pimentel, Hertzberger, Lieverse, van der Wolf, & Deprettere, 2001) and Sesame (Pimentel, Erbas, & Polstra, 2006). Artemis is a methodology for heterogeneous embedded systems modeling, while Sesame is an environment targeted to provide modeling and simulation methods and tools for design space exploration of heterogeneous embedded systems. Koski (Kangas, et al., 2006) is an UML-based MPSoC design flow which provides an automated path from UML design entry to FPGA prototyping, including the functional verification and automated architecture exploration. However, all these approaches still require the designer to manually specify the behavior for each process in the KPN, thus a complete and automatic software synthesis is not supported.

Recently, some design flows follow the MDA approach, thus the designer starts modeling a *platform-independent model* (PIM) using UML for instance and ends by successive refinement in a *platform-specific model* (PSM). This approach is suitable for incremental development processes like RUP (Rational Unified Process) (Kruchten, 2003) and ROPES (Rapid Object-Oriented Process for Embedded Systems) (Douglass, 1998). By using MDA one can rely on automatic DSE tools that perform physical estimation based on high-level models. We refer interested readers to (Gries, 2004) and (Oliveira, Brião, Nascimento, & Wagner, 2007) for more details about these approaches.

All code generation efforts have in common the need for abstraction, in order to reduce the complexity of the specification and allow manual or automatic DSE. However, code abstraction can be more effective if one moves away from the imperative programming model towards the declarative one. In the next section we present an approach for embedded software automation based on a formal language. Our proposal includes automatic code generation from high-level models described in Alloy (a declarative language) and design space exploration to explore different data structures during code generation. The goal is to put together the power of formal verification without loosing time-to-market and code efficiency.

## Software Automation for Embedded Systems: A CASE STUDY

In this chapter, by *software automation* we mean all activities performed and the processing of all assets produced from high level models until the system deployment to the hardware platform. This section illustrates using an example all steps to achieve automation.

## Design Flow for Embedded Software Automation

In order to illustrate all concepts presented in this chapter, we present in this section a complete design flow for embedded software automation. This approach adopts Alloy as specification language, and generates Java code from high-level Alloy models. Figure 1 presents the proposed design flow for embedded software automation. Following the requirements description, an application model is described in Alloy with all functional requirements, which includes structural and behavioral specifications. Using the Alloy Analyzer, the designer can check if the application model complies with its requirements. The Model Translator uses as its input a verified and requirements-compliant Alloy model, generating thus a Java source which implements the modeled application. With the generated Java source and the non-functional requirements at hand, embedded resources such as power, energy and memory footprint are estimated, and an evaluated solution is proposed based on all existing non-functional requirements; this step is currently being performed by hand. Finally, the solution is mapped to the target platform, generating code to FemtoJava processors, whose instructions set are Java bytecodes (Ito, Carro, & Jacobi, 2001).

To enable the use of more elaborate behaviors than those allowed by standard Alloy models, a Java library can be imported and used by the application Alloy model. This library should be verified by means of annotations in AAL, the Alloy annotation language (AAL) (Khurshid, Marinov, & Jackson, 2002). This library would allow for the representation of distinct models of computations. The process of importing methods from this library by means of an automatically generated Alloy model from AAL is currently under development.

*Figure 1. Design flow for embedded software automation*

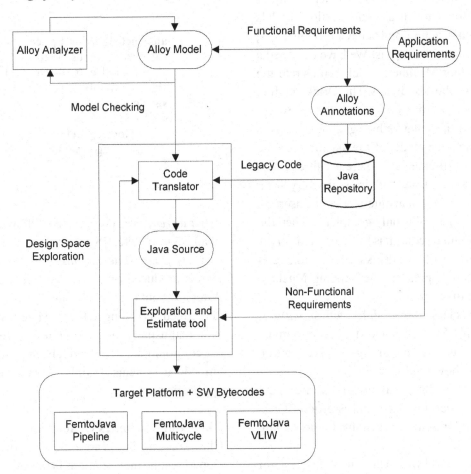

## Alloy Language

Alloy is a declarative language for software specification at high levels of abstraction. It has an object-oriented syntax, and relational operation semantics, being very familiar to software developers (Jackson, 2006). The Alloy Analyzer is a bounded model checker integrated with a model

*Figure 2. Drink vending machine structure in Alloy*

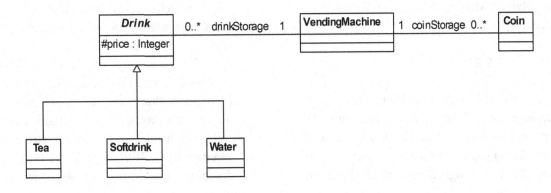

viewer, enabling one to analyze counter-examples generated for a given assertion. Alloy models express both structural and behavioral constructs, as well as model assertions. We have designed a Drink Vending Machine model to illustrate the language and the design flow. This Drink Vending Machine is a reactive embedded system, where the user leads its behavior by signaling options to the machine. Our model of the machine has the following requirements: i) there are three kinds of drink: water, tea, and soft drink; ii) every drink has a price; iii) the machine works by inserting coins in it; iv) a sell is only completed when the needed amount of coins has been inserted; v) the machine does not sell drinks whose storage is empty. Figure 2 presents the Vending Machine UML class diagram.

In Alloy, classes are modeled with s*ignatures,* or simply *sigs.* Sigs introduce a type and a domain. The UML class diagram of Figure 2 is described in Alloy as shown in Figure 3.

One can model behavioral properties with *predicates, functions, facts,* and assertions. Facts are model axioms, and are suitable for describing transition rules.

Contrary to UML, Alloy modeling is not ambiguous; these two languages were designed for different purposes. Alloy was designed to specify software; UML was designed to ease the communication between the development team and stakeholders, as well as a device for system documentation. Obviously, it is possible to use UML for generating code and specifying software, but it will always be a *semiformal* model. For more details in Alloy modeling, we refer interested readers to (Jackson, 2006).

## Model Translator

We have coded a model translator of Alloy models to Java code. This tool was coded with CUP (Hudson, Flannery, & Ananian, 1999) and JFlex (Klein, 2004) parser and scanner generators, respectively. The designed translation algorithms

*Figure 3. Drink vending machine structure in Alloy*

```
abstract sig Drink { price: Int }
sig Water extends Drink {}
sig Softdrink extends Drink {}
sig Tea extends Drink {}
sig Coin {}
sig VendingMachine{
  coinStorage: set Coin,
  drinkStorage: set Drink
}
```

generate *reactive systems* (RS). Often, execution of an RS is infinite. RS are a problem class where there is *finite state machine* (FSM) capturing events produced by internal or external actors. After an event is caught, some data processing is performed according to the FSM next state function, and usually the FSM control is returned to the environment. RS are widely employed in real embedded systems, mainly in control oriented applications.

**Class and Attributes Generation**

Classes and attributes are extracted from declared signatures and their relations in the model, respectively. Signatures containing fields are translated into classes that encapsulate the signature's fields as their attributes; the empty ones are translated into the Java String type. The algorithm for generation of Java classes and attributes is based on the following steps:

*Step 1:* For each *signature S* extracted from the Alloy model, create a Java class *C*, except if this *signature S* does not have fields. If a signature *S'* extends a previously created Java class *C*, create a new Java class *C'* extending *C*. *Exception:* if a signature *S* parameterizes the Alloy library *ordering*, do not create a class even if *S* contains fields.

*Step 2:* For each relation *R* in *S* an attribute is inserted in *C*. If *R* is binary and has as domain a non-empty *signature*, create a

*Figure 4. Drink vending machine structure in Java and Alloy*

**Alloy structural declaration**
```
open util/ordering[State] as ord
abstract sig Drink { price: Int }
sig Water extends Drink {}
sig Softdrink extends Drink {}
sig Tea extends Drink {}
sig Coin {}
sig VendingMachine{
   coinStorage:  set Coin,
   drinkStorage:  set Drink
}
sig State { machine: VendingMachine }
```

**Java generated class structure**
```
public class VendingMachine {
   protected FastList<Drink> drinkStorage;
   protected FastList<String> coinStorage;
   public VendingMachine() {
     this.drinkStorage = new FastList<Drink>();
     this.coinStorage   = new FastList<String>();
   }
   ...
public abstract class Drink { ... }
public class Water extends Drink { ... }
...
```

collection as attribute in *C*; if the *R* domain is empty, create an attribute typed as *String*. If *R* is nth-ary, create a new Java class *C'* in which all *R* columns are *C'* attributes, using the rules described in the beginning of this step.

An example of the above procedure can be seen in Figure 4. The Java classes *vendingmachine*, *Drink*, *Water*, *Softdrink* and *Tea* are created in Step 1. Attributes *drinkstorage* and *coinstorage* are inserted in the class *vendingmachine* in Step 2. Signatures *State* and *Coin* do not generate Java classes due to Step 1 rules.

The exception described in Step 1 occurs because we infer that any signature parameterizing the *ordering* library (*e.g.* In the first line of Figure 4, signature State parameterizes ordering) is actually a state machine. Thus, the parameterizing signature only generates code when the Model Translator synthesizes the application state machine (state machine synthesis is discussed later in this chapter).

The Alloy structural declaration translation was first presented in (Massoni, Gheyi, & Borba, 2004), and the algorithm in this section is very similar with the one presented by these authors.

**Method Generation**

Methods are extracted from predicates and functions declared in the model. Methods extracted

from predicates are typed as void; the ones extracted from functions are typed with the function type declared in the model. The procedure for generating Java methods is:

*Step 1:* For each predicate *P* and for each function *F* having at least two formal parameters typed as *C* which parameterizes the library *ordering*, go to Step 2, else go to Step 3.

*Step 2:* Create a method *M* in Java class *C* with the same name of *P* or *F*. If it is a predicate, set *M* return type as *void*; if it is a function, set *M* return type as the same as *F*. Set *M* visibility access to *public*. Create a method in *C* for each possible type combination of formal parameter extended by another class.

*Step 3:* Create a method *M* in Java class *Main* with the same name of *P* or *F*. If it is a predicate, set *M* return type as *void*; if it is a function, set *M* return type as the same as *F*. Set *M* visibility access to *public static*.

An example of the above procedure can be found in Figure 5. The methods *buydrink_Water*, *buydrink_Softdrink* and *buydrink_Tea* are created in Step 2. Actually, there is only one method (*buydrink(Drink d)*), but *Drink* is extended by *Water*, *Tea* and *Softdrink*. Thus, a method is created for each of these extending classes. The method

*Figure 5. Method generation for the drink vending machine*

**Alloy behavioral declaration**
```
pred buyDrink[m, m': VendingMachine, d: Drink]{
    m'.drinkStorage = m.drinkStorage - d
    #m'.coinStorage = #m.coinStorage - d.price
}
pred addCoin[m, m': VendingMachine, c: Coin]{
    m'.coinStorage = m.coinStorage + c
    m'.drinkStorage = m.drinkStorage
}
```

**Java generated method structure**
```
public class VendingMachine {
...
    public void addCoin(String c) {
        AlloyOperations.alloyUnion(this.coinStorage,c);
    }
    public void buyDrink_Water(Water d) {
        AlloyOperations.alloySubtraction( this.drinkStorage,
            new Water(d));
    }
    public void buyDrink_Softdrink(Softdrink d){
        AlloyOperations.alloySubtraction( this.drinkStorage,
            new Softdrink(d));
    }
    public void buyDrink_Tea(Tea d) {
        AlloyOperations.alloySubtraction( this.drinkStorage,
            new Tea(d));
    }
}
```

*addcoin* is created in Step 2 also, but Coin is not extended by another class; actually, Coin is not a Java class at all.

The Alloy behavioral declaration translation was first presented in (Krishnamurthi, Dougherty, Fisler, & Yoo, 2008), and the algorithm in this section is very similar to the one previously devised by these authors.

## Alloy Built-In Operations Generation

For each built-in Alloy operation we have coded a similar method in Java, in order to maintain the original behavior. Thus, every generated Java code accompanies an automatically generated static class with all Alloy operations called in the model.

## State Machine Inference and Synthesis

The state machine is automatically synthesized from the Alloy model, under the untimed model of computation (untimed MoC) (Jantsch, 2004). In order to generate the state machine under the untimed MoC, the designer just writes the operations that will be added to the state machine with Alloy run commands. The procedure for state machine inference and synthesis is based on the following steps:

*Step 1:* Create a structure $X$ for the state machine. For each run command $E$ in the model, if $E$ calls a predicate $P$ or a function $F$ go to Step 2.

*Step 2:* For each signature $S$ parameterizing the *ordering* library, instantiate $s$ of type $S$ in the *Main* Java class. If some $P$ or $F$ is member of the class $C$ generated from $S$, go to Step 3; else, go to Step 4.

*Step 3:* For each formal parameter $A$ of $P$ or $F$ extending a previously generated Java class, create an option in $X$ for each class extended by $A$. Go to Step 5.

*Step 4:* Create an option in X for $P$ or $F$. Go to Step 5.

*Step 5:* Insert all options in $X$ as if-statement in the *Main* Java class.

An example of the state machine inference and synthesis procedure can be seen in Figure 6. The structure created in Step 1 comprises the I/O constructs generated in order to listen and

*Figure 6. Method generation for the drink vending machine*

**Alloy state machine specification**
```
fact DrinkBuying {
  all s: State, s': ord/next[s] |
    some d: Drink | some c: Coin |
    d.price <= #s.machine.coinStorage =>
      buyDrink[s.machine,s'.machine,d]
      else addCoin[s.machine,s'.machine,c]
}
run addCoin
run buyDrink
```

**Java synthesized state machine**
```
public class Main {
  public static void main(String[] args) {
    VendingMachine machine = new VendingMachine();
    Menu menu_enum = Menu.done;
    InputStreamReader stdin = new
      InputStreamReader(System.in);
    BufferedReader console = new BufferedReader(stdin);
    try {
      while(true){
      if(menu_enum.ordinal()==Menu.addcoin.ordinal())
      {
        try {
          System.out.println("Enter Coin:");
          String c = console.readLine();
          machine.addCoin(c);
        }
        catch (IOException e) { e.printStackTrace(); }
        finally { menu_enum = Menu.done; }
      }
      ...
```

wait for events triggered by an actor, and a Java enumeration called Menu, containing all state machine possible branches. A branch is possible when a *run* Alloy command calls a predicate or function; there is a state machine branch for each called predicate/function.

Based on the generated Java source from *Model Translator*, a tool is used to estimate the embedded resources such as power, energy and memory footprint and evaluate several solutions based on all existing non-functional requirements.

## Estimation Tool and Target Platform

This work uses the DESEJOS (Mattos, & Carro, 2007) tool for physical properties estimation and design space exploration, and adopts the FemtoJava (Ito, Carro, & Jacobi, 2001) processor as embedded platform. This processor is a stack based Java Virtual Machine implementation, executing Java bytecodes natively. We have adopted FemtoJava and DESEJOS due to their use of Java, what makes this design flow general enough to be adapted to other object-oriented based platforms.

The FemtoJava processor implements an execution engine for Java in hardware through a stack machine compatible with Java Virtual Machine (JVM) specification. Our platform uses two different versions of the FemtoJava processor: multicycle and pipeline, which also operate at different frequencies. The multicycle version supports stack operations through stack emulation on their register files. This approach reduces the memory access bottleneck of the stack machine, improving performance. The multicycle version is targeted to low power embedded applications. The second architecture is the pipelined version, which has five stages: instruction fetch, instruction decoding, operand fetch, execution, and write back. Due to the forwarding technique in the stack architecture, the write back stage is not always executed, and hence there are meaningful energy savings when compared to a regular five stages pipeline of a RISC CPU. This version provides better results in terms of performance however dissipating more power than the multicycle one.

Javalution (Dautelle, 2007) was selected as the Java API for data structures, since Java API

*Figure 7. Physical estimate for different solutions and hardware platforms*

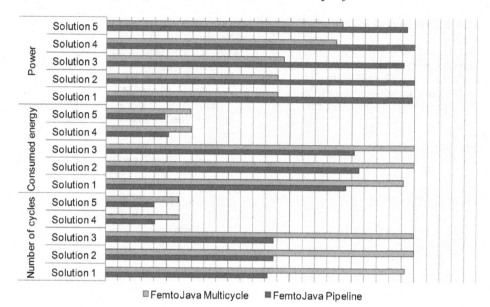

□ FemtoJava Multicycle   ■ FemtoJava Pipeline

(J2SE and J2ME APIs) are not used because their implementations use native code, and the target platform executes Java natively (just executes Java bytecodes). The results of performance, power and energy are measured by the DESEJOS tool using a frequency equal 50 MHz and Vdd equal 3.3V. The tool is calibrated based on a cycle accurate simulator and Synopsis Power Compiler Tool (Synopsys, 2008) from synthesized VHDL descriptions of the processors.

## Experimental Results

Estimates of physical properties have been obtained for the Java code automatically generated from the *Drink Vending Machine* Alloy model introduced earlier. This application is control oriented, being composed of two operations: inserting coins into the machine and buying a drink. The generated Java code contains two *collections*: one storing inserted coins and the other representing the drink storage.

Figure 7 presents the results obtained for estimation of physical properties for five different implementation strategies of the Vending Machine executing both on FemtoJava Multicycle and Pipeline. Each solution has the same FSM; the only variation between them is the assignment of distinct data structures to the two existing collections.

These five generated implementation strategies contain the following pairs of data structures draw from *Javolution*, representing the coin and drink storage, respectively: #1:(*Linked List, Linked List*), #2:(*Linked List, Map*), #3:(*Linked List, Set*), #4:(*Set, Map*) and #5:(*Set, Set*). These results show that only by varying the used data structures, there are significant design tradeoffs between strategies, due to the variation in total number of cycles required to execute the operations under the data structure. Clearly, strategies #4 and #5 take advantage of not using linked lists, reducing algorithmic complexity from $O(n)$ to $O(1)$ when accessing data. These results are coherent, recalling that all solutions have intensive elements insertion and deletion operations over the object collection. Furthermore, Figure 8 shows the program memory overhead of hash-

*Figure 8. Program memory estimate for different solutions*

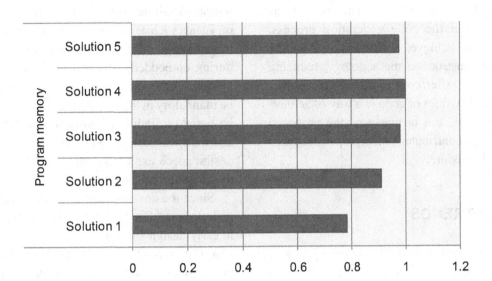

ing data structures (*Map* and *Set*) against linked lists, due to the information needed to maintain a hash function. Since both processors have the same ISA, the program memory occupation is the same in both multicycle and pipeline hardware platforms.

Concerning physical properties only, there are significant tradeoffs between the multicycle and pipeline architectures. Although the multicycle versions present less power consumption than the pipeline ones, there are significant performance and energy improvements in the pipeline versions. If extra power consumption is acceptable, it is very advantageous to adopt the pipeline architecture. Clearly, results presented in Figure 7 and 8 show the importance and the need of design space exploration in order to properly support software automation.

We have performed other experiments to validate our translator and also to measure the abstraction gain achieved by using Alloy as modeling language instead of coding directly in Java. To do so, in addition to the Drink Vending Machine application, we have modeled an Address Book and an Elevator Control System. The Address Book has three operations: adding a new contact in the book, searching for and deleting some existing contact. The Elevator Control System waits for the user to enter the destination floor, moves the elevator to this floor, and returns to the state where it waits for another floor request. The results of these experiments are shown in Table 2

The proposed methodology of generating code from Alloy models is very advantageous when considering the metrics lines of code, mainly due to code synthesis of some constructs not present

*Table 2. Achieved abstraction with Alloy models against Java code*

| Generated Java | Classes | Methods | Lines of Code |
|---|---|---|---|
| Drink Vending Machine | 7 | 18 | 198 |
| Book Address | 4 | 16 | 205 |
| Elevator Control System | 1 | 1 | 53 |

in the Alloy model, but required in the generated Java code. It is worth noting that all applications benefited from the code generation process, because of the achieved abstraction, and for the correct-by-construction methodology, reducing further testing after code synthesis. According to (Kan, 2002), lines of code is a way of achieving abstraction, and in this way, the proposed methodology contributes to the proper design of embedded software.

## FUTURE TRENDS

Due to the complexity and the tendency to join several applications into a single embedded product, an embedded system will support many models of computation, thus we believe that any automation or design space exploration tool must support multiple MoCs to handle heterogeneous systems.

With the increasing use of platform-based design approaches, design derivates are mainly configured by software, thus software automation tools are required. Specification languages should support non-functional requirements and design tools should support design space exploration in order to help designers find a solution that meets the product requirements.

Since only software testing is not sufficient to guarantee that non-functional requirements will be achieved, formal verification will be more and more required due to the complexity of future embedded systems as well as reliability and security concerns.

Using modeling techniques providing high levels of abstraction closer to the problem space makes the design process and implementation easier. Besides, these abstractions provide a very short development time and a lot of code reuse. It is widely known that design decisions taken at higher abstraction levels can lead to substantially superior improvements. Software engineers involved with software configuration of embedded platforms,

however, do not have enough experience to measure the impact of their algorithmic decisions on issues such as performance and power. Thus, methodologies and tools that can help the designer during embedded software development (from modeling to synthesis) are necessary now and will be mandatory in the near future. These tools must be based on traditional software methodologies and the specification, synthesis, verification and design space exploration are important features in the design process.

Since the development focus is moving from code to model, a fast design space exploration in early design steps is desired (Oliveira, Brisolara, Carro, & Wagner, 2006). We believe that in high-level models, where the design effort is now concentrated on modeling decisions, one can achieve substantially superior improvements. However, physical properties estimation from high level models is yet a challenge for some modeling languages as UML.

## CONCLUSION

The growing complexity of embedded systems has claimed for more software solutions in order to reduce the time-to-market. However, while software automation decreases the development time of embedded system functionalities, it must at the same time help the handling of embedded systems tight constraints, like energy, power and memory availability. Traditional software technologies use large amounts of memory, layers of abstraction, elaborate algorithms, and other approaches that are not directly applicable in embedded systems. Thus, the existing software methodologies are not adequate for embedded software development. This development domain is very different from the one used in the traditional environment. Embedded software development should address constraints like memory footprint, real-time behavior, power dissipation and so on. Thus, it is necessary to adapt the available techniques and methodologies, or to create novel approaches that can manipulate embedded systems constraints. We conclude that traditional software engineering processes and models are not enough to manipulate the requirements and constraints of embedded software. To summarize, specifications at higher abstraction levels and tools for software automation, including synthesis and verification, are very important, because reliability and safety are important criteria present in several embedded applications.

In the context of this discussion, this chapter presents a case study of an embedded software design automation tool based on the Alloy language. Following this approach, the high level specification should be described in Alloy, which provides high abstraction and formal verification. After validation, this specification is automatically mapped into different Java codes in order to explore the solution space, and to obtain a final implementation that meets the system's requirements. Using this case study, we shown some steps in the right direction to solve the problems addressed by this chapter. Although we have used the Alloy language as frontend in the design flow, it is possible to use any language, thus inserting the design flow with the MDA principles. For example, there is a tool capable of translating a UML subset into Alloy models (Anastasakis, Bordbar, Georg, & Ray, 2007), enabling to use our design flow with UML instead of Alloy. Moreover, as it has been shown, it is possible to join abstract specification and formal verification together with automatic synthesis and design space exploration, without loss of code efficiency for embedded systems.

As future work we are implementing the Alloy Annotation Language (Khurshid, Marinov, & Jackson, 2002) interpreter as means to provide code reuse; this would provide a checked reusable code assets library. Thus, when an asset is going to be reused, we would use the Alloy Analyzer to check consistence with the application code and asset interface, for instance. To cope with real-time

issues, we plan to introduce annotations in the Alloy model. These annotations would guide the model translator when deciding for a scheduling policy, for example. We are investigating such annotations and we will handle them as future work. As stated before, our approach supports only predicates that incur in some state changing, limiting its usage for reactive systems. We plan to verify the possibilities to handle other predicate types in the near future, and multithread program generation as well as. Besides, we are planning to construct the theoretical proof that our code preserves the Alloy semantics to prove that our set of transformations is sound.

## REFERENCES

Anastasakis, K., Bordbar, B., Georg, G., & Ray, I. (2007). UML2Alloy: A challenging model transformation. In G. Engels, B. Opdyke, D. C. Schmidt & F. Weil (Eds.), *Model driven engineering languages and systems (MoDELS 2007)* (LNCS 4735, pp. 436-450). Nashville: Springer Berlin.

Balarin, F., Chiodo, M., Giusto, P., Hsieh, H., Jurecska, A., & Lavagno, L. (1999). Synthesis of software programs for embedded control applications. *IEEE Transactions on Computer-Aided Design of Integrated Circuits and Systems, 18*(6), 834–849. doi:10.1109/43.766731

Balarin, F., Watanabe, Y., Hsieh, H., Lavagno, L., Passerone, C., & Sangiovanni-Vincentelli, A. (2003). Metropolis: An integrated electronic system design environment. *IEEE Computer, 36*(4), 45–52.

Bengtsson, J., Larsen, K., Larsson, F., Pettersson, P., & Yi, W. (1996). UPPAAL—a tool suite for automatic verification of real-time systems. In *Proceedings of the DIMACS/SYCON Workshop on Hybrid Systems III: Verification and control* (pp. 232-243). New Brunswick: Springer-Verlag New York.

Berry, G., & Gonthier, G. (1992). The esterel synchronous programming language: Design, semantics, implementation. *Science of Computer Programming, 19*(2), 87–152. doi:10.1016/0167-6423(92)90005-V

Bjørner, D., & Jones, C. B. (1978). *The Vienna development method: The metalanguage* (Vol. 61). Heidelberg: Springer Berlin-LNCS.

Brisolara, L. B., Oliveira, M. F., Redin, R., Lamb, L. C., Carro, L., & Wagner, F. (2008). Using UML as front-end for heterogeneous software code generation strategies. *Design* [Munich: IEEE Computer Society Press.]. *Automation and Test in Europe DATE, 08*, 504–509. doi:10.1109/DATE.2008.4484731

Buck, J., Ha, S., Lee, E. A., & Messerschmitt, D. G. (1994). Ptolemy: A framework for simulating and prototyping heterogeneous systems. *International Journal of Computer Simulation, special issue on Simulation Software Development, 4*, 155-182.

Chatzigeorgiou, A., & Stephanides, G. (2002). Evaluating performance and power of object-oriented vs. procedural programming in embedded processors. *7th Ada-Europe International Conference on Reliable Software Technologies* (pp. 65-75). London: Springer-Verlag.

Chen, X., Hsieh, H., & Balarin, F. (2006). Verification approach of metropolis design framework for embedded systems. *International Journal of Parallel Programming, 34*(1), 3–27. doi:10.1007/s10766-005-0002-x

Chen, X., Hsieh, H., Balarin, F., & Watanabe, Y. (2003). Case studies of model checking for embedded system designs. In *Proceedings of the Third International Conference on Application of Concurrency to System Design (ACSD '03)* (p. 20). IEEE Computer Society Press.

Chrissis, M. B., Konrad, M., & Shrum, S. (2003). *CMMI: Guidelines for process integration and product improvement.* Addison-Wesley.

Christopher, B., Edward, A. L., Xiaojun, L., Stephen, N., Yang, Z., & Haiyang, Z. (2008). *Heterogeneous concurrent modeling and design in java (volume 1: introduction to Ptolemy II).* University of California, Berkeley: EECS.

Cockburn, A. (2001). *Agile software development.* Addison-Wesley Professional.

Dautelle, J. (2007). Fully deterministic java. *AIAA SPACE 2007 Conference and Exposition,* CA (pp. 18-20).

Douglass, B. (1998). *Real-time UML: Developing efficient objects for embedded systems.* Boston: Addison-Wesley Professional.

Edwards, S., Lavagno, L., Lee, E. A., & Sangiovanni-Vincentelli, A. (1997). Design of embedded systems: Formal models, validation, and synthesis. *Proceedings of the IEEE, 85*(3), 366–390. doi:10.1109/5.558710

Esterel Technologies (2008). *SCADE tool.* Retrieved on October 7, 2008, from http://www.esterel-technologies.com/products/scade-suite/

Galeotti, J. P., & Frias, M. F. (2007). DynAlloy as a formal method for the analysis of java programs. In A. Schubert & J. Chrząszcz (Eds.), *Software engineering techniques: Design for quality* (Vol. 227/2007, pp. 249-260). Springer Boston.

Gery, E., Harel, D., & Palachi, E. (2002). Rhapsody: A complete life-cycle model-based development system. *Third International Conference on Integrated Formal Methods* (LNCS 2335, pp. 1-10). London: Springer-Verlag.

Gomaa, H. (2000). *Designing concurrent, distributed, and real-time applications with UML.* Boston: Addison-Wesley Professional.

Graaf, B., Lormans, M., & Toetenel, H. (2003). Embedded software engineering: The state of the practice. *IEEE Software, 20*(6), 61–69. doi:10.1109/MS.2003.1241368

Gries, M. (2004). Methods for evaluating and covering the design space during early design development. *Integration, the VLSI Journal, 38*(2), 131-183.

Gu, Z., & Shin, K. G. (2005). Model-checking of component-based event-driven real-time embedded software. In *Proceedings of the 8th IEEE International Symposium on Object-Oriented Real-Time Distributed Computing (ISORC '05)* (pp. 410-417). IEEE Computer Society Press.

LeGuernic, P., Gautier, T., Borgne, M., & Maire, C. (1991). Programming real-time applications with SIGNAL. *Proceedings of the IEEE, 79*(9), 1321–1336. doi:10.1109/5.97301

Halbwachs, N. (1993). *Synchronous programming of reactive systems* (Vol. 215). Springer.

Halbwachs, N., Caspi, P., Raymond, P., & Pilaud, D. (1991). The synchronous data flow programming language LUSTRE. *Proceedings of the IEEE, 79*(9), 1305–1320. doi:10.1109/5.97300

Hall, A. (1990). Using Z as a specification calculus for object-oriented systems. *Third International Symposium of VDM Europe on VDM and Z - Formal Methods in Software Development* (LNCS 428, pp. 290-318). London: Springer-Verlag.

Harel, D. (1987). Statecharts: A visual formalism for complex systems. *Science of Computer Programming, 8*(3), 231–274. doi:10.1016/0167-6423(87)90035-9

Havelund, K., Majumdar, R., & Palsberg, J. (2008). *Model checking software: 15th International SPIN Workshop.* Los Angeles: Springer.

Holzmann, G. J. (1997). The model checker SPIN. *IEEE Transactions on Software Engineering, 23*(5), 279–295. doi:10.1109/32.588521

Honekamp, U., Reidel, J., Werther, K., Zurawka, T., & Beck, T. (1999). Component-node-network: Three levels of optimized code generation with ASCET-SD. *International Symposium on Computer Aided Control System Design* (pp. 243-248). Kohala Coast: IEEE Computer Society Press.

Hudson, S. E., Flannery, F., & Ananian, C. S. (1999). *CUP: Parser generator for java*, 11. Retrieved on October 7, 2008, from http://www2.cs.tum.edu/projects/cup/

Ito, S. A., Carro, L., & Jacobi, R. P. (2001). Making java work for microcontroller applications. *IEEE Design & Test of Computers, 18*(5), 100–110. doi:10.1109/54.953277

Jackson, D. (2006). *Software abstractions–logic, language, and analysis.* Cambridge: The MIT Press.

Jantsch, A. (2004). *Modeling embedded systems and SoC's–concurrency and time in models of computation.* San Francisco: Morgan Kaufmann.

John, K., & Tiegelkamp, M. (2001). *IEC 61131-3: Programming industrial automation systems: Concepts and programming languages, requirements for programming systems, aids to decision-making tools.* Springer.

Kahn, G., & MacQueen, D. B. (1977). Coroutines and networks of parallel processes. *IFIP congress on information processing* (pp. 993-998). Amsterdam: North-Holland. Kan, S. H. (2002). *Metrics and models in software quality engineering* (2nd ed.). Boston: Addison-Wesley Professional.

Kangas, T., Kukkala, P., Orsila, H., Salminen, E., Hännikäinen, M., & Hämäläinen, T. D. (2006). UML-based multiprocessor SoC design framework. [TECS]. *ACM Transactions on Embedded Computing Systems, 5*(2), 281–320. doi:10.1145/1151074.1151077

Khurshid, S., Marinov, D., & Jackson, D. (2002). An analyzable annotation language. *17th ACM SIGPLAN Conference on Object-oriented Programming, Systems, Languages, and Applications (OOPSLA)* (pp. 231-245). Seattle: ACM Press.

Kim, H. (2006). Applying product line to the embedded systems. In M. Gavrilova, O. Gervasi, V. Kumar, C. J. Tan, D. Taniar, A. Laganà, et al. (Eds.), *Computational science and its applications-ICCSA 2006* (LNCS 3982, pp. 163-171). Glasgow: Springer Berlin.

Klein, G. (2004, November). *JFlex: The fast scanner generator for java version 1.4.1.* Retrieved on October 7, 2008, from http://jflex. de Koopman, P. (2007). Reliability, safety, and security in everyday embedded systems. In A. Bondavalli, F. Brasileiro & S. Rajsbaum (Eds.), *Dependable computing* (LNCS 4746, pp. 1-2). Morella: Springer Berlin.

Krishnamurthi, S., Dougherty, D. J., Fisler, K., & Yoo, D. (2008). Alchemy: Transmuting base alloy specifications into implementations. In *Proceedings of the 16th ACM SIGSOFT International Symposium on Foundations of Software Engineering (SIGSOFT '08/FSE-16)* (pp. 158-169). Atlanta: ACM Press.

Kruchten, P. (2003). *The rational unified process: An introduction* (3rd ed.). Boston: Addison-Wesley Professional.

Ledeczi, A., Maroti, M., Bakay, A., Karsai, G., Garrett, J., Thomason, C., et al. (2001). The generic modeling environment. *IEEE International Workshop on Intelligent Signal Processing.* Budapest: IEEE Computer Society Press.

Lee, E. A. (2000). What's ahead for embedded software? *IEEE Computer, 33*(9), 18–26.

Lee, E. A., & Messerschmitt, D. G. (1987). Synchronous data flow. *Proceedings of the IEEE, 75*(9), 1235–1245. doi:10.1109/PROC.1987.13876

Lieverse, P., van der Wolf, P., Deprettere, E., & Vissers, K. (2001). A methodology for architecture exploration of heterogeneous signal processing systems. *Journal of VLSI Signal Processing Systems, special issue on Signal Processing Systems Design and Implementation, 29*(3), 197-207.

Magic, N. *MagicDraw UML.* Retrieved on October 7, 2008, from http://www.magicdraw.com

Martin, G. (2002). UML for embedded systems specification and design: Motivation and overview. *Design, Automation, and Test in Europe Conference and Exhibition* (pp. 773-775). IEEE Computer Society Press.

Massoni, T., Gheyi, R., & Borba, P. (2004). A UML class diagram analyzer. In J. Jürjens, E. B. Fernandez, R. B. France, B. Rumpe, & C. Heitmeyer (Eds.), *Critical systems development using modeling languages (CSDUML'04): Current developments and future challenges* (pp. 100-114). Springer Berlin.

Mathaikutty, D. A., Patel, H. D., Shukla, S. K., & Jantsch, A. (2006). UMoC++: A C++-based multiMoC modeling environment. In A. Vachoux (Ed.), *Applications of specification and design languages for SoCs* (pp. 115-130). Springer Netherlands.

Mathworks (2008). *Matlab/Simulink*. Retrieved on October 7, 2008, from http://www.mathworks.com

Mattos, J. C., & Carro, L. (2007). Object and method exploration for embedded systems applications. *20th Annual Conference on Integrated Circuits and Systems Design (SBCCI'07)* (pp. 318-323). New York: ACM Press.

Mattos, J. C., Specht, E., Neves, B., & Carro, L. (2005). Object orientation problems when applied to the embedded systems domain. In A. Rettberg, Z. M. C & F. J. Rarnmig (Eds.), *From specification to embedded systems application* (Vol. IFIP 184, pp. 147-156). Manaus: Springer Boston.

CMP Media. (2006). *State of embedded market survey.*

Meenakshi, B., Bhatnagar, A., & Sudeepa, R. (2006). Tool for translating simulink models into input language of a model checker. *8th International Conference on Formal Engineering Methods (ICFEM '06)* (LNCS 4260, pp. 606-620). Macao: Springer Berlin.

Mentor Graphics. *BridgePoint UML suite*. Retrieved on October 7, 2008, from http://www.projtech.com

Miller, J., & Mukerji, J. (2003). *MDA guide version 1.0.1*. Object Management Group.

Mohanty, S., Prasanna, V. K., Neema, S., & Davis, J. (2002). Rapid design space exploration of heterogeneous embedded systems using symbolic search and multigranular simulation. *Joint Conference on Languages, Compilers and Tools For Embedded Systems: Software and Compilers For Embedded Systems (LCTES/SCOPES '02)* (pp. 18-27). New York: ACM Press.

National Instruments (2008). *Labview*. Retrieved on October 7, 2008, from http://www.ni.com/labview/

Naur, P., & Randell, B. (1969). *Software engineering. Report on a conference sponsored by the NATO science committee.* Garmisch: NATO.

Neema, S., Sztipanovits, J., & Karsai, G., & Butts, K. (2003). Constraint-based design-space exploration and model synthesis. In R. Alur & I. Lee (Eds.), *Embedded software: Third International Conference (EMSOFT '03)* (LNCS 2855, pp. 290-305). Heidelberg: Springer Berlin.

Ober, I., Graf, S., & Ober, I. (2004). Validation of UML models via a mapping to communicating extended timed automata. In H. Garavel, S. Graf, G. J. Holzmann, I. Ober & R. Mateescu (Eds.), *Model checking software* (LNCS 2989/2004, pp. 127-145). Springer Berlin / Heidelberg.

Oliveira, M. F., Brião, E. W., Nascimento, F. A., & Wagner, F. R. (2007). Model driven engineering for MPSOC design space exploration. *20th Annual Conference on Integrated Circuits and Systems Design (SBCCI '07)* (pp. 81-86). Rio de Janeiro: ACM Press.

Oliveira, M. F., Brisolara, L. B., Carro, L., & Wagner, F. R. (2006). Early embedded software design space exploration using UML-based estimation. *Seventeenth IEEE International Workshop on Rapid System Prototyping (RSP '06)* (pp. 24-32). Chania: IEEE Computer Society Press.

OMG. (1997). *Unified modeling language specification v. 1.0*. Object Management Group.

OMG. (2007). *MARTE specification beta 1*. Object Management Group.

Osterweil, L. J. (2007). A future for software engineering? *International Conference on Software Engineering* (pp. 1-11). Washington: IEEE Computer Society Press.

Pimentel, A. D., Erbas, C., & Polstra, S. (2006). A systematic approach to exploring embedded system architectures at multiple abstraction levels. *IEEE Transactions on Computers, 55*(2), 99–112. doi:10.1109/TC.2006.16

Pimentel, A. D., Hertzberger, L. O., Lieverse, P., van der Wolf, P., & Deprettere, E. F. (2001). Exploring embedded-systems architectures with artemis. *IEEE Computer, 34*(11). IEEE Computer Society Press.

Pressman, R. (2004). *Software engineering: A practitioner's approach* (6th ed.). McGraw-Hill Science/Engineering/Math.

Sander, I., & Jantsch, A. (2004). System modeling and transformational design refinement in ForSyDe. *Transactions on Computer-Aided Design of Integrated Circuits and Systems, 23*(1), 17–32. doi:10.1109/TCAD.2003.819898

Sangiovanni-Vincentelli, A., & Martin, G. (2001). Platform-based design and software design methodology for embedded systems. *IEEE Design & Test, 18*(6), 23–33. doi:10.1109/54.970421

Selic, B. (2003). Models, software models, and UML. In *UML for Real: Design of Embedded Real-Time Systems* (pp. 1-16). Norwell: Kluwer Academic Publishers.

Sgroi, M., Lavagno, L., & Sangiovanni-Vincentelli, A. (2000). Formal models for embedded system design. *IEEE Design & Test of Computers, 17*(2), 14–27. doi:10.1109/54.844330

Snyder, C. (2003). *Paper prototyping: The fast and easy way to design and refine user interfaces* (1st ed.). San Francisco: Morgan Kaufmann.

Sommerville, I. (2006). *Software engineering* (8th ed.). Boston: Addison Wesley.

Synopsys. *Synopsys power compiler*. Retrieved on October 7, 2008, from http://www.synopsys.com/products/logic/design_compiler.html

Tanenbaum, A. S., Herder, J. N., & Bos, H. (2006). Can we make operating systems reliable and secure? *IEEE Computer, 39*(5), 44–51.

Telelogic, A. G. *Rhapsody*. Retrieved on October 7, 2008, from http://modeling.telelogic.com/products/rhapsody/index.cfm

Turley, J. (2002). *The two percent solution*. Retrieved on October 7, 2008, from http://www.embedded.com/story/OEG20021217S0039

Venture Development Corporation. (2006). *VIII: Embedded systems market statistics-the 2005 embedded software strategic market intelligence program*. Natick: Venture Development Corporation.

Voros, N. S., Snook, C. F., Hallerstede, S., & Masselos, K. (2004). Embedded system design using formal model refinement: An approach based on the combined use of UML and the B language. *Design Automation for Embedded Systems, 9*(2), 67–99. doi:10.1007/s10617-005-1184-6

Zhou, G., Leung, M., & Lee, E. A. (2007). *A code generation framework for actor-oriented models with partial evaluation*. University of California, Berkeley: EECS.

# Chapter 11
# Transaction Level Model Automation for Multicore Systems

**Lucky Lo Chi Yu Lo**
*University of California Irvine, USA*

**Samar Abdi**
*University of California Irvine, USA*

**Daniel Gajski**
*University of California Irvine, USA*

## ABSTRACT

*Model based verification has been the bedrock of electronic design automation. Over the past several years, system modeling has evolved to keep up with improvements in process technology fueled by Moore's law. Modeling has evolved to keep up with the complexity of applications resulting in various levels of abstractions. The design automation industry has evolved from transistor level modeling to gate level and eventually to register transfer level (RTL). These models have been used for simulation based verification, formal verification and semiformal verification. With the advent of multicore systems, RTL modeling and verification are no longer feasible. Furthermore, the software content in most modern designs is growing rapidly. The increasing software content, along with the size, complexity and heterogeneity of multicore systems, makes RTL simulation extremely slow for any reasonably sized system. This has made system verification the most serious obstacle to time to market. The root of the problem is the signal-based communication modeling in RTL. In any large design there are hundreds of signals that change their values frequently during the execution of the RTL model. Every signal toggle causes the simulator to stop and reevaluate the state of the system. Therefore, RTL simulation becomes painfully slow. To overcome this problem, designers are increasingly resorting to modeling such complex systems at higher levels of abstraction than RTL. Transaction level models (TLMs) have emerged as the next level of abstraction for system design. However, well defined TLM semantics are needed for design automation at the transaction level. In this chapter, we present transaction level model automation for multicore systems based on well defined TLM semantics. TLMs replace the traditional signal toggling model of system communication with function calls, thereby increasing simulation speed. TLMs are*

DOI: 10.4018/978-1-60566-750-8.ch011

*already being used for executable specification of multicore designs, for analysis, fast simulation, and debugging. They play an important role in early application development and debugging before the final prototype has been implemented. We discuss essential issues in TLM automation and also provide an understanding of the basic building blocks of TLMs.*

## INTRODUCTION

The rise in complexity, size and heterogeneity of modern embedded system designs has pushed modeling to new abstraction levels above RTL. Transaction level modeling using System-Level Design Languages (SLDL) such as SpecC (Gajski, Zhu, Doemer, Gerstlauer & Zhao, 2000; Gerstlauer, Domer, Peng & Gajski, 2001) or SystemC (OSCI, 2007) is emerging as a new paradigm for system modeling. But the transaction level modeling's concept still has not been fully standardized in the industry. Different people have different notions of how TLMs should appear, both syntactically and semantically. This is because the original TLM definition did not provide any specific structure or semantics. However, the argument for establishing standards in TLMs is a very strong one. The reason is that without standards there is no possibility for sharing of models, for having common synthesis and analysis tools and so on. Ad hoc transaction level modeling may seem attractive for having fast simulation speed for a specific design, but that approach is not conducive to establishing TLM as a viable modeling abstraction like RTL.

## TLM BACKGROUND

In 2003, a paper on establishing taxonomy for TLMs was published (Cai & Gajski, 2003) that opened up the debate on what are the useful system level models and how to position TLMs as an abstraction above RTL. The taxonomy was based on the granularity of detail in modeling the computation and communication for systems with multiple processing elements.

In a TLM, the details of communication amongst computation components are separated from the details of computation components themselves. Communication is modeled by channels, which are simply a repository for communication services. This is very similar to a class in C++. In fact, SystemC uses C++ classes to implement channels. The channel communication services are used by transaction requests that take place by calling interface functions of these channels. Unnecessary details of communication and computation are hidden in a TLM and may be added later in the design process. TLMs speed up simulation and allow exploring and validating design alternatives at a higher level of abstraction. However, the definition of TLMs is not well understood. Without clear definition of TLMs, any predefined TLMs cannot be easily reused. Moreover, the usage of TLMs in the existing design domains, namely modeling, validation, refinement, exploration, and synthesis, cannot be systematically developed. Consequently, the inherent advantages of TLMs don't effectively benefit designers. In order to eliminate some ambiguity of TLMs, several TLMs are defined, each of which may be adopted for different design purpose.

In order to simplify the design process, designers generally use a number of intermediate models. The intermediate models slice the entire design process into several smaller design stages, each of which has a specific design objective. Since the models can be simulated and estimated, the result of each of these design stages can be independently validated. In order to relate different models, the

*Figure 1. System modeling graph*

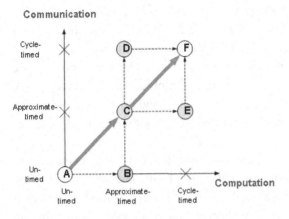

system modeling graph is shown in Figure 1. The X-axis in the graph represents granularity of computation and the Y-axis represents granularity of communication. On each axis, we have three degrees of time accuracy: un-timed, approximate-timed, and cycle-timed. Un-timed computation/communication represents the pure functionality of the design without any implementation details. Approximate-timed computation/communication contains system-level implementation details, such as the selected system architecture and the mapping relations between tasks of the system specification to the processing elements of the system architecture. The execution time for approximate-timed computation/communication is usually estimated at the system level without cycle-accurate RTL /ISS (instruction set simulation) level evaluation. Cycle-timed computation/communication contains implementation details at both system level and the RTL/ISS level, such that cycle-accurate estimation can be obtained.

There are six abstract models in the system-modeling graph based on the timing granularity of computation and communication. These models, labeled A to F, are indicated on the graph by circles. Model A is the specification model that has no notion of timing for either computation or communication. Model B is the component-assembly model that has approximate notion of timing for the

computation part but all communication is modeled to execute in zero time. Model C is the bus-arbitration model where the communication delay due to bus arbitration is factored in. Therefore it models communication timing approximately. Model D is the bus-functional model which reports accurate communication delays by factoring in both arbitration and the detailed bus protocol. However, the computation is still approximately timed. Model E is the cycle-accurate-computation model that reports computation delays at the clock cycle level of accuracy. However, the bus protocols are not modeled which makes the communication timing only an approximation. Finally, model F is dubbed the implementation model because this model is traditionally the starting point for standard design tools. Both communication and computation are modeled down to the cycle accurate level and all transactions are implemented using signal toggling as per the bus protocols. Amongst these models, component-assembly model (B), bus-arbitration model (C), bus-functional model (D), and cycle-accurate computation model(E) are TLMs, and are indicated by shaded circles on the system modeling graph. A system level design process takes a specification model (A) to its corresponding implementation (F). A methodology using TLMs may take any route from A to F via B, C, D and E depending on the type of application, complexity of the platform and the focus of the verification effort. A simple methodology (A→C→F) is highlighted in Figure 1.

## PLATFORM-BASED DESIGN

On the other hand, platform based design (Keutzer, Malik, Newton, Rabaey & Sangiovanni-Vincentelli, 2000; Sangiovanni-Vincentelli, 2007) of multi processor SoCs (MPSoC) is being adapted to combine the best features of top-down and bottom-up system design. Although several SystemC modeling styles for MPSoC have been proposed, no clear semantics for modeling objects

*Figure 2. Design flow*

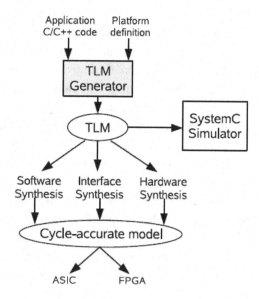

and composition rules have emerged yet. This makes automatic TLM generation difficult. Most surveys point to usage of transaction level models for early system verification and embedded SW development. Therefore, SW developers who use TLM have to understand TL modeling and SystemC semantics. In this chapter, we present a system development framework and TLM generation tool that removes the need for SW developers to understand either the platform communication architecture or to learn new modeling languages like SystemC.

The complete design flow for TL model automation is shown in Figure 2. The inputs are the application C code and the platform definition. The output is a TLM from which the software, hardware and interfaces will be synthesized to construct a Pin Cycle Accurate Model to implement in a FPGA or ASIC. This chapter will be centered on the TLM generator.

The input platform to the generator is a high level net-list of the system consisting of processing elements (PEs), busses and bridges. The bridges interface between busses to allow multi-

hop communication. Each PE consists of one or more processes that can be accessed on the bus. The processes themselves are described using a set of C files that contain the functions implemented for that process. The user would create the input using a Graphic User Interface (GUI), where the PEs, busses and bridges are connected and C processes would be mapped into processes residing in the PEs.

The output is a untimed TL Model of the custom communication platform. The design is the top-level module consisting of sub-modules for each PE, bridge and memory. Processes executing on the PE are modeled as threads inside PE modules. A generic bus channel (GBC) is used to model system busses. A generic bridge module (GBM) models a bridge between two busses. GBM allows for communication between processes/memories that are not connected to a common bus, this may be needed if we have communicating PEs with incompatible bus protocols.

Since the semantics for GBC and GBM are well defined, the TLM can be automatically derived from a set of platform parameters. In order to develop the C code, a standard set of APIs is automatically generated for each process in each PE. These APIs provide communication services for rendezvous communication with other processes in the platform. Software developers need only to use these APIs to construct the TLM, so therefore, the C code developers do not have to understand the communication architecture or write any SystemC code to verify that their code executes on the platform, they need only to use their original C code and adapt it.

## BACKGROUND

TLM has gained a lot of attention recently ever since it was introduced (Grotker, 2002) as part of high level SystemC (OSCI, 2007) modeling initiative. Several use models and design flows (Donlin, 2004; Ghenassia, 2005) have been presented centering on TLM. In (Cai & Gajski, 2003; Schirner & Doemer, 2006), the authors present semantics of different TL models based on timing granularity. Similarly, design optimization and evaluation has also been proposed using practical TLMs (Ogawa, Bayon de Noyer, Chauvet, Shinohara, Watanabe, Niizuma, Sasaki & Takai 2003). These approaches do not clearly separate computation from communication. A generic bus architecture was defined in (Klingauf, Gunzel, Bringmann, Parfuntseu & Burton, 2006), however, none of the above approaches address automatic TLM generation or the designer burden in learning new TLM styles and languages. There have been several approaches to automatically generate executable SystemC code from abstract descriptions. Modeling languages as UML (Bruschi & Di Nitto & Sciuto, 2003) and behavioral descriptions of systems in SystemC (Sarmento, Cesario & Jerraya, 2004) have been proposed. In (Kangas, Kukkala, Orsila, Salminen, Hannikainen, Hamalainen, Riihimaki, & Kuusilinna, 2006), UML is used as a starting specification in order to arrive to a FPGA prototype. These approaches do not address transaction level platform modeling without the need to use another language. The closest work is in SpecC TLM generation for design space exploration (Shin, Gerstlauer, Peng, Doemer, & Gajski, 2006), which still requires designers to understand complex channel modeling in a nonstandard SpecC language. One important difference is that their modeling abstraction requires implementation decisions for synchronization to be already made. Moreover, there is no discussion of modeling communication processes such as bridges and routers.

There have been several other approaches that start from a very high level specification and go to a cycle accurate model or synthesizable model implemented in a FPGA board. Their main difference is the starting point, which generally makes a big difference. For instance, in (Huang, Han, Popovici, Brisolara, Guerin, Li, Yan, Chae, Carro, Jerraya, 2007) the input of the flow is a Simulink

algorithm level, which is eventually converted to a Simulink Combined Algorithm and Architecture level, a Virtual Architecture, Transaction-accurate Model and finally to a Virtual Prototype which is cycle accurate, by the refinement to Instruction Set Simulators. Their main drawback is the need to specify the design in Simulink, before being able to do any transformation/refinement. Another approach that results in a synthesized model mapped to a FPGA-based platform is (Haubelt, Falk, Keinert, Schlichter, Streubuhr, Deyhle, Hader & Teich, 2007). Their work starts with an executable specification written with a subset of SystemC, which is synthesizable, and their target architecture template must be built from components supported by their component library. These two approaches suffer from the same disadvantage mentioned above: the need to learn and use another language in order to generate successive refined models.

The novelty and utility of the presented approach lies in that we require only application C code and provide a programming model that is agnostic of communication architecture. The automation tool presented here is implemented in our Embedded Systems Environment (ESE) tool (CECS, 2008; Yu Lo & Abdi, 2007; Yu Lo & Abdi, 2007).

## PLATFORM MODELING

Each object in the platform is modeled according to a well-defined SystemC template. Busses use the Generic Bus Channel (GBC) template, bridges use Generic Bridge Module (GBM) template, processes are sc_threads and PEs are sc_modules. Figure 3 shows the code organization for the executable TLM. The design is modeled as a top-level sc_module which instantiates all the GBCs, GBMs and PEs as captured in the GUI. We first focus here on one process called p. This process will access its assigned PE's port by using the communication APIs. Each PE is declared also as a sc_module which contains one or more

*Figure 3. Code organization for TLM*

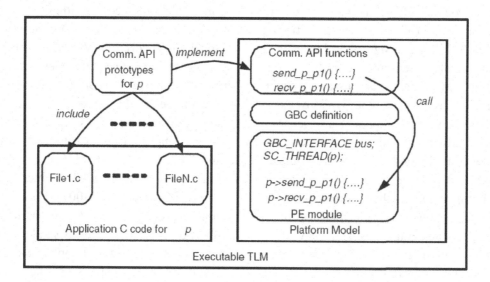

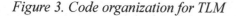

sc_threads representing the C processes of the PE. The communication APIs exported to the application C code are global functions that call the GBC access methods inside the corresponding process' sc_thread. For any process to send or receive data to any other process, a clear semantic is defined, which is independent of the platform defined by the user in the graphical capture. These should be used in the original C code. No further modification to these files is needed after that. The only limitation in the C code is that even if different functions are mapped into different processes in different PEs, they should have different names.

It should be noted that the only alterations on the source files that are needed could be done in a few minutes. The decisions to be made involve:

- What data needs to be transferred from one process to another
- Determining the size of that data
- Choosing the unique name for each send/receive function.

The semantics for the send and receive functions are:

```
{send/receive function name}
(void *pointer, unsigned int
data_size);
```

We present below an example of a simple producer-consumer code:

```
producer.c file
void producer(void){
   int i;
   for (i=0;i<10;i++){
     send_
consumer(&i,sizeof(int));
   }
}
consumer.c file
void consumer(void){
   int data;
   while(1){
     recv_
producer(&data,sizeof(int));
     printf("%d\n",data);
   }
}
```

*Figure 4. Example platform*

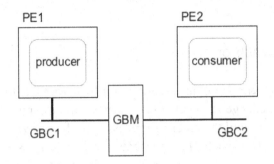

Each file shown above would be mapped into a separate process, which would be named producer and consumer. The functions send_consumer() and recv_producer() are the function calls to the communication API. The names of these functions can be freely chosen by the application developer but should be unique, as the case of the process name. The tool will automatically generate the definition of this API.

The communication API generated depends on the inter-process communication specification in the platform. A GBC send and receive call will be generated for each pair of communicating processes (in the case that they reside in separate PEs). These functions will access the corresponding GBC send/receive functions, even if the destination process is not located in the same GBC as the source process. In this case, the function will route the data through the necessary GBCs and GBMs to arrive at the destination process. All these steps are generated automatically, without the user needing to do anything else except calling the communication APIs. One obvious advantage of this approach is the ease in which the user can modify its platform without modifying again the C source code, facilitating the design space exploration.

A possible platform for this application is shown below.

In Figure 4, the example platform is composed of two Processing Elements (square boxes), each

one hosting one process (rounded boxes). The source files producer.c and consumer.c have been mapped into those two processes. There are two busses connecting the PEs to a bridge (GBM, which is the thin rectangular box). The horizontal lines represent the busses, and the vertical lines represent the connections between the bus and a PE. This platform would be created using the GUI in a couple of minutes, by the use of drag-and-drop of PEs, busses and bridges. The steps to create this platform are: adding a process to each PE, assigning a .c file to each process, and specifying a communicating channel between the producer and consumer. No extra specification of the bridge is needed, except the size of the FIFO.

## Generic Bus Channel

GBC is a channel model that abstracts the system bus as a single unit of communication. GBC provides the basic communication services of synchronization, arbitration and data transfer that are part of a transaction. At the transaction level, we do not distinguish between different bus protocols. The bus is modeled as a sc_channel, implementing a sc_interface which lets the GBC provide five bus communication functions:

1.  Send is the method used by a process to send data to another process using synchronized transaction. The synchronization mode of the sender is selected as initiator, resetter (if determined at compile time) or either (if determined at run time). The parameters are the sender process id, the receiver process id, pointer to data being sent, size of data in bytes and synchronization mode. The receiver process must be connected to the GBC and must execute the Recv function for this transaction. The synchronization mode of the receiver for this transaction must be complementary to sender. That is, if sender mode is initiator then receiver mode must be resetter and vice versa. If sender mode

is either, then receiver mode also must be either.

2. Recv is the method used by a process to receive data from another process using synchronized transaction. The synchronization mode of the receiver is selected as initiator, resetter (if determined at compile time) or either (if determined at run time). The parameters are the receiver process id, the sender process id, pointer to location where received data will be copied, size of data in bytes and synchronization mode. The sender process must be connected to the UBC and must execute the Send function for this transaction. The synchronization mode of the sender for this transaction must be complementary to receiver. That is, if receiver mode is initiator then sender mode must be resetter and vice versa. If receiver mode is either, then sender mode must be either.

3. Write is the method used by a process to write data to a contiguous memory location in a non-blocking fashion. The parameters are the writer process id, the starting memory address, pointer to data that needs to be written and size of data in bytes.

4. Read is the method used by a process to read data from a contiguous memory location in a non-blocking fashion. The parameters are the reader process id, the starting memory address, pointer to local memory where read data will be stored and size of data in bytes.

5. MemoryAccess is the method used by memory controller to service a write or read call from a process connected to the UBC. The parameters are low and high boundaries of the address range for this memory and pointer to start of local memory of device.

There are also 2 private functions, used by the above public functions:

1. ArbiterRequest/ArbiterRelease for selecting the master on the bus
2. Synchronize

## Synchronization

Synchronization is required for two processes to exchange data reliably. A sender process must wait until the receiver process is ready, and vice versa. Synchronization between two processes takes place by one process setting the flag and the other process checking and resetting the flag. We will refer to the process setting the flag as the initiator and the process resetting the flag as resetter. The initiator and resetter processes for a given transaction are determined at compile time. In Figure 5, assume P1 is the initiator process and P2 as the resetter process. Hence, P1 sets the synchronization flag. If P2 is ready before P1, it must keep reading the flag until P1 sets it. P1 notifies this event when it sets the synchronization flag. Once P2 reads the flag as set, it recognizes that P1 is ready and resets the flag.

## Arbitration

After synchronization, the resetter process will attempt to reserve the bus for data transfer. This is necessary since a bus is a shared resource and multiple transactions attempted at the same time must be ordered sequentially. The resetter process will request an arbitration to the bus, and since the GBC model is exclusive for functional verification, the arbiter is modeled as a mutex (which is a sc_mutex in SystemC). An arbitration request corresponds to a mutex lock operation and once the transaction is complete, the process will release the arbitration with a mutex unlock operation.

## Generic Bridge Module

The GBM models the bridge connected to two busses. Its purpose is to facilitate multi-hop transactions, where one process sends data to another

*Figure 5. Flag-based synchronization between processes*

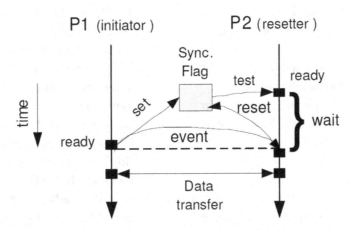

FIFO Channels

process that is not connected directly to the sender via a GBC. The basic functionality of the GBM is to simply receive data from the sender process, store it locally and send it to the receiver process once the latter becomes ready. The receiver can be a processing element or another GBM in the case of multi-hop transactions. There are three types of objects used to model the GBM (shown in Figure 6) as described in this section.

The data in transit via the GBM is stored locally in FIFO channels. The number of such channels is equal to the total number of communication paths through the GBM. The number of such paths can be easily derived from the platform specification. The size of each FIFO can be defined in GUI while parameterizing the bridge. Each FIFO supports four functions as follows:

*Figure 6. TLM for bridge module*

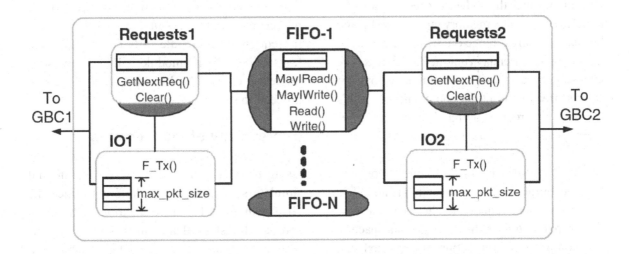

1. MayIWrite returns true if the requested space is available in the FIFO, else returns false;
2. MayIRead returns true if the requested number of bytes are present in the FIFO, else returns false;
3. BufferWrite copies the incoming data to the FIFO buffer and updates the tail pointer;
4. BufferRead copies data from the FIFO buffer to the output and updates the head pointer.

## Request Buffers

In general, before any data is sent/received to/from the GBM, a request must be made such that the GBM interface may check if the internal FIFOs can accommodate the data or supply it. Such a request may be included in the packet itself, but if the packet cannot fit, additional logic is needed in the bridge to reject the packet and in the process to check for rejection and resend it. For simplicity, we will only consider the scenario where the PE writes the request (directly to the exposed memory of the Request buffer), followed by synchronization and data transfer. In case of multiple competing processes, the requests from different processes are arbitrated by the GBM and the communication with the successful process is initiated.

There are two request buffers in the GBM, one for each bus interface. The number of words per request buffer is equal to the number of communication paths through the bridge. The request buffer is modeled as any other memory module in a PE and thus has an address range on the bus. Each word in the request buffer has a unique bus address. The requesting process writes the number of bytes it expects to read/write into the communication path's corresponding request buffer. The request buffer is a module that supports four functions:

1. GetNextReq checks the request words in the buffer in a round-robin fashion. For the chosen, request, it checks if the corresponding FIFO has enough data/space to complete the transaction of requested size

calling the buffers' functions MayIWrite and MayIRead. If the FIFO status check returns TRUE, it returns the request ID and path, else it checks the next pending request.
2. Clear removes the request from the buffer.
3. WriteMem writes to the other request buffer in the same GBM in the case of multi-hop transactions.
4. Write performs the write to the request buffer itself. It is exposed to the other Request Buffer in the GBM (namely to its WriteMem function). In the case of multi-hop transactions the GetNextReady function will call WriteMem in order to write to the next Request Buffer (if the data route continues in the same GBM).

## IO Module

The IO module is the interface function of the GBM that talks to other processes and GBMs on the bus. It consists of a local buffer of the size of maximum data packet and F Tx. It starts by calling the GetNextReady function in the request buffer. Then, for the selected sender or receiver process, it calls the GBC receive or send function respectively. The data received from sender is written to the corresponding FIFO. The data to be sent to the receiver is first read from the corresponding FIFO before calling the GBM send function. Once the requested transaction is completed, the request removed by calling the Clear function in the request buffer module. In the case of multi-hop transactions, the IO module will write the send request to the next GBM in the packet route, and proceed to send it.

## Expressivity of the Elements

Using the GBC and GBM, we can create and simulate several types of platforms. Since the GBC can model synchronization, arbitration and data transfers, that is sufficient for various communication architectures like shared and dedicated busses and NoC links. In the case or our GBM, it can be scaled from a buffer to a bridge to a NoC static router. GBMs can be extended to support dynamic routing by explicitly modeling a routing table.

## AUTOMATIC TLM GENERATION

In this section, we present the procedures for generating the TLM described in Section 3 from the platform specification. For brevity, we will describe generation of GBC, GBM and top level module only.

### GBC Code Generation

The GBC is modeled as a SystemC channel class as described in Section 3.1. For each bus in the platform, a unique GBC channel implementation is generated. Procedure 1 shows the method for creation of the GBC internal structure. Here, we present only the pseudo-code for the send function generation due to lack of space. The receive function is similar to the send function, the read and write functions do not carry the code for synchronization and the memory service function simply executes and endless loop checking for bus address. We start by creating the arbiter, which is an instantiation of the sc mutex module, and create the variable and the event for addressing (lines 2-4). Then, for all the communicating processes defined, we select processes that are directly connected to this GBC and include them in the set Pbus. The interface processes of the GBMs connected to this bus are also included in Pbus. The synchronization and addressing code is generated for all pairs of processes in Pbus (Line 5). We create the synchronization flags and events as described in Section 3.1 for all pairs of processes in Pbus (Line 6). If the sender is an initiator, then code is generated to set the flag and notify the synchronization event (Line 10). Otherwise, we generate code to wait until the flag is set (Lines 11). The

resetter is eventually responsible for acquiring the bus and setting the address. The corresponding code for locking the arbiter mutex and setting the bus address is generated if the sender is resetter (Line 13). If the sender is initiator, code is generated to snoop for the right address for this pair of communicating processes (Line 14). Finally, after the addressing, data transfer is performed by setting the local channel data pointer (DataPtr) to the pointer (data ptr) passed in the send function call, then code is generated to check if the sender is the resetter, and release the bus by unlocking the arbiter mutex.

```
Procedure 1. Generate GBC
1: //Generate GBC flags and
events
2: gen:"sc_mutex arbiter;"
3: gen:"int BusAddr; sc event
AddSet;"
4: Pbus = Set of proc.s on GBC
5: for all p1, p2 Є Pbus do
6:    Declare synchronization
flags and sc_events
7:    //Code gen. for synchroni-
zation
8:    gen:"if (sender==p1 &&
receiver==p2){"
9:    if p1.type = INITIATOR,p2.
type = RESETTER then
10:       Set synchronization flag
and notify sc_event
11:       Wait for AddrSet event
if BusAddress not defined
12:    else
13:       Wait for event if syn-
chronization flag is not set
14:       Arbitration and Bus Ad-
dress set
15:    end if
16: end for
```

## GBM Code Generation

The Generic Bridge Module generated by our tool consists of two sets of modules, one set for each GBC. Each set consists of a FIFO channel, a Request buffer and an IO module as described in Section 3.2. The generation of the GetNextReq function of the Request buffer is shown in the procedure 2. The bridge addresses are uniquely named using the source, destination and address (p1, p2) in each path (Lines 2-6). In the request buffer, the function GetNextReq() checks if any of the request addresses has been modified, and sets the variables {src, dest, size, transfer type} accordingly for the transfer (Lines 9-20). The generator checks each path, and if the current bridge is part of it (Line 10), uses its source and destination (src, dest) to generate the proper process IDs for the pointer assignment (Line 12), and the buffer permission to read or write(Line 13). In order to determine which fifo to read and write, each IO module connection to the busses is checked along with the busses information in each route. This determines which process is assigned to the pointers src and dest. In the same iteration loop, the function Clear described in Section 3.2.2 can be generated. The other modules in the bridge are generated iterating through the FIFOs, and generating the functions MayIWrite, MayIRead, BufferWrite, BufferRead for each of them.

```
Procedure 2. Generate GBM: Ad-
dress labels and GetNextReady()
1: //Bridge addresses generation
2: for each {p1, p2, address} ∈
path do
3:    if bridge ∈ path then
4:       //Bus Addresses genera-
tion using p1 and p2
5:    end if
6: end for
7: //Request:GetNextReq()
8: count = 0
9: for each {src, dest} ∈ path
do
10:    if bridge ∈ path then
11:       gen:"if
(RequestBuffer[count]) {"
12:          Set
source,destination,size and
transfer type
13:       gen:" if(fifo→MayIWrite(
*src,*dest,*size)==Yes)"
14:       if dest is not local to
this bus then
15:          gen:"WriteMem(*src,*de
st,*size,*TransferType);"
16:       end if
17:       gen:" return true; }"
18:    end if
19:    count++
20: end for
```

## Top Module Code Generation

After the GBM and GBC procedures generate the busses and the bridges, Procedure 3 shows the final class generation, where the process, PE, bus and bridge instantiations and connections are made. Instantiations are made for each PE, bus and bridge. Once inside the constructor (Lines 5- 15), a connection is made between its port and the corresponding bus (Line 10), by checking connections (conn) for each PE (Line 9).

```
Procedure 3 Generate Top Module
1: for each {PE, bus, bridge ∈
design} do
2:    Instantiate process in PE
3: end for
4: //Connections inside the con-
structor
5: for each {PE ∈ design} do
6:    for each {proc ∈ PE} do
7:       for each {port ∈ proc} do
```

*Figure 7. Application mapping and platform creation*

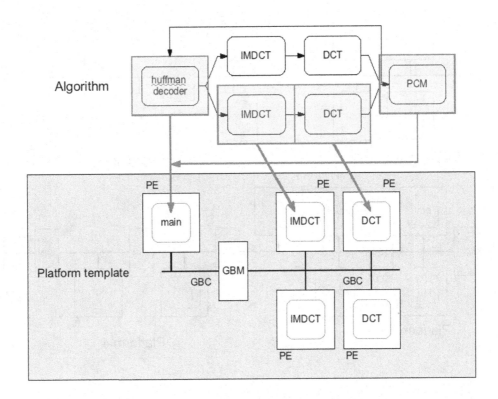

```
8:        for each {conn ∈ de-
sign} do
9:           if conn == PEname
then
10:              gen:"proc inst →
port(*bus inst);"
11:          end if
12:       end for
13:       end for
14:    end for
15: end for
```

## EXPERIMENTAL RESULTS

The procedures shown in Section 4 were implemented in a C++ tool for automatic generation of TLMs from application C code and platform specification. The input to the tool was a high level net-list of the system created with our GUI, with pointers to C code, as described in Section 3. The output is a complete set of executable SystemC files (PEs, GBCs and GBMs).

We selected two large industrial applications namely a MP3 decoder and a H.264 fixed point decoder to test our automatic TLM generation tool. All tests were performed on a Pentium 4, 3 GHz, 1 GB RAM machine running Linux kernel 2.6. The MP3 decoder reference C code (Leslie, 2004) consisted of 9463 lines of C code. The simulation testbench for MP3 was an input file of 138 KB size. The original reference C code for H.264 decoder (Fiedler, 2004) consisted of simplified decoder with 3419 lines of C code and its simulation was performed using a 27 KB clip of frame size 352 by 288 pixels.

In order to create the test platforms, the first step was to decide what functions from the algorithm would reside in separate processes. Then

*Figure 8. Platforms used for MP3 decoder*

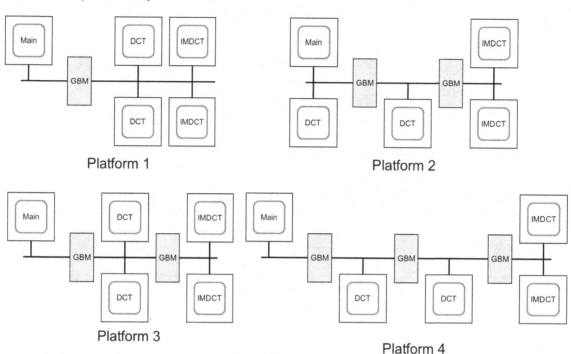

the following step is to add a PE and process for each function, and assign the source file to its process. This is illustrated in Figure 7 for the MP3 decoder.

The decoder algorithm was partitioned into 5 functions: the main decoder, and two sets of DCT and IMDCT filters, each for each stereo channel. For clarity, only the mapping of one set of filters is shown above. The main decoder code (Huffman decoder and PCM code) resides in one process. This process is residing in a PE connected to a bus. The four filters (two DCTs and two IMDCTs) are connected to another bus. The two busses are connected through a bridge (GBM). This platform illustrates the use of two busses and a bridge to represent the case where two communicating PEs have two different bus protocols, in which case a bridge is needed.

In the case of the MP3 decoder, several platforms with different communication architectures, as shown in Figure 8, were used to generate the TLMs. These platforms do not differ on the

number of Processing Elements (the mapping of the processes is the same), but differ on the communication elements that are present. They range between two busses and one bridge to five busses and four bridges. The connections between processing elements and busses also differ. The purpose of testing this variety of platforms lies on the need to stress the generation tool: testing different number of PEs connected to a single bus, communication through one bus to up to four busses and going through several bridges. The complexity of the generation lies mostly on the generation itself of the communication elements (namely the Generic Bus Channels and the Generic Bridge Modules) and not the mapping of C processes onto SystemC modules.

In the case of the H264 decoder, it was partitioned into 6 processes: Main, Get_nal, Input, Mult, IntraDispatch, and Transf. There was also just one process per PE, and several platforms were created, shown in Figure 9.

Table 1 shows the automatic generation re-

*Figure 9. Platforms used for H264 decoder*

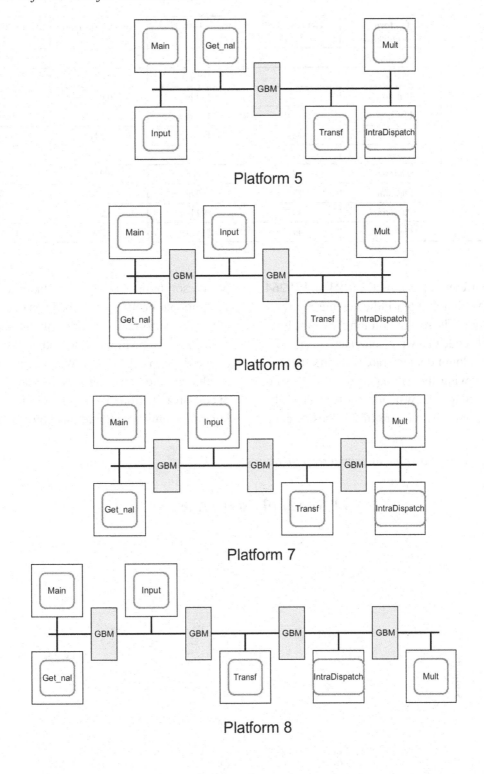

Platform 5

Platform 6

Platform 7

Platform 8

*Table 1. TLM generation time and quality for different MPSoC designs*

| Application | Platform Configuration | Generated SC LOC | Manual est. Time | Generation Time | Simulation Time |
|---|---|---|---|---|---|
| MP3 | reference C | - | - | - | 1.29s |
| | Platform 1 | 2095 | 104 hrs | 0.633s | 3.268s |
| | Platform 2 | 2894 | 144 hrs | 0.661s | 5.519s |
| | Platform 3 | 3148 | 157 hrs | 0.645s | 5.764s |
| | Platform 4 | 3653 | 183 hrs | 0.741s | 7.424s |
| H264 | reference C | - | - | - | 2.027s |
| | Platform 5 | 1722 | 86 hrs | 0.245s | 7.542s |
| | Platform 6 | 2796 | 140 hrs | 0.244s | 9.935s |
| | Platform 7 | 3853 | 192 hrs | 0.267s | 13.326s |
| | Platform 8 | 4910 | 245 hrs | 0.260s | 15.415s |

sults for different platforms for MP3 and H.264 TLMs. The first column indicates the platform configuration. The second column shows the lines of SystemC code that were generated by the tool. The third column demonstrates the productivity gain by showing the estimated time in person-hours for doing this SystemC coding manually. We use an optimistic figure of 20 lines of code per person-hour. The fourth column shows the generation time in seconds for TLM to be created for each platform. The fifth column shows the model simulation time on the testbench described above for each application. We can see from these results that the tool generates thousands of lines of code in a fraction of a second. The manual coding time would cost numerous hours of precious

*Figure 10. Simulation time in example applications*

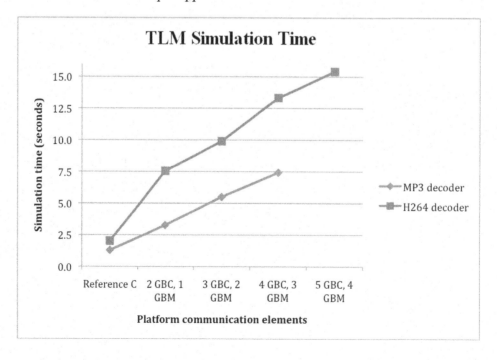

designer time that can be saved using automatic TLM generation.

Another representation of these results (specifically the simulation time) is shown in a graphical form in figure 10.

In the above graph, the y axis represents the simulation time in seconds of the executable SystemC model, and the x axis represents the platforms, groups depending on the number of busses and bridges that form the platform. The reference C model simulation time is included as well for comparison purposes. We see two lines representing the two applications. In the case of the MP3 decoder, there is only three points plus the reference code, since two of the platforms (platform 2 and 3) differ only on the connection of the DCT to a bus.

As the number of busses and bridges in a platform increases, we can see that the simulation time increases accordingly as expected, since depending on the platform, there will be several multi-hop (multi-GBM) transactions, which involve many intermediate steps (synchronization and arbitration in every bus, and read/write and check of every GBM FIFO in the route). Nevertheless, the results show TLM simulation time is of the same order as the reference C simulation. The simulation time also grows linearly with the number of platform components. Thus TLM based design is scalable to support future multicore and many-core systems.

Another important advantage of having automatic generation of TLMs is the productivity gain from the fast generation versus the slow manual implementation. The real advantage is that due to short time needed to produce and test the TLM, the designer can quickly make changes in the platform, application or mapping, and see the result in a matter of seconds. Therefore TLM automation enables fast, early and verifiable design space exploration for multicore systems.

## CONCLUSION, FUTURE TRENDS

In this chapter, we presented a methodology and the procedures to automatically generating TLMs from a graphical capture of platform and application C code. The key differentiation is in the separation of not only computation and communication, but also between application and platform. In other words, with this methodology, there is no need for designers to understand SystemC modeling, event semantics etc. that makes it very attractive for SW developers. Currently synthesis semantics for GBC and GBM are being developed to provide system synthesis from automatically generated TLMs.

Our present work involves refining the current TLM into an approximate-timed TLM in computation and communication (model C in figure 1). This involves adding accurate timing information to the busses, transducers and inside the processes in the PEs, in addition to the modeling of Real-Time Operating Systems in these PEs. The ESE tool incorporating TLM automation is available for download in (CECS, 2008).

In the future, automatic generation of TLMs for application specific NoCs will also be developed. Also, one important goal would be to create the path to go from a system-level model down to a Pin-Cycle Accurate Model, which would involve a complete HW and SW synthesis.

## ACKNOWLEDGMENT

We thank the Center for Embedded Computer Systems (CECS) for supporting this work, Pramod Chandraiah for the MP3 source code, and Yongjin Ahn for the H264 code. The presented TLM concepts have emerged from over fifteen years of System Level Design research in the Embedded System Methodology Groups (ESMG) at the University of California, Irvine. We are thankful for various generations of ESMG group members for their contributions.

# REFERENCES

Baresi, L., Bruschi, F., Di Nitto, E., & Sciuto, D. (2007). SystemC code generation from UML models. In E. Villar & J. Mermet (Eds.), *System specification & design languages* (pp. 161-171). The Netherlands: Kluwer Academic Publishers.

Cai, L., & Gajski, D. (2003). Transaction level modeling: An overview. In *Proceedings of the 1st IEEE/ACM/IFIP International Conference on Hardware/software Codesign and System Synthesis* (pp. 19-24). New York.

Center for Embedded Computer Systems (CECS). (2008). *Embedded systems environment (ESE) (version 1.0)*. Computer software. University of California, Irvine. Retrieved in January 2008, www.cecs.uci.edu/~ese/

Donlin, A. (2004). Transaction level modeling: Flows and use models. In *Proceedings of the 2nd IEEE/ACM/IFIP International Conference on Hardware/ software Codesign and System Synthesis* (pp 75-80). New York.

Fiedler, M. (2004, June). *Implementation of a basic h.264/avc decoder*. Retrieved in January 2007, from http://rtg.informatik.tu-chemnitz.de/docs/da-sa-txt/sa-mfie.pdf

Gajski, D., Zhu, J., Doemer, R., Gerstlauer, A., & Zhao, S. (2000). *SpecC: Specification language and design methodology*. Norwell, MA: Kluwer Academic Publishers.

Gerstlauer, A., Domer, R., Peng, J., & Gajski, D. (2001). *System design: A practical guide with SpecC*. Norwell, MA: Kluwer Academic Publishers.

Ghenassia, F. (2005). *Transaction level modeling with SystemC: TLM concepts and applications for embedded systems*. Dordrecht, The Netherlands: Springer.

Grotker, T. (2002). *System design with SystemC*. Norwell, MA: Kluwer Academic Publishers.

Haubelt, C., Falk, J., Keinert, J., Schlichter, T., Streubuhr, M., Deyhle, A., Hadert, A., & Teich, J. (2007). A SystemC based design methodology for digital signal processing systems. EURASIP Journal on Embedded Systems, (1), 15-37

Huang, K., Han, S., Popovici, K., Brisolara, L., Guerin, X., Li, L., et al. (2007). Simulink-based MPSoC design flow: Case study of motion-JPEG and H.264. In *Proceedings of the Design Automation Conference* (pp. 39-42).

Kangas, T., Kukkala, P., Orsila, H., Salminen, E., Hannikainen, M., & Hamalainen, T. (2006). UML-based multiprocessor SoC design framework. *ACM Transactions on Embedded Computing Systems*, 5(2), 281–320. doi:10.1145/1151074.1151077

Keutzer, K., Malik, S., Newton, R., Rabaey, J., & Sangiovanni-Vincentelli, A. (2000). System level design: Orthogonalization of concerns and platform-based design. IEEE Transactions on Computer-Aided Design of Circuits and Systems, 19(12), 1523–1543

Klingauf, W., Gunzel, R., Bringmann, O., Parfuntseu, P., & Burton, M. (2006) Greenbus-A generic interconnect fabric for transaction level modeling. In *Proceedings of the 43rd Annual Conference on Design Automation* (pp. 905–910). New York: ACM.

Leslie, R. (2004). *MAD fix point mp3 algorithm implementation (version 0.15.1b)*. Computer software. Retrieved in June 2005, from http://sourceforge.net/projects/mad/

Ogawa, O., Bayon de Noyer, S., Chauvet, P., Shinohara, K., Watanabe, Y., Niizuma, H., et al. (2003). A practical approach for bus architecture optimization at transaction level. In I. C. Society (Ed.), *DATE '03: Proceedings of the Conference on Design, Automation, and Test in Europe* (pp. 20176). Washington, DC: IEEE Computer Society.

OSCI. (2007). *SystemC (version 2.2) Computer software. Open systemc initiaitve.* Retrieved in March 2007, from http://www.systemc.org/members/download_files/check_file?agreement=systemc_2-2-0_07-03-14

Sangiovanni-Vincentelli, A. (2007). Quo vadis, SLD? Reasoning about the trends and challenges of system level design. *Proceedings of the IEEE, 95*(3), 467–506. doi:10.1109/JPROC.2006.890107

Sarmento, A., Cesario, W., & Jerraya, A. (2004). Automatic building of executable models from abstract soc architectures made of heterogeneous subsystems. In *Proceedings of the 15th IEEE International Workshop on Rapid System Prototyping* (pp.88-95).

Schirner, G., & Doemer, R. (2006). Quantitative analysis of transaction level models for the amba bus. In *Proceedings of the Design, Automation, and Test Conference in Europe* (pp. 230-235).

Shin, D., Gerstlauer, A., Peng, P., Doemer, R., & Gajski, D. (2006). Automatic generation of transaction-level models for rapid design space exploration. In *Proceedings of the International Conference on Hardware/Software Codesign and System Synthesis* (pp. 64-60).

Yu Lo, L. L. C., & Abdi, S. (2007). Automatic TLM generation for C-based MPSoC design. In *Proceedings of the 2007 IEEE International High-Level Design, Validation, and Test Workshop* (pp.29-36).

Yu Lo, L. L. C., & Abdi, S. (2007) Automatic systemc TLM generation for custom communication platforms. In *Proceedings of the 25th IEEE International Conference on Computer Design* (pp. 41-46).

# Chapter 12
# The Role of Programming Models on Reconfigurable Computing Fabrics

**João M. P. Cardoso**
*University of Porto, Portugal*

**João Bispo**
*Technical University of Lisbon, Portugal*

**Adriano K. Sanches**
*Technical University of Lisbon, Portugal*

## ABSTRACT

*Reconfigurable computing architectures are becoming increasingly important in many computing domains (e.g., embedded and high-performance systems). These architectures promise comparable characteristics to specific hardware solutions with the flexibility and programmability of microprocessor solutions. This chapter gives a comprehensible overview of reconfigurable computing concepts and programming paradigms for the current and future generation of reconfigurable computing architectures. Two paramount aspects are highlighted: understanding how the programming model can help the mapping of computations to these architectures, and understanding also the way new programming models can be used to develop applications to these architectures. We include a set of simple examples to show different aspects of the use of the reconfigurable computing synergies, driven by the initial programming model used.*

## INTRODUCTION

Reconfigurable computing architectures are playing a very important role in specific computing domains (Hauck & DeHon, 2008). In the arena of high-performance computing (HPC), Field-Programmable Gate-Arrays (FPGAs) have exhibited in many cases outstanding performance gains over traditional von-Neumann based computer architectures (El-Ghazawi et al., 2008). In the context of embedded systems, FPGAs are common-place for early prototyping, and more recently even for deployment, given such characteristics as the substantial increase of resources in the high-end FPGAs, the ability to "zero-cost" update of hardware in early timing windows where modifications might have

DOI: 10.4018/978-1-60566-750-8.ch012

*Figure 1. An example of a possible reconfigurable computing fabric which includes general purpose processors (GPPs)*

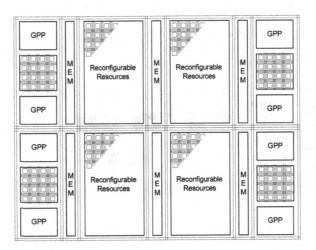

to be done, and the low initial development costs when compared to ASIC (Application-Specific Integrated Circuit) solutions. The aforementioned increase in resource capacity, the extreme flexibility of reconfigurable architectures, and the inherent limitations of traditional computing architectures are allowing reconfigurable architectures to embrace new markets.

Reconfigurable computing fabrics (with FP-GAs being the most notable examples) mainly consist of aggregations of a large number of elements, namely: processing elements (PEs), memory elements (MEs), interconnection resources (IRs), and I/O buffers (IOBs). There are reconfigurable substrates which include microprocessor *hardcores* (*i.e.*, fabricated on-chip processors side-by-side with reconfigurable logic). Examples of this are the Xilinx FPGAs with IBM PowerPC cores. Figure 1 shows a possible block diagram of a reconfigurable computing fabric consisting of GPPs (General Purpose Processors), reconfigurable resources, and memory blocks. The reconfigurable fabrics distinguish themselves according to the granularity of the PEs and IRs. There are fabrics using fine-grained hardware structures, *i.e.*, configurable blocks with small bit-widths (*e.g.*, 4 bits), fabrics using coarse-grained

hardware structures, *i.e.*, configurable blocks with large bit-widths (*e.g.*, 16, 24, 32 bits), and fabrics with a mix of fine- and coarse-grained hardware structures.

The granularity of the fabric constrains the type of computing engines we can implement with its resources (see Figure 2). Fine-grained reconfigurable fabrics implement computing engines using gate-level circuitry descriptions (*e.g.*, AND, OR gates), while coarse-grained reconfigurable fabrics implement computing engines at the word or ALU level. In coarse-grained reconfigurable fabrics we have to recall to a single or a set of pre-defined computing models while in fine-grained reconfigurable fabrics we are able to implement virtually any type of computing model. In the latter case, we can implement static or dynamic (tagged-token) Dataflow Machines, Khan Processor Networks, Petri Nets, Cellular Automata, VLSI (Very Large Scale Integration) and Systolic arrays, von-Neumann processors, SPMD (single-program, multiple-data), SIMD (single-instruction, multiple-data), and MIMD (multiple-instruction, multiple-data) processing engines, ASIPs (Application-Specific Instruction-Set Processors), application specific architectures, etc. This huge flexibility comes with costs: programming is more difficult, takes

*Figure 2. Abstractions of computing structures according to the granularity of the reconfigurable computing fabric*

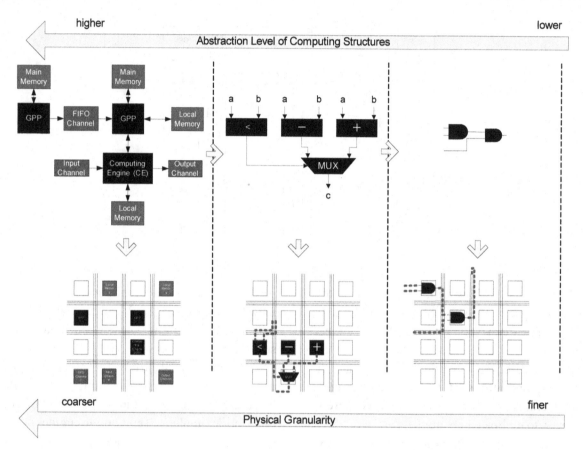

more time, and there is a significant overhead in interconnect-resources, to ensure routing between configurable blocks.

However, the extreme flexibility of fine-grained reconfigurable fabrics establishes them as the dominant technology, and a major part of the work in the reconfigurable computing field has been devoted to them. The programming of fine-grained reconfigurable hardware is softening, but it is still essential to understand digital system design in order to accomplish most requirements. The increasingly complexity of the architectures, the time-to-market pressures, the need for design upgrades and modifications in requirements, strongly indicate the necessity to program this kind of reconfigurable architectures

at higher levels of abstraction. For several years, there have been large efforts on compiling from software programming languages (Cardoso & Diniz, 2008). However, the needed breakthrough advancements seem to have been hampered by the lack of support on FPGAs to help software compilation, their too close to gate-level basic elements, and the maximum clock frequency too dependent on gate-level compilation steps (placement and routing).

The complexity to program reconfigurable computing systems is being exacerbated by their tremendous resource capacity. Thus, research efforts need to be able to master adequate programming paradigms that allow programmers to comfortably understand how to map their applications to these new architectures. These challenges, albeit hard, are not insurmountable. Recent experiences in automatic compilation for reconfigurable architectures provide some evidence that indeed it is possible to overcome these obstacles (Cardoso & Diniz, 2008). This chapter provides an overview about reconfigurable computing, discussing the impact that different programming models and models of computation may have in the final solution.

This chapter is organized as follows. Section 2 introduces some aspects of the design flow for systems with reconfigurable fabrics as the target technology. Section 3 presents some aspects of the mapping from different programming models and comments on the appropriateness of various models of computation to be implemented in reconfigurable computing platforms. Section 4 describes a number of efforts on programming models and languages to assist the mapping of applications to FPGAs and multi-core architectures, which can be also applied to complex reconfigurable fabrics. Section 5 includes some examples showing certain aspects of performance achieved for different implementations in the same reconfigurable fabric. Finally, section 6 concludes this chapter.

## SYSTEMS-ON-A-RECONFIGURABLE FABRIC

Fine-grained reconfigurable fabrics, such as FPGAs (Kuon, Tessier, & Rose, 2008), are ultimately used for implementing full-systems, or most part of them. They can accommodate various microprocessors (GPPs, ASIPs, etc.), acceleration engines, input/output digital interfaces, on-chip memories, all organized in the form more adequate for the functionalities of the system. When using reconfigurable fabrics to implement Systems-on-a-chip (SoCs), the developer may have to face the role of a software programmer, hardware designer, and architect of the system. Traditional decisions con-

sidering hardware/software partitioning (Micheli, Ernst, & Wolf, 2001) are now more complex, also requiring decisions about the type and the number of microprocessors, organization of the system, memory requirements, both in terms of size and number of distributed memories, etc.

Figure 3 illustrates the typical general steps to map applications to a reconfigurable computing platform. The mapping flow is usually accomplished by partitioning the input computations among the components of the target architecture. If those components consist of a typical von-Neumann microprocessor coupled to reconfigurable hardware, one of the important steps is hardware/software partitioning (Micheli et al., 2001), which is usually guided by profiling results. However, the target SoC architectures implemented in reconfigurable fabrics tend to be more complex and to consist of heterogeneous components forming a multi-core architecture. In these architectures, traditional von-Neumann microprocessors can be assisted with application specific and domain specific processing engines. *E.g.*, when processing data streams is required, suitable processing engines become increasingly important and are usually included in the SoC. Reconfigurable hardware tends to be an important component of such engines and therefore developers need to program both software and hardware components.

Reconfigurable fabrics potentiate a true concurrent design from the software application to the organization of the target system's architecture and truly require hardware/software co-design approaches.

### The Potential of Reconfigurable Logic to implement Architectures

Using the fine-grained physical structures of FPGAs one is able to implement a myriad of computing architectures, from the application-specific architectures (also known as non-programmable) to many/multi-core architectures. Figure 4 shows the scenario of architectures usually considered

*Figure 3. Typical programming flow for reconfigurable computing platforms (the two flows on the rightmost identify the fine-grained and the coarse-grained cases, respectively)*

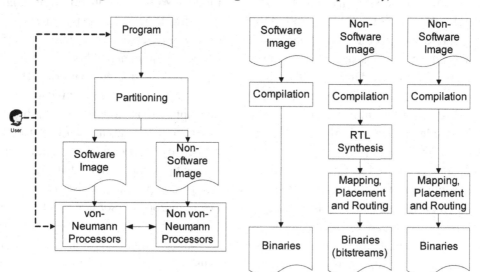

when targeting fine-grained reconfigurable fabrics. Application-specific architectures are usually designed using a Hardware Description Language (HDL) or using a "C-to-Gates"[1] compiler. In this case, a new architecture for each segment of code, algorithm, or application mapped to the FPGA device is employed. Although typical "C-to-Gates" approaches will speed-up the development of an application-specific architecture, the following issues establish fine-grained reconfigurable fabrics solutions as requiring longer development time:

- The lack of a transparent support for standard computer organizations (*e.g.*, external memories coupled to the FPGA);
- The computationally demanding Placement and Routing task;
- The high efforts needed to achieve highly efficient application specific architectures in the case of large designs. This process involves tightening timing constraints and tuning methods.

## The Role of Softcores as Programmable Layers

*Softcores* can be used to mitigate some of the issues referred in the previous section. They are programmable out-of-the-box hardware blocks, sometimes parameterizable, and usually defined in an HDL. They create programming layers and provide multiple computer architectures. Such computing layers are implemented by the physical hardware structures of the FPGAs. *Softcores* can be of the following type:

- General purpose processors (GPPs), such as MicroBlaze from Xilinx (Xilinx) and Nios-II from Altera (Altera);
- Application specific instruction-set processors (ASIPs) (Alomary et al., 1993; Khailany et al., 2001), where configurable processors (Gonzalez, 2000) can be thought as a special case;
- Domain-specific computing layers implemented by physical reconfigurable computing substrates (Jones, Hoare, Kusic,

*Figure 4. Types of architectures in FPGA-based computing platforms*

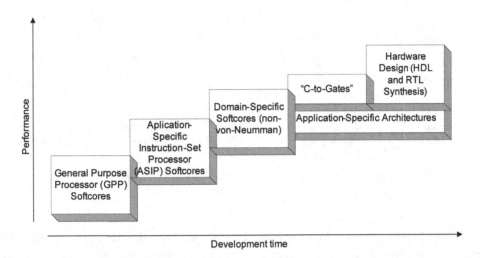

Fazekas, & J, 2005; Wolinski, Gokhale, & McCave, 2002).

## Seamless Software/ Hardware Integration

The integration of components implemented by sections of the reconfigurable fabric coupled to a GPP is an important aspect. This integration should be seamless and portable to different GPPs, for instance. The Molen machine paradigm (Vassiliadis et al., 2004) is one example of an approach including a GPP, reconfigurable logic area, hardware support and specific instructions to interface and deal with the two components (*i.e.*, the GPP and the reconfigurable logic area).

## Architecting the SoC Organization

One of the strengths of implementing systems in fine-grained reconfigurable fabrics is the possibility to use, without substituting the hardware devices, the most suitable architecture and computer organization for a given application or for a domain of applications. Figure 5 illustrates two possible computer organizations. One resembles a typical bus and RAM based organization where

input data are read from I/O components, stored in the memory, processed, and then computed data are written to the memory. The second illustrates an organization suitable to streaming applications. In this latter case, data are consumed by the order it arrives, possible subsets of data can be stored, and output data are produced in sequence. The main idea in streaming processing is based on the fact that the overall data being input may not need to be locally stored and outputs are calculated from input sequences of data elements. Whenever in presence of data streaming processing, there is no need to conform to traditional memory organizations and thus feeding and gathering data to the computing engine can be much more efficient.

The opportunities raised by reconfigurable fabrics are immense. In the development of an application, we have the opportunity to decide about the system organization, the number of cores, local memories, interconnection topologies, customized buffers, acceleration engines, etc. Thus, the distinction between a system designer and a programmer tend to blur with this emergent concept. Integrated Design Environments (IDEs), such as EDK (Embedded Development Kit) from Xilinx with their Platform Studio, and Quartus® II from Altera with their SOPC (system-on-a-programmable-chip)

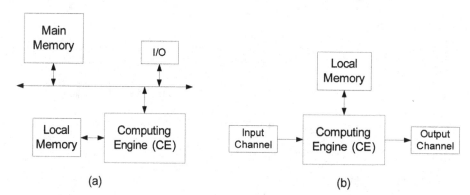

*Figure 5. Distinct computer organizations: (a) based on RAM data storage; (b) based on streaming*

Builder, consist of platform studios which expose to the user the construction of a SoC using both building blocks existent in a library and user's custom blocks. In these environments, all the steps from architecture organization, C programming, and the generation of the *bitstreams* (which define the configuration elements of the target FPGA) are integrated. However, efficient tools to support hardware/software partitioning tasks and "C-to-Gates" compilers are not commonly available. One of the exceptions is the Nios II C-to-Hardware Acceleration Compiler (C2H) (Lau, Pritchard, & Molson, 2006) of Altera that allows automatic generation of a co-processor accelerator for Nios-II, from the input C program.

## MAPPING COMPUTATIONS AND PROGRAMMING MODELS

The programming model used to specify computations not only helps the programming task, but also may permit mapping optimizations not possible with other programming models. As the programming model may effectively and explicitly expose the type of computations, communications, and parallelism, specific computing structures might be used for certain parts of the input descriptions. These specific computing structures are usually based on templates. If the programming model

does not have the capability to explicitly expose those characteristics, they might be hidden by the programming style and by the way the required functionality is represented. In this later case, two options might be available:

- One option consists of advanced analysis techniques to expose certain functionalities hidden in the programming model. Sometimes it is possible for automatic analysis tools to identify, *e.g.*, using pattern matching, segments of code in the input program that can be almost directly mapped to optimized hardware structures already part of the component library of the mapping tool.

- A second option, this one very pragmatic, is to associate directly a hardware component to a certain function in the input program. Usually, in this case, it is revealed to the programming model a library of components with hardware implementations as a form of IP cores. These cores may have parameterization capabilities in order to adapt to certain specific input characteristics and/or might be programmable (processor *soft-cores*). Each time this kind of components is used in the input program, the mapping phase associates those components to the hardware components in the library.

To illustrate the previous two options, consider we have in a library an optimized hardware implementation for matrix multiplication. Each time a function *mat_mult* is used, the mapping tool associates this call to the use of the optimized hardware core existent in the library. The hardware core might have parameters such as the size of the matrixes, the type and precision of data, selection of the unrolling factor and/or of the block size, etc. In a more advanced approach, a pattern matching step might recognize the matrix multiplication pattern and associate to that pattern the hardware core in the library. Although there exist many examples where this might be possible and a finite set of cores might be present in a library, there are also many examples where this is impossible to handle and custom optimizations must be used to deal with the vast idiosyncrasies of the input programs. This is the reason why domain-specific programming languages and optimizations associated to most important descriptions might be of paramount importance. They still ensure the programming capability and flexibility and might be the most feasible approach to achieve optimized computing engines.

## Mapping Applications to Reconfigurable Fabrics

We can distinguish three specific cases when mapping applications to reconfigurable fabrics, namely: programming microprocessor based cores, possibly disposed in a multi-core array, designing an application specific architecture, and programming arrays of ALUs and other elements interconnected using a certain topology.

### Targeting Single- or Multi-Processor Architectures

When considering programmable microprocessor based cores, available as fixed tile-based topologies or implemented using *softcores* (in the latter case, one may define aspects such as their topology in the system, interconnection communication resources, local memory organization, etc), the mapping is accomplished by well-known compilation steps when the input computations do not bring programming model gaps. This is the case when compiling imperative/procedural programming languages, such as C, to GPPs. Programming models with semantic gaps to the target architecture usually require a step known as synthesis which sometimes is accomplished by generating a description of the computations in a close model to the target architecture (*e.g.*, generating C code to be compiled to a GPP). When multi-processors are used, however, the compilation efforts rely on the user expertise to distribute computations and data-structures among the cores and to synchronize the distributed execution.

### Targeting Application-Specific Computing Engines

When targeting application-specific computing engines, one defines for each application a specific computing engine which is implemented by programming the reconfigurable logic. This is traditionally a hardware-only design process responsible to produce data-path and control units. The engine is designed by using HDLs and Register Transfer Level (RTL) synthesis or by using more advanced tools such as high-level synthesis tools or "C-to-gates" compilers, both, however, requiring backend steps of mapping and placement and routing.

The use of HDLs, such as VHDL (VHDL, 1988) and Verilog (Verilog, 2001), is the one permitting to achieve optimal computing engines, but is highly dependent on the designers' expertise not only to design an efficient application-specific architecture, but also to take advantage of specific hardware resources existent in the target reconfigurable fabric (*e.g.*, Block RAMs, multipliers). This type of programming flow is similar to the one used when designing application-specific integrated circuits (ASICs).

Industrial efforts have included the development of Handel-C (Handel-C, 1991-2007) and accompanying tools. Handel-C is used to design computing engines at RTL and can be thought as a HDL with a higher-level of abstraction than the one used in VHDL and Verilog. It is based on the syntax of the C programming language and adds explicit parallelism constructs and other suitable constructs to target hardware resources.

The use of "C-to-gates" has been the focus of many researchers (*e.g.*, see the simple approach used in (Wirth, 1998)). Unfortunately, "C-to-gates" compilers still generically produce efficient solutions only for limited cases. Continuously renewed efforts try to solve such lack of efficiency by including specific optimizations. Besides the numerous academic efforts to develop an efficient "C-to-gates" compiler (see, *e.g.*, (Cardoso & Neto, 2003; Diniz, Hall, Park, So, & Ziegler, 2005; Guo, Buyukkurt, Najjar, & Vissers, 2005; Yankova et al., 2007)), there have been many industrial efforts as well. Some of the most known industrial efforts have been Impulse-C (Pellerin & Thibault, 2005), Catapult Synthesis (Corp), C2H (Lau et al., 2006), and the SRC's Carte Programming Environment (SRC Computers).

There have been efforts addressing FPGA programming flows using, as input, descriptions in graphical programming languages. Viva (StarbridgeSystems) and DSPLogic (uses MATLAB® and the Simulink® environment) (DSPLogic) are two approaches proposed by industry. Graphical languages permit to program systems using blocks representing components and have many adepts, especially in control, signal processing, and communication systems.

## Targeting ALU-Based Reconfigurable Arrays

When targeting reconfigurable computing architectures known as coarse-grained, the programmer has access to pre-existent ALU structures, to interconnect resources between them, and to other hardware resources such as memories. These hardware structures can be available as a reconfigurable fabric or as an abstraction layer implemented with a fine-grained reconfigurable fabric. The mapping usually requires a compiler from high-level languages, such as C (*e.g.*, (Cardoso & Weinhardt, 2002)), or the use of a native programming language which can be either an architecture-specific high-level language (*e.g.*, DIL (Budiu & Goldstein, 1999) and Rapid-C (Cronquist, Franklin, Berg, & Ebeling, 1998)) or a kind of assembly language (as NML, the native programming language of the PACT XPP (XPP-III, 2006)) of the target coarse-grained reconfigurable architecture. Note that in this case the execution model is usually pre-established rather than open to the user.

## Models of Computation and Reconfigurable Fabrics

The way computations are specified may have a great impact on the results a compiler can achieve. The use of domain-specific languages (DSLs), or stylized forms on generic languages, allows very efficient optimizations (*e.g.*, in terms of performance, power dissipation, or energy consumption), which otherwise would not be possible to apply. For example, a Finite Impulse Response (FIR) filter can be represented by the following equation:

$$y[k] = \sum_{n=0}^{N-1} x[k-n] * c[n] \qquad (1)$$

Where $x$ represents the input signal, $y$ the output signal and $c$ the array of $N$ coefficients (taps). The number of samples, *i.e.*, number of elements of $x$ can be either unbound (usually the case when receiving data streams) or can be fixed to a certain number of input samples (*e.g.*, $M$). A typical implementation of the FIR in an imperative programming language such as the C program-

*Figure 6. An 1D FIR (Finite Impulse Response) filter: (a) using a pure C implementation; (b) using a C-based data-streaming implementation*

```
                                         #include "io_ports.h"

                                         #define c0 2
                                         #define c1 4
                  #define c0 2           #define c2 4
                  #define c1 4           #define c3 2
                  #define c2 4
                  #define c3 2           #define M 256

                  #define M 256          #define PORT_A  0x1
                  #define N 4            #define PORT_B  0x2

                  int  c[N] = {c0, c1, c2, c3};   main() {
                                           int x_0, x_1, x_2, x_3, y;
                  main() {                 x_2= receive(PORT_A);
                   for(int j=N-1; j<M; j++) {   x_1= receive(PORT_A);
                     int output=0;         x_0= receive(PORT_A);
                     for(int i=0; i<N; i++) {   for(int j=0; j<M; j++)  // while(1) {
                        output+=c[i]*x[j-i];   x_3=x_2;
                     }                     x_2=x_1;
                     y[j] = output;        x_1=x_0;
                   }                       x_0= receive(PORT_A);
                  }                        y = c0*x_0 + c1*x_1 + c2*x_2 +
                                         c3*x_3;
                                             send(PORT_B, y);
                                           }
                                         }
 (a)                                     (b)
```

ming language is illustrated in Figure 6(a). This implementation resembles a traditional computing system where data is stored in one or more RAMs. When considering a target system, where data are input/output in a streaming way, the C code in Figure 6(b) can be used. These two implementations, albeit with the same functionality, give different opportunities for optimizations.

It is possible to achieve a stream-oriented specification from the RAM model used in Figure 6(a) by applying successive transformations to the code. As an example, Figure 7 shows the transformations/optimizations needed to go from the RAM model specification depicted in Figure 6(a), to a stream-oriented implementation similar to the one presented in Figure 6(b). As an example of the steps performed, Figure 7(d) shows the resultant code after applying data reuse to the code

in Figure 7(c) possibly bearing in mind the use of rotating registers. As can be seen by this simple example, one might need to apply several code transformations and optimizations to achieve, for the same application, a distinct programming model from the one originally used. This is usually a complex task that compilers are not able to cope with, apart from simple cases. The proper sequence of transformations and optimizations can be difficult to expose from the original programming model, and may require the user expertise about the algorithm to be successfully accomplished[2]. This fact more exposes the importance of using abstractions to specify computations.

## Models of Computation and Their Suitability for Reconfigurable Fabrics

A vast number of models of computation (MOCs) have been proposed, see, *e.g.*, (Edwards, Lavagno, Lee, & Sangiovanni-Vincentelli, 1997). Fine-grained reconfigurable fabrics such as FPGAs can implement most of them directly. This fact enables, as an efficient option, the use of the most advantageous computing model for a certain application domain. A selection of a particular model is often based on the suitability of the model to specify the characteristics of the input computations or on the mapping support for the target architecture or target system organization.

Examples of MOCs that can be efficiently mapped to FPGAs are:

- Finite automata, *e.g.*, NFAs (Non-Determinist Finite Automata) or DFAs (Determinist Finite Automata).
- Finite State Machines (FSMs), with or without concurrency, hierarchical support, and data-path extensions (*e.g.*, FSMDs).
- Streaming models of computation such as Kahn Process Networks (KPNs) (Kahn, 1974), Dataflow Process Networks (Lee & Parks, 1995), and Communicating Sequential Processes (CSP) (Hoare, 1978);
- Petri Nets (Murata, 1989), a model used to specify, *e.g.*, control systems and to model scheduling and asynchronous communication;
- Synchronous Reactive (Benveniste & Berry, 1991) such the one used in the Esterel programming language, very suited to specify control-based reactive systems.
- Process Networks consist of concurrent processes communicating directly through channels (see the example in Figure 8). Communication is based on tokens and processes (seen as computing engines in the implementation) are responsible for operations on those tokens. Tokens are usually associated with data elements.
- A special case of Process Networks are Kahn Process Networks (KPNs) (Kahn, 1974). KPNs are networks of concurrent processes which communicate through un-bounded point-to-point FIFO channels (as in the example shown in Figure 8, but with FIFOs for each channel). Communication uses blocking reads and non-blocking writes. Each process is deterministic and sequential and can have internal state. As KPNs capture task parallelism, distributed control and distributed data, they can be efficiently implemented in architectures with support to these characteristics. KPNs are also suitable to specify streaming applications. An implementation with reconfigurable fabrics could consider statically bounded FIFO channels, or FIFO channels with dynamically managed sizes. Due to the characteristics and suitability of KPNs to be implemented using FPGAs, some authors use KPNs as the mapping MOC from programming languages (*e.g.*, from procedural/imperative languages) without KPN underlying mechanisms. One of the examples is the work presented in (Stefanov, Zissulescu, Turjan, Kienhuis, & Deprettere, 2004) which uses KPNs as a computing model to map MATLAB programs to FPGAs.
- Dataflow process networks (Lee & Parks, 1995) are a special case of Process Networks where processes are called "actors" and all arcs between actors represent streams. Actors are activated based on firing rules, and consume data present in their input streams and produce data streams to their outputs. There have been different proposals of dataflow process networks, such as Synchronous, Multidimensional, Static/Dynamic, and Boolean Dataflow processor networks. All of them extend the

*Figure 7. Possible steps to achieve a C-based data-streaming implementation from the original C code*

| | | |
|---|---|---|
| for(int j=3; j<M; j++) {<br>  output=c[0]*x[j];<br>  output+=c[1]*x[j-1];<br>  output+=c[2]*x[j-2];<br>  output+=c[3]*x[j-3];<br>  y[j] = output;<br>} | for(int j=3; j<M; j++) {<br>  output=c0*x[j];<br>  output+=c1*x[j-1];<br>  output+=c2*x[j-2];<br>  output+=c3*x[j-3];<br>  y[j] = output;<br>} | for(int j=3; j<M; j++) {<br>  x_3=x[j];<br>  x_2=x[j-1];<br>  x_1=x[j-2];<br>  x_0=x[j-3];<br>  output=c0*x_3;<br>  output+=c1*x_2;<br>  output+=c2*x_1;<br>  output+=c3*x_0;<br>  y[j] = output;<br>} |
| **(a)** Full Unrolling of inner loop | **(b)** Scalar replacement | **(c)** Auxiliary variables |
| for(int j=3; j<M; j++) {<br>  x_3=x[j];<br>  if(j==3) {<br>    x_2=x[j-1];<br>    x_1=x[j-2];<br>    x_0=x[j-3];<br>  }<br>  output=c0*x_3;<br>  output+=c1*x_2;<br>  output+=c2*x_1;<br>  output+=c3*x_0;<br>  x_0=x_1;<br>  x_1=x_2;<br>  x_2=x_3;<br>  y[j] = output;<br>} | x_0=x[0];<br>x_1=x[1];<br>x_2=x[2];<br><br>for(int j=3; j<M; j++) {<br>  x_3=x[j];<br>  output=c0*x_3;<br>  output+=c1*x_2;<br>  output+=c2*x_1;<br>  output+=c3*x_0;<br>  x_0=x_1;<br>  x_1=x_2;<br>  x_2=x_3;<br>  y[j] = output;<br>} | x_0= **receive**(PORT_A);<br>x_1= **receive**(PORT_A);<br>x_2= **receive**(PORT_A);<br><br>for(int j=3; j<M; j++) {<br>  x_3= **receive**(PORT_A);<br>  output=c0*x_3;<br>  output+=c1*x_2;<br>  output+=c2*x_1;<br>  output+=c3*x_0;<br>  x_0=x_1;<br>  x_1=x_2;<br>  x_2=x_3;<br>  **send**(PORT_B, output);<br>} |
| **(d)** Data reuse | **(e)** Peeling | **(f)** Load/Stores substituted by receive/send primitives |

model with characteristics needed to easily represent certain properties of a system. Dataflow process networks are used by many authors to represent signal processing applications (*e.g.,* multimedia applications) and there have been many implementations using FPGAs. For instance, an approach to map a multidimensional synchronous dataflow model to FPGAs is presented in (McAllister, Woods, Walke, & Reilly, 2004).

- Generically, MOCs explicitly exposing data streaming are efficiently implemented in reconfigurable fabrics (DeHon et al., 2006). Communication channels between computing engines can be implemented with routing and buffer resources, and can be adapted to the characteristics of

*Figure 8. Example of a process network*

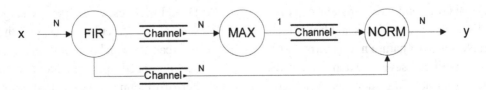

the application. The concurrency and distributed control achieved by reconfigurable fabrics permit to take advantage of coarse-grained pipelining (see Example-A in section Examples). In this kind of pipelining computing engines responsible for the computations of each Process or Actor can execute based on data availability, *i.e.*, processes producing data run concurrently with processes consuming data. The throughput achieved by this pipelining approach is only limited by the producer/consumer order and by the rates of the processes to consume and to produce data. Reconfigurable fabrics give an interesting support to this kind of pipelining as one may customize the buffers between computing engines. The possibility to implement efficient FIFOs, smart buffers, and customized associative memories is of paramount importance in data streaming contexts.

Communicating Sequential Processes (CSP) (Hoare, 1978) is a model consisting of sequential processes which communicate through synchronous message-passing using a *rendezvous* scheme. This model allows non-determinism and does not use buffers for communication between processes. Message passing mechanisms are efficiently implemented in reconfigurable fabrics as point-to-point non-buffered communication channels. This model has been used in various programming languages such as Handel-C (Handel-C, 1991-2007), a language specifically created to program FPGAs.

- Petri Nets (Murata, 1989) model concurrent behavior and are directed bipartite graphs consisting of places and transitions. Petri Nets are per nature non-deterministic. There have been several extensions of the Petri Net model. One such case is the colored Petri Net where the tokens, besides

representing events, also have a value. Due to the concurrent nature of hardware, Petri Nets have been implemented using application-specific architectures by many authors. Fine-grained reconfigurable fabrics allow efficient implementations of Petri Nets. An example of work addressing the mapping of Petri Nets to FPGAs is given in (Chang, Kwon, & Park, 1996).

## Comments on the Support Given by Reconfigurable Architectures

As mentioned before, fine-grained reconfigurable fabrics permit a myriad of models of computation. Obviously, this does not mean that these fabrics should be preferred for every kind of model. As an example, coarse-grained architectures may result in more efficient solutions for streaming applications, and modern GPPs might continue to be the best option for branch-intensive applications. Regarding the data types used in computations, FPGAs are traditionally associated with efficient integer and bit-width specialization and with lower efficiency for floating-point data types (note, however, that there are evidences that this is changing (Craven & Athanas, 2007)). But, independently of the model of computation, fine-grained reconfigurable fabrics may excel other options if the application expresses any of the following characteristics:

- Bit-Level Operations: due to the fine-granularity of FPGAs, this is the kind of computation that bests suit them. It can be exploited in applications that are heavily based on Boolean operators or bit-swapping (*e.g.*, cryptography);
- Deep Pipelines: each pipeline stage can be seen as a different processor. If the execution can be pipelined and streamed, there can be speed-ups equivalent to the number of pipeline stages, when compared to using a single pipeline. For instance, the

architecture for regular expressions in (Bispo, Sourdis, Cardoso, & Vassiliadis, 2006) makes extensive use of pipelining, by implementing a pipeline stage for each character of the regular expression;

- Large amounts of parallelism: the number of operations that can be executed in parallel is only constrained by the size of the FPGA, and by the parallelism in the application.
- Several distributed storage elements: distributing data among memories and registers permits concurrent access to data, and diminishes traditional memory bottlenecks.

Microprocessors are over-provisioned with fixed bit-width types (32, 64 bits). If the problem needs lower data-widths, even if only in specific parts, both fine-grained and coarse-grained reconfigurable fabrics can provide an architecture that is better fitted, which can translate in faster and more efficient execution. Also, because reconfigurable fabrics are not tied to an instruction-based model, an instruction-less accelerator can save the time and energy otherwise spent in fetching and decoding instructions. In the other hand, microprocessors (hardcore or off-the-shelf) can usually run at significantly higher speeds than reconfigurable fabrics, and the instruction-based model makes them easier to program.

*Softcore* processors implemented in reconfigurable hardware are less efficient than *hardcore* processors, but there are situations where the former can still be considered a viable solution:

- To explore solutions with many processors and specialized connections between them;
- To customize the communication scheme between the microprocessor and the accelerator(s);
- To implement the initial solution of a new product, which will be later consolidated in an ASIC design;

- To implement solutions which do not require high clock frequencies.

Coarse-grained reconfigurable fabrics are usually tied to a certain MOC. For instance, the PACT XPP (XPP-III, 2006), a data-driven architecture, uses an implicit static dataflow model. The hardware resources in the architecture behave based on the availability of events and/or data. Operations and data transfers are triggered by a ready/acknowledge handshake protocol which is part of every programmable component and interconnect resource in the architecture. In this case, a given MOC must be mapped to the static dataflow model used in the XPP and the efficiency of this step is of course dependent on how well the input MOC being considered can be represented by a static dataflow model. The programming flow for XPP relies on the mapping of subsets of C programs (imperative model) to the implicit model of the XPP (Cardoso & Weinhardt, 2002) or on the use of a textual native programming language (structural language), making the specific features of the XPP explicitly visible to the programmer.

## PROGRAMMING LANGUAGES

There have been many efforts to help programmers develop applications for reconfigurable fabrics. Due to the wide acceptance of the C programming language in, e.g., embedded systems, most efforts focus on mapping C stylized subsets to reconfigurable fabrics. The following sections briefly describe some prominent programming languages.

### Addressing Application-Specific Computing Engines

Industry recognizes the need to map applications described in high-level languages to reconfigurable fabrics. Herein, we present two recent cases from industry, Mitrion-C (Möhl, 2005) and

CHiMPS (Bennett, Dellinger, Mason, & Sundarajan, 2006; Putnam, Bennett, Dellinger, Mason, & Sundararajan, 2008), which represent efforts on programming languages tailored to target application specific computing engines implemented in reconfigurable fabrics.

Mitrion-C (Möhl, 2005) is an intrinsically parallel programming language for programming reconfigurable architectures. The syntax of the language is somewhat similar to C, and has a development framework which compiles Mitrion-C into the Mitrion Virtual Processor, an abstract machine that can be configured according to the input computations. The Mitrion Virtual Processor is a configurable *softcore*, with non-von Neumann architecture and with support to fine-grained, massive parallelism at the instruction-level. Mitrion-C has specific memory access functions, supports bit-width specification on type declarations (integer, bit, or float), statements with multiple assignments, functions returning multiple scalars, etc. Mitrion-C has explicit instance tokens (implemented as memory references) to order accesses to the same memory. All statements in Mitrion-C return results, even if they are loop and conditional constructs.

Xilinx has recently presented the CHiMPS (Compiling HLL into massively pipelined systems) Target Language (CTL) (Bennett et al., 2006; Putnam et al., 2008) and its associated compiler. CTL code is similar to a dataflow graph description with instructions resembling an assembly language with arithmetic/logic operations, variables defining operands, and special constructs to register variables, demux/mux instructions, wait/sync instructions, etc. CTL targets a static dataflow model of computation.

## Addressing System-Level Design

Languages to assist various phases of system-level design have been proposed. Examples of such languages are System C (Liao, 2000; System C, 2005) and SpecC (Gajski, Zhu, Dömer, Gerstlauer, & Zhao, 2000; SpecC).

System C is a language that extends C++ with libraries for modeling at RTL and system-level. Those libraries include support to arbitrary-length bit vectors, signals, clocked behavior, and concurrency. One of the strengths of System C is the capability to mix, in the same language, architecture components modeled at different abstraction levels. Not surprisingly, the strength of the language is also a source of problems when considering hardware synthesis because the programmer needs to know how to specify synthesizable behaviors.

SpecC (Gajski et al., 2000; SpecC) is another system-level language. As expected, it includes constructions to explicitly specify concurrent statements (with the support of *par {}*, *wait* and *notify*), pipelined execution (using the constructor *pipe(){}*), FSM behavior (using *fsm{}*), arbitrary-length bit vectors, channels (for synchronization and communication between modules), etc. SpecC uses a separation of communication and computation paradigm. SpecC allows the inclusion of temporal information (mainly cycle accuracy information) in the algorithmic level description (see Figure 9). A clause identified by *after* specifies the number of clock cycles a code statement will need to complete in the target application-specific architecture. A clause identified by *piped* assigns a number of pipelining stages to the operations in a code statement. These aspects of the programming model are important in the context of application-specific architectures because they allow the user to explicitly control the scheduling and evaluate different design decisions (such as multi-cycle and pipelined components).

## Addressing Parallel Computers

Recent efforts on programming languages, envisioning the multi-core era, aim at expressing concurrency. Those languages include Cilk

*Figure 9. Specifying clock cycle and pipelining information in SpecC*

```
S1: A = B * C piped 2;
S2: A = A * D after 1;
```

(Cilk, 1998), a language based on C and using a multithreading model, X10 (X10, 2006), a parallel, distributed object-oriented language, Unified Parallel C (UPC) (UPC, 2005), a language extending C with parallel semantics and based on the partitioned global address space model, Fortress (Allen, 2005), a new language with implicit parallelism and support to transactions, and Chapel (Chamberlain, Callahan, & Zima, 2007), a language using a multithreaded parallel programming model, data distribution features and data-driven placement of computations. Although these efforts do not target reconfigurable computing fabrics, by implementing complex multi-core computer organizations with FPGAs we may use the parallel programming languages and their mapping support. Distributing data and computations (and inherently control) over the resources of the reconfigurable fabrics is natural and more efficient. However, models based on the use of shared variables to communicate data can be also easily supported.

Some recent efforts to program multi-core architectures address the use of transactional memories (Harris et al., 2007) by including transactional constructs in the programming model (Carlstrom et al., 2006; Harris & Fraser, 2003). The use of FPGAs gives efficient and customized implementations of configurable transactional memories as shown in (Kachris & Kulkarni, 2007). Notably, the computer architecture research community is currently focusing on FPGAs as a platform to evaluate and test new multi-core architectures (Chung, Nurvitadhi, Hoe, Falsafi, & Mai, 2008). The speedups obtained by prototyping components and cores of the architectures under research are

recognized as of paramount importance to research future parallel computer architectures.

## Domain-Specific Languages

Domain-specific languages (DSLs) seem to be a promising solution to efficiently map computations described in a high-level language. DSLs usually provide constructs with semantic or an underlying MOC suitable for a given domain and thus can be highly expressive. Examples of traditional DSLs are scripting languages (*e.g.*, Perl, Ruby, Python), synchronous programming languages (*e.g.*, Esterel (Boussinot & Simone, 1991) and Silage (Hilfinger & Rabaey, 1992)), Hardware Description Languages (*e.g.*, VHDL (VHDL, 1988) and Verilog(Verilog, 2001)), and languages for modeling and/or specifying certain systems (*e.g.*, MATLAB, Mathematica, and LabVIEW). We believe that DSLs with specific capabilities that can be merged in a more generic programming environment are the ones may contribute more efficiently to the mapping and compilation of high-level programming models to reconfigurable architectures.

There have been efforts to extend traditional languages with domain-specific constructs. Such is the case of CES (C++ for Embedded Systems) (Thrun, 2001), a language that extends C++ with probabilistic computations and machine learning features, to address probabilistic robotics. By helping the programmer with domain-specific constructs, and a semantic close to certain computations in the applications, one is augmenting the productivity, and also may potentiate specific optimizations, otherwise very difficult for a compiler to devise. An intuitive example is the case of a specific domain requiring evaluations of regular expressions. By using traditional programming languages without explicit support to deal with regular expressions requires the programmer to develop the regular expression evaluators or to use specific libraries for this. In this case, it is the role of the compiler to map the descriptions of the regular expression evaluators to the target architecture. Of course that in some cases one may use optimized libraries in terms of software implementations or in terms of specific hardware *softcores* that have been possibly manually optimized for that. On the other hand, when the programming language has explicit constructs to program regular expressions, the compiler may include in its portfolio of optimizations efficient techniques to map those regular expressions to the target architecture. For instance, regular expressions programmed in PCRE (Perl Compatible Regular Expressions) might be translated to custom hardware engines by using a specific synthesis tool (see, *e.g.*, (Bispo et al., 2006) and the Example B in section Examples).

Due to the importance of applications dealing with data-streams, specific languages have been developed. Compilation of streaming computations has already been addressed by many authors. For instance, a stream programming language, StreamC, has been used to program domain-specific processors such as the Imagine Processor (Kapasi et al., 2003), a programmable processor including a stream instruction set. Another streaming programming language is Stream-It (Thies, Karczmarek, & Amarasinghe, 2002) which is being used to map applications to multi-core architectures. Streaming programming languages allow a compiler to generate efficient streaming computing engines. Streaming constructs map naturally to reconfigurable fabrics as illustrated by the work on compiling Stream-C (Gokhale, Stone, Arnold, & Kalinowski, 2000) to FPGAs.

- Dataflow models/languages have also been considered (Johnston, Hanna, & Millar, 2004). They are useful in signal, image and video processing. A dataflow model/language named CAL (CAL Actor Language) (Eker & Janneck, 2003) has been recently developed within the Ptolemy II project. Array-OL (Dumont & Boulet, 2005) is a programming language to handle multidimensional applications. The programming model used in Array-OL is compared to the Multidimensional Synchronous Dataflow model proposed by Murthy and Lee in (Murthy & Lee, 2002). In Array-OL, multidimensional arrays are consumed and produced by tasks. Efforts on mapping applications described in Array-OL into FPGAs are shown in (Beux, Marquet, & Dekeyser, 2007).

- As previously described, the mapping of DSLs to reconfigurable fabrics has been addressed by several authors. The results reported indicate the importance of this path to better accomplish optimizations otherwise difficult to achieve.

## EXAMPLES

We give in this section a number of examples that show some of the potential of reconfigurable fabrics. The experiments compare the performance between single-core versus customized multi-core architectures and between generic versus domain-specific architectures. All the engines were implemented in a Xilinx Virtex-II Pro (xc2vp30ff896-7) FPGA.

### Example-A: Single-core vs. Customized Multi-core Architectures

We present here an example of a typical application consisting of execution stages (see Figure 8). The application receives a digital signal, computes a

*Figure 10. Block diagram for the architectures considered: (a) single core; (b) parallel and pipelined multi-core (2 processors); (c) parallel multi-core (3 processors)*

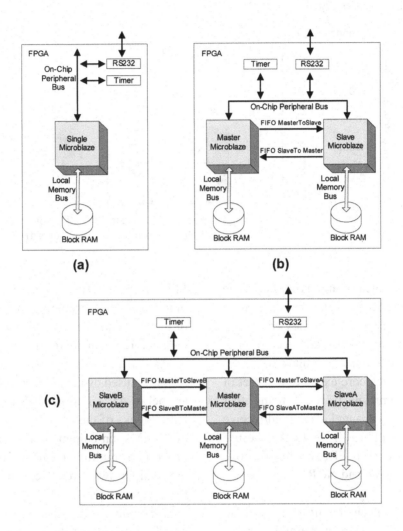

12-tap FIR filter (as the one shown in Figure 6(a)), then computes the maximum value of that signal (MAX stage), and outputs a normalized signal (NORM stage) in floating-point representation (with values ranging from 0 to 1).

To show the flexibility of a fine-grained reconfigurable fabric, we explore three kinds of architectures. All the architectures considered have local memories for data and instructions and include two versions, one considering the existence, and other the absence of a floating-point unit (FPU). The architectures are the following (see Figure 10 for the block diagrams):

- A single-core architecture consisting of a single Xilinx Microblaze softcore. In this architecture all the stages are executed sequentially;

- A parallel multi-core architecture consisting of two and three Xilinx Microblaze *softcores*. In this case data is distributed among the cores and they execute the stages of the application in data chunks, with each data chunk being computed in parallel. In particular we distribute FIR and MAX computations over the cores, then the maximum values calculated by each

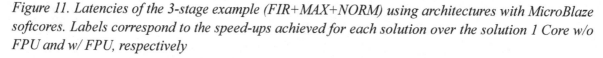

*Figure 11. Latencies of the 3-stage example (FIR+MAX+NORM) using architectures with MicroBlaze softcores. Labels correspond to the speed-ups achieved for each solution over the solution 1 Core w/o FPU and w/ FPU, respectively*

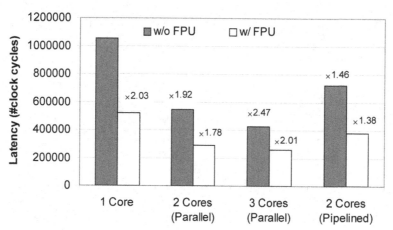

core are combined in the master core. The NORM stage receives then the maximum value and is also split over the cores;

• A pipelining multi-core architecture consisting of two Xilinx Microblaze *softcores*. In this case each core executes a subset of stages and communicate results to the other core by a FIFO channel using send/receive blocking primitives. In particular we use one core to compute FIR and the other one to compute MAX and NORM;

Figure 11 shows the latencies to execute the application using each of the architectures previously presented. The speed-ups presented show that one can achieve a speed-up of 2 by adding a floating-point unit to the single-core architecture. Considering architectures without FPUs, using the parallel multi-core architectures we can achieve speed-ups of 1.92 and 2.47 over the single core architecture for 2 and 3 cores, respectively. When employing architectures with FPUs, the speed-ups using the parallel multi-core architectures decrease to 1.78 and 2.01. Regarding the pipelined multi-core architecture (two cores were used), the speed-ups achieved were 1.46 and 1.38 for the versions without and with

FPUs, respectively. These speed-ups are interesting, especially considering that the MAX stage of the application needs to traverse all the input data before given the result.

As can be seen in Figure 12, the hardware resources used by the more complex architecture are below 45% in terms of Slices (configurable logic blocks of the FPGA), about 70% in terms of BRAMs (on-chip memories), and below 15% in terms of multiplier units (MULT18×18s), of the total hardware resources in the FPGA used for the experiments.

This simple example shows some aspects of the possible multi-core solutions we can expect using fine-grained reconfigurable fabrics. As referred throughout this chapter, one is not constrained by a particular MOC when mapping computations to these reconfigurable devices.

## Example B: Generic vs. Domain-Specific Architectures

In order to show the more powerful specializations achieved by using domain-specific representations and optimizations, we include examples of implementing software and hardware engines for evaluating regular expressions.

*Figure 12. Percentage of hardware resources used in the reconfigurable fabric to implement the multicore architectures*

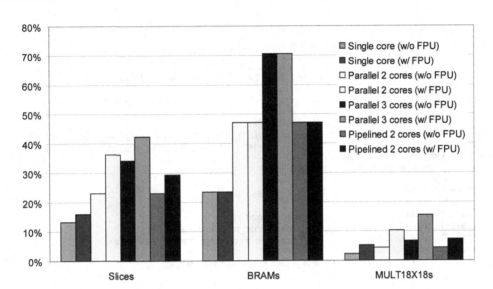

We consider two simple regular expressions and two input strings (one per each regular expression). The regular expressions considered are: a*b+|a+bc*|ef and a+bc*. We measured their performance with the input strings "aaaaaaaaaaaaabccccccccc" (22 characters) and "abc" (3 characters).

For the software implementation we used two versions:

- **SW1:** This solution is based on the code for evaluating regular expressions presented in (Cox, 2007) which uses Thompson NFAs and DFAs. The code compiles the regular expression to NFAs and then simulates the NFA (NFA version) or caches the equivalent DFA on the fly (DFA version). This software implementation only deals with a subset of metacharacters: '|', '*', '+', and '?';
- **SW2:** This implementation represents a customized code for a DFA interpreter with the implementation of the DFA for each regular expression based on tables: next_state = next[current_state, index];

and index = map[char]. A segment of this software implementation is shown in Figure 13(b);

The software versions (SW1 and SW2) use one of the two IBM PowerPC 405 RISC *hardcore* processors existent in the FPGA and we adopted a system with on-chip memories for instructions and data. In the experiments, the programs were compiled with a *gcc* based C compiler and using optimization level O3 and with clock frequency of 300 MHz for the PowerPC.

Both software implementations neither consider substring matching nor overlapped matching. They assume also that the input string is located in the on-chip data memory.

For the hardware engines we use two options:

- **HW1:** This option uses the synthesis approach presented in (Bispo et al., 2006), which takes as input a regular expression[3] (as the one in Figure 13(a)) and outputs the VHDL representation of the hardware engine, ready for logic synthesis. This option

*Figure 13. The example of a regular expression: (a) described in PCRE format; (b) described as a DFA in a customized C program*

```
a*b+|a+bc*|ef

        (a)

...
#define ERR 6

#define NOT_ACCEPT 0
#define ACCEPT 1
...
// can be implemented as a table
int char_map_to_col(char c) {
  switch (c) {
  case 'a' : return 0;
  case 'b' : return 1;
  case 'c' : return 2;
  case 'e' : return 3;
  case 'f' : return 4;
  default : return 5; // others
  }
}
```

```
...
#define S0 0 // begin state
#define S1 1
...
//a, b, c, e, f, others
int next_state[][]={{S2, S1, ERR, S4, S5, ERR},
...
            {ERR, ERR, ERR, ERR, ERR, ERR}
            };

int action[7] = {NOT_ACCEPT, ACCEPT, NOT_ACCEPT, ACCEPT,
            NOT_ACCEPT, ACCEPT, NOT_ACCEPT};
...
// MAIN
...
int current_state = S0;

while(s=get_char()) {
    int index = char_map_to_col(s);
    current_state = next_state[current_state][index];
}
int is_match = action[current_state];
...
```

(b)

can be thought as a domain-specific approach. It leads to customized solutions which support, naturally, and without additional overhead, substring matching and overlapped matching, options that are usually very expensive in software.

- **HW2:** This second option considers the use of state-of-the-art hardware compilation techniques to translate the C code of solution SW2 (Figure 13(b)) in an RTL-VHDL representation of the engine. In this later case, we assume that the arrays are implemented as arrays of constants in VHDL (implemented in the FPGA as glue logic or distributed memories), which leads to more efficient FPGA implementations than the use of RAM modules.

To generate the FPGA bitstreams from the VHDL code - a process requiring logic synthesis, mapping, and placement and routing -, we use the ISE 9.1i framework from Xilinx.

Figure 14 shows the performance in terms of number of clock cycles per input character of

the three solutions. The performance measured for solution SW1 does not take into account the creation of the DFA from the regular expression (a step included in the software code used). The specific hardware engines consider that the input characters are feed to the engines by direct input channels. These engines are both able to process one character per clock cycle. The execution latency to evaluate a regular expression is equal to the number of input characters to be evaluated plus a fixed small number of clock cycles (*e.g.*, 2 clock cycles in the HW1 solution). As can be seen, the hardware engines achieve average speedups of about 700 and 100 over the two software solutions, considering all engines running at the same clock frequency (300 MHz). If maximum operating clock frequencies are used we can expect these speedups increase by about 1.5.

Figure 15 presents the hardware characteristics of the specific hardware engines implemented in the target FPGA. The hardware resources needed for each engine is below 1% of the total FPGA resources. The HW1 solutions are able to achieve 10% (for the regular expression a*b+|a+bc*|ef) and

*Figure 14. The performance results obtained measured in number of clock cycles (#ccs) to process each input character (char)*

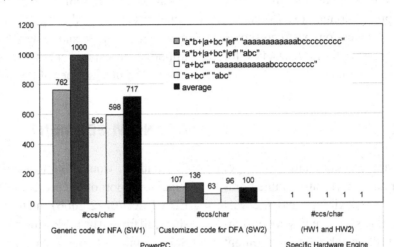

5% (for the regular expression a+bc*) increase in the maximum clock frequency, use less 4-LUTs and more FFs which translate in the overall for these examples into a small increase of required FPGA slices.

The hardware engine obtained (HW2) from the customized software version (SW2) based on DFAs is not as scalable as the solution used for HW1, which uses a hardware engine with structures dedicated to regular expressions. Although the throughput (in number of clock cycles per character) for both hardware solutions can be the same, the operating clock frequency of the solution HW2 decreases with the size of the DFA and with the number of characters used in the DFA (the main structure needs a 2-D matrix). To increase the clock frequency in HW2 engines, one needs to include more aggressively pipelining stages. Using as references the HW2 and HW1 solutions for the small regular expression considered, the more complex regular expression leads to a maximum clock frequency decrease of 8% and 3.5% for the HW2 and HW1 solutions, respectively.

Although the examples shown are simple, they show typical trade-offs among different software and hardware implementations. By using domain-specific optimizations we can achieve better results. These optimizations are in most cases

*Figure 15. FPGA resources for the specific hardware engines for the two examples of regular expressions*

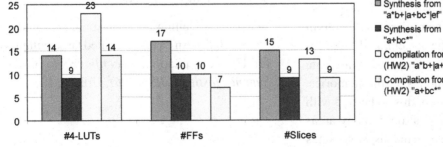

difficult to expose and associate if we start from high-level descriptions without domain-specific constructs. When proper domain extensions are built-in, as the regular expression constructs shown in the latter example, an optimized structure for a specific engine can be used.

## CONCLUSION

No universal model of computation has yet emerged for programming reconfigurable computing platforms. The flexibility and the vast models of computation supported by reconfigurable fabrics allow these fabrics to implement architectures tailored to specific applications. Although using different models of computation may explicitly expose functionalities that can be efficiently mapped to the target reconfigurable fabric, it is expected that most efforts continue to focus on the mapping of the imperative programming model as this model has a large supremacy when programming applications for embedded systems (*e.g.*, the C programming language is seen as the common machine language for general processor architectures). Thus, most research efforts aim at recovering information, *i.e.*, "how to do" aspects, not explicitly expressed or totally absent, when an application is implemented with a software imperative programming language. The emerging of new computing and programming paradigms presents a unique opportunity to close the gap between computations and reconfigurable fabrics.

As complexity increases, it becomes very important to have environments integrating hardware/software partitioning tools, "C-to-Gates" compilers, retargeting compilers for different computing engines in the system, and tools for scheduling and distributing computations and data through the computing engines and the memories. Although an ambitious step, this is the step with the potential to brace innovation in many areas needing high performance demands, sometimes at a lower cost or fulfilling tight constraints (*e.g.*, in embedded systems). Being able to quickly develop custom and adaptable architectures for many situations/scenarios will become critically important to capture market share and to drive innovation in a number of domains.

## ACKNOWLEDGMENT

The authors would like to acknowledge the financial support of the project COBAYA (PTDC/EEA-ELC/70272/2006) and the two PhD fellowships, all funded by the Portuguese Foundation for Science and Technology (FCT). We are grateful to the comments from the anonymous reviewers.

## REFERENCES

X10. (2006). *Report on the experimental language X10, version 1.01*. Retrieved on December 9, 2008, from http://x10.sourceforge.net/

Allen, E. (2005). *The fortress language specification, version 0.618*. Retrieved on November 17, 2008, from http://projectfortress.sun.com/Projects/Community

Alomary, A., Nakata, T., Honma, Y., Sato, J., Hikichi, N., & Imai, M. (1993). PEAS-I: A hardware/software codesign system for ASIPs. *European Design Automation Conference, with EURO-VHDL (EURO-DAC '93)* (pp. 2-7). Hamburg, Germany.

Altera, C. Nios II. Retrieved on November 27, 2008, from http://www.altera.com

Bennett, D., Dellinger, E., Mason, J., & Sundarajan, P. (2006). An FPGA-oriented target language for HLL compilation. *Reconfigurable Systems Summer Institute (RSSI '06)*, Urbana, IL.

Benveniste, A., & Berry, G. (1991). The synchronous approach to reactive and real-time systems. *Proceedings of the IEEE, 79*(9), 1270–1282. doi:10.1109/5.97297

Beux, S. L., Marquet, P., & Dekeyser, J.-L. (2007). *A design flow to map parallel applications onto FPGAs*. Paper presented at the 17th IEEE International Conference on Field Programmable Logic and Applications (FPL'07).

Bispo, J., Sourdis, Y., Cardoso, J. M. P., & Vassiliadis, S. (2006). Regular expression matching for reconfigurable packet inspection. *IEEE International Conference on Field Programmable Technology (FPT'06)* (pp. 119-126). Bangkok, Thailand: IEEE Computer Society Press.

Boussinot, F., & Simone, R. d. (1991). The esterel language. In *Proceedings of the IEEE, 79*(9), 1293-1304.

Budiu, M., & Goldstein, S. C. (1999). Fast compilation for pipelined reconfigurable fabrics. *1999 ACM/SIGDA Seventh International Symposium on Field Programmable Gate Arrays (FPGA'99)* (pp. 195-205). Monterey, CA: ACM New York.

Cardoso, J. M. P., & Diniz, P. C. (2008) Compilation techniques for reconfigurable architectures. Springer.

Cardoso, J. M. P., & Neto, H. C. (2003). Compilation for FPGA-based reconfigurable hardware. *Design & Test of Computers, IEEE, 20*(2), 65–75. doi:10.1109/MDT.2003.1188264

Cardoso, J. M. P., & Weinhardt, M. (2002). XPP-VC: A C compiler with temporal partitioning for the PACT-XPP architecture. *12th International Conference on Field Programmable Logic and Applications (FPL'02)* (pp. 864-874). Montpellier, France.

Carlstrom, B. D., McDonald, A., Chafi, H., Chung, J., Minh, C. C., Kozyrakis, C., et al. (2006). The atomos transactional programming language. *Conference on Programming Language Design and Implementation (PLDI'06)* (pp. 1-13). Ottawa, Ontario, Canada: ACM Press.

Chamberlain, B. L., Callahan, D., & Zima, H. P. (2007). Parallel programmability and the chapel language. *International Journal of High Performance Computing Applications, 21*(3), 291–312. doi:10.1177/1094342007078442

Chang, N., Kwon, W. H., & Park, J. (1996). FPGA-based implementation of synchronous petri nets. *1996 IEEE 22nd International Conference on Industrial Electronics, Control, and Instrumentation (IECON'96)* (pp. 469-474).

Chung, E. S., Nurvitadhi, E., Hoe, J. C., Falsafi, B., & Mai, K. (2008). A complexity-effective architecture for accelerating full-system multiprocessor simulations using FPGAs. *16th International ACM/SIGDA Symposium on Field Programmable Gate Arrays* (pp. 77-86). Monterey, A: ACM.

Cilk (1998). Cilk 5.4.6 *Reference manual, Supercomputing Technologies Group, MIT Laboratory for Computer Science*. Retrieved on December 9, 2008, from http://supertech.lcs.mit.edu/cilk

Computers, S. R. C. I. Retrieved on November 27, 2008, from http://www.srccomp.com/

Corp, M. G. *Catapult synthesis*. Retrieved on December 2, 2008, from http://www.mentor.com/

Cox, R. (2007). Regular expression matching can be simple and fast (but is slow in Java, Perl, PHP, Python, Ruby...). Retrieved on December 2, 2008, from http://swtch.com/~rsc/regexp/regexp1.html

Craven, S., & Athanas, P. (2007). Examining the viability of FPGA supercomputing. *EURASIP Journal of Embedded Systems*.

Cronquist, D. C., Franklin, P., Berg, S. G., & Ebeling, C. (1998). Specifying and compiling applications for RaPiD. *IEEE Symposium on Fpgas for Custom Computing Machines (FCCM'98)* (pp. 116-125). Washington, D.C.: IEEE Computer Society.

DeHon, A., Markovskiy, Y., Caspi, E., Chu, M., Huang, R., & Perissakis, S. (2006). Stream computations organized for reconfigurable execution. *Microprocessors and Microsystems, 30*(6), 334–354. doi:10.1016/j.micpro.2006.02.009

Diniz, P. C., Hall, M. W., Park, J., So, B., & Ziegler, H. E. (2005). Automatic mapping of C to FPGAs with the DEFACTO compilation and synthesis system. *Microprocessors and Microsystems, 29*(2-3), 51–62. doi:10.1016/j.micpro.2004.06.007

DSPLogic. *DSPLogic, Inc*. Retrieved on November 28, 2008, from http://www.dsplogic.com/home/

Dumont, P., & Boulet, P. (2005). Another multi-dimensional synchronous dataflow: Simulating array-OL in ptolemy II. *Research Report RR-5516,* Inria, France.

Edwards, S., Lavagno, L., Lee, E. A., & Sangiovanni-Vincentelli, A. (1997). Design of embedded systems: Formal models, validation, and synthesis. *Proceedings of the IEEE, 85*(3), 366–390. doi:10.1109/5.558710

Eker, J., & Janneck, J. W. (2003). CAL language report: Specification of the CAL actor language. *ERL Technical Memo UCB/ERL M03/48,* University of California at Berkeley, CA.

El-Ghazawi, T., El-Araby, E., Miaoqing, H., Gaj, K., Kindratenko, V., & Buell, D. (2008). The promise of high-performance reconfigurable computing. *Computer, 41*(2), 69–76. doi:10.1109/MC.2008.65

Gajski, D. D., Zhu, J., Dömer, R., Gerstlauer, A., & Zhao, S. (2000). *SpecC: Specification language and methodology*. Boston: Kluwer Academic Publishers.

Gokhale, M. B., Stone, J. M., Arnold, J., & Kalinowski, M. (2000). Stream-oriented FPGA computing in the streams-C high level language. *IEEE Symposium on Field-Programmable Custom Computing Machines (FCCM'00)*. Washington, D.C.: IEEE Computer Society

Gonzalez, R. E. (2000). Xtensa: A configurable and extensible processor. *Micro, IEEE, 20*(2), 60–70. doi:10.1109/40.848473

Guo, Z., Buyukkurt, B., Najjar, W., & Vissers, K. (2005). Optimized generation of data-path from C codes for FPGAs. *ACM/IEEE Design Automation and Test Europe Conference (DATE'05),* Munich, Germany (pp. 112-117).

Handel-C. (1991-2007). *Handel-C language reference manual*. Agility Design Solutions Inc.

Harris, T., Cristal, A., Unsal, O. S., Ayguade, E., Gagliardi, F., & Smith, B. (2007). Transactional memory: An overview. *Micro, IEEE, 27*(3), 8–29. doi:10.1109/MM.2007.63

Harris, T., & Fraser, K. (2003). *Language support for lightweight transactions*. Paper presented at the 18th Annual ACM SIGPLAN Conference on Object-oriented Programing, Systems, Languages, and Applications.

Hauck, S., & DeHon, A. (2008) *Reconfigurable computing: The theory and practice of FPGA-based computation*. Morgan Kaufmann/Elsevier.

Hilfinger, P., & Rabaey, J. (1992). DSP specification using the silage language. In *Anatomy of a Silicon Compiler* (pp. 199-220). Kluwer Academic Publishers.

Hoare, C. A. R. (1978). Communicating sequential processes. *Communications of the ACM, 21*(8), 666–677. doi:10.1145/359576.359585

Johnston, W. M., Hanna, J. P., & Millar, R. J. (2004). Advances in dataflow programming languages. *ACM Computing Surveys, 36*(1), 1–34. doi:10.1145/1013208.1013209

Jones, A. K., Hoare, R., Kusic, D., Fazekas, J., & J, F. (2005). An FPGA-based VLIW processor with custom hardware execution. *ACM International Symposium on Field-Programmable Gate Arrays (FPGA'05),* Monterey, CA (pp. 107-117).

Kachris, C., & Kulkarni, C. (2007). Configurable transactional memory. *15ᵗʰ Annual IEEE Symposium on Field-Programmable Custom Computing Machines* (pp. 65-72). Napa, CA: IEEE Computer Society.

Kahn, G. (1974). The semantics of a simple language for parallel programming. *Information Processing,* 471-475.

Kapasi, U. J., Rixner, S., Dally, W. J., Khailany, B., Jung Ho, A., & Mattson, P. (2003). Programmable stream processors. *Computer, 36*(8), 54–62. doi:10.1109/MC.2003.1220582

Khailany, B., Dally, W. J., Kapasi, U. J., Mattson, P., Namkoong, J., & Owens, J. D. (2001). Imagine: Media processing with streams. *Micro, IEEE, 21*(2), 35–46. doi:10.1109/40.918001

Kuon, I., Tessier, R., & Rose, J. (2008). FPGA architecture: Survey and challenges. In *Foundations and Trends in Electronic Design Automation, 2,* 135-253.

Lau, D., Pritchard, O., & Molson, P. (2006). Automated generation of hardware accelerators with direct memory access from ANSI/ISO standard C functions. *14ᵗʰ Annual IEEE Symposium on Field-Programmable Custom Computing Machines (FCCM '06)* (pp. 45-56).

Lee, E. A., & Parks, T. M. (1995). Dataflow process networks. *Proceedings of the IEEE, 83*(5), 773–801. doi:10.1109/5.381846

Liao, S. Y. (2000). Towards a new standard for system-level design. *Eighth International Workshop on Hardware/Software Codesign,* San Diego, CA (pp. 2-6).

McAllister, J., Woods, R., Walke, R., & Reilly, D. (2004). Synthesis and high level optimisation of multidimensional dataflow actor networks on FPGA. *IEEE Workshop on Signal Processing Systems,* TX (pp. 164-169).

Micheli, G. D., Ernst, R., & Wolf, W. (2001). *Readings in hardware/software codesign (1ˢᵗ ed.).* Morgan Kaufmann.

Möhl, S. (2005). T*he mitrion-C programming language.* Retrieved on November 27, 2008, from http://www.mitrionics.com/

Murata, T. (1989). Petri nets: Properties, analysis, and applications. *Proceedings of the IEEE, 77*(4). doi:10.1109/5.24143

Murthy, P. K., & Lee, E. A. (2002). Multidimensional synchronous dataflow. *IEEE Transactions on Signal Processing, 50*(8), 2064–2079. doi:10.1109/TSP.2002.800830

Pellerin, D., & Thibault, S. (2005). *Practical FPGA programming in C.* Prentice Hall PTR.

Putnam, A. R., Bennett, D., Dellinger, E., Mason, J., & Sundararajan, P. (2008). CHiMPS: A high-level compilation flow for hybrid CPU-FPGA architectures. *16ᵗʰ international ACM/SIGDA Symposium on Field Programmable Gate Arrays (FPGA'08)* (pp. 261-261). Monterey, CA: ACM New York.

SpecC. SpecC technology open consortium. Retrieved on December 2, 2008, from http://www.SpecC.org/

StarbridgeSystems. *Starbridge Systems, Inc*. Retrieved on November 28, 2008, from http://www.starbridgesystems.com

Stefanov, T., Zissulescu, C., Turjan, A., Kienhuis, B., & Deprettere, E. (2004). System design using kahn process networks: The compaan/laura approach. *Design, Automation and Test in Europe conference (DATE'04)* Paris, France (pp. 10340-10346).

SystemC (2005). *Open systemC™ language reference manual, IEEE Std. 1666™*. New York: Institute of Electrical and Electronics Engineers Inc.

Thies, W., Karczmarek, M., & Amarasinghe, S. (2002). StreamIt: A language for streaming applications. *International Conference on Compiler Construction* (LNCS, pp. 179-196). Grenoble, France: Springer.

Thrun, S. (2001). A programming language extension for probabilistic robot programming. *Workshop notes of the IJCAI Workshop on Uncertainty in Robotics (RUR)*. Seattle, WA: IJCAI, Inc.

UPC. (2005). *UPC language specifications. 1.2, a publication of the UPC consortium*. Retrieved on December 9, 2008, from http://upc.lbl.gov/

Vassiliadis, S., Wong, S., Gaydadjiev, G., Bertels, K., Kuzmanov, G., & Panainte, E. M. (2004). The MOLEN polymorphic processor. *Computers . IEEE Transactions*, *53*(11), 1363–1375. doi:10.1109/TC.2004.104

Verilog. (2001). *IEEE standard verilog hardware description language, IEEE Std 1364-2001*. New York: Institute of Electrical and Electronics Engineers Inc.

VHDL. (1988). *IEEE standard VHDL language reference manual, IEEE Std 1076-1987*. New York: Institute of Electrical and Electronics Engineers Inc.

Wirth, N. (1998). Hardware compilation: Translating programs into circuits. *Computer*, *31*(6), 25–31. doi:10.1109/2.683004

Wolinski, C., Gokhale, M., & McCave, K. (2002). A polymorphous computing fabric. *Micro, IEEE*, *22*(5), 56–68. doi:10.1109/MM.2002.1044300

Xilinx, I. *MicroBlaze*. Retrieved on November 27, 2008, from http://www.xilinx.com/

XPP-III. (2006). *XPP-III processors: White paper, version 2.0.1*. XPP Technologies AG.

Yankova, Y., Kuzmanov, G., Bertels, K., Gaydadjiev, G., Lu, Y., & Vassiliadis, S. (2007). DWARV: Delftworkbench automated reconfigurable VHDL generator. *Conference on Field Programmable Logic and Applications (FPL'07)*, Amsterdam, The Netherlands (pp. 697-701).

## ENDNOTES

[1]  We use here the term "C-to-gates" to refer to all the efforts considering the compilation of high-level software programming languages to application specific architectures. Although referred as "C", the programming language does not need to be a general purpose language, and in most cases is in fact a Domain-Specific Language.

[2]  We call the attention of the reader to the fact that a program in a given programming model is already an implementation and transformations from programming models can be, in this case, seen as transformations between implementations.

[3]  The tool accepts regular expressions in the PCRE format.

# Section 5
# Industrial Applications

The fifth and last section includes three chapters that present and discuss several issues that are relevant in real industrial contexts, especially in the automotive domain.

# Chapter 13
# Reconfiguration of Industrial Embedded Control Systems

**Mohamed Khalgui**
*Martin Luther University, Germany*

**Hans-Michael Hanisch**
*Martin Luther University, Germany*

## ABSTRACT

*This research work deals with the development of safety reconfigurable embedded control systems following the international industrial component-based standard IEC61499. According to this standard, a function block (FB) is a functional unit of software and a control application a FB network that has to meet functional and temporal properties described in user requirements. We define in the book chapter a new semantic of the reconfiguration where a crucial criterion to consider is the automatic improvement of the system performance at run-time. If a reconfiguration scenario is applied at run-time, then the FB network implementing the system is totally changed or modified. To handle all possible reconfiguration forms, we propose thereafter an agent-based architecture that applies automatic reconfigurations to adapt the system according to well defined conditions and we model this agent with nested state machines according to the formalism of net condition/event systems which is an extension of the Petri net formalism. In order to satisfy user requirements, we specify the functional and temporal properties with the temporal logic CTL (as well as its extensions ECTL and TCTL) and we apply the model checker SESA to check the whole system behavior. To assign this reconfigurable system into the execution environment, we define thereafter an approach based on the exploration of reachability graphs to construct feasible OS tasks that encode the FB network corresponding to each reconfiguration scenario. Therefore, the system is implemented with sets of OS tasks where each set is to load in memory when the corresponding scenario is applied by the Agent. We developed the tool X-Reconfig to support these contributions that we apply on the FESTO and EnAS benchmark production systems available in our research laboratory.*

DOI: 10.4018/978-1-60566-750-8.ch013

## INTRODUCTION

Nowadays in Manufacturing Industry, the development of Safety Embedded Control Systems is not a trivial activity because a failure can be critical for the safety of human beings. According to user requirements, they have classically to satisfy functional and temporal properties (Baruah & Goossens, 2004) but their time to market has to be shorter than ever. To address all these important requirements, the component-based approach is studied in several academic research works and also in interesting industrial projects to develop modular embedded systems in order to control the design complexity and to support the reusability of already developed components (Bensalem, Bozga, Sifakis & Nguyen, 2008). In industry, several component-based technologies have been proposed to design the application (as a composition of components) (Crnkovic & Larsson, 2002). Among all these technologies, the International Standard IEC61499 is proposed by the International Electrotechnical Commission to design distributed control applications as well as the corresponding execution environment (IEC61499, 2004). In this Standard, a Function Block is an event-triggered component composed of an Interface and an Implementation. The interface contains data/event inputs/outputs supporting interactions with the environment. Events are responsible for the activation of the block, whereas data contain valued information. The Implementation of the block contains algorithms to execute when the corresponding events occur. The selection of an algorithm to execute is performed by a state machine called Execution Control Chart (ECC) which is also responsible for sending output events at the end of the algorithm execution. An IEC61499 application is a network of blocks that have to meet temporal properties defined in this contribution as end-to-end bounds (denoted eertb) which have on one end the input signals from sensors and on the other end the output signals to the corresponding actuators.

Today in academy and industry, rich books have been written (Lewis, 2001; Vyatkin, 2007; Marik, Vyatkin, & Colombo, 2007), many research works have been made (Vyatkin & Hanisch, 2003; Thramboulidis, Perdikis, & Kantas, 2007; Panjaitan & Frey, 2007; Khalgui, Rebeuf, & Simonot-Lion, 2007; Thramboulidis, 2005; Vyatkin, 2006), useful tools (http://www.**isagraf**.com, http://www.**holobloc**.com) have been developed, real industrial platforms (http://www.itia.cnr.it) have been deployed while following this International Standard and finally in our Research Laboratory at the Martin Luther University in Germany, two Benchmark Production Systems FESTO and EnAS are developed according to this component-based technology. On the other hand, the new generation of Industrial Control Systems is addressing today new criteria as flexibility and agility. To reduce their cost, these systems have to be changed and adapted to their environment without any disturbance. Several interesting academic and industrial research works have been made last years to develop Reconfigurable Control Systems. We distinguish in these works two reconfiguration policies: the static and dynamic reconfigurations where the static reconfiguration is applied offline to apply changes before the system cold start (Angelov, Sierszecki & Marian, *2005)*, whereas the dynamic reconfiguration is applied dynamically at run-time. In the last policy, two cases exist: the manual reconfiguration applied by the user (Rooker, Sunder, Strasser, Zoitl, Hummer & Ebenhofer, 2007) and the automatic reconfiguration applied by an Intelligent Agent localized in the system (Al-Safi & Vyatkin, 2007).

In this book chapter, we are interested in the automatic reconfiguration of Industrial Control Systems following the International Standard IEC61499. We define at first time a new semantic of this type of reconfiguration where a crucial criterion to consider is the automatic improvement of the system performance at run-time. We propose thereafter an Agent-based architecture to handle all possible reconfiguration scenarios. Therefore, the system is assumed to be implemented with a set of FB networks where only one is executed when the corresponding scenario is applied at run-time. We model the agent with Net Condition/Event Systems (NCES) proposed by Rausch and Hanisch in (Rausch & Hanisch, 1995) and we use the temporal logic "Computation Tree Logic" (denoted by CTL) as well as its extensions (ECTL and TCTL) to specify functional and temporal properties that we verify with the model checker *SESA* on the different FB networks. Once the network corresponding to each possible scenario is checked, the next step to be addressed is the execution semantic of the system by assigning the corresponding FB networks into a set of OS task sets where each set is to be executed when the corresponding reconfiguration scenario is applied by the Agent at run-time. We give in the following section a useful background before we detail thereafter the book chapter problems and we present our contributions.

## BACKGROUND

We describe in this section the main concepts of the IEC61499 technology before we present the two Benchmark Production Systems FESTO and EnAS that we take as running examples in the following. In addition, we detail the formalism of Net Condition/Event Systems and we present thereafter the temporal Logic "Computation Tree Logic" and its extensions.

### IEC61499 Standard

We present the main concepts of the International Industrial Standard IEC61499 (IEC61499, 2004) used for the development of distributed component-based control systems and which is an extension of the previous Standard IEC61131 used for the development of centralized Programmable Logic Controllers (IEC1131, 1993). According to this standard, a Function Block (FB) (figure 1) is

*Figure 1. An IEC61499 Function Block*

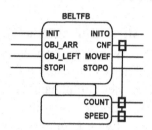

a unit of software supporting functionalities of an application (Lewis, 2001; Vyatkin, 2007; Marik, Vyatkin, & Colombo, 2007). It is composed of an interface and an implementation where the interface contains data/event inputs and outputs supporting interactions with the environment. Events are responsible for the activation of the block while data contain valued information. The implementation of the block contains algorithms to execute when the corresponding events occur. The selection of an algorithm to execute is performed by a state machine called Execution Control Chart (ECC) which is also responsible for sending output events at the end of the algorithm execution. The

ECC is said idle if there is no algorithm to execute and it is busy otherwise. We divide its behavior into the following steps:

- First, it **selects** one event input occurrence according to priority rules,
- It **activates** thereafter the algorithm corresponding to the selected occurrence and **waits** for the processor to start the execution,
- When the execution ends, it **emits** corresponding occurrences of output events.

The ECC is defined as a state machine where each trace is composed of a waiting of an input event, an invocation of a corresponding algorithm and a sending of output events. The block *BELTFB* shown in Figure 1 is a FB used to control conveyer belts (Khalgui & Thramboulidis, 2008). It

*Figure 2. The ECC of the FB BeltFB*

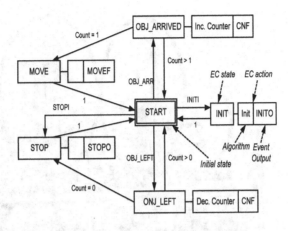

is activated by the input events: *INIT, OBJ_ARR, OBJ_LEFT* and *STOPI*, and responds to the environment by the output events *INITO, CNF, MOVEF* and *STOPO*. When the event *OBJ_ARR* occurs, the state *OBJ_ARRIVED* is activated as shown in Figure 2 to execute the algorithm *Inc. Counter*. Once such execution finishes, the ECC sends the output event *CNF* and activates the states *MOVE* OR *START* depending on the value of the internal variable *Count*. In particular, when the output event *CNF* has to be sent, the block updates the corresponding output data *COUNT* and *SPEED*. According to the Standard IEC61499, a control application is specified by a network of FBs where each event input (resp. output) of a block is linked to an event output (resp. input) by a channel and it corresponds otherwise to a global input (resp. output). Data inputs and outputs follow the same rules. The architecture of the execution environment is well defined by a network of devices where each one is composed of one processing unit and interfaces (with sensors, actuators and the network). Moreover, it is characterized by logical execution unit(s) called resource(s). In the functional level, a resource gathers and serves application blocks, and it is defined in the operational level as an execution unit corresponding to time slots of the processing unit. It defines *the important boundary existing*

between what is within the scope of the IEC61499 model and what is device (OS) and networks (communication protocols) (Lewis, 2001). In this contribution, we assume a centralized control system containing several resources to be considered in the operational level as OS tasks of the execution environment. For more details on the standard concepts, we refer the reader to the book chapters (Hanisch, H.-M., & Vyatkin, V., (2005); Khalgui, Rebeuf & Simonot-Lion, 2006).

## Industrial Case Study

We present the two IEC61499 Benchmark Production Systems FESTO and EnAS available in our research laboratory at the Martin Luther University in Germany.

## FESTO Manufacturing System

FESTO MPS is a well documented laboratory system for research and education purposes (Figure 3). It is composed of three units: the distribution, the test and the processing units. The distribution unit is composed of a pneumatic feeder and a converter to forward cylindrical work pieces from a stack to the testing unit which is composed of the detector, the tester and the elevator. This unit performs checks on work pieces for height, mate-

*Figure 3. The FESTO modular production system*

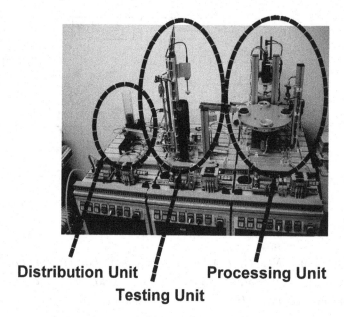

**Distribution Unit**     **Processing Unit**

**Testing Unit**

rial type and color. Work pieces that successfully pass this check are forwarded to the rotating disk of the processing unit, where the drilling of the work piece is performed. We theoretically assume two drilling machines *Drill_machine*1 and *Drill_machine*2 to drill pieces. The result of the drilling operation is next checked by the checking machine and the work piece is forwarded to another mechanical unit. We present in Figure 4 the implementation of this system with IEC61499 Function Blocks distributed on two resources *Resource1* and *Resource2*. The first handles the distribution and the test units, whereas the second handles the processing unit which is activated when pieces are successfully passed from *Ressource1*. In the operational level, each one of these resources corresponds to an OS task where the second task is executed if and only if the first deduces the acceptance of the tested piece.

We assume three FESTO production modes according to the rate of input pieces *number_pieces* into the system (i.e. ejected by the feeder).

- **Case1: High production.** If *number_pieces* $\geq$ *Constante1*, Then the two drilling

machines are used at the same time in order to accelerate the production. In this case, the distribution and the testing units have to forward two successive pieces to the rotating disc before starting the drilling with *Drill_machine*1 AND *Drill_machine*2. In the operation level, the OS task that corresponds to *Resource1* has to be executed twice before the activation of that of *Resource2*: this reason is behind the distribution of FESTO blocks on two resources. On the other hand and for this production mode, the periodicity of input pieces is $p = 11 seconds$.

- **Case2: Medium production.** If *Constante2* $\leq$ *number_pieces* < *Constante1*, Then we use *Drill_machine*1 OR *Drill_machine*2 to drill work pieces. For this production mode, the periodicity of input pieces is $p = 30 seconds$.

- **Case3: Light production.** If *number_pieces* < *Constante2*, Then only the drilling machine *Drill_machine*1 is used. For this production mode, the periodicity of input pieces is $p = 50 seconds$.

*Figure 4. Implementation of the FESTO system with IEC Function Blocks*

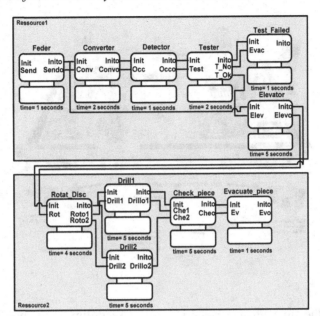

On the other hand, if one of the drilling machines is broken at run-time, then we have to only use the other one. In this case, we reduce the periodicity of input pieces to $p = 40 seconds$. The system is completely stopped in the worst case if the two drilling machines are broken. We present in Figure 4 the times to distribute, test, drill and finally check work pieces (In particular, the drilling operation takes 5 seconds before forwarding the piece into the checking machine). According to the rate of input pieces, the dynamic reconfiguration of the FESTO system is useful to improve the production. This first example shows a new semantic of the reconfiguration in the manufacturing industry: we can automatically change the system configuration to improve its performance even if there is no fault.

## EnAS Manufacturing System

It is assumed that the IEC61499 Benchmark Production System EnAS transports pieces from the production station (i.e. FESTO system) into the storing units (Figure 5). These pieces shall be placed inside tins to close with caps afterwards. Two different production strategies can be applied: we place in each tin one or two pieces according to production rates of pieces, tins and caps. We denote respectively by $nb_{pieces}$, $nb_{tins+caps}$ the production number of pieces and tins (as well as caps) per hour and by *Threshold* a variable (defined in specifications) allowing the choice of the adequate production strategy.

The EnAS system is mainly composed of a belt, two Jack stations ($J1$ and $J2$) and two Gripper stations ($G1$ and $G2$) (figure 6). The Jack stations place new produced pieces and close tins with caps, whereas the Gripper stations remove charged tins from the belt into the storing units. Initially, the belt moves a particular pallet containing a tin and a cap into the first Jack station $J1$. According to the production parameters, we distinguish two cases.

- **The first production policy ($nb\_pieces/$ $_{nbtins+caps} \leq$ Threshold):** the Jack station $J1$ places from the production station a new

*Figure 5. EnAS-Demonstrator in Halle*

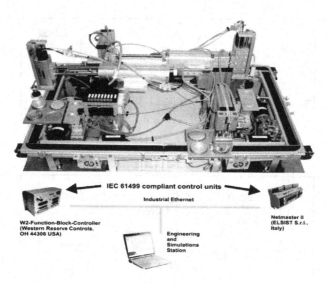

piece and closes the tin with the cap. In this case, the Gripper station *G*1 removes the tin from the belt into the storing station *St*1.

- **The second production policy (*nbpieces/ nbtins+caps > Threshold*)**: the Jack station *J*1 places just a piece in the tin which is moved thereafter into the second Jack station to place a second new piece. Once *J*2 closes the tin with a cap, the belt moves the pallet into the Gripper station *G*2 to remove the tin (with two pieces) into the second storing station *St*2.

According to the production parameters, the dynamic reconfiguration of the transportation system is useful to improve the factory receipt (i.e. to improve the EnAS performance). This second example shows also a new semantic of the reconfiguration in the manufacturing industry: we can change the system configuration to improve the performance even if there is no fault. In the following, we use the FESTO and EnAS systems as examples to explain the book chapter contribution.

*Figure 6. Distribution of the EnAS stations*

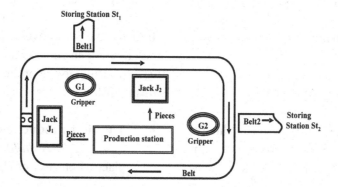

*Figure 7. A module of Net Condition / Event Systems*

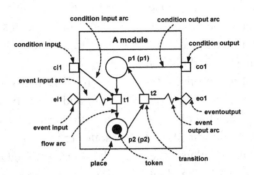

## NCES Formalism: Extension of Petri Net

We use in our work the formalism Net Condition/ Event Systems (NCES) because it provides useful facilities for the specification of any synchronization between modules in a reconfigurable embedded system. This formalism is an extension of the well known Petri net formalism, it was introduced by Rausch and Hanisch in (Rausch & Hanisch, 1995) and further developed through the last years, in particular in (Hanisch & Luder, 1999), according to which a NCES is a place-transition net formally represented as follows (Figure 7):

$S = \{PTN; CN; W_{CN}; I; W_I; EN; em\}$ where:

- $PTN = (P; T; F; K; W_F)$ is a classic Place/ Transition Net,
- $CN \subseteq (P \times T)$ is a set of condition arcs,
- $W_{CN}: CN \rightarrow N^+$ defines a weight for each condition arc,
- $I \subseteq (P \times T)$ is a set of inhibitor arcs
- $WI: I \rightarrow N^+$ defines a weight for each inhibitor arc,
- $EN \subseteq (T \times T)$ is a set of event arcs free of circles, which means:
  - $(t_1; t_2) \in EN: (t_1 = t_2)$,
  - $(t_1; t_2); \dots ; (t_{i-1}; t_i): (t_{i-1}; t_i) \in EN$ with $2 \leq l \leq i \wedge (t_1 = t_i)$.
- $em: T \rightarrow \{\vee, \wedge\}$ is an event mode for every

transition (i.e. if $\wedge$ then the corresponding events have to occur simultaneously before the transition firing, else if $\vee$ then one of them is enough).

The semantics of NCES are defined by the firing rules of transitions. There are several conditions to be fulfilled to enable a transition to fire. First, as it is in ordinary Petri nets, an enabled transition has to have a token concession. That means that all pre-places have to be marked with at least one token. In addition to the flow arcs from places, a transition in NCES may have incoming condition arcs from places and event arcs from other transitions. A transition is enabled by condition signals if all source places of the condition signals are marked by at least one token. The other type of influence on the firing can be described by event signals which come to the transition from some other transitions. Transitions having no incoming event arcs are called *spontaneous*, otherwise *forced*. A forced transition is enabled if it has token concession and it is enabled by condition and event signals (Rausch & Hanisch, 1995).

On the other hand, the NCES formalism is enriched last years to consider time constraints applied to the input arcs of transitions: to every pre-arc of a transition, an interval [eft,lft] of natural numbers is attached with $0 \leq eft \leq w$ ($w$ is a fixed integer). The interpretation is as follows, every place $p$ bears a clock which is running iff the place is marked and switched off otherwise. All running clocks run at the same speed measuring the time the token status of its place has not been changed i.e. the clock on a marked place $p$ shows the age of the youngest token on $p$. If a firing transition $t$ is able to remove a token from the place $p$ or adds a token to $p$ then the clock of $p$ is turned back to 0. In addition, a transition $t$ is able to remove tokens from its pre-places (i.e. to fire) only if for any pre-place $p$ of $t$ the clock at place $p$ shows a time $u(p)$ such that $eft(p, t) \leq u(p) \leq lft(p,t)$. Hence, the firing of transitions is restricted by the clock positions. We note finally that the model-checker SESA is a useful tool to verify functional and temporal properties on NCES (Vyatkin & Hanisch, 2003). We propose to apply it in our work to verify reconfigurable control systems following the standard IEC 61499.

## The Temporal Logic: Computation Tree Logic

The "Computation Tree Logic" CTL offers facilities for the specification of properties to fulfill by the system behavior (Roch, 2000a; Roch, 2000b). In this section, we briefly present this logic, its extension "Extended Computation Tree Logic" (denoted by eCTL) and the "Timed Computation Tree Logic" (denoted by TCTL).

### Computation Tree Logic

In CTL, all formulae specify behaviors of the system starting from an assigned state in which the formula is evaluated by taking paths (i.e. sequence of states) into account. The semantics of formulae is defined with respect to a reachability graph where states and paths are used for the evaluation. A reachability graph $M$ consists of all global states that the system can reach from a given initial state. It is formally defined as a tuple $M = [Z,E]$ where,

- $Z$ is a finite set of states,
- $E$ is a finite set of transitions between states, i.e. a set of edges $(z,z_0)$, such that $z$, $z_0 \in Z$ and $z0$ is reachable from $z$.

In CTL, paths play the key role in the definition and evaluation of formulae. By definition, a path starting in the state $z_0$ is a sequence of states $(z_i) = z_0, z_1,...$ such that for all $j \geq 0$ it holds that there is an edge $(z_j, z_{j+1}) \in E$. In the following, we denote by $(z_i)$ such path. The truth value of CTL formulae is evaluated with respect to a certain state of the reachability graph. Let $z_0 \in Z$ be a state of the reachability graph and $\varphi$ a CTL formula, then the relation ' for CTL formulae is defined inductively.

- Basis:
  - $z_0$ ' $\varphi$ iff the formula $\varphi$ holds in $z_0$,
  - $z_0$ ' *true* always holds,
  - $z_0$ ' *false* iff never holds,
- Steps:
  - $z_0$ ' $EF$ $\varphi$ iff there is a path $(z_i)$ and $j \geq 0$ such that $z_j$ ' $\varphi$,
  - $z_0$ ' $AF$ $\varphi$ iff for all paths $(z_i)$ there exists $j \geq 0$ such that $z_j$ ' $\varphi$,
  - $z_0$ ' $AG$ $\varphi$ iff for all paths $(z_i)$ and for all $j \geq 0$ it holds $z_j$ ' $\varphi$,

### Extended Computation Tree Logic

In CTL, it is rather complicated to refer to information contained in certain transitions between states of a reachability graph. A solution is given in (Roch, 2000a; Roch, 2000b) for this problem by proposing an extension of CTL called Extended Computation Tree Logic ECTL. A transition formula is introduced in ECTL to refer to a transition information contained in the edges of the reachability graph. Since it is wanted to refer not only to state information but also to steps between states, the structure of the reachability graph $M = [Z,E]$ is changed as follows:

- $Z$ is a finite set of states,
- $E$ is a finite set of transitions between states, i.e. a set of labeled edges $(z,s,z')$, such that $z, z' \in Z$ and $z'$ is reachable from $z$ by executing the step $s$.

Let $z_0 \in Z$ be a state of the reachability graph, a transition formula and $\varphi$ an ECTL formula. The relation ' for ECTL formulae is defined inductively:

- $z_0$ ' $E \tau X \varphi$: iff there exists a successor state $z_1$ such that there is an edge $(z_0, s, z_1) \in E$ where $(z_0, s, z_1)$ '$\tau$ and $z_1$ ' $\varphi$ holds,
- $z_0$ ' $A \tau X \varphi$: iff $z_1$ ' $\varphi$ holds for all successors states $z_1$ with an edge $(z_0, s, z_1) \in E$ such that $(z_0, s, z_1) \vDash \tau$ holds,

## Timed Computation Tree Logic

TCTL is an extension of CTL to model qualitative temporal assertions together with time constraints. The extension essentially consists in attaching a time bound to the modalities and we note that a good survey can be found in (Alur & Henzinger, 1992). For a reachability graph $M = [Z,E]$, the state delay D is defined as a mapping $D: Z \rightarrow N_0$ and for any state $z = [m, u]$ the number $D(z)$ is the number of time units which have to elapse at $z$ before firing any transition from this state. For any path $(z_i)$ and any state $z \in Z$ we put:

- $D[(z_i), z] = 0$, if $z_0 = z$,
- $D[(z_i), z] = D(z_0) + D(z_1) + \dots + D(z_{k-1})$, if $z_k = z$ and $z_0, \dots, z_{k-1} \neq z$.

With other words, $D[(z_i), z]$ is the number of time units after which the state $z$ on the path $(z_i)$ is reached the first time, i.e. the minimal time distance from $z_0$. Let $z_0 \in Z$ be a state of the reachability graph and $\varphi$ a TCTL formula. The relation $\vDash$ for TCTL is defined as follows:

- $z_0 \vDash EF[l,h] \varphi$, iff there is a path $(z_i)$ and a $j > 0$ such that $z_j \vDash \varphi$ and $l \leq D((z_i), z_j) \leq h$,
- $z_0 \vDash AF[l,h] \varphi$, iff for all paths $(z_i)$, there is a $j > 0$ such that $z_j \vDash \varphi$ and $l \leq D((z_i), z_j) \leq h$.

## STATE OF THE ART

Today, rich research works have been proposed to develop Reconfigurable Control Systems following the International Industrial Standard IEC61499. In (Angelov, Sierszecki & Marian, 2005), the authors develop reusable Function Blocks to implement a broad range of embedded systems. These blocks are statically reconfigured without any re-programming and this is accomplished by updating the supporting data structure, i.e. a state transition table, whereas the executable code remains unchanged and may be stored in permanent memory. The state transition table consists of multiple-output binary decision diagrams that represent the next-state mappings of various states and the associated control actions. In (Rooker, Sunder, Strasser, Zoitl, Hummer, & Ebenhofer 2007), the authors propose a complete methodology based on the user intervention to dynamically reconfigure control systems and they present in addition an interesting experimentation showing the dynamic change by the user of a Function Block algorithm without disturbing all the system. In (Thramboulidis, Doukas & Frantzis, 2004), the authors use Real-time-UML as a meta-model between the design models of IEC61499 and their implementation models to support a dynamic user-based reconfiguration of control systems. In (Brennan, Fletcher & Norrie, 2001), the authors propose an agent-based reconfiguration approach to save the system when faults occur at run-time. Finally in (Al-Safi & Vyatkin, 2007), the authors propose an ontology-based agent to perform any system reconfiguration that adapts changes in user requirements and also in environment. They are interested in particular to study the reconfiguration of a control system when a hardware fault occurs also at run-time. Although the utility of these interesting contributions in Manufacturing Industry is obvious, we believe in their limitation in particular cases (e.g. to resolve hardware faults or to add new functionalities like the update of an algorithm in a block) without studying all possible reconfiguration scenarios to possibly apply like the performance improvement even if there are no faults. In addition, these contributions do not consider particular reconfiguration techniques to probably apply at run-time like the addition of data/event inputs/outputs in a control system, they do not propose also verification techniques to check the feasibility of the FB network specifying the system for each reconfiguration scenario. The schedulability of such network is not checked in these contributions to verify temporal properties described in user requirements. Finally, the execution semantic of the system .i.e. the assignment of each possible FB network corresponding to a particular reconfiguration scenario into a set of OS tasks of the execution environment is not studied in these contributions.

Nowadays, many research works on the assignment of Function Blocks have been proposed. In (Lastra, Godinho & Tuokko, 2005; Toolkit, 2008), an approach is proposed to assign all the application blocks in only one execution thread. This sequential single-threaded approach seems to be inefficient for complex applications as explained in (Ferrarini & Veber, 2004; Colla & Brusafferri, 2006). In (Thramboulidis & Zoupas, 2005), another solution is proposed by assigning each FB in only one thread. Nevertheless, this approach is limited because it deals with devices containing small numbers of Function Blocks. In (Dukas & Thramboulidis, 2005), an interesting solution is proposed by assigning subsets of application blocks in threads. Each subset is defined as a container handling the execution of the corresponding blocks. Although this approach seems to be efficient and flexible, the assignment does not take into account temporal constraints to

strictly satisfy by the application blocks (Thramboulidis & Dukas, 2006). In addition, there is not a characterization of the ECC behavior to allow an assignment that takes into account all execution scenarios. Finally, we note that all these related works consider mono-resource devices where all the application blocks are injected in only one resource. Since the appearance of the standard (IEC61499, 2004), the only research work dealing with multi-resource devices is that we propose in the current book chapter in which we give solutions for all these problems to develop Safety IEC61499 Reconfigurable Control Systems.

## CONTRIBUTIONS

We define in our book chapter a new semantic of the *automatic reconfiguration* for the development of Manufacturing Control Systems where a crucial criterion to consider is the automatic improvement of their performances at run-time. Indeed, these systems have to dynamically and automatically improve their quality of service according to conditions on their environment or described in user requirements. They have if possible to reduce the energy consumption or the running controllers in order to decrease the production cost. We classify all possible reconfiguration forms to apply at Run-time into three levels where the first level deals with the system architecture, the second with the system control structure and the third with the system data. We propose an Agent-based architecture that we model with Nested Net Condition/Event Systems to handle all these forms by adding, updating or removing Function Blocks under well defined conditions. We assume in the following that no reconfiguration scenario to be incorporated at run-time is unknown previously. Therefore, the system is implemented with different FB networks (i.e. FB compositions) where each one corresponds to a particular reconfiguration scenario to automatically apply at run-time. To check functional and temporal properties defined in user requirements on Function Blocks that implement the System in different scenarios, we use the Computation Tree Logic (denoted by CTL) and its extensions (ECTL and TCTL) to specify these properties and we apply the model checker *SESA* to check the whole system behavior. Once it is correctly checked, the next step that has to be addressed deals with the execution semantic of Reconfigurable IEC61499 Control Systems where the corresponding FB networks have to be assigned into a set of OS task sets of the execution environment. We transform at first time the system blocks into a system of actions with precedence constraints in order to exploit previous interesting results on real-time scheduling (Stankovic, Spuri & Ramamritham, 2005). Therefore, the event-triggered model of each FB network is transformed into a time-triggered one. We use the non-preemptive Earliest Deadline First scheduling policy (denoted by EDF) (Stankovic, Spuri & Ramamritham, 2005) to explore reachability graphs for each network in order to verify the corresponding temporal bounds and we generate static schedulings if these bounds are satisfied. Once the schedulability analysis of the FB network corresponding to each reconfiguration scenario is correctly done, we assign the corresponding processed static schedulings into OS tasks of the execution environment. Therefore the functional architecture of each network is transformed into a set of OS tasks that we have to check their on-line feasibility. An IEC61499 Control System becomes a set of OS task sets such as each set is to execute when the corresponding reconfiguration scenario is automatically applied by the agent at run-time. We apply these different steps on the FESTO and EnAS Benchmark Production Systems that we consider as running examples. The book chapter plan will be as follows, we define in the next section a new semantic of the automatic reconfiguration before we describe in Section6 all possible reconfiguration forms to possibly apply in manufacturing industry. In Section7, an Agent-based architecture is defined

to automatically handle reconfiguration scenarios and we apply in Section8 a SESA-based model checking to verify CTL-based properties defined in user requirements. Before the conclusion and the presentation of our future work, we define in Section9 the assignment of Reconfigurable Control Systems into OS tasks of the execution environment.

## NEW RECONFIGURATION SCENARIO

In the manufacturing industry, a crucial criterion to consider in the new generation of embedded systems is the automatic improvement of their performance at run-time. Indeed, these systems have to dynamically and automatically improve their quality of service according to well defined conditions. In addition, they have if possible to reduce the energy consumption, the number of running controllers or also the traffic on the used communication networks. We define the dynamic reconfiguration in the book chapter as follows.

**Definition.** *According to well defined conditions, a dynamic reconfiguration is any change in software as well as in hardware components to lead the whole embedded system into a better safe state at run-time.*

According to the Standard IEC61499, we mean in this definition by a change in software components any operation that adds, removes or also updates Function Blocks in order to improve the whole system behavior. We mean also by a change in hardware components any operation that adds, removes or also updates devices used in the execution environment. This new definition remains compatible with previous contributions on the reconfiguration of control systems following the Standard IEC61499. Indeed, as defined in (Al-Safi & Vyatkin, 2007), the reconfiguration is applied to save the system when hardware problems occur at run-time. In this case, we have to apply changes in software as well as hardware components to bring the whole system into a better safe state. In addition, as defined in [15], the reconfiguration is manually applied to add new functionalities in the system. Therefore, it corresponds to changes in software and hardware components to bring also the system into a better state. Finally, a dynamic reconfiguration will be any automatic action that saves the system, enriches its behavior or also improves its performance at run-time. To our knowledge, this definition covers all the reconfiguration reasons in the manufacturing industry.

**Running example1.***In our FESTO production system, we dynamically apply the automatic reconfiguration to:*

- *save the whole system if hardware faults occur at run-time. Indeed, If the Drill_machine1 (resp, Drill_machine2) is broken, then the drilling operation will be supported by Drill_machine2 (resp, Drill_machine1),*
- *improve the system productivity. Indeed, if the rate of input pieces is increased, then we improve the production from the light to the medium or from the medium to the high mode.*

**Running example2.***In our EnAS system, we apply the reconfiguration for two reasons:*

- *to save the system when hardware problems occur at run-time. For example, if the Gripper G2 is broken, then we have to follow the first production policy by placing only one piece in each tin,*
- *to improve the production when ($nb_{pieces}$/ $nb_{tins+caps}$ > Threshold). In this case, we apply changes in the system architecture and blocks to apply the second policy. According to these examples, the reconfiguration is not*

only applied to resolve hardware problems as proposed in (Al-Safi & Vyatkin, 2007; Brennan, Fletcher & Norrie, 2001) but also to improve the system performance. This new reconfiguration semantic will be a future issue in the manufacturing industry.

## RECONFIGURATION CASES

We classify in this section all the possible reconfiguration forms to be applied on a control system. We distinguish the following forms:

- **First form.** It deals with the change of the application architecture that we consider as a composition of Function Blocks. In this case, we have possibly to add, to remove or also to change the localization of Function Blocks (from one to another device). This reconfiguration form requires to load new (or to unload old, resp) blocks in (from, resp) the memory.

**Running example1.***In our FESTO manufacturing system, we distinguish two architectures:*

- ***First Architecture (Light production).****We implement the system with the first architecture if we apply the light production mode (i.e. number_pieces < Constante2). In this case, the Function Block Drill2 is not loaded in the memory.*
- ***Second Architecture.****We implement the system with the second architecture if we apply the high or also the medium mode (i.e. number_pieces ≥ Constante2). In this case, we load in the memory the Function Blocks Drill1 and Drill2.*

**Running example2.***In our EnAS manufacturing system, we distinguish two architectures:*

- *First Architecture.We implement the system with the first architecture if we follow the first production policy. In this case, we load in the memory the Function Blocks J1_CTL, Belt_CTL and G1_CTL.*
- *Second Architecture .We implement the system with the second architecture if we follow the second production policy. In this case, we load in the memory the Function Blocks J1_CTL, J2_CTL, Belt_CTL and G2_CTL.*

*If we follow the first production policy and $nb_{pieces}/nb_{tins+caps}$ becomes higher than Threshold, then we have to load the function block G2_CTL in the memory to follow the second production policy.*

- **Second form.** It deals with the reconfiguration of the application without changing its architecture (i.e. without loading or unloading Function Blocks). In this case, we apply changes on the internal structure of blocks or on their composition as follows:
  - we change the ECC structure,
  - we add, update or also remove data/events inputs/outputs,
  - we update algorithms,
  - we change the configuration of connections between blocks

**Running example1.***In our FESTO system, we distinguish for the second architecture the following cases:*

- *High production.If number_pieces ≥ Constante1, Then we have to apply an automatic modification on the ECC of Rotat_Disc in order to use the two drilling machines Drill_machine1 and Drill_machine2.*
- *Medium production. If Constante2 ≤ number_pieces < Constante1, Then we have to apply a new modification on the ECC*

*of Rotat_Disc in order to use one of these machines.*

**Running example2.***In our EnAS system, if we follow the second policy and the Jack station J2 is broken, then we have to change the internal behavior (i.e. the ECC structure) of the block J1_CTL to close the tin with a cap once it places only one piece. The tin will be moved directly thereafter to the Gripper G2. In this example, we do not change the application architecture (e.g. loading or unloading blocks) but we just change the behavior of particular blocks.*

- **Third form.** It simply deals with an easy reconfiguration of the application data (i.e. internal data of blocks or global data of the system).

**Running example1.***In our FESTO system, If we apply the Medium production mode (i.e. the second architecture), Then the production periodicity is 30 seconds, whereas If we apply in the same architecture the High mode Then the periodicity is 11 seconds.*

**Running example2.***In our EnAS system, If a hardware problem occurs at run-time, Then we have to change the value of Threshold to a great number max_value. In this case we will not be interested in the performance improvement but in the rescue of the system to guarantee a minimal level of productivity.*

Finally, this classification covers all possible reconfiguration forms to dynamically bring the system behavior into a safe and better state while satisfying user requirements and environment changes.

## AUTOMATIC RECONFIGURATION OF EMBEDDED SYSTEMS

To apply an automatic reconfiguration, we define in this section an agent-based architecture for embedded systems following the Industrial Standard IEC61499. The agent checks the environment evolution and takes into account user requirements to apply reconfiguration scenarios on the system. It is specified with nested NCES supporting all reconfiguration forms. We specify in addition the system blocks with NCES in order to check with the model checker SESA functional and temporal CTL-based properties described in user requirements.

### Architecture of the Reconfiguration Agent

We define the following units that compose in three levels the agent architecture:

- **First level: (Architecture Unit)** this unit checks the system behavior and changes its architecture (add/remove Function Blocks) when particular conditions are satisfied. We note that *Standardized Manager Function Blocks* are used in this unit to load or unload these blocks in the memory (Lewis, 2001).
- **Second level: (Control Unit)**, for a particular *loaded* architecture and according to well defined conditions, this unit:
  - reconfigures FB compositions (i.e. changes the configuration of connections),
  - adds/removes data/event inputs/outputs,
  - reconfigures the internal behavior of blocks (i.e. modification of the ECC structure or the update of algorithms),
- **Third level: (Data Unit)**, this unit updates data if particular conditions are satisfied.

We model the agent with nested state machines in which we specify the Architecture Unit with an Architecture State Machine (denoted by ASM) where each state corresponds to a particular architecture of the application. Therefore, each transition of the ASM corresponds to the load (resp, or unload) of Function Blocks in (resp, or from) the memory. We construct for each state $S$ of the ASM a particular Control State Machine (denoted by CSM) in the Control Unit. This state machine specifies all the reconfiguration forms to possibly apply when the system architecture corresponding to the state $S$ is loaded (i.e. modification of FB compositions or of their internal behavior). Each transition of any CSM has to be fired if particular conditions are satisfied. Finally, the Data unit is specified also with Data State Machines (denoted by DSMs) where each one corresponds to a state of a CSM or the ASM.

**Notation.** we denote in the following by,

- $n_{ASM}$ the number of states in the *ASM* state machine (i.e. the number of possible architectures implementing the system). $ASM_i$ ($i \in [1,n_{ASM}]$) denotes a state of *ASM* to encode a particular architecture (i.e. particular FB network). This state corresponds to a particular *CSM* state machine that we denote by $CSM_i$ ($i \in [1,n_{ASM}]$),
- $n_{CSMi}$ the number of states in $CSM_i$ and let $CSM_{i,j}$ ($j \in [1,n_{CSMi}]$) be a state of $CSM_i$,
- $n_{DSM}$ the number of Data state machines corresponding to possible reconfiguration scenarios of the system. Each state $CSM_{i,j}$ ($j \in [1,n_{CSMi}]$) is associated to a particular *DSM* state machine $DSM_k$ ($k \in [1, n_{DSM}]$).
- $n_{DSMk}$ the number of states in $DSM_k$. $DSM_{k,h}$ ($h \in [1,n_{DSMk}]$) denotes a state of $DSM_k$ and corresponds to one of the following cases:
  - one or more states of a *CSM* state machine,
  - more than one *CSM* state machine,
  - all the *ASM* state machine,

The agent automatically applies at run-time different reconfiguration scenarios where each scenario denoted by *Reconfiguration*$_{i,j,k,h}$ is implemented by a FB network *fbn*$_{i,j,k,h}$ as follows:

- the architecture *ASM*$_i$ is loaded in the memory,
- the control policy is fixed in the state *CSM*$_{i,j}$,
- the data configuration corresponding to the state *DSM*$_{k,h}$ is applied,

**Running example1.***In our FESTO system, we present inFigure 8the nested state machines implementing the Agent that handles automatic reconfigurations to be applied at run-time. The ASM state machine is composed of two states ASM1 and ASM2 corresponding respectively to the first (i.e. the light production mode) and the second (the high and medium modes) architectures. The state machines CSM1 and CSM2 correspond respectively to the states ASM1 and ASM2. In CSM2 state machine, the states CSM21 and CSM22 correspond respectively to the high and the medium production modes (where the second architecture is loaded). To fire a transition from CSM21 into CSM22, the value of number_pieces has to be in [Constante2, Constante1[. We note that the states CSM12 and CSM25 correspond to the blocking problem where the two drilling machines are broken. Finally the state machines DSM1 and DSM2 correspond respectively to the state machines CSM1 and CSM2. In particular, the state DSM21 encodes the periodicity when we apply the high production mode (i.e. the state CSM21 of CSM2).*

**Running example2.***In our EnAS system, we design the agent with nested state machines as depicted inFigure 9. The first level is specified with the ASM where each state defines a particular architecture of the system (i.e. a particular composition of blocks to load in the memory). The state S1 (resp, S2) corresponds to the sec-ond (resp, first) policy where the stations J1, J2 and G2 (resp, only J1 and G1) are loaded in the memory. We associate for each one of these states a CSM in the Control Unit. Finally, the data unit is specified with a DSM defining the values that Threshold takes under well defined conditions. Note that if we follow the second production policy (state S1) and the gripper G2 is broken, then we have to change the policy and also the system architecture by loading the block G1_CTL to remove pieces into Belt1. On the other hand, we associate in the second level for the state S1 the CSM S1 defining the different reconfiguration forms to apply when the first architecture is loaded in the memory. In particular, when the state S11 is active and the Jack station J1 is broken, then we activate the state S12 in which the Jack station J2 is alone running to place only one piece in the tin. In this case, the internal behavior of the block Belt_CTL has to be changed (i.e. the tin has to be transported directly to the station J2). In the same way, if we follow the same policy in the state S11 and the Jack station J2 is broken, then we have to activate the state S13 where the J1 behavior has to be changed to place a piece in the tin that has to be closed too (i.e. the ECC structure of the block J1_CTL has to be reconfigured). Finally, we specify in the data unit a DSM where we change the value of Threshold when the Gripper G1 is broken (we suppose as an example that we are not interested in the system performance when the Gripper G1 is broken).*

## System Behaviors

The different reconfiguration scenarios applied by the agent define all the possible behaviors to follow by the system when well defined conditions are satisfied. In this work, we specify these behaviors with a unique System State Machine (denoted by SSM) where each state corresponds to a particular behavior of a system block when a corresponding input event occurs.

*Figure 8. The architecture of the agent with Nested State Machines*

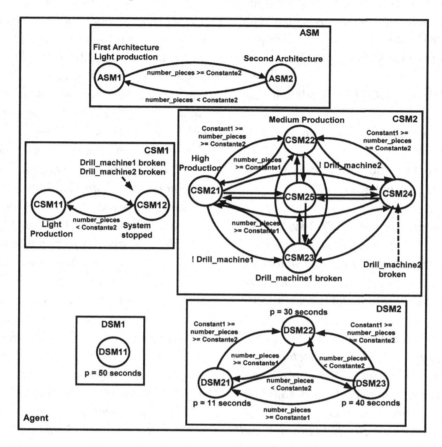

**Running example.***In the EnAS system, we specify in Figure 10 the different system behaviors that we can follow to resolve hardware problems or to improve the system performance. In this example, we distinguish 4 traces encoding 4 different behaviors. The trace trace1 implements the system behavior when the Jack station J1 is broken. The trace trace2 implements the system behavior to apply the second production policy. The trace trace3 implements the system behavior when the Jack station J2 is broken. Finally the last scenario implements the system behavior when the Gripper G2 is broken or when we have to apply the first production policy. Note finally that each state corresponds to a particular behavior of a system block when the corresponding input event occurs.*

## Specification with Net Condition / Event Systems

We use the formalism NCES which provides useful facilities to specify the synchronization between the agent and the system models. We use in particular event/condition signals from the agent to fix the trace to be followed in the SSM (i.e. a reconfiguration) and we use event signals to synchronize the agent state machines: ASM, CSM and DSM.

**Running example.***In our EnAS system, we show inFigure 11the agent and system NCES-based models. The translation from the state machines presented in Figure 9 and Figure 10 into these models is done by adding event/condition signals from the agent to fix the trace to be followed in*

*Figure 9. Behavior of the reconfiguration agent*

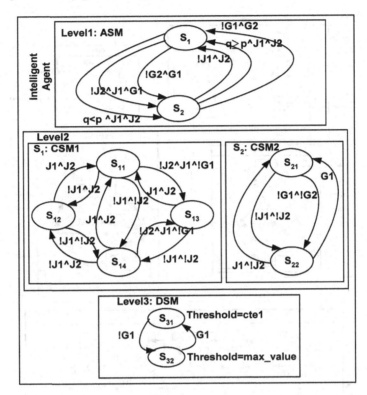

the SSM. According to user requirements, we specify temporal intervals in the transitions of the system model. When the Jack station J1 is broken, the agent activates the place P12 and sends a condition signal to activate the trace trace1 in the system. Note that the architecture and control state machines are communicating by event signals to synchronize the agent behavior. We note finally that the state "Well" represents a deadlock in the system when the Jack stations J1 and J2 are broken.

# VERIFICATION OF CONTROL SYSTEMS FOLLOWING THE STANDARD IEC 61499

We verify functional and extra-functional properties on a reconfigurable control system following the Standard IEC61499 (Artist-Project, 2003). We limit our research work to two types of extra-functional properties: *Temporal* and *QoS* properties that we specify according to the temporal logic CTL and we verify with the model checker

*Figure 10. The system state machine: SSM*

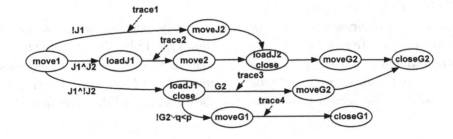

*Figure 11. Design of the reconfigurable system with the NCES formalism*

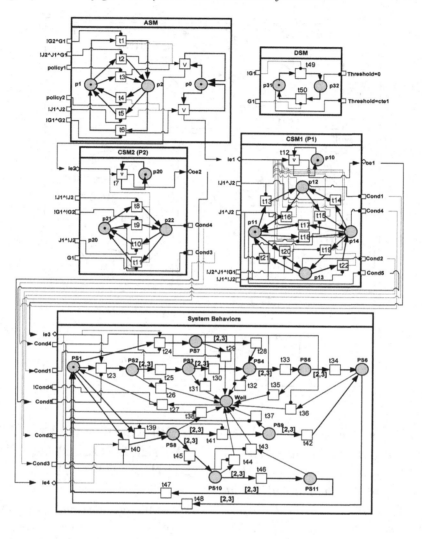

SESA on the reachability graphs generated for all reconfiguration scenarios. The model checking is based on a cross product computation of each reachability graph and the automata of the ECTL (or TCTL) formulae.

**Running example.** *In our EnAS system, we apply the model checker SESA to verify properties on its Function Blocks that implement the different reconfiguration scenarios. We generate with this tool different reachability graphs corresponding to these scenarios. In Figure 12, we present the graph corresponding to the second production*

*policy where the states State1,...State17 encode the behavior of the agent as well as the system blocks when $nb_{pieces}/nb_{tins+caps} > Threshold$. To generate this graph, we only fire the transition t3 and the rest of transitions in the ASM are not firable.*

## Verification of Functional Properties

We verify functional properties on the state machines specifying the agent to prove the correct adaptation of the system to any change in the environment. Moreover, we verify the functional correctness of all the reconfiguration scenarios

*Figure 12. Reachability graph of the second production policy*

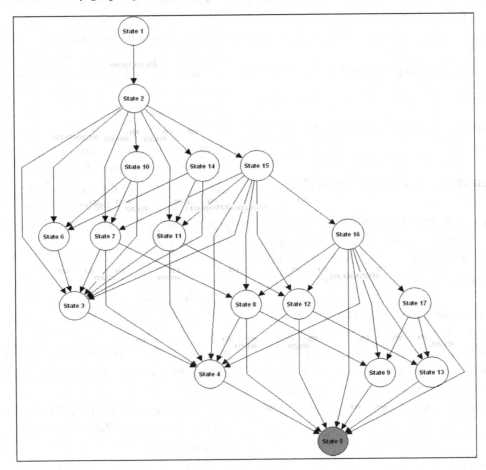

in *SSM* to prove its correction according to user requirements.

**Running example.***In our EnAS system, we check functional properties on the state machines encoding the agent. In particular, we have to check if the system applies the second policy whereas the Gripper station G2 is broken. We propose the following ECTL formula:*

$$z_0 \models AGAt_1 XPS_2$$

*This formula checks with SESA that whenever a state transition fulfilling t1 is possible (i.e. G2 is*

*broken), this transition leads to a successor state in which PS2 holds true in the reachability graph (i.e. we apply the second production policy). This formula is proved to be False. The following formula is proved to be True:*

$$z_0 \models AGAt_1 XPS_8$$

*Indeed, whenever the Gripper G2 is broken, the place $PS_8$ of SSM is activated. On the other hand, to check the behavioral order of the SSM when the Gripper station G2 is broken (i.e. Load a piece and Close the tin in the Jack station J1, then move the Belt to the Gripper station G1 to* remove the product to Belt1), we propose the following ECTL formula,

$$z_0 \vDash AGAt_{40}XAFEt_{45}XAFEt_{46}XTRUE$$

*This formula is proved to be True with the model checker SESA.*

## Verification of Temporal Properties

We verify also temporal properties on the different reconfiguration scenarios of a control system following the Standard IEC 61499. We use in this case the logic TCTL to specify these properties.

**Running example.** *In our EnAS platform, we check temporal properties on the SSM model. When the Gripper station G2 is broken, we have to check if the duration to activate the Gripper station G1 does not exceed 5 time units. Therefore, we apply the following formula:*

$$z_0 \vDash AF[2,5]PS_{11}$$

*This formula is proved to be True with the SESA Model checker. To check if the Gripper station is reachable in 3 time units, we have to verify the following formula:*

$$z_0 \vDash EF[2,3]PS_{11}$$

*It is proved to be False with the SESA model checker.*

## Verification of QoS Properties

The last property to verify according to user requirements is the QoS where we check if the system provides the minimal accepted quality at run-time. We use in this case the CTL logic to specify the QoS formulae.

**Running example.** *In our EnAS platform, we verify if the system provides the minimal accepted QoS. According to the value of $nb_{pieces}/nb_{tins+caps}$, we have to verify if the system applies the best production policy. We propose the following ECTL formula,*

$$z0 \vDash AGAt_3XPS_{11}$$

*Indeed, we have to verify if $nb_{pieces}/nb_{tins+caps} \leq$ Threshold (i.e. the first production policy has to be applied), then the fourth trace of SSM has to be activated (i.e. the state $PS_{11}$ has to be activated). By applying the SESA tool, we find that this formula is True.*

## REAL-TIME ASSIGNMENT

Once the verification of functional and extra-functional properties on the whole reconfigurable system is done, the next step to be addressed is the assignment of the FB network $fbn_{i,j,k,h}$ that implements each reconfiguration scenario $Reconfig_{i,j,k,h}$ ($i \in [1,n_{ASM}], j \in [1,n_{CSMi}], k \in [1,n_{DSM}]$ and $h \in [1,n_{DSMk}]$) into a set of OS tasks of the execution environment. In the following, we assume that $fbn_{i,j,k,h}$ is distributed on a set of resources (denoted by *Resources*) located in a device. To assign the network, we transform the corresponding blocks into a system of actions with precedence constraints in order to exploit previous results in scheduling. We analyze the schedulability of these actions in each resource $Res \in Resources$ and we construct for $Res$ a reachability graph to verify temporal properties (end-to-end bounds). If it is feasible, then we generate a pre-scheduling defining the sequencing of the Function Blocks in $Res$. If all resources are feasible, then we transform the corresponding pre-schedulings into OS tasks (i.e. one resource is transformed into one OS task). To complete the temporal verification of bounds, we check the on-line preemptive feasibility of these tasks by applying a schedulability analysis. This methodology of assignment has different advantages. It reduces the number of tasks to schedule by regrouping blocks of resources in a single task. This advantage is required by several Real Time Operating Systems which restrict such number (Takada & Sakamura, 1995). Thanks to this regrouping, the complexity of the schedulability analysis of OS tasks is reduced and the context switching is minimized at run-time. We present in Figure 13 the different steps to follow in order to assign a reconfigurable control application into feasible OS tasks of the execution environment.

## Formalization of a FB Network

We transform each FB network corresponding to a particular reconfiguration scenario into a system of actions with precedence constraints in which an action is a FB execution when a corresponding input event occurs. Moreover, a trace is a sequence of actions under causality relation in the network.

## Action of a Reconfiguration Scenario

We define an action $act_{i,j,k,h}$ the execution of a FB belonging to $fbn_{i,j,k,h}$ (execution of one or several algorithms) when a particular input event $ie_{i,j,k,h}$ occurs. We denote in the following by $\sigma_{i,j,k,h}$ (resp, $\sigma^{Res}_{i,j,k,h}$) the set of the application actions (resp, the set of actions in a resource $Res$) where we characterize $act_{i,j,k,h} \in \sigma_{i,j,k,h}$ as follows:

- $WCET(act_{i,j,k,h})$ (resp, $BCET(act_{i,j,k,h})$): the Worst (resp, Best) Case Execution Time of the sequence of algorithms corresponding to $ie_{i,j,k,h}$.

- $pred(act_{i,j,k,h})$: the set of actions to execute in the application before the $act_{i,j,k,h}$ execution. These actions belong to FBs producing the output events linked to $ie_{i,j,k,h}$.

- $succ(act_{i,j,k,h})$: a set of action sets. Each actions set corresponds to a possible execution scenario (ie. only one action set between all ones is performed). The actions of a set have to be executed once the execution of $act_{i,j,k,h}$ is finished. These actions belong to blocks activated once the treatment corresponding to $ie_{i,j,k,h}$ finishes.

- $(r_{i,j,k,h}; p_{i,j,k,h}; d_{i,j,k,h})$: the two first parameters characterize the activation first time and the periodicity of $act_{i,j,k,h}$ (Stankovic, Spuri & Ramamritham, 2005). They should be processed while taking into account the execution of $pred(act_{i,j,k,h})$. The deadline $d_{i,j,k,h}$ defines the latest completion date of the execution. To respect temporal bounds, it should be processed while taking into account the deadlines of the $act_{i,j,k,h}$ successors.

Let $first(\sigma_{i,j,k,h})$ (resp, $last(\sigma_{i,j,k,h})$) be a subset of $\sigma_{i,j,k,h}$ such as each action is with no predecessors (resp successors) in $\sigma_{i,j,k,h}$. In particular, we denote by $first(\sigma^{Res}_{i,j,k,h})$ (resp, $last(\sigma^{Res}_{i,j,k,h})$) a subset of $\sigma^{Res}_{i,j,k,h}$ such as each action is with no predecessors (resp successors) in $\sigma^{Res}_{i,j,k,h}$. We denote in addition by $act^{p,q}_{i,j,k,h}$ the $q$-$th$ instance of the action $act^{p}_{i,j,k,h}$ belonging to the FB network $fbn_{i,j,k,h}$.

**Running example.** *In our FESTO system, the successors of the action Rotat of the Function Block Rotat_Disc are as follows:*

- *In the first reconfiguration architecture where only the Function Block Drill is loaded in memory, we activate this block* *when we finish the execution of the action Rotat: $succ(Rotat_{1,1,1,1}) = \{Drill_{1,1,1,1}\}$*

- *In the second reconfiguration architecture where the two blocks Drill1 and Drill2 are loaded in memory, the successors of the action Rotat are as follows,*
  - *If we follow the High production mode, we have to drill two pieces by the machines Drill_machine1 and Drill_machine2. In this case, $succ(Rotat_{2,1,2,1}) = \{Drill1_{2,1,2,1}, Drill2_{2,1,2,1}\}$,*
  - *If we follow the Medium production mode, we have to drill one piece by the machine Drill_machine1 or Drill_machine2. In this case, $succ(Rotat2,1,2,1) = \{\{Drill1_{2,1,2,1}\}, \{Drill2_{2,1,2,1}\}\}$.*

## Trace of a Reconfiguration Scenario

By considering precedence constraints between actions in $fbn_{i,j,k,h}$, we define a trace $tr_{i,j;k;h}$ of $\sigma^{Res}_{i,j,k,h}$ the following sequence,

$$tr_{i,j,k,h} = act^0_{i,j,k,h}, \ldots, act^{n-1}_{i,j,k,h} \text{ such as,}$$

- $\forall p \in [1, n-1], act^{p-1}_{i,j,k,h} = pred(act^p_{i,j,k,h}),$
- $act^0_{i,j,k,h} \in first(\sigma^{Res}_{i,j,k,h})$ and $act^{n-1}_{i,j,k,h} \in last(\sigma^{Res}_{i,j,k,h})$

The execution of the trace $tr_{i,j,k,h}$ has to satisfy an end-to-end response time bound $eertb(tr_{i,j,k,h})$ according to user requirements. In this paper, we consider non reentry traces (Klein, Ralya, Pollack, Obenza & Harbour, 1993): *"the execution of the z-th instance of the trace must not start before the execution end of the (z -1) -th one"*. Therefore, the period of $act^0_{i,j,k,h}$ is greater than $eertb(tr_{i,j,k,h})$. To satisfy all the considered bounds in user requirements, we process deadlines for the different actions of traces in $fbn_{i,j,k,h}$ and we process in particular for the actions of the trace $tr_{i,j,k,h}$ the corresponding deadlines,

- The deadline of the last action $act^{n-1}_{i,j,k,h}$ is as follows: $d(act^{n-1}_{i,j,k,h}) = eertb(tr_{i,j,k,h})$
- The deadline of any action $d(act^p_{i,j,k,h})$, $p \in [0, n-2]$ is processed so that its successors meet also their deadlines as follows, $\forall p \in [0, n-2]$,

$$d(actpi,j,k,h) =$$

$$\min_{s \in succ(act^p_{i,j,k,h})}\{\min_{act^q_{i,j,k,h} \in s}_{(d(act^d_{i,j,k,h}) \leq d(act^q_{i,j,k,h}) act\, d\, i,j,k,h \in s)}\{d(act^q_{i,j,k,h}) - WCET(act^d_{i,j,k,h})\}\}$$

**Running example.***In our FESTO system, we present a trace of actions implementing the second architecture where the Light mode is applied,*

$$tr_{1,1,1,1} = Send_{1,1,1,1}, Conv_{1,1,1,1}, Occ_{1,1,1,1}, Test_{1,1,1,1}, Elev_{1,1,1,1}, Rot_{1,1,1,1}, Drill1_{1,1,1,1}, Che_{1,1,1,1}, Ev_{1,1,1,1}.$$

*This trace has to satisfy the following bound according to user requirements described above: $eertb(tr_{1,1,1,1}) = 35$. On the other hand, the deadline of the action Rot of the Function Block Rotat_Disc depends on the applied production mode.*

- *If we follow the High mode, the two actions Drill1 and Drill2 are executed, therefore, $d(Rot_{2,1,2,1}) = d(Drill2_{2,1,2,1}) - WCET(Drill2_{2,1,2,1}) - WCET(Drill1_{2,1,2,1})$*
- *If we follow the Medium mode, only one is executed at the same time, therefore, $d(Rot_{2,2,2,2}) = \min\{d(Drill2_{2,2,2,2}) - WCET(Drill2_{2,2,2,2}); d(Drill1_{2,2,2,2}) - WCET(Drill1_{2,2,2,2})\}$*

On the other hand, we temporally characterize the actions of $tr_{i,j,k,h}$ as follows: $\forall x \in [1, n-1]$,

*Figure 13. Assignment of Reconfigurable Control Systems into OS tasks of the execution environment*

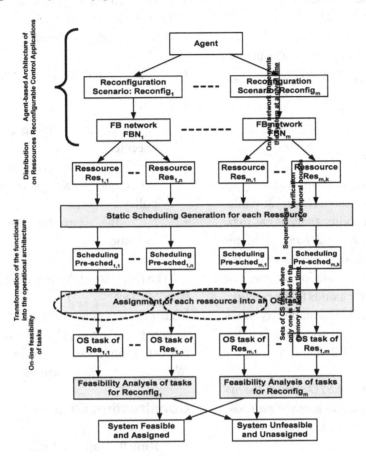

- $r^x_{i,j,k,h} = r^0_{i,j,k,h} + \sum^{d=x-1}_{d=0} BCET(act^d_{i,j,k,h})$: the earliest activation time of the action $act^x_{i,j,k,h}$ in the reconfiguration scenario $Reconfig_{i,j,k,h}$ occurs when each previous action is executed as soon as possible,

- $p^x_{i,j,k,h} = p^0_{i,j,k,h}$: by considering non-reentry traces, all the actions of $tr_{i,j,k,h}$ have the same period.

**Running example.** *In our FESTO system, we characterize in particular the action $Test_{1,1,1,1}$ of the trace $tr_{1,1,1,1}$ that implements the light production mode,*

- $r(Test_{1,1,1,1}) = r(Send_{1,1,1,1}) + BCET(Send_{1,1,1,1})$

- $+ BCET(Conv_{1,1,1,1}) + BCET(Occ_{1,1,1,1})$,
- $p(Test_{1,1,1,1}) = p(Send_{1,1,1,1})$.

## Assignment of a Resource

To assign the blocks of $fbn_{i,j,k,h}$ and located in the resource $Res$ ($Res \in Resources$) into an OS task, we verify at first time the corresponding temporal bounds by generating a reachability graph in a well defined Hyper Period. We apply the scheduling policy "Earliest Deadline First" to construct this graph (Stankovic, Spuri & Ramamritham, 2005) and if it is feasible, then we generate a pre-scheduling as a Direct Acyclic Graph that we assign into an OS task of the execution environment.

## Hyper Period Evaluation for a Reconfiguration Scenario

Let $lcm_{i,j,k,h}$ be the least common multiple of periods of actions in $first(\sigma^{Res}_{i,j,k,h})$. Let $act^{max}_{i,j,k,h} = \{r_{max}, p_{max}, d_{max}\}$ and $act^{min}_{i,j,k,h} = \{r_{min}, p_{min}, d_{min}\}$ be two actions of $first(\sigma^{Res}_{i,j,k,h})$ such as,

$$\forall\ act^{a}_{i,j,k,h} \in first(\sigma^{Res}_{i,j,k,h});\ r_{min} \leq r_a \leq r_{max}$$

By exploiting a previous result on the hyper period for asynchronous systems (Leung & Whitehead, 1982), the schedulability analysis has to be done in $HP^{Res}_{i,j,k,h} = [r_{min}; r_{max} + 2*lcm_{i,j,k,h}]$. In this hyper period, two behavioral modes exist: the stationary mode and the non-stationary one. The non-stationary mode corresponds to the resource behavior during $[r_{min}, r_{max}]$. The stationary mode is performed periodically and corresponds to the behavior during $[r_{max}, r_{max} + 2*lcm_{i,j,k,h}]$.

**Running example.***In our FESTO system, the hyper period for Resource1 is calculated for all possible reconfiguration scenarios. In particular:*

- $HP^{Resource1}_{2,1,2,1} = [0, 22]$ *for the High production mode,*
- $HP^{Resource1}_{2,2,2,2} = [0, 60]$ *for the Medium production mode,*
- $HP^{Resource1}_{1,1,1,1} = [0; 100]$ *for the Light mode.*

## Reachability Graph of a Resource for a Reconfiguration Scenario

The reachability graph $G^{Res}_{i,j,k,h}$ presents all possible execution scenarios of $fbn_{i,j,k,h}$ blocks located in the resource $Res$ when $Reconfiguration_{i,j,k,h}$ is applied. Each trajectory of this graph presents a scheduling of system traces in $Res$. A state $C_{i,j,k,h}$ of a trajectory contains a selected instance of action to execute among all active ones. We apply the static Earliest Deadline First policy (denoted by $EDF$) to perform the selection (Stankovic, Spuri & Ramamritham, 2005). A state $C_{i,j,k,h}$ of $G^{Res}_{i,j,k,h}$ is characterized as follows,

$$C_{i,j,k,h} = \{S_{i,j,k,h},\ act^{m,n}_{i,j,k,h},\ t_{i,j,k,h}\}\ \text{where,}$$

- $S_{i,j,k,h}$: a set of instances of actions to execute,
- $act^{m,n}_{i,j,k,h}$: the selected instance among all active ones of $S_{i,j,k,h}$ according to the $EDF$ policy,
- $t_{i,j,k,h}$: the start time of the $act^{m,n}_{i,j,k,h}$ execution.

The first state of the graph is denoted by $C^{0}_{i,j,k,h} = \{S^{0}_{i,j,k,h},\ act^{min,1}_{i,j,k,h},\ t^{0}_{i,j,k,h}\}$ where $S^{0}_{i,j,k,h}$ contains instances of actions belonging to $first(\sigma^{Res}_{i,j,k,h})$. To construct the reachability graph, the following rules are applied recursively for each state $C_{i,j,k,h} = \{S_{i,j,k,h},\ act^{m,n}_{i,j,k,h},\ t_{i,j,k,h}\}$ without a successor:

## Construction Of $G^{Res}_{i,j,k,h}$

- **Rule 0: stop condition.**

If $t_{i,j,k,h} > r^{max} + 2*lcm_{i,j,k,h}$, Then we reach the limit of $HP^{Res}_{i,j,k,h}$ and the construction of the current trajectory is stopped,

- **Rule 1: Verification of constraints.**

If there exists an instance $act^{p,q}_{i,j,k,h} \in S_{i,j,k,h}$ missing its deadline, then the FB network is unfeasible in the resource $Res$. Otherwise, an instance $act^{m,n}_{i,j,k,h}$ ($act^{m}_{i,j,k,h}$ belongs to $tr_{i,j,k,h}$ in the resource $Res$) is selected by applying the static $EDF$ policy,

- **Rule 2: Construction of new states.**

For each set of $succ(act^{m,n}_{i,j,k,h})$, a new state of $G^{Res}_{i,j,k,h}$ has to be constructed.

If $act^{m}_{i,j,k,h}$ belongs to $last(tr_{i,j,k,h})$, then a new

*Figure 14. Reachability graphs of Resource2 for the High and Medium production modes*

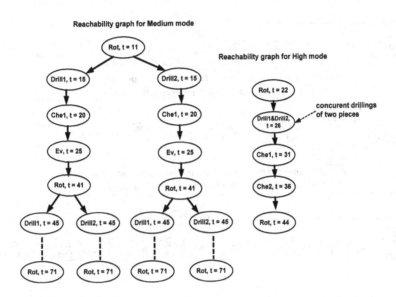

instance of $tr_{i,j,k,h}$ is started,

**Running example.***In our FESTO system, we construct the reachability graph of each resource for each reconfiguration scenario. InFigure 14, we present reachability graphs of Resource2 for the High and the Medium production modes. These graphs are constructed respectively in $HP^{Resource}_{21,2,1}$ and $HP^{Resource2}_{2,2,2}$. In the first mode, we have to execute the two actions Drill1 and Drill2 at t = 26 time units to drill two pieces by Drill_machine1 and Drill_machine2, whereas in the second mode we execute only one of the two actions at t = 15 time units. Finally, we note that initialization actions are not considered in these graphs.*

## Generation of a Resource Pre-scheduling for a Reconfiguration Scenario

If the reachability graph is correctly constructed in the hyper period $HP^{Res}_{i,j,k,h}$ (i.e. all temporal properties are satisfied), then a static scheduling $Stat^{Res}_{i,j,k,h}$ is generated to be used by the OS when the current reconfiguration scenario

$Reconfiguration_{i,h,k,h}$ is applied at run-time. This scheduling is a DAG where each trajectory specifies a possible execution of the system. A state of the graph specifies the execution start time of an action instance selected in the corresponding node of the reachability graph.

**Running example.***In our FESTO system, we generate a pre-scheduling from each reachability graph that we construct in a resource for a particular reconfiguration scenario. InFigure 15, we show portions of pre-schedulings of Resource1 and Resource2 for the High and the Medium production modes. These pre-schedulings are generated in well defined Hyper Periods according to the followed production modes.*

## Assignment of Function Blocks into OS Tasks

We propose a technique to assign the pre-scheduling $Stat^{Res}_{i,j,k,h}$ defining the sequencing of Function Blocks in $Res$ (when the reconfiguration scenario $Reconfiguration_{i,j,k,h}$ is applied) into an OS task. By considering the conditional structure of $Stat^{Res}_{i,j,k,h}$, we exploit the recurring task model

*Figure 15. Pre-schedulings of Resource1 and Resource2 for the High and Medium production modes*

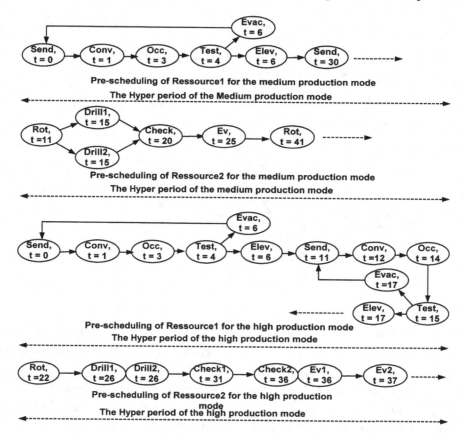

to apply the assignment (Baruah, 2003). This model was introduced to represent conditional real time codes.

**Recurring task:** *a recurring task Γ is characterized by a task graph G(Γ) and a period P(Γ). The task graph G(Γ) is a Direct Acyclic Graph (DAG) with a unique source vertex (denoted by τ⁰) and a unique sink vertex. Each vertex of this DAG represents a subtask (denoted by τ) and each edge represents a possible flow of control. A vertex of Γ is characterized by a WCET and a deadline d. In addition, an edge (τ, τ') is characterized by a real number p(τ,τ') denoting the minimum amount of time that must elapse after vertex τ is triggered (t(τ)) and before vertex τ' can be triggered (t(τ')) (Baruah, 2003).*

In this paper, we encode the graph structure with the set $pred(\tau)$ (resp, $succ(\tau)$) that defines subtasks of Γ such as only one has to be executed before (resp, after) τ . By considering two behavioral modes in the hyper period $HP^{Res}_{i,j,k,h}$, the pre-scheduling $Stat^{Res}_{i,j,k,h}$ has to be transformed into two recurring tasks $\Gamma^{Res}_{i,j,k,h}$ and $\Gamma'^{Res}_{i,j,k,h}$. The task $\Gamma^{Res}_{i,j,k,h}$ implements the stationary behavior whereas the task $\Gamma'^{Res}_{i,j,k,h}$ implements the non-stationary one. Note that $\Gamma^{Res}_{i,j,k,h}$ is periodic with the same period of the stationary mode. A straight-forward transformation consists in associating each subtask to an action instance. Nevertheless, this transformation produces recurring tasks with several subtasks. This transformation increases the complexity of the schedulability analysis (Baruah, 2003). To control this complexity, we merge as a solution a sequence of instances of actions into a unique subtask. To verify all bounds during the feasibility analysis of these OS tasks, an instance $act^{a,b}_{i,j,k,h} \in Stat^{Res}_{i,j,k,h}$ such as $act^a_{i,j,k,h} \in last(\sigma^{Res}_{i,j,k,h})$ must be the last instance of a subtask $\tau_{i,j,k,h}$. According to the EDF policy, the deadline of $\tau_{i,j,k,h}$ is then the deadline of $act^{a,b}_{i,j,k,h}$.

**Notations.** *In the following, $stat\_succ(act^{a,b}_{i,j,k,h})$ (resp $stat\_pred(act^{a,b}_{i,j,k,h})$) denotes the set of instances following (resp preceding) the instance $act^{a,b}_{i,j,k,h}$ in $Stat^{Res}_{i,j,k,h}$.*

A subtask $\tau_{i,j,k,h}$ of $\Gamma^{Res}_{i,j,k,h}$ has to be implemented as follows,

$$\tau_{i,j,k,h} = act^{0,c}_{i,j,k,h}, act^{1,g}_{i,j,k,h} \ldots\ldots, act^{d-1,f}_{i,j,k,h} \text{ such as,}$$

- $\forall \ y \ \in \ [0,d\text{-}2]$, $stat\_succ(act^{y,p}_{i,j,k,h}) = \{act^{y+1,q}_{i,j,k,h}\}$: the sequence implementing $\tau_{i,j,k,h}$ is a sequence of instances in $Stat^{Res}_{i,j,k,h}$,
- $act^{d-1}_{i,j,k,h}$ is an action without successors in $\sigma^{Res}_{i,j,k,h}$ or $act^{d-1,f}_{i,j,k,h}$ has more than one successor in $Stat^{Res}_{i,j,k,h}$,

$$act^{d-1}_{i,j,k,h} \in last(\sigma^{Res}_{i,j,k,h}) \text{ or } cardinality(stat\_succ(act^{d-1,f}_{i,j,k,h})) > 1$$

Let $first(\tau_{i,j,k,h})$ (resp $last(\tau_{i,j,k,h})$) be the first (resp last) instance of the subtask $\tau_{i,j,k,h}$. Moreover, let $first\_stat(Stat^{Res}_{i,j,k,h})$ be the set of instances in $Stat^{Res}_{i,j,k,h}$ with no predecessors to execute in the stationary mode. We apply the following rules to construct the task $\Gamma^{Res}_{i,j,k,h}$. The first rule constructs the first subtask $\tau^0_{i,j,k,h}$ of the recurring task $\Gamma^{Res}_{i,j,k,h}$, whereas the second one is applied recursively to construct the other subtasks,

## Rule 0. Construction of the First Subtask $\tau^0_{i,j,k,h}$ in $\Gamma^{Res}_{i,j,k,h}$.

If $cardinality(first\_stat(Stat^{Res}_{i,j,k,h})) = 1$, Then, $\{\tau^0_{i,j,k,h}\} = first\_stat(Stat^{Res}_{i,j,k,h})$

Otherwise, a virtual subtask $\tau^0_{i,j,k,h}$ in $G(\Gamma^{Res}_{i,j,k,h})$ is constructed as follows:

- $WCET(\tau^0_{i,j,k,h}) = 0$,
- For each state $act^{a,b}_{i,j,k,h} \in first\_stat(Stat^{Res}_{i,j,k,h})$, a subtask $\tau^z_{i,j,k,h}$ such as $(\tau^0_{i,j,k,h}, \tau^z_{i,j,k,h}) \in G(\Gamma^{Res}_{i,j,k,h})$ and $p(\tau^0_{i,j,k,h}, \tau^z_{i,j,k,h}) = 0$ is constructed,

The triggering time of the subtask $\tau^0_{i,j,k,h}$ is equal to the minimum of the execution start times of instances in $first\_stat(Stat^{Res}_{i,j,k,h})$:

$$t(\tau^0_{i,j,k,h}) = \min\{t(act^{a,b}_{i,j,k,h}), act^{a,b}_{i,j,k,h} \in first\_stat(Stat^{Res}_{i,j,k,h})\}$$

Rule 1. construction of subtasks.

Let $\tau^a_{i,j,k,h}$ be a subtask of $\Gamma^{Res}_{i,j,k,h}$ such as $last(\tau^a_{i,j,k,h})$ has a successor in $Stat^{Res}_{i,j,k,h}$,

$$\exists \ act^{0,q}_{i,j,k,h} \in Stat^{Res}_{i,j,k,h}, act^{0,q}_{i,j,k,h} \in stat\_succ(last(\tau^a_{i,j,k,h}))$$

Let $\tau^b_{i,j,k,h}$ be the successor of $\tau^a_{i,j,k,h}$ in $\Gamma^{Res}_{i,j,k,h}$ $(\tau^b_{i,j,k,h} \in succ(\tau^a_{i,j,k,h}))$,

$$\tau^b_{i,j,k,h} = act^{0,q}_{i,j,k,h}, act^{1,w}_{i,j,k,h} \ldots., act^{d-1,p}_{i,j,k,h} \text{ such as,}$$

$$act^{d-1,p}_{i,j,k,h} \text{ in } last(\sigma^{Res}_{i,j,k,h}) \text{ or } cardinality(stat\_succ(act^{d-1,p}_{i,j,k,h})) > 1$$

By considering the recurring task concept as presented in (Baruah, 2003), the following temporal constraints for this new subtask are defined,

- The ready time $t(\tau^b_{i,j,k,h})$ is equal to the earliest possible execution time of the instance $act^{0,q}_{i,j,k,h}$. This time has to take into account the execution of the $act^{0,q}_{i,j,k,h}$ predecessors in $Stat^{Res}_{i,j,k,h}$ and we characterize it as follows,

$$t(\tau^b_{i,j,k,h}) = max\{r(act^{0,q}_{i,j,k,h});$$
$$max^a_{\tau_{i,j,k,h}=pred(\tau_{i,j,k,h})}\{t(\tau^a_{i,j,k,h})+\Sigma_{act^{p,w}_{i,j,k,h} \in \tau^a_{i,j,k,h}}$$
$$BCET(act^p_{i,j,k,h})\}\}$$

- The minimum amount of time $p(\tau^a_{i,j,k,h}, \tau^b_{i,j,k,h})$ is classically equal to the difference between the triggering times of $\tau^b_{i,j,k,h}$ and $\tau^a_{i,j,k,h}$: $p_b = t(\tau^b_{i,j,k,h}) - t(\tau^a_{i,j,k,h})$,
- The deadline $d_b$, corresponds to the deadline of the last instance $act^{d-1,p}_{i,j,k,h}$ of $\tau^b_{i,j,k,h}$,
- The execution requirement $WCET(\tau^b_{i,j,k,h})$ is the sum of the WCETs of the $\tau^b_{i,j,k,h}$ actions,

Finally, we apply the same method to construct the recurring task $\Gamma'^{Res}_{i,j,k,h}$ implementing the non-stationary behavior of the resource *Res* when *Reconfiguration*$_{i,j,k,h}$ is applied by the Agent.

**Running example.** *In our FESTO system, we assign the Function Blocks of each resource for each particular production mode into an OS task. Figure 16 shows the OS tasks* $\Gamma^{Resource1}_{2,2,2,2}$ *and* $\Gamma^{Resource2}_{2,2,2,2}$ *implementing the system in the stationary behavior when the medium production mode is applied by the agent. We show in Figure 17 the OS tasks* $\Gamma^{Resource1}_{2,1,2,1}$ *and* $\Gamma^{Resource2}_{2,1,2,1}$ *implementing the system in the stationary behavior when the high production mode is applied.*

## Verification of OS tasks for a Reconfiguration Scenario

At this step, the FB network $fbn_{i,j,k,h}$ distributed on resources of the set *Resources* is assigned into *independent* OS tasks of the execution environment (each resource is assigned into a recurring task). By considering the transformation technique, the precedence constraints between FB actions of $\sigma^{Res}_{i,j,k,h}$ are not lost. Indeed, the temporal characterization of tasks preserves such dependencies. We apply the schedulability condition defined in

(Baruah, 2003) to check the preemptive on-line feasibility of the tasks implementing $fbn_{i,j,k,h}$ when *Reconfiguration*$_{i,j,k,h}$ is applied. This condition has to be applied in a fixed hyper-period $hp$ as follows,

$$hp_{i,j,k,h} = [0; \Sigma_{\Gamma^{Res}_{i,j,k,h} \in S} 2*E(\Gamma^{Res}_{i,j,k,h}) / 1 - \Sigma_{\Gamma^{Res}_{i,j,k,h} \in S} \rho_{ave}(\Gamma^{Res}_{i,j,k,h})] \text{ where,}$$

- $S$: the set of the recurring tasks of $fbn_{i,j,k,h}$ to validate,
- $E(\Gamma^{Res}_{i,j,k,h})$: denotes the maximum possible cumulative execution requirement on any path from the source node to the sink node of the task graph $G(\Gamma^{Res}_{i,j,k,h})$,
- $\rho_{ave}(\Gamma^{Res}_{i,j,k,h})$: denotes the quantity $E(\Gamma^{Res}_{i,j,k,h})/P(\Gamma^{Res}_{i,j,k,h})$.

The schedulability condition indicates that the system S is feasible if and only if,

$$\forall t \in hp_{i,j,k,h}, \Sigma_{\Gamma Res i,j,k,h \in S} \Gamma^{Res}_{i,j,k,h}.dbf(t) \leq t$$

where, $\Gamma^{Res i,j,k,h}.dbf(t)$ is a function accepting as argument a non negative real number $t$. This function processes the maximum cumulative execution requirement by jobs of $\Gamma^{Res}_{i,j,k,h}$ having both ready times and deadlines within any time interval of duration $t$. Finally, note that (Baruah, 2003) proposes an interesting technique to compute this function in the hyper period $hp_{i,j,k,h}$.

## Generalization: Verification and Assignment of Reconfigurable Control Systems

We generalize the assignment of the FB networks that implement the system in the different reconfiguration scenarios into sets of OS tasks. Each set is to load in memory by the agent if the corresponding reconfiguration scenario is applied.

*Figure 16. The OS tasks implementing the system in the Medium Production Mode*

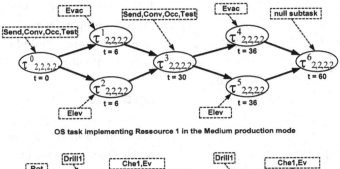

OS task implementing Ressource 1 in the Medium production mode

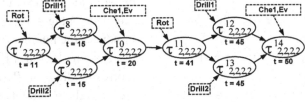

OS task implementing Ressource 2 in the Medium production mode

## Algorithm

To assign a reconfigurable control system into the execution environment, we have to verify end-to-end response time bounds on the FB network $fbn_{i,j,k,h}$ corresponding to each reconfiguration scenario $Reconfiguration_{i,j,k,h}$ ($i \in [1,n_{ASM}]$, $j \in [1,n_{CSMi}]$, $k \in [1; n_{DSM}]$ and $h \in [1; n_{DSMk}]$). This network is distributed on several resources and we have to construct if possible for each one of them a pre-scheduling. If it is feasible, then we assign this pre-scheduling into an OS task that we have to check its on-line feasibility. Finally, if all the FB networks corresponding to the different reconfiguration scenarios are feasible and correctly assigned, then the whole reconfigurable control system is feasible and correctly assigned.

*Algorithm. Verification and Assignment*

*Figure 17. The OS tasks implementing the system in the High Production Mode*

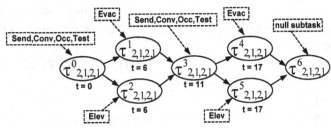

OS task implementing Ressource 1 in the High production mode

OS task implementing Ressource 2 in the High production mode

```
For each Architecture ASM_i; i ∈
[1, n_ASM],
  For each Control policy CSM_i;j ;
j ∈ [1,n_CSMi ],
  For each Data configuration
DSM_k;h; h ∈ [1, n_DSMk ] such as
DSM_k = Data(CSM_i;j),
    Construction Of G^Res_i,j,k,h for
each Res ∈ Resources,
    If a deadline is violated in
fbn_i,j,k,h,
    Then Display(the System is
infeasible),
    Else Generation Of a Pre-
scheduling for each Res ∈ Re-
sources,
    Assignment into an OS task
for each Res ∈ Resources,
    If all constructed OS tasks
meet their deadlines,
      Then Display(fbn_i,j,k,h is cor-
rectly checked and assigned into
the
      execution environment),
    Else Display(the system in
infeasible),
Display(the Reconfigurable sys-
tem is correctly checked and as-
signed),
```

End Algorithm.

To compute the algorithm complexity, we define $n$ a majoration of

$n_{ASM}$,
$\max\{n_{CSMi}, i \in [1, nASM]\}$,
$\max\{n_{DSMk}; k \, 2 \, [1, nDSM]\}$,

The complexity of the algorithm is then in $O(n3)$. In our research group at the Martin Luther University, we developed the tool *X-Reconfig* supporting this algorithm for the verification and assignment of reconfigurable control systems fol-

lowing the standard IEC61499. In addition to the FESTO system, we tested this tool on the EnAS demonstrator and we ask the reader to contact our group for more detailed explanations and documentations (*http://aut.informatik.uni-halle.de*).

## Discussion

The approach that we propose to assign a FB network into the execution environment has different advantages. As required by several RTOS, it reduces the number of OS tasks implementing the system. In our FESTO system, two tasks (corresponding to *Resource*1 and *Resource*2) are enough to support the distribution, the test and the processing units. As shown in Figure 18, this approach reduces also the context switching between tasks at run-time as follows:

- **Case1. High production mode**. if we consider each FB as an OS task (Thramboulidis & Zoupas, 2005), then 22 context switching are applied in the Hyper period. Thanks to our approach where only two tasks implement the whole system, only 2 context switching are applied between them.
- **Case2. Medium and Light production modes**. 18 context switching are applied in the Hyper period if we consider each FB as an OS task (Thramboulidis & Zoupas, 2005). In our approach, only 4 context switching are applied between the two tasks implementing the system.

## FUTURE TRENDS

In our future research work, several problems have to be resolved for the development of Reconfigurable Control Systems following the Standard IEC61499. The minimization criterion of the energy consumption has to be studied in order to control the production cost: is it useful to automatically change the system OS tasks in order to reduce the energy consumption? In addi-

*Figure 18. Context switching for the different production modes of the FESTO Manufacturing System*

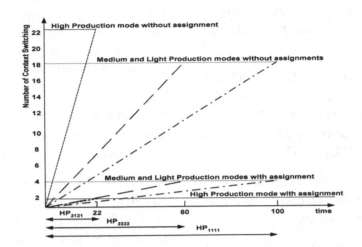

tion, the NCES-based specification and the model checking of critical complex control systems is not trivial in manufacturing industry. Therefore, the refinement-based specification of these systems will be studied from an abstract model into feasible models of elementary Function Blocks. Another problem that has to be resolved in the future deals with the code generation of the FB network that corresponds to each reconfiguration scenario. We plan also to study the simulation of Reconfigurable Control Systems which is known as a non exhaustive approach. To optimize the simulation, it will be useful to apply a fault injection-based technique where errors will be injected in the FB network that implements each scenario in order to generate faults in the whole system behavior. Finally, our important future work is the generalization of our contributions for the development of Heterogeneous Control Systems following different component-based industrial technologies (Crnkovic & Larsson, 2002).

## CONCLUSION

The book chapter deals with the development of Reconfigurable Embedded Systems following a particular industrial technology: the Function Block technology. We define a new semantic that extends previous works to allow automatic reconfigurations of the system for several reasons and to handle all possible reconfiguration forms, we propose an agent-based architecture that we model with nested state machines according to the formalism of NCES. To satisfy user requirements, we apply the model checker SESA for the verification of CTL-based functional and extra-functional properties on the whole system behavior. We propose thereafter an approach to assign Function Blocks that implement the different reconfiguration scenarios into OS tasks of the execution environment. Therefore, the system becomes a set of OS task sets where each one has to be executed under well defined conditions. These contributions are now the subject of negotiations with industrial partners for the next generation of embedded systems in manufacturing industry.

## REFERENCES

Al-Safi, Y., & Vyatkin, V. (2007). An ontology-based reconfiguration agent for intelligent mechatronic systems. In *Third International Conference on Industrial Applications of Holonic and Multi-Agent Systems*. Springer-Verlag.

Alur, R., & Henzinger, T.-A. (1992). Logics and models of real-time: A survey. In *Proceedings of Real-time: Theory in Practice*, (LNCS Vol. 600). Springer-Verlg.

Angelov, C., Sierszecki, K., & Marian, N. (2005). Design models for reusable and reconfigurable state machines, In L.T. Yang, et al. (Eds), *EUC 2005, International Federation for Information Processing* (LNCS 3824, pp. 152-163).

Artist-Project. (2003). *Roadmap:Component-based design and integration platforms*. Retrieved from www.artist-embedded.org

Baruah, S. (2003). Dynamic and static priority scheduling of recurring real-time tasks. *Real-Time Systems, 24*(1). doi:10.1023/A:1021711220939

Baruah, S., & Goossens, J. (2004). Scheduling real-time tasks: Algorithms and complexity. In J. Y.-T. Leung (Ed.), *Handbook of scheduling: Algorithms,models, and performance analysis*. Chapman Hall/CRC press.

Bensalem, S., Bozga, M., Sifakis, J., & Nguyen, T.-H. (2008). Compositional verification for component-based systems and application. *6th International Symposium on Automated Technology for Verification and Analysis, ATVA* (pp. 64-79).

Brennan, R.-W., Fletcher, M., & Norrie, D.-H. (2001). A holonic approach to reconfiguring real-time distributed control systems. In *Multi-Agent Systems and Applications: MASA'01*. Springer-Verlag.

Colla, E.-C.-M., & Brusafferri, A. (2006). Applying the IEC 61499 model to the schoe manufacturing sector. *11th IEEE International Conference on Emerging Technologies and Factory Automation, ETFA'06*.

Crnkovic, I., & Larsson, M. (2002). *Building reliable component-based software systems*. UK: Artech House.

Dukas, G., & Thramboulidis, K. (2005). A real-time linux execution environment for function-block based distributed control applications. *2nd IEEE International Conference on Industrial Informatics, INDIN'05*.

Ferrarini, L., & Veber, C. (2004). Implementation approaches for the execution model of IEC 61499 applications. *2nd IEEE International Conference on Industrial Informatics, INDIN'04*.

Hanisch, H.-M., & Luder, A. (1999). Modular modeling of closed-loop systems. Colloquium on Petri Net Technologies for Modeling Communication Based Systems, Germany (pp. 103-126).

Hanisch, H.-M., & Vyatkin, V. (2005). Achieving reconfigurability of automation systems by using the new international standard IEC 61499: A developer's view. In R. Zurawski (Ed.), *The industrial information technology handbook* (pp. 661-680). USA: CRC Press.

IEC1131. (1993). *Programmable controllers part 3*. In Bureau Central de la Commission Electrotechnique Internationale Switzerland.

IEC61499. (2004). Industrial process measurements and control systems. *International Electro technical Commission (IEC) Committee Draft*.

Khalgui, M., Rebeuf, X., & Simonot-Lion, F. (2006). A static scheduling generator for the deployment of a component based application. In Object-oriented Modeling of Embedded Real-Time Systems. Germany: Heinz-Nixdorf Institute publisher.

Khalgui, M., Rebeuf, X., & Simonot-Lion, F. (2007). A deployment method of component based applications on distributed industrial control systems. *European Jounal of Automated Systems, 41*(6).

Khalgui, M., & Thramboulidis, K. (2008). An IEC61499-based development approach for the deployment of industrial control applications. *International Journal of Modelling, Identification and Control (IJMIC), 4*(2).

Klein, M.-H., Ralya, T., Pollack, B., Obenza, R., & Harbour, M.-G. (1993). *A practioner's handbook for real-time analysis guide to rate monotonic analysis for real-time systems.* Kluwer Academic Booktitle.

Lastra, J.-L.-M., Godinho, L., & Tuokko, R. (2005). An IEC 61499 application generator for scan-based industrial controllers. *3rd IEEE International Conference on Industrial Informatics, INDIN'05.*

Leung, J., & Whitehead, J. (1982). On the complexity of fixed-priority scheduling of periodic real-time tasks. *Real-time Tasks. Performance Evaluation, 2.* doi:10.1016/0166-5316(82)90024-4

Lewis, R. (2001). *Modeling control systems using IEC 61499.* UK: Institution of Engineering and Technology.

Marik, V., Vyatkin, V., & Colombo, A. (2007). *Holonic and multiagent systems in manufacturing* (LNCS 4659). Springer Verlag.

Panjaitan, S., & Frey, G. (2007). Development process for distributed automation systems combining UML and IEC 61499. *International Journal of Manufacturing Research, 2*(1). doi:10.1504/IJMR.2007.013423

Rausch, M., & Hanisch, H.-M. (1995). Net condition/event systems with multiple condition outputs. *Symposium on Emerging Technologies and Factory Automation, 1,* 592-600.

Roch, S. (2000a). Extended computation tree logic. In *Proceedings of the CESP2000 Workshop, No. 140 in Informatik Berichte*, Germany (pp. 225-234).

Roch, S. (2000b). Extended computation tree logic: Implementation and application. In *Proceedings of the AWPN2000 Workshop*, Germany.

Rooker, M. N., Sunder, C., Strasser, T., Zoitl, A., Hummer, O., & Ebenhofer, G. (2007). Zero downtime reconfiguration of distributed automation systems: The CEDAC approach. *Third International Conference on Industrial Applications of Holonic and Multi-Agent Systems.* Springer-Verlag.

Stankovic, J., Spuri, M., & Ramamritham, K. (2005). *Deadline scheduling for real-time systems.* Kluwer Academic Booktitles.

Takada, H., & Sakamura, K. (1995). mu-ITRON for small-scale embedded systems. *IEEE Micro, 15*(6). doi:10.1109/40.476258

Thramboulidis, K. (2005). Model integrated mechatronics-towards a new paradigm in the development of manufacturing systems. *IEEE Transactions on Industrial Informatics, 1.*

Thramboulidis, K., Doukas, G., & Frantzis, A. (2004). Towards an implementation model for FB-based reconfigurable distributed control applications. *In Proceedings of 7th IEEE International Symposium on Object-Oriented Real-Time Distributed Computing* (pp. 193-200).

Thramboulidis, K., & Dukas, G. (2006). IEC61499 execution model semantics. *International Conference on Industrial Electronics, Technology, and Automation, CISSE-IETA'06.*

Thramboulidis, K., Perdikis, D., & Kantas, S. (2007). Model driven development of distributed control applications. [Springer-Verlag.]. *International Journal of Advanced Manufacturing Technology, 33*(3-4), 233–242. doi:10.1007/s00170-006-0455-0

Thramboulidis, K., & Zoupas, A. (2005). Real-time java in control and automation. *10th IEEE International Conference on Emerging Technologies and Factory Automation. ETFA'05.*

Toolkit. (2008). *Rockwell automation.* Retrieved from http://www.holobloc.com

Vyatkin, V. (2006). The potential impact of the IEC 61499 standard on the progress of distributed intelligent automation. *International Journal of Manufacturing Technology and Management, 8*(1). doi:10.1504/IJMTM.2006.008801

Vyatkin, V. (2007). IEC 61499 function blocks for embedded and distributed control systems design. *ISA-o3neida series: Instrumentation, Systems, and Automation Society* (p. 300). USA.

Vyatkin, V., & Hanisch, H.-M. (2003). Verification of distributed control systems in intelligent manufacturing. *International Journal of Manufacturing, 14*(1), 123–136. doi:10.1023/A:1022295414523

# Chapter 14

# Architecture Description Languages for the Automotive Domain

**Sébastien Faucou**
*Université de Nantes, France*

**Françoise Simonot-Lion**
*Nancy Université, France*

**Yvon Trinquet**
*Université de Nantes, France*

## ABSTRACT

*The embedded electronic architecture of a modern vehicle is a distributed system composed of several tenths of nodes. The development of these systems relies on a cooperative process involving several partners (carmakers and several suppliers). In such highly competitive domain, three main factors have to be taken into account: the design and production costs, the performance, comfort, and quality of driving, and several stringent safety requirements. In order to fulfill these requirements in such a context, it is vital for the different stakeholders to master the effects of the different sources of complexity. One way to reach this goal is to provide them with a common modeling language capable of representing the system at all its design steps and a common reference architecture in terms of components and organization. This chapter illustrates this approach. It focuses on EAST-ADL, an architecture description language dedicated to the automotive domain. Its links to the reference architecture defined by the AUTOSAR consortium are given. The chapter focuses especially on the ability offered by EAST-ADL to support the validation and verification (V&V) activities in order to fulfill the safety requirements.*

## INTRODUCTION

Over the past twenty years, the number of computer-based systems embedded in the different functional domains of cars has increased significantly. This trend has been driven by economical and technological factors. Thus, in the 90's and early 00's, the reliability and performance levels of hardware components and the flexibility offered by software technologies led to gradually replacing hydro-me-

DOI: 10.4018/978-1-60566-750-8.ch014

chanical control systems with computer-controlled systems. Today, computer-based systems are used to realize innovative functions in the domain of vehicle and passenger safety, such as "active steering" (introduced in the BMW X5 in 2007). Tomorrow, they are expected to play an important role in reducing fuel consumption. It is expected that the embedded electronic architecture for the next generation of vehicles will be composed of 30 electronic control units (or ECU for short) for low-end vehicles and up to 80 ECU for high-end.

The development of an embedded electronic architecture is a cooperative work involving an OEM (Original Equipment Manufacturer, or carmaker) and several Tier 1 suppliers (a Tier 1 supplier sells its production to OEMs; a Tier 2 supplier sells its production to Tier 1 suppliers; etc.). The result of this work is a complex distributed system, integrating several heterogeneous communication networks, and subject to stringent safety requirements. The importance of the safety concerns will further increase in the next decade because of the emerging ISO 26262 standards (Schubotz, 2008) that are likely to influence the certification process for embedded systems of the automotive domain in terms of dependability guarantee. In a highly competitive domain like the automotive industry, the design and production costs must be kept as low as possible. In this context, it is vital for the different stakeholders to master the complexity of the design of the embedded electronic architecture. One way to reach this goal is to use a modeling language capable of representing the system at all its design steps and common to all the actors involved in the design process. Ideally, this language must be based on a reference architecture defining the target of the design process.

In the last 10 years, the European automotive industry has conducted several R&D projects to define such a modeling language and the accompanying reference architecture. For the modeling language, these efforts have led to the definition of several "Architecture Description Languages"

(or ADL for short) such as AIL_Transport (Elloy and Simonot-Lion, 2002), or EAST-ADL (Freund, Gurrieri, Lönn, Eden, Migge, Reiser, *et al.*, 2004) and its successor EAST-ADL2 (Cuenot *et al.*, 2008). Concerning the reference architecture, it is defined today in the AUTOSAR (AUTomotive Open System Architecture) standards.

This chapter focuses on the modeling language. It is organized as follows: in the next section, an overview of AUTOSAR is given, and the main principles of ADLs are recapitulated. Then, in the following one, the EAST-ADL, an ADL dedicated to the automotive domain, is presented with a focus on the support it provides concerning the validation and verification (V&V) activities. This is illustrated in section "Example: Timing Analysis" with a case study. The last section concludes the chapter.

## BACKGROUND

### Reference Architectures for the Automotive Domain

A reference architecture defines the overall organization and the models of computation and communication used to implement computer-based systems of a certain domain. The most famous reference architecture is the OSI model for networked communication systems.

Concerning critical embedded systems, several reference architectures have been proposed. Similar to the OSI model, they usually rely on a layered architecture style, where each layer offers a set of services to the upper layer that hides the details of the underlying execution platform. The typical organization consists of a top layer that hosts the application components; a middleware layer that abstracts the distribution of the application among the physical nodes; a basic software layer that controls the access to the hardware resources.

Hence, in the domain of avionics systems, the "Integrated Modular Avionics" reference architecture has been proposed (Morgan, 1991). It defines an API (Application Program Interface) to access the hardware and network resources. This API allows developers to design and code the application layer components without having to take into account their deployment. The proposal is based on the standardization of modules named LRMs (Line Replaceable Modules) housed in a cabinet and communicating through back-plane data buses. The operational architecture is then built by connecting several cabinets and existing dedicated avionics units on global multiplexed serial data buses to form an integrated system. An important objective of this approach is the integration of maintenance support facilities.

Another study aimed at similar objectives was carried out within the TTA project, which focused on time-triggered architecture (Scheidler *et al.*, 1997). Their approach targeted a wide range of domains where fault-tolerance, distribution and real-time were critical issues (automotive, aerospace, and railway industries). The proposal was intended to ease "composability" and to provide a transparent implementation of fault-tolerance mechanisms. Within TTA, all activities (tasks, messages) in the system are controlled by the progression of a globally synchronized time-base. This strong design assumption mandates using a network infrastructure capable of providing this global time-base such as TTP/C (TTTech Computertechnik GmbH, 2003) or FlexRay (FlexRay Consortium, 2005; Schätz *et al.*, 2008). This is an important obstacle for adopting TTA into the automotive domain, where the CAN network is still predominant (ISO, 1994; Navet & Simonot-Lion, 2008). Therefore, certain other studies were done to define a less restrictive computation and communication model that, furthermore, would take into account the actual design process of embedded electronic architectures.

The first proposal came from the European project EAST-EEA that identified the main functions of a middleware for embedded electronic architectures. The present business model in the automotive industry is such that the middleware itself is realized by integrating several components, possibly coming from different sources. So, knowing only the behavior and interface of the services, which is provided by the middleware, is not enough; the architecture of the middleware itself has to be carefully mastered in terms of components and the interaction between these components. This is the first objective of the international program AUTOSAR (Fennel *et al.*, 2006; Fürst, 2006; Voget *et al.*, 2008; AUTOSAR, 2008), which gathers the majority of the stakeholders of the automotive industry in the world. One of the goals of the AUTOSAR is to make it possible to separate software from hardware in the design process of a complex distributed technical architecture, thus allowing to master the complexity, the portability of application software components, the flexibility for product modification, upgrade and update, the scalability of solutions within and across product lines, and the improvement of the quality and reliability of embedded systems.

To do so, AUTOSAR specifies the software architecture embedded in an ECU. It is composed of three layers: the application layer, the Run Time Environment (RTE), which provides a computation and communication infrastructure to the application layer, and the basic software, which controls the usage of the hardware resources. An application software component is certified AUTOSAR compliant if its code only calls entry points defined by the RTE. A basic software component has to be of a type specified by AUTOSAR. This means that it must provide its services through the interface formally defined in the specification of its type. This architecture is schematically illustrated in the Figure 1.

Although AUTOSAR defines what the elementary components of an embedded electronic architecture are very precisely, the problems of the deployment of these components, their scaling, the validation of the resulting system, etc. is not addressed. The end of this section introduces

*Figure 1. AUTOSAR reference architecture (adapted from www.autosar.org/)*

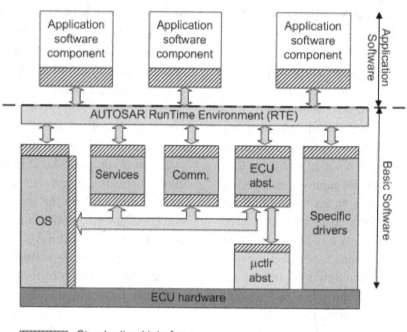

Standardized interfaces

a possible approach for solving these problems. As mentioned in the introduction, this solution is complementary to, and relies on, the existence of a reference architecture such as the one provided by AUTOSAR. The underlying concept is based on the principles of ADLs.

## Concepts of Architecture Description Languages

Architecture Description Languages (ADLs) were proposed in the 90's as a means to specify the overall organization of complex systems. An ADL is a modeling language capable of describing the structure and the abstract behavior of a system. The structure is described as an assembly of components, whose interface and (observable) behavior are specified. The behavior of the whole system is deduced from the behavior of each component and from the properties of the composition operators used to build the assembly. An ADL offers, at minimum, a vertical (or hierarchical) composition operator and a horizontal (or parallel) composition operator. One of the major reasons for using an ADL is having the possibility to generate various analysis models from a common root as well as (a part of) the implementation of the system.

Historically, the ADL approach was developed more or less simultaneously in the software engineering community and in the computer system engineering community. In the software engineering community, it was identified as a solution for mastering the complexity of concurrent and distributed systems. The pioneer works have been conducted with the design of ADLs, such as Wright at Carnegie Mellon University (Allen, 1997), Darwin at Imperial College London (Magee *et al.*, 1995), or Rapide at Stanford University (Luckham *et al.*, 1995). A comparison and classification framework for these proposals (and others) is given in (Medvidovic and Taylor, 2000). In the computer system engineering community, the ADL approach has been identified as a solution to support the exploration of the design space of complex hardware platforms, especially System-on-Chip. In this context, architecture specifications are not only used to generate analysis models and (partial) implementation, but also to generate software tools such as compilers and simulators. A survey of ADLs for hardware platforms is given in (Mishra and Dutt, 2008).

An architecture specification usually starts free from implementation details and is enriched throughout the design process. Therefore, so as to preserve the meaningfulness of early V&V results, it must be possible to maintain or verify the consistency between the different refinements of a specification. To ease this work, one solution consists in defining a virtual platform for each design activity. A virtual platform (Giusto, Brunel, Ferrari, Fourgeau, Lavagno, & Sangiovanni-Vincentelli, 2002) defines an execution environment that abstracts details from the implementation that are irrelevant to the activity. Then, the various abstraction levels at which the components should be described are clearly identified, as well as the correct refinement relationships that should exist between them. Of course, virtual platforms are domain specific artifacts and require the definition of domain specific ADLs.

In the domain of safety-critical real-time embedded systems (which includes in-vehicle embedded systems), several ADLs have been proposed (Hansson *et al.*, 1997; Faucou *et al.*, 2004). The most visible initiatives have been conducted in the avionics domain, leading to the definition of MetaH (Binns & Vestal, 2001) and its successor AADL (Feiler *et al.*, 2003; Feiler *et al.*, 2006). AADL stands for "Architecture Analysis & Design Language". It offers a textual and a graphical syntax to describe software architectures, hardware architectures and the bindings between them. Software architectures are composed of a set of concurrent and communicating threads executing sequences of subprograms within the address space of processes. Hardware architectures are composed of CPU, memory and devices (used to model sensors and actuators)

interconnected through communication buses. The bindings consist in mapping threads to the CPU, processes to memory and communication between distant software components to buses. The model of computation and communication is precisely defined. It includes a timing model, as well as error handling and operating mode handling facilities. Lastly, the language is extensible. Properties can be added to components and exploited by analysis tools. AADL 1.0 has been standardized by the SAE in 2004 (SAE, 2004). AADL 2.0 is on the way (version available in 2008). More information on this language and the associated tools can be obtained from the AADL web site (http://www.aadl.info/).

By providing support for describing both software and hardware architectures, AADL and the other ADL for the domain of safety-critical real-time embedded systems can be classified as system engineering ADLs. However, in their present form, they inherit a lot more from software engineering ADLs than from computer system engineering ADLs. The specification of the hardware architecture is generally very large scale and cannot be used as an input for generating an instruction set simulator or a compiler. This limitation is not an issue as long as the target systems are software-dominant, which is the case of today's in-vehicle embedded systems.

## EAST-ADL: AN ARCHITECTURE DESCRIPTION LANGUAGE FOR THE AUTOMOTIVE INDUSTRY

In the late 90's, the French R&D project AEE, which stands for "Architecture Électronique Embarquée" (or "Embedded Electronic Architecture" in English) defined an ADL named AIL_Transport ("Architecture Implementation Language for Transport"), for mastering the design, modeling and validation of embedded electronic architectures. This language allows for the specification of architectures at different abstraction levels (Elloy

& Simonot-Lion, 2002; Migge & Elloy, 2000). Several tools were developed in order to automate documentation, deployment (SynDEx, 2008) and verification activities. The EAST-EEA project (EAST-EEA, 2004; Freund, Gurrieri, Küster, Lönn, Migge, Reiser, *et al.*, 2004a; Freund, Gurrieri, Lönn, Eden, Migge, Reiser, *et al.*, 2004b; Debruyne *et al.*, 2004*)* was an Eureka-ITEA European project whose objectives were similar to AEE: mastering the complexity of the design of embedded electronic architectures. The main result of the project was the definition of EAST-ADL, an architecture description language capable of being the cornerstone of an ADL-centric design process for the automotive industry. A revised version, named EAST-ADL 2.0, including some adjustments and additions has been defined in the STREP project ATESST (ATESST, 2008; Cuenot *et al.*, 2008; Törner *et al.*, 2008).

The purpose of EAST-ADL is to provide a support for the non-ambiguous description of in-vehicle embedded electronic architectures at each level of their development. EAST-ADL allows capturing all information required and/or produced by each design step, from early analysis down to implementation. It offers common modeling concepts and notations for the architectural artifacts, using a UML2.0 (Booch *et al.*, 2005) compliant approach. The language elements have been defined according to several language domains: structure (structural relations between elements), behavior, requirements and V&V. The grammar of the language is defined within the meta-modeling framework provided by the GME2000 tool (Ledeczi *et al.*, 2001). GME2000 provides also a support for the graphical edition of models in the different language domains listed above. A checker, capable of verifying the consistency of a model according to EAST-ADL semantics, is attached to these editing facilities. The storage format of the models is based on XML.

EAST-ADL provides a framework for the modeling of embedded electronic architectures through 5 abstraction levels (vehicle, analysis, design, implementation, operational) populated by 7 views or artifacts (Vehicle Feature Model, Functional Analysis Architecture, Functional Design Architecture, Function Instance Model, Platform Model, Hardware Architecture, and Allocation Model). Although it provides the necessary concepts to model the interaction between the embedded electronic architecture and its physical environment, it does not allow an explicit modeling of this environment. This structure is illustrated in Figure 2 (Freund, Gurrieri, Küster, Lönn, Migge, Reiser, 2004; Debruyne *et al.*, 2004). All the described views are tightly coupled allowing traceability among the different entities identified during the design process. Besides the structural decomposition, which is typical for any software development or modeling approach, the EAST-ADL also supports the description of "inter-views" entities such as requirements, behavioral description and V&V activities.

## Artifacts in EAST-ADL

Each artifact in EAST-ADL is the result of a specific activity of the design process. The different artifacts are briefly described in the following paragraphs. For further information on this language, the reader can refer to the public manual available at (www.east-eea.net/docs).

## Vehicle Feature Model

This artifact is the top-level view for a vehicle product line; it gathers and structures all the lower levels artifacts (e.g. *Functional Analysis Architecture* objects, *Hardware Architecture* objects, etc.) for this product line. It supports the description of user visible features (*VehicleFeatureModel* objects). Such objects are, for example, Anti-lock Braking System (ABS), windscreen wipers, etc. A *VehicleFeatureModel* instance is composed, on the one hand, of a list of vehicle parameters that are relevant for the configuration of the embedded electronic architectures (e.g. engine size, country,

*Figure 2. Abstraction levels and views in EAST-ADL*

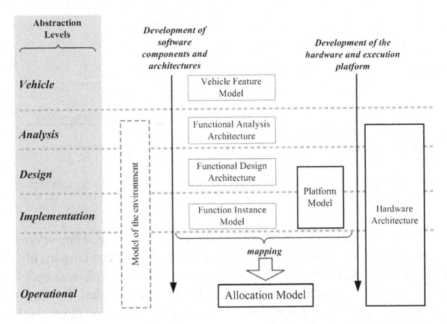

and possible customer choices such as cruise control, etc.) and, on the other hand, of vehicle groups, where a group gathers all the vehicle instances that share common user visible properties (e.g., all vehicles with cruise control and sold in Europe). With these two kinds of parameters, the *VehicleFeatureModel* allows the description of all the variation points among a product line.

## Functional Analysis Architecture

This artifact represents the functions realizing the features, their behavior and how they cooperate. Figure 3-a shows the links between the EAST-ADL entities at this level. The *FunctionalAnalysisArchitecture* defines a top level *AnalysisFunction*. Its purpose is to implement all the functionalities of an embedded electronic architecture, specified at the vehicle level by a *VehicleFeatureModel* instance. There is a 1-to-n mapping between *VehicleFeatureModel* entities and *FunctionalAnalysisArchitecture* ones, i.e. one or several functions realize one feature. In order to be compliant with industrial practices, a *VehicleFeatureModel* can

be directly refined at the design level; in this case, there is no link between a *VehicleFeatureModel* object and a *FunctionalAnalysisArchitecture* one (see Figure 4). An *AnalysisFunction* object can be refined and structured in several *AnalysisFunction* objects. Each *AnalysisFunction* object describes the functionalities at functional analysis level. They can interact with other *AnalysisFunction* objects through *FunctionPort* objects (see Figure 3-b). Furthermore, a behavior specification can complete the description of the object.

## Functional Design Architecture

The *FunctionalDesignArchitecture* is introduced in order to model the refinement of one *FunctionalAnalysisArchitecture* or of one *VehicleFeatureModel* object. It is, in fact, a container for the application software components of an electronic embedded system. A constraint is applied to the meta-model given in Figure 4-a: a *FunctionalDesignArchitecture* is always a top level *CompositeSoftwareFunction* entity.

*Figure 3. Functional Analysis Architecture (meta-model and one instance)*

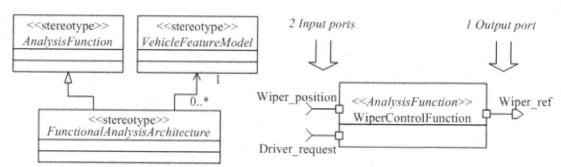

(a) The meta-model

(b) An instance of *AnalysisFunction*

A *CompositeSoftwareFunction* object can be refined in several *CompositeSoftwareFunction* ones. The last refinement produces objects, termed *ElementarySoftwareFunction*. The interactions between *CompositeSoftwareFunction* and / or *ElementarySoftwareFunction* objects are done through ports, termed *SignalFunctionPort* (note that similar ways are provided for the interactions with system services and client/server communica-

tion services through *SystemPort* and *OperationFunctionPort*). Ports are parts of *CompositeSoftwareFunction* or of *ElementarySoftwareFunction* objects. The complete description of a *SignalFunctionPort* or of an *OperationFunctionPort* is achieved by specifying the interface requirement of the port (required / provided - period of the data transmitted through this interface, if necessary). So, *SignalFunctionPortInterface* objects are

*Figure 4. Functional design architecture model*

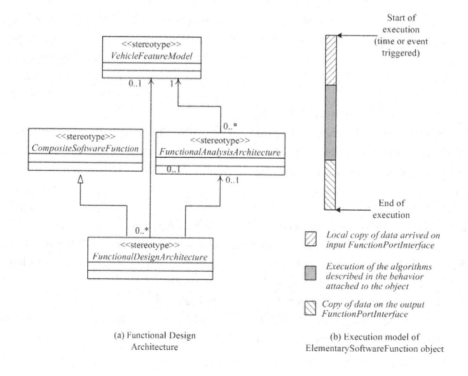

(a) Functional Design Architecture

(b) Execution model of ElementarySoftwareFunction object

defined in Functional Design Architecture. These parameters specify only the input / output of data from a component point of view and so they do not give any information on the data flows into the architecture. Therefore, the *ConnectorSignal* objects complete this specification by a description of the signal types that are exchanged through the port interfaces of *CompositeSoftwareFunction* or *ElementarySoftwareFunction* objects. This allows a unique description for several signals. For example, the vehicle speed is data that is instantiated through several signals in an embedded architecture but each of them refers to the same *ConnectorSignal* object. A data type characterizes each *ConnectorSignal* object. Furthermore, precedence constraints which are imposed on the execution of *ElementarySoftwareFunction* objects can be specified through an association to an object, termed Precedes. Lastly, in EAST-ADL, a behavior is attributed to each *ElementarySoftwareFunction* object: it is assumed to follow the execution model illustrated in Figure 4-b. In the next section, Figure 10 provides an example of a *CompositeSoftwareFunction* (System), broken down into two *ElementarySoftwareFunction* objects (Producer, Consumer) that are connected due to their respective *SignalFunctionPortInterface* and a *ConnectorSignal* object (Vehicle_Speed).

## Function Instance Model

This artifact describes entities that will be used for the deployment of software components and exchanged signals to OS tasks and frames. In fact, if it is possible at the design level to allocate certain objects, such as *ElementarySoftwareFunction*, on a specific ECU, their specification has to be completed in order to deal with, for example, a local scheduling. These additional characteristics are defined by the *FunctionInstance* model, providing an abstraction of the software components to implement on the Platform Model, abstraction that is suited to optimized deployment and tim-

ing analysis. The entities that appear in Function Instance Model are mainly *FunctionInstance*, *SignalInstance* and *LogicalCluster* objects (the specification is partially illustrated in Figure 5).

A *FunctionInstance* represents an instance of an *ElementarySoftwareFunction* while a *Logical-Cluster* object gathers all the *FunctionInstance* objects that have to be statically scheduled within the same *OSTask* (Operating System task). Consequently, a *LogicalCluster* object is allocated on one and only one ECU. *SignalInstance* objects are used for communication within or between *LogicalCluster* objects. A *SignalInstance* object corresponds to a *ConnectorSignal* defined at the upper levels.

In order to model the implementation of a system, EAST-ADL provides, on the one hand, a way for the description of the hardware platforms through the Hardware Architecture artifact and their available services (operating systems, communication protocols, middleware) and, on the other hand, a support for the specification of how a Function Instance Model is distributed onto a platform. For this purpose, three additional views are necessary: the Hardware Architecture, the Platform Model and the Allocation Model.

## Hardware Architecture

The Hardware Architecture artifact defines ECUs, channels, sensors and actuators. The ECU (Electronic Control Unit) models the computer nodes of the embedded system. ECUs consist of processor(s) and memory(ies) and may be connected via channels (serial links, networks) to sensors, actuators and other ECUs (see Figure 6).

## Platform Model

In the *Platform* Model, views of the operating system and/or Middleware API and the services provided (schedulers, frame packing, memory management, I/O drivers, diagnosis software,

*Figure 5. FunctionInstance and SignalInstance specification*

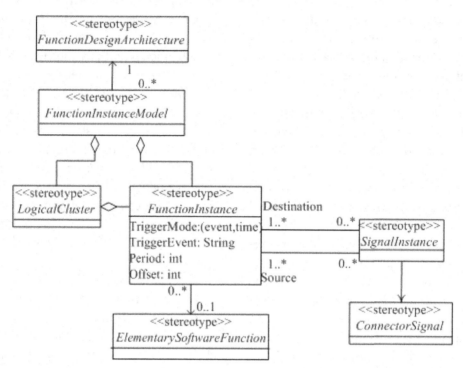

download software etc.) are given. It is, in fact, the programmer's view of the Hardware Architecture.

## Allocation Model

The *Allocation* Model represents the tasks, managed by the operating systems (*OSTask* objects), the frames, managed by the protocols (*Frame* objects) or the communication buffer used for internal communications (*CommunicationBuffer* objects).

It is the result of the deployment of Function Instance artifact objects onto a Platform artifact object. Using a particular policy, specified through a *FunctionDeployment* object (resp. *SignalDeployment* object), a *LogicalCluster* object (resp. a *SignalInstance* object) is assigned to a particular *OSTask* object (resp. a *CommunicationBuffer* or *Frame* object). At this lowest abstraction level, all implementation details are captured. Figure 7 represents the deployment activity.

*Figure 6. Hardware architecture level*

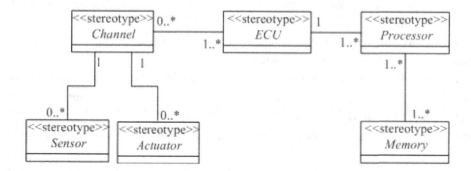

*Figure 7. Deployment model*

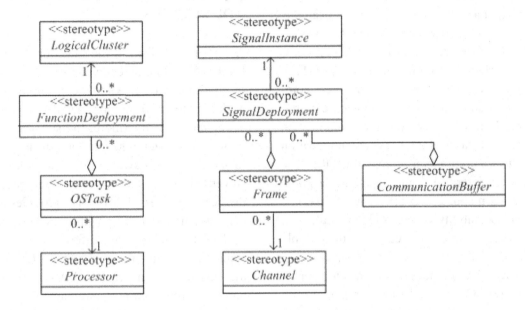

## Association EAST-ADL / AUTOSAR

The final objective of the design of a system is to get an application that executes on the AUTOSAR reference architecture. Therefore, the designer must obtain the real-time tasks, the frames and the communication buffers, as well as the configuration of the various software parts as for example the AUTOSAR OS, the RTE (Run Time Environment), the communication stack etc., in short, the complete configuration of one ECU. This configuration process must be automated to the full, using specific tools in order to minimize the unavoidable errors. In this paragraph we are merely going to give an illustration on how one can use some EAST-ADL objects to construct the software configuration of an ECU.

It is from the *FunctionInstance,* which represents the instances of the *ElementarySoftwareFunction,* that the *OSTasks* (Operating System Task) can be constructed. It can be also necessary to use the *LogicalCluster* objects, which gather the *FunctionInstance* objects, that have to be statically scheduled within the same *OSTask.* From an AUTOSAR point of view we have to use the *Runnable* entity notion. *Runnable* entities are the schedulable parts of the application software components and they have to be mapped to real-time tasks. An application software component provides one or more *Runnable* entities and each *Runnable* entity has an entry point for its activation. All *Runnable* entities are activated by the RTE as a result of "*RTEEvents*" (Timing event, communication event, etc.). The mapping of *Runnable* entities to OSTask must be described by the designer in the ECU Configuration Description. This mapping depends on various attributes of *Runnable* entities, which are the attributes of *FunctionInstances* objects; the mapping is an input of the RTE generator. Depending on the category of a *Runnable* entity (with or without *WaitPoint*) Basic task or Extended Task of the AUTOSAR OS can be used (see AUTOSAR documentation – the RTE part) for more information on the *Runnable* entities mapping).

An AUTOSAR application software component has ports through which the component interacts with other components. A port can be categorized by either a Sender-Receiver interface (message passing) or a Client-Server interface (function invocation). A port is either a p-port (provide port) or a r-port (require port). For example, a p-port of a component typed by an AUTOSAR Sender-Receiver interface can write data elements of this interface. Each communication model can be applied to both intra-ECU component communication and inter-ECU component communication. Intra-ECU component communication includes both cases of intra-task communication (both *Runnable* entities are mapped onto the same *OSTask*) and inter-task communication (*Runnable* entities are mapped onto different *OSTasks*). It is the responsibility of the RTE to implement the communication connections with multiple providers or requirers. For example, with the Sender-Receiver model the RTE has to support 1:n (single sender, multiple receivers). Also, with this model a *Runnable* entity can explicitly use RTE API calls to send and receive data elements (Explicit mode) or the RTE can provide data element to a *Runnable* entity before its invocation (Implicit mode) (see AUTOSAR documentation – RTE part) for more information on communication). In East-ADL, at the design level (Functionnal Design Architecture artifact) the links between software components are achieved using *SignalFunctionPort* (message passing) and *OperationFunctionPort* (function invocation). These objects must be categorized by the interface requirement: required or provided port, and other attributes. At the implementation level (Function Instance Model artifact) the *SignalInstance* object corresponds to a *ConnectorSignal* object, associated with the *SignalFunctionPortInterface* (similar objects are used for the *OperationFunctionPort*). The *SignalInstance* objects (and their attributes) and the *SignalFunctionPortInterface* can be used for the mapping to the ports and the communication data elements managed by the RTE. They also allow the designing of frames used by the AUTOSAR COM part for inter-ECU communication.

## CONSISTENCY OF EAST-ADL MODELS

A system described at the Functional Analysis level may be loosely coupled to hardware based on intuition, various known constraints or as a back annotation from more detailed analysis on lower levels. Furthermore, the structure of the Functional Design architecture and of the Function Instance Model is aware of the Platform Model. Nevertheless, in order to improve the quality of the design process, EAST-ADL provides a way to ensure the consistency within and between the artifacts belonging to the different levels, from a syntactic and semantic point of view (see Figure 8). This leads to making an EAST-ADL-based model a strong and non-ambiguous support for building automatically models suited to formal validation and verification activities.

### Requirements Modeling

EAST-ADL supports the requirements specification and their linking, on the one hand, to objects defined at one or several architectural point of views and, on the other hand, to analysis, design and implementation models (Weber & Weisbrod, 2003). Furthermore, as the validation of embedded systems is a mandatory activity, a formal description of the validation and verification process is provided. The requirements are used for the elaboration of a solution at each development step. Finally, the tracing activities between different requirements or between different versions of requirements can be expressed in this language.

Five requirement types were identified and defined by a textual description possibly completed by a formal one, by an attribute concerned by the tracing activities and by a status which is to be set to specific values according to the result of particular design, validation or verification activities. The requirements types are:

*Figure 8. Links between artifacts as supported by EAST-ADL*

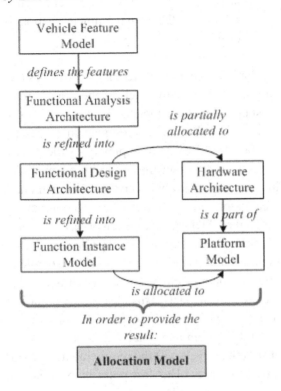

* *EFeature*: describes the required functionalities of an embedded system and is used, mainly, for specifying the system at Vehicle and Functional Analysis Architecture points of view. It may be broke down into sub-features or "variant" features (for a variation point's description).
* *Interaction*: specifies the cooperation modes between *EFeatures* thanks to "Use-Cases", "Message Sequence Charts", etc.
* *FunctionalRequirement*: supports the requirement imposed to the behavior of an EFeatures by means of a set of required properties and can be described, for instance, by "State-Transition Diagrams", "Messages Sequence Charts", or a textual definition.
* *DesignConstraint*: aims at defining how the research field for a solution is constrained; for example, such constraints can impose

a protocol, a given preliminary allocation, a legacy tool for designing the system or criteria to optimize (cost, power consumption, network bandwidth, etc.).
* *QualityRequirement*: expresses extra-functional properties such as performance properties, reliability properties, safety properties, etc.

In this chapter, we focus on the Quality Requirements and on their links to formal validation and verification activities.

## EAST-ADL as a Support for Validation and Verification Activities

### V&V Cases in the Design Process of Embedded Electronic Architecture

In the design process, V&V cases aim at checking with a certain technique that a certain requirement is met or implemented by certain V&V artifacts. In the previous section, the different classes of requirements were recapitulated. Concerning the V&V techniques, three main classes can be identified:

* Formal approaches, i.e. approaches that allow giving a formal answer to a question. A mathematical model of the system is formulated and solved. Depending on the mathematical model, the result produced after resolution can be deterministic or probabilistic. In this class of approach, one finds, for instance, static analysis, model checking, schedulability analysis techniques, etc.
* Simulation. An executable model of the system is formulated and a set of pertinent scenarios is defined statically or generated randomly. The system is run one time for each scenario. The result obtained after simulation is probabilistic. Although the techniques based on simulation are not

able to produce results as strong as the results obtained with formal approaches, they allow taking into account much more complex models.

- Testing. Similar to simulation, a set of scenarios is defined and used to stimulate a part of the real system. The test can target a simple software or hardware component, a (fully or partly) implemented embedded system, etc. Testing is the most widely used V&V technique in the automotive industry.

Concerning the V&V artifacts, three main classes can be identified:

- A functional model that does not take into account the implementation characteristics. Here, the goal of V&V is to check the completeness and coherency of the models with respect to the functional requirements. In EAST-ADL, functional models (with various degrees of abstraction) can be extracted from the following artifacts: *VehicleFeatureModel, FunctionalAnalysisArchitecture, FunctionalDesignArchitecture* and *FunctionInstanceModel*. The corresponding requirements are expressed through the *Efeature, Interaction,* and *FunctionalRequirement* entities.

- An operational model that takes into account the (planned) implementation of the system. Here, the goal of V&V is to check that the implementation choices (choice of the hardware architecture, choice of the allocation of the software architecture onto the hardware architecture) allow the system to meet the required performances. In EAST-ADL, operational models can be extracted from the *AllocationModel* artifact. The corresponding requirements are expressed through *DesignConstraint* and *QualityRequirement* entities.

- A (part of a) real system. With this target class, the goal of V&V is to check that (a part of) the actual implementation is correct.

For each technique, there is a set of tools that can be used. Usually, each of these tools must be supplied with an adequate model, i.e. a set of structured information, presented in a specific format. A part of the complexity of the design process comes from the necessity of maintaining the consistency between the different models created for V&V purposes. One of the important ideas of an ADL-centric design process is to rule out (a part of) this complexity by allowing the automatic creation of V&V models from a common information repository containing all the design architecture artifacts. This idea is fully exploited in EAST-ADL, which supports the description of (i) the system under development at different abstraction levels, (ii) the requirements and (iii) the V&V cases. This last point is explained in the following section, and then followed by an illustration of the joint utilization of these three features given in the form of a case study.

## Modeling of V&V Cases with EAST-ADL

Concerning the modeling of the V&V cases, the EAST-ADL uses some of the ideas already proposed in the UML2 Testing profile. A simplified version of the corresponding part of EAST-ADL meta-model is shown in Figure 9.

The center class is the *V&V_Case*. Each V&V case identified in the design process is modeled with an instance of this class. According to the meta-model, for each V&V case, the designer can specify:

- The requirements (instances of subclasses in the *Requirement* class) that are taken into account. A same V&V case can be used to check more than one requirement and conversely, a requirement can be checked in

*Figure 9. Validation and Verification process modeling*

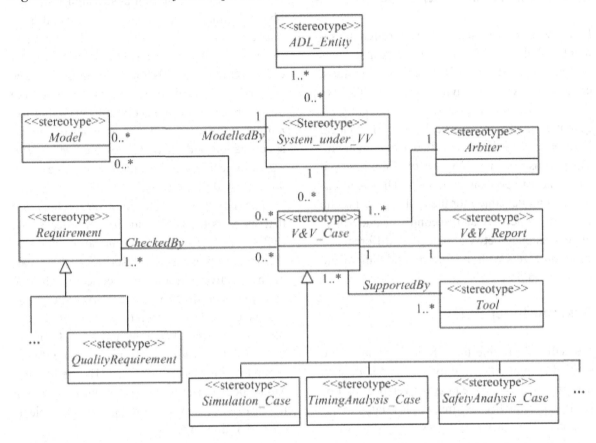

more than one case.

- The design artifacts that are examined. In the meta-model fragment of Figure 9, this corresponds to an instance of the *System_under_VV* class. It gathers the set of instances of the *ADL_Entity* class containing the information relevant with regards to the case. As explained above, so as to be able to use a specific technique to execute a part of the case, this information has to be structured in a set of models, represented by instances of the *Model* class.
- The tools (instances of the *Tool* class) that implement the selected V&V techniques. Each tool exploits one or more of the different models produced for this case.
- The report (*V&V_Report* entity) that gathers the output information produced by the

different tools used to perform the case, and the arbiter (*Arbiter* entity) that exploits this report to evaluate the success of the case.

In the next section, an example of a V&V case is presented. It consists of verifying that a given signal is exchanged between two software components within a specified time frame. This activity shall be modeled by an instance of the *TimingAnalysis_Case* class. The attributes of this class (not shown on Figure 9) allow the designer to document the case through a set of textual descriptions, including the purpose of the case (*Purpose* attribute) and the description of the property under V&V (*PropertyDescription* attribute).

## EXAMPLE: TIMING ANALYSIS

In this section, we illustrate how, through the semantics that the EAST-ADL language associates with artifacts and objects, it is possible to automate certain verification activities. In particular, we focus on the process assessing that a quality requirement, and more specifically for performance, is respected by the system under development. The purpose of this example is twofold; firstly, it shows how to go from an EAST-ADL specification to a model suited for the tool supporting the verification activity and, secondly, it underlines the consistency between objects at different abstraction levels with the formal modeling of the verification process.

### System Under Study

We will not provide the full description of the studied system but will only present the objects that are relevant for the targeted verification objective. The quality requirement is related to the response time of one signal exchanged between two distant embedded software components. For this purpose, we have to consider the frame in which this specific signal is deployed, to identify the network that supports this frame and finally to realize a timing analysis of all the frames sharing this network.

Let us consider a system, and its description at the Design abstraction level, according to the EAST-ADL sysntax. In this system, a set of *CompositeSoftwareFunction* objects have been identified; among them we isolate the Subsystem1, whose refinement provides two *ElementarySoftwareFunction* objects, named Producer and Consumer. These two objects are linked to ports and exchange data through *SignalFunctionPortInterface* objects (PInterface and CInterface). The data flow that connects these interfaces, is defined by the *ConnectorSignal* object *Vehicle Speed* (see Figure 10).

At the implementation abstraction level, the object Producer and Consumer are, each, refined into one *FunctionInstance* object belonging to two *LogicalCluster* objects. The *ConnectorSignal* object Vehicle_Speed is linked to a *SignalInstance* object Signal_Vehicle_Speed. At this level, the designers can specify several attributes. For example, in this case study, he enriches the model specification and characterizes the *FunctionInstance* objects by information about when they are activated (Figure 11).

The specification of the hardware architecture that supports the system identifies, at least, two ECUs connected on a communication network. Figure 12 represents the description of the part of the hardware architecture concerned by the example, according to the EAST-ADL graphical language: two *ECU* objects (PowerTrainECU and SteeringControlECU) connected on a *CAN* object (the *CAN* class is inherited from the *Channel* one), termed CANChassis (CAN, 1994). The Platfom Model does not bring any pertinent information to this example, so we do not present the objects created at this level.

The definition of the objects modeling the system at the implementation abstraction level, according to the Allocation Model, relies on a deployment and mapping activities. In particular, the *LogicalCluster* objects have to be allocated onto *ECU* objects. In the case study, we propose allocating the Group1 *LogicalCluster* objects (resp. Group2) onto the *ECU* objects' PowerTrainECU (resp. SteeringControlECU). Note that these *LogicalCluster* objects have to be deployed into *OSTasks* objects but we will not go into further details about the model in this chapter as it is not useful for the case study. Finally, as the Group1 and Group2 *LogicalCluster* objects are placed in two ECU objects, which represent distant nodes, we have to deal with the allocation / deployment of the Signal_Vehicle_Speed object. The transmission of this signal will obviously be supported by the network on which these ECUs are connected. In

*Figure 10. Architecture of ElementarySoftwareFunction objects*

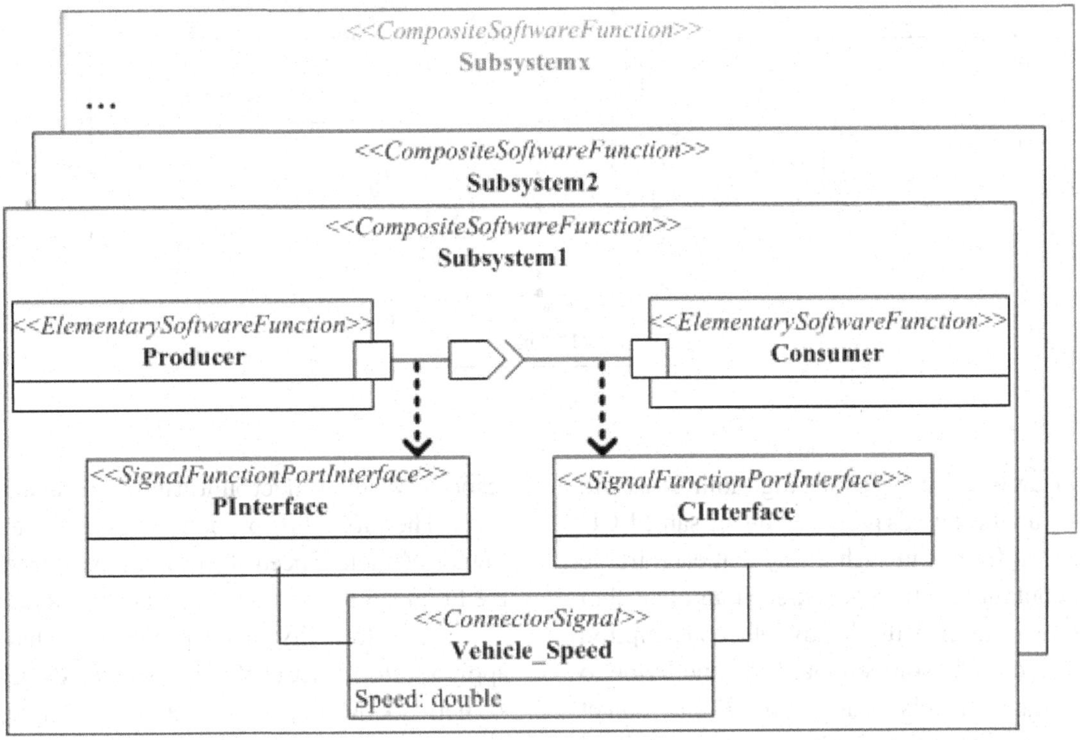

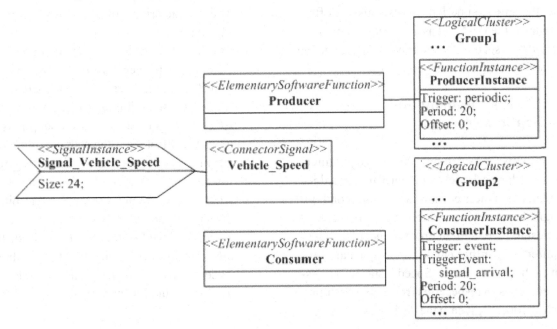

*Figure 11. Objects concerned by the example described according to the InstanceModel (the ProducerInstance object is activated periodically with a period equal to 20ms and no offset; the ConsumerInstance object is activated at each occurrence of event "signal_arrival" with a minimum interarrival equal to 20 ms. and no offset; the length of the Signal_Vehicle_Speed object is equal to 24 bits)*

*Figure 12. The part of the hardware architecture concerned by the case study*

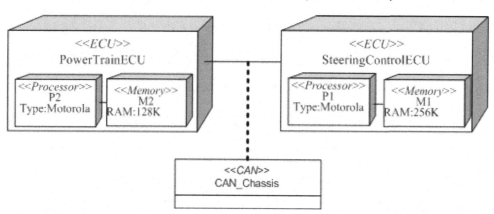

fact, usually, a frame packing algorithm is used to deploy all the signals produced on the same ECU in several frames in such a way that each frame may contain several signals; such an algorithm aims to minimize the bandwidth consumption compared to the solution that links one frame to each signal. In this example, the *Frame* object Frame25 contains two *SignalInstance* objects (Signal_Vehicle_Speed and Signalxx). The model now has to be completed by additional attributes that specify where the *SignalInstance* objects are placed within the *Frame* object that contains them, how long the data field of the *Frame* object is and what the emission period and its emission offset is. Finally, the CAN_Chassis supports the traffic defined by a set of different frames. The model of the deployment is illustrated in Figure 13.

## Quality Requirement and Verification Process

Let us now consider one quality requirement specified during the development of the embedded system: a freshness constraint (2 milliseconds) is assigned to the object Vehicle_Speed modeled at the design level and, in order to meet the safety requirements on the vehicle, the designer imposes that each time a Vehicle_Speed instance is transmitted, it has to respect this freshness constraint. Such a property given at the design level has to be respected by the artifact built at the implementation level. Therefore, this property is assigned to the Signal_Vehicle_Speed object and consequently to the Frame25 that supports its transmission.

In order to verify such a property, we have to apply a performance evaluation of the CAN_Chassis network. More precisely, in this example, we propose evaluating the worst reachable response time of each frame that is transmitted on the network by using the recurrent algorithm whose principle was first given in (Tindell & Burns, 1994). The input for this algorithm is:

- The characteristic of the CAN network (throughput, length).
- The specification of the set of frames: 1- Period: the trigger period (in ms.) represents the nominal period for time-triggered frames and the minimum inter-arrival time for event-triggered ones; 2- Offset (in ms.): gives the offset from the starting time; this attribute is only applied for time-triggered frames; 3- FrameSize (in bits): the total length of the frame; 4- DataSize (in bits): the sum of the size of each *SignalInstance* object deployed in this frame; 5- Priority: the priority according to the Medium Access Protocol; 6- Deadline: the relative deadline value for the frame.

*Figure 13. The deployment of a signal described at the implementation abstraction level*

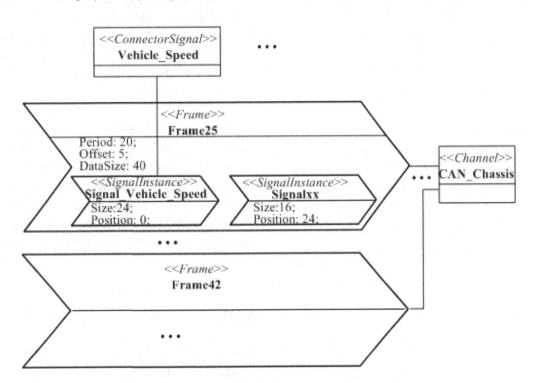

Once the worst case response time for each frame is evaluated, we can compare the one obtained for the object Frame25 to the freshness constraint expressed by the quality requirement and conclude on the feasibility or non-feasibility of this frame.

## EAST Verification Process Applied to the Example

For checking the quality requirement, a verification activity (described by a *V&V_Case* object, specialized in a *TimingAnalysis_Case* and named WorstCaseResponseTime here), can be done by the adhoc algorithm (Tool object, named *Tindell_WorstCase_Evaluator*). The result of this algorithm can then be analyzed and a report that establishes the verdict about the property is produced.

The V&V process is implemented through well-identified steps which are shown in Figure 14.

Figure 15 illustrates how the information required as input of the WorstCaseResponseTime algorithm can be automatically extracted from the EAST-ADL compliant repository of the system through a predefined sequence of parsing activities. The starting point is Vehicle_Speed, a *ConnectorSignal* object; the first parsing activity extracts Signal_Vehicle_Speed, the *SignalInstance* object that is associated to it. The next step is realized by applying another parsing activity that looks for the *Frame* object supporting the Signal_Vehicle_Speed. The result is the *Frame* object Frame25. This result now allows the extraction of the *Channel* object of the Hardware Architecture used to transmit Frame25, which is the CAN_Chassis object. Finally, the worst case response time evaluation needs a description of all the frames sharing the same network; therefore, the last parsing activity extracts this set of frames from the database. This last result is the input data of the Tindell algorithm.

*Figure 14. From EAST-ADL data base to a verdict*

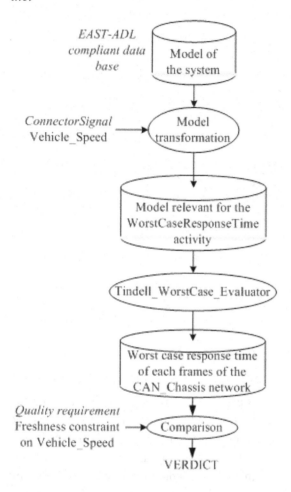

The complexity of the automatic generation of the formal model required for this verification activity depends on the structure of the XML database. In the demonstrator developed in the EAST EEA project, the organization of the XML database was such that it needed:

- to first browse the XML file in order to find the Vehicle_Speed object (*ConnectorSignal* object); the Signal_Vehicle_Speed object (*SignalInstance* object) is then directly referenced,
- to browse the XML file a second time in order to find, among all the *Frame* objects, the one connected to the Signal_Vehicle_Speed;

the object CAN_Chassis (*Channel* object) is then directly referenced,

- to browse the XML file a third time, to extract among the *Frame* objects, all the objects that are connected to the *CAN_Chassis* object.

This example demonstrates that due to the semantics of the objects described according to EAST-ADL, some activities can be automated and that formal links connect objects at different levels. So EAST-ADL is not only a support for the non-ambiguous modeling of an electronic embedded system but also for its development process.

## CONCLUSION

The design of in-vehicle embedded systems is a complex task. The complexity has two main causes. First, the high competitiveness of the market imposes keeping the design and production costs as low as possible and to shorten the time-to-market, while maintaining a high level of quality. Nowadays, the definition of this "high level of quality" tends to be formalized by international standards, for instance, ISO26262 concerning the safety provided to the vehicle and its passengers. Second, the players in the automotive industry have established a business model that imposes a design process which is distributed between the OEM and the Tier-1 suppliers, leading to the distribution of the design information and artifacts, and the heterogeneity of the formalisms and tools that support the design.

To master this complexity, the solution embraced by the automotive industry relies on two concepts: a reference architecture and an architecture description language. A reference architecture defines the structure and the set of rules for the interaction that an implemented system has to follow. In the automotive industry, the reference architecture is provided by the standards edited

*Figure 15. The parsing activities implied by the model transformation of the EAST-ADL database of the case study*

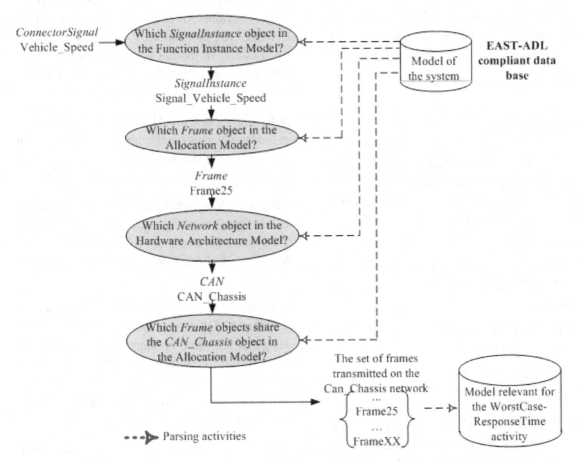

by the AUTOSAR consortium. The second concept is the concept of an architecture description language. An architecture description language is used to specify the structure and the behavior of a system at different abstraction levels. In the context of the automotive industry, the highest abstraction level corresponds to a collection of features that have to be implemented. The lowest abstraction level is an instance of AUTOSAR, the reference architecture.

In this chapter, we have highlighted the benefits obtained by using a domain specific architecture description language for modeling, validation and, more generally, developing automotive embedded systems. We have explained how such a language provides a support for describing and exploiting the information produced at the various design steps. More precisely, we have presented EAST-ADL, an architecture description language defined within the Eureka – ITEA EAST-EEA project (2001-2004). We have focused on the semantics that this language provides, with a focus on two aspects: the requirement specification on the one hand, and the V&V activities on the other. Through a case study, we have demonstrated that EAST-ADL allows specifying how to complete a V&V case. We have also explained how it is possible to automate the extraction of information from design artifacts and the production of a model amenable to a certain analysis technique from such a specification. In the case study, the analysis technique is a schedulability analysis technique, used to check that a signal conveying the current speed of the vehicle is exchanged between a producer and a consumer software component within a specified time frame. Of course, this approach is generic and can be applied to any kind of V&V case.

# REFERENCES

Allen, R. J. (1997). *A formal approach to software architecture*. Unpublished doctoral dissertation (Tech. Rep. No. CMU-CS-97-144), Carnegie Mellon University, Pittsburgh, PA.

ARTIST. (2003). *Component-based design and integration platforms*. (Tech. Rep. W1.A2. N1.Y1). ARTIST-Advanced Real-Time Systems-IST project.

ATESST. (2008). Retrieved on July 1, 2008, from http://www.atesst.org/

AUTOSAR. Retrieved on July 1, 2008 from http://www.autosar.org/

Binns, P., & Vestal, S. (2001). Formalizing software architectures for embedded systems. In T. A. Henzinger & C. M. Kirsch (Eds.), *First international workshop on embedded software* (LNCS 221, pp. 451-468). London: Springer-Verlag.

Booch, G., Rumbaugh, J., & Jacobson, I. (2005). *Unified modeling language user guide, 2nd ed.* Addison Wesley Longman.

Cuenot, P., Frey, P., Johansson, R., Lönn, H., Reiser, M.-O., Servat, D., et al. (2008). Developing automotive products using the EAST-ADL2, and AUTOSAR compliant architecture description language. *4th European Congress ERTS Embedded Real Time Software 2008*, Toulouse, France.

Debruyne, V., Simonot-Lion, F., & Trinquet, Y. (2004). EAST-ADL, an architecture description language–validation and verification aspects. In P. Dissaux, M. Filali Amine, P. Michel & F. Vernadat (Eds.), *IFIP World Computer Congress 2004 – Proceedings of the Workshop on Architecture Description Languages*, Toulouse, France.

DeRemer, F., & Kron, H. (1975). Programming-in-the large versus programming-in-the-small. In *Proceedings of the International Conference on Reliable Software*. Los Angeles, CA: ACM.

Elloy, J.-P., & Simonot-Lion, F. (2002). An architecture description language for in-vehicle embedded system development. In L. Basañez & J. A. de la Puente (Eds.), *15th IFAC World Congress*, Barcelona, Spain.

Faucou, S., Déplanche, A.-M., & Trinquet, Y. (2004). An ADL-centric approach for the formal design of real-time systems. In P. Dissaux, M. Filali Amine, P. Michel & F. Vernadat (Eds.), *IFIP World Computer Congress 2004–Proceedings of the Workshop on Architecture Description Languages*, Toulouse, France.

Feiler, P. H., Gluch, D. P., & Hudak, J. J. (2006). *The architecture analysis & design language (AADL): An introduction* (Tech. Rep. No CMU/SEI-2006-TN-011). Carnegie Mellon University, Pittsburgh, PA.

Feiler, P. H., Lewis, B., & Vestal, S. (2003). The SAE avionics architecture description language (AADL) standard: A basis for model-based architecture-driven embedded systems engineering. In *IEEE Real-Time Application Symposium 2003–Workshop on Model-Driven Embedded Systems*, Washington D.C.

Fennel, H., Bunzel, S., Heinecke, H., Bielefeld, J., Fürstand, S., Schnelle, K. P., et al. (2006, October). Achievements and exploitation of the AUTOSAR development partnership. Paper presented at *Convergence 2006*, Detroit, MI.

FlexRay Consortium. (2005). *FlexRay communications system-protocol specification-version 2.1.* Retrieved from http://www.flexray.com

Freund, U., Gurrieri, O., Küster, J., Lönn, H., Migge, J., Reiser, M.-O., et al. (2004a). An architecture description language for developing automotive ECU-software. In *INCOSE 2004, International Conference On Systems Engineering*, Toulouse, France.

Freund, U., Gurrieri, O., Lönn, H., Eden, J., Migge, J., Reiser, M.-O., et al. (2004b, September). *An architecture description language supporting automotive software product lines.* Presented at Workshop on Solutions for Automotive Software Architectures, satellite event of the Third Software Product Line Conference, SPLC2004, Boston.

Fürst, S. (2006). AUTOSAR for safety-related systems: Objectives, approach, and status. In *Proceedings of 2nd IEE Conference on Automotive Electronics*, London, UK.

Giusto, P., Brunel, J.-Y., Ferrari, A., Fourgeau, E., Lavagno, L., & Sangiovanni-Vincentelli, A. (2002). Automotive virtual integration platforms: Why's, what's, and how's. In *Proceedings of the International Conference of Computation Design*, Freiburg, Germany.

Hansson, H., Lawson, H., Bridal, O., Eriksson, C., Larsson, S., Lönn, H., & Strömberg, M. (1997). Basement: An architecture and methodology for distributed automotive real-time systems. *IEEE Transactions on Computers, 46*(9), 1016–1027. doi:10.1109/12.620482

ISO. (1994). Road vehicles–interchange of digital information–controller area network for high-speed communication, ISO 11898, International Organization for Standardization (ISO).

ISO. (1994). Road vehicles–low-speed serial data communication–part 2: Low-speed controller area network, ISO 11519-2, International Organization for Standardization (ISO).

Ledeczi, A., Maroti, M., Bakay, A., Nordstrom, G., Garrett, J., Thomason, C., et al. (2001). *GME 2000 users manual, v2.0* (Tech. Rep.). Nashville, TN: Vanderbilt University.

Luckham, D. C., Kenney, J. J., Augustin, L. M., Vera, J., Bryan, D., & Mann, W. (1995). Specification and analysis of system architecture using Rapide. *IEEE Transactions on Software Engineering, 21*(4), 336–355. doi:10.1109/32.385971

Magee, J., Dulay, N., Eisenbach, S., & Kramer, J. (1995). Specifying distributed software architectures. In W. Schäfer & P. Botella (Eds.), *5ᵗʰ European Software Engineering Conference* (LNCS 989, pp.137-153). London: Springer-Verlag.

Medvidovic, N., & Taylor, R. (2000). A classification and comparison framework for software architecture description languages. *IEEE Transactions on Software Engineering, 26*(1), 70–93. doi:10.1109/32.825767

Migge, J., & Elloy, J. P. (2000). Embedded electronic architecture. In *Proceedings of 3rd International Workshop on Open Systems in Automotive Networks*, Bad Homburg, Germany.

Mishra, P., & Dutt, N. (2008). *Processor description languages.* Morgan Kaufmann.

Morgan, M. J. (1991). Integrated Modular Avionics for next generation commercial airplanes. *IEEE Aerospace and Electronic Systems Magazine, 6*(8), 9–12. doi:10.1109/62.90950

Navet, N., & Simonot-Lion, F. (2008). A review of embedded automotive protocols. In N. Navet & F. Simonot-Lion (Eds.), *Automotive embedded systems handbook.* Taylor&Francis.

SAE As-2 Embedded Computing System Committee. (2004). Architecture analysis & design language (AADL) (Document Number AS5506).

Schätz, B., Kühnel, C., & Gonschorek, M. (2008). The FlexRay protocol. In N. Navet & F. Simonot-Lion (Eds.), *Automotive embedded systems handbook*. Taylor&Francis.

Scheidler, C., Heiner, G., Sasse, R., Fuchs, E., Kopetz, H., & Temple, C. (1997). Time-triggered architecture (TTA). In *Conference Multimedia, Embedded Systems, and Electronic Commerce Conference-EMMSEC'97*, Florence, Italy.

Schubotz, H. (2008, April). *Experience with ISO WD 26262 in automotive safety projects*. Paper presented at the SAE World Congress & Exhibition, Detroit, MI.

SynDEx. (2008). Retrieved on July 1, 2008, from http://www.rocq-inria.fr/syndex/

SAE. (2004). AADL Standard Info Site. Retrieved on July 12, 2008, from http://www.aadl.info/

Tindell, K., & Burns, A. (1994). Guaranteeing message latencies on controller area network (CAN). *1st International CAN Conference, ICC'94*, Mainz, Germany.

Tomiyama, H., Halambi, A., Grun, P., Dutt, N., & Nicolau, A. (1999). Architecture description languages for system-on-chip design. *6th Asia Pacific Conference on cHip Design Languages, APCHDL'99*, Fukuoka, Japan.

Törner, F., Chen, D. J., Johansson, R., Lönn, H., & Törngren, M. (2008). Supporting an automotive safety case through systematic model based development-the EAST-ADL2 approach. *SAE World Congress*, Detroit, MI.

TTTech Computertechnik GmbH. (2003). Time-triggered protocol TTP/C, high-level specification document, protocol version 1.1. Retrieved from http://www.tttech.com

Voget, S., Golm, M., Sanchez, B., & Stappert, F. (2008). Application of the AUTOSAR standard. In N. Navet & F. Simonot-Lion (Eds.), *Automotive embedded systems handbook*. Taylor & Francis.

Weber, M., & Weisbrod, J. (2003). Requirements engineering in automotive development–experiences and challenges. *IEEE Software*, *20*(1), 16–24. doi:10.1109/MS.2003.1159025

# Chapter 15
# Model–Based Testing of Embedded Systems Exemplified for the Automotive Domain

**Justyna Zander**
*Fraunhofer Institute FOKUS, Germany*

**Ina Schieferdecker**
*Fraunhofer Institute FOKUS & Technische Universität Berlin, Germany*

## ABSTRACT

*The purpose of this chapter is to introduce the test methods applied for embedded systems addressing selected problems in the automotive domain. Model-based test approaches are reviewed and categorized. Weak points are identified and a novel test method is proposed. It is called model-in-the-loop for embedded system test (MiLEST) and is realized in MATLAB®/Simulink®/Stateflow® environment. Its main contribution refers to functional black-box testing based on the system and test models. It is contrasted with the test methods currently applied in the industry that form dedicated solutions, usually specialized in a concrete testing context. The developed signal-feature-oriented paradigm developed herewith allows the abstract description of signals and their properties. It addresses the problem of missing reference signal flows and allows for a systematic and automatic test data selection. Processing of both discrete and continuous signals is possible, so that the hybrid behavior of embedded systems can be handled.*

## INTRODUCTION

### Embedded System Context

An *embedded system* (Broy et al., 1998, Lazić & Velašević, 2004) is a system built for dedicated control functions. *Embedded software* (Lazić & Velašević, 2004; Conrad, 2004) is the software running on an embedded system. Embedded systems have become increasingly sophisticated and their software content has grown rapidly for the last years. Applications now consist of hundreds of thousands or even more lines of code. The requirements that must be fulfilled while developing embedded software are complex in comparison to the standard software. Embedded systems are often produced in large volumes and the software is difficult to be updated once the product is deployed. Embedded systems interact with real-life environment. Hybrid aspects are often expressed via mathematical formu-

DOI: 10.4018/978-1-60566-750-8.ch015

las. In terms of software development, increased complexity of products, shortened development cycles and higher customer expectations of quality implicate the extreme importance and automation need for software testing. Software development activities in every phase are error prone, so the process of defects detection plays a crucial role. The cost of finding and fixing defects grows exponentially in the development cycle. The software testing problem is complex because of the large number of possible scenarios. The typical testing process is a human-intensive activity and, as such, it is usually unproductive and often inadequately done. Nowadays, testing is one of the weakest points of current development practices. According to the study given by Encontre (2003) 50% of embedded systems development projects are months behind schedule and only 44% of designs meet 20% of functionality and performance expectations. This happens despite the fact that approximately 50% of total development effort is spent on testing (Helmerich et al., 2005). The impact of research into test methodologies that reduce this effort is therefore very high and strongly desirable (Helmerich et al., 2005; Bouyssounouse & Sifakis, 2005).

Although a number of valuable efforts in the context of testing already exist, there is still a lot of space to improve the situation. This applies in particular, to the automation potential of the test methods. Also, a systematic, appropriately structured, repeatable and consistent test specification is still an aim to be reached. Furthermore, both abstract and concrete views should be supported so as to improve the readability, on the one hand and assure the executability of the resulting test, on the other hand. The testing method should address all aspects of a tested system – whether a mix of discrete and continuous signals, time constrained functionality or a complex configuration is considered. In order to establish a controlled and stable testing process with respect to time, budget and software quality, the software testing process must be modeled, measured and analyzed. Moreover,

the existence of executable system models opens the potentials for model-based testing (MBT).

## Automotive Domain

Studies show that the strongest impact of embedded systems on the market has to be expected in the automotive industry. The share of innovative electronics and software in the total value of an automobile is currently estimated to be at least 25%, with an expected increase to 40% in 2010 and up to 50% for the time after 2010 (Helmerich et al., 2005; Schäuffele & Zurawka, 2006). Prominent examples of such electronic systems are safety facilities, advanced driver assistance systems (ADAS) or adaptive cruise control (ACC). These functionalities are realized by software within electronic control units (ECUs). A modern car has up to 80 ECUs (Schäuffele & Zurawka, 2006).

Furthermore, the complexity of car software dramatically increases as it implements formerly mechanically or electronically integrated functions. Yet, the functions are distributed over several ECUs interacting with each other. Studies by Maxton & Wormald (2004), Schäuffele & Zurawka (2006), Broy et al. (2007) predict that most innovations in a car will come from its electronic embedded systems and their inherent software. Nowadays, *embedded software* makes up 85% of the value of the entire system, according to Helmerich et al. (2005).

At the same time, it is demanded to shorten time-to-market for a car by making its software components reliable and safe. Additionally, studies provided in DESS deliverable (2001) show that the cost of recalling a car model with a safety critical failure can be more than the cost of thorough testing/verification. Under these circumstances the introduction of quality assurance techniques in the automotive domain becomes obvious and will be followed within this work.

The remainder of this chapter is the following. In Section 2, testing requirements for embedded systems are considered. The test development process, test dimensions and MBT are discussed. Section 3 categorizes the MBT approaches based on a taxonomy. In Section 4, the state of the art is reviewed so as to introduce the proposed test method in Section 5. Section 6 gives a simple case study and Section 7 enlightens the future trends. The chapter is completed with conclusions.

## TESTING OF EMBEDDED SYSTEMS

### Background

Testing, an analytic means for assessing the quality of software (Utting & Legeard, 2006), is one of the most important phases during the software development process with regard to quality assurance. It *„ can never show the absence of failures "* (Dijkstra, 1972), but it aims at increasing the confidence that a system meets its specified behavior. Testing is an activity performed for improving the product quality by identifying defects and problems. It cannot be undertaken in isolation. Instead, in order to be in any way successful and efficient, it must be embedded in adequate software development process and have interfaces to the respective sub-processes.

Testing can lead to the detection of errors, faults and failures. An *error* is a human action that produces an incorrect result as defined in ISTQB Glossary (2006). *Fault* (also called defect) is a flaw in a component or system that can cause the component or system to fail to perform its required function, e.g., an incorrect statement or data definition. A fault, if encountered during execution, may cause a *failure* of the component or system (ISTQB Glossary, 2006). Failures represent the deviation of the component or system from its expected delivery, service, or result.

## Test Development Process

The fundamental test process according to Spillner & Linz (2005), and ISTQB Glossary (2006) comprises (1) planning, (2) specification, (3) execution, (4) recording (i.e., documenting the results), (5) checking for completion, and test closure activities (e.g., rating the final results).

Test planning includes the planning of resources and the laying down of a test strategy: defining the test methods and the coverage criteria to be achieved, the test completion criteria, structuring and prioritizing the tests, and selecting the tool support as well as configuration of the test environment (Spillner & Linz, 2005). In the test specification the corresponding test cases are specified using the test methods defined by the test plan (Spillner & Linz, 2005). Test execution means the execution of test cases and test scenarios. Test records serve to make the test execution understandable for people not directly involved (e.g., customer) and prove afterwards, whether and how the planned test strategy was in actual fact executed. Finally, during the test closure step data is collected from completed test activities to consolidate experience, testware, facts, and numbers. The test process is evaluated and a report is provided in ISTQB Glossary (2006).

In addition, Dai (2006) considers a process of test development. The test development process, related to steps 2 – 4 of the fundamental test process, can be divided into six phases, which are usually consecutive, but may be iterated: test requirements, test design, test specification, test implementation, test execution, and test evaluation.

The test process in the context of automotive embedded systems covers with the fundamental one, although here only steps 2 – 4 are addressed in further considerations. Compared to the approach of Dai (2006) the test development process is modified and shortened. It is motivated by the different nature of the considered *system under test* (SUT). Within traditional software and test

*Figure 1. The five test dimensions for embedded system test*

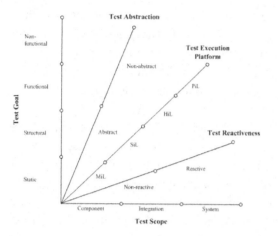

development, phases are clearly separated (Conrad & Hötzer, 1998). For automotive systems a closer integration of the specification and implementation phases occurs. Hence, after defining the test requirements, the test design phase encompasses the preparation of a test harness. The detailed test specification and test implementation are done within one step as the applied modeling language is executable. Further on, test execution and test evaluation are performed sometimes simultaneously (Zander-Nowicka, 2008).

## Hybrid Embedded Systems Test and its Dimensions

Tests can be classified in different levels depending on the characteristics of the SUT and the test system. Neukirchen (2004) aims at testing the communication systems and categorizes testing in the dimensions of test goals, test scope, and test distribution. Dai (2006) replaces the test distribution by a dimension describing the different test development phases, since she is testing both local and distributed systems. In this chapter embedded systems are regarded as SUTs, thus, the test dimensions are modified as shown in Figure 1.

**Test Goal:** During the software development systems are tested with different purposes (i.e.,

goals). They can be categorized into static testing, also called *review*, and dynamic testing, whereas the latter is distinguished between structural, functional, and non-functional testing. In the automotive, after the *review* phase, the test goal is usually to check the functional behavior of the system. Non-functional tests appear in later development stages.

- *Static Test:* Errors can be revealed without execution by just examining its source code (ISTQB Glossary, 2006). Similarly, other development artefacts can be reviewed (e.g., requirements, models or test specification itself). This process is called *static testing. Dynamic testing* in contrast, bases on execution.

- *Structural Test:* Structural tests relate to the dynamic test of the SUT structure (e.g., control or data flow). The internal structure of the system (e.g., code or model) needs to be known. Therefore, structural tests are also called white-box or glass-box tests (Myers, 1979; ISTQB Glossary, 2006).

- *Functional Test:* Functional testing is concerned with assessing the functional behavior of an SUT against the functional requirements. In contrast to structural tests, functional tests do not require any knowledge about system internals. They are therefore called black-box tests (Beizer, 1995). In this category functional safety tests are also included. Their purpose is to determine the safety of a software product. They require a systematic, planned, executed, and documented procedure. At present, safety tests are only a small part of software testing in the automotive area. By introduction of safety standards such as IEC 61508 and ISO 26262 the meaning of software safety tests will, however, increase considerably within the next few years.

- *Non-functional Test*: Similar to functional tests, non-functional tests are performed against requirements specification of the system. In contrast to pure functional testing, non-functional testing aims at the assessment of non-functional, such as reliability, load or performance requirements. Non-functional tests are usually black-box tests. Nevertheless, for retrieving certain information (e.g., internal clock), internal access during test execution is required.

**Test Abstraction:** As far as the abstraction level of the test specification is considered, the higher the abstraction, the better test understandability, readability, and reusability is observed. However, the specified test cases must be executable at the same time. Hence, the abstraction level should not affect the test execution in a negative way. The *non-abstract* tests are supported by a number of tool providers and they do not scale for larger industrial projects (Lehmann & Krämer, 2008).

The approach proposed at the end of this chapter develops a conceptual framework for *abstract* test specification (cf. Section 5); however, simultaneously an *executable* technical framework for a selected platform is built.

**Test Execution Platform:** The test execution is managed by so called test platforms. The purpose of the test platform is to stimulate the test object (i.e., SUT) with inputs, and to observe and analyze the outputs of the SUT.

- *Model-in-the-Loop (MiL):* The first integration level, MiL, is based on the model of the system itself. In this platform the SUT is a functional model or implementation model that is tested in an open-loop (i.e., without any plant model in the first place) or closed-loop test with a plant model (i.e., without any physical hardware) (Kamga et al., 2007; Schäuffele & Zurawka, 2006, Lehmann & Krämer, 2008). The test purpose is basically functional testing in early

development phases in simulation environments such as MATLAB®/Simulink®/Stateflow®.

- *Software-in-the-Loop (SiL):* During SiL the SUT is software tested in a closed or open-loop. The software components under test are usually implemented in C and are either hand-written or generated by code generators based on implementation models. The test purpose in SiL is mainly functional testing (Kamga et al., 2007). If the software is built for a fixed-point architecture, the required scaling is already part of the software.

- *Processor-in-the-Loop (PiL):* In PiL embedded controllers are integrated into embedded devices with proprietary hardware (i.e., ECU). Testing on PiL level is similar to SiL tests, but the embedded software runs on a target board with the target processor or on a target processor emulator. Tests on PiL level are important because they can reveal faults that are caused by the target compiler or by the processor architecture. It is the last integration level which allows debugging during tests in a cheap and manageable way (Lehmann & Krämer, 2008). Therefore, the effort spent by PiL testing is worthwhile in almost all cases.

- *Hardware-in-the-Loop (HiL):* When testing the embedded system on HiL level the software runs on the final ECU. However the environment around the ECU is still a simulated one. ECU and environment interact via the digital and analog electrical connectors of the ECU. The objective of testing on HiL level is to reveal faults in the low-level services of the ECU and in the I/O services (Schäuffele & Zurawka, 2006). Additionally, acceptance tests of components delivered by the supplier are executed on the HiL level because the component itself is the integrated ECU (Kamga et al., 2007). HiL testing requires real-time behavior of the environment model to ensure that the communication with the ECU is the same as in the real application.

- *Car:* Finally, the last integration level is obviously the car itself, as already mentioned. The final ECU runs in the real car which can either be a sample or a car from the production line. However, these tests, as performed only in late development phases, are expensive and do not allow configuration parameters to be varied arbitrarily (Lehmann & Krämer, 2008). Hardware faults are difficult to trigger and the reaction of the SUT is often difficult to observe because internal signals are no longer accessible (Kamga et al., 2007). For these reasons, the number of in-car tests decreases while model-based testing gains more attention.

The approach proposed at the end of this chapter relates mainly to the system design level so as to start testing as early as possible in the development cycle. Thus, the *MiL* platform is researched in detail. The other platforms are not excluded from the methodological viewpoint. However, the portability between different execution platforms is beyond the scope of this work.

**Test Reactiveness:** A concept of *test reactiveness* emerges when test cases are dependent on the system behavior. That is, the execution of a test case depends on what the SUT is doing while being tested. In this sense the system under test and the test driver run in a *'closed loop'*.

In the following, before the *test reactiveness* will be elaborated in detail, the definition of *open-* and *closed-loop system configuration* will be explicitly distinguished:

- *Open-loop System Configuration:* When testing a component in a so-called open-loop the test object is tested directly without any environment or environmental model. This kind of testing is reasonable if the behavior of the test object is described based on the interaction directly at its interfaces (I/O ports). This configuration is applicable for SW modules and implementation sub-models, as well as for control systems with discrete I/O.

- *Closed-loop System Configuration:* For feedback control systems and for complex control systems it is necessary to integrate the SUT with a plant model so as to perform closed-loop tests. In early phases where the interaction between SUT and plant model is implemented in software (i.e., without digital or analog I/O, buses etc.) the plant model does not have to ensure real-time constraints. However, when the HiL systems are considered and the communication between the SUT and the plant model is implemented via data buses, the plant model may include real hardware components (i.e., sensors and actuators). This applies especially when the physics of a system is very crucial for the functionality or when it is too complex to be described in a model.

- *Test Reactiveness:* Reactive tests are tests that apply any signal or data derived from the SUT outputs or test system itself to influence the signals fed into the SUT. With this practice, the execution of reactive test cases varies depending on the SUT behavior. The test reactiveness as such gives the test system a possibility to immediately react to the incoming behavior by modifying the test according to the predefined deterministic criteria. The precondition for achieving the test reactiveness is an online monitoring of the SUT, though. The advantages can be obtained in a number of test specification steps (e.g., an automatic sequencing of test cases, online prioritizing of the test cases).

For example, assume that the adaptive cruise control (ACC) activation should be tested. It is possible to start the ACC only when a certain velocity level has been reached. Hence, the precondition for a test case is the increase of the velocity from *0* up to the point when the ACC may be activated. If the test system is able to detect this point automatically, the ACC may be tested immediately.

A discussion about possible risks and open questions around reactive tests can be found in the work of Lehmann (2003).

**Test Scope:** Finally, the test scope has to be considered. Test scopes describe the granularity of the SUT. Due to the composition of the system, tests at different scopes may reveal different failures as defined in ISTQB Glossary (2006), and D-MINT deliverables (2008). Therefore, they are usually performed in the following order:

- *Component:* At the scope of component testing, the smallest testable component (e.g., a class in an object-oriented implementation or a single ECU) is tested in isolation.
- *Integration:* The scope of integration test is to combine components with each other and test those not yet as a whole system but as a subsystem (i.e., ACC system composed of a speed controller, a distance controller, switches and several processing units). It exposes defects in the interfaces and in the interactions between integrated components or systems (ISTQB Glossary, 2006).
- *System:* In a system test, the complete system (i.e., a vehicle) consisting of subsystems is tested. A complex embedded system is usually distributed; the single subsystems are connected via buses using different data types and interfaces through which the system can be accessed for testing (Hetzel, 1988).

## MODEL-BASED TESTING TAXONOMY

Model-based testing (MBT) relates to a process of test generation from an SUT model by application of a number of sophisticated methods. MBT is the automation of black-box test design (Utting & Legeard, 2006). Several authors such as Bernard, 2004; Campbel et al., 2005; Utting, 2005; Frantzen et al., 2006; Kamga et al., 2007; Tretmans, 2008 define MBT as testing in which test cases are derived in whole or in part from a model that describes some aspects of the SUT based on selected criteria in different contexts. Dai (2006) denotes MBT into model-driven testing (MDT since she proposes the approach in the context of Model Driven Architecture (MDA). Utting et al. (2006) add that MBT inherits the complexity of the domain or, more particularly, of the related domain models.

MBT allows tests to be linked directly to the SUT requirements, makes readability, understandability and maintainability of tests easier. It helps to ensure a repeatable and scientific basis for testing and it may give good coverage of all the behaviors of the SUT (Utting, 2005). Finally, it is a way to reduce the efforts and cost for testing (Pretschner et al., 2005).

The term *MBT* is widely used today with slightly different meanings. Surveys on different MBT approaches are given in Broy (2005), Utting et al. (2005, 2006), D-MINT deliverable (2008). In the automotive industry MBT is used to describe all testing activities in the context of MBD (Conrad et al., 2004; Lehmann & Krämer, 2008). Rau (2002), Lamberg et al. (2004), or Conrad (2004) define MBT as a test process that encompasses a combination of different test methods which utilize the executable model as a source of information. Thus, the automotive viewpoint on MBT is rather process-oriented. A single testing technique is not enough to provide an expected level of test coverage. Hence, different test methods should be combined to complement each other relating to all the specified test dimensions (e.g., functional and structural testing techniques should be combined). If sufficient test coverage has been achieved on model level, the test cases can be reused for testing the control software generated from the model and the control unit within the framework of back-to-back tests (Wiesbrock et al., 2002). With this practice, the functional equivalence between executable model, code and ECUs can be verified and validated (Conrad et al., 2004).

For the purpose of the approach presented in Section 5, the following understanding of MBT is used:

*Model-based testing is testing in which the entire test specification is derived in whole or in part from both the system requirements and a model that describe selected functional aspects of the SUT. In this context, the term entire test specification covers the abstract test scenarios substantiated with the concrete sets of test data and the expected SUT outputs. It is organized in test cases.*

Further on, the resulting test specification is *executed* together with the SUT model so as to provide the test results. In addition, a *test specification model* (also called *test case specification*, *test model* or *test design* in the literature (Pretschner, 2003; Zander et al., 2005; Dai, 2006) is created semi-automatically and concrete test data variants are derived automatically from it.

Furthermore, a graphical form of a test specification will increase its readability. The provided test patterns will considerably reduce the test definition effort and support their reusability. Then, an abstract and common way of describing both discrete and continuous signals will result in automated test signals generation and their evaluation.

Moreover, since the MBT approaches have to be integrated into the existing development processes and combined with the existing methods and tools, a good practice is to select a common framework for both system and test definition.

By that, MBD and MBT are supported using the same environment.

In Section 5, an example of such an MBT understanding is presented. It is called Model-in-the-Loop for Embedded System Test (MiLEST) and is realized in ML/SL/SF environment.

## Model-Based Testing Taxonomy

In the work of Utting et al. (2006) a comprehensive *taxonomy* for MBT identifying its three general *classes*: model, test generation, and test execution is provided. Each of the classes is divided into further *categories*. The model-related ones are subject, independence, characteristics, and paradigm. Further on, the test generation is split into test selection criteria and technology, whereas the test execution partitions into execution options.

In the following work, the *taxonomy* is enriched with an additional *class*, called test evaluation. The test evaluation means comparing the actual SUT outputs with the expected SUT behavior based on a test oracle. Test oracle enables a decision to be made as to whether the actual SUT outputs are correct. It is, apart from the data, a crucial part of a test case. The test evaluation is divided into two *categories*: specification and technology.

Furthermore, in this chapter only one selected class of the system model is investigated. For clarification purposes, its short description based on the options available in the taxonomy of Utting et al. (2006) will be given in the following. The subject is the model (e.g., SL/SF model) that specifies the intended behavior of the SUT and its environment, often connected via a feedback loop. Regarding the independence level this model can be generally used for both test case and code generation. Indicating the model characteristics, it provides deterministic hybrid behavior constrained by timed events, including continuous functions and various data types. Finally, the modeling paradigm combines a history-based, functional data flow paradigm (e.g., the SL function blocks) with a transition-based notation (e.g., SF charts).

*Figure 2. Overview of the taxonomy for model-based testing*

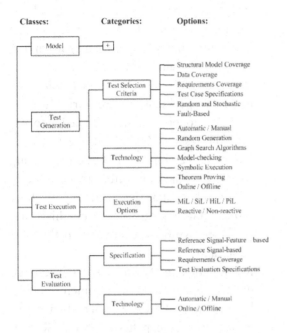

The overview of the resulting, slightly modified and extended MBT *taxonomy* is illustrated in Figure 2. The modification results from the focus of this chapter, which is put on embedded systems. All the categories are split into further instances which influence each other within a given category or between them. The notion of 'A/B/C' at the leaves indicates mutually exclusive options, while the straight lines link further instantiations of a given dimension without exclusion. It is a good practice since, for example, applying more than one test selection criterion and by that, more generation technologies can provide a better test coverage, eventually.

In the next three sections it is referred to the *classes* of the MBT taxonomy and the particular *categories* and *options* are explained in depth. The descriptions of the most important *options* followed in this chapter contain examples of their realization, respectively.

## Test Generation

The process of test generation starts from the system requirements, taking into account the test objectives. It is defined in a given test context and leads to the creation of test cases. Depending on the test selection criteria and generation technology a number of approaches exist. They are reviewed below.

**Test selection criteria:** Test selection criteria define the facilities that are used to control the generation of tests. They help to specify the tests and do not depend on the SUT code (Utting et al., 2006). In the following, the most commonly-used criteria are investigated. Different test methods should be combined to complement each other so as to achieve the best test coverage. Hence, there is no best suitable criterion for generating the test specification.

- *Structural model coverage criteria:* These exploit the structure of the model to select the test cases. They deal with coverage of the control-flow through the model, based on ideas from control-flow through code. Pretschner (2003) shows how test cases can be generated to satisfy the Modified Condition/Decision Coverage (MC/DC) coverage criterion. The idea is to first generate a set of test case specifications that enforce certain variable valuations and then generate test cases for them. Similarly, Safety Test Builder (STB) or Reactis Tester generate test sequences covering a set of SF test objectives (e.g., transitions, states, junctions, actions, MC/DC coverage) and a set of SL test objectives (e.g., boolean flow, look-up tables, conditional subsystems coverage).

- *Data coverage criteria:* The idea is to split the data range into equivalence classes and select one representative from each class. This partitioning is usually complemented by the boundary value analysis (Kosmatov et al., 2004), where the critical limits of the data ranges or boundaries determined by constraints are additionally selected. An example is the MATLAB Automated Testing Tool (MATT) enabling black-box testing of SL models and code generated from it by Real-Time Workshop®. It generally enables the creation of custom test data for model simulations by setting their types for each input. Further on, accuracy, constant, minimum, and maximum values can be provided to generate the test data matrix. Another realization of this criterion is provided by Classification Tree Editor for Embedded Systems (CTE/ES) implementing the Classification Tree Method (CTM) (Grochtmann & Grimm, 1993; Conrad, 2003). The SUT inputs form the classifications in the roots of the tree. Then, the input ranges are divided into classes according to the equivalence partitioning method. The test cases are specified by selecting leaves of the tree in the combination table. A line in the table specifies a test case. CTE/ES provides a way of finding test cases systematically. It breaks the test scenario design process down into steps. Additionally, the test scenario is visualized in a graphical user interface (GUI).

- *Requirements coverage criteria:* These aim to cover all the informal SUT requirements. Traceability of the SUT requirements to the system or test model/code can support the realization of this criterion. It is targeted by almost every test approach.
- *Test case specifications:* When the test engineer defines a test case specification in some formal notation, these can be used to determine which tests will be generated. It is explicitly decided which set of test objectives should be covered. The notation used to express these objectives may be the same as the notation used for the model (Utting et al., 2006). Notations commonly

used for test objectives include Finite State Machines (FSMs), UML Testing Profile (UTP), regular expressions, temporal logic formulas, constraints, and Markov chains (for expressing intended usage patterns). A prominent example of applying this criterion is described in Dai (2006), where the test case specifications are retrieved from UML® models and transformed into executable tests in Testing and Test Control Notation, version 3 (TTCN-3) by using Model Driven Architecture (MDA) methods (Zander, 2005). The work of Pretschner (2003, 2004) is also based on this criterion (see symbolic execution in the next paragraph).

- *Random and stochastic criteria:* These are mostly applicable to environment models, because it is the environment that determines the usage patterns of the SUT. A typical approach is to use a Markov chain to specify the expected SUT usage profile. Another example is to use a statistical usage model in addition to the behavioral model of the SUT (Carter et al., 2008). The statistical model acts as the selection criterion and chooses the paths, while the behavioral model is used to generate the oracle for those paths. Exemplifying, Markov Test Logic (MaTeLo) can generate test suites according to several algorithms. Each of them optimizes the test effort according to the objectives such as boundary values, functional coverage, and reliability level. Test cases are generated in XML/HTML format for manual execution or in TTCN-3 for automatic execution (Dulz & Fenhua, 2003). Another instance, Java Usage Model Builder Library (JUMBL) can generate test cases either as a collection of test cases which cover the model with the minimum cost or by random sampling with replacement, or in order by probability, or by interleaving the events of other test cases. There is also an interactive test case editor for creating test cases by hand.

- *Fault-based criteria:* These rely on knowledge of typically occurring faults, often designed in the form of a fault model (cf. Aichernig, 2005).

**Test generation technology:** One of the most appealing characteristics of model-based testing is its potential for automation. The automated generation of test cases usually necessitates the existence of kind of test case specifications (Utting et al., 2006).

- *Automatic/Manual technology:* Automatic test generation refers to the situation when the test cases are generated automatically from the information source based on the given criteria (cf. Paiva et al., 2003). Manual test generation refers to the situation when the test cases are produced by hand.
- *Random generation:* Random generation of tests is done by sampling the input space of a system. It is easy to implement, but it takes a long time to reach a certain satisfying level of model coverage as Gutjahr (1999) reports.
- *Graph search algorithms:* Dedicated graph search algorithms include node or arc coverage algorithms such as the Chinese Postman algorithm, which covers each arc at least once. For transition-based models, which use explicit graphs containing nodes and arcs, there are many graph coverage criteria that can be used to control test generation. The commonly used are all nodes, all transitions, all transition pairs, and all cycles. The method is exemplified by Lee & Yannakakis (1994), additionally based on structural coverage of FSM models.
- *Model checking:* Model checking is a technology for verifying or falsifying properties of a system. A property typically expresses

an unwanted situation. The model checker verifies whether this situation is reachable or not (Ammann & Black, 2002). It can yield counter examples when a property is not satisfied. If no counter example is found, then the property is proven and the situation has never been reached. Such a mechanism is implemented in CheckMate (Silva et al., 2000), Safety Checker Blockset (SCB) or in Embedded *Validator*. The general idea of test case generation with model checkers is to first formulate test case specifications as reachability properties, for instance, "eventually, a certain state is reached or a certain transition fires". A model checker then yields traces that reach the given state or that eventually make the transition fire. Other variants use mutations of models or properties to generate test suites.

- *Symbolic execution:* The idea of symbolic execution is to run an executable model not with single input values but with sets of input values instead (Marre & Arnould, 2000). These are represented as constraints. With this practice, symbolic traces are generated. By instantiation of these traces with concrete values the test cases are derived. Symbolic execution is guided by test case specifications. These are given as explicit constraints and symbolic execution may be done randomly by respecting these constraints. Pretschner (2003, 2004) presents an approach to test case generation with symbolic execution on the backgrounds of Constraint Logic Programming (CLP) that are initially transformed from the AutoFocus models. He concludes that test case generation for both functional and structural test case specifications limits to finding states in the model's state space. Then, the aim of symbolic execution of a model is then to find a trace representing a test case that leads to the specified state.

- *Theorem proving:* Usually theorem provers are used to check the satisfiability of formulas that directly occur in the models. One variant is similar to the use of model checkers where a theorem prover replaces the model checker. The technique applied in Simulink® Design Verifier™ (SL DV) uses mathematical procedures to search through the possible execution paths of the model so as to find test cases and counter examples.

- *Online/Offline generation technology:* With online test generation, algorithms can react to the actual outputs of the SUT during the test execution. This idea is used for implementing the reactive tests too. Offline testing means that test cases are generated before they are run. A set of test cases is generated once and can be executed many times. Also, the test generation and test execution can be performed on different machines, levels of abstractions or in different environments. Finally, if the test generation process is slower than test execution, then there are obvious advantages to doing the test generation phase only once.

## Test Execution

The test execution options in the context of this chapter have been already described. Hence, in the following only reactive testing and the related work on the reactive/non-reactive option is reviewed.

**Execution options:** Execution options refer to the execution of a test.

- *Reactive/Non-reactive execution:* Reactive tests are tests that apply any signal or data derived from the SUT outputs or test system itself to influence the signals fed into the SUT. Then the execution of reactive test cases varies depending on the SUT behavior, in contrast to the non-reactive test

execution, where the SUT does not influence the test at all.

Reactive tests can be implemented within AutomationDesk. Such tests react to changes in model variables within one simulation step. The scripts run on the processor of the HiL system in real time, synchronously to the model.

The Reactive Test Bench allows for specification of single timing diagram test benches that react to the user's Hardware Description Language (HDL) design files. Markers are placed in the timing diagram so that the SUT activity is recognized. Markers can also be used to call user-written HDL functions and tasks within a diagram.

Dempster & Stuart (2002) conclude that a dynamic test generator and checker are more effective in creating reactive test sequences. They are also more efficient because errors can be detected as they happen. Resigning from the reactive testing methods, a simulation may run for a few hours only to find out during the post-process checking that an error occurred a few minutes after the simulation start.

In the work of Jeannet et al., (2005), in addition to checking the conformance of the implementation under test (IUT), the goal of the test case is to guide the parallel execution towards satisfaction of a test purpose. Due to that feature, the test execution can be seen as a game between two programs: the test case and the IUT. The test case wins if it succeeds in realizing one of the scenarios specified by the test purpose; the IUT wins if the execution cannot realize any test objective. The game may be played offline or online (Jeannet et al., 2005).

## Test Evaluation

The test evaluation, also called the test assessment, is the process that exploits the test oracle. It is a mechanism for analyzing the SUT output and deciding about the test result. As already discussed before, the actual SUT results are compared with the expected ones and a verdict is assigned. An oracle may be the existing system, test specification or an individual's specialized knowledge. The test evaluation is treated explicitly in this chapter since herewith a new concept for the test evaluation is proposed.

**Specification:** Specification of the test assessment algorithms may be based on different foundations that cover some criteria. It usually forms a kind of model or a set of ordered reference signals/ data assigned to specific scenarios. Considering continuous signals the division into reference-based and reference signal-feature – based evaluation becomes particularly important:

- *Reference signal – based specification:* Test evaluation based on reference signals assesses the SUT behavior comparing the SUT outcomes with the previously specified references. An example of such an evaluation approach is realized in the MTest or SystemTest™. The reference signals can be defined using a signal editor or they can be obtained as a result of a simulation. Similarly, test results of back-to-back tests can be analyzed with the help of MEval.
- *Reference signal-feature – based specification:* Test evaluation based on reference signal feature assesses the SUT behavior comparing the SUT outcomes partitioned into features with the previously specified reference values for those features. Such an approach to test evaluation is supported in the Time Partitioning Test (TPT). It is based on the script language Python extended with some syntactic test evaluation functions. By that, the test assessment can be flexibly designed and allows for dedicated complex algorithms and filters to be applied to the recorded test signals. A library containing complex evaluation functions is available.
- *Requirements coverage criteria:* Similar to the case of test data generation, they aim to cover all the informal SUT requirements, but this time with respect to the expected SUT behavior (i.e., regarding the test evaluation scenarios) specified there. Traceability of the SUT requirements to the test model/code can support the realization of this criterion.
- *Test evaluation specifications:* This criterion refers to the specification of the outputs expected from the SUT after the test case execution. Already Richardson et al., (1998) describe several approaches to specification-based test selection and build them up on the concept of test oracle, faults and failures. When the test engineer defines test scenarios in some formal notation, these can be used to determine how, when and which tests will be evaluated.

**Technology:** The technology of the test assessment specification enable an automatic or manual process, whereas the execution of the test evaluation occurs online or offline.

- *Automatic/Manual technology:* The *option* can be understood twofold, either from the perspective of the test evaluation definition, or its execution. Regarding the specification of the test evaluation, when the expected SUT outputs are defined by hand, then it is a manual test specification process. In contrast, when they are derived automatically (e.g., from the behavioral model), then the test evaluation based on the test oracle occurs automatically. Usually, the expected reference signals/data are defined manually; however, they may be facilitated by parameterized test patterns application. The activity of test assessment itself can be done manually or automatically. Manual specification of the test evaluation means is supported in Simulink® Verification and Validation™ (SL VV), where the predefined assertion blocks can be assigned to the test signals defined in the Signal Builder block in SL. With this practice, functional requirements can be verified during model simulation. The evaluation itself then occurs automatically. The tests developed in SystemTest exercise MATLAB (ML) algorithms and SL models. The tool includes predefined test elements to build and maintain standard test routines. Test cases, including test assessment, can be specified manually at a low abstraction level. A set of automatic evaluation means exists and the comparison of obtained signals with the reference ones is done automatically.

- *Online/Offline execution of the test evaluation:* The online (i.e., on the fly) test evaluation happens already during the SUT execution. Online test evaluation enables the concept of test control and test reactiveness to be extended. Offline means the opposite. Hence, the test evaluation happens after the SUT execution.

Watchdogs defined by Conrad & Hötzer, (1998) enable online test evaluation. It is also possible when using TTCN-3. TPT means for online test assessment are limited and are used as watchdogs for extracting any necessary information for making test cases reactive. The offline evaluation is more sophisticated in TPT.

## ANALYSIS OF THE EXISTING APPROACHES FOR THE AUTOMOTIVE DOMAIN

Recently, the application of model-based specifications in development enables more effective and automated process reaching a higher level of abstraction in the automotive domain.

Thereby, model-based testing and platform-independent approaches have been developed such as CTE/ES, MTest, and TPT. As already

mentioned CTE/ES supports the CTM with partition tests according to structural or data-oriented differences of the system to be tested. It also enables the definition of sequences of test steps in combination with the signal flows and their changes along the test. Because of its ease of use, graphical presentation of the test structure and the ability to generate all possible combination of tests, it is widely used in the automotive domain. Integrated with the MTest, test execution, test evaluation, and test management become possible. After the execution, SUT output signals can be compared with previously obtained reference signals. MTest has, however, only limited means to express test behaviors which go beyond simple sequences, but are typical for control systems. The test evaluation bases only on the reference signals which are often not yet available at the early development phase yet and the process of test development is fully manual.

TPT addresses some of these problems. It uses an automaton-based approach to model the test behavior and associates with the states pre- and postconditions on the properties of the tested system (including the continuous signals) and on the timing. In addition, a dedicated run-time environment enables the execution of the tests. The test evaluation is based on a more sophisticated concept of signal feature. However, the specification of the evaluation happens in Python language, without any graphical support. TPT is a dedicated test technology for embedded systems controlled by and acting on continuous signals, but the entire test process is manual and difficult to learn.

Established test tools from, e.g., dSPACE GmbH, Vector Informatik GmbH, MB Tech Group etc. are highly specialized for the automotive domain and usually come together with a test scripting approach which is directly integrated to the respective test device. All these test definitions pertain to a particular test device and by that not portable to other platforms and not exchangeable.

In the following, numerous test approaches are analyzed. Firstly, several, randomly selected academic achievements on testing embedded systems are considered, in general. Then, the test methods applied in the industry are compared.

## Academic Achievements

The approach called Testing-UPPAAL (Mikucionis et al., 2003) presents a framework, a set of algorithms, and a tool for testing of real-time systems based on symbolic techniques used in the UPPAAL model checker. The timed automata network model is extended to a test specification. This one is used to generate test primitives and to check the correctness of system responses. Then, the retrieved timed traces are applied so as to derive a test verdict. Here, online manipulation of test data is an advantage and this concept is partially reused in MiLEST. After all, the state-space explosion problem experienced by many offline test generation tools is reduced since only a limited part of the state space needs to be stored at any point in time. The algorithms use symbolic techniques derived from model checking to efficiently represent and operate on infinite state sets. The implementation of the concept shows that the performance of the computation mechanisms is fast enough for many realistic real-time systems (Mikucionis et al., 2003). However, the approach does not deal with the hybrid nature of the system.

Similar as in MiLEST Bodeveix et al. (2005) consider that a given test case must address a specific goal, which is related to a specific requirement. The proposed approach computes one test case for one specific requirement. This strategy avoids handling the whole specification at once, which reduces the computation complexity. However, here again, the authors focus on testing the timing constraints only, leaving the hybrid behavior testing open.

The same holds for approach presented by Tretmans (2008). Input-output conformance (*ioco*) theory uses labelled transition systems (LTS) as models for specifications, implementations, and

test generation source. *Ioco* defines conformance between implementations and specifications. Similarly as in MiLEST a completeness theorem checking the soundness and exhaustiveness of the *ioco* test method is available. Brandan Briones & Brinksma (2004) extend *ioco* towards testing real-time systems (i.e., *timed-ioco*). It uses timed-LTS and is based on an operational interpretation of the notion of *quiescence*. Frantzen, Tretmans & Willemse (2006) on the other hand, extend *ioco* towards testing based on symbolic execution (i.e., *sioco*). *Sioco* uses symbolic transition systems with an explicit notion of data and data-dependent control flow. The introduction of symbolism avoids the state-space explosion during test generation.

Carter et al. (2008) use two distinct, but complementary concepts of sequence-based specification (SBS) and statistical testing. The system model and the test model for test case generation are distinguished, similar as in MiLEST. The system model is the black-box specification of the software resulting from the SBS process. The test model is the usage model that models the environment producing stimuli for the software system as a result of a stochastic process. The framework proposed in this approach automatically creates Markov chain test models from specifications of the control model (i.e., SF design). The test cases with an oracle are built and statistical results are analyzed. Here, the formerly mentioned JUMBL methods are applied by Prowell (2003). Statistics are used as a means for planning the tests and isolating errors with propagating characteristics. The main shortcoming of this work is that mainly SF models are analyzed, leaving the considerable part of continuous behavior open (i.e., realized in SL design). This is not sufficient for testing the entire functionality of the system.

Philipps et al. (2003) present an approach to generating test cases for hybrid systems automatically. These test cases can be used both for validating models and verifying the respective systems. The method seems to be promising, although as a source of test information two types of system models are used: a hybrid one and its abstracted version in the form of a discrete one. This practice may be very difficult when dealing with the continuous behavior described by differential equations (e.g., purely in SL).

Pretschner et al. (2005) evaluate the efficiency of different MBT techniques. They apply the automotive network controller case study to assess different test suites in terms of error detection, model coverage, and implementation coverage. Here, the comparison between manually or automatically generated test suites both with and without models, at random or with dedicated functional test selection criteria is aimed at. As a result, the test suites retrieved from models, both automatically and manually, detect significantly more requirements errors than handcrafted test suites derived only from the requirements. The number of detected programming errors does not depend on the use of models. Automatically generated tests find as many errors as those defined manually. As the authors claim, a sixfold increase in the number of model-based tests leads to an 11% increase (Pretschner et al., 2005) in detected errors.

Algorithmic testbench generation (ATG) technology (Olen, 2007), though commercially available, is an interesting approach since here the test specification is based on the rule sets. These rule sets show that the high-level testing activities can be performed as a series of lower-level actions. By that, an abstraction is introduced. This hierarchical concept is also used in MiLEST while designing the test system. ATG, similar to MiLEST, supports some aspects of test reactiveness, and includes metrics for measuring the quality of the generated testbench specification. Finally, it reveals cost and time reduction while increasing the quality of the SUT as claimed by Olen (2007).

## Industrial Test Approaches

Considering the test approaches introduced in Table 1, several diversities may be observed. Embedded *Validator* uses model checking as test generation technology and thus, is limited to discrete model sectors. The actual evaluation method offers a basic set of constraints for extracting discrete properties, not addressing continuous signals. Only a few temporal constraints are checked. However, the mentioned properties of the model deal with the concept of signal features, whereas the basic verification patterns contribute to the test patterns and their reusability within the technique proposed in this chapter.

MTest with its CTE/ES gives a good background for partitioning of test inputs into equivalence classes. The data coverage and test case specifications criteria are reused in MiLEST to some extent. Similarly as in SystemTest, the test evaluation is based only on reference signal-based specification, which constitutes a low abstraction level, thus it is not adopted for further development.

MEval is especially powerful for back-to-back-tests and for regression tests, since even very complex reference signals are already available in this case.

Reactis Tester, T-VEC or the method of Pretschner (2003) present approaches for computing test sequences based on structural model coverage. It is searched for tests that satisfy MC/DC criteria. Their value is that the test suites are generated for units (functions, transitions) but also for the entire system or on integration level. The methods seem to be very promising due to their scope and automation grade, they cover only the structural testing criteria, though.

In Reactis Validator only two predefined validation patterns are available. Hence, a systematic test specification is not possible. This gap is bridged in MiLEST that provides *assertion – precondition* pairs. They enable the test evaluation functions to be related with the test data generation.

For SL DV a similar argumentation applies, although another test generation technology is

*Table 1. Classification of the selected test approaches based on the MBT taxonomy*

| MBT Categories, Options Selected Test Tools | Test Generation | | Test Execution | Test Evaluation | |
|---|---|---|---|---|---|
| | *Test Selection Criteria* | *Technology* | *Execution Options* | *Specification* | *Technology* |
| Embedded*Validator* | - does not apply | - automatic generation<br>- model checking | - MiL, SiL<br>- non-reactive | - requirements coverage | - manual specification<br>- does not apply |
| MEval | - does not apply since here back-to-back regression tests are considered | - does not apply | - MiL, SiL, PiL, HiL<br>- non-reactive | - reference signals-based | - manual specification<br>- offline evaluation |
| MTest with CTE/ES | - data coverage<br>- requirements coverage<br>- test case specification<br>- offline generation | - manual generation | - MiL, SiL, PiL, HiL<br>- non-reactive | - reference signals-based | - manual specification<br>- offline evaluation |
| Reactis Tester | - structural model coverage<br>- offline generation | - automatic generation<br>- model checking | - MiL, SiL, HiL<br>- non-reactive | - test evaluation specifications | - automatic specification<br>- offline evaluation |
| Reactis Validator | - structural model coverage<br>- requirements coverage<br>- offline generation | - automatic generation<br>- model checking | - MiL, SiL<br>- non-reactive | - test evaluation specifications | - manual specification<br>- online evaluation |
| Simulink® Verification and Validation™ | - does not apply | - manual generation | - MiL<br>- non-reactive | - requirements coverage | - manual specification<br>- online evaluation |
| Simulink® Design Verifier™ | - structural model coverage<br>- offline generation | - automatic generation<br>- theorem proving | - MiL, SiL<br>- non-reactive | - requirements coverage<br>- test evaluation specifications | - manual specification<br>- online evaluation |
| SystemTest™ | - data coverage<br>- offline generation | - automatic generation | - MiL, SiL, HiL<br>- non-reactive | - reference signals-based | - manual specification<br>- offline evaluation |
| TPT | - data coverage<br>- requirements coverage<br>- test case specification<br>- offline and online generation | - manual generation | - MiL, SiL, PiL, HiL<br>- reactive | - reference signal-feature – based | - manual specification<br>- online and offline evaluation |
| T-VEC | - structural model coverage<br>- data coverage<br>- requirements specification<br>- offline generation | - automatic generation | - MiL, SiL<br>- non-reactive | - test evaluation specifications | - automatic specification<br>- does not apply |

used. An advantage of these three solutions is their possibility to cover both functional and structural test goals, at least to some extent.

SL VV gives the possibility of implementing a test specification directly next to the actual test object, but the standard evaluation functions cover only a very limited functionality range, a test management application is missing and test data must be created fully manually. A similar test assessment method, called 'watchdog' and 'observer', has been introduced by Conrad & Hötzer (1998), Dajani-Brown et al. (2004), respectively.

TPT is platform-independent and can be used at several embedded software development stages, which is not directly supported with MiLEST, although extensions are possible. It is the only tool from the list in Table 1 that enables reactive testing and signal-feature – based specification of the test evaluation algorithms. These concepts are reused and extended in the solution proposed in this chapter.

A classification of the test approaches with respect to the MBT taxonomy is provided in Table 1.

## Analysis Summary

The main *shortcomings* within the reviewed test solutions are the following:

- Automatic generation of test data is based almost only on structural test criteria or state-based models (e.g., SF charts), thus it is not systematic enough.
- For functional testing only manual test data specification is supported, which makes the test development process long and costly.
- The test evaluation is based mainly on the comparison of the SUT outputs with the entire reference signal flows. This demands a so-called *golden device* to produce such references and makes the test evaluation not flexible enough.

- Only a few test patterns exist. They are not structured and not categorized.
- The entire test development process is still almost only manual.
- Abstraction level is very low while developing the test design or selecting the test data variants.

In this chapter, only one selected approach will be provided as a proposal for a concrete MBT realization. This is the method developed by Zander-Nowicka (2008) and serves only as an illustration of the test concepts from the practical viewpoint.

Based on the recognized problems and the criteria that have been proven to be advantageous in the reviewed related work, the first shape of this proposal may be outlined.

- In MiLEST systematic and automatic test data generation process is supported. Here, not only a considerable reduction of manual efforts is advantageous, but also a systematic selection of test data for testing functional requirements including such system characteristics as hybrid, time-constrained behavior is achieved. By that, the method is cheaper and more comprehensive than the existing ones.
- The test evaluation is done based on the concept of signal feature, overcoming the problem of missing reference signals. These are not demanded for the test assessment any more.
- A catalog of categorized test patterns is provided, which eases the application of the methodology and structures the knowledge on the test system being built.
- Some of the steps within the test development process are fully automated, which represents an improvement in the context of the efforts put on testing.
- A test framework enabling the specification of a hierarchical test system on different

abstraction levels is provided. This gives the possibility to navigate through the test system easily and understand its contents immediately from several viewpoints.

A brief description of the MiLEST method is given below, whereas a report on its main contributions will be discussed in the next section in depth.

MiLEST is a test specification framework, including reusable test patterns, generic graphical validation functions (VFs), test data generators, test control algorithms, and an arbitration mechanism collected in a dedicated library. Additionally, transformation functions in the form of ML scripts are available so as to automate the test specification process.

It is a SL add-on exploiting all the advantages of SL/SF application. The application of the same modeling language for both system and test design ensures that the method is relatively clear and it does not force the engineers to learn a completely new language. For running the tests, no additional tool is necessary. The test method handles continuous and discrete signals as well as timing constraints.

## SOLUTION PROPOSAL

### The MiLEST Approach

MiLEST is a method that addresses the goals of a test approach given in Section 1.1 and refers to the selected test dimensions from Section 2.2.

The main innovation of MiLEST is *assuring the quality of embedded system by means of testing at early levels of their development.*

MiLEST is realized in ML/SL/SF. Although technical test extensions of this environment such as Simulink® Design Verifier™, SystemTest™, or MTest already exist, they all encompass the limitations identified above. MiLEST introduces a more efficient approach to test automatically on

model level based on the so called signal-feature – oriented paradigm, specifically suited for functional testing of embedded systems.

## The Test Development Process in MiLEST

The starting point of the MiLEST approach is to design a test specification model. Since at the early stage of system development reference signals are not available, a new method for describing the required SUT behavior is given. Based on a number of so called *signal features*, a novel, abstract understanding of a *signal* is defined.

A signal feature (SigF), also called signal property by Gips & Wiesbrock (2007), Schieferdecker & Großmann (2007, 2008), is a formal description of certain predefined attributes of a signal. In other words, it is an identifiable, descriptive property of a signal. It can be used to describe particular shapes of individual signals by providing means to address abstract characteristics of a signal. Giving some examples – *step response characteristics*, *step*, *minimum* etc. are considerable SigFs (Zander-Nowicka et al., 2006, 2008; Marrero Pérez, 2007).

Graphical instances of SigFs are given in Figure 3. The signal presented on the diagram is fragmented in time according to its descriptive properties resulting in: *decrease*, *constant*, *increase*, *local maximum*, *decrease* and *response*, respectively. This forms the backgrounds of the solution presented in this section.

A feature can be predicated by other features, logical connectives, or timing relations. These can be defined either between features within one signal or throughout more signals, for example Table 2.

Further on, generic test data patterns are retrieved automatically out of marked portions of the test specification. The test data generator concretizes the test data. Its functionality has similarities to the classification tree method and aims at a systematic signal production. The SUT input partitions and boundaries are used to find the meaningful representatives. Additionally, the SUT outputs are considered too. Instead of searching for a scenario that fulfills the test objective it is assumed that this has been already achieved while defining the test specification. Further on, the method enables to deploy a searching strategy for finding different variants of such scenarios and the time points when they should start/stop.

The MiLEST test development process is depicted in Figure 4. Based on the MBD paradigm it is assumed that the SUT model with clearly defined interfaces is available.

Besides the analysis of the SUT specification, proper functional, dynamic testing also requires systematic selection of test stimuli, appropriate test evaluation algorithms, and obviously an execution or simulation environment. If the above assumptions hold, a pattern for generation of a test harness model can be applied on the SUT model as denoted in *step I*. This is done automatically with a MiLEST transformation function, giving a concrete frame for test specification. Further on, the test engineer refines the test specification design (*step II*) using the concept of validation function patterns. Structures for test stimuli and concrete test signals are then generated. This step (*step III*) occurs automatically with application of

*Figure 3. A descriptive approach to signal feature*

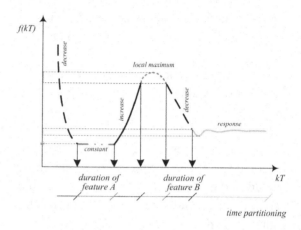

*time partitioning*

the transformations. The test control design can be added automatically too (*step IV*). Finally, the tests may be executed and test results obtained in the form of verdicts (*step V*). At the same time the quality of the test system specification produced is also assessed.

In Figure 5, a generic pattern of the test harness used in MiLEST is presented. The test data (i.e., test signals produced along the test cases), on the left-hand side, are generated within the test data generator. The test specification, on the right-hand side, is constructed by analyzing the SUT functionality requirements and deriving the test objectives from them. It includes the abstract test scenarios, test evaluation algorithms, test oracle and an arbitration mechanism (Zander-Nowicka et al., 2006, 2007, 2008; Marrero Pérez, 2007).

*Figure 4. The MiLEST test development process*

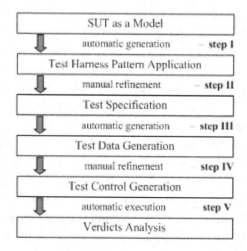

*Table 2. Examples of feature predicates and connectives*

| | |
|---|---|
| - within($A_1$)$A_2$ | - if $SigF\,A_1$ occurs $SigF\,A_2$ occurs at least once whereas $SigF\,A_1$ is active |
| - after(y ms)A&B | - $SigF\,A$ and $SigF\,B$ occur together after $y$ milliseconds |
| - during(A)B | - if $SigF\,A$ occurs $SigF\,B$ occurs continuously during the activation time of $SigF\,A$ |
| - A=v | - a set of $SigFs\,A$ (e.g., maximum) which values are equal to $v$. |

*Figure 5. The MiLEST test harness pattern*

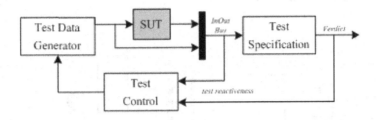

The test specification is built applying the test patterns available in the MiLEST library. It is developed in such a way that it includes the design of a test evaluation as well – opposite to a common practice in the embedded systems domain, where the test evaluation design is considered last. Afterward, based on the already constructed test model, the test data generators are retrieved. These are embedded in a dedicated test data structure and are derived from the test design automatically. The generation of test signal variants, their management and combination within a test case is also supported, similarly as the synchronization of the obtained test stimuli. Finally, the SUT model fed with the previously created test data is executed and the evaluation unit supplies verdicts on the fly.

The first step in the test development process is to identify the test requirements. For that purpose a high level pattern within the test specification unit is applied. The number of test requirements can be chosen in the graphical user interface (GUI) that updates the design and adjusts the structural changes of the test model (e.g., it adjusts the number of inputs in the arbitration unit). The situation is illustrated in Figure 6.

Further on, validation functions (VFs) (Zander-Nowicka et al., 2006; Marrero Pérez, 2007) are introduced to define the test scenarios, test evaluation, and test oracle in a systematic way. VFs serve to evaluate the execution status of a test case by assessing the SUT observations and/or additional characteristics/parameters of the SUT. A VF is created for any single requirement following the generic conditional rule:

*IF preconditions set THEN assertions set (1.1)*

A single informal requirement may imply multiple VFs. If this is the case, the arbitration algorithm accumulates the results of the combined IF-THEN rules and delivers a common verdict. Predefined *verdict* values are pass, fail, none, and error. Retrieval of the local verdicts for a single VF is also possible.

*A preconditions set* consists of at least one extractor for signal feature or temporally and logically related signal features, a comparator for every single extractor, and one unit for preconditions synchronization (PS).

*An assertions set* is similar, it includes, however, at least one unit for preconditions and assertions synchronization (PAS), instead of a PS.

VFs are able to continuously update the verdicts for a test scenario already during test execution. They are defined to be independent of the currently applied test data. Thereby, they can set the verdict for all possible test data vectors and activate themselves (i.e., their assertions) only if the predefined conditions are fulfilled.

An abstract pattern for a VF (shown in Figure 7) consists of a preconditions block which activates the assertions block, where the comparison of actual and expected signal values occurs. The activation, and by that, the actual evaluation proceeds only if the preconditions are fulfilled.

The easiest assertion blocks for feature detection are built following the schema presented in Figure 8.

They include a SigF extraction part, a block comparing the actual values with the expected

*Figure 6. A pattern for the test requirement specification. a) Instantiation for one test requirement. b) Instantiation for three test requirements*

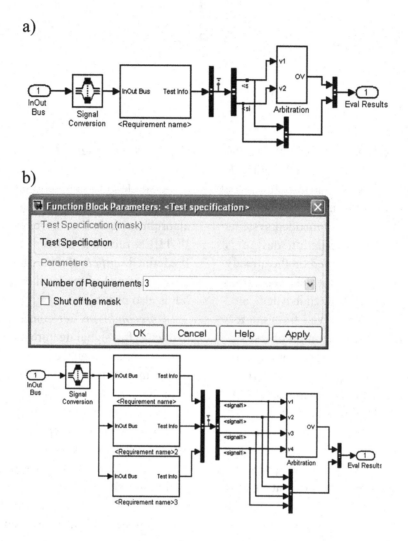

a)

b)

ones and a PAS synchronizer. Optionally, some signal deviations within a permitted tolerance range are allowed. Further schemas are discussed by Marrero Pérez (2007) in detail.

A further step in the MiLEST test development process is the derivation of the corresponding structures for test data sets and the concretization of signal variants. The entire step related to test data generation occurs fully automatically as a result of transformations. Similarly as on the test specification side, a structure on the test require-

ments level for the test data is generated. This is possible due to the knowledge gained from the previous phase. The pattern applied in this step is shown in Figure 9.

Moreover, concrete SigFs on predefined signals are produced afterwards. The test signals are generated following a conditional rule in the form:

*IF preconditions set THEN generations set (1.2)*

*Figure 9. Test requirement level within the test data unit – a pattern*

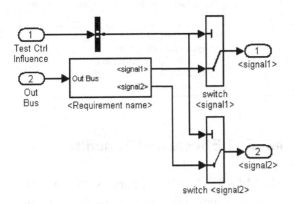

*Figure 7. Structure of a VF – a pattern and its GUI*

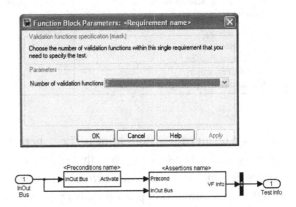

*Figure 8. Assertion block – a pattern*

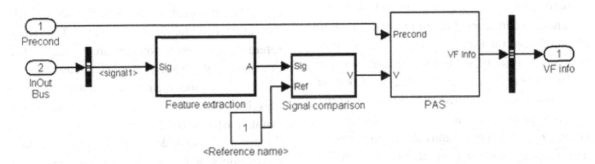

Knowing the SigFs appearing in the preconditions of a VF, the test data can be constructed from them. The preconditions typically depend on the SUT inputs; however, they also may be related to the SUT outputs at some points. Every time a *SigF extractor* occurs for the assertion activation, a corresponding *SigF generator* may be applied for the test data creation. Giving a very simple example – for detection of a given *signal value* in a precondition of a VF, a signal crossing this value during a default time is required. Apart from the feature generation, the SUT output signals may be checked for some constraints, if necessary (cf. Figure 10). The feature generation is activated by a SF diagram sequencing the features in time according to the default temporal constraints (i.e., *after(time1)*). A switch is needed for each SUT

input to handle the dependencies between generated signals. *Initialization & Stabilization* block enables to reset the obtained signal so that there are no influences of one test case on another.

The patterns in Figure 10 and the concrete *feature generators* are collected in a library and associated to the specific test system automati-

*Figure 10. Structure of the test data set – a pattern*

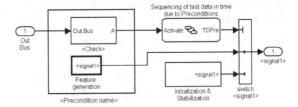

*Table 3. Classification of MiLEST with respect to the MBT taxonomy*

| Test Generation: Selection Criteria and Technology | Test Execution Options | Test Evaluation: Specification and Technology |
|---|---|---|
| - data coverage<br>- requirements coverage<br>- test case specifications<br>- automatic generation<br>- offline and online generation | - MiL<br>- reactive | - reference signal-feature – based<br>- requirements coverage<br>- test evaluation specifications<br>- automatic and manual specification<br>- online evaluation |

cally as a result of transformations. The general principle of the transformation is that if a given *feature or feature dependency extraction* is detected in the source (i.e. preconditions part of a VF), then the action to generate the target (i.e. *feature generator* in the test data structure) is performed. A set of transformation rules has been implemented. Afterwards, the concrete test data variants are constructed based on the generators obtained from the transformations. The assumption and necessary condition for applying the variants generation method is the definition of the *signal ranges* and *partition points* on all the stimuli signals according to the requirements or engineer's experience. Equivalence partitioning and boundary value analysis are used in different combinations to produce then concrete variants for the stimuli.

When a test involves multiple signals, the combination of different signals and their variants has to be computed. Combination strategies are the selection methods where test cases are identified by combining values of different test data parameters according to some predefined criteria. Several combination strategies are known to construct the test cases – *minimal combination, one factor at a time* and *n-wise combination* (Lamberg et al., 2004; Grindal et al., 2005).

After the test specification has been completed, the resulting test design can be executed in SL. Additionally, a report is generated including the applied test data, their variants, test cases, test results, and the calculated quality metrics.

The *options* that MiLEST covers with respect to the MBT taxonomy are listed in Table 3.

## MiLEST Effects and Benefits

The MiLEST *signal feature* approach provides the essential benefit of describing signal flows, their relation to other signal flows and/or to discrete events on an abstract, logical level. This prevents not only the user from error on too technical specifics, but also enables test specification in early development stages. The absence of concrete reference signals is compensated by a logical description of the signal flow characteristics.

This is a fundamental contribution of MiLEST, based on which test case generation and test evaluation have been developed. Numerous signal features have been identified; feature extractors, comparators, and feature generators have been realized in the MiLEST library. The test evaluation can be performed offline but also online, which enables an active test control, opens perspectives for dynamic test generation algorithms and provides extensions of reactive testing. Also, new ways for first diagnosis activities and failure management are possible.

Furthermore, the automated test evaluation reveals a considerable progress, in contrast to the low level of abstraction and the manual assessment means used in the reviewed approaches. The tester can retrieve immediately the test results and is assured about the correct interpretation of the SUT reactions along the tests.

In addition, MiLEST automates the systematic test data selection and generation, providing a better test coverage (e.g., in terms of requirements coverage or test purpose coverage) than manually created test cases.

*Figure 11. SUT – car door*

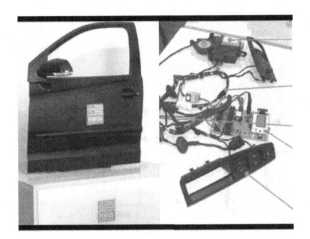

The test specification enables to trace the SUT requirements. The way how it is defined gives the possibility to trace root faults by associating local test verdicts to them, which is a central element in fault management of embedded systems.

Finally, the MiLEST test quality metrics (Zander-Nowicka et al., 2008) reveal the strengths of the approach by providing good analysis

capabilities and high test coverage in different dimensions. The MiLEST projects demonstrated a quality gain of at least 20% (Zander-Nowicka, 2008).

## CASE STUDY

In the following, the functionality of a car door (see Figure 11) is tested with a focus on MiL and SiL level. It has been modeled in ML/SL/SF. The software embedded in a car door controls the position of the window pane and blinking of the light located in the mirror. In the following, a test of one functional requirement will be exemplified.

In Figure 12, the MiLEST test harness for the car door including test data generation and test specification units is presented.

In Figure 13, details of the test specification are highlighted so as to give an insight into the test system that is built in a hierarchical way.

For one of the requirements from Figure 12, *If the blinking is activated, the brightness and darkness period times should equal to 50 ms.'*,

*Figure 12. Test harness for the door*

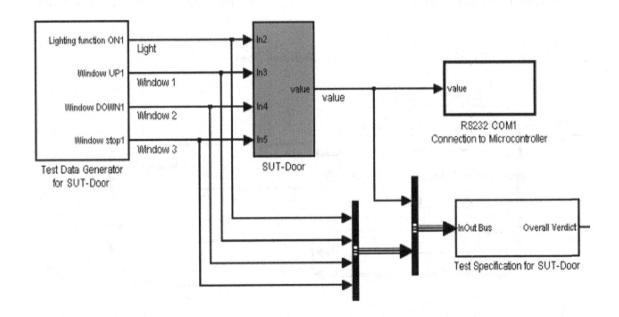

*Figure 13. Test specification view – selected test requirements*

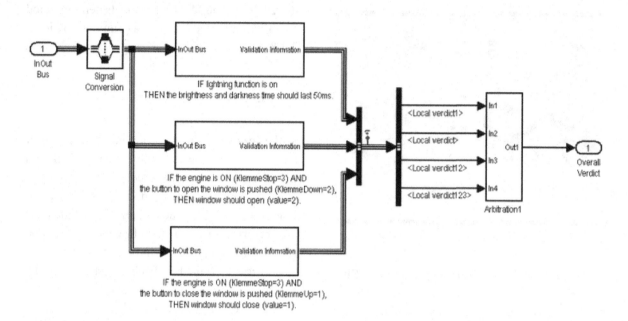

in Figure 13 in the first block at the top, the following IF-THEN rules hold:

IF blinking function is on THEN the brightness period time should last 50 ms.

IF blinking function is on THEN the darkness period time should last 50 ms.

These are modeled in the VFs in Figure 14 so as to consequently enable a systematic and automatic generation of test cases and an automatic test evaluation during the test execution.

As a result, two local verdicts are obtained for this particular requirement, one for each VF. These are presented in Figure 15. The flows of

*Figure 14. Test specification view – selected validation functions*

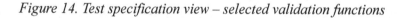

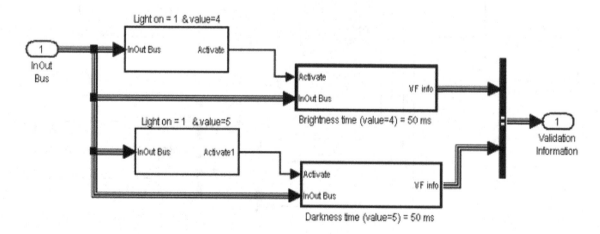

*Figure 15. Test results – two local verdicts*

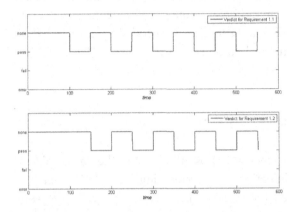

both signals indicate that the test cases passed. This means that the timing of the blinking function is correct.

Additionally, the scenario can be run in connection with the real software on the microprocessor of the door as the test model has been connected to the real SUT via a serial cable. Then, the blinking is observed directly on the door as well.

This example demonstrates the application of the MiLEST on both MiL and SiL level.

## CONCLUSION AND FUTURE TRENDS

In this chapter the test development process in the context of the automotive domain has been discussed. Different test dimensions have been identified. Then, based on the reviewed MBT approaches, a taxonomy has been proposed. Also, MiLEST as an example of MBT method has been introduced and exemplified.

Applying MBT methods considerably less effort is demanded from the test engineer in the context of test generation and test execution, letting focus the attention on the test logic and the corresponding test coverage. By that, the costs of the entire process of software development are cut.

There is still plenty of work concerning future achievements of MBT. For example, in MiLEST the test stimuli generation algorithms can be still refined as not all signal features are included in the realization of the transformation engine. Also, they could be enriched with different extensions applying, in particular, the constraint solver and implicit partitions.

Further work regards the negative testing as well. Here, the test data generation algorithm can be extended so as to produce the invalid input values or exceptions. However, the test engineer's responsibility would be to define what the expected system behavior in such a case is.

An interesting possibility pointed out by Marrero Pérez (2007) would be to take advantage of the reactiveness path for optimizing the generated test data iteratively. In that case, the algorithm could search for the SUT inputs leading to a fail automatically (cf. evolutionary algorithms of Wappler & Wegener, 2006).

Moreover, since software testing alone cannot prove that a system does not contain any defects or that it does have a certain property (i.e., that the signal fulfils a certain signal feature), the proposed VFs could be a basis for developing a verification mechanism based on formal methods in a strict functional context (Lee & Yannakakis, 1994; Amon et al., 1997; Bienmüller et al., 2004; Dajani-Brown et al., 2004). Thus, the perspective of mathematically proving the correctness of a system design remains open for further research within the proposed test framework.

Besides the test quality metrics defined by Zander-Nowicka (2008), also other criteria may be used to assess the test method, the following being only some of them:

- The efficiency of faults detection
- The percentage of test cases / test design / test elements reusability
- Time and effort required for the test engineer to specify the test design

- The percentage of the effective improvement of the test stimuli variants generation in contrast to the manual specification.

Regarding the realization of MiLEST prototype, several GUIs (e.g., for transformation functions, for quality metrics application, for variants generation options or for the test execution) would definitely help the user to apply the method faster and more intuitive.

Furthermore, the support of different test execution platforms for the proposed method has not been sufficiently explored yet. Interesting research questions concern the extent to which the concrete test cases could be reused on various execution levels. Consequently, real-time properties on the run-time execution level (Nicol et al., 2003) in the sense of scheduler, priorities or threads have not been considered.

Current research work aims at designing a new platform independent test specification language, one of the branches called TTCN-3 continuous (Schieferdecker et al., 2006; Bräuer et al., 2007; Großmann, 2008). Its fundamental idea is to obtain a domain specific test language, that is executable and that unifies tests of communicating, software-based systems in all of the automotive subdomains (e.g., telematics, power train, body electronics etc.) integrating the test infrastructure as well as the definition and documentation of tests. It should keep the whole development and test process efficient and manageable. It must address the subjects of test exchange, autonomy of infrastructure, methods and platforms, and the reuse of tests.

This option becomes interesting especially in the context of a new paradigm – AUTomotive Open System Architecture (AUTOSAR) that has been observed as an automotive development trend for the last few years. Traditional TTCN-3 is already in use to test discrete interactions within this architecture. The remaining hybrid or continuous behavior could be tested with TTCN-3 for embedded system.

Another graphical test specification language being already in the development stage is UML Testing Profile for Embedded Systems (UTPes). Its backgrounds root from UTP, TPT, and MiL-EST.

# REFERENCES

Aichernig, B. K. (2005). On the value of fault injection on the modeling level. In N. Plat & P. G. Larsen (Eds.), *Proceedings of the Overture Workshop*, Newcastle Upon Tyne, UK.

Ammann, P., & Black, P. E. (2002). Model checkers. In *Software Testing* (Tech. Rep. NIST-IR 6777). National Institute of Standards and Technology.

Amon, T., Borriello, G., Hu, T., & Liu, J. (1997). Symbolic timing verification of timing diagrams using presburger formulas. In *Proceedings of the 34th Annual Conference on Design Automation* (pp. 226–231). New York: ACM.

Automated Testing Tool, M. A. T. L. A. B. *MATT, the University of Montana, research model-based testing prototype*. Retrieved from http://www.cs.umt.edu/rtsl/matt/

Beizer, B. (1995). *Black-box testing: Techniques for functional testing of software and systems.* John Wiley & Sons, Inc.

Bernard, E., Legeard, B., Luck, X., & Peureux, F. (2004). Generation of test sequences from formal specifications: GSM 11-11 standard case study. *Software Testing, Verification, and Reliability, 34*(10), 915–948.

Bienmüller, T., Brockmeyer, U., & Sandmann, G. (2004). *Automatic validation of simulink/stateflow models, formal verification of safety-critical requirements*. Stuttgart.

Bodeveix, J.-P., Koné, O., & Bouaziz, R. (2005). Test method for embedded real-time systems. In *Proceedings of the European Workshop on Dependable Software Intensive Embedded Systems*, ERCIM, Porto (pp. 1–10).

Brandan Briones, L., & Brinksma, E. (2004). *A test generation framework for quiescent real-time systems.* Internal Report 48975. University of Twente.

Bräuer, J., Kleinwechter, H., & Leicher, A. (2007). μttcn–an approach to continuous signals in TTCN-3. In W.-G. Bleek, H. Schwentner & H. Züllighoven (Eds.), *Proceedings of Software Engineering Workshops, Series LNI* (Vol. 106, pp. 55–64).

Broy, M., Krüger, I. H., Pretschner, A., & Salzmann, C. (2007). Engineering automotive software. *Proceedings of the IEEE, 95*(2), 356–373. doi:10.1109/JPROC.2006.888386

Broy, M., Von der Beeck, M., & Krüger, I. (1998). *Softbed: Problemanalyse Für Ein Großverbundprojekt "Systemtechnik Automobil–Software Für Eingebettete Systeme.* Ausarbeitung für das BMBF. (In German).

BS 7925-2:1998. (1998). *Software testing. Software component testing.* British Standards Institution.

Campbell, C., Grieskamp, W., Nachmanson, L., Schulte, W., Tillmann, N., & Veanes, M. (2005). *Model-based testing of object-oriented reactive systems with spec explorer.* Microsoft Research, MSR-TR-2005-59.

Carnegie Mellon University, Department of Electrical and Computer Engineering. *Hybrid system verification toolbox for MATLAB–checkmate, research tool for system verification.* Retrieved from http://www.ece.cmu.edu/~webk/checkmate/

Carter, J. M., Lin, L., & Poore, J. H. (2008). Automated functional testing of simulink control models. In *Proceedings of the 1st Workshop on Model-Based Testing in Practice, MoTIP 2008.* T. Bauer, H. Eichler, A. Rennoch (Eds.). Berlin, Germany: Fraunhofer IRB Verlag.

Classification Tree Editor for Embedded Systems. *CTE/ES, razorcat development GmbH, commercial tool for testing.* Retrieved from http://www.razorcatdevelopment.de/

Conrad, M. (2004). *A systematic approach to testing automotive control software. SAE technical paper series,* 2004-21-0039. Detroit, MI.

Conrad, M. (2004). *Modell-basierter test eingebetteter software im Automobil: Auswahl und Beschreibung von Testszenarien.* Unpublished doctoral dissertation, Deutscher Universitätsverlag, Wiesbaden (D). (In German).

Conrad, M., Fey, I., & Sadeghipour, S. (2004). Systematic model-based testing of embedded control software–the MB3T approach. In *Proceedings of the ICSE 2004 Workshop on Software Engineering for Automotive Systems*, Edinburgh, United Kingdom.

Conrad, M., & Hötzer, D. (1998). Selective integration of formal methods in the development of electronic control units. *Proceedings of the ICFEM, 1998,* 144.

Copi, I. M., & Cohen, C. (2000). *Introduction to logic, 11th ed.* Upper Saddle River, NJ: Prentice-Hall.

D-MINT Consortium. Deployment of Model-Based Technologies to Industrial Testing. (2007). *Milestone 1, deliverable 2.1–test modeling, test generation and test execution with model-based testing.*

D-MINT Project – Deployment of Model-Based Technologies to Industrial Testing. (2008). Retrieved from http://d-mint.org/ dSpace GmbH. *AutomationDesk, commercial tool for testing*. Retrieved from http://www.dSpace.de/ Goto?Releases dSpace GmbH. Retrieved from http://www.dSpace.de/ww/en/gmb/home.cfm

Dai, Z. R. (2006). *An approach to model-driven testing with UML 2.0, U2TP and TTCN-3*. Doctoral dissertation, Technical University Berlin. Fraunhofer IRB Verlag.

Dajani-Brown, S., Cofer, D., & Bouali, A. (2004). Formal verification of an avionics sensor voter using SCADE. In *Formal Techniques, Modelling, and Analysis of Timed and Fault-Tolerant Systems* (LNCS 3253, pp. 5–20). Springer-Verlag Berlin/ Heidelberg.

Dempster, D., & Stuart, M. (June, 2002). *Verification methodology manual, techniques for verifying HDL designs*. Teamwork International.

DESS–Software Development Process for Real-Time Embedded Software Systems. (2001). The DESS methodology. In S. Van Baelen, J. Gorinsek, & A. Wills (Eds.), *Deliverable D.1, version 01–public*.

Dijkstra, E. W. (1972). Notes on structured programming. In C. A. R. Hoare (Ed.), *Structured programming, Vol. 8 of A.P.I.C. studies in data processing, part 1* (pp. 1–82). Academic Press London/New York.

Dulz, W., & Fenhua, Z. (2003). Matelo–statistical USAge testing by annotated sequence diagrams, Markov chains, and TTCN-3. In *Proceedings of the 3$^{rd}$ International Conference on Quality Software* (p. 336). Washington, D.C.: IEEE Computer Society.

EmbeddedValidator. *OSC–embedded systems AG, commercial verification tool*. Retrieved from http://www.osc-es.de Encontre, V. (2003). *Testing embedded systems: Do you have the guts for it? IBM*. Retrieved from http://www-128.ibm.com/ developerworks/rational/library/459.html

ETSI European Standard (ES) 201 873-1 V3.2.1 (2007-02): *The Testing and Test Control Notation Version 3; Part 1: TTCN-3 Core Language*. European Telecommunications Standards Institute, Sophia-Antipolis, France.

Frantzen, L., Tretmans, J., & Willemse, T. A. C. (2006). A symbolic framework for model-based testing. In *Formal approaches to software testing and runtime verification, 4262*. Springer Berlin / Heidelberg.

Functional Safety and IEC 61508. (2005). Retrieved from http://www.iec.ch/zone/fsafety/ fsafety_entry.htm

Gips, C., & Wiesbrock, H.-W. (2007). Notation und Verfahren zur Automatischen Überprüfung von Temporalen Signalabhängigkeiten und -Merkmalen Für Modellbasiert Entwickelte Software. In M. Conrad, H. Giese, B. Rumpe & B. Schätz (Eds.), *Proceedings of Model Based Engineering of Embedded Systems III*, TU Braunschweig Report TUBS-SSE 2007-01. (In German).

Grindal, M., Offutt, J., & Andler, S. F. (2005). Combination testing strategies: A survey. In *Software Testing, Verification, and Reliability, 15*(3), 167–199. John Wiley & Sons, Ltd.

Grochtmann, M., & Grimm, K. (1993). Classification trees for partition testing. *Verification & Reliability, 3*(2), 63–82. doi:10.1002/ stvr.4370030203

Großmann, J., Schieferdecker, I., & Wiesbrock, H. W. (2008). Modeling property based stream templates with TTCN-3. In *Proceedings of the IFIP 20$^{th}$ Intern. Conf. on Testing Communicating Systems* (Testcom 2008), Tokyo, Japan.

Gutjahr, W. J. (1999). Partition testing vs. random testing: The influence of uncertainty. [NJ: IEEE Press Piscataway.]. *IEEE Transactions on Software Engineering, 25*(5), 661–674. doi:10.1109/32.815325

Helmerich, A., Koch, N., Mandel, L., Braun, P., Dornbusch, P., Gruler, A., et al. (2005). *Study of worldwide trends and R&D programmes in embedded systems in view of maximising the impact of a technology platform in the area.* Final Report for the European Commission, Brussels Belgium.

Hetzel, W. C. (1988). *The complete guide to software testing, second ed.* QED Information Services, Inc.

International Software Testing Qualification Board. (2006). *Standard glossary of terms used in software testing, version 1.2.* E. van Veenendaal (Ed.). The 'Glossary Working Party'.

ISO/NP PAS 26262. Road vehicles-functional safety. Retrieved from http://www.iso.org/iso/iso_catalogue/catalogue_tc/catalogue_detail.htm?csnumber=43464

Java Usage Model Builder Library – JUMBL. Software quality research laboratory, research model-based testing prototype. Retrieved from http://www.cs.utk.edu/sqrl/esp/Jumbl.html

Jeannet, B., Jéron Rusu, V., & Zinovieva, E. (2005). Symbolic test selection based on approximate analysis. In N. Halbwachs & L. Zuck (Eds.), *Proceedings of TACAS 2005* (LNCS 3440, pp. 349–364). Berlin, Heidelberg: Springer-Verlag.

Kamga, J., Herrmann, J., & Joshi, P. (2007). *Deliverable: D-MINT automotive case study–daimler AG, deliverable 1.1, deployment of model-based technologies to industrial testing, itea2 project.*

Kosmatov, N., Legeard, B., Peureux, F., & Utting, M. (2004). Boundary coverage criteria for test generation from formal models. In *Proceedings of the 15th International Symposium on Software Reliability Engineering* (pp. 139–150). Washington, D.C.: IEEE Computer Society.

Lamberg, K., Beine, M., Eschmann, M., Otterbach, R., Conrad, M., & Fey, I. (2004). Model-based testing of embedded automotive software using mtest. In *Proceedings of SAE World Congress*, Detroit, MI.

Lazić, L., & Velašević, D. (2004). Applying simulation and design of experiments to the embedded software testing process. In *Software Testing, Verification, & Reliability, 14*(4), 257–282. Chichester, UK: John Wiley and Sons Ltd.

Lee, T., & Yannakakis, M. (1994). Testing finite-state machines: State identification and verification. *IEEE Transactions on Computers, 43*(3), 306–320. doi:10.1109/12.272431

Lehmann, E. (2003). *Time partition testing, systematischer test des kontinuierlichen verhaltens von eingebetteten systemen.* Unpublished doctoral dissertation, Technical University Berlin (In German).

Lehmann, E., & Krämer, A. (2008). Model-based testing of automotive systems. In *Proceedings of IEEE ICST 08*, Lillehammer, Norway.

Lehmann, E., Krämer, A., Lang, T., Weiss, S., Klaproth, C., Ruhe, J., & Ziech, C. (2006). *Time partition testing manual, version 2.4.*

Markov Test Logic. *Matelo, All4Tec, commercial model-based testing tool.* Retrieved from http://www.all4tec.net/

Marre, B., & Arnould, A. (2000). Test sequences generation from LUSTRE descriptions: Gatel. In *Proceedings of ASE of the 15th IEEE International Conference on Automated Software Engineering*, Grenoble, France (pp. 229–237). Washington, D.C.: IEEE Computer Society.

Marrero Pérez, A. (2007, January). *Simulink test design for hybrid embedded systems.* Diploma thesis, Technical University Berlin.

Maxton, G. P., & Wormald, J. (2004). *Time for a model change: Reengineering the global automotive industry.* Cambridge University Press.

MBTech Group. (2008). Retrieved from http://www.mbtech-group.com/cz/electronics_solutions/test_engineering/provetechta_overview.html

MEval. *IT power consultants, commercial tool for testing* Retrieved from http://www.itpower.de/meval.html

Mikucionis, M., Larsen, K. G., & Nielsen, B. (2003). *Online on-the-fly testing of real-time systems.* BRICS report series, RS-03-49, Denmark.

Model-Based Testing of Reactive Systems. (2005). M. Broy, B. Jonsson, J.-P. Katoen, M. Leucker & A. Pretschner (Eds.), LNCS 3472. Springer-Verlag.

MTest. *dSpace GmbH, commercial MBT tool.* Retrieved from http://www.dspaceinc.com/ww/en/inc/home/products/Sw/expsoft/mtest.cfm

Munich University of Technology, Department of Computer Science. *AutoFocus, research tool for system modelling.* Retrieved from http://autofocus.in.tum.de/

Myers, G. J. (1979). *The art of software testing.* John Wiley & Sons.

Neukirchen, H. W. (2004). Languages, *tools, and patterns for the specification of distributed real-time tests.* Unpublished doctoral dissertation, Georg-August-Universiät zu Göttingen. Retrieved from http://webdoc.sub.gwdg.de/Diss/2004/Neukirchen/Index.html

Nicol, D. M., Liu, J., Liljenstam, M., & Guanhua, Y. (2003). Simulation of large scale networks using SSF. In *Proceedings of the 35th Conference on Winter Simulation: Driving Innovation*, New Orleans, LA (Vol. 1, pp. 650–657). ACM.

Olen, M. (2007). *The new wave in functional verification: Algorithmic testbench technology, white paper.* Mentor Graphics Corporation. http://www.edadesignline.com/showarticle.jhtml?Articleid=197800043 [08/08/08].

OMG. MDA guide v1.0.1. (2003, June). Retrieved from http://www.omg.org/docs/omg/03-06-01.pdf

OMG. UML 2.0 testing profile, version 1.0 formal/05-07-07. (2005). Object Management Group.

Paiva, A. C. R., Faria, J. C. P., & Vidal, R. M. (2003). Specification-based testing of user interfaces. In *Interactive systems, design, specification, and verification.*

Philipps, J., Hahn, G., Pretschner, A., & Stauner, T. (2003). Prototype-based tests for hybrid reactive systems. In *Proceedings of the 14th IEEE International Workshop on Rapid Systems Prototyping* (pp. 78–84). Washington, D.C.: IEEE Computer Society.

Pretschner, A. (2003). Compositional generation of MC/DC integration test suites. In *Proceedings TACOS'03, Electronic Notes in Theoretical Computer Science 6* (pp. 1–11). Retrieved from http://Citeseer.Ist.Psu.Edu/633586.Html

Pretschner, A. (2003). *Zum Modellbasierten Funktionalen Test Reaktiver Systeme*. Unpublished doctoral dissertation, Technical University Munich (In German).

Pretschner, A., Prenninger, W., Wagner, S., Kühnel, C., Baumgartner, M., Sostawa, B., et al. (2005). One evaluation of model-based testing and its automation. In *Proceedings of the 27th International Conference on Software Engineering*, St. Louis, MO (pp. 392–401). New York: ACM New York.

Pretschner, A., Slotosch, O., Aiglstorfer, E., & Kriebel, S. (2004). Model based testing for real– the inhouse card case study. *International Journal on Software Tools for Technology Transfer, 5*, 140–157. doi:10.1007/s10009-003-0128-3

Prowell, S. J. (2003). JUMBL: A tool for model-based statistical testing. In *Proceedings of the 36th Annual Hawaii International Conference on System Sciences (HICSS'03)*, (Vol. 9). Washington, D.C.: IEEE Computer Society.

Rau, A. (2002). *Model-based development of embedded automotive control systems*. Unpublished doctoral dissertation, University of Tübingen.

Reactis Tester. *Reactive Systems, Inc., commercial model-based testing tool*. Retrieved from http://www.reactive-systems.com/tester.msp

Reactis Validator. *Reactive Systems, Inc., commercial validation and verification tool*. Retrieved from http://www.reactive-systems.com/reactis/doc/user/user009.html, http://www.reactive-systems.com/validator.msp

Richardson, D., O'Malley, O., & Tittle, C. (1998). Approaches to specification-based testing. In *Proceedings of ACM SigSoft Software Engineering Notes, 14*(8), 86–96. New York: ACM New York.

Safety Checker Blockset. *TNI-software, commercial model-based testing tool*. Retrieved from http://www.tni-software.com/en/produits/safetychecker blockset/index.php

Safety Test Builder. TNI-software, commercial model-based testing tool Retrieved from http://www.tni-software.com/en/produits/safetytest-builder/index.php

Schäuffele, J., & Zurawka, T. (2006). *Automotive software engineering*. Vieweg.

Schieferdecker, I., Bringmann, E., & Grossmann, J. (2006). Continuous TTCN-3: Testing of embedded control systems. In *Proceedings of the 2006 International Workshop on Software Engineering for Automotive Systems, International Conference on Software Engineering*, Shanghai, China. ACM New York Press.

Schieferdecker, I., & Großmann, J. (2007). Testing embedded control systems with TTCN-3. In *Proceedings Software Technologies for Embedded and Ubiquitous Systems SEUS 2007*, Santorini Island, Greece (LNCS 4761, pp. 125-135). Springer-Verlag Berlin/Heidelberg.

Silva, B. I., Richeson, K., Krogh, B., & Chutinan, A. (2000). Modeling and verifying hybrid dynamic systems using checkmate. In *Proceedings of the 4th International Conference on Automation of Mixed Processes* (ADPM 2000) (pp. 237–242).

Sims, S., & Duvarney, D. C. (2007). Experience report: The reactis validation tool. In *Proceedings of the ICFP '07 Conference, 42*(9), 137–140. New York: ACM New York. Simulink® Design Verifier™, & The MathWorks™, Inc. *Commercial model-based testing tool*. Retrieved from http://www.mathworks.com/products/sldesignverifier Simulink® Verification and Validation™, & The MathWorks™, Inc. *Commercial model-based verification and validation tool*. Retrieved from http://www.mathworks.com/products/simverification/

Spillner, A., & Linz, T. (2005). *Basiswissen Softwaretest, Aus- und Weiterbildung zum Certified Tester Foundation Level nach ASQF- und ISTQB-Standard*. dpunkt. Verlag GmbH Heidelberg (In German).

Test-Bench with Reactive Test Bench. Synapticad, & Waveformer Lite 9.9. *Commercial tool for testing*. Retrieved from http://www.actel.com/documents/reactive_tb_tutorial.pdf SystemTest™, & The MathWorks™, Inc. *Commercial tool for testing*. Retrieved from http://www.mathworks.com/products/systemtest/

Test Vector Tester for Simulink–T-VEC, & T-VEC Technologies, Inc. *Commercial model-based testing tool*. Retrieved from http://www.t-vec.com/solutions/simulink.php

The Artist Roadmap for Research and Development. Embedded Systems Design. (2005). (LNCS 3436). B. Bouyssounouse & J. Sifakis (Eds.)

Time Partitioning Testing–TPT, & PikeTec. Commercial model-based testing tool. Retrieved from http://www.piketec.com/products/tpt.php

Tretmans, J. (2008). Model based testing with labelled transition systems. In *Formal methods and testing* (LNCS 4949, pp. 1–38). Springer Berlin/Heidelberg.

Utting, M. (2005). Model-based testing. In *Proceedings of the Workshop on Verified Software: Theory, Tools, and Experiments, VSTTE 2005*.

Utting, M., & Legeard, B. (2006). *Practical model-based testing: A tools approach*. Elsevier Science & Technology Books.

Utting, M., Pretschner, A., & Legeard B. (2006). *A taxonomy of model-based testing*.

Vector Informatik Gmb, H. Retrieved from http://www.vector-worldwide.com/

Wallmüller, E. (2001). *Software-qualitätsmanagement in der praxis*. Hanser Verlag (in German).

Wappler, S., & Wegener, J. (2006). Evolutionary unit testing of object-oriented software using strongly-typed genetic programming. In *Proceedings of the 8th Annual Conference on Genetic and Evolutionary Computation*, Seattle, WA (pp. 1925-1932). ACM.

Weyuker, E. (1988). The evaluation of program-based software test data adequacy criteria. *Communications of the ACM, 31*(6), 668–675. doi:10.1145/62959.62963

Wiesbrock, H.-W., Conrad, M., & Fey, I. (2002). Pohlheim, ein neues automatisiertes auswerteverfahren für regressions und back-to-back-tests eingebetteter regelsysteme. In *Softwaretechnik-Trends, 22*(3), 22–27 (in German).

Zander, J., Dai, Z. R., Schieferdecker, I., & Din, G. (2005). From U2TP models to executable tests with TTCN-3 -an approach to model driven testing. In *Proceedings of the IFIP 17th Intern. Conf. on Testing Communicating Systems (TestCom 2005)*, Montreal, Canada. Springer-Verlag.

Zander-Nowicka, J. (2007). Reactive testing and test control of hybrid embedded software. In J. Garbajosa, J. Boegh, P. Rodriguez-Dapena, A. Rennoch (Eds.), *Proceedings of the 5th Workshop on System Testing and Validation (STV 2007)* in conjunction with *ICSSEA 2007*, Paris, France (pp. 45–62). Fraunhofer IRB Verlag.

Zander-Nowicka, J. (2008). *Model-based testing of embedded systems in the automotive domain*. Doctoral dissertation. Fraunhofer IRB Verlag.

Zander-Nowicka, J., Marrero Pérez, A., & Schieferdecker, I. (2007). From functional requirements through test evaluation design to automatic test data retrieval–a concept for testing of software dedicated for hybrid embedded systems. In H. R. Arabnia & H. Reza (Eds.), *Proceedings of the IEEE 2007 World Congress in Computer Science, Computer Engineering, & Applied Computing; SERP 2007*, Las Vegas, NV (Vol. II, pp. 347–353). CSREA Press.

Zander-Nowicka, J., Marrero Pérez, A., Schiefer-decker, I., & Dai, Z. R. (2007). Test design patterns for embedded systems. In I. Schieferdecker & S. Goericke (Eds.), *Business Process Engineering. Conquest-Tagungsband 2007–Proceedings of the 10th International Conference on Quality Engineering in Software Technology*, Potsdam, Germany. dpunkt.Verlag GmbH.

Zander-Nowicka, J., Mosterman, J. P., & Schief-erdecker, I. (2008). Quality of test specification by application of patterns. In *Proceedings of the 2nd International Workshop on Software Patterns and Quality (SPAQu 2008)* in conjunction with *15th Conference on Pattern Languages of Programs (PLOP 2008)* colocated with *OOPSLA 2008*, Nashville, TN.

Zander-Nowicka, J., Schieferdecker, I., & Marrero Pérez, A. (2006). Automotive validation functions for online test evaluation of hybrid real-time systems. In *Proceedings of the IEEE 41st Anniversary of The Systems Readiness Technology Conference (Autotestcon 2006)*, Anaheim, CA. IEEE.

Zander-Nowicka, J., Xiong, X., & Schieferdecker, I. (2008). Systematic test data generation for embedded software. In H. R. Arabnia & H. Reza (Eds.), *Proceedings of the IEEE 2008 World Congress in Computer Science, Computer Engineering, & Applied Computing. The 2008 International Conference on Software Engineering Research and Practice (SERP 2008)*, Las Vegas, NV (Vol. I, pp. 164–170). CSREA Press.

# Compilation of References

Achermann, F., Lumpe, M., Jean-Guy, S., & Oscar, N. (2001). Piccola-a small composition language. *Formal methods for distributed processing-a survey of object-oriented approaches*, (pp. 403-426).

Agha, G. A. (1986). *Actors: A model of concurrent computation in distributed systems*. Boston: MIT Press.

Aho, A. V., Lam, M. S., Sethi, R., & Ullman, J. D. (2007). *Compilers: Principles, techniques, and tools*. ED Pearson.

Aichernig, B. K. (2005). On the value of fault injection on the modeling level. In N. Plat & P. G. Larsen (Eds.), *Proceedings of the Overture Workshop*, Newcastle Upon Tyne, UK.

Allen, E. (2005). *The fortress language specification, version 0.618*. Retrieved on November 17, 2008, from http://projectfortress.sun.com/Projects/Community

Allen, R. J. (1997). *A formal approach to software architecture*. Unpublished doctoral dissertation (Tech. Rep. No. CMU-CS-97-144), Carnegie Mellon University, Pittsburgh, PA.

Alloy Website. Retrieved from http://alloy.mit.edu/index.php

Alomary, A., Nakata, T., Honma, Y., Sato, J., Hikichi, N., & Imai, M. (1993). PEAS-I: A hardware/software codesign system for ASIPs. *European Design Automation Conference, with EURO-VHDL (EURO-DAC'93)* (pp. 2-7). Hamburg, Germany.

Al-Safi, Y., & Vyatkin, V. (2007). An ontology-based reconfiguration agent for intelligent mechatronic systems. In *Third International Conference on Industrial Applications of Holonic and Multi-Agent Systems*. Springer-Verlag.

Altera, C. Nios II. Retrieved on November 27, 2008, from http://www.altera.com

Alur, R., & Dill, D. (1994). A theory of timed automata. *ACM Theoretical Computer Science, 126*(2), 183–235. doi:10.1016/0304-3975(94)90010-8

Alur, R., & Henzinger, T.-A. (1992). Logics and models of real-time: A survey. In *Proceedings of Real-time: Theory in Practice*, (LNCS Vol. 600). Springer-Verlg.

Alur, R., Torre, S. L., & Madhusudan, P. (2005). Perturbed timed automata. In M. Morari & L. Thiele (Eds.), *8th International Workshop, Hybrid Systems: Computation and Control, HSCC 2005* (LNCS 3414, pp. 70-85). Springer-Verlag.

Ammann, P., & Black, P. E. (2002). Model checkers. In *Software Testing* (Tech. Rep. NIST-IR 6777). National Institute of Standards and Technology.

Amon, T., Borriello, G., Hu, T., & Liu, J. (1997). Symbolic timing verification of timing diagrams using presburger formulas. In *Proceedings of the 34th Annual Conference on Design Automation* (pp. 226–231). New York: ACM.

Anastasakis, K., Bordbar, B., Georg, G., & Ray, I. (2007). UML2Alloy: A challenging model transformation. In G. Engels, B. Opdyke, D. C. Schmidt & F. Weil (Eds.), *Model driven engineering languages and systems (MoDELS 2007)* (LNCS 4735, pp. 436-450). Nashville: Springer Berlin.

Anceaume, E., & Puaut, I. (1997). A taxonomy of clock synchronization algorithms. *Publication Interne IRISA-PI-97-1103*. IRISA.

Angelov, C., Sierszecki, K., & Marian, N. (2005). Design models for reusable and reconfigurable state machines, In L.T. Yang, et al. (Eds), *EUC 2005, International Federation for Information Processing* (LNCS 3824, pp. 152-163).

Angus, D. (2007). Crowding population-based ant colony optimisation for the multiobjective travelling salesman problem. In *Proceedings of IEEE Symposium on Computational Intelligence in Multicriteria Decision Making* (pp. 333-340). Los Alamitos: IEEE Computer Society Press.

Araújo, J., et al. (2002, October). *Aspect-oriented requirements with UML*. Paper presented at Workshop on Aspect-oriented Modeling with UML, Dresden, Heidelberg.

Arlow, J., & Neustadt, I. (2002). *UML and the Unified Process*. Addison Wesley.

ARM. (2005). *ARM realview development suite*. Retreived from www.arm.com/products/DevTools/RealViewDevSuite.html

ARTIST. (2003). *Component-based design and integration platforms*. (Tech. Rep. W1.A2.N1.Y1). ARTIST-Advanced Real-Time Systems-IST project.

Artist-Project. (2003). *Roadmap:Component-based design and integration platforms*. Retrieved from www.artist-embedded.org

Ascia, G., Catania, V., & Palesi, M. (2004). A GA-based design space exploration framework for parameterized system-on-a-chip platforms. *IEEE Transactions on Evolutionary Computation, 8*(4), 329–346. doi:10.1109/TEVC.2004.826389

ATESST. (2008). Retrieved on July 1, 2008, from http://www.atesst.org/

Atienza, D., Baloukas, C., Papadopoulos, L., Poucet, C., Mamagkakis, S., Hidalgo, J. I., et al. (2007). Optimization of dynamic data structures in multimedia embedded systems using evolutionary computation. *Proceedings of the 10th International Workshop on Software & Compilers for Embedded Systems* (pp. 31-40). Nice, France: ACM.

Atienza, D., Mendias, J. M., Mamagkakis, S., Soudris, D., & Catthoor, F. (2006). Systematic dynamic memory management design methodology for reduced memory footprint. *ACM Transactions on Design Automation of Electronic Systems, 11*(2), 465–489.

Atlee, J. M., France, R., Georg, G., Moreira, A., Rumpe, B., & Zschaler, S. (2007). Modeling in software engineering. In *Proceedings of the International Conference on Software Engineering*.

Automated Testing Tool, M. A. T. L. A. B. *MATT, the University of Montana, research model-based testing prototype*. Retrieved from http://www.cs.umt.edu/rtsl/matt/

AUTOSAR. Retrieved on July 1, 2008 from http://www.autosar.org/

Axelsson, J. (2000, December). Real-world modeling in UML. In *Proceedings of the 13th International Conference on Software and Systems Engineering and their Applications, Paris*.

Babu, E. M. M., Malinowski, A., Suzuki, J., & Matilda. (2005). A distributed UML virtual machine for model-driven software development. In *Proceedings of the World Multi-Conference on Systemics, Cybernetics, and Informatics*.

Baier, C., & Katoen, J. (2008). *Principles of model checking*. MIT Press.

Bailey, B., Martin, G., & Piziali, A. (2007). *ESL design and verification: A prescription for electronic system level methodology*. Morgan Kaufmann

Bakre, S., & Elrad, T. (2007). Scenario based resolution of aspect interactions with aspect interaction charts. *Aspect-Oriented Modeling*.

Bakshi, A., Prasanna, V. K., & Ledeczi, A. (2001). MI-LAN: A model based integrated simulation framework for design of embedded systems. *ACM SIGPLAN Notices, 36*(8), 82–93. doi:10.1145/384196.384210

Balarin, F., Chiodo, M., Giusto, P., Hsieh, H., Jurecska, A., & Lavagno, L. (1999). Synthesis of software programs for embedded control applications. *IEEE Transactions on Computer-Aided Design of Integrated Circuits and Systems, 18*(6), 834–849. doi:10.1109/43.766731

Balarin, F., et al. (1997). *Hardware-software codesign of embedded systems: The polis approach*. Kluwer Academic Publishers.

Balarin, F., Giusto, P., Jurecska, A., Passerone, C., Sentovich, E., Tabbara, B., et al. (1997). *Hardware-software codesign of embedded systems: The POLIS approach*. Springer.

Balarin, F., Watanabe, Y., Hsieh, H., Lavagno, L., Passerone, C., & Sangiovanni-Vincentelli, A. (2003). Metropolis: An integrated electronic system design environment. *IEEE Computer, 36*(4), 45–52.

Balasubramanian, K., Gokhale, A., Karsai, G., Sztipanovits, J., & Neema, S. (2006). Developing applications using model-driven design environments. *IEEE Computer, 39*(2), 33–40.

Baloukas, C., Papadopoulos, L., Mamagkakis, S., Soudris, D. (2007, October 4-5). Component based library implementation of abstract data types for resource management customization of embedded systems. *Embedded Systems for Real-Time Multimedia (ESTIMedia 2007), IEEE/ACM/IFIP Workshop* (pp. 99–104).

Baresi, L., Bruschi, F., Di Nitto, E., & Sciuto, D. (2007). SystemC code generation from UML models. In E. Villar & J. Mermet (Eds.), *System specification & design languages* (pp. 161-171). The Netherlands: Kluwer Academic Publishers.

Bartzas, A., Mamagkakis, S., Pouiklis, G., Atienza, D., Catthoor, F., Soudris, D., et al. (2006). Dynamic data type refinement methodology for systematic performance-energy design exploration of network applications. *DATE '06: Proceedings of the Conference on Design, Automation, and Test in Europe* (pp. 740--745). Munich, Germany: European Design and Automation Association.

Baruah, S. (2003). Dynamic and static priority scheduling of recurring real-time tasks. *Real-Time Systems, 24*(1). doi:10.1023/A:1021711220939

Baruah, S., & Goossens, J. (2004). Scheduling real-time tasks: Algorithms and complexity. In J. Y.-T. Leung (Ed.), *Handbook of scheduling: Algorithms, models, and performance analysis*. Chapman Hall/CRC press.

Batory, D. (2006). Multilevel models in model-driven engineering, product lines, and metaprogramming. *IBM Systems Journal, 45*(3), 527–540.

Batory, D., Sarvela, J. N., & Rauschmayer, A. (2004). Scaling stepwise refinement. *IEEE Transactions on Software Engineering, 30*(6), 355–371. doi:10.1109/TSE.2004.23

Beck, A. C. S., Mattos, J. C. B., Wagner, F. R., & Carro, L. (2003). CACO-PS: A general purpose cycle-accurate configurable power simulator. In *Proceedings 16th Symposium on Integrated Circuits and Systems Design* (pp. 349- 354). Los Alamitos: IEEE Computer Society Press.

Behrmann, G., David, A., & Larsen, K. (2004). A tutorial on UPPAAL. In *Formal methods for the design of real-time systems* (LNCS 3185, pp. 200-236). Springer Verlag.

Beierle, C., Börger, E., Durdanovic, I., Glässer, U., & Riccobene, E. (1995). Refining abstract machine specifications of the steam boiler control to well documented executable code. In Abrial, J.-R., Börger, E., and Langmaack, H., editors, *Formal Methods for Industrial Applications*, volume 1165 of *Lecture Notes in Computer Science*, pages 52–78. Springer.

Beizer, B. (1995). *Black-box testing: Techniques for functional testing of software and systems*. John Wiley & Sons, Inc.

Bengtsson, J., Griffioen, W., Kristoffersen, J., Larsen, K., Larsson, F., Pettersson, P., & Yi, W. (2002). Automated analysis of an audio control protocol using uppaal. *Journal of Logic and Algebraic Programming, 52-53*, 163–181. doi:10.1016/S1567-8326(02)00036-X

Bengtsson, J., Larsen, K., Larsson, F., Pettersson, P., & Yi, W. (1996). UPPAAL—a tool suite for automatic verification of real-time systems. In *Proceedings of the DIMACS/SYCON Workshop on Hybrid Systems III: Verification and control* (pp. 232-243). New Brunswick: Springer-Verlag New York.

Benini, L., & de Micheli, G. (2000). System-level power optimization: Techniques and tools. *ACM Transactions on Design Automation of Electronic Systems, 5*(2), 115–192. doi:10.1145/335043.335044

Benini, L., & de Micheli, G. (Eds.). (2006). *Networks on chip*. Morgan Kaufmann.

Benini, L., Bertozzi, D., Bruni, D., Drago, N., Fummi, F., & Ponzino, M. (2003). SystemC cosimulation and emulation of multiprocessor SoC design. *Computer, 36*(4). IEEE.

Benini, L., Bogliolo, A., Menichelli, F., & Oliveri, M. (2005). MPARM: Exploring the multiprocessor SoC design space with SystemC. *Journal of VLSI Signal Processing, 41*(2). Springer.

Bennett, D., Dellinger, E., Mason, J., & Sundarajan, P. (2006). An FPGA-oriented target language for HLL compilation. *Reconfigurable Systems Summer Institute (RSSI '06)*, Urbana, IL.

Bensalem, S., Bozga, M., Sifakis, J., & Nguyen, T.-H. (2008). Compositional verification for component-based systems and application. *6th International Symposium on Automated Technology for Verification and Analysis, ATVA* (pp. 64-79).

Benveniste, A., & Berry, G. (1991). The synchronous approach to reactive and real-time systems. *Proceedings of the IEEE, 79*(9), 1270–1282. doi:10.1109/5.97297

Berard, B., Bidoit, M., Finkel, A., Laroussinie, F., Petit, A., Petrucci, L., et al. (2001). *Systems and software verification. Model checking techniques and tools*. Berlin/New York: Springer-Verlag.

Berkenkötter, K., Bisanz, S., Hannemann, U., & Peleska, J. (2003). Hybrid UML profile for UML 2.0. In *Proceedings of the UML Workshop on Specification and Validation of UML Models for Real Time and Embedded Systems (SVERTS), San Francisco, USA.*

Bernard, E., Legeard, B., Luck, X., & Peureux, F. (2004). Generation of test sequences from formal specifications: GSM 11-11 standard case study. *Software Testing, Verification, and Reliability, 34*(10), 915–948.

Berry, G., & Gonthier, G. (1992). The esterel synchronous programming language: Design, semantics, implementation. *Science of Computer Programming, 19*(2), 87–152. doi:10.1016/0167-6423(92)90005-V

Berthomieu, B., Lime, D., Roux, O. H., & Vernadat, F. (2007). Reachability problems and abstract state spaces for time petri nets with stopwatches. *Discrete Event Dynamic Systems, 17*(2), 133–158. doi:10.1007/s10626-006-0011-y

Beux, S. L., Marquet, P., & Dekeyser, J.-L. (2007). *A design flow to map parallel applications onto FPGAs*. Paper presented at the 17th IEEE International Conference on Field Programmable Logic and Applications (FPL'07).

Bezivin, J. (2005). On the unification power of models. [SoSym]. *Software and System Modeling, 4*(2), 171–188. doi:10.1007/s10270-005-0079-0

Bézivin, J., Kurtev, I., Jouault, F., & Valduriez, P. (2006). Model-based DSL frameworks. *Companion to the 21st Annual ACM SIGPLAN Conference on Object-Oriented Programming, Systems, Languages, and Applications (OOPSLA)*, Portland, OR (pp. 602-616).

Bhattacharyya, S., Cheong, E., Davis, J., Goel, M., Kienhuis, B., Hylands, C., et al. (2003). *Ptolemy II heterogeneous concurrency modeling and design in java*. Berkeley, CA: University of California Berkeley.

Bichler, L., Radermacher, A., & Schürr, A. (2004). Integrating data flow equations with UML/real-time. *Real-Time Systems, 26*, 107–125. doi:10.1023/B:TIME.0000009308.63403.e6

Bienmüller, T., Brockmeyer, U., & Sandmann, G. (2004). *Automatic validation of simulink/stateflow models, formal verification of safety-critical requirements*. Stuttgart.

Binns, P., & Vestal, S. (2001). Formalizing software architectures for embedded systems. In T. A. Henzinger & C. M. Kirsch (Eds.), *First international workshop on embedded software* (LNCS 221, pp. 451-468). London: Springer-Verlag.

Bispo, J., Sourdis, Y., Cardoso, J. M. P., & Vassiliadis, S. (2006). Regular expression matching for reconfigurable packet inspection. *IEEE International Conference on Field Programmable Technology (FPT'06)* (pp. 119-126). Bangkok, Thailand: IEEE Computer Society Press.

Björklund, D., Lilius, J., & Porres, I. (2005). Code generation for embedded systems. In S. Gérard, J. Babau & J. Champeau (Eds.), *Model driven engineering for distributed real-time embedded systems*. London: Hermes Science.

Bjørner, D., & Jones, C. B. (1978). *The Vienna development method: The metalanguage* (Vol. 61). Heidelberg: Springer Berlin-LNCS.

Blickle, T., Teich, J., & Thiele, L. (1998). System-level synthesis using evolutionary algorithms. *Design Automation for Embedded Systems*, *3*(1), 23–58. doi:10.1023/A:1008899229802

Bocchio, S., Riccobene, E., Rosti, A., & Scandurra, P. (2005) A SoC design flow based on UML 2.0 and SystemC. In *Proc. of the International DAC Workshop UML- SoC'05*. IEEE press.

Bocchio, S., Riccobene, E., Rosti, A., & Scandurra, P. (2008). An Enhanced SystemC UML Profile for Modeling at Transaction-Level. In Villar, E., editor, *Embedded Systems Specification and Design Languages*, pages 211-226. Springer.

Bodeveix, J.-P., Koné, O., & Bouaziz, R. (2005). Test method for embedded real-time systems. In *Proceedings of the European Workshop on Dependable Software Intensive Embedded Systems*, ERCIM, Porto (pp. 1–10).

Boger, M., Sturm, T., & Fragemann, P. (2003). Refactoring browser for UML. In *NODe '02: Revised Papers from the International Conference NetObjectDays on Objects, Components, Architectures, Services, and Applications for a Networked World* (pp. 366–377).

Boldt, R. (2007). Combining the power of MathWorks Simulink and Telelogic UML/SysML-based rhapsody to redefine the model-driven development experience. June, 2006. Telelogic white paper. Retrieved on February 23, 2007, from http://www.ilogix.com/whitepaper-overview.aspx

Bondé, L., Dumoulin, C., & Dekeyser, J.-L. (2004, September). *Metamodels and MDA transformations for embedded systems*. Paper presented at Forum on Design Languages, Lille, France.

Bontempi, G., & Kruijtzer, W. (2002). A data analysis method for software performance prediction. In *Proceedings of the Design, Automation, and Test in Europe Conference and Exhibition* (pp. 971-976). Los Alamitos: IEEE Computer Society Press.

Booch, G. (1993). *Object-oriented analysis and design with applications, 2nd ed.* San Francisco: Benjamin Cummings.

Booch, G. (1999). *The unified modeling language user guide*. Boston: Addison Wesley.

Booch, G., Rumbaugh, J., & Jacobson, I. (2005). *Unified modeling language user guide, 2nd ed.* Addison Wesley Longman.

Börger, E. (2003). The ASM refinement method. *Formal Asp. Comput*, *15*(2-3), 237–257.

Börger, E., & Stärk, R. (2003). *Abstract State Machines: A Method for High-Level System Design and Analysis*. Springer Verlag.

Börger, E., Riccobene, E., & Schmid, J. (2000). Capturing requirements by Abstract State Machines: The light control case study. *J.UCS. Journal of Universal Computer Science*, *6*(7), 597–625.

Boussinot, F., & Simone, R. d. (1991). The esterel language. In *Proceedings of the IEEE*, *79*(9), 1293-1304.

Brandan Briones, L., & Brinksma, E. (2004). *A test generation framework for quiescent real-time systems*. Internal Report 48975. University of Twente.

Brandolese, C., Fornaciari, W., & Sciuto, D. (2000). A multilevel strategy for software power estimation. In *Proc of ISSS*. IEEE.

Brandolese, C., Fornaciari, W., Salice, F., & Sciuto, D. (2001). Source-level execution time estimation of C programs. In *Proc. of CoDes*. IEEE.

Bräuer, J., Kleinwechter, H., & Leicher, A. (2007). μttcn–an approach to continuous signals in TTCN-3. In W.-G. Bleek, H. Schwentner & H. Züllighoven (Eds.), *Proceedings of Software Engineering Workshops, Series LNI* (Vol. 106, pp. 55–64).

Brennan, R.-W., Fletcher, M., & Norrie, D.-H. (2001). A holonic approach to reconfiguring real-time distributed control systems. In *Multi-Agent Systems and Applications: MASA'01*. Springer-Verlag.

Brisolara, L. B., Becker, L. B., Carro, L., Wagner, F. R., Pereira, C. E., & Reis, R. A. L. (2005b). Comparing high-level modeling approaches for embedded systems design. In *Proceedings of the Asia South Pacific Design Automation Conference, ASP-DAC*, Shanghai, China (pp. 986-989).

Brisolara, L. B., Oliveira, M. F., Redin, R., Lamb, L. C., Carro, L., & Wagner, F. (2008). Using UML as front-end for heterogeneous software code generation strategies. *Design* [Munich: IEEE Computer Society Press.]. *Automation and Test in Europe DATE, 08*, 504–509. doi:10.1109/DATE.2008.4484731

Brisolara, L., Becker, L., Carro, L., Wagner, F., & Pereira, C. E. (2005a). A comparison between UML and function blocks for heterogeneous SoC design and ASIP generation. In G. Martin & W. Müller (Eds.), *UML for SoC design* (pp. 199-222). Dordrecht, The Netherlands: Springer.

Broy, M., Krüger, I. H., Pretschner, A., & Salzmann, C. (2007). Engineering automotive software. *Proceedings of the IEEE, 95*(2), 356–373. doi:10.1109/JPROC.2006.888386

Broy, M., Von der Beeck, M., & Krüger, I. (1998). *Softbed: Problemanalyse Für Ein Großverbundprojekt System-technik Automobil Software Für Eingebettete Systeme*. Ausarbeitung für das BMBF. (In German).

Bruschi, F., & Sciuto, D. (2002). SystemC based Design Flow starting from UML Model. In *Proc. of European SystemC Users Group Meeting*.

Bruschi, F., Ferrandi, F., & Sciuto, D. (2005). A framework for the functional verification of systemc models. *International Journal of Parallel Programming, 33*(6), 667–695. doi:10.1007/s10766-005-8908-x

BS 7925-2:1998. (1998). *Software testing. Software component testing*. British Standards Institution.

Bucci, G., Fedeli, A., Sassoli, L., & Vicario, E. (2004). Timed state space analysis of real-time preemptive systems. *IEEE Transactions on Software Engineering, 30*(2), 97–111. doi:10.1109/TSE.2004.1265815

Buck, J., Ha, S., Lee, E. A., & Messerschmitt, D. G. (1994). Ptolemy: A framework for simulating and prototyping heterogeneous systems. *International Journal of Computer Simulation, special issue on Simulation Software Development, 4*, 155-182.

Budhiraja, N. (1993). *The primary-backup approach: Lower and upper bounds*. Ithaca, NY: Cornell University.

Budiu, M., & Goldstein, S. C. (1999). Fast compilation for pipelined reconfigurable fabrics. *1999 ACM/SIGDA Seventh International Symposium on Field Programmable Gate Arrays (FPGA'99)* (pp. 195-205). Monterey, CA: ACM New York.

Burch, J., Clarke, E., McMillan, K., Dill, D., & Hwang, L. (1992). Symbolic model checking: 10^20 states and beyond. *Information and Computation, 98*(2), 142–170. doi:10.1016/0890-5401(92)90017-A

Cai, L., & Gajski, D. (2003). Transaction level modeling: An overview. In *Proceedings of the 1st IEEE/ACM/IFIP International Conference on Hardware/software Codesign and System Synthesis* (pp. 19-24). New York.

Campbell, C., Grieskamp, W., Nachmanson, L., Schulte, W., Tillmann, N., & Veanes, M. (2005). *Model-based testing of object-oriented reactive systems with spec explorer.* Microsoft Research, MSR-TR-2005-59.

Campos, S., & Clarke, E. (1999). Analysis and verification of real-time systems using quantitative symbolic algorithms. *Journal of Software Tools for Technology Transfer, 2*(3), 260–269. doi:10.1007/s100090050033

Cantor, M. (2003). *Rational unified process for systems engineering.* Retrieved on August 15, 2007, from http://www.therationaledge.com/content/aug 03/f rupse mc.jsp

Cardoso, J. M. P., & Diniz, P. C. (2008) Compilation techniques for reconfigurable architectures. Springer.

Cardoso, J. M. P., & Neto, H. C. (2003). Compilation for FPGA-based reconfigurable hardware. *Design & Test of Computers, IEEE, 20*(2), 65–75. doi:10.1109/MDT.2003.1188264

Cardoso, J. M. P., & Weinhardt, M. (2002). XPP-VC: A C compiler with temporal partitioning for the PACT-XPP architecture. *12th International Conference on Field Programmable Logic and Applications (FPL'02)* (pp. 864-874). Montpellier, France.

Carioni, A., Gargantini, A., Riccobene, E., & Scandurra, P. (2008). A Model-driven Technique for Embedded System Validation. In *FDL 08: Proceedings of Forum on Specification and Design Languages,* pp. 191-196. IEEE press.

Carlstrom, B. D., McDonald, A., Chafi, H., Chung, J., Minh, C. C., Kozyrakis, C., et al. (2006). The atomos transactional programming language. *Conference on Programming Language Design and Implementation (PLDI'06)* (pp. 1-13). Ottawa, Ontario, Canada: ACM Press.

Carnegie Mellon University, Department of Electrical and Computer Engineering. *Hybrid system verification toolbox for MATLAB–checkmate, research tool for system verification.* Retrieved from http://www.ece.cmu.edu/~webk/checkmate/

Carter, J. M., Lin, L., & Poore, J. H. (2008). Automated functional testing of simulink control models. In *Pro-ceedings of the 1st Workshop on Model-Based Testing in Practice, MoTIP 2008.* T. Bauer, H. Eichler, A. Rennoch (Eds.). Berlin, Germany: Fraunhofer IRB Verlag.

Carter, K. (2005). *iUML: Intelligent UML.* Retrieved on May 5, 2005, from http://www.kc.com

Castillo, J., Posadas, H., Villar, E., & Martínez, M. (2007). Energy consumption estimation technique in embedded processors with stable power consumption based on source-code operator energy figures. In *Proc. of DCIS.*

Catalysis. The Catalysis process: www.catalysis.org

Catthoor, F. (2007). *Course on metaconcepts and unified system design flow.* Retrieved from http://www.imec.be/tcmwebapp/internet/platform/index.htm

Catthoor, F., & Brockmeyer, E. (2000). Unified metaflow summary for low-power data-dominated applications. In *Unified low-power design flow for data-dominated multimedia and telecom applications.* Boston: Kluwer Academic Publishers.

Catthoor, F., de Greef, E., & Wuytack, S. (1998). *Custom memory management methodology: Exploration of memory organisation for embedded multimedia system design.* Kluwer Academic Publishers.

Center for Embedded Computer Systems (CECS). (2008). *Embedded systems environment (ESE) (version 1.0).* Computer software. University of California, Irvine. Retrieved in January 2008, www.cecs.uci.edu/~ese/

Chamberlain, B. L., Callahan, D., & Zima, H. P. (2007). Parallel programmability and the chapel language. *International Journal of High Performance Computing Applications, 21*(3), 291–312. doi:10.1177/1094342007078442

Chang, N., Kwon, W. H., & Park, J. (1996). FPGA-based implementation of synchronous petri nets. *1996 IEEE 22nd International Conference on Industrial Electronics, Control, and Instrumentation (IECON'96)* (pp. 469-474).

Chatzigeorgiou, A., & Stephanides, G. (2002). Evaluating performance and power of object-oriented vs. procedural programming in embedded processors. *7th Ada-Europe*

*International Conference on Reliable Software Technologies* (pp. 65-75). London: Springer-Verlag.

Chen, R., Sgroi, M., Lavagno, L., Martin, G., Sangiovanni-Vincentelli, A., & Rabaey, J. (2003). Embedded system design using UML and platforms. In L. Lavagno, G. Martin, B. Selic (Eds.), *UML for real: Design of embedded real time systems* (pp. 107-126). Dordrecht: Kluwer Academic Publishers.

Chen, R., Sgroi, M., Martin, G., Lavagno, L., Sangiovanni-Vincentelli, A. L., & Rabaey, J. (2003). Embedded System Design Using UML and Platforms. In *System Specification and Design Languages* (Eugenio Villar and Jean Mermet, eds.), CHDL Series, Kluwer.

Chen, X., Hsieh, H., & Balarin, F. (2006). Verification approach of metropolis design framework for embedded systems. *International Journal of Parallel Programming, 34*(1), 3–27. doi:10.1007/s10766-005-0002-x

Chen, X., Hsieh, H., Balarin, F., & Watanabe, Y. (2003). Case studies of model checking for embedded system designs. In *Proceedings of the Third International Conference on Application of Concurrency to System Design (ACSD '03)* (p. 20). IEEE Computer Society Press.

Chrissis, M. B., Konrad, M., & Shrum, S. (2003). *CMMI: Guidelines for process integration and product improvement.* Addison-Wesley.

Christopher, B., Edward, A. L., Xiaojun, L., Stephen, N., Yang, Z., & Haiyang, Z. (2008). *Heterogeneous concurrent modeling and design in java (volume 1: introduction to Ptolemy II).* University of California, Berkeley: EECS.

Chung, E. S., Nurvitadhi, E., Hoe, J. C., Falsafi, B., & Mai, K. (2008). A complexity-effective architecture for accelerating full-system multiprocessor simulations using FPGAs. *16th International ACM/SIGDA Symposium on Field Programmable Gate Arrays* (pp. 77-86). Monterey, A: ACM.

Cilk (1998). Cilk 5.4.6 *Reference manual, Supercomputing Technologies Group, MIT Laboratory for Computer Science.* Retrieved on December 9, 2008, from http://supertech.lcs.mit.edu/cilk

Clarke, E. M., & Emerson, E. A. (1981). Design and synthesis of synchronization skeletons using branching time logics. In *Logics of Programs: Workshop* (LNCS 131). Springer.

Clarke, E. M., Emerson, E. A., & Sistla, A. P. (1986). Automatic verification of finite-state concurrent systems using temporal logics specifications. *ACM Transactions on Programming Languages and Systems, 8*(2), 244–263. doi:10.1145/5397.5399

Clarke, S., & Baniassad, E. (2005). *Aspect-oriented analysis and design: The theme approach.* Addison-Wesley.

Classification Tree Editor for Embedded Systems. *CTE/ES, razorcat development GmbH, commercial tool for testing.* Retrieved from http://www.razorcatdevelopment.de/

CMP Media. (2006). *State of embedded market survey.*

Cockburn, A. (2001). *Agile software development.* Addison-Wesley Professional.

Colla, E.-C.-M., & Brusafferri, A. (2006). Applying the IEC 61499 model to the schoe manufacturing sector. *11th IEEE International Conference on Emerging Technologies and Factory Automation, ETFA'06.*

Computers, S. R. C. I. Retrieved on November 27, 2008, from http://www.srccomp.com/

Conrad, M. (2004). *A systematic approach to testing automotive control software. SAE technical paper series,* 2004-21-0039. Detroit, MI.

Conrad, M. (2004). *Modell-basierter test eingebetteter software im Automobil: Auswahl und Beschreibung von Testszenarien.* Unpublished doctoral dissertation, Deutscher Universitätsverlag, Wiesbaden (D). (In German).

Conrad, M., & Hötzer, D. (1998). Selective integration of formal methods in the development of electronic control units. *Proceedings of the ICFEM, 1998,* 144.

Conrad, M., Fey, I., & Sadeghipour, S. (2004). Systematic model-based testing of embedded control software–the

MB3T approach. In *Proceedings of the ICSE 2004 Workshop on Software Engineering for Automotive Systems*, Edinburgh, United Kingdom.

Copi, I. M., & Cohen, C. (2000). *Introduction to logic, 11th ed.* Upper Saddle River, NJ: Prentice-Hall.

Corbett, J. C. (1996). Timing analysis of ada tasking programs. *IEEE Transactions on Software Engineering, 22*(7), 461–483. doi:10.1109/32.538604

Corp, M. G. *Catapult synthesis.* Retrieved on December 2, 2008, from http://www.mentor.com/

Cosmas, G., et al. (2002). *3D murale.* Retrieved from http://www.brunel.ac.uk/project/murale/home.html

Cottenier, T., van den Berg, A., & Elrad, T. (2007). Motorola WEAVR: Aspect and model-driven engineering. *Journal of Object Technology, 6*(7), 51–88.

Cox, R. (2007). Regular expression matching can be simple and fast (but is slow in Java, Perl, PHP, Python, Ruby...). Retrieved on December 2, 2008, from http://swtch.com/~rsc/regexp/regexp1.html

Coyle, F. P., & Thornton, M. A. (2005, April). *From UML to HDL: A model driven architectural approach to hardware-software codesign.* Paper presented at Information Systems: New Generations Conference, Las Vegas, NV.

Craven, S., & Athanas, P. (2007). Examining the viability of FPGA supercomputing. *EURASIP Journal of Embedded Systems.*

Crnkovic, I., & Larsson, M. (2002). *Building reliable component-based software systems.* UK: Artech House.

Cronquist, D. C., Franklin, P., Berg, S. G., & Ebeling, C. (1998). Specifying and compiling applications for RaPiD. *IEEE Symposium on Fpgas for Custom Computing Machines (FCCM'98)* (pp. 116-125). Washington, D.C.: IEEE Computer Society.

Cuenot, P., Frey, P., Johansson, R., Lönn, H., Reiser, M.-O., Servat, D., et al. (2008). Developing automotive products using the EAST-ADL2, and AUTOSAR compliant architecture description language. *4th European*

Congress ERTS Embedded Real Time Software 2008, Toulouse, France.

Czarnecki, K., & Eisenecker, U. (2000). *Generative programming: Methods, tools, and applications.* Addison-Wesley.

Dai, Z. R. (2006). *An approach to model-driven testing with UML 2.0, U2TP and TTCN-3.* Doctoral dissertation, Technical University Berlin. Fraunhofer IRB Verlag.

Dajani-Brown, S., Cofer, D., & Bouali, A. (2004). Formal verification of an avionics sensor voter using SCADE. In *Formal Techniques, Modelling, and Analysis of Timed and Fault-Tolerant Systems* (LNCS 3253, pp. 5–20). Springer-Verlag Berlin/Heidelberg.

Dautelle, J. (2007). Fully deterministic java. *AIAA SPACE 2007 Conference and Exposition*, CA (pp. 18-20).

Davis, J. (2003, October 26-30). GME: The generic modeling environment. In R. Crocker & G. L. Steele, Jr. (Eds.), *Companion of the 18th Annual ACM SIGPLAN Conference on Object-Oriented Programming, Systems, Languages, and Applications, OOPSLA 2003, Anaheim, CA* (pp. 82-83). New York: ACM Press.

Daws, C., & Yovine, S. (1995). Two examples of verification of multirate timed automata with Kronos. In *Proceedings of the 16th IEEE Real-Time Systems Symposium (RTSS'95)*, Pisa, Italy (pp. 66-75).

Daws, C., & Yovine, S. (1996). Reducing the number of clock variables of timed automata. In *Proceedings of the 17th IEEE Real Time Systems Symposium.* Washington, D.C.: IEEE Computer Society Press.

Daylight, E. G., Demoen, B., & Catthoor, F. (2004). Formally specifying dynamic data structures for embedded software design: An initial approach. *SPACE 2004: Semantics, Program Analysis, and Computing Environments for Memory Management (Proceedings not published).* Venice, Italy.

de Niz, D., Bhatia, G., & Rajkumar, R. (2006). Model-based development of embedded systems: The sysweaver approach. *IEEE Real-Time and Embedded Technology and Applications Symposium 2006*, San Jose, CA.

Debruyne, V., Simonot-Lion, F., & Trinquet, Y. (2004). EAST-ADL, an architecture description language–validation and verification aspects. In P. Dissaux, M. Filali Amine, P. Michel & F. Vernadat (Eds.), *IFIP World Computer Congress 2004 – Proceedings of the Workshop on Architecture Description Languages,* Toulouse, France.

DeHon, A., Markovskiy, Y., Caspi, E., Chu, M., Huang, R., & Perissakis, S. (2006). Stream computations organized for reconfigurable execution. *Microprocessors and Microsystems, 30*(6), 334–354. doi:10.1016/j.micpro.2006.02.009

Dempster, D., & Stuart, M. (June, 2002). *Verification methodology manual, techniques for verifying HDL designs.* Teamwork International.

DeRemer, F., & Kron, H. (1975). Programming-in-the-large versus programming-in-the-small. In *Proceedings of the International Conference on Reliable Software.* Los Angeles, CA: ACM.

DESS–Software Development Process for Real-Time Embedded Software Systems. (2001). The DESS methodology. In S. Van Baelen, J. Gorinsek, & A. Wills (Eds.), *Deliverable D.1, version 01–public.*

Dibble, P. (2008). *Real-time specification for Java.* Addison-Wesley.

Dick, R. P., & Jha, N. K. (1998). MOGAC: A multiobjective genetic algorithm for hardware-software cosynthesis of distributed embedded systems. *IEEE Transactions on Computer-Aided Design of Integrated Circuits and Systems, 17*(10), 920–935. doi:10.1109/43.728914

Dijkstra, E. W. (1972). Notes on structured programming. In C. A. R. Hoare (Ed.), *Structured programming, Vol. 8 of A.P.I.C. studies in data processing, part 1* (pp. 1–82). Academic Press London/New York.

Diniz, P. C., Hall, M. W., Park, J., So, B., & Ziegler, H. E. (2005). Automatic mapping of C to FPGAs with the DEFACTO compilation and synthesis system. *Microprocessors and Microsystems, 29*(2-3), 51–62. doi:10.1016/j.micpro.2004.06.007

D-MINT Consortium. Deployment of Model-Based Technologies to Industrial Testing. (2007). *Milestone 1, deliverable 2.1–test modeling, test generation and test execution with model-based testing.*

D-MINT Project – Deployment of Model-Based Technologies to Industrial Testing. (2008). Retrieved from http://d-mint.org/ dSpace GmbH. *AutomationDesk, commercial tool for testing.* Retrieved from http://www.dSpace.de/Goto?Releases dSpace GmbH. Retrieved from http://www.dSpace.de/ww/en/gmb/home.cfm

do Nascimento, F. A. M., Oliveira, M. F. S., & Wagner, F. R. (2007). ModES: ES Design Methodology and Tools based on MDE. In *Fourth International workshop on Model-based Methodologies for Pervasive and Embedded Software (MOMPES'07).* IEEE Press.

Donlin, A. (2004). Transaction level modeling: Flows and use models. In *Proceedings of the 2nd IEEE/ACM/IFIP International Conference on Hardware/ software Codesign and System Synthesis* (pp 75-80). New York.

Douglass, B. (1998). *Real-time UML: Developing efficient objects for embedded systems.* Boston: Addison-Wesley Professional.

Douglass, B. (2003). *Real-time design patterns: Robust scalable architecture for real-time systems.* Boston: Addison Wesley.

Douglass, B. P. (2004). *Real time UML: Advances in the UML for real-time systems, 3rd ed.* Boston: Addison Wesley.

DSPLogic. *DSPLogic, Inc.* Retrieved on November 28, 2008, from http://www.dsplogic.com/home/

Dukas, G., & Thramboulidis, K. (2005). A real-time linux execution environment for function-block based distributed control applications. *2nd IEEE International Conference on Industrial Informatics, INDIN'05.*

Dulz, W., & Fenhua, Z. (2003). Matelo–statistical USAge testing by annotated sequence diagrams, Markov chains, and TTCN-3. In *Proceedings of the 3rd International Conference on Quality Software* (p. 336). Washington, D.C.: IEEE Computer Society.

Dumont, P., & Boulet, P. (2005). Another multidimensional synchronous dataflow: Simulating array-OL in ptolemy II. *Research Report RR-5516,* Inria, France.

Duzan, G., Loyall, J., Schantz, R., Shapiro, R., & Zinky, J. (2004). Building adaptive distributed applications with middleware and aspects. *International Conference on Aspect-Oriented Software Development (AOSD),* Lancaster, UK (pp. 66-73).

Dwivedi, B. K., Kumar, A., & Balakrishnan, M. (2004). Automatic synthesis of system on chip multiprocessor architectures for process networks. In A. Orailoglu, P. H. Chou, P. Eles & A. Jantsch (Eds.), *Proceedings of the 2nd IEEE/ACM/IFIP International Conference on Hardware/Software Codesign and System Synthesis* (pp 60-65). New York: ACM Press.

Edwards, M., & Green, P. (2003). UML for hardware and software object modeling. In L. Lavagno, G. Martin & B. Selic (Eds.), *UML for real: Design of embedded real-time systems* (pp. 127-147). Norwell, USA: Kluwer Academic Publishers.

Edwards, S., Lavagno, L., Lee, E. A., & Sangiovanni-Vincentelli, A. (1997). Design of embedded systems: Formal models, validation, and synthesis. *Proceedings of the IEEE, 85*(3), 366–390. doi:10.1109/5.558710

Eker, J., & Janneck, J. W. (2003). CAL language report: Specification of the CAL actor language. *ERL Technical Memo UCB/ERL M03/48,* University of California at Berkeley,CA.

El-Ghazawi, T., El-Araby, E., Miaoqing, H., Gaj, K., Kindratenko, V., & Buell, D. (2008). The promise of high-performance reconfigurable computing. *Computer, 41*(2), 69–76. doi:10.1109/MC.2008.65

Elloy, J.-P., & Simonot-Lion, F. (2002). An architecture description language for in-vehicle embedded system development. In L. Basañez & J. A. de la Puente (Eds.), *15th IFAC World Congress,* Barcelona, Spain.

Elrad, T., Aldawud, A., & Bader, A. (2002). Aspect-oriented modeling: Bridging the gap between modeling and design. *Generative Programming and Component Engineering (GPCE),* Pittsburgh, PA (pp. 189-201).

Embedded Validator. *OSC—embedded systems AG, commercial verification tool.* Retrieved from http://www.osc-es.de Encontre, V. (2003). *Testing embedded systems: Do you have the guts for it? IBM.* Retrieved from http://www-128.ibm.com/developerworks/rational/library/459.html

Erbas, C., Erbas, S. E., & Pimentel, A. D. (2003). A multiobjective optimization model for exploring multiprocessor mappings of process networks. In R. Gupta, Y. Nakamura, A. Orailoglu & P. H. Chou (Eds.), *Proceedings of the 1st IEEE/ACM/IFIP International Conference on Hardware/Software Codesign and System Synthesis* (pp 182-187). New York: ACM Press.

Esterel Technologies (2008). *SCADE tool.* Retrieved on October 7, 2008, from http://www.esterel-technologies.com/products/scade-suite/

ETSI European Standard (ES) 201 873-1 V3.2.1 (2007-02): *The Testing and Test Control Notation Version 3; Part 1: TTCN-3 Core Language.* European Telecommunications Standards Institute, Sophia-Antipolis, France.

Extessy (2007). Exite tool. Retrieved on May 25, 2007, from http://www.extessy.com/

Faucou, S., Déplanche, A.-M., & Trinquet, Y. (2004). An ADL-centric approach for the formal design of real-time systems. In P. Dissaux, M. Filali Amine, P. Michel & F. Vernadat (Eds.), *IFIP World Computer Congress 2004–Proceedings of the Workshop on Architecture Description Languages,* Toulouse, France.

Feiler, P. H., Gluch, D. P., & Hudak, J. J. (2006). *The architecture analysis & design language (AADL): An introduction* (Tech. Rep. No CMU/SEI-2006-TN-011). Carnegie Mellon University, Pittsburgh, PA.

Feiler, P. H., Lewis, B., & Vestal, S. (2003). The SAE avionics architecture description language (AADL) standard: A basis for model-based architecture-driven embedded systems engineering. In *IEEE Real-Time Application Symposium 2003–Workshop on Model-Driven Embedded Systems,* Washington D.C.

Fennel, H., Bunzel, S., Heinecke, H., Bielefeld, J., Fürstand, S., Schnelle, K. P., et al. (2006, October). Achievements and exploitation of the AUTOSAR development partnership. Paper presented at *Convergence 2006*, Detroit, MI.

Fernandes, J., Machado, R., & Santos, H. (2000). Modeling industrial embedded systems with UML. In F. Vahid & J. Madsen (Eds.), *Proceedings of the Eighth International Workshop on Hardware/Software Codesign* (pp. 18-22). New York: ACM Press.

Ferrarini, L., & Veber, C. (2004). Implementation approaches for the execution model of IEC 61499 applications. *2nd IEEE International Conference on Industrial Informatics, INDIN'04*.

Fersman, E., Pettersson, P., & Yi, W. (2002). Timed automata with asynchronous processes: Schedulability and decidability. In *Proceedings of 8th International Conference on Tools and Algorithms for the Construction and Analysis of Systems TACAS 2002* (LNCS 2280, pp.67-82). Berlin/New York: Springer-Verlag.

Fersman, E., Pettersson, P., & Yi, W. (2003). Schedulability analysis using two clocks. In *Proceedings of 9th International Conference on Tools and Algorithms for the Construction and Analysis of Systems TACAS 2003* (LNCS 2619, pp. 224-239). Berlin/New York: Springer-Verlag.

Fiedler, M. (2004, June). *Implementation of a basic h.264/avc decoder*. Retrieved in January 2007, from http://rtg.informatik.tu-chemnitz.de/docs/da-sa-txt/sa-mfie.pdf

Filman, R. E., Elrad, T., Clarke, S., & Aksit, M. (2004). *Aspect-oriented software development*. Boston: Addison-Wesley.

Filman, R., & Friedman, D. (2000). Aspect-oriented programming is quantification and obliviousness. *OOPSLA Workshop on Advanced Separation of Concerns*, Minneapolis, MN.

FlexRay Consortium. (2005). *FlexRay communications system-protocol specification-version 2.1*. Retrieved from http://www.flexray.com

Fowler, M. (1999). *Refactoring: Improving the design of existing code*. Boston: Addison-Wesley Longman Publishing Co., Inc.

Frantzen, L., Tretmans, J., & Willemse, T. A. C. (2006). A symbolic framework for model-based testing. In *Formal approaches to software testing and runtime verification, 4262*. Springer Berlin / Heidelberg.

Fredette, A. N., & Cleaveland, R. (1993). RTSL: A language for real-time schedulability analysis. In *Proceedings of the Real-Time Systems Symposium* (pp 274-283). IEEE Computer Society Press.

Fredkin, E. (1960). Trie memory. *Communications of the ACM, 3*(9), 490–499.doi:doi:10.1145/367390.367400

Freitas, E. P., Wehrmeister, M. A., da Silva Junior, E. T., Carvalho, F., Pereira, C. E., & Wagner, F. R. (2007, March 13). DERAF: A high-level aspects framework for distributed embedded real-time systems design. In A. Moreira (Ed.), *Early Aspects: Current Challenges and Future Directions, 10th International Workshop on Early Aspects,* Vancouver, Canada (LNCS 4765, pp. 55-74). Berlin, Heidelberg: Springer-Verlag.

Freund, U., Gurrieri, O., Küster, J., Lönn, H., Migge, J., Reiser, M.-O., et al. (2004a). An architecture description language for developing automotive ECU-software. In *INCOSE 2004, International Conference On Systems Engineering*, Toulouse, France.

Freund, U., Gurrieri, O., Lönn, H., Eden, J., Migge, J., Reiser, M.-O., et al. (2004b, September). *An architecture description language supporting automotive software product lines.* Presented at Workshop on Solutions for Automotive Software Architectures, satellite event of the Third Software Product Line Conference, SPLC2004, Boston.

Functional Safety and IEC 61508. (2005). Retrieved from http://www.iec.ch/zone/fsafety/fsafety_entry.htm

Fürst, S. (2006). AUTOSAR for safety-related systems: Objectives, approach, and status. In *Proceedings of 2nd IEE Conference on Automotive Electronics*, London, UK.

Gajski, D. D., Zhu, J., Dömer, R., Gerstlauer, A., & Zhao, S. (2000). *SpecC: Specification language and methodology*. Boston: Kluwer Academic Publishers.

Galeotti, J. P., & Frias, M. F. (2007). DynAlloy as a formal method for the analysis of java programs. In A. Schubert & J. Chrząszcz (Eds.), *Software engineering techniques: Design for quality* (Vol. 227/2007, pp. 249-260). Springer Boston.

Gamma, E., Helm, R., Johnson, R., & Vlissides, J. (1995). *Design patterns: Elements of reusable object-oriented software*. Boston: Addison-Wesley Longman Publishing Co., Inc.

Ganesan, S., & Prevostini, M. (2006). *Bridging the gap between SysML and design space exploration*. Paper presented at Forum on Design Languages, Darmstadt, Germany.

Gargantini, A., Riccobene, E., & Rinzivillo, S. (2003). Using Spin to Generate Tests from ASM Specifications. In *Proc. of the 10th Int. Workshop on Abstract State Machines*. LNCS 2589, p. 263-277. Springer.

Gargantini, A., Riccobene, E., & Scandurra, P. (2007). A metamodel-based simulator for ASMs. In *Proc. of the 14th Int. ASM Workshop*.

Gargantini, A., Riccobene, E., & Scandurra, P. (2008). A language and a simulation engine for abstract state machines based on metamodelling. In [Springer.]. *Journal of Universal Computer Science*, *14*(12), 1949–1983.

Gargantini, A., Riccobene, E., & Scandurra, P. (2008). A scenario-based validation language for ASMs. In *Proc. of First International Conference on Abstract State Machines, B and Z (ABZ 2008)*. LNCS 5238, pp. 71–84, Springer.

Geilen, M. C. W. (2001). Modeling and specification using SHE. *Journal of Computer Languages*, *27*(1-3), 19–38. doi:10.1016/S0096-0551(01)00014-5

Gerstlauer, A., Domer, R., Peng, J., & Gajski, D. (2001). *System design: A practical guide with SpecC*. Norwell, MA: Kluwer Academic Publishers.

Gerstlauer, A., Yu, H., & Gajski, D. D. (2003). *RTOS modeling for system level design*. In *Proc. of DATE*. IEEE.

Gery, E., Harel, D., & Palachi, E. (2002). Rhapsody: A complete life-cycle model-based development system. *Third International Conference on Integrated Formal Methods* (LNCS 2335, pp. 1-10). London: Springer-Verlag.

Ghenassia, F. (2005). *Transaction level modeling with SystemC: TLM concepts and applications for embedded systems*. Dordrecht, The Netherlands: Springer.

Gheyi, R., Massoni, T., & Borba, P. (2005). A rigorous approach for proving model refactorings. In *ASE '05: Proceedings of the 20th IEEE/ACM International Conference on Automated Software Engineering* (pp. 372–375).

Gips, C., & Wiesbrock, H.-W. (2007). Notation und Verfahren zur Automatischen Überprüfung von Temporalen Signalabhängigkeiten und -Merkmalen Für Modellbasiert Entwickelte Software. In M. Conrad, H. Giese, B. Rumpe & B. Schätz (Eds.), *Proceedings of Model Based Engineering of Embedded Systems III*, TU Braunschweig Report TUBS-SSE 2007-01. (In German).

Giusto, P., Brunel, J.-Y., Ferrari, A., Fourgeau, E., Lavagno, L., & Sangiovanni-Vincentelli, A. (2002). Automotive virtual integration platforms: Why's, what's, and how's. In *Proceedings of the International Conference of Computation Design*, Freiburg, Germany.

Givargis, T., & Vhid, F. (2002). Platune: A tuning framework for system-on-a-chip platforms. *IEEE Transaction on Computer-aided Design of Integrated Circuits and Systems*, *21*(11), 1317–1327. doi:10.1109/TCAD.2002.804107

Goering, R. (2002, November). Platform-based design: A choice, not a panacea. *EEDesign of EETimes*. Retrieved in September 2008, from http://www.eetimes.com/story/OEG20020911S0061

Gokhale, A., Balasubramanian, K., Krishna, A., Balasubramanian, J., Edwards, G., & Deng, G. (2008). Model-driven middleware: A new paradigm for developing distributed real-time and embedded systems. *Science of Computer Programming*, *73*(1), 39–58. doi:10.1016/j.scico.2008.05.005

Gokhale, M. B., Stone, J. M., Arnold, J., & Kalinowski, M. (2000). Stream-oriented FPGA computing in the streams-C high level language. *IEEE Symposium on Field-Programmable Custom Computing Machines (FCCM'00)*. Washington, D.C.: IEEE Computer Society

Gomaa, H. (2000). *Designing concurrent, distributed, and real-time applications with UML*. Boston: Addison-Wesley.

Gomaa, H. (2000). *Designing concurrent, distributed, and real-time applications with UML*. Boston: Addison-Wesley Professional.

Gonzalez, R. E. (2000). Xtensa: A configurable and extensible processor. *Micro, IEEE, 20*(2), 60–70. doi:10.1109/40.848473

Gorp, P. V., Stenten, H., Mens, T., & Demeyer, S. (2003). Towards automating source-consistent UML refactorings. In *Proceedings of UML* (pp. 144–158).

Graaf, B., Lormans, M., & Toetenel, H. (2003). Embedded software engineering: The state of the practice. *IEEE Software, 20*(6), 61–69. doi:10.1109/MS.2003.1241368

Gray, J., Bapty, T., Neema, S., & Tuck, J. (2001). Handling crosscutting constraints in domain-specific modeling. *Communications of the ACM, 44*(10), 87–93. doi:10.1145/383845.383864

Gray, J., Lin, Y., & Zhang, J. (2006). Automating change evolution in model-driven engineering. *IEEE Computer, 39*(2), 41–48.

Gray, J., Sztipanovits, J., Schmidt, D., Bapty, T., Neema, S., & Gokhale, A. (2004). Two-level aspect weaving to support evolution of model-driven synthesis. In *Aspect-Oriented Software Development*, (pp. 681-710). Addison-Wesley.

Gray, J., Tolvanen, J.-P., Kelly, S., Gokhale, A., Neema, S., & Sprinkle, J. (2007). Domain-specific modeling. In *Handbook on dynamic system modeling* (pp. 7-1–7-20). CRC Press.

Green, P. A., Jr. (1997). The art of creating reliable software-based systems using off-the-shelf software components. In *SRDS '97: Proceedings of the 16ᵗʰ Symposium on Reliable Distributed Systems (SRDS '97)*, Washington, D.C. (p. 118). IEEE Computer Society.

Green, P. N., & Edwards, M. D. (2002). The modeling of embedded systems using HASoC. In *Proceedings of the Design, Automation, and Test in Europe Conference and Exhibition* (pp. 752-759). Los Alamitos: IEEE Computer Society Press.

Green, P. N., & Essa, S. (2004). Integrating the synchronous dataflow model with UML. In *Proceedings of the Design, Automation, and Test in Europe, DATE*. IEEE Press.

Gries, M. (2004). Methods for evaluating and covering the design space during early design development. *Integration, the VLSI Journal, 38*(2), 131-183.

Grindal, M., Offutt, J., & Andler, S. F. (2005). Combination testing strategies: A survey. In *Software Testing, Verification, and Reliability, 15*(3), 167–199. John Wiley & Sons, Ltd.

Griswold, W., Shonie, M., Sullivan, K., Song, Y., Tewari, N., & Cai, Y. (2006). Modular software design with crosscutting interfaces. *IEEE Software, 23*(1), 51–60. doi:doi:10.1109/MS.2006.24

Grochtmann, M., & Grimm, K. (1993). Classification trees for partition testing. *Verification & Reliability, 3*(2), 63–82. doi:10.1002/stvr.4370030203

Gröetker, T., Liao, S., Martin, G., & Swan, S. (2002). *System Design with SystemC*. Kluwer Academic Publisher.

Großmann, J., Schieferdecker, I., & Wiesbrock, H. W. (2008). Modeling property based stream templates with TTCN-3. In *Proceedings of the IFIP 20ᵗʰ Intern. Conf. on Testing Communicating Systems* (Testcom 2008), Tokyo, Japan.

Grotker, T. (2002). *System design with SystemC*. Norwell, MA: Kluwer Academic Publishers.

Gu, Z., & Shin, K. G. (2005). Model-checking of component-based event-driven real-time embedded software. In *Proceedings of the 8ᵗʰ IEEE International Symposium on Object-Oriented Real-Time Distributed*

*Computing (ISORC '05)* (pp. 410-417). IEEE Computer Society Press.

Guo, Z., Buyukkurt, B., Najjar, W., & Vissers, K. (2005). Optimized generation of data-path from C codes for FPGAs. *ACM/IEEE Design Automation and Test Europe Conference (DATE'05),* Munich, Germany (pp. 112-117).

Gutjahr, W. J. (1999). Partition testing vs. random testing: The influence of uncertainty. [NJ: IEEE Press Piscataway.]. *IEEE Transactions on Software Engineering, 25*(5), 661–674. doi:10.1109/32.815325

Guttag, J. (1977). Abstract data types and the development of data structures. *Communications of the ACM, 20*(6), 396–404.doi:doi:10.1145/359605.359618

Habibi, A., & Tahar, S. (2006). Design and verification of systemc transaction-level models. *IEEE Transactions on VLSI Systems, 14,* 57–68. doi:10.1109/TVLSI.2005.863187

Halbwachs, N. (1993). *Synchronous programming of reactive systems* (Vol. 215). Springer.

Halbwachs, N., Caspi, P., Raymond, P., & Pilaud, D. (1991). The synchronous dataflow programming language LUSTRE. *Proceedings of the IEEE, 79*(9), 1305–1320. doi:10.1109/5.97300

Hall, A. (1990). Using Z as a specification calculus for object-oriented systems. *Third International Symposium of VDM Europe on VDM and Z - Formal Methods in Software Development* (LNCS 428, pp. 290-318). London: Springer-Verlag.

Handel-C. (1991-2007). *Handel-C language reference manual.* Agility Design Solutions Inc.

Hanisch, H.-M., & Luder, A. (1999). Modular modeling of closed-loop systems. Colloquium on Petri Net Technologies for Modeling Communication Based Systems, Germany (pp. 103-126).

Hanisch, H.-M., & Vyatkin, V. (2005). Achieving reconfigurability of automation systems by using the new international standard IEC 61499: A developer's view. In

R. Zurawski (Ed.), *The industrial information technology handbook* (pp. 661-680). USA: CRC Press.

Hansson, H., Lawson, H., Bridal, O., Eriksson, C., Larsson, S., Lönn, H., & Strömberg, M. (1997). Basement: An architecture and methodology for distributed automotive real-time systems. *IEEE Transactions on Computers, 46*(9), 1016–1027. doi:10.1109/12.620482

Harel, D. (1987). Statecharts: A visual formalism for complex systems. *Science of Computer Programming, 8*(3), 231–274. doi:10.1016/0167-6423(87)90035-9

Haroud, M., Blazevic, L., & Biere, A. (2004). HW accelerated ultra wide band mac protocol using sdl and systemc. In *IEEE Radio and Wireless Conference,* pp. 525–528.

Harris, T., & Fraser, K. (2003). *Language support for lightweight transactions.* Paper presented at the 18th Annual ACM SIGPLAN Conference on Object-oriented Programing, Systems, Languages, and Applications.

Harris, T., Cristal, A., Unsal, O. S., Ayguade, E., Gagliardi, F., & Smith, B. (2007). Transactional memory: An overview. *Micro, IEEE, 27*(3), 8–29. doi:10.1109/MM.2007.63

Hassan, M. A., Sakanushi, K., Takeuchi, Y., & Imai, M. (2005B). Enabling RTOS simulation modeling in a system level design language. *Proc. of ASP-DAC.* IEEE.

Hassan, M. A., Yoshinori, S. K., Takeuchi, Y., & Imai, M. (2005A). RTK-Spec TRON: A simulation model of an ITRON based RTOS kernel in SystemC. In *Proc of DATE.* IEEE.

Haubelt, C., Falk, J., Keinert, J., Schlichter, T., Streubuhr, M., Deyhle, A., Hadert, A., & Teich, J. (2007). A SystemC based design methodology for digital signal processing systems. EURASIP Journal on Embedded Systems, (1), 15-37

Hauck, S., & DeHon, A. (2008) *Reconfigurable computing: The theory and practice of FPGA-based computation.* Morgan Kaufmann/Elsevier.

Havelund, K., Majumdar, R., & Palsberg, J. (2008). *Model checking software: 15th International SPIN Workshop.* Los Angeles: Springer.

He, Z., Mok, A., & Peng, C. (2005). Timed RTOS modeling for embedded system design. In *Proc. of RTAS*. IEEE.

Heidenreich, F., Johannes, J., & Zschaler, S. (2007). Aspect orientation for your language of choice. *Aspect-Oriented Modeling*.

Helmerich, A., Koch, N., Mandel, L., Braun, P., Dornbusch, P., Gruler, A., et al. (2005). *Study of worldwide trends and R&D programmes in embedded systems in view of maximising the impact of a technology platform in the area*. Final Report for the European Commission, Brussels Belgium.

Henzinger, T. A., Kopke, P. W., Puri, A., & Varaiya, P. (1998). What's decidable about hybrid automata? *Journal of Computer and System Sciences, 57*, 94–124. doi:10.1006/jcss.1998.1581

Henzinger, T. A., Nicollin, X., Sifakis, J., & Yovine, S. (1992). Symbolic model checking for real-time systems. In *Proceeding of the 7th Annual IEEE Symposium on Logic in Computer Science*.

Hergenhan, A., & Rosenstiel, W. (2000). Static timing analysis of embedded software on advanced processor architectures. In *Proc. of DATE*. IEEE.

Hetzel, W. C. (1988). *The complete guide to software testing, second ed*. QED Information Services, Inc.

Hewitt, C. (1977). Viewing control structures as patterns of passing messages. Journal of Artificial Intelligence.

Hilfinger, P., & Rabaey, J. (1992). DSP specification using the silage language. In *Anatomy of a Silicon Compiler* (pp. 199-220). Kluwer Academic Publishers.

Hoare, C. A. R. (1978). Communicating sequential processes. *Communications of the ACM, 21*(8), 666–677. doi:10.1145/359576.359585

Holzmann, G. J. (1997). The model checker SPIN. *IEEE Transactions on Software Engineering, 23*(5), 279–295. doi:10.1109/32.588521

Honekamp, U., Reidel, J., Werther, K., Zurawka, T., & Beck, T. (1999). Component-node-network: Three levels of optimized code generation with ASCET-SD. *International Symposium on Computer Aided Control System Design* (pp. 243-248). Kohala Coast: IEEE Computer Society Press.

Huang, K., Han, S., Popovici, K., Brisolara, L., Guerin, X., Li, L., et al. (2007). Simulink-based MPSoC design flow: Case study of motion-JPEG and H.264. In *Proceedings of the Design Automation Conference* (pp. 39-42).

Hudson, S. E., Flannery, F., & Ananian, C. S. (1999). *CUP: Parser generator for java*, 11. Retrieved on October 7, 2008, from http://www2.cs.tum.edu/projects/cup/

IBM. (2008). *IBM rational software architect, version 7.0*. Retrieved on May 10, 2008, from www.ibm.com

IEC1131. (1993). *Programmable controllers part 3*. In Bureau Central de la Commission Electrotechnique Internationale Switzerland.

IEC61499. (2004). Industrial process measurements and control systems. *International Electro technical Commission (IEC) Committee Draft*.

IEEE. (2004). Standard for information technology-portable operating system interface (POSIX). Base definitions, IEEE Std 1003.1, 2004 ed. *The Open Group Technical Standard Base Specifications, 6*.

IEEE. *1666 -2005 standard LRM*. Retrieved from http://www.systemc.org/downloads/lrm

InterDesign Technologies. *FastVeri™ (SystemC-based high-speed simulator) product overview*. Retrieved from http://www.interdesigntech.co.jp/english/

International Software Testing Qualification Board. (2006). *Standard glossary of terms used in software testing, version 1.2*. E. van Veenendaal (Ed.). The 'Glossary Working Party'.

Iqbal, A., & Elrand, T. (2006). Modeling timing constraints of real-time systems as crosscutting concerns. *Aspect-Oriented Modeling Workshop*.

Isermann, R., Schwarz, R., & Stolzl, S. (2002). Fault-tolerant drive-by-wire systems. *Control Systems Magazine, IEEE*, 64-81.

ISO. (1994). Road vehicles–interchange of digital information–controller area network for high-speed communication, ISO 11898, International Organization for Standardization (ISO).

ISO. (1994). Road vehicles–low-speed serial data communication–part 2: Low-speed controller area network, ISO 11519-2, International Organization for Standardization (ISO).

ISO/NP PAS 26262. Road vehicles-functional safety. Retrieved from http://www.iso.org/iso/ iso_catalogue/ catalogue_tc/catalogue_detail.htm?csnumber=43464

Ito, S. A., Carro, L., & Jacobi, R. P. (2001). Making java work for microcontroller applications. *IEEE Design & Test of Computers, 18*(5), 100–110. doi:10.1109/54.953277

ITRS. (2007*). ITRS-executive summary.*Retrieved from http://www.itrs.net/Links/2007ITRS/Home2007.htm

ITRS. (2007). *ITRS-design.* International Technology Roadmap for Semiconductors. Retrieved from http:// www.itrs.net/Links/2007ITRS/Home2007.htm

Ivers, J., Sinha, N., & Walnau, K. (2002). *A basis for composition language CL.* Pittsburgh, PA: Software Engineering Institute-Carnegie Mellon University.

Jackson, D. (2006). *Software abstractions–logic, language, and analysis.* Cambridge: The MIT Press.

Jacobson, I., & Ng, P.-W. (2005). *Aspect-oriented software development with use cases.* Boston: Addison-Wesley.

Jacobson, I., Christerson, M., Jonsson, P., & Overgaard, G. (1992). *Object-oriented software engineering: A use case driven approach.* Boston: Addison-Wesley.

Jantsch, A. (2004). *Modeling embedded systems and SoC's–concurrency and time in models of computation.* San Francisco: Morgan Kaufmann.

Java Usage Model Builder Library – JUMBL. Software quality research laboratory, research model-based testing prototype. Retrieved from http://www.cs.utk.edu/ sqrl/esp/Jumbl.html

Jeannet, B., Jéron Rusu, V., & Zinovieva, E. (2005). Symbolic test selection based on approximate analysis. In

N. Halbwachs & L. Zuck (Eds.), *Proceedings of TACAS 2005* (LNCS 3440, pp. 349–364). Berlin, Heidelberg: Springer-Verlag.

Jerraya, A., & Wolf, W. (Eds.). (2005). *Multiprocessor systems on chip.* Morgan Kaufmann.

John, K., & Tiegelkamp, M. (2001). *IEC 61131-3: Programming industrial automation systems: Concepts and programming languages, requirements for programming systems, aids to decision-making tools.* Springer.

Johnston, W. M., Hanna, J. P., & Millar, R. J. (2004). Advances in dataflow programming languages. *ACM Computing Surveys, 36*(1), 1–34. doi:10.1145/1013208.1013209

Jones, A. K., Hoare, R., Kusic, D., Fazekas, J., & J, F. (2005). An FPGA-based VLIW processor with custom hardware execution. *ACM International Symposium on Field-Programmable Gate Arrays (FPGA'05),* Monterey, CA (pp. 107-117).

Kachris, C., & Kulkarni, C. (2007). Configurable transactional memory. *15th Annual IEEE Symposium on Field-Programmable Custom Computing Machines* (pp. 65-72). Napa, CA: IEEE Computer Society.

Kahn, G. (1974). The semantics of a simple language for parallel programming. *Information Processing,* 471-475.

Kahn, G., & MacQueen, D. B. (1977). Coroutines and networks of parallel processes. *IFIP congress on information processing* (pp. 993-998). Amsterdan: North-Holland. Kan, S. H. (2002). *Metrics and models in software quality engineering* (2nd ed.). Boston: Addison-Wesley Professional.

Kaiya, H., & Saeki, M. (2004). Weaving multiple viewpoint specification in goal-oriented requirements analysis. In *Proceedings of the 11th Asia Pacific Software Engineering Conference* (pp. 418-427). Washington, D.C.: IEEE Computer Society.

Kalavade, A., & Lee, E. A. (1993). Hardware/software codesign using ptolemy: A case study. In *Proceeding of First IFIP International Workshop Hardware/Software*

*Codesign* (pp. 84-87). Los Alamitos: IEEE Computer Society Press.

Kamga, J., Herrmann, J., & Joshi, P. (2007). *Deliverable: D-MINT automotive case study–daimler AG, deliverable 1.1, deployment of model-based technologies to industrial testing, itea2 project.*

Kandemir, M., Ramanujam, J., & Choudhary, A. (1999). Improving cache locality by a combination of loop and data transformations. *IEEE Transactions on Computers, 48*(2), 159–167. doi:10.1109/12.752657

Kangas, T., Kukkala, P., Orsila, H., Salminen, E., Hannikainen, M., & Hamalainen, T. (2006). UML-based multiprocessor SoC design framework. *ACM Transactions on Embedded Computing Systems, 5*(2), 281–320. doi:10.1145/1151074.1151077

Kangas, T., Kukkala, P., Orsila, H., Salminen, E., Hännikäinen, M., & Hämäläinen, T. D. (2006). UML-based multiprocessor SoC design framework. *Transactions on Embedded Computing Systems, 5*(2), 281–320. doi:10.1145/1151074.1151077

Kangas, T., Kukkala, P., Orsila, H., Salminen, E., Hännikäinen, M., & Hämäläinen, T. D. (2006). UML-based multiprocessor SoC design framework. [TECS]. *ACM Transactions on Embedded Computing Systems, 5*(2), 281–320. doi:10.1145/1151074.1151077

Kapasi, U. J., Rixner, S., Dally, W. J., Khailany, B., Jung Ho, A., & Mattson, P. (2003). Programmable stream processors. *Computer, 36*(8), 54–62. doi:10.1109/MC.2003.1220582

Karr, D., Rodrigues, C., Loyall, J., Schantz, R., Krishnamurthy, Y., Pyarali, I., & Schmidt, D. (2001). Application of the QuO quality-of-service framework to a distributed video application. *International Symposium on Distributed Objects and Applications*, Rome, Italy (pp. 299-309).

Karsai, G., Maroti, M., Lédeczi, A., Gray, J., & Sztipanovits, J. (2004). Composition and cloning in modeling and metamodeling languages. *IEEE Transactions on Control Systems Technology, 12*(2), 263–278. doi:10.1109/TCST.2004.824311

Karsai, G., Sztipanovits, J., Ledeczi, A., & Bapty, T. (2003). Model-integrated development of embedded software. [Washington, D.C.: IEEE Computer Society.]. *Proceedings of the IEEE, 91*, 145–164. doi:10.1109/JPROC.2002.805824

Kempf, T., Karur, K., Wallentowitz, S., & Meyr, H. (2006). A SW performance estimation framework for early SL design using fine-grained instrumentation. In *Proc. of DATE*. IEEE.

Keutzer, K., Malik, S., Newton, R., Rabaey, J., & Sangiovanni-Vincentelli, A. (2000). System level design: Orthogonalization of concerns and platform-based design. IEEE Transactions on Computer-Aided Design of Circuits and Systems, 19(12), 1523–1543

Keutzer, K., Newton, A. R., Rabaey, J. M., & Sangiovanni-Vincentelli, A. (2000). System-level design: Orthogonalization of concerns and platform-based design. *IEEE Transactions on Computer-Aided Design of Integrated Circuits and Systems, 19*(12), 1523–1543. doi:10.1109/43.898830

Khailany, B., Dally, W. J., Kapasi, U. J., Mattson, P., Namkoong, J., & Owens, J. D. (2001). Imagine: Media processing with streams. *Micro, IEEE, 21*(2), 35–46. doi:10.1109/40.918001

Khalgui, M., & Thramboulidis, K. (2008). An IEC61499-based development approach for the deployment of industrial control applications. *International Journal of Modelling, Identification and Control (IJMIC), 4*(2).

Khalgui, M., Rebeuf, X., & Simonot-Lion, F. (2006). A static scheduling generator for the deployment of a component based application. In Object-oriented Modeling of Embedded Real-Time Systems. Germany: Heinz-Nixdorf Institute publisher.

Khalgui, M., Rebeuf, X., & Simonot-Lion, F. (2007). A deployment method of component based applications on distributed industrial control systems. *European Journal of Automated Systems, 41*(6).

Khurshid, S., Marinov, D., & Jackson, D. (2002). An analyzable annotation language. *17th ACM SIGPLAN Conference on Object-oriented Programming, Systems,*

*Languages, and Applications (OOPSLA)* (pp. 231-245). Seattle: ACM Press.

Kiczales, G., et al. (1997). Aspect-oriented programming. In M. Aksit & S. Matsuoka (Eds.), *Proceedings of European Conference for Object-Oriented Programming* (pp. 220-240) (LNCS 1241). Berlin, Heidelberg: Springer-Verlag.

Kiczales, G., Lamping, J., Mendhekar, A., Maeda, C., Lopes, C., Loingtier, J.-M., & Irwin, J. (1997). Aspect-oriented programming. *European Conference on Object-Oriented Programming (ECOOP)*, Jyväskylä, Finland (pp. 220-242).

Kienhuis, B., Deprettere, E., Vissers, K., & van der Wolf, P. (1997). An approach for quantitative analysis of application-specific dataflow architectures. In *Proceedings of 11ᵗʰ International Conference on Application-specific Systems, Architectures, and Processors* (pp. 338-350). Los Alamitos: IEEE Computer Society Press.

Kim, H. (2006). Applying product line to the embedded systems. In M. Gavrilova, O. Gervasi, V. Kumar, C. J. Tan, D. Taniar, A. Laganà, et al. (Eds.), *Computational science and its applications-ICCSA 2006* (LNCS 3982, pp. 163-171). Glasgow: Springer Berlin.

Kishi, T., & Noda, N. (2004, March). *Aspect-oriented context modeling for embedded systems.* Paper presented at Early Aspects 2004: Aspect-Oriented Requirements Engineering and Architecture Design Workshop, Lancaster, Lancashire.

Klein, G. (2004, November). *JFlex: The fast scanner generator for java version 1.4.1.* Retrieved on October 7, 2008, from http://jflex.de Koopman, P. (2007). Reliability, safety, and security in everyday embedded systems. In A. Bondavalli, F. Brasileiro & S. Rajsbaum (Eds.), *Dependable computing* (LNCS 4746, pp. 1-2). Morella: Springer Berlin.

Klein, J., & Kienzle, J. (2007). Reusable aspect models. *Aspect-Oriented Modeling.*

Klein, J., Hélouët, L., & Jezequel, J.-M. (2006). Semantic-based weaving of scenarios. In R. Filman (Ed.), *Proceedings of the 5ᵗʰ International Conference on Aspect-Oriented Software Development* (pp. 27-38). New York: ACM Press.

Klein, M.-H., Ralya, T., Pollack, B., Obenza, R., & Harbour, M.-G. (1993). *A practioner's handbook for real-time analysis guide to rate monotonic analysis for real-time systems.* Kluwer Academic.

Klingauf, W., Gunzel, R., Bringmann, O., Parfuntseu, P., & Burton, M. (2006) Greenbus-A generic interconnect fabric for transaction level modeling. In *Proceedings of the 43ʳᵈ Annual Conference on Design Automation* (pp. 905–910). New York: ACM.

Kogel, T., Doerper, M., Kempf, T., Wieferink, A., Leupers, R., Ascheid, G., & Meyr, H. (2004). Virtual architecture mapping: A systemc based methodology for architectural exploration of system-on-chip designs. In Pimentel, A. D. and Vassiliadis, S., editors, *Computer Systems: Architectures, Modeling, and Simulation, Third and Fourth International Workshops, SAMOS*, volume 3133 of *Lecture Notes in Computer Science*, pp. 138–148.

Kopetz, H. (1997). *Real-time systems: Design principles for distributed embedded applications.* Kluwer Academic Press.

Kopetz, H., & Bauer, G. (2003). The time-triggered architecture. *Proceedings of the IEEE, 91*(1), 112–126. doi:10.1109/JPROC.2002.805821

Kosmatov, N., Legeard, B., Peureux, F., & Utting, M. (2004). Boundary coverage criteria for test generation from formal models. In *Proceedings of the 15ᵗʰ International Symposium on Software Reliability Engineering* (pp. 139–150). Washington, D.C.: IEEE Computer Society.

Kotz, D., & Essien, K. (2005). Analysis of a campus-wide wireless network. *Wireless Networks, 11*(1-2), 115–131. doi:doi:10.1007/s11276-004-4750-0

Krčál, P., & Yi, W. (2004). Decidable and undecidable problems in schedulability analysis using timed automata. In *Proceedings of 10ᵗʰ International Conference on Tools and Algorithms for the Construction and Analysis of Systems TACAS* (LNCS 2988, pp. 236-250). Berlin/New York: Springer-Verlag.

Krčál, P., Mokrushin, L., Thiagarajan, P. S., & Yi, W. (2004). Timed vs. time triggered automata. In *Proceedings of the 15th International Conference on Concurrency Theory CONCUR'04* (LNCS 3170, pp. 340-354). Berlin/ New York: Springer-Verlag.

Krishnamurthi, S., Dougherty, D. J., Fisler, K., & Yoo, D. (2008). Alchemy: Transmuting base alloy specifications into implementations. In *Proceedings of the 16th ACM SIGSOFT International Symposium on Foundations of Software Engineering (SIGSOFT '08/FSE-16)* (pp. 158-169). Atlanta: ACM Press.

Kruchten, P. (1995). Architectural bluprints-the "4+1" view model of software architecture. *IEEE Software*, *12*(6), 42–50.doi:doi:10.1109/52.469759

Kruchten, P. (1999). *The Rational Unified Process*. Addison Wesley.

Kruchten, P. (2003). *The rational unified process: An introduction* (3rd ed.). Boston: Addison-Wesley Professional.

Kuon, I., Tessier, R., & Rose, J. (2008). FPGA architecture: Survey and challenges. In *Foundations and Trends in Electronic Design Automation, 2*, 135-253.

Lamberg, K., Beine, M., Eschmann, M., Otterbach, R., Conrad, M., & Fey, I. (2004). Model-based testing of embedded automotive software using mtest. In *Proceedings of SAE World Congress*, Detroit, MI.

Larsen, K. G., Pettersson, P., & Yi, W. (1997). UPPAAL in a nutshell. *International Journal on Software Tools for Technology Transfers, 1*(1-2), 134–152. doi:10.1007/s100090050010

Larsen, K. G., Pettersson, P., & Yi, W. (1997). UPPAAL: Status & developments. In *Proceedings of the 9th International Conference on Computer Aided Verification*, Haifa, Israel (pp. 22-25).

Lastra, J.-L.-M., Godinho, L., & Tuokko, R. (2005). An IEC 61499 application generator for scan-based industrial controllers. *3rd IEEE International Conference on Industrial Informatics, INDIN'05*.

Lau, D., Pritchard, O., & Molson, P. (2006). Automated generation of hardware accelerators with direct memory access from ANSI/ISO standard C functions. *14th Annual IEEE Symposium on Field-Programmable Custom Computing Machines (FCCM '06)* (pp. 45-56).

Laurent, J., Senn, E., Julien, N., & Martin, E. (2002). Power consumption estimation of a c-algorithm: A new perspective for software design. In *Proc. of LCR*. ACM.

Lavagno, L., Martin, G., & Selic, B. (Eds.). (2003). *UML for real: Design of embedded real-time systems*. Dordrecht, The Netherlands: Kluwer Academic.

Lavagno, L., Martin, G., Vincentelli, A. S., Rabaey, J., Chen, R., & Sgroi, M. (2003). UML and Platform based Design. *UML for Real Design of Embedded Real-Time Systems*.

Lazić, L., & Velašević, D. (2004). Applying simulation and design of experiments to the embedded software testing process. In *Software Testing, Verification, & Reliability, 14*(4), 257–282. Chichester, UK: John Wiley and Sons Ltd.

Le Guennec, A., & Dion, B. (2006). Esterel technologies, bridging UML and safety-critical software development environments. In *Proceedings of the European Congress Embedded Real Time Software, ERTS*.

Ledeczi, A., Bakay, A., Maroti, M., Volgyesi, P., Nordstrom, G., & Sprinkle, J. (2001). Composing domain-specific design environments. *Computer, 34*(11), 44–51. doi:10.1109/2.963443

Ledeczi, A., Davis, J., Neema, S., & Agrawal, A. (2003). Modeling methodology for integrated simulation of embedded systems. *ACM Transactions on Modeling and Computer Simulation, 13*(1), 82–103. doi:10.1145/778553.778557

Ledeczi, A., Maroti, M., Bakay, A., Karsai, G., Garrett, J., Thomason, C., et al. (2001). The generic modeling environment. *IEEE International Workshop on Intelligent Signal Processing*. Budapest: IEEE Computer Society Press.

Ledeczi, A., Maroti, M., Bakay, A., Nordstrom, G., Garrett, J., Thomason, C., et al. (2001). *GME 2000 users manual, v2.0* (Tech. Rep.). Nashville, TN: Vanderbilt University.

Lee, E. A. (2000). What's ahead for embedded software? *IEEE Computer, 33*(9), 18–26.

Lee, E. A., & Messerschmitt, D. G. (1987). Synchronous data flow. *Proceedings of the IEEE, 75*(9), 1235–1245. doi:10.1109/PROC.1987.13876

Lee, E. A., & Parks, T. M. (1995). Dataflow process networks. *Proceedings of the IEEE, 83*(5), 773–801. doi:10.1109/5.381846

Lee, T., & Yannakakis, M. (1994). Testing finite-state machines: State identification and verification. *IEEE Transactions on Computers, 43*(3), 306–320. doi:10.1109/12.272431

Leeman, M., Atienza, D., Deconinck, G., Florio, V., Mendias, J. M., & Ykman-Couvreur, C. (2005). Methodology for refinements and optimisation of dynamic memory management for embedded systems in multimedia applications. *VLSI Signal Processing, 40*, 383–396. doi:10.1007/s11265-005-5272-4

LeGuernic, P., Gautier, T., Borgne, M., & Maire, C. (1991). Programming real-time applications with SIGNAL. *Proceedings of the IEEE, 79*(9), 1321–1336. doi:10.1109/5.97301

Lehmann, E. (2003). *Time partition testing, systematischer test des kontinuierlichen verhaltens von eingebetteten systemen.* Unpublished doctoral dissertation, Technical University Berlin (In German).

Lehmann, E., & Krämer, A. (2008). Model-based testing of automotive systems. In *Proceedings of IEEE ICST 08,* Lillehammer, Norway.

Lehmann, E., Krämer, A., Lang, T., Weiss, S., Klaproth, C., Ruhe, J., & Ziech, C. (2006). *Time partition testing manual, version 2.4.*

Leslie, R. (2004). *MAD fix point mp3 algorithm implementation (version 0.15.1b).* Computer software. Retrieved in June 2005, from http://sourceforge.net/projects/mad/

Leung, J., & Whitehead, J. (1982). On the complexity of fixed-priority scheduling of periodic real-time tasks. *Real-time Tasks. Performance Evaluation, 2.* doi:10.1016/0166-5316(82)90024-4

Lewis, R. (2001). *Modeling control systems using IEC 61499.* UK: Institution of Engineering and Technology.

Liao, S. Y. (2000). Towards a new standard for system-level design. *Eighth International Workshop on Hardware/Software Codesign,* San Diego, CA (pp. 2-6).

Lieberherr, K. (1997). Demeter and aspect-oriented programming. *STJA.*

Lieverse, P., Wolf, P. V., Vissers, K., & Deprettere, E. (2001). A methodology for architecture exploration of heterogeneous signal processing systems. *Journal of VLSI Signal Processing Systems, 29*(3), 197–207. doi:10.1023/A:1012231429554

Lime, D., & Roux, O. H. (2004). A translation based method for the timed analysis of scheduling extended time petri nets. In *Proceedings of the 25th IEEE International Real-Time Systems Symposium* (pp. 187-196). IEEE Computer Society Press.

Lin, Y. (2007). *A model transformation approach to automated model evolution.* Unpublished doctoral dissertation, University of Alabama at Birmingham, Department of Computer and Information Sciences. Retrieved from http://www.cis.uab.edu/softcom/dissertations/LinYuehua.pdf

Lin, Y., Gray, J., & Jouault, F. (2007). DSMDiff: A differentiation tool for domain-specific models. *European Journal of Information Systems, 16*(4), 349–361. doi:10.1057/palgrave.ejis.3000685

Lin, Y., Gray, J., Zhang, J., Nordstrom, S., Gokhale, A., Neema, S., & Gokhale, S. (2008). Model replication: Transformations to address model scalability. *Software, Practice & Experience, 38*(14), 1475–1497. doi:10.1002/spe.876

Lin, Y., Zhang, J., & Gray, J. (2005). A framework for testing model transformations. In *Model-driven software development,* (pp. 219-236). Springer.

Liu, C., & Layland, J. (1973). Scheduling algorithms for multiprogramming in hard real-time environment. Journal of the ACM.

Liu, J. W. S. (2000). *Real-time systems*. Upper Saddle River, NJ: Prentice-Hall.

Loyall, J., Schantz, R., Zinky, J., Pal, P., Shapiro, R., Rodrigues, C., et al. (2001). Comparing and contrasting adaptive middleware support in wide-area and embedded distributed object applications. *IEEE International Conference on Distributed Computing Systems (ICDCS)*, Phoenix, AZ (pp. 625-634).

Lu, T., Turkay, E., Gokhale, A., & Schmidt, D. C. (2003, October). *CoSMIC: An MDA tool suite for application deployment and configuration*. Paper presented at Workshop on Generative Techniques in the Context of Model Driven Architecture in Conference on Object Oriented Programming Systems Languages and Applications, Anaheim, CA.

Luckham, D. C., Kenney, J. J., Augustin, L. M., Vera, J., Bryan, D., & Mann, W. (1995). Specification and analysis of system architecture using Rapide. *IEEE Transactions on Software Engineering, 21*(4), 336–355. doi:10.1109/32.385971

Lundqvist, K., & Asplund, L. (2003). A ravenscar-compliant run-time kernel for safety-critical systems. *Real-Time Systems, 24*(1), 29–54. doi:10.1023/A:1021701221847

Magee, J., Dulay, N., & Kramer, J. (1993). Structuring parallel and distributed programs. *IEEE Software Engineering Journal*.

Magee, J., Dulay, N., Eisenbach, S., & Kramer, J. (1995). Specifying distributed software architectures. In W. Schäfer & P. Botella (Eds.), *5th European Software Engineering Conference* (LNCS 989, pp.137-153). London: Springer-Verlag.

Magic, N. *MagicDraw UML*. Retrieved on October 7, 2008, from http://www.magicdraw.com

Mamagkakis, S., Atienza, D., Poucet, C., Catthoor, F., Soudris, D. & Mendias, J. M. (2004). Custom design of multilevel dynamic memory management subsystem for embedded systems. *In Proceedings of the IEEE Workshop on Signal Processing Systems (SIPS)* (pp. 170-175). IEEE Press.

Marchal, P., Gomez, J., Atienza, D., Mamagkakis, S., & Catthoor, F. (2005). Power aware data and memory management for dynamic applications. *IEE Proceedings. Computers and Digital Techniques, 152*(2), 224–238. doi:10.1049/ip-cdt:20045077

Marik, V., Vyatkin, V., & Colombo, A. (2007). *Holonic and multiagent systems in manufacturing* (LNCS 4659). Springer Verlag.

Markov Test Logic. *Matelo, All4Tec, commercial model-based testing tool*. Retrieved from http://www. all4tec.net/

Marre, B., & Arnould, A. (2000). Test sequences generation from LUSTRE descriptions: Gatel. In *Proceedings of ASE of the 15th IEEE International Conference on Automated Software Engineering*, Grenoble, France (pp. 229–237). Washington, D.C.: IEEE Computer Society.

Marrero Pérez, A. (2007, January). *Simulink test design for hybrid embedded systems*. Diploma thesis, Technical University Berlin.

MARTE (2008). OMG, UML Profile for Modeling and Analysis of Real-time and Embedded Systems, ptc/08-06-08.

Martin, C. (1999). UML and VCC. White paper, Cadence Design Systems, Inc.

Martin, G. (2002). UML for embedded systems specification and design: Motivation and overview. *Design, Automation, and Test in Europe Conference and Exhibition* (pp. 773-775). IEEE Computer Society Press.

Martin, G., & Mueller, W. (Eds.). (2005). *UML for SoC design, v. 1*. Dordrecht, The Netherlands: Springer.

Martin, G., Lavagno, L., & Louis-Guerin, J. (2001). Embedded UML: A merger of real-time UML and codesign. In *Proceedings of the International Workshop on Hardware/Software Codesign, CODES* (pp. 23-28).

Massoni, T., Gheyi, R., & Borba, P. (2004). A UML class diagram analyzer. In J. Jürjens, E. B. Fernandez,

R. B. France, B. Rumpe, & C. Heitmeyer (Eds.), *Critical systems development using modeling languages (CS-DUML'04): Current developments and future challenges* (pp. 100-114). Springer Berlin.

Mathaikutty, D. A., Patel, H. D., Shukla, S. K., & Jantsch, A. (2006). UMoC++: A C++-based multiMoC modeling environment. In A. Vachoux (Ed.), *Applications of specification and design languages for SoCs* (pp. 115-130). Springer Netherlands.

Mathaikutty, D., Ahuja, S., Dingankar, A., & Shukla, S. (2007). Model-driven test generation for system level validation. *High Level Design Validation and Test Workshop, 2007. HLVDT 2007. IEEE*, pp. 83–90.

Mathworks (2008). *Matlab/Simulink.* Retrieved on October 7, 2008, from http://www.mathworks.com

Mattos, J. C., & Carro, L. (2007). Object and method exploration for embedded systems applications. *20th Annual Conference on Integrated Circuits and Systems Design (SBCCI'07)* (pp. 318-323). New York: ACM Press.

Mattos, J. C., Specht, E., Neves, B., & Carro, L. (2005). Object orientation problems when applied to the embedded systems domain. In A. Rettberg, Z. M. C & F. J. Rarnmig (Eds.), *From specification to embedded systems application* (Vol. IFIP 184, pp. 147-156). Manaus: Springer Boston.

Maxton, G. P., & Wormald, J. (2004). *Time for a model change: Reengineering the global automotive industry.* Cambridge University Press.

MBTech Group. (2008). Retrieved from http://www.mbtech-group.com/cz/electronics_solutions/test_engineering/provetechta_overview.html

McAllister, J., Woods, R., Walke, R., & Reilly, D. (2004). Synthesis and high level optimisation of multidimensional dataflow actor networks on FPGA. *IEEE Workshop on Signal Processing Systems,* TX (pp. 164-169).

Medvidovic, N., & Taylor, R. (2000). A classification and comparison framework for software architecture description languages. *IEEE Transactions on Software Engineering, 26*(1), 70–93. doi:10.1109/32.825767

Meenakshi, B., Bhatnagar, A., & Sudeepa, R. (2006). Tool for translating simulink models into input language of a model checker. *8th International Conference on Formal Engineering Methods (ICFEM '06)* (LNCS 4260, pp. 606-620). Macao: Springer Berlin.

Mellor, S., & Balcer, M. (2002). *Executable UML: A foundation for model driven architecture.* Boston: Addison-Wesley.

Mellor, S., Scott, K., Uhl, A., & Weise, D. (2004). *MDA Distilled, Principles of Model Driven Architecture.* Addison-Wesley Professional.

Memik, G., Mangione-Smith, W. H., & Hu, W. (2001). NetBench: A benchmarking suite for network processors. *ICCAD '01: Proceedings of the 2001 IEEE/ACM International Conference on Computer-aided Design* (pp. 39-42). San Jose, CA: IEEE Press.

Mens, T., Wermelinger, M., Ducasse, S., Demeyer, S., Hirschfeld, R., & Jazayeri, M. (2005). Challenges in Software Evolution. In *Proc. of the International Workshop on Software Evolution.* IEEE.

Mentor Graphics. *BridgePoint UML suite.* Retrieved on October 7, 2008, from http://www.projtech.com

Merlin, P., & Faber, D. J. (1976). Recoverability of communication protocols. *IEEE Transactions on Communications, 24*(9), 1036–1043. doi:10.1109/TCOM.1976.1093424

Mernik, M., Heering, J., & Sloane, A. (2005). When and how to develop domain-specific languages. *ACM Computing Surveys, 37*(4), 316–344. doi:10.1145/1118890.1118892

MEval. *IT power consultants, commercial tool for testing* Retrieved from http://www.itpower.de/meval.html

Micheli, G. D., Ernst, R., & Wolf, W. (2001). *Readings in hardware/software codesign (1st ed.).* Morgan Kaufmann.

Migge, J., & Elloy, J. P. (2000). Embedded electronic architecture. In *Proceedings of 3rd International Workshop on Open Systems in Automotive Networks,* Bad Homburg, Germany.

Mihal, A., Kulkarni, C., Moskewicz, M., Tsai, M., Shah, N., & Weber, S. (2002). Developing architectural platforms: A disciplined approach. *IEEE Design & Test of Computers, 19*(6), 6–16. doi:10.1109/MDT.2002.1047739

Mikucionis, M., Larsen, K. G., & Nielsen, B. (2003). *Online on-the-fly testing of real-time systems*. BRICS report series, RS-03-49, Denmark.

Miller, J., & Mukerji, J. (2003). *MDA guide version 1.0.1*. Object Management Group.

Milligan, M. (2005). *The ESL ecosystem-ready for deployment*. Retrieved from http://www.esl-now.com/pdfs/eco_presentation.pdf

Milner. (1989). *Communication and concurrency*. Prentice-Hall.

Mishra, P., & Dutt, N. (2008). *Processor description languages*. Morgan Kaufmann.

Mitola, J. I. (2002). *Software radio architecture*. Wiley InterScience.

Moby Games. *A game documentation and review project*. Retrieved from http://www.mobygames.com/

Model-Based Testing of Reactive Systems. (2005). M. Broy, B. Jonsson, J.-P. Katoen, M. Leucker & A. Pretschner (Eds.), LNCS 3472. Springer-Verlag.

Mohanty, S., Prasanna, V. K., Neema, S., & Davis, J. (2002). Rapid design space exploration of heterogeneous embedded systems using symbolic search and multi-granular simulation. *Joint Conference on Languages, Compilers and Tools For Embedded Systems: Software and Compilers For Embedded Systems (LCTES/SCOPES '02)* (pp. 18-27). New York: ACM Press.

Möhl, S. (2005). T*he mitrion-C programming language*. Retrieved on November 27, 2008, from http://www.mitrionics.com/

Moore, T., Vanderperren, Y., Sonck, G., van Oostende, P., Pauwels, M., & Dehaene, W. (2002). A Design Methodology for the Development of a Complex System-On-Chip using UML and Executable System Models. In *Forum on Specification and Design Languages, ECSL*.

Morgan, M. J. (1991). Integrated Modular Avionics for next generation commercial airplanes. *IEEE Aerospace and Electronic Systems Magazine, 6*(8), 9–12. doi:10.1109/62.90950

Moser, E., & Nebel, W. (1999). Case study: System model of crane and embedded control. In *Proceedings of the Design, Automation, and Test in Europe, DATE*, Munich, Germany.

Moussa, I., Grellier, T., & Nguyen, G. (2003). Exploring SW performance using SoC transaction-level modeling. In *Proc. of DATE*. IEEE.

Mpeg4. *Iso/iec jtc1/sc29/wg11 mpeg-4 standard features overview*. Retrieved from http://www.chiariglione.org/mpeg/standards/mpeg-4/mpeg-4.htm

MSC. (1999). Message Sequence Charts (MSC). ITU-T Recommendation Z.120 International Communication Union.

MTest. *dSpace GmbH, commercial MBT tool*. Retrieved from http://www.dspaceinc.com/ww/en/inc/home/products/Sw/expsoft/mtest.cfm

Mueller, W., Rosti, A., Bocchio, S., Riccobene, E., Scandurra, P., Dehaene, W., & Vanderperren, Y. (2006). UML for ESL design—basic principles, tools, and applications. In *Proceedings of the International Conference on Computer Aided Design, ICCAD* (pp. 73-80).

Munich University of Technology, Department of Computer Science. *AutoFocus, research tool for system modelling*. Retrieved from http://autofocus.in.tum.de/

Murata, T. (1989). Petri nets: Properties, analysis, and applications. *Proceedings of the IEEE, 77*(4). doi:10.1109/5.24143

Murthy, P. K., & Lee, E. A. (2002). Multidimensional synchronous dataflow. *IEEE Transactions on Signal Processing, 50*(8), 2064–2079. doi:10.1109/TSP.2002.800830

Myers, G. J. (1979). *The art of software testing*. John Wiley & Sons.

Narashimhan, P. (1999). *Transparent fault-tolerance for CORBA*. Unpublished doctoral dissertation, Santa

Barbara, CA: Electrical and Computer Engineering, University of California Santa Barbara.

Nascimento, F. A., Oliveira, M. F. S., & Wagner, F. R. (2007). ModES: Embedded systems design methodology and tools based on MDE. In *Fourth International Workshop on Model-Based Methodologies for Pervasive and Embedded Software -MOMPES* (pp.6-76). Los Alamitos: IEEE Computer Society Press.

National Instruments (2008). *Labview.* Retrieved on October 7, 2008, from http://www.ni.com/labview/

Naur, P., & Randell, B. (1969). *Software engineering. Report on a conference sponsored by the NATO science committee.* Garmisch: NATO.

Navet, N., & Simonot-Lion, F. (2008). A review of embedded automotive protocols. In N. Navet & F. Simonot-Lion (Eds.), *Automotive embedded systems handbook.* Taylor&Francis.

Neema, S., Bapty, T., Gray, G., & Gokhale, A. (2002). Generators for synthesis of QoS adaptation in distributed real-time embedded systems. *Generative Programming and Component Engineering (GPCE)*, Pittsburgh, PA (pp. 236-251).

Neema, S., Sztipanovits, J., & Karsai, G. (2003, October 13-15). Constraint-based design-space exploration and model synthesis. In R. Alur & I. Lee (Eds.), *Embedded Software: Third International Conference, EMSOFT 2003,* Philadelphia, PA (pp 290-305) (LNCS 2855). Berlin, Heidelberg: Springer-Verlag.

Neema, S., Sztipanovits, J., & Karsai, G., & Butts, K. (2003). Constraint-based design-space exploration and model synthesis. In R. Alur & I. Lee (Eds.), *Embedded software: Third International Conference (EMSOFT '03)* (LNCS 2855, pp. 290-305). Heidelberg: Springer Berlin.

Neema, S., Sztipanovits, J., Karsai, G., & Butts, K. (2003). Constraint-based design-space exploration and model synthesis. *International Conference on Embedded Software (EMSOFT)*, Philadelphia, PA (pp. 290-305).

Neukirchen, H. W. (2004). Languages, *tools, and patterns for the specification of distributed real-time tests.* Un-

published doctoral dissertation, Georg-August-Universiät zu Göttingen. Retrieved from http://webdoc.sub.gwdg.de/Diss/2004/ Neukirchen/Index.html

Nguyen, K., Sun, Z., Thiagarajan, P., & Wong, W. (2005). Model-Driven SoC Design: The UML-SystemC Bridge. *UML for SOC Design.*

Nicol, D. M., Liu, J., Liljenstam, M., & Guanhua, Y. (2003). Simulation of large scale networks using SSF. In *Proceedings of the 35th Conference on Winter Simulation: Driving Innovation*, New Orleans, LA (Vol. 1, pp. 650–657). ACM.

Nierstrasz, O., Arevalo, G., Cucasse, S., Wuyts, R., Black, A., Muller, P., et al. (2002). A component model for field devices. *First International IFIP/ACM Working Conference on Component Deployment,* Berlin, Germany (LNCS).

NoMagic. (2008). Retrieved on June 10, 2008, from www.magicdraw.com

Nuseibeh, B., Kramer, J., & Finkelstein, A. (1994). A framework for expressing the relationship between multiple views in requirements specification. *IEEE Transactions on Software Engineering, 20*(10), 760–773. doi:10.1109/32.328995

Ober, I., Graf, S., & Ober, I. (2004). Validation of UML models via a mapping to communicating extended timed automata. In H. Garavel, S. Graf, G. J. Holzmann, I. Ober & R. Mateescu (Eds.), *Model checking software* (LNCS 2989/2004, pp. 127-145). Springer Berlin / Heidelberg.

OCCN. OCCN Project: http://occn.sourceforge.net/

Ogawa, O., Bayon de Noyer, S., Chauvet, P., Shinohara, K., Watanabe, Y., Niizuma, H., et al. (2003). A practical approach for bus architecture optimization at transaction level. In I. C. Society (Ed.), *DATE '03: Proceedings of the Conference on Design, Automation, and Test in Europe* (pp. 20176). Washington, DC: IEEE Computer Society.

Olen, M. (2007). *The new wave in functional verification: Algorithmic testbench technology, white paper.* Mentor Graphics Corporation. http://www.edadesignline.com/showarticle.jhtml?Articleid=197800043 [08/08/08].

Oliveira, M. F. S., Briao, E. W., Nascimento, F. A., & Wganer, F. R. (2008). Model driven engineering for MPSoC design space exploration. *Journal of Integrated Circuits and Systems, 3*(1), 13–22.

Oliveira, M. F. S., Brisolara, L. B., Carro, L., & Wagner, F. R. (2006). Early embedded software design space exploration using UML-based estimation. In *Proceedings 17ᵗʰ IEEE International Workshop on Rapid System Prototyping: Vol. 1. Shortening the Path from Specification to Prototype* (pp. 24-30). Los Alamitos: IEEE Computer Society Press.

Oliveira, M. F., Brião, E. W., Nascimento, F. A., & Wagner, F. R. (2007). Model driven engineering for MPSOC design space exploration. *20ᵗʰ Annual Conference on Integrated Circuits and Systems Design (SBCCI '07)* (pp. 81-86). Rio de Janeiro: ACM Press.

Oliveira, M. F., Brisolara, L. B., Carro, L., & Wagner, F. R. (2006). Early embedded software design space exploration using UML-based estimation. *Seventeenth IEEE International Workshop on Rapid System Prototyping (RSP '06)* (pp. 24-32). Chania: IEEE Computer Society Press.

OMG. (1997). *Unified modeling language specification v. 1.0.* Object Management Group.

OMG. (2002). *UML profile for schedulability, performance, and time.* (OMG document no. ptc/02-03-02). Retrieved on March 15, 2004, from http://www.omg. org

OMG. (2003). *Model driven architecture.* (OMG document om/03-06-01) Retrieved on January 5, 2007, from http://www.omg.org/mda/

OMG. (2004). QoS&FT: *UML profile for modeling quality of service and fault tolerance characteristics and mechanisms.* (OMG document ptc/04-09-01). Retrieved on January 5, 2007, from http://www.omg.org

OMG. (2005). *UML SPT–UML profile for schedulability, performance, and time v1.1.* Retrieved on December 2, 2005, from http://www.omg.org

OMG. (2006). *CCM–CORBA component model.* Retrieved on December 12, 2006, from http://www.omg. org

OMG. (2006). *CORBA component model specification version 4.0.* Object Management Group.

OMG. (2006, January). *MOF: Metaobject facility (MOF) 2.0 specification.* Retrieved October 20, 2008, from http://www.omg.org/mof

OMG. (2006, August). *UML profile for SoC specification, v1.0.1.* Retrieved on May 5, 2008, from http://www.omg.org/technology/documents/formal/profile_soc.htm

OMG. (2007). *Model driven architecture guide.* Retrieved on December 15, 2007, from http://www.omg.org/mda

OMG. (2007). *Unified modeling language specification 2.1.1.* Retrieved from http://www.omg.org/spec/UML/2.1.1/

OMG. (2007). *MARTE specification beta 1.* (OMG document: ptc/07-08-04). Retrieved on June 2, 2008, from http://www.omg.org

OMG. (2007). *UML–Unified modeling language.* Retrieved on November 15, 2007, from http://www.omg.org/uml

OMG. (2007). *MOF QVT-queryviews/transformations.* Retrieved on December 4, 2007, from http://www.omg.org

OMG. (2007, September). *Systems modeling language (SysML) specification, version 1.0.* Retrieved on December 15, 2007, from http://www.omgsysml.org/

OMG. (2007). *Meta object facility (MOF) 2.0 core specification.* Retrieved on December 4, 2007, from http://www.omg.org

OMG. (2007, November). *UML specification, version 2.1.2.* (OMG document: formal/2007-11-04). Retrieved on February 25, 2008, from www.omg.org/

OMG. (2007). *UML profile for modeling and analysis of real-time and embedded systems (MARTE).* Retrieved on March 4, 2008, from http://www.omgmarte.org/

OMG. (2008, January 23). *The official OMG MARTE Web site*. Retrieved on November 3, 2008, from www.omgmarte.org

OMG. MDA guide v1.0.1. (2003, June). Retrieved from http://www.omg.org/docs/omg/03-06-01.pdf

OMG. Object Management Group. (1997). *Unified modeling language specification, v. 1.0*. Retrieved on May 2002, from http://www.omg.org

OMG. UML 2.0 testing profile, version 1.0 formal/05-07-07. (2005). Object Management Group.

Open SystemC Initiative. (2008). http://www.systemc.org.

OSCI. (2007). *SystemC (version 2.2) Computer software. Open systemc initiaitve*. Retrieved in March 2007, from http://www.systemc.org/members/download_files/check_file?agreement=systemc_2-2-0_07-03-14

OSEK Group. (2005). *OSEK/VDX operating system specification 2.2.3*. Retrieved from http://www.osek-vdx.org/

Osterweil, L. J. (2007). A future for software engineering? *International Conference on Software Engineering* (pp. 1-11). Washington: IEEE Computer Society Press.

Oyamada, M. S., Zschornack, F., & Wagner, F. R. (2008). Applying neural networks to performance estimation of embedded software. *Journal of Systems Architecture*, *54*(1-2), 224–240. doi:10.1016/j.sysarc.2007.06.005

Paige, R. F., Kolovos, D. S., & Polack, F. A. (2005). Refinement via consistency checking in MDA. *Electronic Notes in Theoretical Computer Science*, *137*(2), 151–161. doi:10.1016/j.entcs.2005.04.029

Paiva, A. C. R., Faria, J. C. P., & Vidal, R. M. (2003). Specification-based testing of user interfaces. In *Interactive systems, design, specification, and verification*.

Panjaitan, S., & Frey, G. (2007). Development process for distributed automation systems combining UML and IEC 61499. *International Journal of Manufacturing Research*, *2*(1). doi:10.1504/IJMR.2007.013423

Papyrus, U. M. L. (Ed.). home page. (2008). *Papyrus for MARTE*. Retrieved on June 2, 2008, from http://www.papyrusuml.org/

Pasricha, S., Dutt, N., & Ben-Romdhane, M. (2004). Fast exploration of bus-based on-chip communication architectures. In *Proc. of CODES/ISSS*. IEEE.

Patel, H. D., & Shukla, S. K. (2007). Model-driven validation of systemc designs. In *DAC '07: Proc. of the 44th annual conference on Design automation*, pp. 29–34, New York, NY, USA. ACM.

Paulin, P. G., Pilkington, C., & Bensoudane, E. (2002). StepNP: A system-level exploration platform for network processors. *IEEE Design & Test of Computers*, *19*(6), 17–26. doi:10.1109/MDT.2002.1047740

Pellerin, D., & Thibault, S. (2005). *Practical FPGA programming in C*. Prentice Hall PTR.

Pender, T. (2004). *UML bible*. New York: Wiley publishing.

Philipps, J., Hahn, G., Pretschner, A., & Stauner, T. (2003). Prototype-based tests for hybrid reactive systems. In *Proceedings of the 14th IEEE International Workshop on Rapid Systems Prototyping* (pp. 78–84). Washington, D.C.: IEEE Computer Society.

Pimentel, A. D., Erbas, C., & Polstra, S. (2006). A systematic approach to exploring embedded system architectures at multiple abstraction levels. *IEEE Transactions on Computers*, *55*(2), 99–112. doi:10.1109/TC.2006.16

Pimentel, A. D., Hertzberger, L. O., Lieverse, P., van der Wolf, P., & Deprettere, E. F. (2001). Exploring embedded-systems architectures with artemis. *IEEE Computer*, *34*(11). IEEE Computer Society Press.

Pons, C., & Garcia, D. (2006). An OCL-Based Technique for Specifying and Verifying Refinement-Oriented Transformations in MDE. In *MoDELS*, pp. 646–660.

Pons, C., & Kutsche, R.-D. (2003). Using UML-B and U2B for formal refinement of digital components. In *Proc. of Forum on specification and design languages, Frankfurt, 2003*.

Pons, C., & Kutsche, R.-D. (2004). Traceability Across Refinement Steps in UML Modeling. In *Proc. of WiSME@ UML 2004*.

Posadas, H., Adámez, J., Sánchez, P., Villar, E., & Blasco, P. (2006). POSIX modeling in SystemC. In *Proc. of ASP-DAC*. IEEE.

Posadas, H., Herrera, F., Sánchez, P., Villar, E., & Blasco, F. (2004). System-level performance analysis in systemc. In *Proc. of DATE*. IEEE.

Posadas, H., Quijano, D., Villar, E., & Martínez, M. (2007). TLM interrupt modelling for HW/SW cosimulation in SystemC. In *Proc. of DCIS*.

Poucet, C., Atienza, D., & Catthoor, F. (2006). Template-based semiautomatic profiling of multimedia applications. *Proceedings of the International Conference on Multimedia and Expo (ICME 2006)* (pp. 1061 - 1064). Toronto, Canada: IEEE Computer, IEEE Signal Processing, IEEE System & IEEE Communications Society.

Pressman, R. (2004). *Software engineering: A practitioner's approach* (6th ed.). McGraw-Hill Science/Engineering/Math.

Pretschner, A. (2003). Compositional generation of MC/DC integration test suites. In *Proceedings TACOS'03, Electronic Notes in Theoretical Computer Science 6* (pp. 1–11). Retrieved from http://Citeseer.Ist.Psu.Edu/633586. Html

Pretschner, A. (2003). *Zum Modellbasierten Funktionalen Test Reaktiver Systeme*. Unpublished doctoral dissertation, Technical University Munich (In German).

Pretschner, A., Prenninger, W., Wagner, S., Kühnel, C., Baumgartner, M., Sostawa, B., et al. (2005). One evaluation of model-based testing and its automation. In *Proceedings of the 27th International Conference on Software Engineering*, St. Louis, MO (pp. 392–401). New York: ACM New York.

Pretschner, A., Slotosch, O., Aiglstorfer, E., & Kriebel, S. (2004). Model based testing for real–the inhouse card case study. *International Journal on Software Tools for Technology Transfer, 5*, 140–157. doi:10.1007/s10009-003-0128-3

Prowell, S. J. (2003). JUMBL: A tool for model-based statistical testing. In *Proceedings of the 36th Annual Hawaii International Conference on System Sciences (HICSS'03)*, (Vol. 9). Washington, D.C.: IEEE Computer Society.

Putnam, A. R., Bennett, D., Dellinger, E., Mason, J., & Sundararajan, P. (2008). CHiMPS: A high-level compilation flow for hybrid CPU-FPGA architectures. *16th international ACM/SIGDA Symposium on Field Programmable Gate Arrays (FPGA'08)* (pp. 261-261). Monterey, CA: ACM New York.

Queille, J.-P., & Sifakis, J. (1982). Specification and verification of concurrent systems in CESAR (LNCS 137). Springer-Verlag.

QVT (2007). OMG, MOF Query/Views/Transformations, ptc/07-07-07.

Rajkumar, R., Gaglardi, M., & Sha, L. (1995). The real-time publisher/subscriber interprocess communication model for distributed real-time systems: Design and implementation. *Real-Time Technology and Application Symposium*. IEEE.

Ramchandani, C. (1974). *Analysis of asynchronous concurrent systems by timed petri nets* (Tech. Rep. No. 120). Cambridge, MA: Massachusetts Institute of Technology.

Rashid, A., Moreira, A., & Araújo, J. (2003). Modularization and composition of aspectual requirements. *International Conference on Aspect-Oriented Software Development (AOSD)*, Boston (pp. 11-20).

Rashid, A., Sawyer, P., Moreira, A., & Araujo, J. (2002). Early aspects: A model for aspect-oriented requirements engineering. In S. Greenspan, J. Siddiqi, E. Dubois & K. Pohl (Eds.), *IEEE Joint International Conference on Requirements Engineering* (pp. 199-202). Washington, D.C.: IEEE Computer Society.

Rau, A. (2002). *Model-based development of embedded automotive control systems*. Unpublished doctoral dissertation, University of Tübingen.

Rausch, M., & Hanisch, H.-M. (1995). Net condition/event systems with multiple condition outputs. *Symposium on Emerging Technologies and Factory Automation, 1*, 592-600.

Reactis Tester. *Reactive Systems, Inc., commercial model-based testing tool.* Retrieved from http://www.reactive-systems.com/tester.msp

Reactis Validator. *Reactive Systems, Inc., commercial validation and verification tool.* Retrieved from http://www.reactive-systems.com/reactis/doc/user/user009.html, http://www.reactive-systems.com/validator.msp

Real-Time Innovation. (2007). *Constellation framework.* Retrieved on March 25, 2007, from http://www.rti.com/

Reddy, Y., Ghosh, S., France, R., Straw, G., Bieman, J., & McEachen, N. (2006). Directives for composing aspect-oriented design class models. *Transactions on Aspect-Oriented Software Development, 1*(1), 75–105. doi:10.1007/11687061_3

Reichmann, C., Kühl, M., Graf, P., & Müller-Glaser, K. D. (2004). GeneralStore-a CASE-tool integration platform enabling model level coupling of heterogeneous designs for embedded electronic systems. In *Proceedings of the IEEE International Conference and Workshop on the Engineering of Computer-Based Systems, ECBS* (pp. 225- 232).

Reyneri, L. M., Cucinotta, F., Serra, A., & Lavagno, L. (2001). A hardware/software codesign flow and IP library based on simulink. In J. Rabaey (Ed.), *Proceedings of the 38th Design Automation Conference* (pp. 593-598). New York: ACM Press.

Riccobene, E., Scandurra, P., Rosti, A., & Bocchio, S. (2005). A SoC Design Methodology Based on a UML 2.0 Profile for SystemC. In *Proc. of Design Automation and Test in Europe (DATE 05), IEEE Computer Society.

Riccobene, E., Scandurra, P., Rosti, A., & Bocchio, S. (2005). A UML 2.0 profile for SystemC: toward high-level SoC design. In *EMSOFT '05: Proceedings of the 5th ACM international conference on Embedded Software* (pp. 138-141). ACM Press.

Riccobene, E., Scandurra, P., Rosti, A., & Bocchio, S. (2006). A Model-driven Design Environment for Embedded Systems. In *DAC '06: Proc. of the 43rd annual conference on Design automation* (915-918). ACM Press.

Riccobene, E., Scandurra, P., Rosti, A., & Bocchio, S. (2007). A Model-driven co-design flow for Embedded Systems. In (Sorin A. Huss ed.) *Advances in Design and Specification Languages for Embedded Systems.* Springer.

Riccobene, E., Scandurra, P., Rosti, A., & Bocchio, S. (2007). Designing a Unified Process for Embedded Systems. In *MOMPES '07: Proceedings of Fourth international workshop on model-based methodologies for pervasive and embedded software.* IEEE Press.

Riccobene, E., Scandurra, P., Rosti, A., Bocchio, S. (2005). A UML 2.0 Profile for SystemC. STMicroelectronics Technical Report, AST-AGR-2005-3.

Richardson, D., O'Malley, O., & Tittle, C. (1998). Approaches to specification-based testing. In *Proceedings of ACM SigSoft Software Engineering Notes, 14*(8), 86–96. New York: ACM New York.

Rioux, L., Saunier, T., Gerard, S., Radermacher, A., de Simone, R., Gautier, T., et al. (2005). MARTE: A new Profile RFP for the Modeling and Analysis of Real-time ES. In *UML for SoC Design workshop at DAC '05.*

Roch, S. (2000). Extended computation tree logic. In *Proceedings of the CESP2000 Workshop, No. 140 in Informatik Berichte*, Germany (pp. 225-234).

Roch, S. (2000). Extended computation tree logic: Implementation and application. In *Proceedings of the AWPN2000 Workshop*, Germany.

Rodriguez-Navas, G., Proenza, J., & Hansson, H. (2006). An UPPAAL model for formal verification of master/slave clock synchronization over the controller area network. In *Proc. of the 6th IEEE International Workshop on Factory Communication Systems*, Torino, Italy.

Rodriguez-Navas, G., Roca, S., & Proenza, J. (2008). Orthogonal, fault-tolerant, and high-precision clock synchronization for the controller area network. *IEEE Transactions on Industrial Informatics, 4*(2).

Roll, W. (2003). Towards model-based and CCM-based applications for real-time systems. *International Symposium on Object-Oriented Real-Time Distributed Computing (ISORC)*, Hokkaido, Japan (pp. 75-82).

Rooker, M. N., Sunder, C., Strasser, T., Zoitl, A., Hummer, O., & Ebenhofer, G. (2007). Zero downtime reconfiguration of distributed automation systems: The CEDAC approach. *Third International Conference on Industrial Applications of Holonic and Multi-Agent Systems*. Springer-Verlag.

Rumbaugh, J., Blaha, M. R., Lorensen, W., Eddy, F., & Premerlani, W. (1991). *Object-oriented modeling and design*. New Jersey: Prentice Hall.

Russell, J. T., & Jacome, M. F. (2003). Architecture-level performance evaluation of component based embedded systems. In I. Getreu, L. Fix & L. Lavagno (Eds.), *Proceedings of the 40th Design Automation Conference* (pp. 396-401). New York: ACM Press.

SAE As-2 Embedded Computing System Committee. (2004). Architecture analysis & design language (AADL) (Document Number AS5506).

SAE. (2004). AADL Standard Info Site. Retrieved on July 12, 2008, from http://www.aadl.info/

Safety Checker Blockset. *TNI-software, commercial model-based testing tool*. Retrieved from http://www.tni-software.com/en/produits/safetychecker blockset/index.php

Safety Test Builder. TNI-software, commercial model-based testing tool Retrieved from http://www.tni-software.com/en/produits/safetytestbuilder/index.php

Sander, I., & Jantsch, A. (2004). System modeling and transformational design refinement in ForSyDe. *Transactions on Computer-Aided Design of Integrated Circuits and Systems, 23*(1), 17–32. doi:10.1109/TCAD.2003.819898

Sangiovanni-Vincentelli, A. (2002, February). Defining platform-based design. *EEDesign of EETimes.* Retrieved in August 2007, from http://www.gigascale.org/pubs/141.html

Sangiovanni-Vincentelli, A. (2007). Quo vadis, SLD? Reasoning about the trends and challenges of system level design. *Proceedings of the IEEE, 95*(3), 467–506. doi:10.1109/JPROC.2006.890107

Sangiovanni-Vincentelli, A., & Martin, G. (2001). Platform-based design and software design methodology for embedded systems. *IEEE Design & Test of Computers, 18*(6), 23–33. doi:10.1109/54.970421

Sarmento, A., Cesario, W., & Jerraya, A. (2004). Automatic building of executable models from abstract soc architectures made of heterogeneous subsystems. In *Proceedings of the 15th IEEE International Workshop on Rapid System Prototyping* (pp.88-95).

Scandurra, P. (2005). Model-driven Language Definition: metamodelling methodologies and applications. PhD thesis, Catania (Italy), December 2005.

Schantz, R., & Schmidt, D. (2001). Middleware for distributed systems: Evolving the common structure for network-centric applications. In *Encyclopedia of Software Engineering*. John Wiley and Sons.

Schantz, R., Loyall, J., Atighetchi, M., & Pal, P. (2002). Packaging quality of service control behaviors for reuse. *International Symposium on Object-oriented Real-time Distributed Computing (ISORC)*, Washington, D.C. (pp. 375-385).

Schattkowsky, T., Muller, W., & Rettberg, A. (2005). A generic model execution platform for the design of hardware and software. In G. Martin & W. Müller (Eds.), *UML for SoC design* (pp. 33-68). New York: Kluwer Academic Publishers.

Schätz, B., Kühnel, C., & Gonschorek, M. (2008). The FlexRay protocol. In N. Navet & F. Simonot-Lion (Eds.), *Automotive embedded systems handbook*. Taylor&Francis.

Schauerhuber, A., et al. (2006, March). *Towards a common reference architecture for aspect-oriented modeling.* Paper presented at 8th International Workshop on Aspect-Oriented Modeling, Bonn, North Rhine-Westphalia.

Schäuffele, J., & Zurawka, T. (2006). *Automotive software engineering*. Vieweg.

Scheidler, C., Heiner, G., Sasse, R., Fuchs, E., Kopetz, H., & Temple, C. (1997). Time-triggered architecture (TTA). In *Conference Multimedia, Embedded Systems, and Electronic Commerce Conference-EMMSEC'97*, Florence, Italy.

Schieferdecker, I., & Großmann, J. (2007). Testing embedded control systems with TTCN-3. In *Proceedings Software Technologies for Embedded and Ubiquitous Systems SEUS 2007*, Santorini Island, Greece (LNCS 4761, pp. 125-135). Springer-Verlag Berlin/Heidelberg.

Schieferdecker, I., Bringmann, E., & Grossmann, J. (2006). Continuous TTCN-3: Testing of embedded control systems. In *Proceedings of the 2006 International Workshop on Software Engineering for Automotive Systems, International Conference on Software Engineering*, Shanghai, China. ACM New York Press.

Schirner, G., & Doemer, R. (2006). Quantitative analysis of transaction level models for the amba bus. In *Proceedings of the Design, Automation, and Test Conference in Europe* (pp. 230-235).

Schirner, G., & Domer, R. (2007). Result oriented modeling, a novel technique for fast and accurate TLM. *Transactions on Computer-Aided Design of Integrated Circuits, 26*(9). IEEE.

Schmidt, D. C. (2006). Model-driven engineering. *IEEE Computer, 39*(2), 25–31.

Schneider, F. (1987). *Understanding protocols for Byzantine clock synchronization* (Tech. Rep. 87-859). Dept of Computer Science, Cornell University.

Schnerr, J., Bringmann, O., Viehl, A., & Rosenstiel, W. (2008). High-performance timing simulation of embedded software. In *Proc. of DAC*.

Schubotz, H. (2008, April). *Experience with ISO WD 26262 in automotive safety projects*. Paper presented at the SAE World Congress & Exhibition, Detroit, MI.

Sciuto, D., Salice, F., Pomante, L., & Fornaciari, W. (2002, May). *Metrics for design space exploration of geterogeneous multiprocessor embedded systems*. Paper presented at 10th International Symposium on Hardware/Software Codesign, Estes Park, USA.

Selic, B. (2003). A Generic Framework for Modeling Resources with UML. In *Proceedings of the 16th Symposium on Integrated Circuits and Systems Design (SBCCI'03)*. 33:64–69, IEEE Computer Society.

Selic, B. (2003). Models, software models, and UML. In *UML for Real: Design of Embedded Real-Time Systems* (pp. 1-16). Norwell: Kluwer Academic Publishers.

Selic, B. (2006). UML 2: A model-driven development tool. Model-driven software development. *IBM Systems Journal, 45*(3), 607–620.

SGI. (2006). *Standard template library*. Retrieved from http://www.sgi.com/tech/stl

Sgroi, M., Lavagno, L., & Sangiovanni-Vincentelli, A. (2000). Formal models for embedded system design. *IEEE Design & Test of Computers, 17*(2), 14–27. doi:10.1109/54.844330

Sharma, P., Loyall, J., Heineman, G., Schantz, R., Shapiro, R., & Duzan, G. (2004). Component-based dynamic QoS adaptations in distributed real-time and embedded systems. *International Symposium on Distributed Objects and Applications (DOA)*, Agia Napa, Cyprus (pp. 1208-1224).

Shin, D., Gerstlauer, A., Peng, P., Doemer, R., & Gajski, D. (2006). Automatic generation of transaction-level models for rapid design space exploration. In *Proceedings of the International Conference on Hardware/Software Codesign and System Synthesis* (pp. 64-60).

Shreedhar, M., & Varghese, G. (1995). Efficient fair queuing using deficit round robin. *SIGCOMM*. Cambridge.

Silva, B. I., Richeson, K., Krogh, B., & Chutinan, A. (2000). Modeling and verifying hybrid dynamic systems using checkmate. In *Proceedings of the 4th International Conference on Automation of Mixed Processes* (ADPM 2000) (pp. 237–242).

Sims, S., & Duvarney, D. C. (2007). Experience report: The reactis validation tool. In *Proceedings of the ICFP '07*

*Conference, 42*(9), 137–140. New York: ACM New York. Simulink® Design Verifier™, & The MathWorks™, Inc. *Commercial model-based testing tool.* Retrieved from http://www.mathworks.com/products/sldesignverifier Simulink® Verification and Validation™, & The Math-Works™, Inc. *Commercial model-based verification and validation tool.* Retrieved from http://www.mathworks.com/products/simverification/

Singhoff, F., Legrand, J., Nana, L., & Marcé, L. (2004). Cheddar: A flexible real time scheduling framework. *ACM SIGAda Ada Letters, 24*(4), 1-8. New York: ACM Press.

SkyEye. (2005). *SkyEye user manual.* Retreived from www.skyeye.org

Smaragdakis, Y., & Batory, D. (2001). Mixin-based programming in C++. (LNCS 163).

Snyder, C. (2003). *Paper prototyping: The fast and easy way to design and refine user interfaces* (1st ed.). San Francisco: Morgan Kaufmann.

Sodagar, I. (1999, March). Scalable wavelet coding for synthetic and natural hybrid images. *IEEE Transactions on Circuits and Systems for Video Technology, 9*(2), 244–254.doi:doi:10.1109/76.752092

Sommerville, I. (2006). *Software engineering* (8th ed.). Boston: Addison Wesley.

Sousa, G., Soares, S., Borba, P., & Castro, J. (2004, March). *Separation of crosscutting concerns from requirements to design: Adapting a use case driven approach.* Paper presented at Early Aspects 2004: Aspect-Oriented Requirements Engineering and Architecture Design Workshop, Lancaster, Lancashire.

SpecC. SpecC technology open consortium. Retrieved on December 2, 2008, from http://www.SpecC.org/

Spillner, A., & Linz, T. (2005). *Basiswissen Softwaretest, Aus- und Weiterbildung zum Certified Tester Foundation Level nach ASQF- und ISTQB-Standard.* dpunkt. Verlag GmbH Heidelberg (In German).

Spinczyk, O., Gal, A., & Schröder-Preikschat, W. (2002). AspectC++: An aspect-oriented extension to the C++ programming language. In J. Potter, J. Noble, & B. Meyer (Eds.), *ACM International Conference Proceeding Series: Vol. 21. Proceedings of the Fortieth International Conference on Tools Pacific: Objects for Internet, Mobile, and Embedded Applications* (pp. 53-60). Darlinghurst, NSW: Australian Computer Society.

Stankovic, J. A., et al. (2003). VEST: An aspect-based composition tool for real-time system. In R. Bettati, D. Locke, G. Bollella & D. Schmidt (Eds.), *9th IEEE Real-Time and Embedded Technology and Applications Symposium* (pp. 70-77). Washington, D.C.: IEEE Computer Society.

Stankovic, J., Nagaraddi, P., Yu, Z., He, Z., & Ellis, B. (2004) Exploiting prescriptive aspects: A design time capability. *International Conference on Embedded Software (EMSOFT)*, Pisa, Italy (pp. 165-174).

Stankovic, J., Spuri, M., & Ramamritham, K. (2005). *Deadline scheduling for real-time systems.* Kluwer Academic Booktitles.

StarbridgeSystems. *Starbridge Systems, Inc.* Retrieved on November 28, 2008, from http://www.starbridgesystems.com

Stefanov, T., Zissulescu, C., Turjan, A., Kienhuis, B., & Deprettere, E. (2004). System design using kahn process networks: The compaan/laura approach. *Design, Automation and Test in Europe conference (DATE'04)* Paris, France (pp. 10340-10346).

Stein, D., Hanenberg, S., & Unland, R. (2002). A UML-based aspect-oriented design notation for aspect. In H. Ossher & G. Kiczales (Eds.), *Aspect-oriented software development: Proceedings of the 1st International Conference on Aspect-oriented Software Development* (pp. 106-112). New York: ACM Press.

Stein, D., Hanenberg, S., & Unland, R. (2006). Expressing different conceptual models of join point selections in aspect-oriented design. In R. Filman (Ed.), *Proceedings of 5th International Conference on Aspect-Oriented Software Development* (pp. 15-26). New York: ACM Press.

Steinke, S., Wehmeyer, L., Lee, B., & Marwedel, P. (2002). Assigning program and data objects to scratchpad for energy reduction. In *DATE '02: Proceedings of the Conference on Design, Automation, and Test in Europe*, Washington, D.C. (p. 409). IEEE Computer Society.

Stewart, D., Volpe, R., & Khosla, P. (1997). Design of dynamically reconfigurable real-time software using port-based objects. *IEEE Transactions on Software Engineering*.

Sunye, G., Pollet, D., Traon, Y. L., & Jezequel, J.-M. (2001). Refactoring UML models. In *UML 200-the unified modeling language: Modeling Languages, Concepts, and Tools. 4th International Conference* (LNCS 2185, pp. 134–148).

Swan, S., et al. (2002). *Functional specification for systemc 2.0*. Retrieved from http://www.systemc.org/

SynDEx. (2008). Retrieved on July 1, 2008, from http://www.rocq-inria.fr/syndex/

Synopsys. *Synopsys power compiler*. Retrieved on October 7, 2008, from http://www.synopsys.com/products/logic/design_compiler.html

SysML (2007). OMG, SysML, Version 1.0, formal/2007-09-01. http://www.omgsysml.org/.

SystemC (2005). *Open systemC™ language reference manual, IEEE Std. 1666™*. New York: Institute of Electrical and Electronics Engineers Inc.

SystemC (2006). SystemC Language Reference Manual. IEEE Std 1666-2005, 31 March 2006.

Sztipanovits, J., & Karsai, G. (1997). Model-integrated computing. *IEEE Computer, 30*(4), 10–12.

Takada, H., & Sakamura, K. (1995). mu-ITRON for small-scale embedded systems. *IEEE Micro, 15*(6). doi:10.1109/40.476258

Tanenbaum, A. (2001). *Modern operating systems, 2nd ed.* Prentice Hall.

Tanenbaum, A. S., Herder, J. N., & Bos, H. (2006). Can we make operating systems reliable and secure? *IEEE Computer, 39*(5), 44–51.

Tannenbaum, A. S. (2005). *Modern operating systems* (p. 992). Upper Saddle River, NJ: Prentice-Hall, Inc.

Tarr, P. (2003). Toward a more piece-ful world. *Generative Programming and Component Engineering (GPCE)*, Erfurt, Germany (pp. 265-266).

Tarr, P., Ossher, H., Harrison, W., & Sutton, S. (1999). N degrees of separation: Multidimensional separation of concerns. *International Conference on Software Engineering (ICSE)*, Los Angeles, CA (pp. 107-119).

Telelogic (2004). *Telelogic tau architecture/development*. Retrieved on October 24, 2004, from http://www.telelogic.com/

Telelogic (2008). *Telelogic rhapsody*. Retrieved on June 24, 2008, from http://www.telelogic.com/

Telelogic, A. G. *Rhapsody*. Retrieved on October 7, 2008, from http://modeling.telelogic.com/products/rhapsody/index.cfm

Temmerman, M. (2008). *An ADT Profile*. Retrieved from http://www.lore.ua.ac.be/Research/Artefacts/

Temmerman, M. (2008). *Optimizing abstract data type models for dynamic and data-dominant embedded applications*. Unpublished doctoral dissertation, Antwerp.

Temmerman, M., Daylight, E., Catthoor, F., Demeyer, S., & Dhaene, T. (2007). Optimizing data structures at the modeling level in embedded multimedia. [JSA]. *Journal of Systems Architecture, 53*(8), 539–549. doi:doi:10.1016/j.sysarc.2006.11.008

Test Vector Tester for Simulink–T-VEC, & T-VEC Technologies, Inc. *Commercial model-based testing tool*. Retrieved from http://www.t-vec.com/solutions/simulink.php

Test-Bench with Reactive Test Bench. Synapticad, & Waveformer Lite 9.9. *Commercial tool for testing*. Retrieved from http://www.actel.com/documents/reactive_tb_tutorial.pdfSystemTest™, & The MathWorks™, Inc. *Commercial tool for testing*. Retrieved from http://www.mathworks.com/products/systemtest/

The Artist Roadmap for Research and Development. Embedded Systems Design. (2005). (LNCS 3436). B. Bouyssounouse & J. Sifakis (Eds.)

The ASMETA toolset. (2007). http://asmeta.sf.net/

Thies, W., Karczmarek, M., & Amarasinghe, S. (2002). StreamIt: A language for streaming applications. *International Conference on Compiler Construction* (LNCS, pp. 179-196). Grenoble, France: Springer.

Thramboulidis, K. (2005). Model integrated mechatronics-towards a new paradigm in the development of manufacturing systems. *IEEE Transactions on Industrial Informatics, 1.*

Thramboulidis, K., & Dukas, G. (2006). IEC61499 execution model semantics. *International Conference on Industrial Electronics, Technology, and Automation, CISSE-IETA'06.*

Thramboulidis, K., & Zoupas, A. (2005). Real-time java in control and automation. *10th IEEE International Conference on Emerging Technologies and Factory Automation. ETFA'05.*

Thramboulidis, K., Doukas, G., & Frantzis, A. (2004). Towards an implementation model for FB-based reconfigurable distributed control applications. *In Proceedings of 7th IEEE International Symposium on Object-Oriented Real-Time Distributed Computing* (pp. 193-200).

Thramboulidis, K., Perdikis, D., & Kantas, S. (2007). Model driven development of distributed control applications. [Springer-Verlag.]. *International Journal of Advanced Manufacturing Technology, 33*(3-4), 233–242. doi:10.1007/s00170-006-0455-0

Thrun, S. (2001). A programming language extension for probabilistic robot programming. *Workshop notes of the IJCAI Workshop on Uncertainty in Robotics (RUR).* Seattle, WA: IJCAI, Inc.

Time Partitioning Testing–TPT, & PikeTec. Commercial model-based testing tool. Retrieved from http://www.piketec.com/products/tpt.php

Tindell, K., & Burns, A. (1994). Guaranteeing message latencies on controller area network (CAN). *1st International CAN Conference, ICC'94*, Mainz, Germany.

Tolvanen, J., & Rossi, M. (2003). MetaEdit+: Defining and using domain-specific modeling languages and code generators. *Conference on Object Oriented Programming Systems Languages and Applications,* Anaheim, CA (pp. 92-93). ACM.

Tomiyama, H., Halambi, A., Grun, P., Dutt, N., & Nicolau, A. (1999). Architecture description languages for system-on-chip design. *6th Asia Pacific Conference on cHip Design Languages, APCHDL'99*, Fukuoka, Japan.

Toolkit. (2008). *Rockwell automation.* Retrieved from http://www.holobloc.com

Törner, F., Chen, D. J., Johansson, R., Lönn, H., & Törngren, M. (2008). Supporting an automotive safety case through systematic model based development-the EAST-ADL2 approach. *SAE World Congress*, Detroit, MI.

Tretmans, J. (2008). Model based testing with labelled transition systems. In *Formal methods and testing* (LNCS 4949, pp. 1–38). Springer Berlin/Heidelberg.

Tri-Pacific Software. (2008). *RapidRMA.* Retrieved on June 20, 2008, from http http://www.tripac.com/

TTTech Computertechnik GmbH. (2003). Time-triggered protocol TTP/C, high-level specification document, protocol version 1.1. Retrieved from http://www.tttech.com

Turley, J. (2002). *The two percent solution.* Retrieved on October 7, 2008, from http://www.embedded.com/story/OEG20021217S0039

UML. (2005). Unified Modeling Language, Version 2.0, 2005. http://www.uml.org/

UPC. (2005). *UPC language specifications. 1.2, a publication of the UPC consortium.* Retrieved on December 9, 2008, from http://upc.lbl.gov/

USoC (2005). Fujitsu Limited, IBM, NEC. A UML Extension for SoC. Draft RFC to OMG, 2005-01-01.

Utting, M. (2005). Model-based testing. In *Proceedings of the Workshop on Verified Software: Theory, Tools, and Experiments, VSTTE 2005.*

Utting, M., & Legeard, B. (2006). *Practical model-based testing: A tools approach.* Elsevier Science & Technology Books.

Utting, M., Pretschner, A., & Legeard B. (2006). *A taxonomy of model-based testing.*

van den Berg, K., Conejero, J. M., & Chitchyan, R. (2005). *AOSD ontology 1.0-public ontology of aspect-orientation* (Tech. Rep. AOSD-Europe-UT-01). Retrieved in June 2008 from http://eprints.eemcs.utwente.nl/10220/

van Ommering, R., van der Linden, F., Kramer, J., & Magee, J. (2000). The koala component model for consumer electronics software. *Computer, 33*(3), 78–85. doi:doi:10.1109/2.825699

Vanderperren, Y., & Dehaene, W. (2006). From UML/SysML to Matlab/Simulink: Current state and future perspectives. In *Proceedings of the Design, Automation, and Test in Europe Conference, DATE* (pp.93-93).

Vandevoorde, D., & Josuttis, N. M. (2003). *C++ templates, the complete guide.* London: Addison Wesley.

Vardi, M. Y. (2007). Formal techniques for SystemC verification; position paper. In *DAC '07: Proc. of the 43rd annual conference on Design automation*, (pp. 188–192). IEEE.

Vassiliadis, S., Wong, S., Gaydadjiev, G., Bertels, K., Kuzmanov, G., & Panainte, E. M. (2004). The MOLEN polymorphic processor. *Computers . IEEE Transactions, 53*(11), 1363–1375. doi:10.1109/TC.2004.104

Vector Informatik Gmb, H. Retrieved from http://www.vector-worldwide.com/

Venture Development Corporation. (2006). *VIII: Embedded systems market statistics-the 2005 embedded software strategic market intelligence program.* Natick: Venture Development Corporation.

Verilog. (2001). *IEEE standard verilog hardware description language, IEEE Std 1364-2001.* New York: Institute of Electrical and Electronics Engineers Inc.

Veríssimo, P. (1997). On the role of time in distributed systems. In *Proceedings of the 6th Workshop on Future Trends of Distributed Computing Systems.*

VHDL. (1988). *IEEE standard VHDL language reference manual, IEEE Std 1076-1987.* New York: Institute of Electrical and Electronics Engineers Inc.

Viaud, E., Pecheux, F., & Greiner, A. (2006). *An efficient TLM/T modeling and simulation environment based on conservative parallel discrete event principles.* In *Proc. of DATE.* IEEE.

Voget, S., Golm, M., Sanchez, B., & Stappert, F. (2008). Application of the AUTOSAR standard. In N. Navet & F. Simonot-Lion (Eds.), *Automotive embedded systems handbook.* Taylor & Francis.

Voros, N. S., Snook, C. F., Hallerstede, S., & Masselos, K. (2004). Embedded system design using formal model refinement: An approach based on the combined use of UML and the B language. *Design Automation for Embedded Systems, 9*(2), 67–99. doi:10.1007/s10617-005-1184-6

Vyatkin, V. (2006). The potential impact of the IEC 61499 standard on the progress of distributed intelligent automation. *International Journal of Manufacturing Technology and Management, 8*(1). doi:10.1504/IJMTM.2006.008801

Vyatkin, V. (2007). IEC 61499 function blocks for embedded and distributed control systems design. *ISA-o3neida series: Instrumentation, Systems, and Automation Society* (p. 300). USA.

Vyatkin, V., & Hanisch, H.-M. (2003). Verification of distributed control systems in intelligent manufacturing. *International Journal of Manufacturing, 14*(1), 123–136. doi:10.1023/A:1022295414523

Wallmüller, E. (2001). *Software-qualitätsmanagement in der praxis.* Hanser Verlag (in German).

Wang, S., & Shin, K. (2000). An architecture for embedded software integration using reusable components. *International Conference on Compilers, Architecture, and Synthesis for Embedded Systems,* San Jose, CA.

Wappler, S., & Wegener, J. (2006). Evolutionary unit testing of object-oriented software using strongly-typed genetic programming. In *Proceedings of the 8th Annual Conference on Genetic and Evolutionary Computation,* Seattle, WA (pp. 1925-1932). ACM.

Warmer, J., & Kleppe, A. (1998). *The object constraint language: Precise modeling with UML*. Addison-Wesley.

Warmer, J., & Kleppe, A. (1998). *The object-constraint language: Precise modeling with UML* (p. 112). Boston: Addison-Wesley.

Waszniowski, L. (2006). *Formal verification of multitasking applications based on a timed automata model*. Unpublished doctoral dissertation, Czech Technical University in Prague, Czech Republic.

Waszniowski, L., & Hanzálek, Z. (2005). Timed automata model of preemptive multitasking applications. In *Preprints of the 16ᵗʰ World Congress of the International Federation of Automatic Control* [CD-ROM]. Praha: IFAC.

Waszniowski, L., & Hanzálek, Z. (2008). Formal verification of multitasking applications based on timed automata model. *Real-Time Systems, 38*(1), 39–65. doi:10.1007/s11241-007-9036-z

Weber, M., & Weisbrod, J. (2003). Requirements engineering in automotive development–experiences and challenges. *IEEE Software, 20*(1), 16–24. doi:10.1109/MS.2003.1159025

Wehrmeister, M. A., Becker, L. B., Wagner, F. R., & Pereira, C. E. (2005). An object-oriented platform-based design process for embedded real-time systems. In *8ᵗʰ IEEE International Symposium on Object-Oriented Real-Time Distributed Computing–ISORC* (pp. 125-128). Los Alamitos: IEEE Computer Society.

Wehrmeister, M. A., Freitas, E. P., Orfanus, D., Pereira, C. E., & Rammig, F. J. (2008). A case study to evaluate pros/cons of aspect- and object-oriented paradigms to model distributed embedded real-time systems. In *5ᵗʰ International Workshop on Model-based Methodologies for Pervasive and Embedded Software–MOMPES* (pp. 44-54). Los Alamitos: EEE Computer Society Press.

Wehrmeister, M. A., Freitas, E. P., Pereira, C. E., & Rammig, F. J. (2008). GenERTiCA: A tool for code generation and aspects weaving. In *11ᵗʰ IEEE Symposium on Object Oriented Real-Time Distributed Computing–ISORC* (pp. 234-238). Los Alamitos: IEEE Computer Society.

Wehrmeister, M. A., Freitas, E. P., Pereira, C. E., & Wagner, F. R. (2007). An aspect-oriented approach for dealing with nonfunctional requirements in a model-driven development of distributed embedded real-time systems. In *10ᵗʰ IEEE International Symposium on Object and Component-Oriented Real-Time Distributed Computing* (pp. 428-432). Washington: IEEE Computer Society.

Wehrmeister, M., Freitas, E., Pereira, C., & Rammig, F. (2008). GenERTiCA: A tool for code generation and aspects weaving. *International Symposium on Object Oriented Real-Time Distributed Computing (ISORC)*, Orlando, FL (pp. 234 – 238).

Weichsel, P. M. (1962). The Kronecker product of graphs. *Proceedings of the American Mathematical Society, 13*(1), 47–52. doi:10.2307/2033769

Weyuker, E. (1988). The evaluation of program-based software test data adequacy criteria. *Communications of the ACM, 31*(6), 668–675. doi:10.1145/62959.62963

Wiesbrock, H.-W., Conrad, M., & Fey, I. (2002). Pohlheim, ein neues automatisiertes auswerteverfahren für regressions und back-to-back-tests eingebetteter regelsysteme. In *Softwaretechnik-Trends, 22*(3), 22–27 (in German).

Wirth, N. (1998). Hardware compilation: Translating programs into circuits. *Computer, 31*(6), 25–31. doi:10.1109/2.683004

Wolinski, C., Gokhale, M., & McCave, K. (2002). A polymorphous computing fabric. *Micro, IEEE, 22*(5), 56–68. doi:10.1109/MM.2002.1044300

Wood, D. (1993). *Data structures, algorithms, and performance*. USA: Addison-Wesley Longman Publishing Co.

X10. (2006). *Report on the experimental language X10, version 1.01*. Retrieved on December 9, 2008, from http://x10.sourceforge.net/

Xilinx, I. *MicroBlaze*. Retrieved on November 27, 2008, from http://www.xilinx.com/

XPP-III. (2006). *XPP-III processors: White paper, version 2.0.1*. XPP Technologies AG.

Yankova, Y., Kuzmanov, G., Bertels, K., Gaydadjiev, G., Lu, Y., & Vassiliadis, S. (2007). DWARV: Delft workbench automated reconfigurable VHDL generator. *Conference on Field Programmable Logic and Applications (FPL'07)*, Amsterdam, The Netherlands (pp. 697-701).

Yi, Y., Kim, D., & Ha, S. (2003). Fast and time-accurate cosimulation with OS scheduler modeling. *Design Automation of Embedded Systems, 8*(2-3). Springer.

Yoo, S., Nicolescu, G., Gauthier, L. G., & Jerraya, A. A. (2002). Automatic generation of fast timed simulation models for operating systems in SoC design. In *Proc. of DATE*. IEEE.

Yovine, S. (1997). KRONOS: A verification tool for real-time systems. [STTT]. *International Journal on Software Tools for Technology Transfer, 1*(1-2), 123–133.

Yu Lo, L. L. C., & Abdi, S. (2007) Automatic SystemC TLM generation for custom communication platforms. In *Proceedings of the 25th IEEE International Conference on Computer Design* (pp. 41-46).

Yu Lo, L. L. C., & Abdi, S. (2007). Automatic TLM generation for C-based MPSoC design. In *Proceedings of the 2007 IEEE International High-Level Design, Validation, and Test Workshop* (pp.29-36).

Yu, Y., Leite, J. C. S. P., & Mylopoulos, J. (2004). From goals to aspects: Discovering aspects from requirements goal models. In N. Aoyama, M. Saeki & N. Maiden (Ed.), *12th IEEE International Requirements Engineering Conference* (pp. 38-47). Los Alamitos, CA: IEEE Computer Society.

Zander, J., Dai, Z. R., Schieferdecker, I., & Din, G. (2005). From U2TP models to executable tests with TTCN-3 -an approach to model driven testing. In *Proceedings of the IFIP 17th Intern. Conf. on Testing Communicating Systems (TestCom 2005)*, Montreal, Canada. Springer-Verlag.

Zander-Nowicka, J. (2007). Reactive testing and test control of hybrid embedded software. In J. Garbajosa, J. Boegh, P. Rodriguez-Dapena, A. Rennoch (Eds.), *Proceedings of the 5th Workshop on System Testing and Validation (STV 2007)* in conjunction with *ICSSEA 2007*, Paris, France (pp. 45–62). Fraunhofer IRB Verlag.

Zander-Nowicka, J. (2008). *Model-based testing of embedded systems in the automotive domain*. Doctoral dissertation. Fraunhofer IRB Verlag.

Zander-Nowicka, J., Marrero Pérez, A., & Schieferdecker, I. (2007). From functional requirements through test evaluation design to automatic test data retrieval–a concept for testing of software dedicated for hybrid embedded systems. In H. R. Arabnia & H. Reza (Eds.), *Proceedings of the IEEE 2007 World Congress in Computer Science, Computer Engineering, & Applied Computing; SERP 2007*, Las Vegas, NV (Vol. II, pp. 347–353). CSREA Press.

Zander-Nowicka, J., Marrero Pérez, A., Schieferdecker, I., & Dai, Z. R. (2007). Test design patterns for embedded systems. In I. Schieferdecker & S. Goericke (Eds.), *Business Process Engineering. Conquest-Tagungsband 2007–Proceedings of the 10th International Conference on Quality Engineering in Software Technology*, Potsdam, Germany. dpunkt.Verlag GmbH.

Zander-Nowicka, J., Mosterman, J. P., & Schieferdecker, I. (2008). Quality of test specification by application of patterns. In *Proceedings of the 2nd International Workshop on Software Patterns and Quality (SPAQu 2008)* in conjunction with *15th Conference on Pattern Languages of Programs (PLOP 2008)* colocated with *OOPSLA 2008*, Nashville, TN.

Zander-Nowicka, J., Schieferdecker, I., & Marrero Pérez, A. (2006). Automotive validation functions for online test evaluation of hybrid real-time systems. In *Proceedings of the IEEE 41st Anniversary of The Systems Readiness Technology Conference (Autotestcon 2006)*, Anaheim, CA. IEEE.

Zander-Nowicka, J., Xiong, X., & Schieferdecker, I. (2008). Systematic test data generation for embedded software. In H. R. Arabnia & H. Reza (Eds.), *Proceedings of the IEEE 2008 World Congress in Computer Science, Computer Engineering, & Applied Computing. The 2008 International Conference on Software Engineering Re-*

*search and Practice (SERP 2008)*, Las Vegas, NV (Vol. I, pp. 164–170). CSREA Press.

Zhang, L., & Liu, R. (2005). Aspect-oriented real-time system modeling method based on UML. In R. Bettati, D. Locke, G. Bollella & D. Schmidt (Eds.), *11ᵗʰ IEEE International Conference on Embedded and Real-Time Computing Systems and Applications* (pp. 373-376). Washington, D.C.: IEEE Computer Society.

Zhang, T., Jouault, F., Bézivin, J., & Zhao, J. (2008). A MDE Based Approach for Bridging Formal Models. In Proc. 2nd IFIP/IEEE *International Symposium on Theoretical Aspects of Software Engineering*. IEEE Computer Society.

Zhe, M., Marchal, P., Scarpazza, D., Yang, P., Wong, C., Gomez, J. I., et al. (2007). *Systematic methodology for real-time cost effective mapping of dynamic concurrent task-based systems on heterogeneous platforms*. Springer.

Zhou, G., Leung, M., & Lee, E. A. (2007). *A code generation framework for actor-oriented models with partial evaluation*. University of California, Berkeley: EECS.

Zhu, Q., Nakata, T., Mine, M., & Kuroki, K. Endo, & Hasegawa, T. (2004). Integrating UML into SoC design process. In *UML for SoC Design Workshop*.

Zhu, Q., Oishi, R., Hasegawa, T., & Nakata, T. (2004). System-on-Chip Validation using UML and CWL. In *Proc. of CODES*.

# About the Contributors

**Luís Gomes** has been since 1987 with the Faculty of Sciences and Technology, Universidade Nova de Lisboa, Portugal, where he currently is associate professor at the Department of Electrical Engineering, and has been a researcher with the UNINOVA Institute, Caparica, Portugal (a not-for-profit R&D institution aimed at technology transfer). From 1984 to 1987, he was with the R&D Engineering Department of EID, a Portuguese medium enterprise in the area of electronic system design. He was made a "Profesor Onorific", at Transilvanea University of Brasov, Romania in 2007. His main scientific interests include the usage of formal methods for embedded systems co-design, such as Petri nets and other concurrency models, emphasizing reconfigurable computing platforms based implementations. He is author of more than 100 papers published in journals, books and conference proceedings. He was co-editor of the books "Hardware Design and Petri Nets" (Kluwer Academic Publishers, 2000), and of "Advances on Remote laboratories and E-Learning Experiences" (University of Deusto, 2007). He served as general co-chair for the Int. Symp. on Industrial Embedded Systems (SIES 2007, SIES 2008) and the IEEE Int. Conf. on Emerging Technologies and Factory Automation (ETFA 2003) and organizer of the Int. Conf. on Application and Theory of Petri nets (ATPN 1998). Dr. Gomes has been an associate editor for the *IEEE Transactions on Industrial Informatics*, since 2005, and a member of the editorial board of LNCS ToPNoC - Transactions on Petri Nets and Other Models of Concurrency, since 2006.

**João M. Fernandes** is an associate professor at the Dept. Informatics, Universidade do Minho. He conducts his research activities in software engineering, with a special interest in software modeling, requirements engineering, and embedded software. In May 2000, he finished his PhD dissertation, where he proposed a UML-based approach to develop embedded systems. During his PhD and now as part of his research and teaching activities, his work is focused on the methodological and technologic aspects related with the use of a multi-perspective, model-driven approach for developing embedded systems. From Sep/2002 until Feb/2003, he was a post-doctoral researcher at the Embedded Systems Laboratory, TUCS, in Turku, Finland, and from Sep/2006 until Jun/2007, he was an invited assistant professor at Dept. Computer Science, Aarhus University, Denmark. He is author of more than 70 papers published in journals, books and conference proceedings. Dr. Fernandes is member of the editorial review board of the *Journal of Information Technology Research*, IGI Publishing, since Jun/2007. He has been involved in the organization of various international events, including the 3rd Int. Conf. on Application of Concurrency to System Design (ACSD 2003), the 5th IFIP Int. Conf. on Distributed and Parallel Embedded Systems (DIPES 2006), the 3rd Int. Summer School on Generative and Transformational Techniques in Software Engineering (GTTSE 2009), and the Model-Based Methodologies for Pervasive and Embedded Software (MOMPES) workshops series.

\* \* \*

**Samar Abdi** is a project scientist at the Center for Embedded Computer Systems (CECS) at University of California, Irvine. He is also a faculty member in the Gigascale Systems Research Center (GSRC), a focus center of the Semiconductor Research Corporation (SRC). He received his PhD from UC Irvine and BTech from IIT Kharagpur, but in computer science. He is also the architect and lead developer of Embedded System Environment (ESE), a framework for automatic transaction level modeling and prototyping of embedded systems. He has written over 15 journal and conference papers in ESL design of embedded systems.

**Christos Baloukas** received his Diploma and MSc degree in electrical and computer engineering from the Democritus University of Thrace, Greece, in 2004 and 2006, respectively. He is currently a PhD researcher in the VLSI Design and Testing Center in the Democritus University of Thrace. His research interests include dynamic access and storage optimization on communications applications for low power and high performance, embedded systems and high-level design optimizations.

**Ted Bapty** is a research associate professor and senior researcher at the Institute for Software Integrated Systems at Vanderbilt University. He is interested in and leads research projects in model-integrated systems as applied to: Large-scale, distributed embedded systems, C4ISR systems, digital signal processing and instrumentation systems, parallel embedded systems, aspect-oriented design, architecture modeling and analysis, autonomous systems, and tools for rapid system prototyping and system integration. Current projects include large-scale, service oriented systems for military and space applications, system integration tools and infrastructure, and embedded DSP systems.

**Gaurav Bhatia** is a research staff member in the Electrical and Computer Engineering Department at Carnegie Mellon University in Pittsburg, USA. He received his BS and MS degrees in electrical and computer engineering from Carnegie Mellon University in 2002 and 2003 respectively. His research interests include the design, implementation and analysis of compute systems in the areas of distributed, networked and embedded systems with a specifc focus on automotive systems.

**João Bispo** received a 5-year engineering degree in computer systems and informatics from the University of Algarve, Portugal, in 2006. He is working towards the PhD degree from IST / Technical University of Lisbon at INESC-ID, Lisbon. In 2006, he spent a period working at the Computer Engineering Department of the Delft University of Technology, the Netherlands. His research interests include reconfigurable computing, automatic generation of hardware for specific applications, and architecture design exploration.

**Lisane Brisolara de Brisolara** is graduated from Catholic University of Pelotas in computer science in 1999. She received the MSc and Dr degrees from Federal University of Rio Grande do Sul, UFRGS, Brazil, in 2002 and 2007, respectively, all in computer science. She is presently a professor at the Computer Science Department at the Federal University of Pelotas (UFPel), in charge of software engineering and information systems disciplines at the undergraduate levels. Her research interests include embedded systems modeling, design, validation, automation and test, and embedded software development.

**João M. P. Cardoso** received a 5-year engineering degree in telecommunications and electronics from the University of Aveiro in 1993, and an MSc and a PhD degree in electrical and computer engineering from the IST, Lisbon, Portugal in 1997 and 2001, respectively. He is currently associate professor at the Department of Informatics Engineering, Faculty of Engineering of the University of Porto. Before, he was with the IST/Technical University of Lisbon (2006-2008) and with the University of Algarve (1993-2006). He is a senior researcher at INESC-ID in Lisbon. In 2001/2002, he worked for PACT XPP Technologies, Inc., Munich, Germany. He has participated in the organization of a number of conferences (FPL'03, FPL'07, FPL'08, ARC'05, ARC'06 and ARC'07) and he serves as a program committee member for various international conferences (e.g., IEEE FPT, FPL, IC-SAMOS, ACM SAC, ARC). He is co-author of a Springer book and co-editor of two Springer LNCS volumes. He has (co-)authored over 70 scientific publications (including journal/conference papers and patents) on subjects related to compilers, embedded systems, and reconfigurable computing. He is a member of IEEE, IEEE Computer Society and ACM. His research interests include reconfigurable computing, compilers for domain- and application-specific architectures, and design automation for embedded systems.

**Luigi Carro** received the Dr degree from Universidade Federal do Rio Grande do Sul (UFRGS), Brazil, in 1996 after a period working at ST-Microelectronics (from 1989 to 1991), Agrate, Italy, in the R&D group. He is presently a professor at the Applied Informatics Department at the Informatics Institute of UFRGS. His primary research interests include embedded systems design, validation, automation and test, fault tolerance for future technologies and rapid system prototyping. He has advised more than 20 graduate students (Master and Dr levels). He has published more than 150 technical papers on those topics and is the author of the book "Digital Systems Design and Prototyping" (2001-in Portuguese) and co-author of "Fault-Tolerance Techniques for SRAM-based FPGAs" (2006-Springer).

**Juan Castillo** graduated in telecommunication engineering from the University of Cantabria in 2006, with specialization in microelectronic and radiocommunications. Currently, he is complementing his educational background with the degree of technical engineering in computer systems and a Master in computation science. He started is career in the University of Cantabria, where he is currently working in European projects and collaborating as teacher assistant. His areas of research are focused on embedded systems design and verification.

**Francky Catthoor** received the engineering degree and a PhD in electrical engineering from the Katholieke Universiteit Leuven, Belgium in 1982 and 1987 respectively. Between 1987 and 2000, he has headed several research domains in the area of high-level and system synthesis techniques and architectural methodologies at the Inter-university Micro-Electronics Center (IMEC), Heverlee, Belgium. Currently he is an IMEC fellow. He is part-time full professor at the EE department of the K.U.Leuven. In 1986 he received the Young Scientist Award from the Marconi International Fellowship Council. He has been associate editor for several IEEE and ACM journals, like *Trans. on VLSI Signal Processing, Trans. on Multi-media*, and *ACM TODAES*. He was the program chair of several conferences including ISSS'97 and SIPS'01. He has been elected an IEEE fellow in 2005.

**Érika Cota** is currently an adjunct professor at the Computer Science Dept. of Universidade Federal do Rio Grande do Sul (UFRGS), in Porto Alegre, Brazil, where she participates in the Test and Reliability of Integrated Systems Group and in the Embedded Systems Laboratory. Érika got her BS in computer science in 1994 from Universidade Federal de Minas Gerais. Subsequently she got her Masters and Doctorate in computer science from Universidade Federal do Rio Grande do Sul in 1997 and 2003, respectively. Her research interests include the test and design for test of hardware and software systems, test of embedded systems, test planning, and fault tolerance of integrated systems. She has published over 50 papers in international journals and conferences on these topics. She is currently serving as vice-chair of LA-TTTC.

**Dionisio de Niz** is a senior member of the technical staff of the Software Engineering Institute at Carnegie Mellon University working on the evolution of the SAE AADL standard. He holds a computer engineering PhD from Carnegie Mellon University. His research interest includes model-based engineering of embedded real-time systems and real-time systems in general.

**Serge Demeyer** is a professor at the University of Antwerp (Department of Mathematics and Computer Science) where he leads a research group investigating the theme of "software reengineering" (LORE - Lab On REengineering). His main research interest concerns software engineering (more precisely, reengineering in an object-oriented context) but due to historical reasons he maintains a heavy interest in hypermedia systems as well. He is an active member of the international research community, serving in various conference organization and program committees. He has writen a book entitled "Object-Oriented Reengineering" en edited a book entitled "Software Evolution". He also authored a considerable amount of peer reviewed articles, some of them in highly respected scientific journals. He completed his MSc in 1987 and his PhD in 1996, both at the Vrije Universiteit Brussel. After his PhD, he worked for three years in Switzerland, where he served as a technical co-ordinator of an European research project.

**Sébastien Faucou** is an assistant professor of computer science at Nantes Université (France). He is member of the real-time system team of the Institute of Research in Communications and Cybernetics of Nantes (IRCCyN). He received his MSc from Ecole Centrale de Nantes in 1999 and his PhD in control and applied computer science from the University of Nantes in 2002. His research interests are in architecture description languages for distributed real-time embedded systems, schedulability analysis of real-time systems, and design of operating systems for real-time embedded applications, with a focus on the automotive domain. He takes an active part in the development of Trampoline, an open-source real-time operating system for in-vehicle embedded applications.

**Víctor Fernández** got his PhD in electronics from the University of Cantabria in 1998 where he's associate professor since 2003 at the Electronics Technology, Automatics and Systems Engineering Department. He has been responsible of several projects related with HW design, especially for space applications, with emphasis in channel coding and modulation. Current areas of interest are VLSI design (especially in adaptive coding and modulation systems) and HW/SW co-design.

**Ronaldo Ferreira** is currently pursuing the BS degree in computer science at the Universidade Federal do Rio Grande do Sul (UFRGS), Brazil. His research interests are on programming languages and software engineering for embedded software, as well as formal methods and software abstraction. He is an ACM student member.

**Daniel Gajski**, a leader in the areas of embedded systems, design methodologies and languages, headed research teams that created new design methodologies, tools and languages. He was instrumental in developing formalisms and algorithms for high-level synthesis, the definition of the finite-state-machine with data (FSMD), system level languages such as SpecCharts and SpecC, and design tools such as SpecSyn and System-on-Chip Environment. Many of these concepts have been adapted by academia and industry in the last 25 years. Prof. Gajski directs the Center for Embedded Computer Systems at UC Irvine, with a research mission to incorporate embedded systems into automotive, communications, and medical applications. He has authored over 300 papers and numerous textbooks, and he holds a doctoral degree in computer and information sciences from the University of Pennsylvania, Philadelphia. After 10 years as professor at the University of Illinois he joined UCI, where he presently holds The Henry Samueli Endowed Chair in computer system design.

**Angelo Gargantini** was born in Bergamo in 1969. He graduated in electronic engineering in 1994. He holds one PhD from the Politecnico di Milano, and another from the University of Catania. He worked as visiting researcher at the NRL Naval Research Laboratory in Washington DC, as technician at the University of Catania, and now he is assistant professor at the University of Bergamo, where he teaches basic and advanced courses of software design and programming. His research interests are centered on languages, methods and tools for the specification, analysis, validation, verification, design, and testing of critical, real-time, embedded computer-based systems. Keywords of his research are: formal methods, abstract state machines, SCR, model checking, theorem proving, model based testing, combinatorial testing.

**Aniruddha S. Gokhale** is an assistant professor of computer science and engineering in the Department of Electrical Engineering and Computer Science at Vanderbilt University. He received his BE (Computer Engineering) from Pune University in 1989; MS (Computer Science) from Arizona State University in 1992; and DSc (computer science) from Washington University in 1998. Prior to joining Vanderbilt, he was a member of technical staff at Bell Labs, Lucent Technologies. Dr. Gokhale is a member of IEEE and ACM. His research combines model-driven engineering and middleware for distributed, real-time and embedded systems.

**Jeff Gray** is an associate professor in the Department of Computer and Information Sciences from the University of Alabama at Birmingham (UAB), where he co-directs research in the Software Composition and Modeling (SoftCom) Laboratory. His funding from NSF, DARPA, and IBM has supported research in model-driven engineering, aspect-oriented software development, domain-specific languages, and clone refactoring. A 2007 recipient of an NSF CAREER award, Jeff was also named the 2008 Alabama Professor of the Year by the Carnegie Foundation. He is the chair of the Alabama IEEE Computer Society and performs outreach to children in elementary through high school to raise the awareness of computer science and technology. Jeff has published over 120 book chapters, journal articles, and conference papers and is one of the founders of the OOPSLA Workshop on Domain-Specific Modeling and the International Conference on Model Transformation.

**Hans-Michael Hanisch** is the professor and the head of the Research Laboratory on Automation Technology at the Martin Luther University in Germany. He obtained in 1982 the diploma degree on chemical engineering (specialization process systems engineering) with Excellence, and in 1987 the PhD diploma with "summa cum laude" on "Mathematical Modeling of Discrete Control Tasks in Chemical Process Systems" at the Polytechnical Institute of Leuna Merseburg in Germany. Between 1991 and 1993, Prof. Hanisch followed researches at the Process Control Laboratory at the University of Dortmund in Germany to prepare the Habilitation which is successfully obtained in 1995 on "Modeling, Analysis, and Controller Design in Hierarchical Discrete Control Systems". Prof. Hanisch is an active member in several scientific international organizations and supervizes different R&D projects. He wrote more than 160 papers in reviewed Journals and Conference Proceedings. In his research laboratory, more than 15 PhD students finished or are following research activities.

**Hans Hansson** (born Aug 8, 1957) is professor in computer engineering, specialising in real-time systems, at Mälardalen University since 1997. He is director of research at the School of Innovation, Design and Engineering, director of Mälardalen Real-Time Research Centre, the PROGRESS national strategic research centre, and the national graduate school SAVE-IT. He received an MSc (engineering physics), a Licentiate degree (computer science), a BA (business administration), and a Doctor of Technology degree (computer science) from Uppsala University, Sweden, in 1981, 1984, 1984 and 1992, respectively. He was appointed "docent" in computer systems at Uppsala University 1998. Prof. Hansson was previously director of the national research programme ARTES, visiting professor and department chairman at the Department of Computer Systems, Uppsala University, and researcher and scientific advisor at the Swedish Institute of Computer Science in Stockholm, Sweden. Research interests and contributions include component-based design of safety-critical real-time embedded systems, modelling and analysis of real-time communication, real-time testing and debugging, execution-time analysis, development of automotive control SW, and formal modeling of timing and probability. Prof. Hansson is associate editor of the *IEEE Tr. on Industrial Informatics* and Springer's *Journal of Real-Time Systems*.

**Zdeněk Hanzálek** is a member of the IEEE and the IEEE Computer Society. He obtained the Diploma in electrical engineering from the Czech Technical University (CTU) in Prague in 1990. He obtained his PhD degree in control engineering from the CTU in Prague and PhD degree in industrial informatics from the Universite Paul Sabatier Toulouse. He was with LAAS - Laboratoire d'Analyse et d'Architecture des Systemes in Toulouse (1992 to 1997) and with LAG INPG - Institut National Polytechnique de Grenoble (1998 to 2000). In 2005, he obtained Doc. degree at the Czech Technical University in Prague. His research interests include real-time systems and scheduling.

**Anne Keller** received her Diploma in media systems in 2006 from the Bauhaus-University, Weimar. She did her thesis on "Optimizing Abstract Data Types in Embedded Applications at Modeling Level" at IMEC vzw, Leuven. She is currently pursuing a PhD at the University of Antwerp. Her research interests include model-driven engineering, with a particular focus on inconsistency management and inconsistency resolution.

**Mohamed Khalgui** is a full time researcher in computer science at the Martin Luther University in Germany and a member of the Mosic Research Laboratory in Tunisia. He was a part time researcher at the ITIA-CNR Institute in Italy and a temporary lecturer at the Henri Poincaré University in France. Dr. Khalgui obtained the Bachelor degree in computer science at the Tunis University in 2001, the master degree was obtained in telecommunication and services at the Henri Poincaré University in 2003. He made research activities in computer science at the INRIA Institute to obtain the PhD at the French

Polytechnical Institute of Lorraine in 2007. Dr. Khalgui activates in several European projects and also in other interesting international collaborations.

**Marcio Eduardo Kreutz** is graduated from University of Ijuí, Brazil, in Computer Science in 1994. He received the Msc and Dr. degrees from Federal University of Rio Grande do Sul, UFRGS, Brazil, in 1997 and 2005, respectively, all in Computer Science. He is presently a professor at the Computer Science Department at the University of Santa Cruz do Sul (UNISC), in charge of Computer Architecture and Digital Systems Design disciplines at the undergraduate level and Embedded Systems at the graduate level. His research interests include heterogeneous embedded systems modeling and evaluation and communication and processing architectures design and optimization.

**Yuehua ("Jane") Lin** received a PhD degree in computer science from the University of Alabama at Birmingham in 2007, where she conducted research in model-driven engineering and aspect-oriented software development with a focus on model transformation and supporting tools, mode transformation testing and model differentiation. Her thesis was entitled, "A Model Transformation Approach to Automated Model Evolution." Dr. Lin joined Honda Manufacturing of Alabama, LLC as a senior software engineer in 2007. She currently designs and develops distributed systems for automatic production tracking and supply chain management.

**Stylianos Mamagkakis** received his Master and PhD degree in electrical and computer engineering from the Democritus Uni. Thrace (Greece) in 2004 and 2007, respectively. Since 2006, he coordinates a team of PhD students within the NES division at IMEC, Leuven, Belgium. His research activities mainly belong to the field of system-level exploration, with emphasis on MPSoC run-time resource management, design for reliability and system integration. He has published more than 35 papers in International Journals and Conferences. He was investigator in 9 research projects in the embedded systems domain funded from the EC as well as national governments and industry. He is member of the IEEE.

**Marcos Martínez** received an MS degree in telecommunications engineering in 1998 from the Polytechnic University of Valencia. From 1999 to 2003, he worked for Alcatel Microelectronics in Paris, where he participated in the design of high performance embedded systems in the automotive, DSL and Optical access sectors. In 2003 he joined ST Microelectronics in Paris as system engineer to participate in the advanced R&D programs for next generation passive optical networks in the framework of several European projects. In 2005, he joined DS2 as senior engineer to participate in the R&D activities of the company in the framework of different cooperation programs.

**Júlio Carlos Balzano de Mattos** is currently a professor at the Computer Science Department at the Universidade Federal de Pelotas (UFPel), in Pelotas, Brazil. Júlio did his BS in Computer Science in 1997 from Universidade Federal de Pelotas, Brazil. Subsequently he got his Master's and Doctorate in computer science from Universidade Federal do Rio Grande do Sul (UFRGS), Brazil, in 2000 and 2007, respectively. His primary research interests include embedded systems design, validation and automation and test, embedded architectures, embedded software development and rapid system prototyping.

**Francisco Nascimento** is a PhD candidate in the Informatics Institute at Federal University of Rio Grande do Sul in Porto Alegre, RS, Brazil. He is also assistant professor in the Integrated Faculties of

Taquara, Brazil, where he teaches courses on computer architecture, distributed systems, and performance evaluation of computer systems. His research interests include formal methods to the design automation of distributed, real time embedded systems, more specifically co-synthesis techniques and tools based on concepts from model driven engineering. He received a MSc in computer science from Federal University of Rio Grande do Sul.

**Sandeep Neema** is a research assistant professor of electrical engineering and computer science at Vanderbilt University, and senior research scientist at the Institute for Software-Integrated Systems at Vanderbilt. He has over eleven years of experience in modeling and synthesis of embedded, distributed, real-time systems. His research interests include architecture analysis and synthesis of large scale system-of-systems; design space exploration and constraint based synthesis of distributed, real-time, embedded systems; modeling of distributed, real-time, embedded systems; dynamic reconfiguration of hardware and software in embedded real-time systems; and fault tolerances in large-scale computing clusters. Dr. Neema received his BTech from the Indian Institute of Technology, New Delhi in 1995, MS from Utah State University, in 1997, and PhD. from Vanderbilt University in 2001, all in electrical and computer engineering. He has published over 60 research papers.

**Marcio F. da S. Oliveira** received his BS degree in computer science (major in real time and embedded systems) from Catholic University of Petropolis, Brazil (2004) and MSc degree in computer science from Federal University of Rio Grande do Sul, Brazil (2006). Currently he is PhD candidate at the Informatics Institute of Federal University of Rio Grande do Sul. His research interests are real-time and embedded system development methods, design automation and model-driven engineering, which focus on model-based design space exploration and estimation for embedded system design.

**Carlos E. Pereira** received his DrIng degree from University of Stuttgart, Germany - 1995, his MSc and BS EE degree in 1990 and 1987 from the Federal University of Rio Grande do Sul (UFRGS) in Brazil. He is an associate professor of the Electrical Engineering Department at the UFRGS in Brazil. From 2000 to 2001 he was a visiting researcher at the United Technologies Research Center (UTRC) in Hartford/CT USA. Since 2005 has acted as Technical Director for CETA – an applied research center, whose goal is to promote innovative applied research projects between academia and industry, focusing on the areas of industrial automation, information and communication technologies. Prof. Pereira's research focuses on methodologies and tool support for the development of distributed real-time embedded systems, with special emphasis on industrial automation applications. He is chair of the IFAC Technical Committee on Manufacturing Plant Control (TC 5.1) and is associate editor of the Journal "Control Engineering Practice" – Elsevier and AtP International - Oldenbourg. He has more than 150 technical publications on conferences and journals.

**Paul Pettersson** (born May 19, 1967) is professor in real-time systems (specialised in modelling and verification) and leader of the Division of Embedded Systems at Mälardalen University in Sweden. He received a PhD in computer systems from Uppsala University in 1999 for his thesis on theory and practice of modeling and verification of real-time systems. After a post doc period at Aalborg University in Denmark, he joined the Department of Information Technology at Uppsala University in 2000 as Senior Lecturer. He was appointed "Docent" in computer science at Uppsala University in 2006. He also joined Mälardalen University in 2006. His current research interests include component-based design, analysis, and verification of embedded and real-time systems. He is co-founder of serveral tools, including UPPAAL (for model-checking of timed systems), TIMES (for schedulability analysis of real-time systems), and Cover (for model-based testing of timed systems), and of the company UP4ALL International AB.

**Hector Posadas** received his Bachelor (2002) and Master (2005) in telecommunication engineering from the University of Cantabria. He also received the Bachelor in computer engineering from then UNED in 2005. In 2003 he was hired as researcher at the University of Cantabria, where he later achieved a grant to start the PhD studies. Currently, Hector Posadas is a PhD student and teacher assistant at this university since 2006, collaborating in several European projects. His areas of interest are centered on co-simulation and co-design, specially in fast prototyping and modeling of HW/SW systems, where he is working on high-level OS modeling and fast system performance estimation.

**Julián Proenza** received the first degree in physics and the doctorate in informatics from the University of the Balearic Islands (UIB), Palma de Mallorca, Spain, in 1989 and 2007, respectively. He is currently holding a permanent position as a lecturer in the Department of Mathematics and Informatics at the UIB. His research interests include dependable and real-time systems, fault-tolerant distributed systems, clock synchronization, dependable communication topologies and field-bus networks such as CAN (controller area network).

**David Quijano** was born on 1982 in Santander, Spain. He graduated from the University of Cantabria in 2005 in telecommunication engineering with specialization in microelectronics. A few months later, in 2006, he graduated from National University of Distance Education in technical engineering in computer systems. For finishing his actual studies, in 2007, he began a Master in computation science degree. Professionally, he joined to the University of Cantabria immediately after the finalization of his first degree to collaborate on the developing of design tools. The investigation area, in which he is focused on, is design and verification of HW/SW embedded systems, for three different projects: LoMoSA+, Atenea and SPICES.

**Ragunathan (Raj) Rajkumar** is a professor of electrical and computer engineering and of Robotics Institute at Carnegie Mellon University. At Carnegie Mellon, he directs the Real-Time and Multimedia Systems Laboratory, and co-directs the General Motors - Carnegie Mellon Vehicle Information Technology Collaborative Research Laboratory and the General Motors - Carnegie Mellon Autonomous Driving Collaborative Research Laboratory. He obtained his BE (Hons) degree from the University of Madras in 1984, and his MS and PhD from Carnegie Mellon University in 1986 and 1989 respectively. His research interests include cyber-physical systems, embedded real-time systems, wireless sensor networks and automotive systems.

**Elvinia Riccobene** is associate professor in computer science at the Information Technology Dept., University of Milan. She received her degree in mathematics and her PhD degree from the University of Catania (Italy). She holds visiting position at the Centre For High Assurance Computer System (Washington DC), at the Univ. of Bristol (UK), at the Univ. of Karlsruhe (Germany). Her research interests include formal methods and analyses techniques for complex software systems and embedded systems, integration between formal and semi-formal methods, model-driven engineering. She is the scientific coordinator of national research projects and she participated to various European and Italian research projects. She serves as member of the program committee of international conferences. She published several papers in International journals and in proceedings of international conferences.

**Guillermo Rodríguez-Navas** received the telecommunication engineer degree from the University of Vigo, Vigo, Spain, in 2002. He is currently pursuing the PhD degree in computer science at the University of the Balearic Islands (UIB), Palma de Mallorca, Spain. He is a member of the System, Robotics, and Vision (SRV) research group at UIB. His research is focused on dependable and real-time distributed embedded systems. In particular, he has addressed various issues related to the CAN field-bus, such as fault tolerance, clock synchronization, and response time analysis.

**Adriano Kaminski Sanches** received his BSc in computer science from Universidade Estadual de Maringa, Brazil in 2002, and the MS degrees in computer science from ICMC/Universidade de São Paulo (USP), Brazil in 2006. He worked during one year (2006/2007) for Siemens VDO Automotive developing embedded software in automotive systems. He is a PhD candidate in computer science and engineering in IST/Technical University of Lisbon, and a member of INESC-ID, Lisbon. His research interests include reconfigurable computing, compilation techniques and computer architectures applied to embedded systems and image compression.

**Patrizia Scandurra** received the degree in computer science from the University of Catania (Italy) on July 26th 2002 and the PhD degree in computer science from the same university on March 17th 2006. In 2006, she got a post-doc research position at the Department of Information Technologies (DTI) of the University of Milan (Italy). Currently, she is assistant professor (researcher) at the Department of Information Engineering and Mathematical Methods of the University of Bergamo (Italy), where she teaches basic courses of software design/programming and operating systems. Her research interests includes: aspects pertaining to the integration of formal and semi-formal modelling languages; formal methods and behavioural specifications; formal verification; model-driven engineering (MDE); model-driven methodologies; techniques and tools for the design and analysis of embedded systems and systems on chip (SoC). She is a member of the abstract state machines (ASM) community.

**Ina Schieferdecker** studied mathematical computer science at Humboldt-University Berlin and did her PhD in 1994 at Technical University Berlin. She is heading the Competence Center Modeling and Testing for Systems and Service Solutions at the Fraunhofer Institute for Open Communication Systems. She is professor on engineering and testing of telecommunication systems at TU Berlin since 2003. Prof. DrIng Ina Schieferdecker is an active member in the standardization of TTCN-3 by ETSI and of the UTP by OMG. She is co-founder of the Testing Technologies IST GmbH, Berlin and member of the German Testing Board. She received in 2004 the Alfried Krupp von Bohlen and Halbach Award for Young Professors and in 2005 the ITEA Achievement Award.

**Douglas C. Schmidt** is a professor of computer science and associate chair of the Computer Science and Engineering program at Vanderbilt University. He has published 9 books and over 400 technical papers that cover a range of research topics, including patterns, optimization techniques, and empirical analyses of software frameworks and domain-specific modeling environments that facilitate the development of distributed real-time and embedded (DRE) middleware and applications running over high-speed networks and embedded system interconnects. Dr. Schmidt has served as a program manager at DARPA, where he led the national R&D effort on middleware for DRE systems. In addition to his academic research and government service, Dr. Schmidt has over fifteen years of experience leading the development of ACE, TAO, and CIAO, which are widely used, open-source DRE middleware frameworks that contain a rich set of components and domain-specific languages that implement patterns and product-line architectures for high-performance DRE systems.

**Françoise Simonot-Lion** is a professor of computer science at Nancy Université (France). Since 1997, she is the scientific leader of the Real Time and InterOperability (TRIO) research team, an INRIA project at LORIA laboratory in Nancy (France). During 4 years (2001-2004), she was responsible of CARA-MELS, a joint research team with PSA Peugeot Citroën funded by the French Ministry for Research and Technology. She has participated in the French Embedded Electronic Architecture project (AEE, 1999-2001), and in the European project ITEA EAST-EEA (2001-2004). The purpose of ITEA EAST was to define an industry-wide layered software architecture, including a communication middleware, and a common architecture description language supporting a formal description of in-vehicle embedded systems (EAST-ADL). She is involved in several research collaboration with automotive industry and she is co-chair of the subcommittee "Automotive Electronic and Embedded Systems" of the IEEE Industrial Electronic Society (IES) - TCFA.

**Dimitrios Soudris** received his Diploma in electrical engineering from the University of Patras, Greece, in 1987. He received the PhD degree in electrical engineering, from the University of Patras in 1992. He is currently working as assistant professor in Department of Computer Science, School of Electrical and Computer Engineering, National Technical University of Athens, Greece. His research interests include low power design, parallel architectures, embedded systems design, and VLSI signal processing. He has published more than 180 papers in international journals and conferences, and he (co-)authored/edited four books. He was leader and principal investigator in numerous research projects funded from the Greek Government and Industry as well as the European Commission (ESPRIT II-III-IV and 5th, 6th and 7th IST). He has served as general chair and program chair for the International Workshop on Power and Timing Modelling, Optimisation, and Simulation (PATMOS) and General Chair IEEE/CEDA VLSI-SOC 2008. He received an award from INTEL and IBM for the project results of LPGD #25256 (ESPRIT IV). He is a member of the IEEE, the VLSI Systems and Applications Technical Committee of IEEE CAS and the ACM.

**Emilena Specht** got her computer engineering and MS in computer science degrees at the Universidade Federal do Rio Grande do Sul (UFRGS), Brazil, in 2005 and 2008, respectively. Her research interests include embedded software automation, code generation, and design space exploration.

**Marijn Temmerman** received the MSc degree in computer science from the Katholieke Universiteit (KU) Leuven, Belgium in 1980, and the PhD degree at the University of Antwerp in 2008. Since 1980, she is a professor at the Karel de Grote University College (Departement of Applied Engineering). Her research focuses on modeling and optimization of embedded software, and embedded software engineering.

**Yvon Trinquet** is a professor in the University of Nantes in France. He is also member of the IRC-CyN laboratory (joint research unit from CNRS (National Scientific Resarch Center), the University of Nantes, the Ecole Centrale de Nantes and the Ecole des Mines de Nantes). Since 1995 he is the head of "real-time systems" team of IRCCyN. His research interests are in the design of real-time systems and more particularly: real-time scheduling, real-time executive kernels and architecture description languages. He participated in the French project AEE (1999-2001) on embedded electronic architectures, as well as in the European project ITEA EAST-EEA (2001-2004) in which has been defined the EAST-ADL language presented in this paper. Currently he is involved in several projects in collaboration with the main actors of the French automotive industry on topics as the mastery of the execution times and the robustness of real-time kernels. He takes an active part in the development of Trampoline, an open-source OSEK-compliant real-time operating kernel for in-vehicle embedded applications.

**Eugenio Villar** got his PhD in electronics from the University of Cantabria in 1984 where he is currently the responsible for the area of HW/SW Embedded Systems Design at the Microelectronics Engineering Group. Since 1992 is full professor at the Electronics Technology, Automatics and Systems Engineering Department of the University of Cantabria. His research activity has been always related with system specification and modeling. He participated actively in the standardization process of VHDL where he contributed to the definition of the synthesis subset. His current research interests cover system specification and performance estimation using SystemC. He is author of more than 100 papers in international conferences, journals and books in the area of specification and design of embedded electronic systems. Prof. Villar served in several technical committees of international conferences like the VHDL Forum, Euro-VHDL, EuroDAC, DATE, and FDL. He has participated in several international projects in electronic system design under the FP5, FP6 and FP7, Itea and Medea programs. He is the representative of the University of Cantabria in the ArtemisIA JU.

**Flávio R. Wagner** received the DrIng degree in computer engineering from the University of Kaiserslautern, Germany, in 1983, the MSc degree in computer science in 1977 and the BS degree in electrical engineering in 1975, both from the Federal University of Rio Grande do Sul (UFRGS), in Porto Alegre, Brazil. He is a full professor of the Institute of Informatics at UFRGS. His main research interest is the design and architecture of embedded systems, with special emphasis on high-level hardware/software design space exploration. He has been the chair of the IFIP (International Federation for Information Processing) Working Group 10.5, on Design and Engineering of Electronic Systems, from 2001 to 2007, and is an associate editor of the journal *Design Automation for Embedded Systems*, from Springer/Kluwer. He served in the board of directors of the Brazilian Computer Society (SBC) for 12 years, from which he was the president in two consecutive terms, from 1999 to 2003.

**Libor Waszniowski** graduated in technical cybernetics from the Czech Technical University in Prague (CTU) in 2000 and received the PhD degree in electrical engineering and informatics from CTU in 2006. Currently, he is a researcher with the Center for Applied Cybernetics at CTU. His main research activities are in real-time systems, formal methods for real-time systems design and analysis and rapid application development. He worked on several industrial projects focusing on development of tools supporting model-based design and validation of control systems.

**Marco Aurélio Wehrmeister** received his MSc degree in computer science in 2005 from the Federal University of Rio Grande do Sul. Currently, he is PhD candidate at the same university. His research focuses on design of embedded and real-time systems with emphasis on Model-Driven Design using UML and concepts of aspect-oriented development. Moreover, he works with code generation, aspects weaving, and platform customization. Besides these topics, his interests also include Java and the real-time specification for Java for embedded systems, models transformation and synthesis, and RTOS.

**Lochi Yu** is a PhD student at the Center for Embedded Computer Systems (CECS) at the University of California, Irvine. His research focus include automatic TLM generation and communication estimation at transaction level. He received his MSc in electrical engineering from Stanford University, and a MD and BSEE from the University of Costa Rica.

**Justyna Zander** holds Doctorate of Engineering Science (2008) and Master of Science (2005) in the fields of computer science and electrical engineering from Technical University Berlin in Germany, and Bachelor of Science in environmental protection and management from Gdansk University of Technology in Poland (2003). Currently, she is a postdoctoral research scientist at the Fraunhofer Institute for Open Communication Systems. She was a visiting scholar at the University of California in San Diego, CA, USA (2007) and at The MathWorks in Natick, MA, USA (2008). For her scientific efforts she received grants from such institutions as Polish Prime Ministry (1999), Polish Ministry of Education and Sport (2001-2004), Hertie Foundation (2004), IFIP TC6 (2005), IEEE (2006), Siemens (2007), Metodos y Tecnologia (2008), or Singularity University at NASA Ames (2009). Her doctoral thesis on model-based testing was supported by German National Academic Foundation. She is certified by International Software Quality Institute.

**Jing Zhang** is a senior research engineer at Motorola Applied Research and Technology Center (ARTC), where she is responsible for conducting research and implementing prototype for policy-based management systems and service orchestration platforms. Jing is also a part-time PhD student in the Department of Computer and Information Sciences at the University of Alabama at Birmingham. Her PhD research is focused on techniques that combine model transformation and program transformation in order to assist in evolving large legacy software systems. Jing's research interests are in model-driven software engineering, aspect-oriented software development, business rule management and service-oriented architecture.

# Index